D1783639

International Organizations Before National Courts

This book investigates in a radically empirical way how national courts 'react' to disputes involving international organizations. Comprehensively analyzing both national courts' attitudes and techniques and underlying policy reasons, it first describes various legal approaches that result in adjudication or non-adjudication of disputes concerning international organizations. Secondly, it discusses policy issues *pro* and *contra* the adjudication of such disputes. It scrutinizes the rationale for immunizing international organizations from domestic litigation, especially the 'functional' need for immunity, and substantially debates the implications of a human rights-based right of access to a court on the immunizing of international organizations against the jurisdiction of national courts. The book finally identifies contemporary trends, seeking to ascertain whether a more flexible principle exempting certain types of disputes from domestic adjudication might substitute for the traditional immunity concept, which would simultaneously guarantee the functioning and independence of international organizations without impairing private parties' access to a fair dispute settlement procedure.

AUGUST REINISCH is Professor of Public International Law and EC Law at the University of Vienna Law School, and a lecturer at the Austrian Diplomatic Academy in Vienna and at the SAIS/ Johns Hopkins University in Bologna.

CAMBRIDGE STUDIES IN INTERNATIONAL AND COMPARATIVE LAW

This series (established in 1946 by Professors Gutteridge, Hersch Lauterpacht and McNair) is a forum for studies of high quality in the fields of public and private international law and comparative law. Although these are distinct legal subdisciplines, developments since 1946 confirm their interrelationship. Comparative law is increasingly used as a tool in the making of law at national, regional and international levels. Private international law is increasingly affected by international conventions, and the issues faced by classical conflicts rules are increasingly dealt with by substantive harmonisation of law under international auspices. Mixed international arbitrations, especially those involving state economic activity, raise mixed questions of public and private international law. In many fields (such as the protection of human rights and democratic standards, investment guarantees, international criminal law) international and national systems interact. National constitutional arrangements relating to 'foreign affairs', and to the implementation of international norms, are a focus of attention.

Professor Sir Robert Jennings edited the series from 1981. Following his retirement as General Editor, an editorial board has been created and Cambridge University Press has recommitted itself to the series, affirming its broad scope.

The Board welcomes works of a theoretical or interdisciplinary character, and those focusing on new approaches to international or comparative law or conflicts of law. Studies of particular institutions or problems are equally welcome, as are translations of the best work published in other languages.

A list of books in the series can be found at the end of this volume

International Organizations Before National Courts

AUGUST REINISCH

CAMBRIDGE
UNIVERSITY PRESS

CAMBRIDGE UNIVERSITY PRESS
Cambridge, New York, Melbourne, Madrid, Cape Town, Singapore, São Paulo

Cambridge University Press
The Edinburgh Building, Cambridge CB2 8RU, UK

Published in the United States of America by Cambridge University Press, New York

www.cambridge.org
Information on this title: www.cambridge.org/9780521653268

First published 2000
This digitally printed version 2008

A catalogue record for this publication is available from the British Library

Library of Congress Cataloguing in Publication data

Reinisch, August.
International organizations before national courts / August Reinisch.
   p. cm.
ISBN 0 521 65326 6 (hb)
1. International agencies.   2. International and municipal law.
3. Jurisdiction.   I. Title
KZ4850.R45   1999
341.5′5 – dc21   99-11072   CIP

ISBN 978-0-521-65326-8 hardback
ISBN 978-0-521-06364-7 paperback

Contents

Preface

My interest in the subject-matter of this book arose rather incidentally when I attended the 1992 Centre for Studies and Research seminar of the Hague Academy of International Law on 'The External Debt'. It was my task there to focus on responsibility issues concerning debt rescheduling and the international debts crisis; one of the side issues that emerged from this investigation was whether international organizations could be made responsible or liable for part of the crisis and, if so, whether international or national fora would be available to adjudicate such claims. As far as the latter were concerned, it was apparent that immunity from jurisdiction could impede the enforcement of liability. At first, I simply assumed that international organizations would enjoy a similar degree of immunity as states. After a second look, I realized, however, that most applicable international agreements and domestic statutes provided for functional and/or absolute immunity without making explicit what this difference implied. Later on, I found that some national courts, in particular, in the US and Italy, are in fact using a state immunity standard. It appeared that no predictions about any judicial outcomes could be readily made.

To some extent my book is an attempt to find answers to this puzzle. Its subject was soon broadened to include all the various types of reasoning employed by national courts when they have to decide whether or not they will hear cases involving international organizations. It also reflects my preference for 'real world' problems which should hopefully make it a useful companion for the practitioner. At the same time it will evidence my attempt to use strict systematic standards in classifying the types and rationales of judicial responses. If it thereby combines elements of a Common Law inspired case analysis with a more formal Civil Law approach, this was not wholly unintended.

I have attempted to make the study current to spring 1998. This inevitably implies that important later developments could not be covered.

August Reinisch

Acknowledgements

This study was submitted as 'Habilitationsschrift' to the Law Faculty of the University of Vienna in 1997. I wish to express my gratitude to all friends and colleagues at the Institute of International Law and International Relations in Vienna who helped me during the various stages of preparing it.

My main debt of gratitude goes to Professor Hanspeter Neuhold, who did not only take up the arduous task of presiding over the faculty committee which accepted my thesis in 1998, but who also gave me constant encouragement and practical advice, initially, when delimiting the scope of my study and, later, when confirming my decision to wind it up without venturing into news fields. Equally, I benefited from the wise counsel and valuable comments of Professors Karl Zemanek and Gerhard Hafner. Special mention must also be made of emeritus Professor Ignaz Seidl-Hohenveldern from whose unique experience in the particular subject-matter of my work I benefited when discussing with him various aspects of my work.

I also greatly appreciated the critical remarks and comments of numerous other professors at the University of Vienna among them: Ena-Marlies Bajons, Peter Böhm, Peter Fischer, Christoph Grabenwarter, Hans Hoyer, Theo Öhlinger, Walter Rechberger, and Hannes Tretter. I should also like to thank the external member of the faculty committee, Professor Martti Koskenniemi, whose 'deconstruction' of my policy approach did not only enliven the thesis defense before the faculty committee, but whose suggestions were most helpful and were thus incorporated in the final version.

As regards my work in Washington D.C., particular thanks must go to Professor Christoph Schreuer, with whom I had many discussions on the legal status of international organizations and whose hospitality at the Paul H. Nitze School of Advanced International Studies, Johns Hopkins University, enabled me to immediately start with my research. This work was further facilitated by the SAIS staff, all of whom I would like to thank, singling out Betty Glover for a particular recognition of her help.

I should also like to express my gratitude to Charlotte Ku for the American Society of International Law and to Michael Byers for the British Branch of the International Law Association for inviting me to present parts of my still unfinished study at Tillar House, Washington D.C., and at Jesus College, Oxford. These presentations and the ensuing debates helped me to develop and improve the arguments contained in this book.

My gratitude is further extended to Professor James Crawford, who carefully read my original manuscript, provided a wealth of highly valuable suggestions, which I have largely followed, and did not exasperate over my persistent objections to some others. I can only guess that his role in the decision of the Press Syndicate of Cambridge University Press to include my study in the International and Comparative Law Series was all but marginal. Likewise, I am indebted to the anonymous Reader A who also reviewed my draft manuscript for Cambridge University Press. His valuable comments helped to improve the book. I am particularly grateful to Finola O'Sullivan for preparing the publication of this book in a most efficient and professional manner. And my sincere admiration goes to Martin Gleeson, who helped me to avoid many technical imperfections of the text at the copy-editing stage.

Of course, all the errors and mistakes remain my exclusive responsibility. On the institutional side, I would like to express my gratitude to the Paul H. Nitze School of Advanced International Studies of Johns Hopkins University in Washington D.C. where I was invited to do research as a visiting scholar in 1995/96. The Erwin-Schrödinger-scholarship, which was awarded to me by the Austrian Science Fund, was a sine qua non for carrying out this research plan in the United States. Equally, the assistance of the Emil-Boral-Foundation has been instrumental in enabling me to complete my study.

On a personal level, I have relied very much on the support of my family. I am grateful to my mother and father, Herta and August Reinisch, who have enabled me to pursue my studies and who have always encouraged me in my work. Finally, and most importantly, I have to express my thanks to my wife, Elisabeth, for her support and patience with which she endured my passion for tracking down obscure case-quotations and cryptic footnotes which often made me less available for my family than I wished to be, especially during our 1995/96 stay in Washington D.C. This book is dedicated to her and to our wonderful children, Johanna and August, who have grown up splendidly, while I was writing, without having to worry about 'international organizations before national courts'.

August Reinisch

Table of cases

Argentine

Araya v. *Institute for Latin-American Integration/Inter-American Development Bank*, Labour Court, 1974; A. N. Vorkink and M. C. Hakuta, *Lawsuits Against International Organizations – Cases in National Courts Involving Staff and Employment* (Washington DC, World Bank Legal Department, 1985), 25

Bergaveche v. *United Nations Information Centre*, Juzgado del Trabajo No. 17, Buenos Aires, 7 February 1956, *Annual Report of the Secretary-General*, 12 UN GAOR, Supp. (No. 1) 124, UN Doc. A/3594; Camara Nacional de Apelaciones del Trabajo de la Capital Federal, 19 March 1958, (1959) 94 *Revista Juridica Argentina La Ley* 585; (1958–II) 26 ILR 620; A. N. Vorkink and M. C. Hakuta, *Lawsuits Against International Organizations – Cases in National Courts Involving Staff and Employment* (Washington DC, World Bank Legal Department, 1985), 17; summarized in United Nations Secretariat, The Practice of the United Nations, the Specialized Agencies and the International Atomic Energy Agency Concerning Their Status, Privileges and Immunities, 1967, UN Doc. A/CN.4/L.118 and Add. 1–2, *Yearbook of the International Law Commission* (1967), vol. II, 224

Dutto v. *United Nations High Commissioner for Refugees*, Labour Court of Appeals, 31 May 1989, Case No. 87.803, *La Ley* (1989), D, 532; (1990) 117 *Journal de droit international* (Clunet) 448; (1992) 89 ILR 90–2

Ezcurra de Mann v. *Inter-American Development Bank*, Labour Court, 15 August 1978, Court of Appeals, 11 June 1979; A. N. Vorkink and M. C. Hakuta, *Lawsuits Against International Organizations – Cases in National Courts Involving Staff and Employment* (Washington DC, World Bank Legal Department, 1985), 36

Colombia

Egypt

France

Greece

India

Ireland

Italy

Luxembourg

Malaysia

Mexico

Netherlands

Spain

Switzerland

Syria

United States

European Commission of Human Rights

European Court of Human Rights

European Court of Justice

Inter-American Commission on Human Rights

International Court of Justice

OAS Administrative Tribunal

OECD Administrative Tribunal

Permanent Court of International Justice

UN Administrative Tribunal

UN Human Rights Committee

World Bank Administrative Tribunal

Table of legal instruments

Constituent instruments

CERN Convention: Convention for the Establishment of a European Organization for Nuclear Research (CERN), Paris, 1 July 1953, 200 UNTS 149

Common Fund for Commodities Agreement: Agreement Establishing the Common Fund for Commodities, Geneva, 27 June 1980, UN Doc. TC/IPC/CF/CONF/24, reprinted in (1980) 19 ILM 896

EC Treaty: Treaty Establishing the European Economic Community, Rome, 25 March 1957, 298 UNTS 11

ELDO Convention: Convention for the Establishment of a European Launcher Development Organization, London, 29 March 1962, 507 UNTS 177

ESA Convention: Convention for the Establishment of a European Space Agency, Paris, 30 May 1975, (1975) 14 ILM 855

ESRO Convention: Convention for the Establishment of a European Space Research Organization, Paris, 14 June 1962, 528 UNTS 33

Eurocontrol Convention: International Convention Relating to Co-operation for the Safety of Air Navigation, Brussels, 13 December 1960, 523 UNTS 117

Eurofima Convention: Convention on the Establishment of Eurofima, European Company for the Financing of Railway Rolling Stock, Berne, 20 October 1955, 378 UNTS 225

FAO Constitution: Constitution of the Food and Agriculture Organization of the United Nations, 16 October 1945, (1946–7) *United Nations Yearbook* 693

IAEA Statute: Statute of the International Atomic Energy Agency, UN Headquarters, 26 October 1956, 276 UNTS 3

IBRD Articles of Agreement: Articles of Agreement of the International Bank for Reconstruction and Development, Washington DC, 27 December 1945, 2 UNTS 134

ICAO Convention: Convention on International Civil Aviation, Chicago, 7 December 1944, 15 UNTS 295

IDA Articles of Agreement: Articles of Agreement of the International Development Association, Approved for Submission to Governments by the Executive Directors of IBRD, 26 January 1960, 439 UNTS 249

ILO Constitution: Instrument for the Amendment of the Constitution of the International Labour Organisation, Montreal, 9 October 1946, 15 UNTS 35

Institute for Intellectual Cooperation: Letter from the French Government to the President of the Council of the League of Nations, 8 December 1924, including a Statute of the Institute and Resolution of the Council of the League of Nations, 13 December 1924, *League of Nations Official Journal*, February 1925, 285; reprinted in Franz Knipping, Hans von Mangoldt and Volker Rittberger (eds.), *The United Nations System and its Predecessors. Statutes and Legal Acts*, 3 vols (Berne and Munich, 1995), vol. II, 1064

IMF Articles of Agreement: Articles of Agreement of the International Monetary Fund, Washington DC, 27 December 1945, 2 UNTS 40

IMO Convention: Convention on the International Maritime (Consultative) Organization, Geneva, 6 March 1979, 289 UNTS 48

Inmarsat Convention: Convention on the International Maritime Satellite Organization (Inmarsat), London, 3 September 1976, 1143 UNTS 105

Intelsat Agreement: Agreement relating to the International Telecommunications Satellite Organization, Washington, DC, 20 August 1971, TIAS No. 7532, reprinted in (1971) 10 ILM 909

International Bureau of Weights and Measures: Convention internationale du mètre, Paris, 20 May 1875, 20 *US Statutes at Large* 709, reprinted in Franz Knipping, Hans von Mangoldt and Volker Rittberger (eds.), *The United Nations System and its Predecessors. Statutes and Legal Acts*, 3 vols (Berne and Munich, 1995), vol. II, 180

International Office for Dealing with Contagious Diseases of Animals: Agreement for the Creation of an International Office for Dealing with Contagious Diseases of Animals, Paris, 24 January 1924, 57 LNTS 135

International Wine Office: Agreement for the Creation of an International Wine Office, Paris, 29 November 1924, 80 LNTS 293

International Institute of Agriculture: Convention for the Creation of an International Institute of Agriculture, Rome, 7 June 1905, reprinted in (1908) 2 *American Journal of International Law*, Supplement, 358

International Institute of Refrigeration: Convention for the Creation of an International Institute of Refrigeration, Paris, 21 June 1920, 8 LNTS 66

IRO Constitution: UN General Assembly Resolution 62(I), 15 December 1946, 18 UNTS 3

ITC Agreement: Sixth International Tin Agreement, Geneva, 26 June 1982, 1282 UNTS 205

League of Nations Covenant: The Covenant of the League of Nations, 28 June 1919, 225 CTS 195

MIGA Convention: Convention Establishing the Multilateral Investment Guarantee Agency, Seoul, 11 October 1985, (1985) 24 ILM 1605

OAS Charter: Charter of the Organization of American States, Bogotá, 30 April 1948, 119 UNTS 3

UN Charter: Charter of the United Nations, San Francisco, 26 June 1945, (1946–7) *United Nations Yearbook* 831

UNESCO Constitution: Constitution of the United Nations Educational, Scientific and Cultural Organization, London, 16 November 1945, 4 UNTS 275

UNRRA Agreement: Agreement for United Nations Relief and Rehabilitation Administration, Washington, 9 November 1943, British Command Paper, Cmd. 6491 (1943), reprinted in (1944) 38 *American Journal of International Law*, Supplement, 33

UPU Constitution: Constitution of the Universal Postal Union, 10 July 1964; text in Franz Knipping, Hans von Mangoldt and Volker Rittberger (eds.), *The United Nations System and its Predecessors. Statutes and Legal Acts*, 3 vols (Berne and Munich, 1995), vol. I/2, 992

WHO Constitution: Constitution of the World Health Organization, New York, 22 July 1946, 14 UNTS 185

WIPO Convention: Convention Establishing the World Intellectual Property Organization, Stockholm, 14 July 1967, 828 UNTS 3

WTO Agreement: Agreement Establishing the WTO: General Agreement on Tariffs and Trade: Multilateral Trade Negotiations Final Act Embodying the Results of the Uruguay Round of Trade Negotiations, Marrakesh, 15 April 1994, reprinted in (1994) 33 ILM 13

Multilateral privileges and immunities treaties

Council of Europe Privileges and Immunities Agreement: General Agreement on Privileges and Immunities of the Council of Europe, Paris, 2 September 1949, 250 UNTS 14

EC Privileges and Immunities Protocol: Protocol on the Privileges and Immunities of the European Communities, Brussels, 8 April 1965, 13, 1348 UNTS 54

ECSC Privileges and Immunities Protocol: Protocol on the Privileges and Immunities of the (European) Community (for Coal and Steel), Paris, 18 April 1951, 261 UNTS 238

ELDO Protocol on Privileges and Immunities: Protocol on the Privileges and Immunities of the ELDO, London, 29 June 1964, 605 UNTS 370

EPO Privileges and Immunities Protocol: Protocol on Privileges and Immunities of the European Patent Organization, 1065 UNTS 199

IAEA Privileges and Immunities Agreement: Agreement on the Privileges and Immunities of the International Atomic Energy Agency, Approved by the Board of Governors, 1 July 1959, 374 UNTS 147

UN General Convention: Convention on the Privileges and Immunities of the United Nations 1946, Adopted by the General Assembly of the United Nations on 13 February 1946, 1 UNTS 15

UN Special Convention: Convention on the Privileges and Immunities of the Specialized Agencies 1947, Approved by the General Assembly of the United Nations on 21 November 1947, 33 UNTS 261

Bilateral agreements

Agence de Cooperation Culturelle et Technique Headquarters Agreement: Agreement between the Government of the French Republic and the Agency for Cultural and Technical Co-operation Concerning the Headquarters of the Agency and its Privileges and Immunities in French Territory, Paris, 30 August 1972, 961 UNTS 272

EMBL Headquarters Agreement: Headquarters Agreement Between the Federal Republic of Germany and the European Molecular Biology Laboratory, 10 December 1974, *Bundesgesetzblatt* 1975 II 933

EPO Sub-Office Headquarters Agreement: Agreement Between the Republic of Austria and the European Patent Organization Concerning the Headquarters of the Vienna Sub-Office of the European Patent Office, Vienna, 2 July 1990, *Bundesgesetzblatt* No. 672/1990

FAO Headquarters Agreement: Agreement Regarding the Headquarters of the FAO, Washington, 31 October 1950, *Gazzeta Ufficiale*, 27 January 1951, No. 22; 1409 UNTS 521

FAO–Italy Exchange of Notes, Rome, 20/23 December 1986; reprinted in FAO, 'Constitutional and General Legal Matters, Annex I' (1986) *United Nations Juridical Yearbook* 156

ILO–Swiss Agreement 1946: Agreement Between the Swiss Federal Council and the ILO Concerning the Legal Status of the International Labour Organisation in Switzerland, 11 March 1946, reprinted in Martin Hill, *Immunities and Privileges of International Officials, The Experience of the League of Nations* (Washington DC, 1947), 248

ITC Headquarters Agreement: Headquarters Agreement Between the Government of the United Kingdom and the International Tin Council, London, 9 February 1972, 834 UNTS 287

Iran–United States Claims Tribunal Host State Agreement: Dutch Host State Agreement with the Iran–United States Claims Tribunal, The Hague, 6/24 September 1990, (1990) 29 *Tractatenblad Jaargang* No. 1, No. 150

League of Nations Swiss *modus vivendi*: Communications from the Swiss Federal Council Concerning Diplomatic Immunities to be Accorded to the Staff of the League of Nations, Geneva, 18/20 September 1926, (1926) *League of Nations Official Journal* 1422, reprinted in Martin Hill, *Immunities and Privileges of International Officials, The Experience of the League of Nations* (Washington DC, 1947), 138

OPEC Fund Headquarters Agreement 1981: Agreement Between the Republic of Austria and the OPEC Fund for International Development Regarding the Headquarters of the Fund, Vienna, 21 April 1981, *Bundesgesetzblatt* No. 248/1982

UN Headquarters Agreement 1947: Agreement Between the United Nations and the United States of America Regarding the Headquarters of the United Nations at Lake Success, 26 June 1947, 11 UNTS 11

UN–Swiss Interim Arrangement 1946: Interim Arrangement on Privileges and Immunities of the United Nations Concluded Between the Secretary-General of the United Nations and the Swiss Federal Council, Berne and New York, 11 June–1 July 1946, 1 UNTS 163

UN Economic Commission for Latin America–Chile Agreement: Agreement Between Chile and the UN Economic Commission for Latin America, 16 February 1953, 314 UNTS 49

UNIDO Headquarters Agreement 1967: Agreement Between the United Nations and the Republic of Austria Regarding the Headquarters of the United Nations Industrial Development Organization, New York, 13 April 1967, 600 UNTS 93

WHO–Egypt Agreement: Agreement Between the WHO and Egypt for the Purposes of Determining the Privileges, Immunities and Facilities to be Granted in Egypt by the Government to the Organization, Cairo, 25 March 1951, 223 UNTS 90

WHO–Philippines Host Agreement: Agreement Between the WHO and the Government of the Philippines on the Privileges, Immunities and Facilities to be Granted by the Government of the Philippines to the WHO, Manila, 22 July 1951, 149 UNTS 198

Other treaties

Brussels Convention on Jurisdiction and the Enforcement of Judgments in Civil and Commercial Matters 1968, OJ No. 304/1978

European Convention for the Protection of Human Rights and Fundamental Freedoms, Rome, 4 November 1950, 213 UNTS 221

European Convention on State Immunity of 1972, UNTS Reg. No. 25699, reprinted in (1972) 11 ILM 420

Hague Convention on the Recognition of the Legal Personality of Foreign Companies, Associations and Foundations, 1 June 1956, *Recueil des Conventions de la Haye adoptés par les 7e, 8e et 9e sessions* (1961), 28

International Covenant on Civil and Political Rights, Adopted by the UN General Assembly, 16 December 1966 (UN General Assembly Resolution 2200), 999 UNTS 171

Vienna Convention on Consular Relations, 24 April 1963, 596 UNTS 261

Vienna Convention on Diplomatic Relations, 18 April 1961, 500 UNTS 95

Vienna Convention on the Law of Treaties, 23 May 1969, 1155 UNTS 331

Vienna Convention on the Law of Treaties Between States and International Organizations and Between International Organizations, 21 March 1986; reprinted in (1986) 25 ILM 543

Statutes of international tribunals

ICJ Statute: Statute of the International Court of Justice, 26 June 1945, (1946–7) *United Nations Yearbook* 843

ILO Administrative Tribunal Statute: Statute of the Administrative Tribunal of the International Labour Organisation, adopted by the International Labour Conference on 9 October 1946 and amended on June 1949 and 17 June 1986, reprinted in C. de Cooker (ed.), *International Administration* (looseleaf, The Hague, Boston and London, 1989–), DOC.3

UN Administrative Tribunal Statute: Statute of the UN Administrative Tribunal, adopted by General Assembly Resolution 351 A (IV), 24 November 1949, amended by General Assembly Resolution 782 B (VIII), 9 December 1953 and General Assembly Resolution 957 (X), 8 November 1955

World Bank Administrative Tribunal Statute: Statute of the World Bank Administrative Tribunal, adopted by the Boards of Governors of the IBRD, the IDA and the IFC on 30 April 1980

Other international documents

Amicus curiae brief of the UN in *Marvin R. Broadbent et al.* v. *OAS et al.*, reprinted in (1980) *United Nations Juridical Yearbook* 227

Amicus curiae brief of the US in *Marvin R. Broadbent et al.* v. *OAS et al.*, reprinted in part in (1978) *Digest of US Practice in International Law* 115

General Comment Nos. 7 and 20, 'Article 7', adopted by the Human Rights Committee under Article 40(4) of the International Covenant on Civil and Political Rights, 37 UN GAOR Supp. (No. 40) Annex V, 94, para. 1 (1982) and UN Doc. No. CCPR/C/21/Rev.1/Add.3, 7 April 1992

ILC Draft Articles on Jurisdictional Immunities of States and Their Property and Commentary Thereto, UN Doc. A/46/10, reprinted in *Yearbook of the International Law Commission* (1991), vol. II, Part Two, 12–62

ILC Draft Articles and Report on Relations Between States and International Organizations in Leonardo Díaz-González (Special Rapporteur), 'Fourth Report on Relations Between States and International Organizations (Second Part of the Topic)' (UN Doc. A/CN.4/424) *Yearbook of the International Law Commission* (1989), vol. II, Part One, 153–68

Statement of the Austrian delegate to the 44th UN General Assembly concerning Draft Article 7 submitted by the ILC Special Rapporteur on Relations Between States and International Organizations (Second Part of the Topic) reprinted in 'Recent Austrian Practice in International Law', Part B, in (1991) 42 *Austrian Journal of Public and International Law* 542

UN Regulation No. 4, General Assembly Resolution 41/210, reprinted in Szasz, 'The United Nations Legislates to Limit its Liability' (1987) 81 *American Journal of International Law* 739–44 at 742, note 14

Universal Declaration of Human Rights, 10 December 1948, UN General Assembly Resolution 217 (III 1948)

US State Department's Tate Letter of 1952, (1952) 26 *Department of State Bulletin* 984

National legislation

Australia

Foreign States Immunities Act 1985, reprinted in (1985) 25 ILM 715

Austria

Cartel Law 1988, *Bundesgesetzblatt* No. 600/1988

Code of Civil Procedure, *Reichsgesetzblatt* No. 113/1895

Constitution

Introductory Law to the Norms on Jurisdiction, *Reichsgesetzblatt* No. 110/1895

Law on the Granting of Privileges and Immunities to International Organizations, Federal Act of 14 December 1977, *Bundesgesetzblatt* No. 677/1977, English text in (1977) *United Nations Juridical Yearbook* 3

Canada

State Immunity Act 1982, reprinted in (1982) 21 ILM 798

Denmark

Constitution

France

Constitution

Germany

Basic Law

Law on the Accession of the Federal Republic of Germany to the Special Convention and on the Granting of Privileges and Immunities to other International Organizations, *Bundesgesetzblatt*, 1954 II, 639

Second Regulation on Privileges and Immunities for Eurocontrol of 29 August 1979

India

Diplomatic Privileges (Extension) Act 1944

Italy

Constitution

Japan

Constitution

Spain

Constitution

United Kingdom

Diplomatic Privileges (Extension) Act 1944

Inmarsat (Immunities and Privileges) Order 1979, SI 1979 No. 187, reprinted in (1979) 50 *British Yearbook of International Law* 307

International Organisations Act 1968

International Tin Council (Immunities and Privileges) Order 1972, SI 1972 No. 120

State Immunity Act 1978, reprinted in (1978) 17 ILM 1123

United States

Constitution

Foreign Sovereign Immunities Act 1975, 90 Stat. 2891, 28 USCA §§ 1330 *et seq*

International Organizations Immunities Act 1945, 59 Stat. 669, 22 USCA §§ 288 *et seq*

Abbreviations

Add.	Addendum
All ER	*All England Law Reports*
AMF	Arab Monetary Fund
AOI	Arab Organization for Industrialization
App.	Appellate
ASECNA	Agence pour la sécurité de la navigation aérienne en Afrique et à Madagascar
BGE	*Entscheidungen des Bundesgerichts (Decisions of the Federal Supreme Court)* (Switzerland)
BVerfGE	*Entscheidungen des Bundesverfassungsgerichts (Decisions of the Federal Constitutional Court)* (Germany)
BVerwGE	*Entscheidungen des Bundesverwaltungsgerichts (Decisions of the Federal Administrative Court)* (Germany)
CA	Court of Appeal(s)
CDI	Centre pour le développement industriel
CERN	(Conseil) Organisation Européenne pour la Recherche Nucléaire / European Organization for Nuclear Research
CMLR	*Common Market Law Reports*
Comsat	Communications Satellite Corporation
Ct	Court
Ct Cl.	Court of Claims
CTS	*Consolidated Treaty Series*
EBRD	European Bank for Reconstruction and Development
EC	European Community/Communities
ECJ	European Court of Justice
ECOSOC	(United Nations) Economic and Social Council
ECR	*European Court Reports*

ECSC	European Coal and Steel Community
EEC	European Economic Community
EEOC	Equal Employment Opportunity Commission
EFTA	European Free Trade Association
ELDO	European Launcher Development Organization
EMBL	European Molecular Biology Laboratory
EPO	European Patent Organization
ESA	European Space Agency
ESRO	European Space Research Organisation
EU	European Union
Euratom	European Atomic Energy Community
Eurocontrol	European Organization for the Safety of Air Navigation
F. 2d	*Federal Reporter* (Second Series)
F. Supp.	*Federal Supplement*
FAO	Food and Agriculture Organization
FSIA	(US) Foreign Sovereign Immunities Act 1976
GAOR	*Official Records of the (UN) General Assembly*
GATT	General Agreement on Tariffs and Trade
General Convention	Convention on the Privileges and Immunities of the United Nations 1946
HAFSE	Headquarters Allied Forces Southern Europe
IAEA	International Atomic Energy Agency
IATA	International Air Transport Association
IBRD	International Bank for Reconstruction and Development
ICAO	International Civil Aviation Organization
ICC	International Chamber of Commerce
ICCPR	International Covenant on Civil and Political Rights
ICEM	Intergovernmental Committee for European Migration
ICJ	International Court of Justice
ICRC	International Committee of the Red Cross
ICRISAT	International Crops Research Institute for the Semi-Arid Tropics
IDA	International Development Association
IDB	Inter-American Development Bank
IDI	Institut de droit international
IFC	International Finance Corporation
ILA	International Law Association
ILC	International Law Commission
ILM	*International Legal Materials*
ILO	International Labour Organisation

ILR	*International Law Reports*
IMF	International Monetary Fund
IMO	International Maritime Organization
Inmarsat	International Maritime Satellite Organization
Intelsat	International Telecommunications Satellite Organization
Interpol	International Criminal Police Organization
IOC	International Olympic Committee
IOIA	(US) International Organizations Immunities Act 1945
IRO	International Refugee Organization
ITC	International Tin Council
ITU	International Telecommunication Union
LNTS	*League of Nations Treaty Series*
MIGA	Multilateral Investment Guarantee Agency
NATO	North Atlantic Treaty Organization
NGO	non-governmental organization
NLRB	National Labor Relations Board
OAS	Organization of American States
OAU	Organization of African Unity
OECD	Organization for Economic Cooperation and Development
OEEC	Organization for European Economic Cooperation
OGH	Oberster Gerichtshof (Supreme Court) (Austria)
OGH/Z	*Entscheidungen des Obersten Gerichtshofs in Zivilsachen (Decisions of the Supreme Court in Civil Matters)* (Austria)
OJ	*Official Journal of the European Communities*
OPEC	Organization of Petroleum Exporting Countries
PAHO	Pan American Health Organization
PCIJ	Permanent Court of International Justice
Special Convention	Convention on the Privileges and Immunities of the Specialized Agencies 1947
Stat.	Statute
Supp.	Supplement
TIAS	(United States) *Treaties and other International Acts Series*
UNCIO	*United Nations Conference on International Organization*
UNDP	United Nations Development Programme
UNESCO	United Nations Educational, Scientific and Cultural Organization
UNHCR	United Nations High Commissioner for Refugees
UNIDO	United Nations Industrial Development Organization
UNRRA	United Nations Relief and Rehabilitation Administration

UNRWA	United Nations Relief and Works Agency for Palestine Refugees in the Near East
UNTS	United Nations Treaty Series
UPU	Union Postale Universelle / Universal Postal Union
USCA	*United States Code Annotated*
WEU	Western European Union
WHO	World Health Organization
WIPO	World Intellectual Property Organization
WLR	*Weekly Law Reports*
WTO	World Trade Organization

1   Purpose, subject and methodology of this study

Introduction

Studies of international organizations as parties to legal proceedings before national courts have been dealt with in the past mainly using traditional concepts, the two most important of which have focused on the domestic legal personality of international organizations and their immunity from suit. This study is broader in scope. It does not limit itself to issues of immunity or personality and thus does not view the issue from a preconceived legal point of view. Rather, it takes a primarily phenomenological approach: it describes how courts respond to international organizations in proceedings before them.

Although this study focuses on decided cases, it will also analyze scholarly writings and, in particular, the work of the International Law Commission (ILC), the Institut de droit international (IDI), the International Law Association (ILA) and other scholarly bodies entrusted with the codification and development of international law. However, in view of the abundant literature on issues concerning the legal personality of international organizations and their privileges and immunities, theoretical reflections will be kept to a minimum. An effort will be made to address the problems relevant to deciding actual cases. The emphasis is on the way decision-makers handle such problems in the real world of national courts. Therefore, this study will focus on national case law as well as on other legal documents potentially manifesting state practice. This study will not, however, confine itself to analyzing 'how national judges behave' in settling particular types of disputes involving international law. Rather, the comparative analysis will provide a basis for finding 'desired models of [judicial] behavior' for the specific kinds of problems at issue.[1]

---

[1] *Cf.* the similar approach taken by the Institut de droit international in 'The Activities of

The purpose of analyzing the relevant case law should not be limited to elaborating whether a consistent practice can be found – which in turn might help to ascertain possible customary rules[2] – or to see whether the international obligations of states have been fulfilled. Rather, this study concentrates on how domestic courts actually deal with such cases and investigates whether certain trends might ultimately lead to new ways of approaching disputes involving international organizations, that is, to a method that is different from the currently predominant party-focused immunity.[3] In this respect, a number of questions are raised: how do domestic courts resolve questions concerning the legal personality of international organizations and their immunity from suit? What are the policy issues underlying immunity claims and are they made explicit by the parties and/or by the courts? What kinds of legal tools are employed to solve such problems? Do courts actively seek to adjudicate disputes involving international organizations or are they rather trying to abstain from them?

This study focuses on the attitudes of and techniques used by national courts when confronted with disputes involving international organizations. Under what circumstances they exercise or refrain from exercising their adjudicatory jurisdiction and their justifications for so doing, are matters which lie at the core of this investigation. Thus, decisions of international courts and tribunals are, in principle, outside the scope of this study. However, such decisions will be analyzed in so far as they contain elements relevant to the question of how national courts should treat international organizations, for example international decisions addressing issues of domestic legal personality or immunities and privileges of international organizations.[4]

National Judges and the International Relations of Their State' (1993 I) 65 *Annuaire de l'Institut de Droit International* 327–448 at 329.

[2] In the course of this investigation national court decisions will be viewed as potential 'sources' of international law, not only in the sense of Article 38(1)(d) of the Statute of the ICJ as a supplementary source and evidence of international law, but rather as relevant state practice for the formation, or – to be proven – the confirmation, of customary law. *Cf.* Antonio Cassese, 'L'immunité de juridiction civile des organisations internationales dans la jurisprudence italienne' (1984) 30 *Annuaire français de droit international* 556–66 at 566; Sir Hersch Lauterpacht, 'Decisions of Municipal Courts as a Source of International Law' (1929) 10 *British Yearbook of International Law* 65–95 at 67; Karl Zemanek, 'What is "State Practice" and Who Makes It?' in Ulrich Beyerlin, Michael Bothe, Rainer Hofmann and Ernst-Ulrich Petersmann (eds.), *Recht zwischen Umbruch und Bewahrung. Festschrift für Rudolf Bernhardt* (Berlin, 1995), 289–306 at 294. *Cf.* also the discussion of potential customary personality and immunity standards at pp. 45*ff* below.

[3] See, in particular, Parts I and III of this study.

[4] Thus, decisions of international tribunals such as the International Court of Justice, the

In a broader sense, this analysis of national case law will also contribute to the issue of international law before national tribunals,[5] since issues of the domestic legal personality and judicial immunity of international organizations stand at the intersection between domestic and international law.[6] In fact, most of the legal problems involved concern the interpretation and application of treaty or customary law. Although the majority of cases arise from routine employment or contractual disputes between international organizations and private parties, these cases sometimes have strong political implications.

This book is divided into three major parts. Part I analyzes the attitudes of national courts towards disputes involving international organizations. It describes the various legal approaches taken by courts when confronted with international organizations as parties to legal proceedings. It discusses the applicable legal norms resulting in the adjudication or non-adjudication of such disputes and it focuses on the legal techniques used to avoid such cases or to confront them. Among those legal techniques, jurisdictional immunity is certainly the most prominent but it is by no means the only one: issues concerning the legal personality of international organizations and, in particular, the scope of their personality under domestic law are of particular relevance, as are also the various non-justiciability doctrines.

Part II discusses the policy issues *pro* and *contra* the adjudication of disputes involving international organizations by national courts. It analyzes the rationale for immunizing international organizations from domestic litigation, especially the frequently asserted functional need for immunity. It will also devote substantial space to a discussion of the burden immunity places upon third parties, and the question of how far such a burden can be tolerated.

Part III summarizes the conclusions and seeks to present some suggestions for the future development of this area of the law. It identifies

European Court of Justice or international arbitral bodies, of human rights organs, such as the European Commission of Human Rights and the European Court of Human Rights, as well as of administrative tribunals of international organizations, such as the World Bank Administrative Tribunal, or the OAS and the UN Administrative Tribunals, will be analyzed as far as they prove to be relevant for the main topic.

[5] *Cf.* recent ILA Committee work. Committee on International Law in Municipal Courts, ILA, *Report of the 66th Conference, Buenos Aires* (1994), 326ff. See also Thomas M. Franck and Gregory H. Fox (eds.), *International Law Decisions in National Courts* (Irvington-on-Hudson, NY, 1996).

[6] See also Bernhard Schlüter, *Die innerstaatliche Rechtsstellung der internationalen Organisationen unter besonderer Berücksichtigung der Rechtslage in der Bundesrepublik Deutschland* (Cologne, Berlin, Bonn and Munich, 1972), 1, for issues of domestic legal personality.

trends in the case law, and asks whether some of them could substitute for or modify the presently predominant immunity concept with a more flexible principle exempting certain types of dispute from domestic adjudication – a principle that would at the same time guarantee the functioning and independence of international organizations and not unduly impair the access of private parties to a fair dispute settlement procedure.

Subject of the study

The subject of this study is the public international organization before domestic courts. Since national courts sometimes treat other entities, not falling under a strict definition of international organizations, as if they were international organizations, these will also be covered with the necessary caution in mind.[7]

Some clarification is therefore needed of the entities regarded as genuine international organizations as opposed to those other entities also receiving attention in this study. Some terminological explanation of such crucial terms as 'personality', 'immunity', 'privilege' and related notions is also required.

International organizations

The need to define international organizations arises not only from the scholarly tradition of limiting and clarifying the issues and topics set out for detailed discussion in the course of a learned investigation. For this particular purpose – ascertaining rules concerning the international and domestic legal personality of international organizations that might be relevant for domestic courts in deciding cases involving international organizations – some clarification of the nature of the subject of the investigation might prove valuable for the insights it will give into the factors which may be decisive for the way courts treat international organizations.

This study focuses on what are called 'intergovernmental organiz-

---

[7] Such similar treatment might result from an erroneous qualification of certain entities as international organizations, or from a specific legal rule calling for the application of rules relating to international organization to non-international organizations, or from the fact that national courts consider them to be in a similar situation. *Cf.* pp. 11 and 171–2 below.

ations',[8] 'inter-state organizations'[9] or 'public international organizations',[10] which will be referred to hereinafter for convenience simply as
'international organizations'.[11] Although there is no generally accepted
definition of international organizations,[12] there seems to be wide consensus on their constitutive elements.[13] International organizations are
entities consisting predominantly of states, created by international
agreements, having their own organs, and entrusted to fulfil some
common (usually public) tasks.[14] Sometimes the possession of a legal
personality distinct from its member states is included in definitions of
an international organization.[15] However, this distinction appears to be

---

[8] *Cf.* the definition of international organizations as 'intergovernmental organizations' in
Article 2(1)(i) of the Vienna Convention on the Law of Treaties and in Article 2(1)(i) of the
Vienna Convention on the Law of Treaties Between States and International Organiz-
ations or Between International Organizations.

[9] Michel Virally, 'La notion de fonction dans la théorie de l'organisation internationale' in
La Communauté Internationale. Melanges offerts à Charles Rousseau (Paris, 1974), 277–300 at 277.

[10] Henry G. Schermers, *International Institutional Law* (Alphen aan den Rijn and Rockville, 2nd
edn, 1980), 8; Louis Henkin, Richard C. Pugh, Oscar Schachter and Hans Smit, *International
Law* (2nd edn, St Paul, MN, 1987), 318. See also the definition of international organization 'as public international organization in which the United States participates
pursuant to any treaty' under section 1 of the US IOIA.

[11] It is important to distinguish the notion of international organizations as legal entities
from the concept of 'international organization' (usually in the singular) which describes
inter-state cooperation or generally refers to the framework and structure of the international society (of states). Georges Abi-Saab (ed.), *The Concept of International Organization*
(Paris, 1981), 9. Mario Bettati, *Le droit des organisations internationales* (Paris, 1987), 9. This
term is mainly used in Anglo-American international relations theory. The few examples
of German usages of this concept (e.g., Hans Wehberg, 'Entwicklungsstufen der internationalen Organisation' (1953–5) 52 *Friedens-Warte* 193–218) have not been widely adopted.

[12] The ILC deliberately omitted a definition of international organizations when it began
considering the now-abandoned topic of relations between states and international
organizations (second part of the topic) 'in order to avoid starting interminable discussions on theoretical and doctrinal questions, on which there were conflicting opinions in the Commission and the General Assembly, as was only natural'. Díaz-González in
Yearbook of the International Law Commission (1985), vol. I, 284.

[13] Schermers, *International Institutional Law*, 5.

[14] Rudolf Bindschedler, 'International Organizations, General Aspects' in Rudolf Bernhardt
(ed.), *Encyclopedia of Public International Law* (2nd edn, 1995), vol. II, 1289–309 at 1289; Enno
J. Harders, 'Haftung und Verantwortlichkeit Internationaler Organisationen' in Rüdiger
Wolfrum (ed.), *Handbuch Vereinte Nationen* (2nd edn, Munich, 1991), 248–58 at 248; Karl
Zemanek, *Das Vertragsrecht der internationalen Organisationen* (Vienna, 1957), 9ff; *Restatement
(Third) of the Law, The Foreign Relations Law of the United States* (ed. American Law Institute, St
Paul, MN, 1987), § 221.

[15] *Cf* Bettati, *Le droit des organisations internationales*, 12. See also the definition of an
international organization in the IDI draft resolution on 'The legal consequences for
member states of the non-fulfilment by international organizations of their obligations
toward third parties', Article 1(a) of the Draft Resolution in (1995 I) 66 *Annuaire de l'Institut
de Droit International* 465.

rather a consequence than a constitutive criterion of an international organization.[16] Also, the existence of an independent will of the organization and of permanent organs competent to express that will as a 'basic criterion for distinguishing an international organization from other entities'[17] seems to focus more on the result than on the constitutive elements of an international organization.[18]

International organizations are created by states, and more recently sometimes with the participation of other international organizations.[19] There is some controversy among legal commentators over whether two states by themselves could set up an international organization or whether at least three states are required.[20] In practice, domestic courts do not seem to be aware of this scholarly debate and have been willing to accept without hesitation that, for instance, bilateral commissions or tribunals can be regarded as international organizations.[21]

---

[16] See pp. 57ff below.

[17] Lacleta Muñoz in *Yearbook of the International Law Commission* (1985), vol. I, 296.

[18] See also the definition of an international organization in the IDI draft resolution on 'The legal consequences for member states of the non-fulfilment by international organizations of their obligations toward third parties' requiring the existence of an organization's 'own will'. Article 2(b) provides: 'The existence of a *volonté distincte*, as well as capacity to enter into contracts, to own property and to sue and be sued, is evidence of international legal personality.' Draft Resolution, (1995 I) 66 *Annuaire de l'Institut de Droit International* 465.

[19] For instance, the EEC became a member of the (Sixth) International Tin Council in 1982; the League of Nations was a founding member of the International Institute for the Unification of Private Law (Unidroit) in 1926. *Cf.* Henry G. Schermers, 'International Organizations as Members of Other International Organizations' in Bernhardt, Geck, Jaenicke and Steinberger (eds.), *Völkerrecht als Rechtsordnung, Internationale Gerichtsbarkeit, Menschenrechte, Festschrift Mosler* (Berlin, Heidelberg and New York, 1983), 823–37 at 823ff; Ignaz Seidl-Hohenveldern and Gerhard Loibl, *Das Recht der Internationalen Organisationen einschließlich der Supranationalen Gemeinschaften* (6th edn, Cologne, Berlin, Bonn and Munich, 1996), 6.

[20] Zemanek, *Das Vertragsrecht der internationalen Organisationen*, 11, argues that it is part of the essential nature of international organizations that they are formed by a multilateral treaty. This view would require at least three participating states in order to form an international organization. Seidl-Hohenveldern and Loibl, *Das Recht der Internationalen Organisationen*, 5, on the other hand, expressly state that at least two states must participate in an organization. See also Rudolph Bernhardt, 'Qualifikation und Anwendungsbereich des internen Rechts internationaler Organisationen' (1973) 12 *Berichte der Deutschen Gesellschaft für Völkerrecht* 7–46 at 7; and Sucharitkul in *Yearbook of the International Law Commission* (1985), vol. I, 287.

[21] In *Soucheray et al. v. Corps of Engineers of the United States Army et al.*, US District Court WD Wisconsin, 7 November 1979, a US district court held that the US–Canadian International Joint Commission regulating the water level of the Great Lakes (an 'international agency' in the words of the court) was immune from suit under the IOIA – a finding that presupposes that the Commission is an international organization. Even more explicitly the US Court of Claims held that 'the International Joint Commission is an international organization' enjoying immunity. *Edison Sault Electric Co. v. United States*, US Court of

International organizations are normally set up by international agreement,[22] usually by formal written agreements, i.e. by treaties. The terminology used – whether the constituent treaty is called convention, charter, constitution, statute, etc. – is irrelevant. However, international organizations can also be founded by implicit agreement which might be expressed through identical domestic legislation (e.g., the Nordic Council),[23] or by a resolution adopted during an inter-state conference (e.g., Comecon).[24]

It is further commonly thought that international organizations require a certain institutional minimum, i.e. organs that perform the tasks entrusted to the organization.[25] In practice it is sometimes difficult to distinguish organs of international organizations from mere 'treaty administering organs'[26] set up by international agreements falling short of true international organization status.[27]

Finally, it has been asserted that only those inter-state entities which meet an 'official public purpose' test can qualify as international organizations.[28] It seems, however, that this requirement is no longer generally

Claims, 23 March 1977, reaffirmed in *Erosion Victims of Lake Superior Regulation, etc.* v. *United States*, US Court of Claims, 25 March 1987. See also the Dutch case of *AS* v. *Iran–United States Claims Tribunal*, Local Court of The Hague, 8 June 1983; District Court of The Hague, 9 July 1984; Supreme Court, 20 December 1985, involving the bilateral Iran–United States Claims Tribunal which was treated as an international organization as far as immunity was concerned.

[22] Peter H. F. Bekker, *The Legal Position of Intergovernmental Organizations. A Functional Necessity Analysis of Their Legal Status and Immunities* (Dordrecht, Boston and London, 1994), 39; Schermers, *International Institutional Law*, 9; and Zemanek, *Das Vertragsrecht der internationalen Organisationen*, 9.

[23] Axel Berg, 'Nordic Council and Nordic Council of Ministers' in Rudolf Bernhardt (ed.), *Encyclopedia of Public International Law* (1983), vol. VI, 261–3 at 261.

[24] Schermers, *International Institutional Law*, 9.

[25] Article 1(a) of the Draft Resolution, (1995 I) 66 *Annuaire de l'Institut de Droit International* 465; Zemanek, *Das Vertragsrecht der internationalen Organisationen*, 13.

[26] Waldemar Hummer, 'Reichweite und Grenzen unmittelbarer Anwendbarkeit der Freihandelsabkommen' in Hans-Georg Koppensteiner (ed.), *Rechtsfragen der Freihandelsabkommen der Europäischen Wirtschaftsgemeinschaft mit den EFTA-Staaten* (Vienna, 1987), 43–83 at 44.

[27] *Restatement (Third)*, § 221, Comment b. *Cf.* also the diverging qualification of the nature of the 'joint committees' administering the 1972 Free Trade Agreements between EFTA states and the EEC. While Hummer, 'Reichweite und Grenzen', 44, calls them 'treaty administering organs' (*Vertragsanwendungsorgane*), Theo Ohlinger, 'Rechtsfragen des Freihandelsabkommens zwischen Osterreich und der EWG' (1974) 34 *Zeitschrift für ausländisches öffentliches Recht und Völkerrecht* 655–88 at 681, note 79, seems to be ready to regard them as organs of an (unnamed) international organization created by the Free Trade Agreements.

[28] Ignaz Seidl-Hohenveldern, 'The Legal Personality of International and Supranational Organizations' (1965) 21 *Revue egyptienne de droit international* 35–72 at 37; and Ignaz Seidl-Hohenveldern, *Corporations in and under International Law* (Cambridge, 1987), 72.

accepted.[29] If the public purpose test were upheld, this would have important implications for the present discussion. According to its adherents, inter-state entities which pursue an aim 'which under domestic law the States concerned would fulfil as subjects of private law rather then as subjects of public law' could not be labelled international organizations.[30] The issues of domestic legal personality and immunity from national jurisdiction, however, frequently arise in contexts where international organizations act like 'subjects of private law'. If all those entities that are acting in a private law setting were excluded from the range of international organizations, few issues of interest here would arise in practice. It seems, however, that even the adherents of a 'public purpose requirement' do not always support this result of eliminating inter-state entities acting like private parties from the definition of international organizations. They do not dispute that international organizations might engage in private law affairs in the course of their activities. What they obviously want to exclude from the range of international organizations are entities which fulfil no public purpose at all and are exclusively charged with 'private law tasks'.[31] This restricted view, however, faces two major practical problems. First, from a theoretical point of view, the dichotomy of public/private law activities is difficult to rationalize on an international law level. It is true that international law has to make the distinction in various fields, especially in the sovereign immunity context or for attributing acts to states for the purposes of state responsibility, but it is still far from being a generally accepted distinction. Secondly, with the rise of international organizations entrusted with market regu-

---

[29] Rosalyn Higgins, 'The Legal Consequences for Member States of the Non-Fulfilment by International Organizations of Their Obligations Toward Third Parties – Preliminary Exposé and Draft Questionnaire' (1995 I) 66 *Annuaire de l'Institut de Droit International* 249–89 at 254; and Shihata, 'Réponse' (1995 I) 66 *Annuaire de l'Institut de Droit International* 311. *Cf.* also the differentiation made by Schermers, *International Institutional Law*, 8*ff*, between public and private international organizations who – although speaking of public international organizations – states only three requirements (established by international agreement, having organs, established under international law) that have to be fulfilled by an entity in order to qualify as 'public' international organization.

[30] Seidl-Hohenveldern, 'The Legal Personality of International and Supranational Organizations', 37. In his more recent book on international corporations, Seidl-Hohenveldern maintains this distinction and uses an even more pertinent dichotomy when he differentiates between organizations *iure imperii* and organizations *iure gestionis* with the latter being mere intergovernmental enterprises lacking international personality. In the former group he includes those, the acts of which, if done by a single state, would be acts *iure imperii* while the latter comprises entities with a commercial focus which he calls 'common inter-state enterprises'. Seidl-Hohenveldern, *Corporations*, 109*ff*.

[31] See p. 10 below.

latory functions to be carried out either by directly dealing on the marketplace (organizations administering commodity agreements)[32] or by regulating its members' market behaviour (certain export-regulating organizations),[33] the issue of whether these organizations should be seen as private or public actors has become increasingly difficult.[34] Moreover, even undisputedly 'public' international organizations undoubtedly perform a number of private law acts.

Other international bodies

Although this study is devoted to international organizations, other 'international' bodies should not be overlooked where decisions dealing with such entities might prove relevant for the subject of this book. The two most important groups of such other international entities are international tribunals and so-called international public corporations. International non-governmental organizations and transnational corporations – although also frequently associated when dealing with international organizations – are of less importance in the present context.

International tribunals

International tribunals[35] are in many respects comparable to international organizations. As far as the specific topics of personality and immunity are concerned, it is interesting to note that, in fact, many international tribunals have been accorded such status and prerogative either by international agreement or express domestic legislation or even implicitly.[36] Some international courts and tribunals are, of course, part of larger organizations and derive their legal status from them. Nevertheless, there are also frequently specific instruments addressing their privi-

---

[32] E.g., the International Tin Council. See pp. 118*ff* below.

[33] E.g., OPEC. See also Henkin, Pugh, Schachter and Smit, *International Law*, 343.

[34] *Cf.* the difficulty of US courts in characterizing OPEC's activities as *iure imperii* or *iure gestionis* in *International Association of Machinists* v. *OPEC*, US District Court CD Cal., 18 September 1979, *affirmed on other grounds*, US Court of Appeals 9th Cir., 6 July–24 August 1981. See p. 91 below.

[35] *Cf.* Christian Tomuschat, 'International Courts and Tribunals' in Rudolf Bernhardt (ed.), *Encyclopedia of Public International Law* (2nd edn, 1995), vol. II, 1108–15 at 1108*ff*.

[36] For instance, the instrument establishing the Iran–US Claims Tribunal, the Claims Settlement Declaration of Algiers, 19 January 1981, mentions neither the Tribunal's international nor its domestic legal personality. In the view of the Dutch Foreign Ministry, the Tribunal, having been created by an instrument under international law, 'is therefore a joint institution of the two States involved, and has legal personality derived from international law'. Reply to written questions asked in Parliament about the status in the Netherlands of the Iran–US Claims Tribunal in the absence of a treaty between the three countries, Minister for Foreign Affairs, (1984) 15 *Netherlands Yearbook of International Law* 356.

leges and immunities. Decisions by national courts concerning international tribunals may thus be directly relevant for the analysis of their treatment of international organizations.[37]

International public corporations

Common inter-state enterprises,[38] joint international state or quasi-state enterprises,[39] international public corporations,[40] or intergovernmental companies and consortia[41] are interesting intermediate entities between international organizations and private corporations operating internationally. Like international organizations, they are created by states or state bodies and possess their own organs. However, the major distinguishing factor lies in the nature of their tasks, which are generally of a commercial, although not necessarily profit-making, character.[42] Such corporate entities are frequently formed on the basis of a treaty and then established in accordance with a national corporate law.[43] They may be relevant for present purposes where their constitutive agreements expressly provide for a legal status similar to that of an international organization and for comparable privileges and immunities.[44]

[37] For instance, the recognition of the domestic personality of the Iran–US Claims Tribunal by Dutch courts in the *AS* v. *Iran–United States Claims Tribunal* decisions, Local Court of The Hague, 8 June 1983; District Court of The Hague, 9 July 1984. See p. 82 below.

[38] Seidl-Hohenveldern, *Corporations*, 109*ff*; Ignaz Seidl-Hohenveldern, 'Le droit applicable aux entreprises internationales communes, étatiques ou paraétatiques' (1983 I) 60 *Annuaire de l'Institut de Droit International* 1–37 and 97–102 at 1*ff*.

[39] IDI Resolution on the law applicable to joint international state or quasi-state enterprises of an economic nature, adopted at its Helsinki Session 1985, (1986 II) 61 *Annuaire de l'Institut de Droit International* 269.

[40] *Restatement (Third)*, § 221, Comment d.

[41] Henkin, Pugh, Schachter and Smit, *International Law*, 341.

[42] Seidl-Hohenveldern stresses their *iure gestionis* character. Seidl-Hohenveldern, *Corporations*, 109. The IDI Resolution on the law applicable to joint international state or quasi-state enterprises of an economic nature characterizes their tasks as 'for purposes of general economic interest principally through private law procedures'. Article 1(b), (1986 II) 61 *Annuaire de l'Institut de Droit International* 271.

[43] For instance, the creation of Eurofima, the European Company for the Financing of Railway Rolling Stock, was provided for in a treaty of 20 October 1955 between a number of European states. It was then established as a company according to Swiss law. Michael Kenny, 'European Company for the Financing of Railway Rolling Stock (EUROFIMA)' in Rudolf Bernhardt (ed.), *Encyclopedia of Public International Law* (2nd edn, 1995), vol. II, 178–80 at 178*ff*; See also Ignaz Seidl-Hohenveldern, 'Gemeinsame zwischenstaatliche Unternehmen' in Friedrich-Wilhelm Baer-Kaupert, Georg Leistner and Herwig Schwaiger (eds.), *Liber Amicorum Bernhard C. H. Aubin* (Kehl am Rhein and Strasbourg, 1979), 193–216 at 193*ff*, discussing various forms of such entities.

[44] This is the case with Intelsat, the International Telecommunications Satellite Organization, established in 1973 by treaty. See also James Fawcett and Gunnar Schuster, 'Intelsat' in Rudolf Bernhardt (ed.), *Encyclopedia of Public International Law* (2nd edn, 1995), vol. II, 1000–4 at 1000*ff*.

International non-governmental organizations

International non-governmental organizations[45] (NGOs), usually formed by private persons operating on a transnational level, but regularly associated under a domestic system of law,[46] lie beyond the scope of the present study. As it happens, however, they may sometimes also be accorded privileges and immunities and thus be treated by national legal systems similar to international organizations proper. National court decisions reflecting such a legal situation will thus be taken into account in this study.[47]

Transnational corporations

Transnational corporations, sometimes also called multinational companies, are commercial entities organized under a specific national company law that are commercially active in more than one state, commonly through subsidiaries.[48]

In the past, some of these corporations have been accorded privileges and immunities, including immunity from local jurisdiction, by territorial sovereigns, in particular, in the older type of oil concession agreements.[49] In this very limited respect, national case law involving such

[45] Article 71 of the UN Charter.
[46] According to the UN Economic and Social Council which 'may make suitable arrangements' with NGOs (Article 71 of the UN Charter), '[a]ny international organization which is not established by international agreement shall be considered as a non-governmental organization for the purposes of these arrangements'. Resolution 288 B (X), para. 8, 27 February 1950, ECOSOC, Official Records, Fifth Year, Tenth Session. See also ECOSOC Resolution 1296 (XLIV), 23 May 1968.
[47] Cf. *International Catholic Migration Commission* v. *Pura Calleja*, Philippine Supreme Court, 28 September 1990; and *Kapisanan Ng Manggagawa AT Tac Sa IRRI (International Rice Research Institute)* v. *Secretary of Labor and Employment*, Philippine Supreme Court, 28 September 1990, involving NGOs that enjoy special privileges and immunities as a matter of national law. See pp. 171f note 9 below. Cf. also the Swiss practice to conclude fiscal agreements with 'quasi-governmental' international organizations, like IATA or the Union internationale pour la conservation de la nature et de ses ressources, conferring certain privileges and immunities upon them. On IATA, see *Jenni, Mouvement Vigilance et Groupe Vigilant du Grand Conseil Genevois* v. *Conseil d'Etat du canton de Genève*, Federal Tribunal, 4 October 1978; on the Union see (1986) 42 *Annuaire suisse de droit international* 72ff. See also p. 171 below.
[48] See Peter Fischer, 'Transnational Enterprises' in Rudolf Bernhardt (ed.), *Encyclopedia of Public International Law* (1985), vol. VIII, 515–19 at 515; Waldemar Hummer, 'Politisch bedeutsame transnationale Akteure an oder unter der Schwelle der Völkerrechtssubjektivität' in Hanspeter Neuhold, Waldemar Hummer and Christoph Schreuer (eds.), Osterreichisches Handbuch des Völkerrechts (2nd edn, Vienna, 1991), 201–16 at 207.
[49] Peter Fischer, *Die internationale Konzession* (Vienna and New York, 1974), 321; see also Wilhelm Karl Geck, 'Konzession' in Strupp and Schlochauer (eds.), *Wörterbuch des Völkerrechts* (1961), vol. II, 301–7 at 301; and Hummer, 'Politisch bedeutsame transnationale Akteure', 210.

corporations may be relevant in elucidating principles applicable to international organizations. Today, however, such far-reaching concessions are rarely made. Thus, transnational corporations are largely irrelevant to the subject of this study.

Some further terminological clarifications

This book investigates legal problems involving international organizations before national courts in general; a major part of it will be devoted to questions of their personality under domestic law and their immunity from the jurisdiction of national courts. It seems appropriate therefore to outline the terminological use of the notions of 'personality' and 'immunity' as well as the relationship between immunity and different forms of state jurisdiction.

'Personality' is normally regarded as the capability of an entity to possess rights and obligations under a specific legal system. National courts frequently refer to these notions as employed in the applicable domestic and international norms, i.e. mainly domestic legislation and constituent treaties of international organizations, as well as headquarters agreements and treaties concerning their privileges and immunities. The majority of these sources speaks of 'legal'[50] or 'juridical'[51] 'personality', or of 'legal'[52] or 'juridical'[53] 'capacity'. Courts and legal writers mainly use the expression 'legal personality', although the other terms are used as well. In most cases, 'personality' is understood as a more fundamental concept relating to the existence of an entity as a subject of law within a specific legal order, whereas 'capacity' is more often regarded as a qualification of personality indicating specific legal powers possessed by an entity having personality. In the course of this

---

[50] *Cf.* Draft Article 5 of the ILC Draft on relations between states and international organizations (second part of the topic) according to which '[i]nternational organizations shall enjoy legal personality under international law and under the internal law of their member States'. Leonardo Díaz-González (Special Rapporteur), 'Fourth Report on Relations Between States and International Organizations (Second Part of the Topic)' (UN Doc. A/CN.4/424) *Yearbook of the International Law Commission* (1989), vol. II, Part One, 153–68 at 157.

[51] *Cf.* Article I(1) of the General Convention providing that '[t]he United Nations shall have juridical personality'. According to Article 2 of the 1976 Agreement Establishing the Arab Monetary Fund, the organization has 'independent juridical personality'.

[52] *Cf.* Article 104 of the UN Charter, according to which '[t]he Organization shall enjoy in the territory of each of its Members such legal capacity as may be necessary for the exercise of its functions and the fulfillment of its purposes'. Article 211 of the EC Treaty provides: 'In each of the Member States, the Community shall enjoy the most extensive legal capacity'.

[53] *Cf.* Article 6, second sentence of the ECSC Treaty stating that 'the Community shall enjoy the most extensive juridical capacity'.

study, this broad distinction will prove relevant for the analysis of two very fundamental avoidance techniques concerning the non-recognition of an organization's personality,[54] on the one hand, and the non-recognition of an organization's capacity to perform certain acts,[55] on the other.

It is always important, however, to keep in mind that personality, capacity, etc. are legal concepts deeply rooted in the various national legal systems, and that different legal systems can differ substantially in the way they define and apply these concepts. Thus, the terminology used by courts and in the legal doctrine of different countries has to be treated with a degree of caution. In particular, it cannot be assumed that the underlying notions are readily transferable.

Both in legal doctrine and in case law, the distinction between 'immunity' and 'privilege' is often blurred. Frequently, one encounters a synonymous use of the two terms.[56] One author has even concluded that "no such distinction [between privileges and immunities] has gained general acceptance.[57] But, even if the terminology used might remain at variance, a clear differentiation of substance can and should be made between the two terms.

In the older literature on the subject, one finds attempts to differentiate according to some material criterion. Some authors associate the term 'immunity' with legal notions such as guarantees or the necessary standard for functioning, while they ascribe to privileges the status of prestige, honour, protocol or courtesy.[58] This approach has not been further pursued, however.

Today's predominantly accepted definition of and differentiation between immunity and privilege concerns issues of the appropriate forum and the applicable law: 'Immunities, as distinct from privileges, confer no substantive exemption from local law but give only procedural protec-

---

[54] See pp. 37ff below.   [55] See pp. 70ff below.

[56] E.g., *Yearbook of the International Law Commission* (1967), vol. II, 222; *Yearbook of the International Law Commission* (1989), vol. II, Part One, 161; *Restatement (Third)*, §467, para. 1. See also *Mendaro* v. *World Bank*, US Court of Appeals, 27 September 1983, calling for an exemption from the application of national employment/labour law (*cf.* H. J. Steiner, D. F. Vagts and H. H. Koh, *Transnational Legal Problems: Materials and Text* (4th edn, Westbury, NY, 1994), 1013); and *Alpha Lyracom Space Communications Inc.* v. *Communications Satellite Corp.*, US District Court SDNY, 13 September 1990, where an 'immunity' from anti-trust law was in fact an exemption from the applicable US competition rules.

[57] Bekker, *The Legal Position*, 97. Similarly, Michael Akehurst, *The Law Governing Employment in International Organizations* (Cambridge, 1967), 117.

[58] *Cf.* Ake Hammarskjöld, 'Les immunités des personnes investies de fonctions internationales' (1936 II) 56 *Recueil des Cours* 107–211 at 137; Josef L. Kunz, 'Privileges and Immunities of International Organizations' (1947) 41 *American Journal of International Law* 828–62 at 847.

tion from legal process of adjudication and enforcement.'[59] Using the terminology of the US *Restatement (Third) of Foreign Relations Law*, with its division of a state's jurisdiction into the jurisdiction to prescribe, the jurisdiction to adjudicate and the jurisdiction to enforce, one could characterize immunity as an exception from a state's jurisdiction to adjudicate and/or jurisdiction to enforce, while a privilege can be viewed as an exemption from a state's jurisdiction to prescribe.[60] Normally an international organization is immune only in respect of adjudicative and enforcement jurisdiction, i.e. it remains liable to obey the law of the state where it is operating, and is merely exempt from judicial process to enforce that law.[61] But there are some areas of national law which regularly do not apply to an international organization, e.g. customs, tax, immigration, financial (e.g., foreign exchange) controls, work permit regulations, etc. These areas should properly be referred to as privileges of international organizations.[62]

The precise scope of these privileges is beyond the scope of this study.[63] However, a few remarks on the subject seem appropriate, in particular since the issues of applicable law and adjudicative jurisdiction are frequently intertwined in cases involving international organizations. Employment disputes have proven especially difficult in this respect. Many decisions in this area fail to differentiate correctly between questions of applicable law and jurisdictional questions.

While issues concerning privileges are normally governed and regulated by international agreements, the question also arises – as in the case of personality and immunity – of whether such privileges are exclus-

---

[59] Eileen Denza, 'Diplomatic Agents and Missions, Privileges and Immunities' in Rudolf Bernhardt (ed.), *Encyclopedia of Public International Law* (2nd edn, 1992), vol. I, 1040–5 at 1042. *Cf.* Bekker, *The Legal Position*, 182; and Hans Fasching, *Lehrbuch des österreichischen Zivilprozeßrechts* (Vienna, 1984), 37. See also the definition of immunity in the ILC Commentary on state immunity covering not only an 'exemption from the exercise of the power to adjudicate', but also the 'non-exercise of all other administrative and executive powers in relation to a judicial proceeding'. Commentary to Draft Article I on 'Jurisdictional immunities of states and their property', *Yearbook of the International Law Commission* (1991), vol. II, Part Two, 13.

[60] Thus, it is certainly a confusing use of terms when the *Restatement* argues that it seems necessary to consider also a potential 'immunity' from a state's jurisdiction to prescribe. *Cf. Restatement (Third)*, § 467, Comment c.

[61] Harders, 'Haftung und Verantwortlichkeit Internationaler Organisationen', 249.

[62] *Cf.* Schermers, speaking of the non-applicability of certain national legal provisions (and government activities based thereon) as issues of privileges. Schermers, *International Institutional Law*, 179 and 792ff.

[63] For a detailed appraisal of these issues, see C. Wilfred Jenks, *The Proper Law of International Organizations* (London and Dobbs Ferry, NY, 1962).

ively determined by treaty law or whether there is customary law on the subject as well. Some authors seem to support a 'general rule of international institutional law' requiring the non-applicability of national legislation to international organizations where that could negatively affect their proper functioning.[64] Generally, however, a more restrictive view prevails. It is usually acknowledged that immunity from suit does not free an international organization from obedience to the local law and that international organizations remain subject to the applicable domestic law unless issues of a purely internal nature are concerned[65] or unless exceptions are expressly provided for, as may be the case in headquarters agreements or specific conventions on privileges and immunities such as the Convention on the Privileges and Immunities of the United Nations 1946[66] (hereinafter the 'General Convention'[67]) or the Convention on the Privileges and Immunities of the Specialized Agencies 1947[68] (hereinafter the 'Special Convention').

A specific exemption from the otherwise applicable law may result from an international organization's power to substitute its own law for the law of the host country. It is an interesting feature of a few headquarters agreements that they recognize the international organization's power to legislate in certain fields. If this power is granted, the international organization's own law will replace the otherwise applicable law of the host state. Most notably the UN has this power and has acted upon it.[69] But

---

[64] Schermers, for instance, seems to be a proponent of a school of thought which advocates some customary principles in this field. Schermers, *International Institutional Law*, 794. In corroboration of this submission, he refers to the UN's refusal to comply with national publication law. (1970) *United Nations Juridical Yearbook* 167.

[65] Hans Peter Kunz-Hallstein, 'Privilegien und Immunitäten internationaler Organisationen im Bereich nicht hoheitlicher Privatrechtsgeschäfte' (1992) *Neue Juristische Wochenschrift* 3069–73 at 3070.

[66] Adopted by the General Assembly of the United Nations on 13 February 1946.

[67] This use conforms to the typical definition used in various headquarters agreements: 'The expression "General Convention" means the Convention on the Privileges and Immunities of the United Nations approved by the General Assembly of the United Nations on 13 February 1946.' *Cf.* section 1(c) of the UN Headquarters Agreement 1947; and section 1(i) of the UNIDO Headquarters Agreement 1967.

[68] Approved by the General Assembly of the United Nations on 21 November 1947.

[69] For instance, section 7(b) of the UN Headquarters Agreement 1947 provides that 'except as otherwise provided the federal, state and local law of the United States shall apply within the headquarters district'. The 'exception' of this norm refers to the power of the UN 'to make regulations, operative within the headquarters district, for the purpose of establishing therein conditions in all respects necessary for the full execution of its functions' (section 8). If this power has been exercised, the agreement provides that '[n]o federal, state or local law or regulation of the United States which is inconsistent with a regulation of the United Nations authorized by this section shall, to the extent of such

other organizations may also avail themselves of similar legislative powers.[70]

Immunity from legal process or immunity from jurisdiction are usually broadly understood as an exemption both from the adjudicative and from the enforcement procedures of national courts. It is probably an English peculiarity to regard the phrase 'immunity from legal process' to refer more narrowly only to immunity from executive or enforcement measures and immunity from jurisdiction to refer only to the adjudicative stage of court proceedings.[71]

When dealing with the immunities of international organizations, the notion of 'international immunities' is widely used. Most frequently, it appears to denote the privileges and immunities enjoyed by international organizations and their staff.[72] In an attempt to restrict the term

inconsistency, be applicable within the headquarters district' (*ibid.*). The UN has 'legislated' upon this provision in the early 1950s by adopting Regulation No. 1 concerning a social security system for its staff members, Regulation No. 2 regarding qualifications and requirements for the performance of professional services (e.g., legal and medical services) within the headquarters district, and Regulation No. 3 concerning hours of operation of any services and facilities or retail establishments with the headquarters district. In 1986, the UN adopted Regulation No. 4 limiting the liability of the organization in tort actions in respect of acts occurring within the headquarters district in order to avoid excessive damages awards under US law. Regulation No. 4, General Assembly Resolution 41/210, reprinted in Paul C. Szasz, 'The United Nations Legislates to Limit its Liability' (1987) 81 *American Journal of International Law* 739–44 at 742, note 14. It has been stressed correctly that such 'legislative' action must be clearly differentiated from reliance on the UN's jurisdictional immunity. Szasz, 'The United Nations Legislates', 744. By the adopted legislation, the UN does not try to hide behind the shield of immunity. In view of the provisions of the headquarters agreement, it rather remains under the obligation to waive its immunity or – in the alternative – to provide for other dispute settlement procedures in cases where legal claims are brought by private parties. Any competent forum, however – be it a US or another country's court or an arbitral tribunal – would be bound to apply the UN's regulation as applicable law. For US courts this obligation would specifically result from the headquarters agreement; in other states it should be the result of applying the *loci delicti* choice of law rule.

[70] CERN, for instance, issued its own workplace security code as well as a radiation manual. Franz Schmid and Jean-Marie Dufour, 'Le CERN, exemple de coopération scientifique européenne' (1976) 103 *Journal de droit international* 46–104 at 100. See also the general overview on 'internal legislation of intergovernmental organizations' by Finn Seyersted, 'Jurisdiction over Organs and Officials of States, the Holy See and Intergovernmental Organisations' (1965) 14 *International and Comparative Law Quarterly* 31–82 and 493–527 at 52*ff*, who even submits that international organizations have a general power to legislate in their internal matters, whether or not their constitutions so provide. *Ibid.*, 57.

[71] According to *Arab Banking Corporation* v. *International Tin Council and Algemene Bank Nederland and others (Interveners) and Holco Trading Company Ltd (Interveners)*, High Court, Queen's Bench Division, 15 January 1986, '[i]mmunity from jurisdiction only refers to the adjudicative process'. (1988) 77 ILR 1 at 6. See pp. 219*f* below as to the facts of this case.

[72] C. Wilfred Jenks, *International Immunities* (London and New York, 1961), *passim*.

'international immunities' to those of the international organization itself, the expressions 'organizational immunities'[73] or 'institutional immunit[ies]'[74] are sometimes used. It is this latter concept, concerning the immunity of international organizations from domestic courts, that is relevant to the present study.

Survey of existing material and literature
Court decisions and other relevant practice

This study discusses judicial decisions involving international organiz ations rendered by national courts from all regions of the world as far as they were available. It cannot claim to include all relevant decisions.[75]

The majority of cases analyzed in this book[76] are US (over fifty) and Italian (some forty). The abundance of Italian cases largely stems from litigation involving the FAO and NATO, but also some less well-known organizations such as the Bari Institute of the International Centre for Advanced Mediterranean Agronomic Studies or the Intergovernmental Committee for European Migration. In the US, at some point, most of the

---

[73] Bekker, *The Legal Position*, 153.

[74] Romana Sadurska and Christine M. Chinkin, 'The Collapse of the International Tin Council: A Case of State Responsibility?' (1990) 30 *Virginia Journal of International Law* 845–90 at 854.

[75] To make such a claim to exhaustive treatment would ignore the limited accessibility and the sometimes – as a practical matter – very difficult access to the judicial opinions which form the main 'subject' of this study. In order to gain material in a fashion as comprehensive as possible, the classic 'sources' of international practice have been used: digests of (internationally relevant domestic) court decisions, international case reports (annual digests, the *International Law Reports*, the *International Legal Materials*, etc.), collections of state practice (such as the *American Journal of International Law*, the *Austrian Journal of Public and International Law*, the *British Yearbook of International Law*, the *Netherlands Yearbook of International Law*, etc.), and other documents have been consulted – both in traditional hard-bound form as well as on computer databases (such as Westlaw, Lexis-Nexis, various internet sites, etc.). In addition, less orthodox methods of gaining access were pursued. For countries which do not regularly publish practice reports or where access to domestic cases is otherwise hardly feasible, the assistance of legal advisor's offices of their foreign ministries was sought through written inquiries for domestic cases involving international organizations. The author addressed more than seventy countries through their diplomatic missions in Washington DC (correspondence on file with the author). The expectedly modest result – as far as 'new cases' are concerned (of seventy-seven missions contacted, twenty-three replied; seven of them informed the author that no domestic cases involving international organizations were known, while four reported cases, two of which were previously unknown to the author) – was not necessarily disappointing. To know that the courts of some countries were not (yet) confronted with lawsuits involving international organizations is fundamentally different from not knowing whether they were or not.

[76] See the Table of cases, pp. xi–xlvii above.

larger organizations having their seat there (the IBRD, the IFC, Intelsat, the OAS and the UN) have been targets of judicial proceedings or have themselves sought legal remedies from US courts. Due to the rather restrictive attitude of US courts to the availability of judicial recourse against international organizations, attempts to 'hail them into court' have not been frequent.

Apart from the Tin Council litigation, there are only a few UK decisions concerning either organizations of which the United Kingdom is a member state or 'foreign' international organizations. A fair number of French decisions are relevant in the present context; their brevity, however, as far as legal reasoning is concerned, makes their analysis quite difficult.[77] Surprisingly few cases have been heard by courts in other western European states with a civil law tradition: in particular, Austrian and Swiss cases are not very numerous. The number of German decisions increased only recently. Relevant judgments of national courts other than European or US seem rare – or at least their availability is rather limited. Among those that are available are a number of employment-related disputes involving UN agencies in Latin American countries and in the Middle East, such as the cases brought against UNRWA in Egypt, Jordan, the Lebanon and Syria.

A few remarkable conclusions can be drawn already from this overview. For instance, the number of cases in a particular country does not appear to have any correlation to the number of international organizations having their seat there. On this assumption, one might have expected a large number of Swiss court decisions, and some at least in Austria and the United Kingdom. The host state factor alone does not prove to be a decisive aspect. Furthermore, while it might not be that surprising that a number of US cases deal with international organizations, it is certainly remarkable that almost every international organization setting foot on Italian soil has been sued there – and even more unexpectedly that Italian courts have frequently asserted their jurisdiction over them. The relatively high number of US cases probably has to do with the well-known litigiousness of US society. One should, however, also consider that it is less the cultural differences in the perception of courts as dispute settlement mechanisms and their willingness to address them, than the specific case law that has developed in that country that might be an incentive or disincentive for potential claimants to sue. Thus, the Italian inclination to treat international organizations – as far

---

[77] See p. 317 below as to the quality of the reasoning in the cases analysed here.

as immunity is concerned – like states[78] and the US indeterminacy of whether under the applicable US law international organizations should be treated like states[79] that probably accounts for the high number of cases in these countries.

Apart from actual court decisions, other state practice will be scrutinized as well,[80] in particular such documents as opinions of foreign ministries, opinions of the legal advisors to international organizations and – of particular relevance in the context of this study – *amicus curiae* briefs in court proceedings in those jurisdictions which allow them.[81]

Literature

The predominance of the traditional legal concepts of personality and immunity of international organizations, in the study of international organizations before domestic courts is clearly reflected by the existing literature. The issue of the domestic legal personality of international organizations has been addressed in a number of law journal articles, but has rarely been dealt with in a comprehensive fashion. Among the few exceptions are the 1969 report for the German Society of International Law by Beitzke[82] and the 1983 Hague lecture of Barberis[83] as well as the treatises on the domestic legal status of international organizations in the Federal Republic of Germany by Schlüter[84] and in Switzerland by

---

[78] See pp. 186*ff* below.   [79] See pp. 197*ff* below.

[80] *Cf.* Karl Zemanek, 'What is "State Practice"', 296*ff*, concerning new forms of state practice.

[81] Thus, a very valuable source of these manifestations of state practice and/or *opinio iuris* are the documents published in the sections on diplomatic practice of various national collections of state practice as well as those contained in the *United Nations Juridical Yearbook* and to a certain extent the updated volumes of the *Repertory of Practice of United Nations Organs*. Apart from selected national court decisions involving the UN and other organizations of the 'UN family', the *Juridical Yearbook* contains legal opinions of UN lawyers that are sometimes relevant to the pre-lawsuit stage. The *Repertory*, however, is of limited value for the purposes of this study, since it is 'confined to the practice of United Nations organs [and] does not deal with enabling legislation of individual States and decisions of national courts relating to the privileges and immunities of the United Nations'. *Repertory of Practice of United Nations Organs*, Supplement No. 1, vol. II, 415, Articles 104 and 105.

[82] Günther Beitzke, 'Zivilrechtsfähigkeit von auf Staatsvertrag beruhenden internationalen Organisationen und juristischen Personen' (1969) 9 *Berichte der Deutschen Gesellschaft für Völkerrecht* 77–119.

[83] Julio A. Barberis, 'Nouvelles questions concernant la personalité juridique internationale' (1983 I) 179 *Recueil des Cours* 145–304.

[84] Bernhard Schlüter, *Die innerstaatliche Rechtsstellung der internationalen Organisationen unter besonderer Berücksichtigung der Rechtslage in der Bundesrepublik Deutschland* (Cologne, Berlin, Bonn and Munich, 1972).

Hug.[85] All of them analyze the issue on a highly theoretical level. However, they rarely address any relevant case law.

As far as the second fundamental doctrinal view point is concerned, there are a number of broader scholarly works on the issue of privileges and immunities of international organizations. The classical studies are those by Lalive,[86] Jenks,[87] Ahluwalia,[88] Michaels,[89] and Dominicé.[90] Among the more recent studies are those by de Bellis,[91] Bekker[92] and Wenckstern.[93] However, all three generally lay emphasis on aspects other than those focused on in this book.

Compared to the wealth of literature on state immunity, the topic of immunity of international organizations remains to be surveyed. For reasons that will be analyzed and critically discussed in-depth below, a direct analogy or reference to those principles of sovereign immunity is generally regarded as inappropriate.[94] As a consequence, questions concerning the immunity of international organizations are usually excluded when state immunity is dealt with. For instance, the Schauman report for the German Society of International Law 1968,[95] the ILC codification of the law of state immunity,[96] and the work of the sovereign immunity committee of the ILA[97] all consider the immunity of interna-

---

[85] Dieter Hug, *Die Rechtsstellung der in der Schweiz niedergelassenen internationalen Organisationen* (Berne, Frankfurt am Main, Nancy and New York, 1984).

[86] Jean-Flavien Lalive, 'L'immunité de juridiction des états et des organisations internationales' (1953 III) 84 *Recueil des Cours* 205–396.

[87] Jenks, *International Immunities*.

[88] Kuljit Ahluwalia, *The Legal Status, Privileges and Immunities of the Specialized Agencies of the United Nations and Certain Other International Organizations* (The Hague, 1964).

[89] David B. Michaels, *International Privileges and Immunities. A Case for a Universal Statute* (The Hague, 1971).

[90] Christian Dominicé, 'L'immunité de juridiction et d'exécution des organisations internationales' (1984 IV) 187 *Recueil des Cours* 145–238.

[91] Saverio de Bellis, *L'immunità delle organizzazioni internazionali dalla giurisdizione* (Bari, 1992).

[92] Bekker, *The Legal Position*.

[93] Manfred Wenckstern, *Die Immunität internationaler Organisationen. Handbuch des Internationalen Zivilverfahrensrechts* (Tübingen, 1994), vol. II/1.

[94] *Cf.* pp. 347*ff* below.

[95] W. Schaumann, 'Die Immunität ausländischer Staaten nach Völkerrecht' in (1968) 8 *Berichte der Deutschen Gesellschaft für Völkerrecht* 1–57 at 6, expressly excluding any comments on the immunity of international organizations.

[96] ILC Draft Article 1 on 'Jurisdictional immunities of states and their property' limits the scope of applicability to 'the immunity of a State and its property from the jurisdiction of another State'. *Yearbook of the International Law Commission* (1991), vol. II, Part Two, 12–62 at 13.

[97] In the Revised Draft Articles for a Convention on State Immunity adopted at the ILA's Buenos Aires meeting in 1994, Article IX(A)(2) expressly provides that '[t]his Convention is without prejudice to [t]he rules of international law relating to the immunities of

tional organizations as expressly or implicitly outside their scope.[98] There are, however, some indications that, with the finalization of current codification tasks on state immunity within the aforementioned expert bodies, issues concerning international organizations before domestic courts might gain or regain importance.[99]

Methods
Overall solutions versus topical jurisprudence

There is, of course, a certain temptation to look for an overall solution, a sort of magic formula, that provides a universally applicable rule to determine the position of international organizations before national courts. In this respect, as in other respects, the parallel to state immunity is evident. The rule that a state has absolute immunity from the domestic courts of another state was accepted for a long time.[100] With the growing awareness of the inadequacies and injustices of this rule in a modern, increasingly commercial environment, the predominance of the rule was cast into doubt. Significantly, specific exceptions, relating *inter alia* to

international organisations'. ILA, *Report of the 66th Conference, Buenos Aires* (1994), 28. In its explanatory report, the Committee considered this savings clause necessary to reflect the basic difference between state immunity and immunities of international organiz ations. The Committee even considered the rules on immunities of international organ izations a ' "self-contained regime" separate from state immunity'. ILA, *Report of th e 66th Conference, Buenos Aires* (1994), 474.

[98] Even the IDI Commission on 'The legal consequences for member states of the non-fulfilment by international organizations of their obligations toward third parties' regards the topic of the jurisdictional immunity of international organizations as beyond its scope. Rosalyn Higgins, 'The Legal Consequences for Member States of the Non-Fulfilment by International Organizations of Their Obligations Toward Third Parties – Provisional Report' (1995 I) 66 *Annuaire de l'Institut de Droit International* 373–420 at 382.

[99] For instance, while the ILA Committee on State Immunity was wound up after the Buenos Aires meeting 1994, it has been suggested that the ILA should set up a new committee dealing with issues of the jurisdictional immunities of international organizations. (1994) *ILA Newsletter*, No. 3, 4. To date no such action has been taken. Instead, a committee reflecting on the accountability of international organizations is to be formed. (1995) *ILA bNewsletter*, No. 5, 2. It is likely that such a committee, which will probably address the issue of liability under both international and domestic law, will also deal with immun ity questions. Between 1975 and 1992 the ILC addressed aspects of the issue under the topic of 'relations between states and international organizations'. See Díaz-González, 'Fourth Report', 153–68. In 1992 the topic was deleted from the Commission's work programme. *Cf.* Peter H. F. Bekker, 'The Work of the International Law Commission on "Relations Between States and International Organizations" Discontinued: An Assess ment' (1993) 6 *Leiden Journal of International Law* 3–16 at 4.

[100] *Cf. Oppenheim's International Law* (9th edn, ed. by Robert Jennings and Arthur Watts, 1992), vol. I, 357*ff*.

vessels, real property in the forum state, certain torts, etc., were develop-ed by the judiciary in various states.[101] Still, the quest for an equally broad general rule to substitute for the now abandoned absolute immun-ity led to attempts to formulate a rule of restrictive immunity that would incorporate these exceptions into a single straightforward theory. And, indeed, most of the judge-made exceptions seemed to fit into the newly created theoretical dichotomy of 'private' *versus* 'public' acts, of *acta iure gestionis* and *acta iure imperii*.[102]

More recent developments, however, have demonstrated that there are intrinsic weaknesses in such a general formula, in particular in its inabil-ity to solve problems stemming from certain factual situations. This has led to a growing scepticism against the all-encompassing rule[103] and to arguments in favour of developing specific rules for specific categories of cases.[104]

These doctrinal hesitations, coupled with the strong emphasis on sov-ereignty by a few, mostly developing states, have resulted in a re-emerg-ence of a topical approach to state immunity in the most prominent recent codification efforts of the law on state immunity, the ILC's Draft Articles on Jurisdictional Immunities of States and Their Property[105] and the ILA's Revised Draft Articles for a Convention on State Immunity.[106] The latter relies more heavily upon the *iure gestionis/iure imperii* distinc-

---

[101] *Cf. Oppenheim's International Law*, 355*ff*. See also the overview in the ILC commentary to its Draft Articles on jurisdictional immunities of states and their property, *Yearbook of the International Law Commission* (1991), vol. II, Part Two, 12 at 36*ff*.

[102] The *iure gestionis/iure imperii* dichotomy not only purports to serve as a general key to solving state immunity issues, it has another feature that makes it very attractive both to judges sitting over actual disputes and to state representatives who would officially have to uphold or dispense with the standard, namely its 'neutrality' or rather its perceived neutrality. Because it appears to apply a general test in a mechanical way without having regard to or even taking into consideration policy arguments, etc., it seems to be highly impartial and thus most appropriate for judicial dispute resolution in particular cases. This unbiased 'blindness', however, frequently fails to take into account the specifics of some cases.

[103] See Ian Brownlie, 'Contemporary Problems Concerning the Jurisdictional Immunity of States – Supplementary Report' (1989 I) 63 *Annuaire de l'Institut de Droit International* 13–30 at 14*ff*.

[104] *Cf.* James Crawford, 'International Law and Foreign Sovereigns: Distinguishing Immune Transactions' (1983) 54 *British Yearbook of International Law* 75–118 at 114: 'The better approach is to deal with the specific categories and classes of case[s] that have arisen in practice and to elaborate specific rules for each such category, taking into account the reasons for extending immunity or asserting jurisdiction in that context.'

[105] Draft Articles on 'Jurisdictional immunities of states and their property', *Yearbook of the International Law Commission* (1991), vol. II, Part Two, 12–62.

[106] Revised Draft Articles for a Convention on State Immunity, ILA, *Report of the 66th Conference, Buenos Aires* (1994), 22*ff*.

tion by providing for immunity – in principle – 'for acts performed . . . in the exercise of . . . sovereign authority, i.e. jure imperii'.[107] It continues to provide for specific exceptions relating to commercial activity, employment disputes, disputes concerning immovable property in the forum state, certain tort actions, etc.[108] The ILC Draft Convention also retains the *iure gestionis/iure imperii* dichotomy. However, it does not exclusively rely on it as a determining criterion for solving immunity questions but, in effect, replaces it by very detailed and casuistic examples of 'official' *versus* 'commercial' acts.[109] Significantly, this is also the approach taken by a number of other codifications. The European Convention on State Immunity, the US Foreign Sovereign Immunities Act 1975, the UK State Immunity Act 1978, the Canadian State Immunity Act 1982 and the Australian Foreign States Immunities Act 1985 all generally follow this concept.

Topical method as policy- and interest-based approach

This peculiar development in the field of state immunity points towards a broader jurisprudential issue that might be relevant for the evaluation of the subject matter of this study, the decisions of domestic courts, and the conclusions one might attempt to draw from them for the study of international organizations before domestic courts. This broader issue concerns the proper choice of methods used to classify and evaluate the judgments and to develop criteria for future decision-making in cases involving international organizations before national courts.

It seems that one of the most developed areas of the law of immunity, state immunity law, provides guidance for such a shift from a systematic to a topical legal reasoning. Topical jurisprudence is understood here as a method of legal reasoning that focuses on weighing the advantages and disadvantages for and against a specific result in a specific situation by using legal *topoi* in the sense of relatively specific legal rules, sometimes commonplaces, maxims, etc., instead of relying pri-

---

[107] *Ibid.*, Draft Article II.   [108] *Ibid.*, Draft Article III.
[109] The ILC Draft Articles on 'Jurisdictional immunities of states and their property' provide in their Article 5 for a state's immunity from the jurisdiction of the courts of another state as a general principle. Articles 10–17 state exceptions for commercial transactions, certain contracts of employment, personal injuries and damage to property, ownership, possession and use of property, intellectual and industrial property, participation in companies and other collective bodies, ships owned or operated by a state, and the effect of an arbitration agreement. *Cf.* also Donald W. Greig, 'Specific Exceptions to Immunity Under the International Law Commission's Draft Articles' (1989) 38 *International and Comparative Law Quarterly* 560–88 at 560*ff.*

marily on systematic and logical deductions from abstract rules.[110] A topical jurisprudence has thus been characterized as mainly problem-oriented legal reasoning.[111]

Topical legal reasoning has formed part of the legal techniques applied by jurists since ancient times. Despite attempts to portray it as diametrically opposed to a systematic legal reasoning, it is probably rather a question of degree how intensely one or the other method is used. Nevertheless, there seems to be a certain stronger affinity to it in legal systems based on a case law tradition, whereas codified-law-oriented legal traditions appear to prefer a systematic reasoning.

A topical jurisprudence, however, does not only rely on legal *topoi*, in the sense of particular concepts, rules, etc. It always tries to stay close to the actual problems to be solved. To cope with this task, this jurisprudence tends to develop factual *topoi* which call for legal solution; it extracts certain types of cases which require judicial decision-making. It is this second aspect of topical legal reasoning that will in particular be useful in discussing the merits of decision-making by national courts in disputes involving international organizations.

Types of cases involving international organizations before domestic courts

When taking a phenomenological approach towards international organizations before domestic courts, a certain recurrent pattern will soon become evident, both in terms of frequency and of characteristics, in the disputes arising and the circumstances leading to them. If one supplements the actual cases with a number of theoretical cases, i.e. potential cases that have not so far been brought before domestic courts at all, but might conceivably find their way to them, a certain typology of cases becomes apparent. This categorization does not serve so much as a tool to group the various cases for analytical purposes;[112] rather, it will prove valuable at a later stage for assessing possible solutions. If a topical solution is to be proposed, these groups of cases are the likely *topoi* framing the field of reference. However, without prejudging this issue, even if an all-encompassing immunity rule should ultimately be discovered, it will have to be tested against the

---

[110] Gerhard Struck, *Topische Jurisprudenz* (Frankfurt am Main, 1971), 14*ff*; Theodor Viehweg, *Topik und Jurisprudenz* (5th edn, Munich, 1974), 14.

[111] Viehweg, *Topik und Jurisprudenz*, 31.

[112] Part I will rather analyze the existing case law according to the 'avoidance' or 'engagement' approaches taken by the deciding courts.

topical background of actual and potential lawsuits involving international organizations.

Personal services rendered to international organizations

The most frequent source of legal disputes seeking a domestic judicial forum are probably services rendered by individuals to international organizations. Those services are provided on the basis of either regular employment relations or of more *ad hoc* relationships, as is frequently the case with professional services. Within the employment relations, services are usually rendered either by persons integrated within the international organization system (its regular staff, officers, etc.) or by persons contracted on the basis of a looser relationship. A legal consequence of this differentiation can be found in the distinction between, on the one hand, an internal administrative law for staff members who are appointed officials and, on the other hand, the applicability of the respective local labour law to persons hired by international organizations on the basis of contracts. A substantial amount of litigation has arisen in this field mainly addressing the problematic distinction between these two types of legal relationships.[113]

Among the more *ad hoc* rendering of services by external persons are typically professional services,[114] but also other services, such as the

---

[113] See, for instance, the Italian cases concerning the *iure imperii* or *iure gestionis* character of employment relationships with the Bari Institute leading to different immunity decisions in *Bari Institute of the International Centre for Advanced Mediterranean Agronomic Studies v. Jasbez*, Corte di Cassazione, 21 October 1977, and in *Bari Institute of the International Centre for Advanced Mediterranean Agronomic Studies v. Scivetti*, Tribunale di Bari, 23 December 1975. See pp. 186*f* and 192*f* below. See also *Chirico v. Istituto di Bari del Centre International de Hautes Etudes Agronomiques Méditerranéennes (CIHEAM)*, Tribunale di Bari, 10 October 1985, and *Nacci v. Istituto di Bari*, Corte di Cassazione, 8 June 1994. See also *ICEM v. Di Banella Schirone*, Corte di Cassazione, 8 April 1975. *Cf.* pp. 113*f* and 190*f* below. See also the specific difficulties arising from the correct classification of persons working for NATO: *cf. Bruno v. USA*, Corte di Cassazione, 25 January 1977, *Conte v. HAFSE*, Tribunale Napoli, 28 September 1967; *HAFSE v. Di Castro e Atlantic Office*, Corte di Cassazione, 24 November 1978; *HAFSE v. Ferrero, Sanità and INPS*, Pretore di Verona, 17 May 1975; Corte di Cassazione, 6 February 1978; *HAFSE v. Pastena*, Corte di Cassazione, 24 March 1980; *HAFSE v. Sindicato FILTAT-CISL Vicenza*, Corte di Cassazione, 7 July 1978; *Lo Franco et al. v. NATO*, Corte di Cassazione, 22 March 1984; *Mazzanti v. HAFSE and Ministry of Defence*, Tribunale Firenze, 2 January 1954; Court of Appeals of Florence, 4–23 August 1955.

[114] Such as legal services rendered to NATO (*cf. Allied Headquarters in Southern Europe [HAFSE] v. Capocci Belmonte*, Corte di Cassazione, 5 June 1976; see pp. 193*f* below) or to PAHO (*cf. Tuck v. Pan American Health Organization*, US District Court DC, 17 November 1980, US Court of Appeals DC Cir., 13 November 1981; see p. 200 below), or medical services rendered to the IRO (*Maida v. Administration for International Assistance*, Corte di Cassazione, 27 May 1955; see pp. 210 and 224*f* below).

construction of buildings,[115] the transport of goods,[116] the design of computer software,[117] etc.[118]

Provision of movable and immovable property

Cases concerning the provision of movable and immovable property might typically arise from the sale of goods or the lease of office, storage and other space to international organizations.[119] The type of movable property provided to international organizations will depend on the kind of organization involved. While all organizations will need office equip-

---

[115] *Cf.* the Canadian case of *International Civil Aviation Organization* v. *Tripal Systems Pty Ltd et al.*, Superior Court, 9 September 1994, concerning the construction of an airport (see p. 109 below); the French case of *Dumont & Besson* v. *Association de la Muette*, Court of Appeal of Paris, 11 June 1966, regarding the erection of office buildings for the OECD (see p. 174 below); the Swiss litigation in *Groupement d'entreprises Fougerolle & consorts* v. *CERN*, Swiss Federal Tribunal, 21 December 1992, arising from the construction of a large circular tunnel for CERN (see p. 163 below); or the US case of *Dupree Associates Inc.* v. *OAS*, US District Court DC, 31 May 1977, 22 June 1977, involving the construction of a building for the OAS (see pp. 202 below). Suits related to the construction of buildings are the challenge to the plan to construct additional buildings for the IMF in *Loughran et al.* v. *United States*, US Court of Appeals DC Cir., 18 April 1963 (see p. 162 below), or a similar challenge directed against the enlargement of the test sites of CERN in *Girod de l'Ain*, Conseil d'Etat, 25 July 1986 (see p. 297 below). A similar problem was in issue in *Procurateur Général près de la Cour de Cassation* v. *Société Immobilière Alfred Dehodencq*, Cour de Cassation, 6 July 1954, where suit was brought to enjoin the construction of office buildings for the OEEC, (see p. 204 below). Also in *Curran* v. *City of New York et al.*, Supreme Court, Special Term, Queens County, 29 December 1947, the plaintiff sought to prevent the establishment of UN headquarters on a particular site in New York city (see pp. 94 and 125 below).

[116] *Cf.* the Philippine case of *United States Lines Inc.* v. *World Health Organization*, Intermediate Appellate Court, 30 September 1983 (see p. 178 below); and the US case of *IRO* v. *Republic Steamship Corp.*, US District Court D. Maryland, 8 July 1950; US Court of Appeals 4th Cir., 11 May/11 July 1951 (see p. 69 below), both concerning shipping contracts.

[117] *Cf. International Finance Corporation* v. *GDK Systems Inc. and Hogan Systems Inc.*, US District Court DC, 14 April 1989, arising from the provision of special software for international banking systems (see p. 70 below).

[118] *Cf. Branno* v. *Ministry of War*, Corte di Cassazione, 14 June 1954, concerning the provision of canteen facilities by a private individual for NATO staff (see pp. 196*f* below). *Cf.* also *Food and Agriculture Organization of the United Nations* v. *Ente Nazionale di Previdenza e di Assistenza per i Lavoratori dello Spettacolo (ENPALS)*, Pretore di Roma, 20 October 1982, a dispute arising from work as a film editor for the FAO.

[119] *Cf.* the cases concerning the lease of office space in Austria (*E GmbH* v. *European Patent Organization*, Austrian Supreme Court, 11 June 1992; see pp. 211*ff* below), Italy (*Food and Agriculture Organization* v. *Istituto Nazionale di Previdenza per i Dirigenti di Aziende Industriali (INPDAI)*, Corte di Cassazione, 18 October 1982; *Istituto Nazionale di Previdenza per i Dirigenti di Aziende Industriali (INPDAI)* v. *Food and Agriculture Organization*, Pretore di Roma, 4 April 1984; see pp. 131*ff* and 187*f* below), or the English case of *Safehaven Investments Inc.* v. *Springbok Ltd*, Chancery Division, 18 May 1995, involving the lease of premises to an international organization in a very indirect way (see p. 258 below).

ment, personal computers, typewriters, paper, etc., some will engage in far more diverse acquisitions. 'Instrumental' international organizations such as international commodity organizations will buy and sell sugar, tin, cocoa, etc., while technical organizations such as satellite operators will have to acquire expensive technical equipment. 'Political' organizations, such as, for instance, the UN when engaged in peacekeeping operations, will have to make provisions for logistic support, e.g. lease of aircraft, etc.

Apart from contracts for the purchase of goods, organizations will sometimes also conclude loan agreements. Although mainly financed by the contributions of their member states, certain international organizations enter into large loan agreements either for the purpose of refinancing, such as the international banks, or to cover their operational expenses, as is the case with a number of commodity agreements.[120]

Both in the case of rendering services and of providing property, international organizations are usually in a recipient position. However, it might well be that they are the provider of the services. An international organization may provide professional advice to its member states or to third parties;[121] it may render services based on its technical expertise;[122] or it may provide educational services.[123] An international organization might also sell office buildings or other tangible property it possesses, etc.

---

[120] The breakdown of the Tin Council and the ensuing litigation is illustrative of this fact (see pp. 118ff below). Apart from the various English cases, other national courts were also confronted with lawsuits involving the attempts of the Tin Council's creditors to recover their loans, e.g. in Malaysia (*Bank Bumiputra Malaysia Bhd* v. *International Tin Council and another*, High Court, 13 January 1987; see p. 196 below) and in the United States (*International Tin Council* v. *Amalgamet Inc.*, Supreme Court, New York County, 25 January 1988; see pp. 90 and 181f below). See also the attempt to hold the EEC as a member of the Tin Council responsible in an action brought before the ECJ, *Maclaine Watson and Co. Ltd* v. *Council and Commission of the European Communities*, Case 241/87, ECJ, 10 May 1990 (see pp. 84f below).

[121] E.g., the economic advisory functions of the World Bank Group.

[122] Such as the tasks of securing the air space fulfilled by regional international organizations such as Eurocontrol or ASECNA. Their services and in particular the collection of charges for their services has given rise to some litigation in national courts, e.g., in Germany (*Eurocontrol-Flight Charges cases*, Federal Administrative Court, 16 September 1977; Federal Constitutional Court, Second Chamber, 23 June 1981; see pp. 107f and 291ff below) and in the Netherlands (*Trans-Mediterranean Airways* v. *Eurocontrol*, Royal Decree (administrative decision of the Crown), 16 January 1974; see pp. 184 and 291 below).

[123] *Cf.* the lawsuits brought before Belgian courts in order to collect outstanding tuition fees referred to in *European School Mol* v. *Hermans-Jacobs and Heuvelmans-Van Iersel*, Court of Arbitration, 3 February 1994 (see p. 176 below).

Tortious contacts

Disputes might arise not only from a consensual relationship between an international organization and private parties, but could also result from incidents causing harm to either the organization or to a third party as a consequence of the organization's activities. Apart from the routine cases of automobile accidents,[124] other torts have occurred or are conceivable. International organizations have infringed upon the personal property rights of private persons;[125] international organizations might be accused of libel or slander,[126] even of false imprisonment,[127] of infringing other property rights,[128] of causing harm by violating competition (antitrust) rules,[129] or domestic employment legislation.[130]

---

[124] *Cf. Robert A. Mitishen v. Otis Elevator Company, IBRD*, US District Court DC, 19 September 1990, US Court of Appeals DC Cir., 22 July 1992, concerning an elevator accident (see pp. 184ff below); and *Wencak v. United Nations*, Supreme Court of New York, Special Term, 18 January 1956, concerning an unspecified accident for which UNRRA was contended to be responsible.

[125] *Cf.* the famous *Manderlier* case involving the infliction of damages by UN forces in the course of the Congo operation. *Manderlier v. Organisation des Nations Unies and Etat Belge (Ministre des Affaires Etrangères)*, Civil Tribunal of Brussels, 11 May 1966; and *Manderlier v. Organisation des Nations Unies and Etat Belge*, Brussels Appeals Court, 15 September 1969. See pp. 39, 99 and 279 below. *Cf.* also the arbitral proceedings brought against the UN in *Starways Ltd v. United Nations*, Arbitral Award, 24 September 1969, for damages suffered in the course of the civil war in the Congo. See also the similar claims arising from UN involvement in Cyprus brought before English courts in *Attorney-General v. Nissan*, House of Lords, 11 February 1969; see pp. 97f below.

[126] *Cf.* the US defamation actions brought in *William Douglas Clark et al. v. Alejandro Orfila et al.*, US Court of Appeals DC Cir., 8 September 1977; and in *Steinberg v. International Criminal Police Organization*, US Court of Appeals DC Cir., 23 October 1981; see pp. 152ff below.

[127] *Cf. Morgan v. IBRD*, US District Court DC, 13 September 1990, a tort action against the World Bank for libel, slander, infliction of emotional distress and false imprisonment. See pp. 165 and 200 below.

[128] In two English lawsuits brought against Eurocontrol, the plaintiffs claimed, *inter alia*, damages for the unlawful detention of aircraft. *Irish Aerospace (Belgium) NV v. European Organisation for the Safety of Air Navigation and Civil Aviation Authority*, Queen's Bench Division (Commercial Court), 6 June 1991; *Internationale Nederlanden Aviation Lease BV and others v. Aviation Authority and the European Organisation for the Safety of Air Navigation (Eurocontrol)*, Queen's Bench Division (Commercial Court), 11 June 1996; see p. 184 below.

[129] *Cf.* the suits brought against Eurocontrol alleging abuse of a dominant position in Belgian and English courts: *Soc. dr. allem. Sat Fluggesellschaft mbH v. Eurocontrol*, Cour d'appel de Bruxelles, 4 October 1990; and *Irish Aerospace (Belgium) NV v. European Organisation for the Safety of Air Navigation and Civil Aviation Authority*, Queen's Bench Division (Commercial Court), 6 June 1991 (see p. 184 below). See also the US lawsuits involving international organizations in *Alpha Lyracom Space Communications Inc. v. Communications Satellite Corp.*, US District Court SDNY, 13 September 1990 (see p. 175 below) and *International Association of Machinists v. OPEC*, US District Court CD Cal., 18 September 1979, *affirmed on other grounds*, US Court of Appeals 9th Cir., 6 July–24 August 1981, where a US labour union sued OPEC and its individual member states asking for damages and injunctive relief for alleged price-fixing (see p. 90ff below).

In some cases the alleged violation of personal rights might be so grave as to amount to an abrogation of an individual's fundamental rights.[131] Sometimes lawsuits, styled as tort actions, are brought against international organizations or individuals acting on their behalf in order to challenge the organizations' activities.[132]

[130] *Cf. Camera confederale del lavoro and Sindicato scuola CGIL* v. *Istituto di Bari del Centro internazionale di alti studi agronomici mediterranei*, Pretore di Bari, 15 February 1974; Corte di Cassazione, 27 April 1979, involving the alleged infringement of employees' rights such as the right to strike and to join a trade union under Italian legislation and *HAFSE* v. *Sindicato FILTAT-CISL Vicenza*, Corte di Cassazione, 7 July 1978, alleging that the defendant had impeded various trade union activities. See pp. 112f below. See also an English lawsuit alleging unlawful racial discrimination in rejecting his application for employment: *Mukoro* v. *European Bank for Reconstruction and Development and another*, Employment Appeal Tribunal, 19 March 1994. See pp. 207f below. Also in *Boimah* v. *United Nations General Assembly*, US District Court EDNY, 24 July 1987, suit was brought alleging employment discrimination under the US Civil Rights Act. See pp. 206f below. *Cf.* the similar claim raised in *Mendaro* v. *World Bank*, US Court of Appeals DC Cir., 27 September 1983, alleging sexual discrimination (see p. 152 below); and in *Novak* v. *World Bank*, US District Court DC, 12 June 1979; US District Court DC, 23 October 1979; US Court of Appeals DC Cir., 28 April 1980; US District Court DC, 4 February 1982; VS Court of Appeals DC Cir., 1 April 1983, alleging age discrimination.

[131] *Cf. Confédération Française démocratique du Travail* v. *European Communities*, European Commission of Human Rights, Application No. 8030/77, 10 July 1978, an attempt to hold the EC directly liable for fundamental rights violations before an international tribunal. See p. 302 below. A number a domestic court decisions addressed the difficulty of differentiating between tort and abrogation of fundamental rights by official acts. In various *Eurocontrol* cases, German courts qualified the activities of Eurocontrol as official acts of an international organization, not of German organs, thus excluding their reviewability under German constitutional law. *Cf. Hetzel* v. *Eurocontrol*, Administrative Court Karlsruhe, 5 July 1979, Appellate Administrative Court Baden-Württemberg, 7 August 1979; Federal Constitutional Court, 10 November 1981 (see pp. 104ff and 291f below).

[132] *Cf. Zoernsch* v. *Waldock et McNulty*, Court of Appeal, 24 March 1964, an attempt to question a decision of the European Commission of Human Rights by suing one of its individual members for negligence. In *Lutcher SA Celulose e Papel* v. *Inter-American Development Bank*, US Court of Appeals DC Cir., 13 July 1967, a Brazilian corporation brought suit for damages and sought an injunction against the Inter-American Development Bank arguing that loans made or about to be made to the plaintiff's competitors violated an 'implied obligation' of its own loan agreement with the Bank to act prudently in considering loan applications from competitors. See p. 216 below. *Cf. Miller* v. *United States*, US Court of Appeals DC Cir., 31 August 1978, where a tort action was brought against the US as a member of the International Joint Commission regulating water levels in the boundary lakes between Canada and the US. *Cf.* also *Donald* v. *Orfila*, US District Court DC, 30 July 1985, *affirmed* US Court of Appeals DC Cir., 18 April 1986, an employment dismissal suit brought against the OAS Secretary-General, complaining of unlawful interference with the plaintiff's employment contract. See p. 207 below. Similarly, in *Kissi* v. *De Larosiere*, US District Court DC, 23 June 1982, an employment discrimination suit was brought against the managing director of the IMF. See p. 207 below. *Cf.* also *De Luca* v. *United Nations Organization, Perez de Cuellar, Gomez, Duque, Annan et al.*, US District Court SDNY, 10 January 1994, an attempt to sue for damages for a failure to reimburse the plaintiff, a UN employee, for income taxes withheld in accordance with the normal UN reimbursement schemes. See p. 201 below.

Secondary disputes

International organizations may also become involved in lawsuits that do not arise directly out of a substantive dispute, but rather result from an attack on its institutional structure or relate only indirectly to a quarrel with a private party. Examples of such 'secondary disputes' are the attempt to annul a judgment of an organization's administrative tribunal,[133] the challenge of a decision of the European School requiring a pupil to repeat a school year[134] or the indirect attack against the European Patent Office's revocation of a patent.[135] A taxpayer seeking to enjoin the establishment of the UN headquarters in New York also falls into this category.[136]

Consequences for the methods employed

It can be seen that the three parts of this book, the contents of which have been briefly outlined above,[137] require a specific methodological approach. Part I of this book undertakes to present the arguments and the reasoning used by domestic courts when faced with cases involving an international organization in a primarily descriptive fashion. Normative arguments, critique of the legal reasoning employed, and policy considerations as to the appropriateness of the solutions found, will be kept to a minimum and incorporated only where necessary for a better understanding of the cases. Thus Part I might justifiably be called a 'phenomenology' of legal reasoning. The important point, however, is that it should illustrate how diverse judicial interpretations of a comparatively simple problem can be and that the issue of immunity – normally considered of paramount importance – does not in fact enjoy such exclusive prominence. This deliberately descriptive approach requires a considerable amount of patience on the part of the reader to defer questions relating to the legal value, correctness and usefulness of the decisions analyzed and to the author's own evaluation, critique and proposals to a later stage.

---

[133] *Cf. Popineau* v. *Office Europeen des Brevets*, Conseil d'Etat, 15 February 1995, where a former employee of the European Patent Office tried to 'appeal' a decision of the ILO Administrative Tribunal, confirming his employment termination, to the French Conseil d'Etat. See p. 123 below.

[134] *Dalfino* v. *Governing Council of European Schools and European School of Brussels I*, Conseil d'Etat, 17 November 1982. See p. 213 below.

[135] *Lenzing AG's European Patent*, Queen's Bench Division (Crown Office List), 20 December 1996. See p. 214 below.

[136] *Cf. Curran* v. *City of New York et al.*, Supreme Court, Special Term, Queens County, 29 December 1947. See pp. 94 and 125 below.

[137] See pp. 3*f* above.

Part II will revert to a normative discussion analyzing the underlying rationales that may require the abstention or engagement of domestic courts. The label 'normative' is used here in a broad sense and is not limited to strictly 'legal' reasoning as conceived by any particular legal system. Rather, it will focus on the broader policy reasons for and against abstention or engagement. These policy considerations are based on an analysis of the interests of the parties involved (international organizations and their potential opponents as well as the forum state) and will then be supported by more legal considerations.[138] This is not to suggest that there is a clear-cut distinction between 'legal' and 'political' reasoning: rather, it emphasizes a difference in degree.

Part III will shift the emphasis to a more genuinely legal discussion. Drawing from the lessons of how courts actually deal with disputes involving international organizations and taking into account and evaluating the interests identified in Part II, Part III will attempt to examine possible solutions as to how courts should approach such disputes. At the same time this part will critically assess some of the key concepts used in the cases analyzed, such as functional or restrictive immunity, as well as lack of jurisdiction models.

---

[138] See pp. 278*ff* below for the parallel between a potential human right and an interest in access to court.

Part I
Descriptive analysis

2   Avoidance techniques

In practice, national courts frequently decline to exercise jurisdiction over disputes involving international organizations either as plaintiffs or defendants, even when the international organizations are only involved peripherally, whether as third parties or as persons whose acts might be decisive for a legal dispute between other parties. Courts may decline to exercise jurisdiction for a number of reasons that could be termed 'internal' or 'domestic' in so far as their jurisprudential rationale or legal-political purpose clearly has roots within the domestic realm. Distribution of powers arguments, underlying the 'political questions' doctrine, rank here next to 'case' or 'controversy' requirements intended to further the efficacy of the administration of justice. Courts may, however, also use 'international' reasons or policy arguments that relate to the 'external', international relations of a forum state. The most prominent among them is, of course, the grant of immunity to international organizations which is normally perceived as a requirement under international law, conventional or customary. Certain strategies might also involve both internal and external rationales. The US-type act of state doctrine is a good example resting on internal power distribution rationales as well as on external comity considerations.

Apart from official high-level rationales to decline jurisdiction over certain disputes, domestic courts can have considerably more mundane reasons to avoid disputes involving international organizations.[1] Lacking

---

[1] The term 'avoidance' is used here in a non-evaluative fashion. Although a court might, of course, 'avoid' deciding a dispute before it by employing any of the methods or doctrines discussed below, Part I focuses on a descriptive analysis of the legal reasoning leading courts to refrain from deciding cases. An evaluation as to the propriety or impropriety of declining jurisdiction might follow an analysis of the international legal requirements either under fundamental rights considerations or under immunity standards. But here

35

familiarity with the issues involved, ready to seize an opportunity to get rid of another case that awaits decision, courts may have a number of 'avoidance' strategies. Much depends upon cultural differences between judicial systems and those involved in the administration of justice. For judges willing to abandon a case, however, the employment of one of the avoidance doctrines discussed below might prove an effective and simple way to free themselves of part of their heavy case load. Considering the rarity of disputes concerning international immunity issues, in particular those involving international organizations, the benefit – in numerical terms – might not appear very great. However, the gain of abandoning some of the harder cases – at least from the perspective of the judges confronted with them and not familiar with the issues contained therein – should not be underestimated.[2]

Where the relationship between international organizations and national courts is discussed, attention usually focuses on the problem of their jurisdictional immunity.[3] Immunity is certainly the doctrinal and jurisprudential centrepiece of this relationship. However, judicial practice evidences that the issue of immunity from suit is but one aspect of the sometimes very sophisticated approaches domestic courts take when addressing legal disputes before them that involve international organizations.

One reason for the inherently limited usefulness of the concept of immunity is that, essentially, it works only in suits brought against an international organization and cannot lead to judicial abstention if an international organization chooses to bring suit. Another, probably increasingly important reason for avoiding immunity and replacing it by other avoidance doctrines might lie in the fact that the concept of immunity appears to be regarded as increasingly inappropriate, as a relic of traditional international law favouring its 'subjects' improperly *vis-à-vis* individuals.[4] Thus, other avoidance doctrines have resurfaced, in par-

---

again the rationales for judging whether judicial abstention from adjudicating is proper or not must be differentiated from the correct application of the *lex lata*.

[2] To a certain extent the enthusiasm of some national courts in Europe to refer EC law problems to the ECJ according to Article 177 of the EC Treaty may also evidence a willingness on the part of such courts to avoid deciding issues of non-domestic law. There are, however, considerable differences in the frequency with which national courts ask for preliminary rulings. While German and Dutch courts seem to be very willing to do so, French and English courts tend to be more reluctant. *Cf.* Waldemar Hummer, Bruno Simma, Christoph Vedder and Frank Emmert, *Europarecht in Fällen* (2nd edn, Baden-Baden, 1994), 27.

[3] *Cf.* the large body of literature focusing on individual cases, frequent case notes, etc. Compare, however, the rare systematic treatment of the subject. *Cf.* p. 20 above.

[4] *Cf.* pp. 278*ff* below on human rights considerations requiring a restriction of immunity.

ticular those which appear to be neutral in the sense of not to favour specific persons. Clearly, immunity for a certain group of persons is not neutral, but rather unilaterally places the burden upon the party seeking judicial redress.[5]

Among those other doctrines may be included 'non-recognition' theories, relating to a concept of the legal personality of international organizations or to the legal significance of their activities; procedural law requirements, relating to the ripeness or justiciability of a dispute that might disqualify certain issues from judicial scrutiny;[6] and the 'political questions', 'act of state' or similar doctrines.

Compared to these broader and not necessarily international-law-related concepts, the issue of immunity is more concrete and will serve as a method of last resort for courts to avoid adjudication of a claim against an international organization.

Non-recognition as a legal person under domestic law

Legal personality is generally regarded as the capability to possess rights and duties under a specific system of law.[7] An international organization's status as a 'legal', 'juridical' or 'juristic' person[8] under domestic law is a prerequisite not only for entering into legal relationships,[9] but

---

[5] The subsequent analysis will try to show that the *prima facie* neutrality of other 'avoidance doctrines' is not necessarily impartial in all cases.

[6] Those requirements of domestic (procedural) law generally apply to cases with an 'international' aspect as well as to domestic cases. E.g., it appears well accepted in the US that principles as to jurisdiction, standing, mootness, ripeness, etc. apply to 'foreign relations cases' as to others. *Restatement (Third) of the Law, The Foreign Relations Law of the United States* (ed. American Law Institute, St Paul, MN, 1987), §1, Reporters' Note 4. The conclusion seems well founded, since these adjudicative principles relate to a court's power of decision-making in general.

[7] Klaus F. Röhl, *Allgemeine Rechtslehre* (Cologne, Berlin, Bonn and Munich, 1994), 471; see also the ICJ's definition of the international personality of the United Nations as an entity 'capable of possessing international rights and duties'. *Reparation for Injuries Suffered in the Service of the United Nations*, Advisory Opinion, (1949) *ICJ Reports* 174 at 179.

[8] All these terms are used in treaties, legislation and the literature on the subject. *Cf.* pp. 12*ff* above. It appears, however, that the expression 'legal' person or personality is predominant. It will thus mainly be used here.

[9] Günther Beitzke, 'Zivilrechtsfähigkeit von auf Staatsvertrag beruhenden internationalen Organisationen und juristischen Personen' (1969) 9 *Berichte der Deutschen Gesellschaft für Völkerrecht* 77–119 at 84. Friedrich Schröer, 'Die Anwendung von Landesrecht auf völkerrechtliche Zweckverbände' (1965) 25 *Zeitschrift für ausländisches öffentliches Recht und Völkerrecht* 617–56 at 620. *Cf.* also the case of the International Commission for the Northwest Atlantic Fisheries recounted by J. E. Carroz and A. G. Roche, 'The Proposed International Commission for the Conservation of Atlantic Tunas' (1967) 61 *American Journal of International Law* 673–702 at 697*ff*. Like most other intergovernmental fisheries organizations, its

also for being a party to legal proceedings before domestic courts. Thus, only an international organization endowed with domestic legal personality can be subjected to judicial proceedings in national courts. Only then is a potential exemption *ratione personae*[10] (for example, immunity) or *ratione materiae*[11] (for example, lack of adjudicative power) of interest.

Accordingly, the most radical method available to national courts in order to avoid adjudication of a dispute involving an international organization is to regard international organizations as non-entities, unable to bring suit or to be sued. Usually this kind of non-recognition or de-recognition will be framed in the language of lack of personality. Immunity might clearly become secondary, or even irrelevant, if no domestic personality is granted to an international organization, because then there is no possibility of suing the non-entity in domestic courts.[12] Only if an entity can be considered a legal person under the forum state's law, may it play a role before its courts. An entity that does not legally exist cannot sue or be sued before domestic courts. This argument seems universally applicable and of a compellingly simple logic. Nevertheless, it has only rarely entered the actual case law, not at least because the arguments, if raised at all, appear very artificial.

Thus, the issue of legal personality, both international and domestic, of international organizations – although there are scholarly disputes over whether this is an objective or merely a derivative personality[13] – has to be addressed in an inquiry focusing on immunity and other jurisdictional issues. Since many authors consider that there is a direct link between international and domestic legal personality – that is, that the first is a precondition of the second – and since the issue of the scope or extent of the personality of international organizations will show similarities, the issue of international legal personality will be dealt with as well. To address the

---

constituent agreement was silent on the issues of (domestic) legal personality. When the organization intended to contract for an insurance plan for its staff, it was advised by Canada as headquarters state that it was considered not to have legal authority to enter into a contract. *Cf.* also the criticism by Seidl-Hohenveldern, *Corporations*, 102, qualifying this Canadian ruling as an 'astonishing exercise of legal positivism'.

[10] *Cf.* pp. 127*ff* below.   [11] *Cf.* pp. 99*ff* below.

[12] Christian Dominicé, 'L'immunité de juridiction et d'exécution des organisations internationales' (1984 IV) 187 *Recueil des Cours* 145–238 at 164: '[A]ccorder des immunitiés à une organisation qui n'aurait pas, en droit interne, la personnalité juridique, n'aurait pas grand sens, car ce ne serait pas l'organisation qui, par exemple, devrait être assignée en justice.' See also Michael Singer, 'Jurisdictional Immunity of International Organizations: Human Rights and Functional Necessity Concerns' (1995) 36 *Virginia Journal of International Law* 53–165 at 67, arguing that the question of legal personality precedes that of jurisdictional immunity.

[13] See pp. 57*ff* below.

issue of personality is further useful in view of the intrinsic parallelism between a functional personality and a functional immunity concept.[14]

The problem before the courts

A number of cases evidence that domestic legal personality is required for an international organization to be a party to legal proceedings before a national court. Although they usually stop short of de-recognizing or failing to recognize the legal personality of international organizations, their reasoning clearly demonstrates the essential importance of the personality of an international organization in order to enable a domestic court to adjudicate the underlying dispute.

The well-known case of *Manderlier v. Organisation des Nations Unies and Etat Belge (Ministre des Affaires Etrangères)*[15] illustrates this point aptly. Although finally holding that the UN could not be sued before the Belgian courts because of its absolute immunity in accordance with the General Convention, the Civil Tribunal of Brussels explicitly reasoned that the UN was competent to appear in legal proceedings in Belgium as a result of the legal personality it enjoyed in the territory of each member state by virtue of Article 104 of the UN Charter.

In another Belgian case, *Centre pour le développement industriel (CDI) v. X*,[16] the legal personality of an international organization as a prerequisite to bring suit was also discussed. CDI, an international organization with its seat in Brussels, was set up within the framework of the Lomé Conventions in order to facilitate the development of the industrial sector in the African, Caribbean and Pacific states. The defendant worked as a marketing advisor for CDI. When his employment contract was unilaterally terminated by his employer, he sought and obtained an arbitral award granting him substantial damages. Thereupon CDI sued him in Belgian courts seeking to annul the arbitral award that the employee had obtained in his favour and to annul a lower Belgian court's *exequatur* of the award, permitting its enforcement in Belgium. The defendant claimed, *inter alia*, that the action should be declared inadmissible because of the

---

[14] *Cf.* Edwin H. Fedder, 'The Functional Basis of International Privileges and Immunities: A New Concept in International Law and Organization' (1960) 9 *American University Law Review* 60–9 at 63: 'The reliance on the functional principle in determining the extent of protection for international organizations . . . did not stop at legal status. The change from previous practice is also evident in the privileges and immunities accorded to the organizations.' See also Bekker, *The Legal Position of Intergovernmental Organizations: A Functional Neccessity Analysis of Their Legal Status and Immunities* (Dordrecht, Boston and London, 1994).

[15] Civil Tribunal of Brussels, 11 May 1966; Brussels Appeals Court, 15 September 1969. See pp. 279*f* below for the facts of this case.

[16] Tribunal Civil de Bruxelles, 13 March 1992.

claimant's lack of domestic legal personality. The Belgian court rejected this contention on the basis that CDI's legal personality was expressly recognized in the headquarters agreement with Belgium and probably also implicitly recognized as an automatic result of the CDI's international legal personality.[17] The court ironically questioned how the defendant might have entered into an employment contract if CDI had lacked legal personality.[18]

A similar situation arose in two legal proceedings instituted by the UN and UNRRA against former employees in order to recover moneys paid to them in excess of the amount due. Both in *United Nations and UNRRA v. B*[19] and in *UNRRA v. Daan*,[20] the defendants contended that the plaintiff organizations did not have the legal personality required to bring suit in the domestic courts. Both courts rejected this argument. In the former case, brought by the UN and UNRRA collectively in order to recover payments erroneously made to the defendant, without specifically referring to the domestic legal personality clauses contained in the treaty establishing UNRRA[21] or to the UN Charter, a Belgian court simply stated that Belgium had ratified both instruments and that such 'public international establishments, recognized by Belgian law, had thus juridical personality in Belgium'.[22] In *UNRRA v. Daan*, a Dutch court found that, as a result of a treaty provision according to which UNRRA had the power to acquire and transfer property, to conclude contracts and to perform all legal acts appropriate to the fulfilment of its tasks, 'it must also be considered a legal person under Dutch law, and as such competent to act as a party to legal proceedings'.[23]

In *Arab Monetary Fund v. Hashim (No. 3)*[24] the plaintiff organization almost failed in the English courts because of the uncertainty involving its legal status under English law. In the course of this litigation, which went all the way to the House of Lords, the Court of Appeal actually denied its adjudicative power over the dispute as a result of what it perceived as the Fund's lack of legal personality under domestic law.[25]

---

[17] See pp. 59*ff* below.   [18] (1992) *Actualités du droit* 1377 at 1381.

[19] Tribunal Civil of Brussels, 27 March 1952.

[20] Cantonal Court Amersfoort, 16 June 1948, District Court Utrecht, 23 February 1949, Supreme Court, Decision of 19 May 1950.

[21] Agreement for United Nations Relief and Rehabilitation Administration, Washington, 9 November 1943.

[22] (1953) *Pasicrisie Belge* III, 66: 'que ces établissements publics internationaux, étant reconnus par la loi Belge, ont donc la personnalité juridique en Belgique.'

[23] (1949) 16 ILR 337.

[24] Chancery Division, 9–12 October, 14 November 1989; Court of Appeal, 26–27 March, 9 April 1990; House of Lords, 26–28 November 1990, 21 February 1991.

[25] See pp. 64*ff* below for a detailed discussion.

In practice, courts may employ a number of different methods to de-recognize an international organization's domestic legal personality and its capacity to claim or defend its rights and obligations in a domestic forum: courts might feel empowered to regard the legal personality of an international organization as non-existent if there is no explicit or implicit international rule bestowing such personality or if any such rule is not directly applicable under domestic law. They may also do so if there is no corresponding domestic rule implementing it or if there are no conflict of laws rules allowing a domestic forum to recognize the 'foreign' personality of an international organization, etc.

Before discussing these specific avoidance techniques, the normal case where personality clearly exists should be analyzed. Since this issue usually depends upon the existence of a domestically applicable rule attributing personality to international organizations, it largely becomes a question of the sources of personality of international organizations.

The normal approach to domestic legal personality

The following will provide an overview of how domestic legal personality, as a prerequisite to appearing in national courts, may become relevant in various national legal orders. Since it is frequently asserted that there is an intrinsic relationship between such domestic legal personality and international legal personality the latter will also be addressed.

Different approaches between member and non-member states

There seems to be a fundamental difference between where the issue of the domestic legal personality of an international organization is raised before a court of a member state of that organization or before a court in a third country. In general, member states are under an international obligation to accord such personality to an organization – pursuant to its constituent treaty or possibly under customary international law[26] – while non-member states – in the absence of specific treaty obligations[27] – remain free to recognize an organization as a legal person under their domestic law. Member states may fulfil their international law obligations by regarding the treaty or customary requirements to confer personality as directly applicable in the sphere of domestic law; non-member states are likely to rely on their domestic legislation or on other rules of domestic law to allow them to recognize the legal personality of an international organization.

The cases analyzed will show, however, that it is rarely a problem of

---

[26] See pp. 45f below.   [27] See pp. 43f below.

whether national courts are willing to accept the domestic legal personality of international organizations where they are obliged to do so, but rather one of their ability to recognize it where they are not obliged to do so. Therefore, it is not surprising that most cases where the existence of domestic legal personality was an issue arose in the context of organizations before courts of non-member states as in *Arab Monetary Fund* v. *Hashim (No. 3)*,[28] *Westland Helicopters Ltd* v. *Arab Organisation for Industrialisation*,[29] *International Association of Machinists* v. *OPEC*[30] and *Re Jawad Mahmoud Hashim et al.*[31]

The predominance of English decisions among those where domestic legal personality caused serious problems and the fact that it was in issue also in cases involving organizations of which the UK is a member, like the *Tin Council* proceedings, shows, however, that these difficulties are apparently not primarily a result of the UK's non-membership of the organization in question but rather of its specific rules of private international law and of its peculiar treatment of norms of international origin within the domestic realm.[32]

Moreover, courts are quite reluctant to distinguish between organizations of which the forum state is a member and organizations of which it is not – as a matter of principle – when confronted with an issue of domestic legal personality. Thus, the distinction between member and non-member states will be dealt with incidentally in the following sections.

Sources of domestic legal personality

As in the case of international legal personality,[33] a treaty norm or possibly a rule of customary international law may form the basis for the domestic legal personality of an international organization. In addition, domestic law may – even independently of a possible international requirement to this effect – provide for such personality. Since questions of domestic legal personality become relevant primarily before domestic law-applying and law-enforcing organs (courts and administrative authorities), the determinative rules must be ones that are applicable under national law. Thus, it will frequently be an issue regarding the incorporation and applicability of international rules into and within the

---

[28] Chancery Division, 9–12 October, 14 November 1989; Court of Appeal, 26–27 March, 9 April 1990; House of Lords, 26–28 November 1990, 21 February 1991.

[29] High Court, Queen's Bench Division, 3 August 1994.

[30] US District Court CD Cal., 18 September 1979, *affirmed on other grounds*, US Court of Appeals 9th Cir., 6 July–24 August 1981.

[31] US Bankruptcy Court D. Arizona, 15 August 1995.   [32] See pp. 46*f* below.

[33] See pp. 53*ff* below.

national legal order that is decisive to the question of domestic legal personality of international organizations. In this sense it is certainly justified to say that the methods of granting domestic legal personality depend primarily upon the domestic legal order.[34]

Treaties

Frequently, international agreements (founding treaties of international organizations, headquarters agreements, etc.) contain an express stipulation either directly granting legal personality[35] or imposing an obligation to provide for it domestically.[36] Most treaties constituting international organizations contain explicit provisions on the domestic legal personality of the organization in question.[37]

---

[34] Beitzke, 'Zivilrechtsfähigkeit', 84; See also C. F. Amerasinghe, 'International Legal Personality Revisited' (1955) 47 *Austrian Journal of Public and International Law* 123–45 at 125: 'Whether personality is recognized in municipal law will depend primarily on the municipal legal system and law concerned.' See, however, pp. 59*ff* below concerning the declarative or constitutive character of the domestic grant of domestic legal personality.

[35] See pp. 72*ff* below for examples. In a monist legal system, such treaty provisions are likely to be regarded as self-executing, thus being able to be relied upon without domestic legal implementation. See pp. 46*ff* below.

[36] For instance, the Agreement Between the United Nations and Austria for the Establishment of the European Centre for Social Welfare Training and Research of 24 July 1974 contained the following clearly non-self-executing obligation for Austria: 'The host Government shall take the necessary steps to establish the Centre as an autonomous non-profitmaking entity, having legal personality under Austrian law.' (cited in (1974) *United Nations Juridical Yearbook* 21). A similar provision was contained in the Agreement Between the United Nations and Austria to Continue the European Centre for Social Welfare Training and Research of 7 December 1978: 'The host Government shall take the necessary steps to ensure the Centre's status as an autonomous non-profitmaking entity having legal personality under Austrian law.' (cited in (1978) *United Nations Juridical Yearbook* 32). In a less explicit way, the personality provision of the Agreement Establishing the WTO could also be understood in this way. Article VIII(1) provides that: 'The WTO . . . shall *be accorded by each of its Members* such legal capacity as may be necessary for the exercise of its functions.' (emphasis added).

[37] E.g., Article 104 of the UN Charter, Article IX(2) of the IMF agreement, Article VII(2) of the IBRD agreement, Article XVI of the FAO agreement, Article 39 of the ILO agreement, Article 66 of the WHO agreement, Article 107 of the ITU agreement, Article 27 of the WMO agreement, Article 9 of the CERN agreement, Article 35 of the EFTA agreement and Article 12 of the WIPO agreement. For the exact wording of these provisions see pp. 72*ff* below. In some cases the relevant provision does not specify exactly whether it refers to international or domestic personality. For instance, Article IX(2) of the IMF Articles of Agreement and Article VII(2) of the IBRD Articles of Agreement merely provide that the Fund/Bank 'shall possess full juridical personality'. In such situations, a clarification can frequently be found by referring to the 'object and purpose' provision, normally preceding such a grant of personality. Article IX(1) of the IMF Articles of Agreement and Article VII(1) of the IBRD Articles of Agreement start out thus: 'To enable the [Fund/Bank] to fulfil the functions with which it is entrusted the status, immunities and privileges set forth in

The domestic legal personality of an international organization might also be provided for in agreements other than those establishing an international organization. Multilateral treaties, such as the UN General Convention[38] and Special Convention,[39] bilateral headquarters agreements and other treaties relating to the recognition of an international organization's status by a member or – more importantly – by a non-member country are examples.[40]

It has been argued that some constituent treaties of international organizations not containing any provision dealing with domestic legal personality[41] must be deemed to have implicitly conferred such personality.[42] Indeed, one might reason that certain functions entrusted to an international organization which can only be carried out by acting in the area of private law can be seen as an implicit grant of domestic legal personality.[43] This argument closely resembles the implied powers doctrine pertinent at the level of international legal personality.[44] Provisions

this article shall be accorded to the fund *in the territories of each member*.' (emphasis added). As a result it is a commonly shared view that these provisions relate to domestic juridical personality only. *Cf.* Arghyrios A. Fatouros, 'The World Bank's Impact on International Law – A Case Study in the International Law of Cooperation' in Gabriel M. Wilner (ed.), *Jus et Societas. Essays in Tribute to Wolfgang Friedmann* (The Hague, Boston and London, 1979), 62–95 at 65, for the IBRD. In a similar vein, the provision on the FAO's legal status in its Constitution, Article XVI, is not very explicit. Article XVI(1) provides: 'The organization shall have the capacity of a legal person to perform any legal act appropriate to its purpose which is not beyond the powers granted to it by this Constitution.' There is no explicit provision dealing with international legal personality. So this could apply to either form of personality. However, since Article XVI(2) deals with the 'immunities and facilities' of the FAO to be granted by its member states, one can infer that it is domestic personality that is referred to in Article XVI(1).

[38] Article I(1) of the General Convention.   [39] Article II(3) of the Special Convention.

[40] E.g., Article 7 of the OPEC Fund Headquarters Agreement with Austria of 1981 according to which '[t]he Government recognizes the juridical personality of the Fund and, in particular, its capacity . . .'. See also Article I(1) of the 1946 Interim Arrangement Between the UN and Switzerland providing that '[t]he Swiss Federal Council recognizes the international personality and legal capacity of the United Nations'. See also p. 61 below.

[41] For instance, the Universal Postal Union (UPU). The same is also true for some other older organizations, e.g. the International Institute of Agriculture.

[42] Hug – disputing any general customary rule conferring personality upon international organizations – submits that the UPU's domestic legal personality can be deduced from the explicit assignment of certain functions – among them the publishing of notes on international postal services, the printing of postal ID's and of intentional response cards as well as the publication of a journal (according to Articles 113, 115 and 117 of the UPU Rules of Procedure) – which clearly require legal capacity to enter into the necessary contractual relationships. Dieter Hug, *Die Rechtsstellung der in der Schweiz niedergelassenen internationalen Organisationen* (Berne, Frankfurt am Main, Nancy and New York, 1984), 65*ff*.

[43] Beitzke, 'Zivilrechtsfähigkeit', 88.

contained in a treaty establishing an international organization concerning separate property of the international organization, concerning the representation of the international organization, or providing for the capability to own property, to receive gifts or legacies, etc., provide evidence of such an implicit legal personality.[45]

Custom

Since most constitutive treaties expressly provide for the domestic legal personality of international organizations, the issue of a potential customary source of such personality may seem rather theoretical. It might become relevant, however, in two types of situations: (1) the rare case where the constituent treaty contains no provisions on domestic legal personality at all; and (2) where an international organization's potential legal personality in a non-member state is concerned.

1. As far as the first situation is concerned, where the constituent treaty contains no provisions on domestic legal personality, the majority opinion seems to deny a customary obligation of states to recognize that an international organization enjoys legal personality under their domestic law.[46] However, for practical purposes, the theory of an implicit conferment of domestic legal personality[47] will effectively replace the need to postulate a customary law duty.
2. Regarding the latter situation, where an international organization's potential legal personality in a non-member state is concerned, a duty for non-member states to recognize or accord domestic legal

---

[44] See pp. 72ff below.

[45] Cf. the treaty provision regulating UNRRA's capacities which does not expressly mention the organization's personality: 'The Administration shall have power to acquire, hold and convey property, to enter into contracts and undertake obligations, to designate or create agencies and to review the activities of agencies so created, to manage undertakings and in general to perform any legal act appropriate to its objects and purposes.' Article I(1) of the Agreement for United Nations Relief and Rehabilitation Administration (UNRRA). The Dutch district court's conclusion that, as a result of these specific powers, '[UNRRA] must also be considered a legal person under Dutch law, and as such competent to act as a party to legal proceedings' can be counted as an acknowledgment of an implicit conferment of domestic legal personality on UNRRA. UNRRA v. Daan, District Court Utrecht, 23 February 1949, (1949) 16 ILR 337.

[46] Beitzke, 'Zivilrechtsfähigkeit', 86; Schlüter, Die innerstaatliche Rechtsstellung, 63ff; Karl Zemanek, Das Vertragsrecht der internationalen Organisationen (Vienna, 1957), 131ff; see, however, Jean-Flavien Lalive, 'L'immunité de juridiction des états et des organisations internationales' (1953 III) 84 Recueil des Cours 205–396 at 304ff, arguing in favour of such a customary rule. See also the possibly different position of a seat state as discussed by Josef L. Kunz, 'Privileges and Immunities of International Organizations' (1947) 41 American Journal of International Law 828–62 at 849.

[47] See pp. 44f above.

personality to an international organization is generally denied by reference to the *res inter alios acta* rule.[48] Most authors seem – at least implicitly – to share that assumption.[49] It appears, however, again for practical purposes, that the readiness of third countries to recognize the domestic legal personality of international organizations in their respective legal orders as a result of their private international law/choice of law rules[50] or pursuant to domestic legislation[51] lessens the relevance of this question.

National legal rules

For a national court, confronted with the issue of the domestic legal personality of an international organization, it is a rule of *domestic* law that determines the legal status of such an entity within the domestic legal sphere. Even if this rule is of international origin,[52] to become operative for the purpose of determining an international organization's precise legal status under domestic law, the rule must form part of domestic law. Thus, only domestic law can define or attribute the status of domestic legal personality.

The incorporation of international rules concerning domestic legal personality may be achieved through various techniques such as adoption, general or specific transformation, etc.[53] Normally the relevant treaties leave it to the states parties how they implement a duty to confer domestic personality.[54] Frequently, domestic legislation on the issue of

---

[48] E.g., Hug, *Die Rechtsstellung*, 51, denying any relevance of the provisions of the UN Charter and of the constituent treaty of OIPC (Organisation internationale pour la protection civile) on the legal personality of these oriorganizations in Switzerland as a non-member country.

[49] Hug, *Die Rechtsstellung*, 65 with further references. According to Hug, an older doctrine seems to have held so: Lalive, 'L'immunité de juridiction', 303*ff*; Philippe Cahier, *Etude des accords de siège conclus entre les organisations internationales et les états où elles résident* (Milan, 1959), 71, 113.   [50] *Cf.* pp. 50*ff* below.

[51] Ignaz Seidl-Hohenveldern and Gerhard Loibl, *Das Recht der Internationalen Organisationen einschließlich der Supranationalen Gemeinschaften* (6th edn, Cologne, Berlin, Bonn and Munich, 1996), 53, give the example of Austrian legislation protecting the signs of Comecon and of the Commonwealth against private use as trademarks as examples of non-member states recognizing the domestic legal personality of international organizations.

[52] *Cf.* pp. 42*ff* above.

[53] See in general Ian Brownlie, *Principles of Public International Law* (4th edn, 1990), 43; Felix Ermacora, 'Völkerrecht und Landesrecht' in Hanspeter Neuhold, Waldemar Hummer and Christoph Schreuer (eds.), *Österreichisches Handbuch des Völkerrechts* (2nd edn, Vienna, 1991), 115–25 at 117*ff*; and Knut Ipsen, *Völkerrecht* (3rd edn, Munich, 1990), 1078*ff*.

[54] *Cf.* 13 UNCIO, Doc. 803, IV/2/A/7 (1945), 817, regarding Article 104 of the UN Charter: 'The Committee has preferred to express no opinion on the procedures of internal law necessary to assure this result [i.e., to provide for a juridical status permitting the UN to exercise its function]. These procedures may differ according to the legislation of each member State.'

the personality of international organizations will be part of the implementing legislation of treaty obligations. However, it may also be that, in
the absence of such explicit or implicit duties, states confer domestic
personality upon international organizations by genuinely domestic
norms. Moreover, domestic personality could also result from the application of the rules of private international law of a particular state.

If – in a monist system – international law, in particular treaty law,
forms part of national law, then domestic legal personality, provided for
in a treaty, will directly operate as a grant of such domestic personality.
On the other hand, in a dualist system – where international law is
incorporated into the domestic sphere only by implementing legislation
– a treaty provision stipulating the domestic legal personality of an
international organization does not *eo ipso* have this effect. Examples
taken from cases determining domestic legal personality of international
organizations clearly demonstrate these distinctive methods.

Domestic legal systems, allowing for the direct application of rules of
international law in principle, will see no obstacles to permitting the
direct invocation of and reliance on treaty norms (or rules of customary
international law) providing for domestic legal personality of international organizations. The requirement of a sufficiently clear and precise
quality of the international norms in issue under doctrines of direct
applicability[55] or concerning the self-executing character of international norms[56] will be fulfilled in most cases.

For the US, as member state of an international organization, it seems
well settled that self-executing international agreements containing provisions on the legal personality or capacity of such international organizations constitute domestic (federal) law.[57] Accordingly, in *Balfour, Guthrie
& Co. Ltd et al. v. United States et al.*,[58] a US court affirmed the UN's capacity
to institute legal proceedings in the US based on Article 104 of the UN
Charter which – as a treaty ratified by the US – formed 'part of the
supreme law of the land. No implementing legislation would appear to be

---

[55] *Cf.* Waldemar Hummer, 'Reichweite und Grenzen unmittelbarer Anwendbarkeit der
Freihandelsabkommen' in Hans-Georg Koppensteiner (ed.), *Rechtsfragen der Freihandelsabkommen der Europäischen Wirtschaftsgemeinschaft mit den EFTA-Staaten* (Vienna, 1987), 43–83
at 43*ff*; and August Reinisch, 'Zur unmittelbaren Anwendbarkeit von EWR-Recht' (1993)
34 *Zeitschrift für Rechtsvergleichung, internationales Privatrecht und Europarecht* 11–30 at 16.
[56] *Restatement (Third)*, § 111, Comment h.
[57] Frederic L. Kirgis, *International Organizations in Their Legal Setting* (2nd edn, St Paul, MN,
1993), 19.
[58] USDC ND Cal., 5 May 1950. In this case the UN brought an action for damages arising out
of loss of and damage to cargo shipped on behalf of a UN agency on a US-owned vessel.

necessary to endow the United Nations with legal capacity in the United States.'[59]

Similarly, in a number of other countries, where (mostly constitutional) national rules provide for the domestic applicability of international norms, treaty provisions on the domestic legal personality of international organizations have been usually given direct effect.

This was apparently the solution of the Dutch Supreme Court in *UNRRA v. Daan*.[60] The district court rejected the defendant's argument that UNRRA had no legal personality required to bring suit in domestic courts because neither the UNRRA Constitution nor Dutch law specifically provided for such personality. The court held that, as a result of the treaty provision, as UNRRA had the power to acquire and transfer property, to conclude contracts and to perform all legal acts appropriate to the fulfilment of its tasks 'it must also be considered a legal person under Dutch law, and as such competent to act as a party to legal proceedings'. The Supreme Court affirmed and explicitly stated that '[t]he question whether such a body must be recognized as a legal entity in an action in Holland did not depend on any provision of Netherlands law'.[61]

In the Belgian *Manderlier v. Organisation des Nations Unies and Etat Belge (Ministre des Affaires Etrangères)* case[62] the direct application of the UN Charter provision on the organization's domestic legal personality was taken for granted. According to a Brussels court:

The United Nations was set up by the San Francisco Charter of 26 January 1945, approved in Belgium by the Law of 14 December 1945. By Article 104 of that Charter the organization enjoys in the territory of each of its Members such legal capacity as may be necessary to it. The defendant is consequently competent to appear in legal proceedings in Belgium.[63]

On the other hand, domestic legal systems may preclude the direct applicability of treaties. A prominent example is the UK system where the conclusion of treaties is regarded as a prerogative of the Crown and the domestic implementation of such treaties as an exclusive right of the Parliament.[64] The extensive Tin Council litigation[65] as well as the judicial pronouncements in *Arab Monetary Fund v. Hashim (No. 3)*[66] provide ample evidence of this approach. International rules providing for the domestic

---

[59] (1950) 17 ILR 323 at 324.
[60] Cantonal Court Amersfoort, 16 June 1948, District Court Utrecht, 23 February 1949, Supreme Court, 19 May 1950. See also p. 40 above.
[61] (1949) 16 ILR 337.   [62] Civil Tribunal of Brussels, 11 May 1966.
[63] (1972) 45 ILR 446 at 450.   [64] See, in general, Brownlie, *Principles*, 47.
[65] See pp. 118*ff* below.   [66] See pp. 64*ff* below.

legal personality of international organizations become legally relevant in the English legal order only when they are expressly incorporated by an Act of Parliament. It results from this dualist approach that the domestic legal personality of international organizations entirely depends upon the existence of domestic rules providing for such personality.

Provisions of domestic legislation conferring legal personality are not infrequent in international practice. Many countries have enacted special legislation enabling them to confer domestic legal personality upon international organizations.[67] In dualist countries these provisions are necessary to implement international obligations to that effect because, even if domestic legal personality is granted in a treaty, this grant becomes operative only upon national implementing measures.[68] In the UK, for instance, an Order in Council on the basis of the International Organisations Act 1968 may grant the 'legal capacity of a body corporate'[69] to any organization of which the UK and one or more foreign states are members. Similar statutory law exists in Australia, Canada and New Zealand.[70] It is more surprising to have such legislation in countries which can be counted among those of a monist tradition, where treaties are the 'supreme law of the land' and where custom is also regarded as law of the land. This is the case, for example, in the US where – despite the direct applicability of personality provisions contained in most constituent agreements of international organizations – section 2(a) of the International Organizations Immunities Act 1945 (IOIA)[71] provides for domestic legal status to be accorded to international organizations. In such monist systems, specific legislation might safeguard the possibility of granting personality to international organizations in which the legislating state does not participate[72] or where agreements with international organizations do not address the issue or have not been concluded.

---

[67] E.g., the IOIA in the US, the International Organisations Act 1968 in the UK, etc. For a comprehensive overview, see United Nations, *Legislative Texts and Treaty Provisions Concerning the Legal Status, Privileges and Immunities of International Organizations*, vol. I (1959) and vol. II (1961).

[68] Dominicé, 'L'immunité de juridiction', 164.

[69] Section 2(a) of the International Organisations Act 1968.

[70] *Cf.* Díaz-González (Special Rapporteur), 'Second Report on Relations Between States and International Organizations (Second Part of the Topic)' in *Yearbook of the International Law Commission* (1985), vol. II, Part One, 109.

[71] See p. 74 note 190 below.

[72] *Cf.* the IOIA provisions allowing the extension of legal capacities and immunities provided therein to organizations of which the US is not a member. See 22 USCA § 288f-1, § 288f-2, § 288f-3 and § 288h relating to the ESA, the Organization of Eastern Caribbean States, the OAU, the ICRC and the Commission of the European Communities.

Interestingly, there is no specific legislation in Switzerland,[73] although Switzerland, as a non-member of a number of international organizations that are operating in Switzerland, certainly has a need to regulate this issue. It seems, however, that the web of Swiss bilateral agreements concluded with such organizations provides a viable alternative. Another valid reason to enact specific legislation lies in the potentially wider reach of such domestic rules that might enable a country to confer domestic legal personality to entities not fitting into the exact definition of international organizations.[74]

Finally, the domestic legal personality of international organizations is frequently recognized as a result of the application of rules of private international law. It has been argued that one of the two main reasons for granting domestic legal personality to international organizations[75] lies in the fact that an 'organization has been *lawfully established* by foreign States and according to the rules of *private international law* legal personality acquired abroad is accepted'.[76] This technique of accepting the legal personality of foreign juridical persons is inspired by the provisions of the 1956 Hague Convention on the Recognition of the Legal Personality of Foreign Companies, Associations and Foundations[77] and the 1968 Brussels Convention on the Mutual Recognition of Corporations and Juridical

---

[73] Hug, *Die Rechtsstellung*, 58.

[74] *Cf.* the 1983 designation of Interpol as an organization entitled to enjoy the privileges (including domestic legal personality), exemptions and immunities conferred by the IOIA by Presidential Executive Order No. 12425, 48 *Federal Register* 28069. See, however, the Austrian Law on the Granting of Privileges and Immunities to International Organizations, which does not contain any reference to domestic legal personality, probably because of the direct applicability of international law within the domestic legal sphere and because domestic legal personality is not viewed a privilege or immunity in a technical sense by the Austrian legislator. *Cf.* Zemanek, *Das Vertragsrecht der internationalen Organisationen*, 131, note 2.

[75] The other one would be the result of the recognition of the international legal personality of an international organization since 'legal personality under domestic law follows from personality under public international law'. Bekker, *The Legal Position of Intergovernmental Organizations*, 63. *The assumption that international legal personality directly entails domestic legal personality is, however, not undisputed. See pp. 59ff below.*

[76] Bekker, *The Legal Position*, 63, mainly relying on Henry G. Schermers, *International Institutional Law* (Alphen aan den Rijn and Rockville, 2nd edn, 1980), 791. See also Georges van Hecke, 'Contracts Between International Organizations and Private Law Persons' in Rudolf Bernhardt (ed.), *Encyclopedia of Public International Law* (2nd edn, 1992), vol. I, 812–14 at 812, who speaks of the possibility that international organizations enjoy legal personality in third states 'either upon the basis of a specific treaty to that effect . . . or upon the basis of the third country's rules on the recognition of foreign legal persons' without referring to custom.

[77] Hague Convention on the Recognition of the Legal Personality of Foreign Companies, Associations and Foundations, 1 June 1956.

Persons,[78] as well as by domestic private international law/conflict of laws principles evidencing the same approach.[79]

There seems to be abundant evidence that member states of international organizations in general recognize the legal personality of international organizations under their domestic law also in cases where no explicit treaty provision to that effect exists.[80] In non-member countries, the legal personality of international organizations is also usually recognized, either by deducing it from the organizations' international legal personality or by the application of the private international law rule on the recognition of legal personality acquired abroad.[81]

The analogy to the recognition of foreign juridical persons, however, is not unproblematic. International organizations are created by international agreement among subjects of international law; they are not created according to the law of any one state. Thus they have no legal personality 'acquired abroad' in the strict sense. As an English court put it with regard to the Tin Council, strictly speaking that organization 'is neither an English nor a foreign corporation, but the creation of a treaty'.[82] Thus, it has been proposed to regard the internal law of an organization as its *lex personalis*.[83] In a variation on the latter view, it has been said that one could 'regard the treaty provisions as the national law of the organization. An international organization will thus exist in the domestic law of member and non-member states alike as a *societé sans loi nationale*.'[84]

---

[78] See Gerhard Kegel, *Internationales Privatrecht* (5th edn, Munich, 1985), 347ff.

[79] Bernhard Grossfeld, *Praxis des Internationalen Privat- und Wirtschaftsrechts* (Hamburg, 1975), 26. See also IDI Resolution on 'Les sociétés anonymes en droit international privé', adopted at its Warsaw Session 1965, (1965 II) 51 *Annuaire de l'Institut de Droit International* 263.

[80] As to the domestic legal personality of the UN Specialized Agencies, see *Yearbook of the International Law Commission* (1967), II, 299ff; see also Schermers, *International Institutional Law*, 790.

[81] Schermers, *International Institutional Law*, 791.

[82] *Re International Tin Council*, High Court, Chancery Division, 22 January 1987; (1988) 77 ILR 18–41 at 27. As a consequence, the High Court thought that an organization's 'recognition by the courts of a member state is a matter, not of that state's private international law, but of its constitutional law'. *Ibid.*, 28.

[83] *Cf.* Finn Seyersted, 'Applicable Law in Relations Between Intergovernmental Organizations and Private Parties' (1967 III) 122 *Recueil des Cours* 427–616 at 569: 'the lex personalis of an [intergovernmental organization] is its own internal law, in the same manner as the lex personalis of a State is its own municipal law'. Ignaz Seidl-Hohenveldern, *Corporations in and under International Law* (Cambridge, 1987), 108, suggests 'regard[ing] the treaty provisions as the national law of the organization'. A similar approach is taken by Amerasinghe, 'Réponse', in (1995 I) 66 *Annuaire de l'Institut de Droit International* 349.

[84] Seidl-Hohenveldern, *Corporations*, 108.

This view was firmly upheld by the panel of arbitrators in *Westland Helicopters Ltd* v. *Arab Organization for Industrialization, United Arab Emirates, Kingdom of Saudi Arabia, State of Qatar, Arab Republic of Egypt and Arab British Helicopter Company*.[85] When addressing the nature of the defendant organization, it rejected the view 'that no legal person may exist without a legal foundation within a national legal order'.[86] In the tribunal's view:

it is, from the outset, impossible to attribute to it, *a posteriori*, an applicable law according to the rules of private international law, that is to say to submit this entity to the law of either the place where the centre of its business activities lies, or the place of its management, or any other place . . . whereas it is true that an individual cannot set up a legal entity without the authorization of a State or a State law, sovereign States may themselves dispense with such a basis. Their acts have the force of law, and if a State alone can create by its acts (even without recourse to its legislation previously in force) a legal person, several States clearly have the same power when they act together and with common intent.[87]

The relevance of the international legal personality of international organizations for their domestic personality

It has been suggested that the domestic legal personality of an international organization could somehow directly flow from its international legal personality.[88] Accordingly, the legal personality of an international organization under domestic law would be entirely dependent upon its international legal personality. This idea of an 'implicit' domestic recognition of personality has caused some confusion among writers.

It is important to distinguish this concept from the question of an 'implied recognition of international organizations' by other persons of

---

[85] Interim Arbitration Award Regarding Jurisdiction of 5 March 1984, 8 June 1982, 5 March 1984, 25 July 1985. The Arab Organization for Industrialization (AOI) was established by treaty between the four defendant states in the arbitral proceedings in order to contribute to a joint arms industry. In 1978, the AOI entered into a 'Shareholders' Agreement' with Westland Helicopters Ltd, an English company, and formed a joint stock company, Arab British Helicopter Company, for the manufacturing and marketing of helicopters developed by Westland. This contract contained an explicit arbitration clause concerning 'any controversy or dispute which may arise between the parties in connection with the interpretation, application or effect of this Agreement'. Following the Camp David peace accord between Israel and Egypt, the three other AOI member states announced the liquidation of the AOI's existence, while Egypt provided for its further existence under domestic law. Westland filed a request for arbitration claiming UK£126 million from AOI and its member states. In its interim award of 5 March 1984, the arbitral tribunal held that, in the absence of any express exclusion of liability of the member states, it had to be inferred that the states were liable for the obligations of the organization including the contractual duty to arbitrate and thus upheld its jurisdiction.
[86] (1989) 80 ILR 595 at 611.   [87] *Ibid.*   [88] For more detail, see pp. 59*ff* below.

international law which can be raised on the international plane only. In the latter context, one would ask whether the international legal personality of an international organization might be recognized by other subjects of international law through the performance of certain acts, e.g. the conclusion of a treaty, the establishment of official relations, etc.[89] The question of an implied recognition of the domestic legal personality of international organizations, however, refers to the issue of whether the recognition of their international legal personality automatically includes a recognition of their personality on the domestic level or merely entails a duty to recognize them domestically.[90]

International legal personality

The international legal personality of international organizations, their existence as subjects of international law, is widely recognized today. The fierce scholarly debate over the (international) personality of international organizations, reflecting the sharp political divide between Communist and Western capitalist states,[91] has yielded to a more or less generally accepted view that international organizations are, or at least can be, subjects of international law capable of enjoying a legal personality of their own which is distinct from the personalities of their member states.[92]

What remains subject to dispute in many cases are the legal grounds for and the extent of such personality. The first aspect relates to questions such as why organizations can be considered subjects of international law at all and what exactly the legal reason for enjoying that status is. These issues are to be determined again primarily by ascertaining the applicable sources of law and will be dealt with in this section. The second

---

[89] *Cf.* Seidl-Hohenveldern and Loibl, *Das Recht der Internationalen Organisationen*, 86.

[90] It has been suggested, for instance, that a seat state is under a legal obligation to grant personality under domestic law to an international organization 'in so far as it is necessary for the fulfillment of its functions and not beyond the powers granted to it by its Constitutions'. Kunz, 'Privileges and Immunities', 849.

[91] Mario Bettati, *Le droit des organisations internationales* (Paris, 1987), 20; Christopher O. Osakwe, 'Contemporary Soviet Doctrine on the Juridical Nature of Universal International Organizations' (1971) 65 *American Journal of International Law* 502–21 at 502*ff*; and Schermers, *International Institutional Law*, 779. The vigorous denial of legal personality of international organizations was, however, not only supported by Soviet doctrine, but also by a number of Italian scholars.

[92] *Cf.* Bardo Faßbender, 'Die Völkerrechtssubjektivität internationaler Organisationen' (1986) 37 *Osterreichische Zeitschrift für öffentliches Recht und Völkerrecht* 17–47 at 17*ff*; Heribert Franz Köck and Peter Fischer, *Internationale Organisationen* (3rd edn, Eisenstadt, 1997), 565*ff*; Schermers, *International Institutional Law*, 779; and Seidl-Hohenveldern and Loibl, *Das Recht der Internationalen Organisationen*, 40.

aspect relates to the extent of their legal personality, to the question of whether international organizations occupy a status in international law similar to that of individual states and, if not, which types of activities they can legally perform. Although this aspect is certainly dependent upon the applicable sources of law as well, it will be dealt with in a separate section dealing with the consequences of a regularly 'functionally' limited personality.[93]

International legal personality is usually conferred upon an organization in its founding treaty. Unfortunately, unlike many express provisions as to the domestic legal personality, this grant of international legal personality to international organizations is rarely made in an explicit manner in the relevant constituent instruments.[94] While, for instance, Article 210 of the EC Treaty and Article 6 of the ECSC Treaty expressly provide for the international legal personality of the respective Communities,[95] no such provision is made in the UN Charter. Its Article 104 clearly refers to domestic personality only.[96] In such cases, the most frequent guidance used to ascertain an organization's international legal personality are certain legal capacities that are expressly provided for in the constitutional texts of international organizations, most prominently among them a treaty-making power, but also privileges and immunities, etc. Common opinion – supported by the explicit *travaux préparatoires* of the UN Charter – is ready to accept the aggregate of these capacities or powers in the constituent treaty as an implicit conferment of international legal personality.[97]

As far as the UN is concerned, the ICJ has more or less authoritatively resolved this issue in the *Reparations* case[98] where it affirmed the 'implicit

---

[93] See pp. 71ff below.

[94] Amerasinghe, 'International Legal Personality Revisited', 125; Christoph H. Schreuer, 'Internationale Organisationen' in Hanspeter Neuhold, Waldemar Hummer and Christoph Schreuer (eds.), *Österreichisches Handbuch des Völkerrechts* (2nd edn, Vienna, 1991), 157–99 at 163; and Seidl-Hohenveldern, *Corporations*, 86.

[95] Although Article 210 of the EC Treaty only speaks of legal personality in an unqualified way, it is clear from the context (according to Article 211 the Community possesses legal capacities in *the member states*) that international legal personality is meant.

[96] Article 104 of the UN Charter speaks of the organization's legal capacity 'in the territory of each of its Members'.

[97] See the report on Article 104 of the UN Charter: 'As regards the question of international legal personality, the Subcommittee has considered it superfluous to make this the subject of a text. In effect, it will be determined implicitly from the provisions of the Charter taken as a whole.' 13 UNCIO, Doc. 803, IV/2/A/7 (1945), 817. For the IBRD, see Fatouros, 'The World Bank's Impact', 65.

[98] *Reparation for Injuries Suffered in the Service of the United Nations*, Advisory Opinion, (1949) *ICJ Reports* 174.

conferment' view. The case arose from the 1948 assassination by Israeli terrorists of the UN mediator in Palestine, the Swedish Count Folke Bernadotte, while on duty in Jerusalem.[99] The UN General Assembly requested an advisory opinion from the ICJ, asking whether the UN had the capacity to bring an international claim against the responsible state in order to obtain reparation for damage caused to itself and to the victim, represented by his relatives. If this question were answered in the affirmative, it was further asked how a request for reparation by the UN could be reconciled with the rights of the victim's national state. These issues were unclear because the particular capacity to make an international claim was not expressly provided for in the UN Charter and because, under traditional international law, diplomatic protection could only be exercised by the state of which the victim was a national. Although the ICJ was only asked whether the UN had 'the capacity to bring an international claim', the ICJ interpreted this question as relating to the issue of whether the organization possessed international personality. The ICJ concluded, on the basis of the rights of the UN to require member states to assist it and to accept and carry out Security Council decisions and on the basis of the UN's privileges and immunities and its power to conclude agreements, that 'the Organization was intended to exercise and enjoy, and is in fact exercising and enjoying, functions and rights which can only be explained on the basis of the possession of a large measure of international personality and the capacity to operate upon an international plane'.[100]

However, the 'indicative' approach of assuming an implicit conferment of international legal personality carries with it an inherent danger of circular argument.[101] Even the ICJ in the *Reparations* case did not escape circularity: the ICJ inferred from the specific powers bestowed on the UN that it had international personality and then went on to deduce from the existence of such personality that it had the specific power to bring an international claim for one of its officials.[102] This danger also becomes apparent in views such as a 'wide contractual theory' according to which not only the explicitly enumerated rights and duties in the relevant constitutional text, but also – following the implied powers doctrine –

---

[99] See for the background of these facts, Kati Marton, *A Death in Jerusalem: The Assassination by Jewish Extremists of the First Arab/Israeli Peacemaker* (New York, 1994).

[100] (1949) *ICJ Reports* 174 at 179.

[101] Derek W. Bowett, *The Law of International Institutions* (4th edn, London, 1982), 337.

[102] *Reparation for Injuries Suffered in the Service of the United Nations*, Advisory Opinion, (1949) *ICJ Reports* 174 at 179 and 182–4.

those implicitly bestowed upon it, will be constitutive for the legal personality of an international organization.[103]

For the UN, again the *Reparations* opinion clarified the matter. According to the ICJ, by entrusting certain functions to the UN, its members intended that the UN possess the competence to discharge those functions effectively. In the specific case this included the capacity to bring diplomatic claims and to afford effective protection for its agents in order to ensure the efficient and independent performance of UN missions. The ICJ summed up this aspect of the UN's personality in the by now classical formulation of the implied powers doctrine stating that:

under international law, the Organization must be deemed to have those powers which, though not expressly provided in the Charter, are conferred upon it by necessary implication as being essential to the performance of its duties.[104]

The question of whether the holding of the *Reparations* opinion could be applied to other intergovernmental organizations as well is not uncontroversial.[105] This scepticism might be justified as far as the ICJ addressed the capacity of the UN to bring an international claim against non-member states.[106] Otherwise, however, the implicit personality

---

[103] *Cf.* the references in Faßbender, 'Die Völkerrechtssubjektivität internationaler Organisationen', 49.

[104] *Reparation for Injuries Suffered in the Service of the United Nations*, Advisory Opinion, (1949) *ICJ Reports* 174 at 182.

[105] Note, 'Federal Jurisdiction over International Organizations' (1952) 61 *Yale Law Journal* 111–17 at 112, note 4. According to the author of this note, a similar reasoning would be appropriate for UN specialized agencies only. See also Arangio-Ruiz in *Yearbook of the International Law Commission* (1985), vol. I, 289; and McCaffrey in *Yearbook of the International Law Commission* (1985), vol. I, 293. See, however, Seidl-Hohenveldern, *Corporations*, 88, who thinks that the ICJ's finding of the UN's 'objective international personality *erga omnes*' constitutes an 'exception granted to it alone'.

[106] Rosalyn Higgins, 'The Legal Consequences for Member States of the Non-Fulfilment by International Organizations of Their Obligations Toward Third Parties – Provisional Report' (1995) 66 *Annuaire de l'Institut de Droit International* 373–420 at 384. In order to allow for this extension, the ICJ developed an 'objective personality' theory by holding that 'fifty States, representing the vast majority of the members of the international community, had the power, in conformity with international law, to bring into being an entity possessing objective international personality, and not merely personality recognized by them alone, together with capacity to bring international claims'. *Reparation for Injuries Suffered in the Service of the United Nations*, Advisory Opinion, (1949) *ICJ Reports* 185. This concept should be kept apart from the 'objective international personality' concept developed by Seyersted which finds a basis for the legal personality of international organizations not in the 'subjective' will derived from treaties, but rather in either the 'objective' circumstance of their existence or in custom. *Cf.* Finn Seyersted, 'Objective International Personality of Intergovernmental Organizations: Do Their Capacities Really Depend Upon the Conventions Establishing Them?' (1964) 34 *Nordisk Tidsskrift for International Ret* 1–112 at 1.

concept appears to be quite well adaptable to other international organizations. In practice, the indicative approach seems to be generally accepted today and is also applied to many other international organizations.[107]

According to most authors,[108] however, a conferment of international legal personality by the member states in the founding treaty – even if only implicitly – is still necessary. This 'traceability' to the will of the founding members might also account for the notion of a 'derivative' international legal personality of international organizations.[109]

While the above-mentioned approaches all rely – to at least some degree – on the will of the states creating an international organization to bestow international personality upon it (as can be directly or indirectly deduced from treaty provisions), a broader theory relies on objective criteria – independent of the subjective will of the states concerned – in order to ascertain the international legal personality of international organizations. According to the most prominent version of this theory of the 'objective international personality' of international organizations, a rule of customary international law confers international legal personality upon international organizations which fulfil certain objective requirements. Most importantly, an organization must have at least one organ which can express a will of the organization itself:

Such organizations have an inherent capacity to perform any sovereign and international act which they are in a practical position to perform, even if their constitution contains no relevant provision and even if there is no evidence of any relevant intention of their drafters or of any previous practice by or in respect of the Organization. [They are thus] general subjects of international law, *ipso facto* and on the basis of general and customary international law, in basically the same manner as States.[110]

This objective legal personality theory finds some corroboration in the work of the ILC on relations between states and international organiz-

---

[107] Schermers, *International Institutional Law*, 778.

[108] Seidl-Hohenveldern and Loibl, *Das Recht der Internationalen Organisationen*, 38*ff*; Alfred Verdross and Bruno Simma, *Universelles Völkerrecht, Theorie und Praxis* (3rd edn, Berlin, 1984), 216*ff*; Bruno Simma and Christoph Vedder, 'Art. 210' in Eberhard Grabitz (ed.), *Kommentar zum EWG-Vertrag* (Munich, 1983), Article 210(1).

[109] '*Abgeleitete Völkerrechtsfähigkeit*' (Simma and Vedder, 'Art. 210' in Grabitz, *Kommentar zum EWG-Vertrag*, Article 210(2)) or '*abgeleitete Völkerrechtssubjekte*' in the sense of being derived from the will of its founding members, the sovereign states. See also Seidl-Hohenveldern and Loibl, *Das Recht der Internationalen Organisationen*, 43.

[110] Seyersted, 'Objective International Personality', 99*ff*; see also Zemanek, 'Réponse', in (1995 I) 66 *Annuaire de l'Institut de Droit International* 325.

ations.[111] Its Draft Article 5 provides quite generally that: 'International organizations shall enjoy legal personality under international law'. From the determination of the capacity to conclude treaties, probably the most important aspect of international legal personality, one might infer that the legal personality does not exclusively result from the will of the states creating the organization, but might be a consequence of (customary) international law. Draft Article 6 clarifies that the treaty-making power of an international organization is determined 'by the relevant rules of that organization *and* by international law'.[112] The Draft Articles define the 'relevant rules of the organization' as the constitutive treaties plus the organization's decisions and practice.[113] Since the treaty-making power is thus not exclusively a matter of the constitutive treaty, but also of an organization's practice and of international law in general, it appears that customary rules might be relevant as well.

In addition to these unfinished and now shelved ILC Draft Articles on the relations between states and international organizations,[114] the completed codification – or, for that matter, progressive development – achieved by the ILC in its Convention on the Law of Treaties between States and International Organizations or Between International Organizations[115] might support the objective legal personality theory. Article 6 of this Convention provides: 'The capacity of an international organization to conclude treaties is governed by the rules of that organization.' These rules are defined as 'the constituent instruments, decisions and resolutions adopted in accordance with them, and established practice of the organization'.[116] The Convention's preambular paragraph 11 reads: 'Noting that international organizations possess the capacity to conclude treaties which is necessary for the exercise of their functions

---

[111] *Cf.* Leonardo Díaz-González (Special Rapporteur), 'Fourth Report on Relations Between States and International Organizations (Second Part of the Topic)' (UN Doc. A/CN.4/424) *Yearbook of the International Law Commission* (1989), vol. II, Part One, 153–68.

[112] *Ibid.* (emphasis added).

[113] According to Draft Article 1(1)(b) 'relevant rules of the organization' 'means, in particular, the constituent instruments of the organization, its decisions and resolutions adopted in accordance therewith and its established practice'. *Ibid.*

[114] *Cf.* Report of the ILC on the work of its forty-fourth session, *Yearbook of the International Law Commission* (1992), vol. II, Part Two, 1, at 53 'deciding not to pursue consideration of the topic further . . . unless the General Assembly should decide otherwise'. See also Peter H. F. Bekker, 'The Work of the International Law Commission on "Relations Between States and International Organizations" Discontinued: An Assessment' (1993) 6 *Leiden Journal of International Law* 3–16 at 3*ff.*

[115] 1986 Vienna Convention on the Law of Treaties Between States and International Organizations or Between International Organizations.

[116] *Ibid.*, Article 2(1)(j).

and the fulfilment of their purposes.' This could be understood as an affirmation of the view that international organizations enjoy certain capacities – constitutive for their international legal personality – independently from an express conferment of them by their member states. One may thus, for instance, still maintain that the treaty-making capacity of an international organization itself flows from general international law.[117]

However, the theory that international organizations enjoy international legal personality as a matter of customary law is not generally accepted.[118] It still remains the majority view that personality is determined – either expressly or implicitly – by an organization's constituent instrument.[119] In practice the sharp theoretical divide between the two views is mitigated by the result of an expansive interpretation of the implied powers doctrine. Where specific capacities – and arguably the personality – of an international organization are regarded as resulting from an implied will of the founding member states, recourse to custom as a source of personality becomes superfluous.

The declarative or constitutive character of the conferment of domestic legal personality

If the existence of international legal personality of an international organization directly implied that such an international organization also enjoyed legal personality under domestic law, any specific treaty, customary or domestic rule to that effect would be superfluous. It is exactly this automatic consequence of international legal personality within domestic law that is claimed by a group of scholars adhering to a

---

[117] Finn Seyersted, 'Treaty Making Capacity of Intergovernmental Organizations: Article 6 of the International Law Commission's Draft Articles on the Law of Treaties Between States and International Organizations or Between International Organizations' (1983) 34 *Osterreichische Zeitschrift für öffentliches Recht und Völkerrecht* 261–7 at 266. See also Karl Zemanek, 'The United Nations Conference on the Law of Treaties Between States and International Organizations or Between International Organizations: The Unrecorded History of its "General Agreement" in Karl-Heinz Böckstiegel, Hans-Ernst Folz, Jörg Manfred Mössner and Karl Zemanek (eds.), *Völkerrecht – Recht der Internationalen Organisationen – Weltwirtschaftsrecht. Festschrift für Ignaz Seidl-Hohenveldern* (Cologne, Berlin, Bonn and Munich, 1988), 665–79 at 671, who thinks that the textual compromise arrived at in the 1986 Vienna Convention on the Law of Treaties Between States and International Organizations or Between International Organizations lends itself to the interpretation 'that international organizations possess treaty-making capacity by virtue of general (customary) international law, if that capacity is necessary for the exercise of their functions and the fulfilment of their purposes' which 'comes very close to, if it is not identical with the theory which *Finn Seyersted* has defenced [sic] for many years'.

[118] *Cf.* Ipsen, *Völkerrecht*, 68.   [119] Higgins, 'Provisional Report', 380.

'declarative' view as to the effect of domestic law provisions of legal personality.[120] They are opposed by scholars upholding a 'constitutive' view[121] who treat the issue of international legal personality separately from the question of personality under domestic law and would dispute the assumption that domestic personality could be directly deduced from international personality.[122]

However, on closer scrutiny, the effect of international legal personality within domestic law can be considered under two aspects: on the one hand, the relationship between international legal personality and domestic legal personality; and, on the other hand, the relationship between domestic legal personality as required by international law and domestic legal personality as accorded under domestic law. In both situations one could adopt a declarative or a constitutive view.

In the first context, it could be argued that international legal personality automatically implies that an entity should also have domestic legal personality and would thereby adhere to a declarative view; whereas if one argued that domestic legal personality was a separate issue that might or might not be attributed to an entity enjoying international legal personality, one would follow a constitutive view.

As far as the second aspect is concerned, a declarative view would maintain that the fact that a norm of international law provides for domestic legal personality automatically means that this domestic personality is given under domestic law. Under a constitutive view, it could be argued that, though an international norm might oblige states to provide for domestic legal personality, its actual existence, however, depends upon the domestic legal order.

The debate concerning declarative and constitutive views is problematic mainly because these different aspects are rarely considered separately and a combination of them is often used in drawing certain conclusions. Frequently, a combination of both aspects is understood to support either a declarative or a constitutive theory. Under such a combined declarative view, some authors think that the domestic legal personality of an international organization directly results from its interna-

---

[120] Kuljit Ahluwalia, *The Legal Status, Privileges and Immunities of the Specialized Agencies of the United Nations and Certain Other International Organizations* (The Hague, 1964), 60; Dominicé, 'L'immunité de juridiction', 165; C. Wilfred Jenks, 'The Legal Personality of International Organizations' (1945) 22 *British Yearbook of International Law* 267–75 at 270ff.

[121] Bekker, *The Legal Position*, 74, speaks of a 'scholarly dispute' between the declaratory and the constitutive views.

[122] Beitzke, 'Zivilrechtsfähigkeit', 86; Hug, *Die Rechtsstellung*, 65; Hans Kelsen, *The Law of the United Nations: A Critical Analysis of its Fundamental Problems* (London, 1950), 336.

tional legal personality, for instance by holding that the juridical capacity under domestic law is nothing but 'le reflet, la conséquence nécessaire et inéluctable, de sa qualité de sujet de droit international'[123] or that, in the absence of treaty provisions or domestic legislation, 'personality under domestic law should follow by implication from the existence of the organization'.[124] Consequently, any treaty provisions granting domestic legal personality would be merely declarative. In support of such a declarative view, certain treaty provisions recognizing the legal personality of international organizations under domestic law are sometimes cited – among them, for instance, Article I(1) of the 1946 Interim Arrangement between the UN and Switzerland providing that [t]he Swiss Federal Council recognizes the international personality and legal capacity of the United Nations[125] – suggesting that it is only possible to recognize something already existing.[126] This would imply that international organizations enjoying international legal personality are automatically legal persons of domestic law. The conclusions drawn from these provisions, however, appear to go a little too far. To take the example of Switzerland, it definitely had to recognize the international personality of the UN of which it is not a member state. As a matter of legal logic it could not bestow international personality upon the UN because it was not one of its founding members. Assuming that 'legal capacity' of the UN refers indeed to domestic legal personality,[127] it still seems that such recogni-

---

[123] Dominicé, 'L'immunité de juridiction', 165 ('the mirror, the necessary and unavoidable consequence of its quality as a subject of international law').

[124] Bekker, *The Legal Position*, 62. He tries to affirm this implicit personality concept by the following argument: if such domestic personality were not implied, the organization would depend upon the common action of all the member states together in order to carry out its activities 'which would clearly impede the unhampered exercise of functions, as dictated by considerations of functional necessity'.

[125] A similar provision can be found in Article 2 of the 1946 Agreement between the Swiss Federal Council and ILO according to which '[t]he Swiss Federal Council recognises the international personality and legal capacity in Switzerland of the International Labour Organisation'.

[126] Dominicé, 'L'immunité de juridiction', 165, alludes, in particular, to this UN–Swiss agreement.

[127] This seems to be true for the ILO by virtue of the explicit reference to 'legal capacity in Switzerland', but it might be doubted in the UN arrangement which – concluded only shortly later – does not contain the clarifying reference 'in Switzerland'. On the other hand, the fact that the Interim Arrangement of 1946 broadly deals with privileges and immunities of the UN in Switzerland and follows closely the ILO agreement indicate that the 'recognition' of legal capacity refers to domestic legal personality. Also the term 'legal capacity' – if understood as referring to international legal capacity – could be seen as tautological, since international personality is expressly mentioned in the same sentence.

tion by Switzerland has a constitutive character for the Swiss legal order.[128]

According to the constitutive view, domestic legal personality ultimately depends upon a (constitutive) domestic legal act.[129] In other words, domestic legal personality only stems from the domestic law of the respective countries concerned, not directly from any treaties the member states might have concluded[130] or from the organization's international legal personality. Accordingly, the presence or absence of international personality does not necessarily determine the legal personality of an international organization under the domestic law of member or non-member states. One rather has to look into the domestic law of a particular state, including its international agreements that might have direct domestic legal effect, in order to ascertain whether a particular international organization enjoys domestic legal personality.

While the constitutive view appears to rest on firm ground – embodying a 'safe-track approach' – the declarative view contains a number of problematic elements.

The declarative view – understood as a legal assessment that domestic law automatically grants domestic legal personality to international legal persons – is probably not correct. The present structure and development of international law does not require that international legal rules are automatically effective within the domestic legal order. Such an effect could be envisaged as an extreme form of monism,[131] but there is no evidence that the relationship between international law and domestic law has actually developed in that direction. Presently, international law requires from states only that international obligations are carried out. Whether they do so by giving direct effect to them or by means of implementing legislation is, in general, open to the obligated state.[132] Only in specific cases might there be an obligation under international

---

[128] Hug, *Die Rechtsstellung*, 62, recounts a Swiss tradition in all its headquarters agreements with international organizations to 'recognize' their international legal personality.

[129] Kelsen, *The Law of the UN*, 336; Simma and Vedder, 'Art. 211' in Grabitz (ed.), *Kommentar zum EWG-Vertrag*, Art 211(1); Ushakov in *Yearbook of the International Law Commission* (1985), vol. I, 295, maintaining that '[e]very State was completely free to accept or not to accept, in its internal law, the legal capacity of other States or of international organizations. The recognition by a State of the legal capacity of international organizations . . . could depend on legislation enacted by that State or on commitments to other States to recognize that capacity in its internal law. International law did not impose any such recognition on States.'

[130] Beitzke, 'Zivilrechtsfähigkeit', 94.

[131] *Cf.* Ignaz Seidl-Hohenveldern, *Völkerrecht* (Cologne, Berlin, Bonn and Munich, 1987), 138.

[132] Ipsen, *Völkerrecht*, 1078*ff*.

law to apply directly certain international norms in the domestic legal order, but whether this obligation is fulfilled, and whether certain international rules are part of the domestic legal order, still depends upon domestic law, usually constitutional law. In general international law there is simply nothing comparable to the 'direct effect' doctrine in European Community law. The crucial difference between direct applicability in international law and the autonomous European Community law direct effect lies in the concept that the direct effect (sometimes also called 'direct applicability') of European Community law is ultimately not a question of national law, but rather a characteristic of the special legal order of the European Community.[133]

If the declarative view is meant to be a factual, empirical statement, saying that – in all domestic orders – legal personality of international organizations automatically attaches to their international personality, it is open to falsification. In fact, many domestic legal systems make the recognition of domestic legal personality dependent upon an applicable provision of domestic law and thus refuse to grant personality to international legal persons automatically. Ample evidence here comes from the dualist approach taken in the UK. In the course of the Tin Council proceedings,[134] the House of Lords clearly rejected the proposition that the International Tin Council's domestic legal personality directly resulted from the Sixth Tin Agreement which provided, *inter alia*, that '[t]he Council shall have legal personality. It shall in particular have the capacity to contract, to acquire and dispose of movable and immovable property and to institute legal proceedings.'[135] Rather, the House of Lords relied exclusively on the domestic legal provision granting personality contained in the International Tin Council (Privileges and Immunities) Order 1972[136] and held that '[w]ithout the Order in Council the ITC had no existence in the law of the United Kingdom and no significance save in the name of an international body created by a treaty between sovereign states which was

---

[133] *Cf. van Gend en Loos*, Case 26/62, ECJ, 5 February 1963; *Costa v. ENEL*, Case 6/64, ECJ, 15 July 1964; *Amministrazione delle Finanze dello Stato* v. *Simmenthal*, Case 106/77, ECJ, 9 March 1978. See also Bengt Beutler, Roland Bieber, Jörn Pipkorn and Jochen Streil, *Die Euro-päische Union. Rechtsordnung und Politik* (Baden-Baden, 4th edn, 1993), 60*ff*; Albert Bleckmann, 'Self-Executing Treaty Provisions' in Rudolf Bernhardt (ed.), *Encyclopedia of Public International Law* (1984), vol. VII, 414–17 at 414; Peter Fischer and Heribert Franz Köck, *Europarecht* (3rd edn, Vienna, 1997), 343; Stefan Griller, *Die Übertragung von Hoheitsrechten auf zwischenstaatliche Einrichtungen: eine Untersuchung zu Art. 9 Abs. 2 des Bundes-Verfassungs-gesetzes* (Vienna, 1989).

[134] See pp. 118*ff* below.

[135] Article 16 of the Sixth International Tin Agreement, 26 June 1982.

[136] Article 5 of the International Tin Council (Privileges and Immunities) Order 1972.

not justiciable by municipal courts'.[137] In the lengthy *Arab Monetary Fund* v. *Hashim (No. 3)*[138] litigation, the recognition of the AMF depended upon the existence of an English rule of private international law that allowed the Fund to be recognized as a 'foreign' person incorporated under the laws of a foreign state. The courts clearly rejected the idea that the provision of the agreement establishing the AMF which conferred domestic legal personality upon it could have any immediate effect in England.

The admission that 'municipal legislation may be necessary to secure effective recognition of this capacity for municipal purposes'[139] by authors considered to adhere to the declarative view[140] might be nothing but the insight that ultimately only municipal law can determine the recognition of legal personality for domestic purposes even if states may be internationally obligated to do so. This conclusion, however, lies at the heart of the constitutive view.

A number of arguments support this concept of two different, unrelated types of personality which implicitly reinforces the constitutive view. As a matter of positive treaty law, domestic legal personality is not necessarily attributed to entities which enjoy international legal personality.[141] Also, the different scope of personality attributed to international organizations on the international and domestic levels points towards the lack of an intrinsic relationship between the two concepts. Frequently, international organizations are bestowed with functionally limited international personality, while at the same time it is provided that they should be attributed with a far broader domestic personality.[142] This discrepancy clearly militates against the assumption of a necessary connection between the international and the domestic legal personality of international organizations.

Based on the legal irrelevance of international legal personality for domestic personality, the theory of a 'pluri-national domestic legal personality' of international organizations was developed.[143] According to this view, international organizations enjoy 'parallel' domestic legal

---

[137] *Maclaine Watson & Co. Ltd* v. *International Tin Council*, House of Lords, 26 October 1989, [1990] 2 AC 418 at 510.

[138] Chancery Division, 9–12 October, 14 November 1989; Court of Appeal, 26–27 March, 9 April 1990; House of Lords, 26–28 November 1990, 21 February 1991. See pp. 65*ff* below for the details of the case.

[139] Jenks, 'The Legal Personality of International Organizations', 270.

[140] Ahluwalia, *The Legal Status*, 60.   [141] Schermers, *International Institutional Law*, 788.

[142] Beitzke, 'Zivilrechtsfähigkeit', 87. He cites as examples Article 6 of the ECSC Treaty as well as Articles 210 and 211 of the EC Treaty.

[143] Beitzke, 'Zivilrechtsfähigkeit', 94*ff*.

personalities in all member states. The content of these legal personalities depends upon the respective domestic legal order. However, this content may, of course, have to comply with some internationally agreed upon provisions, i.e. those contained in a founding charter or in specific other treaties like headquarters agreements, etc. It is important to note that this concept of a pluri-national domestic legal personality does not imply the existence of different legal persons, but rather presupposes one single and identical subject of law, whose legal personality and capability might be treated differently in the respective states.[144] In *Arab Monetary Fund v. Hashim (No. 3)* the defendant tried to attack the plaintiff's contention that the foreign-incorporated AMF should be regarded as possessing domestic legal personality enabling it to sue before the English courts by arguing that if English law treated a foreign decree as having created a distinct legal person it must follow that there were as many distinct persons as there were participating states which had by municipal legislation accorded legal personality to the AMF. This view was clearly rejected by the House of Lords stating that 'though the fund was incorporated by 21 states and has multiple incorporation and multiple nationality there is only one fund'. In the opinion of the House of Lords, [i]t may safely be assumed that no one except Dr Hashim and the other respondents has doubted that the fund is a separate corporate entity or has conceived the fanciful notion of the existence of more than one fund.[145] This view was followed in *Westland Helicopters Ltd v. Arab Organisation for Industrialisation*: 'The fact that several states have accorded to [the AOI the legal] capacity [of a corporation] under their law does not mean that there is more than one international organisation for the English courts to recognise, but merely that there is more than one factual basis upon which recognition can be accorded to the same organisation'.[146]

Judicial practice of avoiding dispute settlement by de-recognizing the domestic legal personality of international organizations

The best-known case where the alleged lack of domestic legal personality of an international organization was in issue is *Arab Monetary Fund v. Hashim (No. 3)*.[147] In the course of this litigation the Court of Appeal

---

[144] *Ibid.*

[145] *Arab Monetary Fund v. Hashim (No. 3)*, House of Lords, 26–28 November 1990, 21 February 1991, [1991] 1 All ER 871 at 877.

[146] High Court, Queen's Bench Division, 3 August 1994, [1995] 2 All ER 387 at 404.

[147] Chancery Division, 9–12 October, 14 November 1989; Court of Appeal, 26–27 March, 9 April 1990; House of Lords, 26–28 November 1990, 21 February 1991.

actually refused to adjudicate on the merits as a consequence of the plaintiff organization's perceived lack of personality under English law. In this case the AMF's personality under English law was a legal pre-requisite for the organization in order to sue its former director-general who had allegedly embezzled US$70 million. This personality of the AMF, an international organization of which the UK was not a member state, was finally accepted by the House of Lords, but its perceived lack served as a reason for the Court of Appeal to avoid deciding the case.

The AMF was created by international agreement in 1976 between twenty Arab states and the PLO and incorporated under the law of the United Arab Emirates where it also had its head offices. According to Article 2 of the 1976 Agreement, the AMF was to have 'independent juridical personality' and 'in particular, the right to own, contract and litigate' which was given effect in the domestic legal systems of the member states. When the AMF instituted legal proceedings in the UK, the defendant ex-director-general of the AMF sought dismissal of the action on the ground that the AMF 'did not exist in English law and therefore could not sue [him]'.[148]

The case depended largely on a number of legal features peculiar to English law. On the one hand, as a dualist system requiring domestic incorporation of international law, English courts are not in a position to enforce international agreements.[149] Under English law '[t]he making of a treaty is an act of the executive, not of the legislature, and it is therefore a fundamental principle of [the] constitution that the terms of a treaty do not by virtue of the treaty alone, have the force of law in the United Kingdom'.[150] On the other hand, *Arab Monetary Fund* v. *Hashim (No. 3)* was largely decided on English private international law principles governing the recognition of foreign corporate entities.[151] The issue was further complicated by a decision handed down by the House of Lords in the course of the Tin Council litigation while *Arab Monetary Fund* v. *Hashim (No. 3)* was pending. That precedent[152] was understood to establish the prin-

---

[148] [1990] 1 All ER 685.
[149] *Oppenheim's International Law* (9th edn, ed. by Robert Jennings and Arthur Watts, 1992), vol. I, 58ff.
[150] *Re International Tin Council*, High Court, Chancery Division, 22 January 1987; (1988) 77 ILR 18–41 at 26.
[151] *Cf.* Cheshire and North, *Private International Law* (ed. by P. M. North and J. J. Fawcett, 11th edn, London, 1987) at 173 and 901ff.
[152] *J. H. Rayner (Mincing Lane) Ltd* v. *Department of Trade and Industry*, House of Lords, 26 October 1989.

ciple that an international organization created under international law could not be treated as having legal personality in English law without statutory authorization.

The court of first instance in the *Arab Monetary Fund* case held that:

Where [an] international organisation had been accorded legal personality under a foreign system of domestic law of a contracting state [i.e., to the treaty establishing the international organization] it was to be regarded as being constituted under that law as a separate *persona ficta* and as such was entitled to recognition under English conflict of laws rules as an ordinary foreign juridical entity.[153]

The Court of Appeal[154] reversed this decision, finding that it was prevented from applying the conflict of laws rule adopted by the lower court, since the AMF was created by public international law and not by the law of the United Arab Emirates whose legislative recognition of the AMF was irrelevant. The Court of Appeal held:

An international organisation constituted under international law by a treaty between foreign sovereign states to which the United Kingdom was not a party and which was not the subject of any United Kingdom legislation would not be recognised as a foreign juridical person with the capacity to bring proceedings in the English courts, even though it had been accorded independent juridical personality as a *persona ficta* by one of the signatory states in line with its obligations under international law to give direct effect to the treaty as part of its own municipal law, since, as a matter of English private international law, the legislation conferring personality under the law of the signatory state was to be regarded as purely territorial in scope, its purpose being solely to give effect to the treaty within that state's own territory and not to create a separate entity capable of recognition abroad. Accordingly the plaintiff was not entitled to recognition as a foreign municipal juridical person with the capacity to bring proceedings in the English courts. The appeals would therefore be allowed and the plaintiff's action struck out.[155]

The House of Lords in turn reversed the Court of Appeal.[156] It held that there was no rule under English law which would prevent the courts from recognizing an international organization without the legislative authority of the International Organisations Act 1968 or another enactment. While the 1976 AMF treaty in itself was not sufficient to create personality under English law, the foreign incorporation led to the application of the normal conflicts rule that English courts recognize legal personalities

---

[153] [1990] 1 All ER 686.   [154] [1990] 1 All ER 769; [1990] 3 WLR 139, Court of Appeal.
[155] [1990] 1 All ER 769.   [156] [1991] 1 All ER 871; [1991] 2 WLR 729, House of Lords.

created under the law of foreign states.[157] In spite of this 'face-saving' by the House of Lords, the case in general and the appellate decision in particular shows how a national court may successfully abstain from adjudicating upon disputes involving international organizations because it denies the legal personality of an international organization under domestic law.

After the 1994 decision in *Westland Helicopters Ltd* v. *Arab Organisation for Industrialisation*[158] the danger of de-recognizing international organizations of which the UK is not a member has been reduced. This judgment closely followed the private international law solution of recognizing the foreign incorporation of an international organization as it was pursued by the House of Lords in *Arab Monetary Fund* v. *Hashim (No. 3)*. The High Court held:

that English law will only recognise a foreign entity as having legal personality and therefore a capacity to sue or be sued if such body has been accorded legal personality under the law of a foreign state recognised by this country . . . In the case of an international organisation one looks to see whether it has been accorded the legal capacity of a corporation under the law of any of the member states or the state where it has its seat, if that state is not a member state. Where some or all of the member states have accorded to it the legal capacity of a corporation the English courts will also treat it as having the legal capacity of a corporation.[159]

With the 1995 decision in *Re Jawad Mahmoud Hashim et al.*[160] it is also unlikely that judicial de-recognition might threaten a foreign international organization in the US. This case is in many respects a continuance of the English *Arab Monetary Fund* v. *Hashim (No. 3)* litigation. After the English courts had entered judgment in favour of the AMF in 1993 and 1994, Dr Hashim and his family left England and finally settled in Arizona where they voluntarily filed for bankruptcy protection before the AMF could bring suit to enforce the English judgment. They listed the AMF as a creditor whose claims they disputed and – relying on arguments similar

---

[157] The House of Lords held that '[a]lthough when sovereign states entered into an agreement by treaty to confer legal personality on an international organisation the treaty did not create a corporate body with capacity to sue and be sued in English courts, the registration of that treaty in one of the sovereign states conferred legal personality on the international organisation and thus created a corporate body which the English courts could and should recognise, since by comity the courts of the United Kingdom recognised corporate bodies created by the law of a foreign state recognised by the Crown'. [1991] 1 All ER 871 at 872.

[158] High Court, Queen's Bench Division, 3 August 1994. See pp. 121f below for the details of this case.

[159] [1995] 2 All ER 387 at 403ff.   [160] US Bankruptcy Court D. Arizona, 15 August 1995.

to those brought forward in the English proceedings – they specifically contended that the AMF lacked capacity to sue in the US and that it could not participate in any way in the debtors' bankruptcy cases. In a special order concerning 'standing and capacity of Arab Monetary Fund' a US bankruptcy judge rejected the Hashims' argument. He basically followed the reasoning of the House of Lords combining a private international law and customary personality concept, since it was clear that the AMF, as a regional international organization in which the US did not participate and which was not specifically designated under the US International Organizations Immunities Act 1945 (IOIA), could not derive its legal status from domestic legislation. Rather, the court held that:

the AMF is a juridical person (a corporation, a *persona ficta*, an entity capable of legal battle) under United Arab Emirates law . . . Once this has been decided, capacity follows under American law as a matter of 'customary law'.[161]

There are other problems, however, if international organizations try to sue in US federal courts. In *IRO* v. *Republic Steamship Corp.*[162] the International Refugee Organization (IRO) brought suit against a Panamanian company for breach of a shipping charter. The action was dismissed by the lower federal court for lack of jurisdiction since it saw no 'federal question' giving rise to federal jurisdiction.[163] This dismissal, however, was reversed by the appellate court. The Fourth Circuit court held that by providing in the (IOIA) that international organizations such as the IRO 'shall posses the capacity . . . to institute legal proceedings' the US has discharged its obligation under Article 13 of the Constitution of the IRO requiring that the organization shall enjoy in the territory of each of its member states such legal capacity as may be necessary for the exercise of its functions and the fulfilment of its purposes. According to the Fourth Circuit court, this 'means, by necessary implication, that Congress has opened the doors of the federal courts to suits by such international organizations'.[164]

[161] 188 Bankr. 633 at 649 (D. Arizona 1995).
[162] US District Court D. Maryland, 8 July 1950, US Court of Appeals 4th Cir., 11 May/11 July 1951.
[163] Thus, an amendment to the IOIA has been suggested by including an express provision granting original jurisdiction of federal district courts over international organizations. *Cf.* Note, 'Federal Jurisdiction over International Organizations' (1952) 61 *Yale Law Journal* 111–17 at 114.
[164] 189 F. 2d 858 at 860 (4th Cir. 1951). *United Nations Korean Reconstruction Agency* v. *Glass Production Methods Inc. et al.*, US District Court SDNY, 3 August 1956, confirmed this result but held that a UN subsidiary organ bringing a contract claim was obliged to comply with venue requirements. Similar problems were addressed in *International Finance*

A concept related to the notion of not accepting the legal personality of an international organization for the purposes of domestic law can be found in the US case of *International Association of Machinists* v. *OPEC.*[165] There a US labour union brought suit against OPEC and its individual member states in US courts asking for damages and injunctive relief for alleged price-fixing of crude oil prices in violation of US antitrust law. On appeal the case was decided and dismissed mainly on act of state reasons applied to the collective acts of OPEC's member states.[166] As far as the case against the organization itself was concerned, the courts did not hesitate to dismiss the plaintiff's suit because OPEC 'could not be and had not been legally served with process'.[167] The two potential legal bases for service of process, the US Foreign Sovereign Immunities Act 1976 (FSIA) and the IOIA, were both held inapplicable since 'FSIA applies only to foreign sovereigns, which OPEC is not; and, IOIA applies only to those international organizations in which the United States participates and the United States does not participate in OPEC'.[168] Although the dismissal was justified on the technical ground of lack of a possibility to serve the organization with process, this comes close to a non-recognition of foreign international organizations as persons amenable to suit under domestic law.

The paucity of cases demonstrates, however, that in general this most radical method of avoidance is rarely used by national courts.

Non-recognition of a particular act of an international organization – *ultra vires* acts and non-attributability

Even if the domestic legal personality of an international organization is recognized by a national court,[169] it might avoid adjudication upon a specific dispute involving such international organization as a result of the peculiar 'functionally limited' scope of an organization's personality. This notion could be used to regard acts that go beyond this functional realm, i.e. acts frequently denoted as *ultra vires*, as acts that cannot be

---

Corporation v. *GDK Systems Inc. and Hogan Systems Inc.*, US District Court DC, 14 April 1989 where the deciding US court confirmed that section 282f of the IOIA provided a proper basis for a federal court's jurisdiction over the IFC's claim without violating the constitutional prohibition on expanding the jurisdiction of federal courts beyond Article III(2) of US Constitution.

[165] US District Court CD Cal., 18 September 1979, *affirmed on other grounds*, US Court of Appeals 9th Cir., 6 July–24 August 1981.

[166] See the discussion on pp. 90*ff* below.   [167] 477 F. Supp 560.   [168] *Ibid.*

[169] See pp. 37*ff* above.

attributed to them. In other words, a strict interpretation of the concept of 'functional personality' of international organizations could imply that international organizations cannot be sued for *ultra vires* acts.

Scope of domestic legal personality

In general, the notion of 'scope of personality' might have a twofold meaning: one referring to the extent of the specific rights and duties of the international organization concerned; and another referring to the 'personal' scope, against whom the personality is valid/opposable.[170] This section is concerned with 'scope of personality' in the first sense, dealing with the extent of specific rights and duties of international organizations.

Frequently this issue is also referred to as one of legal capacity, i.e. of what an entity is legally empowered to do.[171] However, it appears to be mostly a matter of terminology whether one prefers to speak of 'personality', which in itself might have differing degrees, or whether one adheres to the concept of one – more or less undefined – broad personality which is then specified by differing rights and duties, a certain scale of 'capacities' (or even of subgroups like 'competencies' and 'powers'),[172] which answer the concrete issues of legal relevance. Of course, as noted above, 'personality', 'capacity', etc. are legal concepts, usually deeply rooted in the various domestic legal systems, that may differ substantially from each other.[173] Thus, the terminology used by courts and in legal doctrine has to be treated with a degree of caution. The very notion of the widely used term 'functional personality' subscribes to the first usage since it already assumes a qualified personality concept. In the course of this investigation this understanding will be followed with the awareness that different terms might denote the same or a similar concept.

Sources determining the scope of domestic legal personality

In order to delimit precisely the exact scope of the functional personality of international organizations it is necessary first to look at the specific

---

[170] This second meaning is closely connected to the notion of 'objective international personality' as used by the ICJ in its Advisory Opinion in the so-called *Reparations* case. *Reparation for Injuries Suffered in the Service of the United Nations*, Advisory Opinion, (1949) *ICJ Reports* 174 at 185. There, it more or less signifies that personality is valid also *vis-à-vis* non-member states and does not depend upon recognition. Seyersted uses the same term in a slightly different way, referring to 'objective international personality' as arising from the fact of an international organization's existence regardless of explicit or implicit conferment of personality in the constituent instrument. *Cf.* Seyersted, 'Objective International Personality', 1*ff*. See also pp. 57*ff* above.

[171] Bekker, *The Legal Position*, 63.   [172] *Ibid.*, 71.   [173] *Cf.* pp. 13 and 37 note 8 above.

legal sources containing provisions relevant for the scope of an international organization's (domestic) personality.

Treaties

Some treaties, such as the constituent instruments of CERN,[174] ELDO[175] and ESRO,[176] as well as of their successor organization, ESA,[177] etc., simply speak of (domestic) legal 'personality' without qualifying its scope. In general, however, two types of standard formulations can be encountered in international agreements: on the one hand, 'functional personality clauses', and, on the other, 'descriptive personality concepts', listing certain activities international organizations are legally capable of performing in a demonstrative fashion. There are variations on them, but these two are by far the most frequently used provisions.

According to a typical functional personality clause an international organization enjoys the 'legal capacity necessary to exercise its functions'. The prototype of a functional personality clause is Article 104 of the UN Charter according to which '[t]he Organization shall enjoy in the territory of each of its Members such legal capacity as may be necessary for the exercise of its functions and the fulfilment of its purposes'. Many other constituent texts of international organizations also contain such clauses[178] or incorporate them by reference.[179] A number of treaties contain variations on this functionally limited personality concept.[180]

The classic and widely used form of a 'descriptive' personality clause adds to a general conferment of personality specific legal capacities: 'The international organization shall possess legal personality and have the capacity to contract, to acquire and dispose of immovable and movable property and to institute legal proceedings.'[181] It is generally understood

---

[174] Article IX of the Convention for the Establishment of a European Organization for Nuclear Research (CERN) provides that '[t]he Organization shall have legal personality in the metropolitan territories of all members States'.

[175] Article 20 of the Convention for the Establishment of a European Launcher Development Organization.

[176] Article XIV(1) of the Convention for the Establishment of a European Space Research Organization.

[177] Article XV(1) (Article I of Annex I) of the Convention for the Establishment of a European Space Agency.

[178] *Cf.* Article 66 of the WHO Constitution; Article XV of the IAEA Statute; similarly Article 139 of the OAS Charter; Article VIII(1) of the Agreement Establishing the WTO.

[179] Article XII of the UNESCO Constitution.

[180] Article XVI(1) of the FAO Constitution. See p. 44 note 37 above.

[181] Similarly, Article I(1) of the General Convention. See also Article 5 of the ILC Draft on relations between states and international organizations (second part of the topic).

that the three types of legal capacities are a non-exhaustive, demonstrative listing only, even if this is not always clear from the texts.[182]

A provision granting 'full juridical personality' to organizations is frequently used in order to lay down the scope of the domestic legal personality of international financial institutions. The classic example can be found in the Articles of Agreement of the International Monetary Fund and of the World Bank:[183] 'The [Fund/Bank] shall possess full juridical personality and, in particular, the capacity: (i) to contract; (ii) to acquire and dispose of immovable and movable property; and (iii) to institute legal proceedings.' The only sensible reading of such provisions seems to be one viewing the specifically enumerated capacities as *typical* powers that are only descriptively added and to regard the grant of full personality as the important operative part. Still, the redundancy of a provision which sets out to confer 'full personality' and then goes on to particularize three capacities certainly included in the concept of 'full personality' has been rightly criticized.[184]

European Community law also contains a particular variation of a grant of full personality. The EC Treaty provides: 'In each of the Member States, the Community shall enjoy the most extensive legal capacity accorded to legal persons under their laws.'[185]

Custom

According to authors following a concept of 'objective personality' of international organizations, a principle of customary law of intergovernmental organizations provides that they can 'profit from a full range of international *and* domestic capacities' unless explicit restrictions have been laid down and subject to specific functions and purposes of the international organization in question.[186]

Apart from the question of whether custom can be a source proper of

---

[182] Seidl-Hohenveldern and Loibl, *Das Recht der Internationalen Organisationen*, 50; Zemanek, *Das Vertragsrecht der internationalen Organisationen*, 132.

[183] Article IX(2) of the IMF Articles of Agreement; Article VII(2) IBRD of the Articles of Agreement.

[184] Jenks, 'The Legal Personality of International Organizations', 271.

[185] Article 211 of the EC Treaty. See also the similar provisions in Article 185 of the Euratom Treaty; Article 6, second sentence of the ECSC Treaty; and Article 4 of the Eurocontrol Convention.

[186] Bekker, *The Legal Position*, 71. He relies expressly on Finn Seyersted, 'International Personality of Intergovernmental Organizations: Do Their Capacities Really Depend Upon Their Constitutions?' (1964) 4 *Indian Journal of International Law* 1–74 at 19. In the passage referred to, however, Seyersted only deals with the scope of the 'international personality' of international organizations.

personality,[187] it can also be asked whether customary rules might provide for a 'normal' extent of personality where such personality is granted by either treaties or domestic legal rules. According to some scholars, the broad uniformity of treaty provisions expressly granting domestic legal personality to international organizations allows the inference of a customary content of the legal status of international organizations in domestic law.[188] In this sense, while not technically being the source of domestic legal personality, customary law could provide the content in order to determine the scope of the domestic legal personality of an international organization granted by other sources.

Domestic legislation

Domestic legislation[189] frequently provides for the legal personality of international organizations in a 'descriptive' fashion. For instance, the US International Organizations Immunities Act 1945 contains such a legal personality clause along the lines of the General Convention.[190]

The UK International Organisations Act 1968, on the other hand, foresees the conferment of 'the legal capacities of a body corporate' by Order in Council.[191] The respective Orders in Council usually only repeat this language without specifying the exact capacities enjoyed by such organizations.[192] Similar legislation has been enacted in Australia, Canada and New Zealand.[193]

Resulting legal capacities in the domestic sphere

To define the precise scope of the legal personality resulting from the above-mentioned provisions remains in most cases a difficult task which has given rise to varying interpretations. In a minority of international organizations, and more frequently for 'international public corpor-

---

[187] See pp. 45ff above.
[188] Karl Zemanek, 'Die Rechtsstellung der internationalen Organisationen in Osterreich' (1958) 13 *Osterreichische Juristenzeitung* 380–1 at 380.
[189] See the overview in United Nations, *Legislative Texts and Treaty Provisions Concerning the Legal Status, Privileges and Immunities of International Organizations*.
[190] Section 2(a) of the IOIA provides: 'International organizations shall, to the extent consistent with the instrument creating them, possess the capacity (i) to contract; (ii) to acquire and dispose of real and personal property; (iii) to institute legal proceedings.'
[191] Section 2(a) of the International Organisations Act 1968.
[192] *Cf.* Article 5 of the International Tin Council (Privileges and Immunities) Order 1972, providing that the International Tin Council shall have 'the legal capacities of a body corporate'.
[193] *Cf. Yearbook of the International Law Commission* (1985), vol. II, Part One, 109.

ations' or 'common inter-state enterprises',[194] this question was settled by – more or less directly – providing in the applicable treaty for a legal personality according to a specific domestic legal order.[195]

It seems that for those international organizations which are accorded either 'full', 'to the greatest extent', or simply 'personality' the exact scope of personality depends upon the respective domestic legal system.[196] The answer appears to be more difficult, however, in the large number of cases where domestic personality is – already on the international level – 'functionally' qualified. In these cases, the functional limitation of their international legal personality seems to be relevant for the determination of the scope of domestic legal personality as well.

Scope of functional international legal personality

It is generally agreed that international organizations, by virtue of being subjects of international law and of enjoying international legal personality, do not have all the rights and duties under international law that states have.[197] This is mostly taken for granted as a matter of practical necessity. In the absence of their own territories and citizens, international principles concerning jurisdiction over territory and citizens – the examples usually given in this context[198] – are regarded to be inapplicable to international organizations. Certain capacities, however, are normally attributed to international organizations in a general fashion. Among them rank a treaty-making power, international responsibility, the right

---

[194] Cf. p. 10 above.

[195] For instance, the Bank of International Settlements, Eurochemic or Eurofima. Beitzke, 'Zivilrechtsfähigkeit', 91. Cf. Article 1 of the Convention for the Establishment of 'Eurofima', 20 October 1955: 'The Governments which are Parties to this Convention approve the formation of the Company which shall be governed by Statutes appended to this Convention . . . and subsidiarily by the Law of the State in which the Head Office is situated, in so far as this Convention does not provide otherwise.'

[196] Beitzke, 'Zivilrechtsfähigkeit', 104, deduces this from his concept of a 'pluri-national' legal personality whose precise scope might be defined differently according to the relevant domestic legal order. Schröer, 'Die Anwendung', 622, considers Article 211 of the EC Treaty granting 'the most extensive legal capacity accorded to legal persons under [the member states'] laws' as a kind of national treatment clause which would require that international organizations had to be treated like national corporate entities.

[197] See the famous phrase of the ICJ in the Reparations case with regard to the UN: 'The subjects of international law are not necessarily identical in their nature or in the extent of their rights, and their nature depends upon the needs of the community.' Reparation for Injuries Suffered in the Service of the United Nations, Advisory Opinion, (1949) ICJ Reports 174 at 178.

[198] E.g., Beitzke, 'Zivilrechtsfähigkeit', 87.

to make international claims, the right to establish diplomatic relations (*ius legationis*), the right to enjoy privileges and immunities, etc.[199]

The personality of international organizations is generally regarded as a 'functional personality' as opposed to the general personality of the primary subjects of international law, the individual states.[200] The exact scope of the 'functional limitation' of such personality, however, remains unclear. A number of theories attempt to determine the exact functional scope of an international organization's international legal personality.

A strict view on the functional nature of international organizations holds that – regardless of a general grant of international personality – only those rights and duties specifically conferred upon international organizations in their constituent treaties can be exercised by them.[201] In UN practice this approach found strong support by Soviet doctrine.[202] Also with regard to the EC's legislative powers this view has been upheld in principle under the label of the doctrine of 'enumerated powers' both in legal writing as well as in the jurisprudence of the ECJ. However, the broad grant of powers to the Community as evidenced in Articles 100a and 235 of the EC Treaty has been an effective counterweight to this limiting concept.[203]

---

[199] Bekker, *The Legal Position*, 64, also notes a right to recognize other subjects of international law and refers to the non-recognition by the UN of the Federal Republic of Yugoslavia (or de-recognition of the Socialist Federal Republic of Yugoslavia) as expressed in UN Security Council Resolution 777 (1992).

[200] See Rudolf Bindschedler, 'International Organizations, General Aspects' in Rudolf Bernhardt (ed.), *Encyclopedia of Public International Law* (2nd edn, 1995), vol. II, 1289–309 at 1299: 'In contrast to States, which are characterized by unlimited legal personality, the legal personality of organizations exists only within the limits of their objects and functions, since it is defined not by general international law but on the basis of the constituent treaty.' Similarly, Simma and Vedder state that the European Communities, like all international organizations, are 'functionally limited' in their international legal capacity. Simma and Vedder, 'Art. 210, ' in Grabitz (ed.), *Kommentar zum EWG-Vertrag*, Article 210(5).

[201] Faßbender, 'Die Völkerrechtssubjektivität internationaler Organisationen', 28. See also the dissenting opinion of Judge Hackworth in the *Reparation for Injuries* opinion stating that '[t]here can be no gainsaying the fact that the [UN] is one of delegated and enumerated powers. It is to be presumed that such powers as the Member States desired to confer upon it are stated either in the Charter or in complementary agreements concluded by them'. *Reparation for Injuries Suffered in the Service of the United Nations*, Advisory Opinion, (1949) *ICJ Reports* 174 at 198.

[202] Grigory I. Tunkin, 'The Legal Nature of the United Nations' (1966 III) 119 *Recueil des Cours* 7–66 at 20*ff*.

[203] Heribert Franz Köck, 'Die "implied powers" der Europäischen Gemeinschaften als Anwendungsfall der 'implied powers' internationaler Organisationen überhaupt' in Karl-Heinz Böckstiegel, Hans-Ernst Folz, Jörg Manfred Mössner and Karl Zemanek (eds.),

In general, however, the 'implied powers' doctrine leads to an important enlargement of the functional personality concept of international organizations. According to this theory, the rights and duties of an international organization follow not only from capacities explicitly bestowed upon it, but also from the tasks and functions of an international organization.[204] In the course of the *Reparations* case it has been, on the whole successfully, argued before the ICJ that 'fonction implique capacité'.[205] The ICJ stated that:

Under international law, the Organization must be deemed to have those powers which, though not expressly provided in the Charter, are conferred upon it by necessary implication as being essential to the performance of its duties.[206]

The legal effects of non-functional acts performed by international organizations as domestic legal persons in theory

For the purposes of clarifying the potential role of non-functional acts for avoiding the adjudication of disputes involving international organizations before national courts, the legal consequences of non-functional acts of international organizations under domestic law are even more important than the precise scope of a functionally limited domestic personality. The issue to be addressed here relates to the exact meaning and effects of a qualified personality concept such as 'functional personality'. Thus, one has, first and foremost, to address the problem of non-functional acts and their legal effects.

The literature dealing with the legal personality of international organizations is usually very cautious about hinting at the legal consequences of

Völkerrecht – Recht der Internationalen Organisationen – Weltwirtschaftsrecht. Festschrift für Ignaz Seidl-Hohenveldern (Cologne, Berlin, Bonn and Munich, 1988), 279–99 at 279*ff*; Gert Nicolaysen, 'Zur Theorie von den implied powers in den Europäischen Gemeinschaften' (1966) 1 *Europarecht* 129–42 at 129*ff*.

[204] *Cf.* Jerzy Makarczyk, 'The International Court of Justice on the Implied Powers of International Organizations' in J. Makarczyk (ed.), *Essays in Honour of Judge Manfred Lachs* (The Hague, Boston and Lancaster, 1984), 501–18 at 501*ff*; Manuel Rama Montaldo, 'International Legal Personality and Implied Powers of International Organizations' (1970) 44 *British Yearbook of International Law* 111–55 at 111*ff*; Bernard Rouyer-Hameray, *Les compétences implicites des organisations internationales* (Paris, 1962); and Manfred Zuleeg, 'International Organizations, Implied Powers' in Rudolf Bernhardt (ed.), *Encyclopedia of Public International Law* (2nd edn, 1995), vol. II, 1312–14 at 1312*ff*.

[205] *Reparation for Injuries Suffered in the Service of the United Nations*, Statement of Mr Kaeckenbeeck, (1949) *ICJ Pleadings* 98 ('function implies capacity').

[206] *Reparation for Injuries Suffered in the Service of the United Nations*, Advisory Opinion, (1949) *ICJ Reports* 174 at 182.

non-functional acts.[207] One might wonder why this is the case. If it is indeed an organization's legal personality itself which is limited by functional criteria, it is logically almost impossible to see how such a legal person could validly act in fields not covered by its functional personality. Thus, it has been concluded that international organizations do not enjoy legal personality for acts clearly beyond their constitutional competencies. Accordingly, such *ultra vires* transactions would be null and void.[208] This non-attributability solution, however, has not been generally followed.

Some authors assert that the functional personality concept of international organizations itself can be traced back to the Anglo-American *ultra vires* doctrine.[209] There is indeed a very close interrelation. In the common law, the *ultra vires* doctrine has its origin in company law, but is also very strongly relied upon in the field of administrative law.[210] Meanwhile, a certain, albeit rather limited, *ultra vires* literature has also emerged in international legal doctrine.[211]

Content of domestic law *ultra vires* doctrine

In English and US corporate law an *ultra vires* act (or contract) is one that is beyond the powers expressly or implicitly conferred upon a juridical

[207] When speaking of the World Bank's functional legal personality, Fatouros maintains that as a consequence 'institutional actions which go beyond functional requirements may be denied international legal validity'. Fatouros, 'The World Bank's Impact', 64.

[208] Hans Peter Kunz-Hallstein, 'Die Beteiligung Internationaler Organisationen am Rechts- und Wirtschaftsverkehr, unter besonderer Berücksichtigung der Probleme des Schutzes des geistigen und gewerblichen Eigentums' (1987) *Gewerblicher Rechtsschutz und Urheberrecht (Internationaler Teil)* 819–33 at 825.

[209] Beitzke, 'Zivilrechtsfähigkeit', 105, thinks that it is in fact the Anglo-American *ultra vires* doctrine which is meant by the functional personality provisions in some treaties and which is thereby 'so to speak internationalized'. See also Hug, *Die Rechtsstellung*, 71.

[210] *Cf.* Ebere Osieke, '*Ultra Vires* Acts in International Organizations – The Experience of the International Labour Organisation' (1976–7) 48 *British Yearbook of International Law* 259–80 at 259, who focuses on 'constitutional' *ultra vires* acts in international organizations, i.e. from a public international law point of view.

[211] (1973) 55 *Annuaire de l'Institut de Droit International* 214 at 263*ff*; Bekker, *The Legal Position*, 802, note 364; Philippe Cahier, 'Les charactéristiques de la nullité en droit international' (1972) 76 *Revue générale de droit international public* 645–97 at 645*ff*; Elihu Lauterpacht, 'The Development of the Law of International Organisations by the Decisions of International Tribunals' (1976 IV) 152 *Recueil des Cours* 377–478 at 407 and 409; Elihu Lauterpacht, 'The Legal Effects of Illegal Acts of International Organisations' in *Cambridge Essays in International Law – Essays in Honour of Lord McNair* (London and New York, 1965), 88–121 at 88*ff*; Ebere Osieke, 'The Legal Validity of Ultra Vires Decisions of International Organizations' (1983) 77 *American Journal of International Law* 239–56 at 293*ff*; Osieke, '*Ultra Vires* Acts', 259; Ebere Osieke, 'Unconstitutional Acts in International Organizations: The Law and Practice of the ICAO' (1979) 28 *International and Comparative Law Quarterly* 1–26 at 1*ff*; and Seyersted, 'International Personality of Intergovernmental Organizations', 23*ff*.

person, typically a corporate entity.[212] The powers of a corporation are defined by its charter and the law. The traditional common law rule was one of non-enforceability in the case of *ultra vires* contracts.[213] This rule was justified because the party dealing with the corporation was deemed to know that the corporation had no power to contract, since the capacities of an incorporated entity were laid down in its charter of incorporation. This doctrine mainly served the purpose of protecting shareholders and beneficiaries of a company from liability for unauthorized actions of the company (i.e., its management) over which they usually had little control. Soon, however, a number of exceptions to this rule were developed:[214] they were of statutory character or relied on traditional notions like estoppel where contracts had been partially or totally performed and where the defence of *ultra vires* was unconscionable or would work injustice in the circumstances.

It is important to realize, however, that – contrary to commonly held views – the *ultra vires* doctrine, as outlined above, is not a peculiar feature of Anglo-American common law. Civil law systems, like German or Austrian law, generally reject the *ultra vires* concept for juridical persons of private law, i.e. corporations and other companies that are formed usually by contractual agreement between private persons, because they consider the protection of innocent third parties to be an overriding principle.[215] They do, however, recognize a functionally limited legal personality of juridical persons of a public law character.[216] Consequently, such persons are generally considered to be able to act only within the functional scope of their competencies.[217] While this *ultra vires* inspired concept is certainly used with regard to their public law activities, it seems that when such entities act like a private person, i.e. in the field of contracts and torts, the protection of third parties frequently leads to a broader attributability of their acts. Thus, a German case holding an *ultra vires* contract of a juridical person of public

---

[212] American Jurisprudence, *Corporations* (2nd edn, Rochester, NY and San Francisco, 1985), vol. 18B, paras 1168–2168 at para. 2009.

[213] *Ashbury Railway Carriage & Iron Co.* v. *Riche*, (1875) 33 NS *Law Times Reports* 450.

[214] *Cf.* American Jurisprudence, *Corporations*, para. 2015.

[215] Karl Schiemer, Peter Jabornegg and Rudolf Strasser, *Kommentar zum Aktiengesetz* (Vienna, 1993), 12.

[216] 'Juristische Personen des öffentlichen Rechts'. *Cf.* Bernhard Raschauer, *Allgemeines Verwaltungsrecht* (Vienna and New York, 1998), 47ff.

[217] 'Grundsätzlich existiert eine juristische Person im Umfang ihrer Verbandskompetenzen; jenseits dieses Bereiches ("*ultra vires*") ist Zurechnung nicht vorgesehen'. Raschauer, *Allgemeines Verwaltungsrecht*, 47.

law character to be void appears to be rather an exception than the rule.[218]

International *ultra vires* doctrine

Ultra vires acts on the international level are especially problematic since most rules of international organizations do not contain specific procedural provisions regulating how to invoke, to react to and to determine *ultra vires* acts.[219] This ultimately leaves the authority to decide whether a specific act was *ultra vires* or *intra vires* to the member states.

In order to mitigate the resulting danger of divergent (national) interpretations of borderline acts of international organizations the scope of their powers is usually interpreted widely. The actual practice of international organizations evidences that irregular acts have rarely been deemed null or void – either by way of subsequent ratification[220] or by way of a broad interpretation of an international organization's competence having recourse to the concept of implied powers.[221] Also the distinction between acts *ultra vires* an organ and *ultra vires* an organization – elaborated on in the ICJ's not entirely unambiguous opinion in the *Certain Expenses* case[222] – contributes to the result that acts are rarely regarded as unattributable to an organization. Another facet of this

[218] *Cf. X v. Hauptgeschäftsstelle Fischwirtschaft*, BGH, 28 February 1956, where an *ultra vires* contract of a legal person of a public law character was held to be absolutely ineffective ('*schlechthin unwirksam*'): '*Juristische Personen des öffentlichen Rechts sind jedenfalls grundsätzlich nur im Rahmen des ihnen durch Gesetz oder Satzung zugewiesenen Aufgaben- und Wirkungsbereichs zu einem rechtswirksamen Handeln befugt. Sie können nur innerhalb des durch die Zwecke und Aufgaben bestimmten, sachlich und räumlich beschränkten Lebenskreises handeln. Außerhalb ihres Funktionsbereichs liegende Handlungen entbehren schlechthin der Rechtswirksamkeit*'. (1956) *Neue Juristische Wochenschrift* 746 at 748.

[219] See, however, Article 173 of the EC Treaty as one of the rare exceptions.

[220] The acts of the incorrectly assembled Intergovernmental Maritime Consultative Organization's Maritime Security Committee (*Constitution of the Maritime Safety Committee of the Inter-Governmental Maritime Consultative Organization*, Advisory Opinion, (1960) *ICJ Reports* 150) were subsequently (re-)confirmed by the correctly assembled organ. Osieke, 'The Legal Validity', 244.

[221] As in the case of UN peacekeeping operations. *Cf. Certain Expenses of the United Nations*, Advisory Opinion, 20 July 1962, (1962) *ICJ Reports* 151 at 168. A similar argument can be found in Sadurska and Chinkin's discussion of the ITC's potential liability for tortious acts where they view the buffer stock manager's 'imprudent transactions' – as risky as they were from an economic point of view – as probably not *ultra vires*, because they could be regarded authorized by the implied powers doctrine. Romana Sadurska and Christine M. Chinkin, 'The Collapse of the International Tin Council: A Case of State Responsibility?' (1990) 30 *Virginia Journal of International Law* 845–90 at 886.

[222] *Certain Expenses of the United Nations*, Advisory Opinion of 20 July 1962, (1962) *ICJ Reports* 151.

important case leading to the view that only acts manifestly *ultra vires* should be regarded void *ab initio* and thus not attributable to an international organization[223] works in the same direction and seems to be an appropriate response to protect the justified expectations and good faith of third parties.[224]

Explicitly addressing domestic legal personality

The most prominent policy argument militating against an automatic nullity of non-functional acts of international organizations is one of legal certainty and the proper allocation of risk.

The underlying assumption of the *ultra vires* doctrine that third parties have knowledge of the functionally limited personality of the corporate entity they are dealing with proves untenable in practice both in domestic corporate law[225] and probably even more so in the context of international organizations.[226] This is particularly true in cases where the concept of functional personality is found in the constituent text only and where the seat state, not being itself a member of the international organization concerned, has entered into a headquarters agreement containing no similar restriction which speaks only of 'legal personality'.[227] In such situations it appears very difficult to argue that a private party relying on the headquarters agreement's grant of legal personality

---

[223] *Ibid.*, Separate Opinion of Judge Morelli, (1962) *ICJ Reports* 223.

[224] Rudolph Bernhardt, 'Qualifikation und Anwendungsbereich des internen Rechts internationaler Organisationen' (1973) 12 *Berichte der Deutschen Gesellschaft für Völkerrecht* 7–46 at 34; Mosche Hirsch, *The Responsibility of International Organizations Toward Third Parties* (Dordrecht, Boston and London, 1995), 88*ff*; Kegel, *Internationales Privatrecht*, 340; Erhard Klotz, 'Beschränkter Wirkungskreis der juristischen Personen des öffentlichen Rechts. Grenzen der privatrechtlichen Rechtsfähigkeit der juristischen Personen des öffentlichen Rechts' (1964) 17 *Die Offentliche Verwaltung* 181–89 at 188.

[225] Arguing under US domestic law, Hamilton considers the fact that articles of incorporation are on public file to be only a 'superficially plausible justification' for the *ultra vires* doctrine which proves from a business standpoint 'unrealistic' because 'it assumes people will check articles of incorporation when in fact they do not, and that when they do check the articles, they will make business judgments based on a reading of what often is essentially boiler-plate legalese'. Robert W. Hamilton, *Cases and Materials on Corporations* (4th edn, St Paul, MN, 1990), 208.

[226] Thus, Shihata opines that '[t]he liability of an international organization for its acts does not seem to depend on whether the act is *intra* or *ultra vires* as much as on whether it is a violation of a contractual obligation'. He concludes that '[a]n international organization may not invoke its charter as justification for its failure to perform a conflicting contractual legal duty unless it has reserved the right to do so in the contractual arrangement'. Shihata, 'Réponse' (1995 I) 66 *Annuaire de l'Institut de Droit International* 314.

[227] This is actually the case in the relation of Switzerland *vis-à-vis* some international organizations. See Hug, *Die Rechtsstellung*, 81.

should have been aware of the functionally limited character of such personality since one might well interpret the unqualified legal personality standard as one that does not hint at the possibility of *ultra vires* acts.[228]

Avoiding dispute settlement by referring to the limited scope of domestic legal personality in practice

National courts have infrequently taken recourse to a concept of *ultra vires* acts, of acts beyond the functionally limited personality of an international organization, in order to avoid the adjudication of disputes involving international organizations. They sometimes pay lip-service to the concept in general by affirming the functionally limited domestic personality of international organizations; however, they normally do not engage in any serious discussion on this point.

The reasoning of the Belgian *Manderlier* v. *Organisation des Nations Unies and Etat Belge (Ministre des Affaires Etrangères)*[229] case, for instance, demonstrates that courts are willing to infer a competence of international organizations to appear before domestic courts from their general grant of functional domestic legal personality without any need to refer to a specific capacity to sue, as contained, for instance, in the demonstrative clauses of some of the immunity instruments. The court in that case was able to invoke Article 104 of the UN Charter, according to which the UN enjoys such legal capacity in the territory of each member state as may be necessary. The court went on to say that the UN 'is consequently competent to appear in legal proceedings in Belgium'.[230]

Another good example of this attitude of accepting a rather broad scope of functional personality is the lower court's decision in the Dutch case of *AS* v. *Iran–United States Claims Tribunal*[231] where the Local Court of The Hague considered the conclusion of an employment contract with a Dutch citizen calling for translating and interpreting services covered by the tribunal's functional personality. The court expressly recognized that an international organization, in that case the Iran–US Claims Tribunal, 'can act only in performance of the tasks for which is has been instituted, and that the agreement between the Tribunal and the plaintiff was made in order to serve the help of the plaintiff in the performance of these tasks'.[232]

---

[228] *Cf.* pp. 72*ff* above.
[229] *Manderlier* v. *Organisation des Nations Unies and Etat Belge (Ministre des Affaires Etrangères)*, Civil Tribunal of Brussels, 11 May 1966.
[230] (1972) 45 ILR 446 at 450.   [231] Local Court of The Hague, 8 June 1983.
[232] (1984) 15 *Netherlands Yearbook of International Law* 431.

As already indicated, however, courts are very reluctant to use the consequences of a strict functionally limited personality concept which would provide them with a tool to abstain from adjudicating disputes involving international organizations. They have not accepted the offer made by learned authors who argue that international organizations cannot act beyond the scope of their functional personality with the result that any such (attempted) acts would be non-attributable to the organization. In fact, an explicit reliance on such a concept is totally exceptional.

One of the very rare cases where a national court relied on a concept of an organization's limited scope of personality – although in a very peculiar and indirect way and only as a supplementary reason next to deciding on immunity grounds – is the relatively recent Italian Supreme Court decision in *FAO* v. *Colagrossi*.[233] That case, an employment dispute between an international organization and a national of the forum state, was actually dismissed mainly on the ground of the FAO's immunity from Italian jurisdiction. However, as a supplementary argument, the Italian Supreme Court used an interesting reasoning inspired by the idea that an international organization enjoys only such capacities as are specifically bestowed upon it. Since the FAO's capacity was limited 'to institute legal proceedings', it was considered not to encompass the capacity to be sued. The Supreme Court expressly rejected the employee's argument that the grant of 'immunity from every form of legal process' in Article 16 of the FAO–Italy Headquarters Agreement might be limited by the recognition of the FAO's capacity to be a party to legal proceedings in Article 14. It considered this view a misunderstanding that might have resulted from the Italian version of Article 14 speaking of the organization's capacity 'di stare in giudizio' which could be understood broadly as 'being a party to a lawsuit'. The Supreme Court, however, pointed out that the English version – which speaks of the FAO's capacity 'to institute legal proceedings' – correctly accentuated the aspect of actively bringing suit.[234] What is even more important for the present context is that it saw therein an implicit exclusion of the passive aspect, of being subjected to a lawsuit, as long as there was no waiver.[235] Thus, the FAO could not be sued. It seems, however, that the Supreme Court's recognition of a waiver possibility

---

[233] Corte di Cassazione, 18 May 1992. See also pp. 162f below.
[234] The Corte di Cassazione speaks of the 'profilo attivo della legittimazione'. (1992) 75 *Rivista di diritto internazionale* 407 at 409.
[235] In the Corte di Cassazione's words: 'con l'implicazione di escludere la soggezione a quello passivo' adding 'salva la eventuale, espressa rinunzia all'immunità'. *Ibid.*

already shows that a strict functionally limited personality concept, limited to the FAO's active standing as opposed to its passive one, would be inconsistent as a matter of legal logic. By waiving its immunity, it could not 'gain' a passive capacity to be sued, if this capacity did not exist before.

Prudential judicial abstention through doctrines concerning act of state, political questions, and non-justiciability

In a number of states the judiciary has developed 'prudential rules of judicial self-restraint'[236] that serve to avoid the adjudication of disputes which are perceived properly to belong to non-judicial, mainly political, dispute resolution processes. If followed in the context of a lawsuit involving international organizations, such doctrines can in effect serve as alternatives to immunity in so far as they might form a valid reason for a court to deny its jurisdiction.

Among the most important and well known of these 'prudential abstention doctrines'[237] are the political questions and the act of state doctrine as developed by US courts. Although mainly associated with US case law, they are not only applied by US courts. The act of state doctrine has been used by the House of Lords – frequently under the term of 'non-justiciability'[238] – and finds application in other common law jurisdictions as well.[239] Still, the act of state doctrine seems to be a jurisprudential maxim mainly employed by common law courts that has not gained broader acceptance. The 'political questions' doctrine, on the other hand, appears to have its counterparts on a far broader basis. Even if frequently dealt with under 'non-justiciability' or other labels in civil law traditions the idea that certain highly political disputes are not to be settled by the judiciary is current in many legal systems.[240]

---

[236] Louis Henkin, Richard C. Pugh, Oscar Schachter and Hans Smit, *International Law* (2nd edn, St Paul, MN, 1987), 162.

[237] These kinds of avoidance techniques have also been termed 'passive virtues' of courts. *Cf.* Michael Robert Tyler, 'IAM v. OPEC: 'Acts of States' and 'Passive Virtues'' (1982) 5 *Loyola of Los Angeles International and Comparative Law Journal* 159–71 at 159.

[238] *Buttes Gas & Oil Co.* v. *Hammer*, [1981] All ER 616; [1982] AC 888 (House of Lords).

[239] For instance, in South Africa courts will not sit in judgment over acts of state – acts which include the 'official acts of recognized foreign entities'. A. J. G. M. Sanders, 'Non-Justiciability of Foreign Policy Matters' in W. A. Joubert (ed.), *The Law of South Africa* (Durban and Pretoria, 1981), vol. XI, *International Law*, para. 350.

[240] *Cf.* the extensive comparative survey of Advocate-General Darmon in *Maclaine Watson and Co Ltd* v. *Council and Commission of the European Communities*, Case 241/87, ECJ, 10 May 1990. As a consequence of an out-of-court settlement the case was removed from the register of the court before judgment was rendered. However, the opinion of Advocate-General

What is important for the purpose of ascertaining their actual use and potential usefulness (with particular regard to the consequences of disputes involving international organizations) is an investigation into the effects of the application of these doctrines, whether they lead to judicial abstention or rather to an implicit affirmation of acts that are not to be scrutinized by judicial abstention, in other words whether there will be no judicial forum or a forum that does not question the foreign act of state or the political act in issue. This aspect of the application of both the act of state doctrine and the political questions doctrine does not always seem to be quite clear.[241] Only in the first case might the invocation of the act of state or political questions doctrine effectively substitute for immunity in so far as it also provides a justification to deny a court's jurisdiction.[242]

The act of state doctrine

The act of state doctrine[243] as primarily developed in English and US courts shows some important parallels to the concept of immunity. Both

Darmon is of particular interest because it extensively deals with the issue of a potential bar to adjudication as a result of a non-justiciability or political questions doctrine. Since Maclaine Watson's claim under Article 215 of the EEC Treaty against the EEC as a member of the ITC corresponded to a tort action before a domestic court, the Advocate-General's deliberations on an abstention doctrine based on the common tradition of the member states can be used in the present context. The case arose from a continuation of the lengthy Tin Council litigation in the UK. While pursuing legal remedies in English courts against the Tin Council and its member states, Maclaine Watson also brought an action against the Council and Commission of the EEC asking for compensation for damage arising from the acts and omissions of the EEC as a member of the Tin Council. After reviewing the laws of the EEC member states relating to the 'question of judicial control of external relations', Advocate-General Darmon concluded that a non-justiciability doctrine or 'concept analogous to "act of the government" which would render inadmissible in principle actions for damages in respect of the institutions in the field of external relations' was not truly a principle common to the laws of the member states. [1990] ECR I-1797 at 1813.

[241] Restatement (Third), § 1, Reporters' Note 4; Louis Henkin, Foreign Affairs and the United States Constitution (2nd edn, Oxford, 1996), 146. See pp. 88ff below.

[242] In Maclaine Watson and Co Ltd v. Council and Commission of the European Communities, Case 241/87, ECJ, 10 May 1990, the defendant Community organs obviously invoked a theory of non-justiciability in order to prevent the ECJ's adjudication of a dispute for which the EEC would not have enjoyed immunity. According to Article 178 of the EC Treaty the ECJ is the exclusive forum for Article 215 disputes relating to compensation for damage.

[243] See, in general, Barry E. Carter and Phillip R. Trimble, International Law (Boston, New York, Toronto and London, 2nd edn, 1995), 669ff; J.-P. Fonteyne, 'Acts of State' in Rudolf Bernhardt (ed.), Encyclopedia of Public International (2nd edn, 1992), vol. I, 17–20 at 17ff; Hans-Ernst Folz, Die Geltungskraft fremder Hoheitsäußerungen (Baden-Baden, 1975); Henkin, Pugh, Schachter and Smit, International Law, 162ff; Restatement (Third), § 443; and Ignaz Seidl-Hohenveldern, 'Völkerrechtswidrige Akte fremder Staaten vor innerstaatlichen Gerichten' in Carl Hermann Ule, (ed.), Recht im Wandel. Festschrift zum 150jährigen Bestehen des Carl Heymanns Verlages (Cologne, Berlin, Bonn and Munich, 1965), 591–619 at 591ff.

have been termed expressions of judicial restraint whereby judges manage to avoid dealing with foreign and international law issues.[244] It is
generally thought that the application of the act of state doctrine is not
required by international law, but is rather a matter of domestic law and
policy – at best an expression of comity.[245] The avoidance rationale points
to an important common root of immunity from suit and act of state
principles – at least in the perception of common law courts – that is, the
concept that both doctrines help to prevent a court from becoming
involved in disputes which might lead to friction between a foreign state
and their own country.[246] This notion that the judicial branch should
abstain from any possible interference with the executive's tasks – frequently affirmed in act of state decisions – rests on a deeply rooted
separation of powers rationale.[247]

The US act of state doctrine prevents its courts from questioning the
validity of a foreign act of state committed by a recognized foreign
sovereign within its own territory.[248] Thus, in effect, the application of
the act of state doctrine normally leads to the uncontested assumption of
the validity of such acts.[249] Under US law it is not wholly clear what
exactly constitutes an act of state giving rise to judicial abstention from
scrutinizing it. The traditional types of acts of state contemplated by this
doctrine are expropriations. However, it is generally accepted that other
acts may also qualify.[250] The definitions given as 'acts by which a state has

---

[244] H. J. Steiner, D. F. Vagts and H. H. Koh, *Transnational Legal Problems: Materials and Text* (4th edn, Westbury, NY, 1994), 780.

[245] *Restatement (Third)*, § 443, Reporters' Note 12. Moreover, the missing 'hard law' character of the principles embodied in the act of state doctrine is also frequently acknowledged. C. T. Oliver, E. B. Firmage, C. L. Blakesley, R. F. Scott and S. A. Williams, *The International Legal System: Cases and Materials* (4th edn, Westbury, NY, 1995), 623, speak of 'matters that are not as yet governed by widely-accepted rules of public international law'.

[246] Steiner, Vagts and Koh, *Transnational Legal Problems*, 780. According to Oliver, Firmage, Blakesley, Scott and Williams, *The International Legal System*, 624, application of the act of state doctrine avoids the risk of 'being enmeshed in matters of foreign affairs which could risk embarrassment to the executive'.

[247] *Banco Nacional de Cuba v. Sabbatino*, 376 US 398 at 423 (1964) reflects the 'strong sense of the Judicial Branch that its engagement in the task of passing on the validity of foreign acts of state may hinder' the conduct of foreign affairs.

[248] *Restatement (Third)*, § 443, para. 1, relying mainly on *Underhill v. Hernandez*, 168 US 250 (1897), and *Banco Nacional de Cuba v. Sabbatino*, 376 US 398 (1964); Fonteyne, 'Acts of State', 17.

[249] See, however, pp. 88f below.

[250] *Cf.* the *Restatement's* formulation that 'courts in the United States will generally refrain from examining the validity of a taking by a foreign state of property within its own territory, or from sitting in judgment on other acts of a governmental character done by a foreign state within its own territory and applicable there'. *Restatement (Third)*, § 443, para. 1.

exercised its jurisdiction to give effect to its public interests',[251] as 'official acts',[252] 'acts of a governmental character',[253] 'formal acts of sovereign authority',[254] 'acts of general application decided by the executive or legislative branches of the acting state'[255] are all imprecise.[256] Examples of act of state cases may be more helpful. However, most US decisions deal with expropriations. Nevertheless, the classic US act of state case, *Underhill v. Hernandez*,[257] concerned an informal action by a military commander.[258] Some cases seem to suggest that the distinction between acts of state and activities not giving rise to the application of the doctrine follows the distinction between acts *iure imperii* and acts *iure gestionis* in the field of sovereign immunity. In *Alfred Dunhill of London Inc.* v. *Republic of Cuba*,[259] the Supreme Court held that the repudiation of a Cuban state agency to repay sums paid by cigar importers into the US was no act of state. In clarifying the essentials of an act of state, the Supreme Court stated that it may take the form of a decree, a statute or a comparable instrument, or of a statement made by someone with authority to exercise sovereign power; however, a mere default on a contract or repudiation of an obligation would not suffice.[260] Some of the justices in the case even explicitly considered a commercial exception to the act of state doctrine, analogous to the commercial activity exception to the sovereign immunity doctrine.[261] However, in *International Association of Machinists* v. *OPEC*,[262] a US circuit court acknowledged that '[w]hile purely commercial activity may not rise to the level of an act of state, certain seemingly commercial activity will trigger act of state considerations.'[263] It was of the opinion that 'the act of state doctrine remains available when such caution [i.e., to avoid an affront to a foreign state's sovereignty] is appro-

---

[251] Steiner, Vagts and Koh, *Transnational Legal Problems*, 781.

[252] *W. S. Kirkpatrick & Co. Inc.* v. *Environmental Tectonics Corporation, Int.*, 493 US 400, (1990).

[253] *Restatement (Third)*, § 443, para. 1.

[254] *Alfred Dunhill of London Inc.* v. *Republic of Cuba*, 425 US 682 (1976).

[255] *Restatement (Third)*, § 443, Reporters' Note 10.

[256] It is interesting to note how strongly US law relies on the public/private distinction for act of state purposes although it is generally believed – at least in some non-common law countries – to be hostile to such a dichotomy.

[257] 168 US 250 (1897).

[258] A Venezuelan general denied a US citizen travel documents required to leave the country.

[259] 425 US 682 (1976).

[260] *Alfred Dunhill of London Inc.* v. *Republic of Cuba*, 425 US 682 at 693–5 (1976).

[261] See also *Restatement (Third)*, § 443, Reporters' Note 6.

[262] US District Court CD Cal., 18 September 1979, *affirmed on other grounds*, US Court of Appeals 9th Cir., 6 July–24 August 1981.

[263] 649 F. 2d 1354 at 1360 (9th Cir. 1981).

priate, regardless of any commercial component of the activity involved', expressly adding that '[t]he act of state doctrine is not diluted by the commercial activity exception which limits the doctrine of sovereign immunity'.[264]

Despite these uncertainties there seems to be a growing convergence between acts or activities triggering the application of both the sovereign immunity doctrine and the act of state doctrine. The development of the restrictive immunity concept[265] and its adoption by US courts and ultimately the US legislature in the FSIA according to which, in principle, only *acta iure imperii* give rise to the sovereign immunity defence have certainly paved the way for this increasing similarity.

In two respects, however, the two concepts clearly differ. While the sovereign immunity defence is open only to foreign states (and under some conditions to their instrumentalities), the act of state doctrine can be invoked in disputes between private parties as well. One could therefore rightly say that the sovereign immunity doctrine is *party*-focused, whereas the act of state doctrine is *activity*-focused.[266] The second and crucial distinction, however, seems to lie in its operation and effect. While a finding of sovereign immunity results in the domestic court's lack of jurisdiction and thus prevents it from inquiring any further into the merits of a dispute, the act of state doctrine normally excludes any scrutiny of the foreign sovereign act, thereby implicitly upholding it on the merits.[267] At least this appears to be the traditional view.

The historic leading case of *Underhill* v. *Hernandez*[268] used language closely reminiscent of the classical *par in parem non habet imperium* rationale and seems to be close to jurisdictional abstention doctrines: 'Every sovereign state is bound to respect the independence of every other sovereign state, and the courts of one country will not sit in judgment on the acts of the government of another, done within its own territory.'[269] The statement that US courts will 'not sit in judgment' seems to imply

---

[264] *Ibid.*   [265] See pp. 335 note 58 and 349*ff* below.

[266] Steiner, Vagts and Koh, *Transnational Legal Problems*, 781.

[267] This difference had been less apparent than one would expect probably because the act of state doctrine was frequently invoked and applied in expropriation contexts where it led to the same result for expropriated ex-owners by precluding their right of recovery. But the important distinction remained that, where this right had been precluded for sovereign immunity reasons, the courts denied jurisdiction thereby avoiding dealing with the rights of the claimants at all, while under act of state doctrine decisions they implicitly affirmed the foreign expropriatory act by not questioning it which, in effect, leads to judgment for the defendants.

[268] 168 US 250 (1897).   [269] 168 US 250 at 252 (1897).

that they will abstain from adjudication.[270] Normally, however, the judicial abstention required by the act of state doctrine has received a narrower meaning. Courts applying it have usually upheld their jurisdiction and passed judgment on the merits. They only abstained from invalidating a foreign act of state – which in effect meant that they assumed its validity.

There are, however, act of state precedents that suggest that the application of the doctrine may lead to abstaining from adjudicating the dispute brought before the court. In *International Association of Machinists* v. *OPEC*,[271] the court noted that applying the act of state doctrine did 'not compel dismissal as a matter of course', but rather suggested that 'dismissal is appropriate'.[272] Also, the English affirmation of the validity of the act of state doctrine in *Buttes Gas & Oil Co.* v. *Hammer*[273] points in the same direction. Instead of implicitly acknowledging the validity of the foreign act of state, the House of Lords expressly declined to decide the issue at all.[274] The House of Lords held that 'there exists in English law a more general principle that the courts will not adjudicate on the transactions of foreign sovereign states. Though I would prefer to avoid argument on terminology, it seems desirable to consider this principle, if existing, not as a variety of act of state but one for judicial restraint or abstention.'[275]

Act of state considerations in abstaining from adjudicating lawsuits involving international organizations

In order to work as a potential reason for refraining from adjudicating disputes involving international organizations, the act of state doctrine must be considered – at least potentially – applicable to acts of international organizations. Although on its face and by definition the act of

---

[270] See also Advocate-General Darmon's opinion in *Maclaine Watson and Co Ltd* v. *Council and Commission of the European Communities*, Case 241/87, ECJ, 10 May 1990, comparing various abstention doctrines with 'similar solutions as part of the act of State doctrine' of US courts. [1990] ECR I-1797 at 1811.

[271] US District Court CD Cal., 18 September 1979, *affirmed on other grounds*, US Court of Appeals 9th Cir., 6 July–24 August 1981.

[272] 649 F. 2d 1354 at 1361 (9th Cir. 1981). For more detail, see pp. 90ff below.

[273] [1981] All ER 616; [1982] AC 888 (House of Lords).

[274] This defamation suit arose from a dispute between two competing US oil companies claiming that they had both been validly granted oil concessions for the same area in the Persian Gulf by two different rulers. The House of Lords decided not to decide this dispute which was intrinsically interwoven with the main dispute involving the validity of foreign acts of state.

[275] *Buttes Gas & Oil Co.* v. *Hammer*, [1981] All ER 616 at 628.

state doctrine seems to be limited to 'state' acts,[276] there is some authority in the case law that acts of international organizations could also
trigger its application.

In *International Tin Council* v. *Amalgamet Inc.*,[277] a US follow-up to the Tin
Council litigation in England, a New York court had to deal with, *inter
alia*, the issue of act of state as a potential bar to arbitration. The ITC had
moved to stay arbitration proceedings in New York brought against it by
Amalgamet Inc. for not honouring contractual liabilities. The ITC argued
that since it enjoyed immunity from legal process it should not be
amenable to arbitral proceedings as well and, in the alternative, that the
issue involved amounted to something like an act of state which could
not form the subject of arbitral scrutiny. It is interesting that the court
held the act of state argument inapplicable because it could not find any
exercise of 'sovereign' functions in the entering into contracts for the
purchase of tin. Thus, it must have at least implicitly thought that an
international organization could act in a sovereign fashion over which
domestic courts would have to refrain from sitting in judgment. In a
short case note the decision was criticized for using an act of state test at
all, because this doctrine was considered inapplicable for the simple
reason that the ITC was not a foreign state.[278] While this assessment
appears convincing on its face, the underlying rationale asking whether
there might be something comparable, like an 'act of the international
organization', is worth discussing. The court's language – reasoning that
the doctrine 'is involved where the dispute is intrinsically involved with
some sovereign function of a foreign entity so that political as well as
purely private commercial issues are implicated'[279] – already suggests
that a modification of the act of state doctrine could gain wider applicability.

The *International Association of Machinists* v. *OPEC* court also relied upon
the act of state doctrine. Technically, however, it did not apply it to OPEC,
but rather to the collective acts of its member states. Still, this case seems
to show that the act of state doctrine may be applicable to acts of
international organizations. In *International Association of Machinists* v.
OPEC[280] a US labour union brought suit against OPEC and its individual

---

[276] *Cf.* Steven R. Ratner, 'Sovereign Immunity – International Organizations – Act of State
    Doctrine – Recognition of Foreign Laws – Arbitration Clauses, International Tin Council
    v. Amalgamet Inc. . . .' (1988) 82 *American Journal of International Law* 837–40 at 839.

[277] New York County, Supreme Court, 25 January 1988.

[278] Ratner, 'Sovereign Immunity', 839.   [279] 524 NYS 2d 971 at 974 (1988).

[280] US District Court CD Cal., 18 September 1979, *affirmed on other grounds*, US Court of
    Appeals 9th Cir., 6 July–24 August 1981.

member states in US courts asking for damages and injunctive relief for alleged price-fixing of crude oil prices in violation of US antitrust law. As far as the case against the organization itself was concerned, the courts did not hesitate to dismiss the plaintiff's suit because OPEC was not and could not legally be served in the US – either under the IOIA or under the FSIA.[281] As far as the other defendants named in the claim were concerned, the courts differed in their reasoning for dismissing the suit. While the court of first instance based its dismissal on sovereign immunity reasons[282] and on antitrust law requirements which have not been met,[283] the appellate court embarked on an interesting act of state analysis which led it to abstain from adjudicating the dispute. Although, technically, the circuit court did not have to address the issue of OPEC's amenability to suit in the US courts (because it affirmed the district court's dismissal on grounds of lack of service of process), its discussion of the act of state doctrine is so broad and sometimes indeterminate that it seems to apply as well to international organizations. While the court clearly saw that the remedy sought was an 'injunction against the OPEC nations',[284] it frequently referred to the organization in its legal analysis, noting that 'OPEC's price fixing activity has a significant sovereign component',[285] contemplating the possibility that 'the court [could] hold that OPEC's actions are legal',[286] and at some point speaking of the 'injunction against OPEC's alleged price-fixing activity'.[287] The Court of Appeals did not explicitly affirm the lower court's decision to qualify the price-fixing activity within OPEC as 'sovereign' and thus requiring immunity for its

---

[281] 477 F. Supp 553 at 560 (CD Cal. 1979). Although the dismissal was justified on the technical ground of the lack of a possibility of serving the organization with process, this came close to a de-recognition of foreign international organizations. *Cf.* p. 70 above.

[282] It qualified the setting of crude oil prices as a governmental, as opposed to a commercial, activity. The court noted that 'the nature of the activity engaged in by each of these OPEC member countries is the establishment by a sovereign state of the terms and conditions for the removal of a prime natural resource – to wit, crude oil – from its territory'. 477 F. Supp 553 at 567 (CD Cal. 1979). It went on to regard the 'defendants' control over their oil resources [as] an especially sovereign function because oil, as their primary, if not sole, revenue-producing resource, is crucial to the welfare of their nations' peoples'. It rejected the plaintiffs' assertion that the 'actions of the OPEC nations in coming together to conspire to fix prices is commercial and, thus, not immune' with the following words: 'It is ridiculous to suggest that the essentially governmental nature of an activity changes merely by the act of two or more countries coming together to agree upon how they will carry out that activity.' 477 F. Supp. 553 at 569 (CD Cal. 1979).

[283] The court held that foreign states were not persons amenable to suit under US anti-trust law (477 F. Supp. 553 at 572) and that indirect purchasers, like plaintiffs, could not seek damages (477 F. Supp. 553 at 574).

[284] 649 F. 2d 1354 at 1361 (9th Cir. 1981).   [285] *Ibid.*, 1360.   [286] *Ibid.*, 1361.   [287] *Ibid.*

participants. That it probably had some doubts about this qualification is evidenced by its differentiation between activities triggering act of state considerations and activities leading to sovereign immunity. The court in effect suggested that a broader range of activities might give rise to act of state concerns than to sovereign immunity.[288] Applying the act of state doctrine, the court ultimately held that it did 'not compel dismissal as a matter of course', but that 'dismissal [was] appropriate'.[289] The court arrived at this conclusion not merely by qualifying the price-fixing activity of OPEC as an act of state, but rather by following a balancing approach suggested in the *Sabbatino* case[290] which looks at the content of the specific act of state in question. It held that the issuance of the injunction against the OPEC countries sought would not only insult the OPEC nations, but thereby also interfere with foreign relations efforts of the US political branches of the highest importance. The court further thought that in an area 'so void of international consensus' regarding the condemnation of cartels, royalties and production agreements, judicial interference should be allowed only reluctantly.[291] It thus affirmed the district court's dismissal of the suit.

Political questions doctrine

A 'political questions' doctrine – as most vigorously applied by the US courts – may also serve as a tool to abstain from deciding cases involving international organizations before national courts. Although developed in the context of executive determinations on the recognition of states and related issues concerning territorial sovereignty, of presidential decisions to engage in hostilities, of executive declarations on sovereign immunity to be accorded or denied to foreign states, etc.,[292] there is no reason why it could not be applied to disputes involving international organizations.[293]

The difficulty rather lies in determining the political element. What constitutes a 'political question' is almost as difficult to define as to define what constitutes an act of state. At the national level the leading

---

[288] See pp. 87f above.   [289] 649 F. 2d 1354 at 1361 (9th Cir. 1981).

[290] There the Supreme Court stated that 'the less important the implications of an issue are for our foreign relations, the weaker the justification for exclusivity in the political branches'. *Banco Nacional de Cuba* v. *Sabbatino*, 376 US 398 at 428 (1964).

[291] 649 F. 2d 1354 at 1361 (9th Cir. 1981).   [292] *Cf. Restatement (Third)*, § 1, Reporters' Note 4.

[293] Given the rationales put forward in the OPEC case (*cf.* pp. 90ff above), it almost seems that it was rather *political questions* than *act of state* that had been applied; this can also be deduced from the result reached in the OPEC case which led to a denial of jurisdiction, not to a validation of OPEC's activities.

case is *Baker* v. *Carr*[294] where the US Supreme Court enumerated an illustrative list of aspects involving political questions, including:

a textually demonstrable constitutional commitment of the issue to a coordinate political department; or a lack of judicially discoverable and manageable standards for resolving it; or the impossibility of deciding without an initial policy determination of a kind clearly for nonjudicial discretion; or the impossibility of a court's undertaking independent resolution without expressing lack of the respect due coordinate branches of government; or an unusual need for unquestioning adherence to a political decision already made; or the potentiality of embarrassment from multifarious pronouncements by various departments on one question.[295]

As with the act of state doctrine the legal effect of the application of the political questions doctrine is not free from ambiguity.[296] While some cases seem to lead to judicial abstention by denying the courts' jurisdiction to adjudicate,[297] others rather hint towards judicial abstention by generally upholding political decisions.[298]

Court decisions using a political questions doctrine

A political questions rationale as a reason to deny their adjudicative power over disputes involving international organizations is rarely used by domestic courts. However, in some cases involving international organizations, such a reasoning was accepted in order to justify the courts' adherence to immunity decisions made by the executive. This clearly followed the practice in the context of sovereign immunity determinations. For decades it was the executive branch which determined whether the immunity claimed by a foreign state should be respected or not.[299] If the determination was in the negative, the dispute would be judicially

---

[294] 369 US 186 (1962).   [295] *Baker* v. *Carr*, 369 US 186 at 217 (1962).

[296] *Restatement (Third)*, § 1, Reporters' Note 4; Henkin, *Foreign Affairs*, 146.

[297] In *Oetjen* v. *Central Leather Co.*, 246 US 297 at 302 (1918), the Supreme Court held that '[t]he conduct of the foreign relations of our Government is committed by the Constitution to the Executive and Legislative – the "political" – Departments of the Government, and the propriety of what may be done in the exercise of this political power is not subject to judicial inquiry or decision'.

[298] Classical examples are cases where the recognition of foreign states and governments is considered binding on courts. E.g., *Jones* v. *United States*, 137 US 202 at 212 (1890): 'Who is the sovereign, *de jure* or *de facto*, of a territory is not a judicial, but a political question, the determination of which by the legislative and executive departments of any government conclusively binds the judges.'

[299] *Cf. Restatement (Third)*, 392, Introductory Note to § 451. There is a general trend, however, towards a free evaluation of immunity issues by the courts themselves. See p. 129 below.

resolved. The rationale for the traditional view to defer to the executive's opinion corresponded exactly to a kind of political questions doctrine.[300] This practice also illustrates that the non-justiciability of certain issues need not necessarily lead to the ousting of certain disputes from judicial settlement.

In the *Curran* case,[301] the court saw the 'wisdom of the rule' (that the State Department finally and binding for the courts decided on the immunity of states and international organizations before domestic courts) in leaving to the executive branch 'delicate questions pertaining to the foreign policy of the United States'.[302] *Curran*, however, could also be viewed as an example of an emerging jurisprudence of avoiding the adjudication of certain disputes properly considered as political. In the court's view these disputes 'should be addressed to the political branch of the government not the judicial'.[303] Another rare case involving – at least indirectly – an international organization that was decided on a political questions rationale is *Soucheray et al. v. Corps of Engineers of the United States Army et al.*[304] There a US court denied the relief requested, *inter alia*, on grounds of non-justiciability because – in its view – the heart of the matter was a political, foreign policy issue. The plaintiffs had claimed damages for inundation resulting from the International Joint Commission's regulation of water levels of Lake Superior. They had not directed their suit against the Commission itself, a US–Canadian bilateral institution, enjoying privileges and immunities like an international organization, but rather against the US member of the Board of Control, an organ of the Commission, and against other US defendants claiming that the US was responsible for the Commission's activities. The court still felt that granting the relief sought would in effect infringe upon the tasks of the Commission. It held that:

questions regarding the Commission's regulation of the boundary waters under the Treaty of 1909 may not be appropriate for judicial resolution. These questions contain issues of foreign relations, for which the Constitution gives Congress and the Executive primary responsibility.[305]

---

[300] See also *Ex parte Republic of Peru*, 318 US 578 at 588–9 (1943), where the Supreme Court held that executive 'suggestions of immunity' 'must be accepted by the courts as a conclusive determination by the political arm of the government' and that adjudication would 'interfere with the proper conduct of our foreign relations'.

[301] *Curran v. City of New York et al*, Supreme Court, Special Term, Queens County, 29 December 1947.

[302] 77 NYS 2d 206 at 209 (S. Ct 1947).   [303] *Ibid.*, 213. For more detail, see p. 125 below.

[304] US District Court WD Wisconsin, 7 November 1979.

[305] 483 F. Supp. 352 at 356 (WD Wisconsin 1979).

Relying among others on *Baker* v. *Carr*,[306] the leading political questions precedent, the court thought there was an 'obvious' potential for conflict and multiple decisions where domestic courts would interfere with the activities of an international organization.[307]

In another interesting suit which did not involve an international organization proper but rather the International Olympic Committee (IOC), which is a private, non-profit organization established under the laws of Switzerland,[308] the political questions rationale was considered in a similar fashion. In *Martin* v. *International Olympic Committee*,[309] a suit alleging sex discrimination, a US Circuit Court found:

> persuasive the argument that a court should be wary of applying a state statute to alter the content of the Olympic Games. The Olympic Games are organized and conducted under the terms of an international agreement – the Olympic Charter. We are extremely hesitant to undertake the application of one state's statute to alter an event that is staged with competitors from the entire world under the terms of that agreement.[310]

The court certainly overestimated the legal relevance of the Olympic Charter which is not exactly an international agreement in the sense of an agreement under international law. However, the court's concern that the unilateral imposition of national policies might hamper the internationally governed rules of the IOC seem justly to reflect a foreign-affairs-based political questions rationale that is equally applicable to international organizations proper. The court, rightly, did not consider whether the IOC could enjoy immunity from suit in the US

---

[306] 369 US 186 (1962). *Cf.* p. 93 above.

[307] 483 F. Supp. 352 at 356 (WD Wisconsin 1979).

[308] *Cf.* Bruno Simma, 'The Court of Arbitration for Sport' in Karl-Heinz Böckstiegel, Hans-Ernst Folz, Jörg Manfred Mössner and Karl Zemanek (eds.), *Völkerrecht – Recht der Internationalen Organisationen – Weltwirtschaftsrecht. Festschrift für Ignaz Seidl-Hohenveldern* (Cologne, Berlin, Bonn and Munich, 1988), 573–85 at 574*ff*; and Christoph Vedder, 'The International Olympic Committee: An Advanced Non-Governmental Organization and the International Law' (1984) 27 *German Yearbook of International Law* 233–85 at 245*ff*.

[309] US District Court of California, 16 April 1984, US Court of Appeals, 21 June 1984. A number of female athletes brought suit against the IOC alleging that its failure to include 5,000-metre and 10,000-metre track events for women constituted gender-based discrimination in violation of US federal and state law, US constitutional law and international law. The district court denied the preliminary injunctive relief sought by the applicants. This decision was upheld by the appellate court. It found no abuse of discretion or erroneous legal reasoning by the lower court. The circuit court shared the view that the IOC's decision not to organize certain sporting events for women did not constitute unlawful discrimination.

[310] 740 F. 2d 670 at 677 (9th Cir. 1984).

courts.[311] The IOC's amenability to suit was taken for granted and it was not treated any differently from any other foreign-incorporated legal person that was not an international organization.

Non-justiciability or acte de gouvernement doctrines

Other legal systems contain doctrines that are closely related to the US political questions and also the act of state doctrine which may also be used in the context of abstaining from adjudicating disputes involving international organizations. The French doctrine of *acte de gouvernement* tends to immunize against challenging governmental acts relating to the conduct of foreign affairs, in particular, those involving the negotiation, conclusion and implementation of international agreements because such acts are considered to be non-justiciable by their nature.[312] The French Conseil d'Etat, however, introduced an important limitation to this abstention doctrine. It allowed tort actions of individuals against the French government claiming damages arising from a duly published international agreement provided that the damage is abnormal and special and that the reparation is not precluded by the agreement itself.[313] In this context it is interesting to note that in *Ministre des Affaires Etrangères y. Dame Burgat*,[314] the Conseil d'Etat even went as far as to award damages to an individual who was deprived of the possibility of suing a person enjoying jurisdictional immunity as a result of the headquarters agreement between France and UNESCO.

Similarly, Italian courts tend to abstain from ruling on political

---

[311] See, however, James G. Goettel, 'Is the International Olympic Committee Amenable to Suit in a United States Court?' (1984) 7 *Fordham International Law Journal* 61–82 at 68*ff*, regarding the IOC as an entity possessing international legal personality. In Goettel's view, the only reason why it did not enjoy immunity was that it 'is probably not a public international organization because, although it is created by governments, it maintains independence from all governmental control. Even if the IOIA could apply, the IOC has not been designated by the President as an exempt organization.' *Ibid.*, 71. This commentator may have been deceived by rule 11(2) of the Olympic Rules that form part of the Olympic Charter which describes the IOC as 'a body corporate by international law having juridical status and perpetual succession'. This rather misleading wording does not alter the fact that the IOC's status amounts only to an entity enjoying legal personality under Swiss private law. *Cf.* Simma, 'The Court of Arbitration for Sport', 574.

[312] See Rusen Ergec, 'Le contrôle juridictionnel de l'administration dans les matières qui se rattachent aux rapports internationaux: actes de gouvernement ou réserve du pouvoir discrétionaire' (1986) 68 *Revue de droit international et de droit comparé* 72–134 at 72*ff*. *Cf.* also Advocate-General Darmon's opinion in *Maclaine Watson and Co Ltd* v. *Council and Commission of the European Communities*, Case 241/87, ECJ, 10 May 1990.

[313] *Compagnie générale d'énergie radio-électrique*, Conseil d'Etat, 30 March 1966.

[314] Conseil d'Etat, 29 October 1976. See pp. 296*f* below for details of the case.

measures. With particular relevance for international acts, the Corte di Cassazione held in *De Langlade* v. *Ministero tesoro*[315] that the responsibility of governmental organs for international acts was political and could not be raised before judicial organs but only by using the means and institutions for the implementation of political control of the government.

The English variation on the act of state doctrine, frequently discussed under the more appropriate heading of non-justiciability, is also very close to the French concept of *acte de gouvernement*.[316] It was used by the House of Lords in a case concerning the liability of national contingents of UN peacekeeping forces for damages caused to British subjects in Cyprus. In *Attorney-General* v. *Nissan*,[317] the House of Lords did not directly consider the applicability of the act of state or non-justiciability doctrine to the UN[318] because it did not regard the UN as possessing the quality of a state. Rather it expressly held that '[t]he United Nations is not a super-State nor even a sovereign state'.[319] However, the House of Lords discussed at length whether such a principle could preclude them from 'taking cognisance of certain acts . . . of the Crown done under the prerogative in the sphere of foreign relations'.[320] While a majority of judges thought that the acts complained of, taking possession of hotel premises on Cyprus owned by a British subject in the course of peacekeeping operations, could not be qualified as acts of state and would thus not prevent them from deciding an action for damages, one judge reached the same result by holding that a British subject 'can never be deprived of his legal right to redress by any assertion by the Crown or decision of the court that the acts of which he complains were acts of State'.[321] The majority, however, seemed to agree on the principle that English courts may have no jurisdiction over certain English and foreign acts of state, understood mainly as 'transactions of independent States between each other',[322] such as the making of treaties, the recognition of foreign states or conquest and annexation.[323] The House of Lords finally held that the

---

[315] Corte di Cassazione, 12 July 1968. *Cf.* (1969) 52 *Rivista di diritto internazionale* 583 at 586.

[316] See P. Cane, 'Prerogative Acts, Acts of State and Justiciability' (1980) 29 *International and Comparative Law Quarterly* 684*ff.*

[317] House of Lords, 11 February 1969.

[318] In a material sense, however, the court did so. *Cf.* Jochen A. Frowein, 'Diskussionsbeitrag' in Bernhardt and Miehsler, 'Qualifikation und Anwendungsbereich des internen Rechts internationaler Organisationen' (1973) 12 *Berichte der Deutschen Gesellschaft für Völkerrecht* 111–12 at 112. Since a potential liability of the UN was not sought by the plaintiff, the privileges and immunities of the UN were also not discussed.

[319] Lord Pearce at [1969] 1 All ER 647; (1972) 44 ILR 359 at 377.

[320] Lord Wilberforce, (1972) 44 ILR 359 at 384.   [321] Lord Reid, *ibid.*, 370.

[322] *Ibid.*, 373.   [323] *Ibid.*, 371.

UK government was liable in principle for damages caused to a British subject by British troops both before and after they joined the United Nations peace-keeping force in Cyprus since – even as forces serving with the UN – they continued to be British soldiers for whom the Crown remained exclusively liable.

In Germany the discussion revolves around 'acts of government' or 'non-justiciable acts' ('*justizfreie Hoheitsakte*').[324] In a well-publicized decision of the Federal Constitutional Court concerning nuclear missiles, the jurisdictional consequence of a non-justiciability issue was considerably restricted. In a challenge to the German government's so-called *Pershing* decision to authorize the installation of nuclear missiles,[325] the Federal Constitutional Court acknowledged that certain claims could not give rise to judicial review because of the public authorities' discretion in the conduct of foreign affairs. It went on, however, to examine on the merits whether a general principle of international law – becoming part of German law *via* Article 25 of the Basic Law – prohibited the possession or use of nuclear arms.

Acte de gouvernement and non-justiciability considerations in abstaining from adjudicating lawsuits involving international organizations

There appear to be no cases involving international organizations where courts denied their adjudicative power exclusively on the ground that the questions were *actes de gouvernement* or otherwise non-justiciable for political reasons. However, some of the cases analyzed at least consider these reasons among others.

An example where a domestic court justified its abstention from adjudicating an employment dispute involving an international organization and one of its employees, *inter alia*, on the ground of the political nature of the issues concerned is *Weiss* v. *Institute for Intellectual Cooperation*.[326] The Conseil d'Etat thought that an examination of the action in question – which lay not only against the Institute but also against the French state[327] – 'necessarily implies an appreciation of French government acts

---

[324] *Cf.* H. Schneider, 'Gerichtsfreie Hoheitsakte' (1951) 169 *Staat und Recht* 47.
[325] German Federal Constitutional Court, 16 December 1983.
[326] Conseil d'Etat, 20 February 1953.
[327] The former legal adviser of the Institute, a body established under the auspices of the League of Nations and subsequently incorporated into UNESCO, claimed that actions of the French Minister of Foreign Affairs led to his dismissal in 1941 and prevented him from obtaining execution of an award rendered in his favour by the League of Nations Administrative Tribunal as well as from obtaining a comparable post at UNESCO. Thus

in its relations with international bodies or with foreign states and the Conseil d'Etat [has] therefore no jurisdiction in these matters'.[328]

In a similar way the English High Court refused to make a winding-up order against the International Tin Council in *Re International Tin Council*.[329] The court considered it obvious that such an order would 'compel the government of the United Kingdom either to be in breach of its treaty obligations or to seek to withdraw from the Agreement [Establishing the Sixth International Tin Council]'.[330] In the court's opinion '[s]uch questions are not justiciable by domestic courts. They must be solved by diplomacy, not by domestic litigation.'[331]

The well-known Belgian *Manderlier* v. *Organisation des Nations Unies and Etat Belge*[332] decision, famous for its grant of absolute immunity to the UN,[333] also contains a reference to a political questions abstention rationale holding that 'the courts have no power to assess diplomatic action taken by the executive'.[334]

Lack of adjudicative power of domestic courts

A further reason to dismiss lawsuits involving international organizations on grounds other than immunity is used when domestic courts declare themselves not 'competent' to address certain types of disputes. This legal 'incompetence' to deal with certain disputes might be phrased in concepts like 'lack of jurisdiction', 'lack of judicial competence', etc.; a case might be perceived to lie beyond the cognizance of a particular court; the particular lawsuit might be considered to lie outside the subject matter jurisdiction of the court resorted to, etc. The terms and exact legal concepts will depend upon the procedural (and partly substantive) law of the forum state. However, there appear to be certain similarities (as evidenced by the actual cases decided) that allow one to discover common features underlying these (nationally) different con-

the claim seems to have been directed first of all against the French government (the brevity of this decision is not particularly helpful for analytical purposes). Nevertheless, the Conseil d'Etat stated that the claimant was 'an official of a body with an international character, consequently the Conseil d'Etat has no jurisdiction, in the matter of a claim, in respect of difficulties between said international body and one of its officials'. (1954) 81 *Journal de droit international* (Clunet) 747.

[328] *Ibid.*
[329] High Court, Chancery Division. 22 January 1987. See p. 118 below for details of this decision.
[330] (1988) 77 ILR 18 at 30.   [331] *Ibid.*, 31.
[332] Brussels Appeals Court, 15 September 1969.   [333] See pp. 214 and 179f below.
[334] (1969) *Pasicrisie Belge* 247 at 249.

cepts. Since most of the legal concepts of jurisdiction, *compétence*, *Gerichtsbarkeit*, etc., are deeply rooted in specific legal traditions, the expression 'adjudicative power' of domestic courts will be used as a neutral term. The common denominator behind many of the various ways of reasoning appears to be a certain specific concept of the adjudicative power of domestic courts and its limits. Some kinds of disputes involving international organizations are simply perceived to lie beyond those powers.

At the outset the relationship and distinction between 'lack of jurisdiction' and 'immunity' as well as the terminological use of the two notions need to be clarified. Although there appear to be some similarities between the concept of 'lack of jurisdiction' and the notion of 'immunity *ratione materiae*' – and in fact there might be a growing convergence that could ultimately lead to a development where a 'lack of jurisdiction' theory could replace immunity considerations[335] – the two concepts should be kept apart.

In a sense immunity is a secondary issue, an issue that becomes relevant only when a domestic court is competent or has jurisdiction in the first place.[336] Immunity is a specific reason for hindering further proceedings. The lack of adjudicative power of domestic courts, however, can serve as a primary tool to avoid disputes involving international organizations. If a court finds that it lacks adjudicative power to sit in judgment over a certain dispute, the immunity issue does not even arise.[337]

---

[335] See Part III below.

[336] *Cf.* Lalive, 'L'immunité de juridiction', 293: 'L'immunité présuppose un tribunal territorial qui serait normalement compétent.' See also the distinction made by Finn Seyersted, 'Jurisdiction over Organs and Officials of States, the Holy See and Intergovernmental Organisations' (1965) 14 *International and Comparative Law Quarterly* 31–82 and 493–527 at 39, between 'immunity *rationae personae*' and 'incompetence *ratione materiae*' which results from the exclusive 'organic' jurisdiction of a foreign state or an international organization.

[337] The German case of *Hetzel v. Eurocontrol* is probably one of the clearest examples demonstrating the irrelevance of the immunity issue in cases where the lack of jurisdiction can be justified by the availability of alternative methods of legal redress. For more detail, see pp. 104ff below. The Verwaltungsgerichtshof (Administrative Court) Baden-Württemberg expressly held that it could leave the question of Eurocontrol's immunity undecided, since it could deduce its lack of jurisdiction from the grant of exclusive jurisdiction for employment disputes to the ILO Administrative Tribunal. Appellate Administrative Court Baden-Württemberg, 7 August 1979; see also Federal Constitutional Court, 10 November 1981, BVerfGE 59, 63 at 93. See also the express statement of the English High Court in *Re International Tin Council*, High Court, 22 January 1987, concluding that '[it] had no jurisdiction to wind up the ITC. This makes it unnecessary to consider the question of immunity, for there is no need for immunity from a jurisdiction which does not exist.' (1988) 77 ILR 18 at 36.

In most legal systems the adjudicative power of courts is primarily based on territorial and personal links between the forum state and the dispute/litigants.[338] Rules on territorial and *in personam* jurisdiction in many countries' procedural law clearly evidence this.[339] There is, however, also a third aspect of adjudicative power that relates to the subject matter of a dispute. The jurisdiction or competence of a domestic court is usually limited to certain subject matters. Although these subject matters are normally defined in a sufficiently broad and encompassing way that their inherently limiting quality is hardly perceived, they do determine the adjudicative power of courts.

Many domestic legal systems confine the subject matter adjudicative power of their courts to the determination of 'civil rights and obligations'. Thereby they usually exclude administrative or public law issues from the cognizance of courts. Civil law countries in particular have supplemented the basic distinction between substantive private and public law with a corresponding dichotomy of civil and administrative procedure to adjudicate and enforce claims arising from the two distinct bodies of law. Also common law countries which have no such strong tradition of differentiating between public and private law seem to have increasingly developed special administrative procedures to adjudicate issues that would be considered of a public law nature. A clear example for the limits of the adjudicative power of courts – one that is of particular relevance to the present study – can be found in employment law. Most legal systems exclude public employment relations from the jurisdiction of ordinary courts and empower special administrative courts or tribunals or administrative organs with the adjudication of disputes arising from such employment relations. It is frequently asserted that domestic courts lack adjudicative power to deal with the internal law of an international organization,[340] in particular with employment issues governed by staff rules and regulations.[341] The main reason for this view

---

[338] *Cf.* Harold J. Berman, William R. Greiner and Samir N. Saliba, *The Nature and Functions of Law* (Westbury, NY, 1996), 134*ff*.

[339] See *Restatement (Third)*, § 421, para. 2, setting out the connecting factors entitling a state to exercise jurisdiction to adjudicate.

[340] *Cf.* Rudolph Bernhardt, 'International Organizations, Internal Law and Rules' in Rudolf Bernhardt (ed.), *Encyclopedia of Public International Law* (2nd edn, 1995), vol. II, 1314–18 at 1314*ff*; and Rudolph Bernhardt, 'Qualifikation und Anwendungsbereich des internen Rechts internationaler Organisationen' (1973) 12 *Berichte der Deutschen Gesellschaft für Völkerrecht* 7–46 at 7*ff*.

[341] Questions concerning the validity and content of an international organization's employment and administrative law are usually regarded as issues of an internal nature. Hans Peter Kunz-Hallstein, 'Privilegien und Immunitäten internationaler

seems to lie in the parallel between employment relations within international organizations and the civil service of foreign states.[342] This, however, also implies an inherent limitation on the lack of jurisdiction argument. Only in so far as one can speak of an international administration, the exclusivity of special (administrative) fora can be justified. Where an employment relationship is based on a (private) contractual relationship outside the specific internal regulations, the exclusion of domestic courts does not seem to be warranted.

It has also been argued that international organizations possess an organizational power to regulate their internal affairs in an autonomous fashion.[343] This organizational power should comprise a personal jurisdiction over their staff, which in turn implies that states lack any jurisdiction *ratione materiae* to legislate or exercise adjudicative jurisdiction over such relations.[344]

Apart from the basic distinction between private and public law disputes which may have to be handled by different fora, many legal systems seem to show a certain awareness that some disputes involving issues of international law or subjects of international law might lie beyond the adjudicative power of their courts. Courts may be reluctant to deal with disputes relating to 'constitutional' issues of international law, such as use of force, or with disputes that do not affect rights and obligations of individuals but rather of states only, etc. They might also refrain from adjudicating issues which they consider to belong properly to the realm of other states or other subjects of international law.

Another important limitation of a domestic court's adjudicative power stems from the respect of the litigants' autonomy. Courts might, thus, see their power to adjudicate limited by the free will of the litigants whose choice of forum selection they will respect in general.

Organisationen im Bereich nicht hoheitlicher Privatrechtsgeschäfte' (1992) *Neue Juristische Wochenschrift* 3069–73 at 3070. See also Michael Akehurst, *The Law Governing Employment in International Organizations* (Cambridge, 1967), 12; Zemanek, 'Die Rechtsstellung', 381.

[342] Akehurst, *The Law Governing Employment*, 12, compares such a situation to 'an English court trying to judge a dispute between the French Government and one of its officials'.

[343] The difference from a juridical person under domestic law whose internal (legal) system (statutes, charter of incorporation, etc.) is regularly subject to domestic law is evident. Dominicé, 'L'immunité de juridiction', 167.

[344] *Cf.* Seyersted, 'Jurisdiction over Organs', 69 and 505*ff*; Kunz-Hallstein, 'Die Beteiligung', 823*ff*: 'Aufgrund der Organisationsgewalt der Internationalen Organisationen [comprising *Personalhoheit*] sind ihre inneren Angelegenheiten der Legislationsgewalt der Staaten und deren Gerichtsbarkeit der Sache nach (*ratione materiae*) unmittelbar entzogen.'

Judicial practice of abstention through respect for an exclusively competent forum

A number of court decisions adopted the view that they were required to abstain from adjudicating disputes involving international organizations as a result of their obligation to respect an alternative, exclusively competent forum. Courts have consequently denied their jurisdiction based on the exclusivity of an internal system of (administrative) legal recourse within an international organization. They sometimes show an inclination to avoid their jurisdiction over disputes involving international organizations by referring to a concept of subject-matter jurisdiction which they consider they do not possess in certain employment disputes.

For instance, a decision of the French Cour de Cassation in the case *Bellaton* v. *Agence spatiale européenne*[345] apparently dismissed an employment suit at least on the alternative ground that it was already subject to internal administrative proceedings.[346]

In a recent English employment case, in *Bertolucci* v. *European Bank for Reconstruction and Development and others*,[347] the domestic tribunal – holding that EBRD's scope of immunity was clear – expressly 'sympathise[d] with Ms Bertolucci but her remedy, if any, [was] against the Bank under its grievance and appeals procedure and, if that is ineffectual, by way of representation to the Governors and Secretary-General of the Bank'.[348]

Also in Italian cases the jurisdiction of other tribunals has been a determinative factor in the decision of national courts to abstain from exercising their own jurisdiction. In *Marré* v. *Istituto internazionale per l'unificazione del diritto privato (Unidroit)*[349] the existence of an administrative tribunal competent to handle employment disputes was one of the reasons taken into consideration by the Tribunale di Roma in upholding Unidroit's immunity from suit before the Italian courts.

One of the best documented and most thoroughly commented domestic cases of a suit against an international organization – although frequently

---

[345] Cour de Cassation, 24 May 1978.

[346] The Cour de Cassation affirmed the dismissal by the Paris Court of Appeal of a suit brought by a former employee against the European Space Agency. The organization had not expressly waived its immunity, and the termination of Mr Bellaton's employment contract was already the subject of administrative proceedings within the European Space Agency's Appeals Commission.

[347] Employment Appeal Tribunal, EAT/276/97, 19 August 1997.   [348] Lexis transcript.

[349] Tribunale Roma, 12 June 1965. See also p. 368 note 188 below. See also *Commissione delle Comunità europee* v. *Beditti*, Corte di Cassazione, 2 February 1987, and *Commissione delle Comunità europee* v. *Ucchiara*, Corte di Cassazione, 9 February 1987, concerning the exclusive jurisdiction of the ECJ over EURATOM staff disputes.

discussed under the heading immunity of international organizations[350] – was in fact decided under a lack of adjudicative power rationale. In *Hetzel* v. *Eurocontrol*,[351] a German appellate administrative court held that as a result of the possibility of having legal recourse to the ILO Administrative Tribunal under Eurocontrol staff rules, German courts lacked jurisdiction for Eurocontrol employment disputes. It particularly stressed the need for a single employment law and an equally exclusive jurisprudence formed by a single court as elements guaranteeing the proper functioning of the international organization. The Federal Constitutional Court rejected a constitutional challenge to this decision.[352]

Hetzel v. *Eurocontrol* is not the only case where a domestic court resorted to a lack of jurisdiction concept rather than to immunity from suit. A number of employment disputes concerning Eurocontrol were brought before various domestic courts in different countries. The issue of whether domestic courts are competent to hear such cases was complicated by a peculiarity of Eurocontrol's conventional framework which does not provide for the organization's immunity from suit[353] but includes a number of confusing provisions giving rise to potentially conflicting conclusions.

Eurocontrol, like most international organizations, employed personnel according to two different categories, unilaterally appointed officials (*fonctionnaires internationaux*) and persons hired on the basis of contract. While employment relationships of the first type were governed

---

[350] *Cf.* the published legal opinions of Bleckmann and Seidl-Hohenveldern for these legal proceedings: Albert Bleckmann, *Internationale Beamtenstreitigkeiten vor nationalen Gerichten, Materialien zum Recht der internationalen Organisationen und zur Immunität, Rechtsgutachten für die Union Syndicale, Section Eurocontrol* (Berlin, 1981); and Ignaz Seidl-Hohenveldern, *Die Immunität internationaler Organisationen in Dienstrechtsstreitfällen, Rechtsgutachten für Eurocontrol. Schriften zum Völkerrecht* (Berlin, 1981), vol. 71.

[351] Administrative Court Karlsruhe, 5 July 1979, Appellate Administrative Court Baden-Württemberg, 7 August 1979.

[352] Federal Constitutional Court, 10 November 1981. The appellant had argued that the exclusivity of the ILO Administrative Tribunal violated the minimum requirements of the rule of law principle contained in the German Constitution. He maintained that he had a claim to the jurisdiction of German administrative courts as a constitutionally guaranteed right. The Constitutional Court, however, held that the constitutional guarantee related only to acts of German authorities, and that, since Eurocontrol did not exercise 'German' authority, German administrative courts were not by constitutional necessity competent to hear the plaintiff's claim. This rejection was clearly based on earlier decisions limiting the right of access to German administrative courts as guaranteed by Article 19 of the German Basic Law to actions directed against acts of 'German' authority. See the two *Eurocontrol-Flight Charges* cases at pp. 107f below.

[353] Article 27 of the Eurocontrol Convention only provides for a limited immunity from enforcement measures.

by the organization's staff regulations, its internal administrative law, the latter were subject to local labour law. It also appeared unproblematic to assume that domestic courts had jurisdiction to adjudicate disputes arising from the second type of employment relationships. The competent forum to decide disputes arising from the first type of employment was harder to ascertain. The applicable administrative law provided:

Any dispute between the Agency [i.e., the Air Traffic Services Agency, one of two main organs of Eurocontrol] and any person to whom these Conditions of Employment . . . apply regarding non-observance, in substance or form, of the provisions of the present Conditions of Employment . . . shall be referred to the Administrative Tribunal of the International Labour Organisation, in the absence of a competent national jurisdiction.[354]

Furthermore, a provision in the Protocol of Signature stipulated that:

Nothing in the Convention or the Statute annexed thereto shall be deemed to restrict the jurisdiction of national courts in respect of disputes between the Organization and the personnel of the Agency.[355]

These provisions gave rise to conflicting interpretations as far as the issue of the jurisdiction of domestic courts over such employment relations with appointed officials were concerned. The issue turned on the correct interpretation of the phrase 'in the absence of a competent national jurisdiction' and in particular on whether this should be regarded as a 'normative' or a purely 'explanatory' statement. Those advocating the adjudicative power of domestic courts interpreted it in a 'normative' fashion, implying that the ILO Administrative Tribunal should be competent only subsidiarily where no national court would have jurisdiction.[356] Adherents of the 'explanatory' view regarded the controversial phrase as a causal explanation of the fact that national courts were not competent to hear such disputes.[357] Since they were not, the Article provided for the jurisdiction of the ILO Administrative Tribunal. The provision in the Protocol of Signature, according to which national courts' jurisdiction is deemed unrestricted in employment disputes too,

---

[354] Article 92(1) of the General Conditions of Employment entering into force on 15 December 1969; Article 93(1) of the Staff Regulations entering into force on 13 June 1964, cited in (1985) 16 *Netherlands Yearbook of International Law* 468ff.
[355] Section 5 of the Protocol of Signature of the Convention, cited in (1985) 16 *Netherlands Yearbook of International Law* 468ff.
[356] Bleckmann, *Internationale Beamtenstreitigkeiten*, 38, 77 and 116.
[357] Seidl-Hohenveldern, *Die Immunität internationaler Organisationen*, 15ff and 99.

should be interpreted as a temporary waiver of Eurocontrol's immunity valid only from the assumption of its operations in 1963 to the entry into force of the controversial provisions of the Staff Regulations in 1964 providing for the jurisdiction of the ILO Administrative Tribunal. It can be argued that the jurisdiction of domestic courts was intended only during the period where no international tribunal was competent to hear staff cases. In *Hetzel* v. *Eurocontrol*[358] German courts denied their adjudicative power by relying on this 'explanatory' interpretation of the controversial provisions.[359]

A similar employment dispute was brought in the Dutch courts. In *Eckhardt* v. *Eurocontrol*[360] the court of first instance affirmed its jurisdiction over an employment dispute between Eurocontrol and one of its staff members. The plaintiff had applied to the national court seeking an annulment of Eurocontrol's decision to terminate his employment. The court dismissed the petition as a matter of substantive law holding that the employment was not governed by Dutch labour law, but rather by the defendant's administrative law, i.e. the convention establishing the organization, staff regulations, etc., and that the plaintiff had failed to show that Eurocontrol had infringed these provisions. The court based its finding of jurisdiction on a normative interpretation of the above cited provisions concluding that they 'clearly show[ed] that national courts (in this case the Local Court, since a labour dispute is involved) have jurisdiction in respect of such a dispute'.[361]

The appellate court in *Eckhardt* v. *Eurocontrol*[362] reversed the jurisdictional decision and dismissed the case on the ground of the lack of jurisdiction of the Dutch courts. It qualified the employment relationship between the plaintiff and Eurocontrol as an 'administrative law relationship' and held that Eurocontrol was 'empowered to autonomously establish legal provisions relating to its personnel, which implies a right . . . to designate an exclusive Tribunal'.[363] As to the controversial consequence

---

[358] Administrative Court Karlsruhe, 5 July 1979, Appellate Administrative Court Baden-Württemberg, 7 August 1979.

[359] The Constitutional Court accepted the appellate Administrative Court's reasoning to understand section 5 of the Protocol of Signature of the Convention as a provision of only temporary applicability (on which the applicant could not rely) and considered it plausible to understand the phrase 'in the absence of a competent national jurisdiction' as one merely restating the existing legal situation and not providing for a subsidiary jurisdiction of the ILO Administrative Tribunal. BVerfGE 59, 63 at 94*ff*.

[360] Local Court of Sittard, 25 June 1976.

[361] (1978) 9 *Netherlands Yearbook of International Law* 277.

[362] District Court of Maastricht, 12 January 1984.

[363] (1985) 16 *Netherlands Yearbook of International Law* 470.

of the applicable provisions, it clearly followed the 'explanatory' interpretation.

In *Strech* v. *Eurocontrol*,[364] a staff dispute where an employee of the defendant organization sought a court order requiring his employer to make payments to the German unemployment and pension insurance system, the significance of section 5 of the Protocol of Signature of the Convention was of crucial importance. The labour court at first instance, although recognizing that Eurocontrol was a supranational organization with its own international legal personality, denied its claim to immunity from suit. It thought that such an immunity was precluded by the explicit reservation of national jurisdiction as expressed in the protocol. Upholding the jurisdiction of the German courts, it referred the case to the competent court of social security matters. This decision was reversed by the appellate court.[365] It did not so much rely on the explanatory interpretation of section 5 of the Protocol but rather on a provision of German domestic law contained in the Second Regulation on Privileges and Immunities for Eurocontrol of 29 August 1979. In the court's view, Germany had thereby renounced its jurisdiction over employment disputes concerning Eurocontrol. The court furthermore based its finding upon the fact that the provisions of the Eurocontrol staff rules on means of recourse were exclusively applicable. Thus, the German courts did not have jurisdiction to hear social security disputes.[366]

Two other prominent disputes involving Eurocontrol, concerning its flight charges, were also left undecided by the German courts on grounds of lack of jurisdiction. In *Eurocontrol-Flight Charges I*,[367] a German air transportation company brought suit against Eurocontrol challenging the legality of the latter's competence to collect flight charges. The German Federal Administrative Court upheld the reasoning of the lower courts which had decided that German courts had no jurisdiction to scrutinize flight charges of Eurocontrol, because such jurisdiction was

---

[364] Labour Court Karlsruhe, 5 December 1978; State Labour Court Baden-Württemberg, 28 September 1979.

[365] State Labour Court Baden-Württemberg, 28 September 1979.

[366] 'Der Ausschluß der deutschen Rechtsvorschriften über das öffentlich-rechtlichen Sozialversicherungswesen hat zur Folge, daß die nationalen deutschen Gerichte von Bediensteten der Beklagten, die deutsche Staatsangehörige sind, zur Klärung von Streitigkeiten über Ansprüche der sozialen Sicherheit und Versorgung nicht angerufen werden können. Es gelten vielmehr insoweit ausschließlich die Bestimmungen der ABB [allgemeinen Beschäftigungsbedingungen für die Bediensteten der Eurocontrol-Zentrale Maastricht] über Beschwerdeweg und Rechtsschutz'. State Labour Court Baden-Württemberg, 28 September 1979, 6 Sa 33/79 (unpublished).

[367] Federal Administrative Court, 16 September 1977.

vested exclusively in Belgian courts as a result of Eurocontrol's internal law. It emphasized that – since Belgian courts would adequately guarantee a fair trial – the lack of German jurisdiction posed no constitutional law problems.[368]

In *Eurocontrol-Flight Charges II*,[369] the Federal Constitutional Court rejected the contention of the claimants that the exclusive jurisdiction of the Belgian courts violated principles of the German Basic Law. It held that the German constitution did not provide a subsidiary jurisdiction of German courts in disputes over flight charges of Eurocontrol since the provision invoked, Article 19(4) of the Basic Law, provides for legal recourse only against acts of German authorities, not of intergovernmental institutions. It reiterated its view – already enunciated in the famous *Solange* decisions – according to which the constitutional licence to transfer sovereign rights to international organizations under Article 24(1) of the Basic Law is limited by the respect for the core elements of the German Constitution. Among those range fundamental rights which may not be ousted by such a transfer of sovereignty. The German court was, however, clearly of the opinion that the option of legal recourse at hand offered by Belgian courts satisfied the requirements of a broad and effective legal protection.

Respecting choice of forum clauses providing for arbitration or other fora

National courts may also deny their power to adjudicate out of respect for the parties' freedom to select a competent forum. As such this abstention rationale is in no way peculiar to international organizations or other subjects of international law.

In *Viecelli v. IRO*,[370] an Italian court dismissed a claim brought by one of the IRO's employees for lack of jurisdiction, basing its finding on the existence of an alternative dispute settlement mode, rather than on the organization's functional immunity.[371] The court grounded its lack of jurisdiction on the express choice of forum clause contained in the

---

[368] BVerwGE 54, 291 at 304.   [369] Federal Constitutional Court, 23 June 1981.

[370] Tribunale Trieste, 20 July 1951.

[371] The court not only disregarded the applicable conventional norms of immunity (Riccardo Monaco, 'Capacités de droit privé des organisations internationales' in Caemmerer, Ernst von *et al.* (eds.), *Festschrift für Pan Zepos* (Athens and Freiburg, 1973), 475–90 at 475), but also failed to consider a possible basis in customary law: On the assumption that only sovereign international persons could enjoy immunity, it denied such a possibility for the IRO: 'L'IRO . . . non può venire riconosciuta quale ente sovrano avendo una limitata capacità giuridica internazionale ed alla quale, pertanto, non può venire riconosciuta l'immunità giurisdizionale.' (1953) 36 *Rivista di diritto internazionale* 471. Subsequent Italian cases show that international organizations are considered to enjoy immunity from suit as a result of their international legal personality. *Cf.* pp. 194ff below.

employment contract between Viecelli and the IRO which provided for arbitration in cases of dispute.

In a very indirect way, the Canadian decision in *International Civil Aviation Organization* v. *Tripal Systems Pty Ltd et al.*[372] is also based on the respect for the competence of an arbitral tribunal in which a domestic court should not interfere. The ICAO entered into a contract for the construction of an airport in Vietnam which contained an arbitration clause and at the same time stated that nothing in it should be construed as a waiver of its immunity. When a dispute arose and the ICAO's partner demanded arbitration, the ICAO contested the arbitral tribunal's competence on the ground of immunity. The tribunal rejected this claim qualifying it as premature. The ICAO then sought a declaratory judgment from a Canadian court which would confirm that it enjoyed 'absolute immunity from judicial process of every kind', including obviously also from arbitration. The Canadian court refused to adjudicate on this request which it considered an attempt to circumvent the work of the arbitral tribunal. It strictly interpreted the legal condition under which a domestic court was entitled to supervise arbitral proceedings and concluded that the relief sought did not fall under these categories.[373]

Judicial practice of abstention vis-à-vis *foreign public law cases*

In a number of primarily employment-related disputes national courts refused to adjudicate because they thought that the issues to be decided were part of public law and that they were not the appropriate fora to pass judgment upon them. For instance, in *De Bruyn* v. *European Parliamentary Assembly*,[374] a domestic arbitral tribunal in Luxembourg decided that it had no jurisdiction over a complaint concerning the dismissal of a former employee of the European Parliamentary Assembly since that employment relationship existed in public law. The dispute was subsequently decided by the ECJ serving as the administrative tribunal of the staff of Community officials in *De Bruyn* v. *European Parliamentary Assembly*.[375] The ECJ upheld the plaintiff's claim for unlawful termination of his employment contract.

Some Italian cases brought against NATO, its sub-units or other NATO member states were also decided on the basis of treaty-transformed principles providing that certain types of employment relations were considered to be public law relations over which Italian courts had no

---

[372] Superior Court, 9 September 1994.
[373] (1994) *Recueil de Jurisprudence du Québec* 2560–75.
[374] Employment Arbitration Tribunal, 22 January 1960.
[375] Case 25/60, ECJ, 1 March 1962.

jurisdiction. The conventions governing the civil personnel employed by NATO and its member states basically divided this staff into two categories, one of 'international civilian personnel', whose contracts of employment were directly governed by NATO rules and which lay outside the jurisdiction of the receiving state; and another of 'local civilian labour', whose employment relationships were subject to the jurisdiction of the receiving state.[376] Under the Convention Between the Parties to the North Atlantic Treaty Regarding the Status of Their Forces[377] and the Protocol on the Status of International Military Headquarters set up pursuant to the North Atlantic Treaty,[378] and various North Atlantic Council decisions, only persons not nationals of, or resident in, the receiving state, remunerated in accordance with NATO-established rules and holding permanent administrative assignments, i.e. persons whose functions had a direct connection with the structure and functioning of NATO, could qualify as 'international civilian personnel'.[379] Italian courts, however, frequently disregarded these treaty-based nationality requirements and have decided cases brought by Italian nationals merely on the basis of whether a particular employment relationship fell under a public law relationship with NATO or one of the other NATO member states. In their view the difference between 'local civilian labour' and 'international civilian personnel' more or less 'incorporated the distinction between the private and public nature of the employment relationship'[380] which frequently allowed them to apply *iure gestionis/iure imperii* criteria to decide such cases.[381]

[376] See in general Rosa Maria Battaglia, 'Jurisdiction over NATO Employees' (1978–9) 4 *Italian Yearbook of International Law* 166–73 at 166ff.

[377] London, 19 June 1951, 199 UNTS 67.   [378] Paris, 28 August 1952, 200 UNTS 340.

[379] Battaglia, 'Jurisdiction over NATO Employees', 167.

[380] *United States* v. *Porciello*, Corte di Cassazione, 1977, (1978–9) 4 *Italian Yearbook of International Law* 174 at 176. See also *Pelizon* v. *SETAF Headquarters*, Corte d'Appello di Velezio, 19 April 1973. In another decision the supreme court held that the distinction between 'local civilian labour' and 'international civilian personnel' 'is based on the well-known rule that not all the work relations brought into being by a subject of international law within the territory of another entity form an integral part of the typical organization of that subject and thus subject to its substantive and jurisdictional regulation'. *HAFSE* v. *Trotta*, Corte di Cassazione, 1978, (1978–9) 4 *Italian Yearbook of International Law* 179, upholding the jurisdiction of the Italian courts over a labour dispute involving a member of the 'local civilian labour' of Italian nationality. See also *Baruffati* v. *SACLANT ASW Research Center*, Pretore La Spezia, 4 February 1977, where an Italian court upheld its jurisdiction over an unjust employment termination suit brought by an Italian–British double-national employed as a school-teacher by an organ of NATO's Atlantic Allied Command.

[381] See, however, *United States* v. *Gereschi*, Corte di Cassazione, 14 October 1977, where the Italian Supreme Court did not rely on the general distinction between the private or public law character of the employment relationship, but rather correctly concluded that the plaintiff as a result of the applicable treaty law could not be qualified as part of the international civil personnel of NATO. Thus, disputes concerning his position as part

This problematic disregard for certain treaty requirements is evident in *Conte* v. *HAFSE*,[382] an employment suit against Allied Headquarters in Southern Europe (HAFSE), by an Italian national who worked as an administrative clerk and later as librarian for the intelligence division of NATO. In this case the defendant organization successfully claimed that such suits were excluded from the jurisdiction of domestic courts. The court found that one could not doubt that the plaintiff fulfilled administrative tasks that are strictly inherent in the organization of military duties.[383] Conte tried to rely upon the distinction within NATO law between 'international civilian personnel' subject to NATO rules and jurisdiction and 'local civilian labour' subject to local law and jurisdiction.[384] The Italian court, however, regarded the differentiation as only exemplary and did not think that it excluded a third category of civilian employees who – although of Italian nationality or residing there – would be exclusively subject to NATO jurisdiction in so far as their tasks were truly administrative. The court remarked quite generally that administrative activities of a permanent character in the military headquarters – whether principal or auxiliary – are always to be considered as an activity inherent in the organization of military duties.[385] It continued to see a direct link between the administrative tasks and the functioning of an international organization stating that the administrative activities are destined to make the functioning of these (military) duties possible in a direct and immediate way and that they respond to the constant and essential exigencies of the organization.[386] The Naples court, thus, refused to decide on the merits.

of the 'local civilian labour' would not be excluded from the jurisdiction of Italian courts. Although *United States* v. *Gereschi* did not address issues of the immunity of international organizations, this decision is relevant for the Italian Supreme Court's view of the relationship between treaty and general international law of jurisdictional immunities. The court expressly held that general principles of international law governing state immunity were not applicable where a specific international treaty governed the matter. (1978–9) 4 *Italian Yearbook of International Law* 173.

[382] Tribunale Napoli, 28 September 1967.

[383] 'Non può dubitarsi che il Conte espletasse stabilente manisioni amministrative, in quanto tali strettamente inerenti all'organizzazione dell'ufficio militare'. (1968) 51 *Rivista di diritto internazionale* 718.

[384] Based on the 1951 London Convention and the 1961 Paris Agreement. See p. 110 notes 377 and 378 above.

[385] 'Le attività amministrative svolte con carattere di permanenza nei Quartieri generali militari, siano esse principali o ausiliari, sono sempre da considerarsi come attività inerenti all'organizzazione interna degli uffici militari'. (1968) 51 *Rivista di diritto internazionale* 717.

[386] '[E]sse sono destinate a rendere possibile in modo diretto e immediato il funzionamento di questi uffici e rispondono ad esigenze costanti ed essenziali dell'organizzazione' (1968) 51 *Rivista di diritto internazionale* 717.

In *Mazzanti* v. *HAFSE and Ministry of Defence*[387] the Tribunal of Florence held already that it had no jurisdiction over an employment dispute between an Italian national and HAFSE which was an 'international legal person' and had entered into the labour contract in the exercise of its 'public law capacity'. The Court of Appeals of Florence affirmed the decision, specifically qualifying the employment relationship between HAFSE and the plaintiff as one of a public law character subject to the legal code established by HAFSE and thus exempt from the jurisdiction of the Italian courts.[388] On the basis of these principles, the Italian Supreme Court confirmed in *HAFSE* v. *De Raffaele*[389] and in *HAFSE* v. *Gardi and INPS*[390] that Italian courts lacked jurisdiction over employment disputes between NATO and its 'international civil personnel' even if they were Italian nationals.

In *HAFSE* v. *Sindicato FILTAT-CISL Vicenza*[391] the true reason for denying jurisdiction in a suit brought by local trade unions seemed to have been the concept of a lack of subject matter jurisdiction. The court apparently considered that, while Italian 'private' labour law was applicable to certain NATO staff, Italian trade union law was not.[392] It concluded from this substantive finding that the relevant agreements did not provide for the application of Italian trade union legislation, and that these matters were also outside the jurisdiction of Italian courts.

Similarly, in *Camera confederale del lavoro and Sindicato scuola CGIL* v. *Istituto di Bari del Centro internazionale di alti studi agronomici mediterranei*[393] the Italian Supreme Court held that the Italian courts lacked

---

[387] Tribunal of Florence, 2 January 1954; Court of Appeals of Florence, 4–23 August 1955.

[388] Court of Appeals of Florence; A. N. Vorkink and M. C. Hakuta, *Lawsuits Against International Organizations – Cases in National Courts Involving Staff and Employment* (Washington DC, World Bank Legal Department, 1985), 14.

[389] Corte di Cassazione, 24 November 1978.   [390] Corte di Cassazione, 7 July 1978.

[391] Corte di Cassazione, 7 July 1978.

[392] The plaintiff, an Italian trade union, instituted proceedings against the Headquarters of the Allied (NATO) Forces in Southern Europe (HAFSE) alleging that they had hindered their activities in various ways. On a preliminary appeal from the Pretore of Vicenza, the Supreme Court denied jurisdiction. It arrived at this conclusion by interpreting the applicable treaty law governing the stationing of NATO forces in Italy. These agreements, distinguishing between 'international staff members' and 'local staff', subjected the latter to the jurisdiction of the receiving state regarding their conditions of employment. The Court, however, viewed the regulation of employment and the regulation of trade unions as entirely different matters. Adhering to a restrictive treaty interpretation, the Court refused to extend the jurisdiction in the former field to the latter. (1988) 77 ILR 630.

[393] Pretore di Bari, 15 February 1974; Corte di Cassazione, 27 April 1979. Two Italian trade unions brought suit against the Bari Institute claiming that it had seriously infringed its employees' rights such as the right to strike and to join a trade union. The director of the Institute claimed that he had acted under the authority of the staff rules of the

jurisdiction in a suit brought by two Italian trade unions claiming that the rights to strike and to join a union of the employees of the defendant international organization had been seriously infringed. Although the Supreme Court expressly relied on a sovereign immunity rationale,[394] it appeared to reason with broader jurisdictional principles. The court made a clear distinction between relationships of employment (concerning rights and duties of employer and employee) and labour relationships (concerning the trade unions *vis-à-vis* the Centre) and held that 'general international law would not allow a State to have jurisdiction over the labor relations between foreign States and their employees'.[395] The Supreme Court expressly referred to states, although it clearly decided an issue concerning the labour relations between an organization and its employees. This decision was followed in *Sindicato scuola UIL (Bari Branch)* v. *Istituto di Bari del Centro internazionale di alti studi agronomici mediterranei*[396] where an order of annulment sought by a trade union against internal restructuring measures of the Bari Institute was held inadmissible because it would have unduly interfered with the organization's rights of self-organization.[397]

In general, it seems that decisions that purport to base their conclusion on immunity from suit concepts also frequently use a reasoning that is more akin to a 'lack of jurisdiction for foreign employment disputes' rationale. In *ICEM* v. *Chiti*[398] the Italian Supreme Court recognized the immunity of an international organization sued by a secretarial employee of Italian nationality under a contract of employment which it qualified as one falling under a *iure imperii* category. The Court of Cassation, however, also reasoned that acts by which an international organization arranges its internal structure, including staff employment relations, were manifestations of the organization's powers under international law:

Case law has also upheld that acts of self-organization and the regulation of organizational relations, amongst which are those of public employment, are an

---

organization and that since they fell under the internal administrative powers of the Institute they were not amenable to suit in Italian courts. While the court of first instance upheld its jurisdiction under a very strict functional immunity standard, the Corte di Cassazione granted immunity arguing, *inter alia*, that trade union labour relations fell outside the scope of Italian jurisdiction in a way similar to the law of foreign public officials which could not be adjudicated by the Italian courts.

[394] A result of Italy's reservation to the applicable treaty provision calling for 'absolute' immunity. See pp. 186ff below.

[395] (1985) 6 *Italian Yearbook of International Law* 185.   [396] Corte di Cassazione, 4 June 1986.

[397] (1992) 87 ILR 37 at 38.   [398] Corte di Cassazione, 7 November 1973.

expression of the sovereign power of the international law subject in the same way that they are, in Italy, the expression of the sovereign power of the Italian State and are governed by public law . . . [These were] governed exclusively by the international organization's own rules and consequently not subject to the Italian legal system and exempt from the jurisdiction of Italian courts.[399]

A recent German court decision also confirms the view that international organizations are not subject to the jurisdiction of German courts because they are not subject to local law as far as the regulation of their employment and administrative law is concerned. These are considered matters of internal affairs. In *X et al. v. European School Karlsruhe*,[400] the German Federal Administrative Court affirmed the decision of a lower administrative court which refused to hear a dispute concerning the remuneration of a teacher employed by the European School in Karlsruhe on the ground of a lack of jurisdiction. The court reasoned that the school was autonomous in regulating its internal affairs including its staff relations and that this autonomy comprised the competence to set up a system of legal recourse which may exclude the jurisdiction of national courts.[401]

Judicial practice of abstention vis-à-vis *subjects of international law and matters of international law*

In other employment disputes, national, in particular French, courts have used a slightly different reasoning to deny their adjudicative power. They stressed less the public law character of the disputes than the fact that it involved subjects and matters of international law. A typical case is in *Re Dame Adrien and others*[402] where the French Conseil d'Etat stated that it had no competence to hear a petition directed against an international reparations commission because the 'petitioners belonged to an international organisation and their position was determinable only by international public law'.[403] This French abstention practice *vis-à-vis* international bodies has a long tradition. In a number of older Conseil d'Etat decisions the lack of jurisdiction of French courts over employment

---

[399] (1976) 2 *Italian Yearbook of International Law* 350f. See also *C v. ICEM*, Corte di Cassazione, 7 June 1973.

[400] Federal Administrative Court, 29 October 1992.

[401] 'Diese Regelungsbefugnis [die Bestimmung des Rechtsschutzes und der Rechtsschutzgewährung bei Streitigkeiten dienstrechtlicher Art], die namentlich auch die Einrichtung eines den nationalen Rechtsweg ausschließenden besonderen Rechtsschutzsystems umfaßt.' *X et al. v. European School Karlsruhe*, Federal Administrative Court, 29 October 1992, BVerwGE 91, 126 at 129.

[402] Conseil d'Etat, 17 July 1931. French officials of the Reparations Commission had requested the French Minister of Foreign Affairs for their official classification in the service. The Conseil d'Etat upheld the latter's refusal to do so.

[403] (1931–2) 6 *Annual Digest of Public International Law Cases* 33.

disputes with international agencies and organizations was established. In *Re Antin*[404] and in *Re Marthoud*,[405] the Conseil d'Etat dismissed two employment complaints brought against the railroad administration in the occupied territory considering that it did not constitute an 'administration or establishment of the [French] State',[406] but rather an international organization over which France had no jurisdiction. In a dispute concerning retirement payments, in *Re Courmes*,[407] the Conseil d'Etat upheld the decision of the French Ministry of Health not to pay indemnities to someone who was not a 'French' agent, but rather an employee of the port of the principality of Monaco who rendered his services according to a bilateral agreement between the two states.[408] In *Re Lamborot*[409] the Conseil d'Etat confirmed the French Ministry of War's decision not to pay a salary to the plaintiff while he served as French representative to the Inter-Allied Commission; while in *Re Godard*[410] the Conseil d'Etat refused to reimburse the plaintiff's moving costs from a post at the same Commission since service with it was with an 'international organization', not with the French government.[411]

In *Chemidlin* v. *Bureau international des Poids et Mesures*,[412] a French civil court stated that – even in the absence of any treaty provisions conferring immunity – it had no jurisdiction *ratione materiae* over an employment dispute of a French national with an international organization. A former employee of the International Bureau of Weights and Measures, established by the Metre Convention[413] in 1875, brought suit against the 'defendant organisation'[414] claiming that he was entitled under French legislation concerning ex-soldiers and prisoners of war to damages for breach of contract and failure to be reinstated in his former position. Chemidlin had left the Bureau in 1937 to perform his military service duties and continued to serve in the French army during World War II until he was taken prisoner of war. The French court followed the Bureau's contention that it was entitled to rely on its own particular statutes regulating the issue outside French law. The constituent treaty, the 1875 Metre Convention, did not contain any immunity provisions. It

---

[404] Conseil d'Etat, 1928.   [405] Conseil d'Etat, 1929.
[406] Vorkink and Hakuta, *Lawsuits Against International Organizations*, 8.
[407] Conseil d'Etat, 1928.
[408] Vorkink and Hakuta, *Lawsuits Against International Organizations*, 8.
[409] Conseil d'Etat, 1928.   [410] Conseil d'Etat, 1930.
[411] Vorkink and Hakuta, *Lawsuits Against International Organizations*, 9.
[412] Tribunal Civil of Versailles, 27 July 1945.   [413] Article 3 of the Metre Convention.
[414] The Tribunal Civil held that the 'international character of the defendant organisation ha[d] been established'. (1943–5) 12 *Annual Digest of Public International Law Cases* 281 at 282.

did, however, provide that the Bureau should function under the exclusive direction and supervision of an international committee. This case also shows the interrelation between applicable law and the jurisdiction of courts, between the issue of jurisdiction to prescribe and jurisdiction to adjudicate. The French court deduced from the absence of the first the lack of the second. It stated that:

International civil servants, it is generally admitted, exercise their functions in the public interest but under international authority and outside the legal system of the State to which they belong. The French State not having been, in this case, charged by the international Convention with the duty of assisting officials recruited thereunder, it would appear that the conventions and rules to which recourse is to be had to settle Chemidlin's claim must be outside the framework of French law so that they retain their purely international character. Hence French law is not, in all the circumstances, applicable.[415]

In *Weiss* v. *Institute for Intellectual Cooperation*,[416] the Conseil d'Etat reasoned in a very short opinion that the claimant was 'an official of a body with an international character, consequently the Conseil d'Etat has no jurisdiction, in the matter of a claim, in respect of difficulties between said international body and one of its officials'.[417] The defendant institution, the International Institute for Intellectual Cooperation created in 1924,[418] did not expressly enjoy any immunity. On the contrary, its statute provided quite generally that '[i]n legal proceedings and in all matters of civil law the Institute shall be represented by the President'.[419] The statute, however, also provided that '[t]he International Institute shall be independent of the authorities of the country in which it is established'[420] and the constitutive Letter from the French Government provided, *inter alia*, that the staff of the International Institute 'shall be subject only to the rules laid down in the organic statutes and in the regulations approved and decisions adopted by the Committee on Intellectual Co-operation'.[421]

In *Klarsfeld* v. *L'office franco-allemand pour la jeunesse*,[422] a bilingual secre-

[415] *Ibid.*   [416] Conseil d'Etat, 20 February 1953.

[417] (1954) 81 *Journal de droit international* (Clunet) 747. See pp. 98*f* above for details of the case.

[418] Letter from the French Government to the President of the Council of the League of Nations, 8 December 1924, including a Statute of the Institute and Resolution of the Council of the League of Nations, 13 December 1924.

[419] Article 9 of the Statute of the International Institute for Intellectual Cooperation.

[420] *Ibid.*, Article 3.

[421] Letter from the French Government to the President of the Council of the League of Nations, 8 December 1924, para. 4.

[422] Tribunal d'Instance Paris, 19 February 1968, Cour d'Appel Paris, 18 June 1968.

tary of the French–German Youth Office disputed the lawfulness of the organization's termination of her employment contract before the French courts. Both the court of first instance and the appellate court declared that domestic courts were not competent to decide this kind of dispute. Relying primarily on *Re Dame Adrien and others*[423] and *Chemidlin v. Bureau international des Poids et Mesures*,[424] they considered the Office an international legal person 'escaping' the internal law of France,[425] in particular as far as the relations with its staff were concerned. The dispute was subsequently heard by the internal grievance board (*commission de recours*) of the Office.[426]

A number of Italian cases also seem to rely primarily upon a concept of 'lack of jurisdiction' over international organizations in order to avoid the adjudication of certain disputes. For instance, in *Institut international pour l'agriculture v. Profili*,[427] an employment dispute was held to be outside the Italian courts' jurisdiction because the defendant institute was an 'international administrative union' which was 'free, as regards its internal affairs, from interference by the sovereign power of the States composing the Union, except when it consented thereto'.[428] The Italian Supreme Court could not rely on a concept of immunity since the Institute's constituent agreement, the Convention for the Creation of an International Institute of Agriculture,[429] did not contain any provision concerning its legal personality or immunity.[430] Subsequent Italian decisions continued this line of reasoning. They are frequently very close in their arguments to the cases avoiding adjudication because of the 'public law' quality of the issues involved. In an *obiter dictum* the Italian Supreme Court said in *Branno v. Ministry of War*[431] that '[t]he Italian courts will not exercise jurisdiction with respect to cases arising out of public law activities of a subject of international law possessing both *jus imperii* and a legal system

---

[423] Conseil d'Etat, 17 July 1931.   [424] Tribunal Civil of Versailles, 27 July 1945.

[425] The Cour d'Appel Paris, 18 June 1968, (1968) 14 *Annuaire français de droit international* 373, qualified the Office as a 'personne morale de droit international échappant aux règles de droit interne'.

[426] *Cf.* David Ruzié, 'De l'obligation de réserve des fonctionnaires internationaux et des conditions de leur licenciement a propos de l'affaire Klarsfeld' (1970) 16 *Annuaire français de droit international* 417–28 at 417.

[427] Tribunal of Rome, 1 February 1930; Corte di Cassazione, 26 February 1931.

[428] Corte di Cassazione, (1929–30) 5 *Annual Digest of Public International Law Cases* 413 at 414.

[429] 7 June 1905, reprinted in (1908) 2 *American Journal of International Law* Supplement, 358.

[430] Only during pending proceedings domestic Italian law conferred diplomatic immunities to the Institute's higher officials. (1929–30) 5 *Annual Digest of Public International Law Cases* 414.

[431] Corte di Cassazione, 14 June 1954.

of its own [referring to NATO]'.[432] In the already mentioned case of *Camera confederale del lavoro and Sindicato scuola CGIL* v. *Istituto di Bari del Centro internazionale di alti studi agronomici mediterranei*,[433] the Italian Supreme Court was of the opinion that a dispute with an organization concerning the right to strike and to join a union of the employees of the defendant international organization was completely outside Italian jurisdiction because it fell within the Bari Institute's organizational autonomy:

> If the international body's power to organize itself by means of rules in a given way is queried, this power, as pertaining to the public subjectivity of that body, falls totally outside the sphere of Italian law, and Italian courts . . . cannot inquire into the congruity and necessity (as far as the operative purposes for which immunity from jurisdiction is granted to the international body) of the results of an exercise of that power, in as much as it is embodied in a specific norm and implemented by a given organizational structure.[434]

One of the most prominent examples of national decisions where courts abstained from deciding disputes involving a subject of international law and matters of international law by declaring that they lacked jurisdiction is in *Re International Tin Council*.[435] Following the ITC's insolvency, Amalgamated Metal Trading Ltd, one of the ITC's creditors, having previously obtained an arbitration award against the ITC, presented a petition for the compulsory winding up of the ITC according to English law. The court refused to grant the remedies sought. It held that English legislation implementing the Sixth International Tin Agreement and the Tin Council's Headquarters Agreement did not confer the legal status of a body corporate on the ITC, but only the capacities of such a body.[436] In the court's view, the ITC was an international legal person and although English insolvency law could exceptionally be applied to foreign corporations such law was in principle inapplicable to international organizations. As an additional reason to strike out the petition, the court held that the ITC enjoyed immunity under the International Tin Council (Immunities and Privileges) Order 1972. This Order contained an exception from immunity for the enforcement of an arbitration award. However, since insolvency proceedings were regarded as going beyond measures to enforce an arbitral award, the exemption was not granted. The petitioner's appeal against the High Court's decision was dismissed in *Re International Tin Council*.[437]

[432] (1955) 22 ILR 757.
[433] Pretore di Bari, 15 February 1974; Corte di Cassazione, 27 April 1979. See p. 112 above.
[434] Corte di Cassazione, 27 April 1979, (1985) 6 *Italian Yearbook of International Law* 187.
[435] High Court, Chancery Division, 22 January 1987.   [436] (1988) 77 ILR 18 at 25.
[437] Court of Appeal, 27 April 1988.

The best-known of the Tin Council actions, addressing the issue of the ITC member states' liability for the debts of the organization, were mainly decided – or rather not decided, but dismissed – for even more fundamental avoidance reasons. The courts refused to follow the demands of the Tin Council's creditors either to appoint a receiver who should determine the member states' liability for the organization's debts (the so-called receivership action) or to hold the members directly liable (the so-called direct actions). The essence of this refusal lay in the particular English doctrine of incorporation. The courts held that the rights which they thought derived from treaty law and which had not been incorporated into domestic law were not justiciable in English courts.

In the receivership action of *Maclaine Watson & Co. Ltd* v. *International Tin Council*,[438] Maclaine Watson, one of the ITC's creditors, had an enforceable arbitration award against its debtor. Since the Tin Council was unable to meet its obligations and refused to demand contributions from its member states, Maclaine Watson applied for the appointment of a receiver under English law by way of equitable execution over the ITC's assets. The applicant considered that the ITC had a right to be indemnified by its member states in order to meet its obligations. The High Court dismissed this application, holding that applicant failed to show that the ITC had an arguable cause of action against its member states which could have been upheld by a receiver. It held that, even if such a right to contribution could be deduced from the Sixth International Tin Agreement, such a treaty provision was not justiciable in the English courts. The dismissal of this application was affirmed by the Court of Appeal in *Maclaine Watson & Co. Ltd* v. *International Tin Council*[439] and finally upheld by the House of Lords.[440] In the appellate court's view, the rights of the ITC against its members were derived not from the contracts between the ITC and the applicant but from the Sixth International Tin Agreement and thus were not justiciable in the English courts.

The 'direct actions' were largely decided on grounds of non-enforcement of non-incorporated treaties. The case of *J. H. Rayner (Mincing Lane) Ltd* v. *Department of Trade and Industry and others*[441] is a good example. Failing to recover their loans from the insolvent ITC itself, the organization's creditors tried to bring legal proceedings against the ITC's individual member states directly. One of the creditors, J. H. Rayner (Mincing Lane) Ltd, after having obtained a valid arbitration award, sued the

---

[438] High Court, Chancery Division, 13 May 1987.   [439] Court of Appeal, 27 April 1988.
[440] House of Lords, 26 October 1989.
[441] High Court, Queen's Bench Division (Commercial Court), 24 June 1987; Court of Appeal, 27 April 1988; House of Lords, 26 October 1989.

Department of Trade as the relevant governmental department of the UK together with twenty-two other ITC member states and the EEC. The plaintiff claimed the liability of the members on the alternative grounds (1) that the ITC was not a separate legal person from its members so that its contracts were in fact those of the member states; (2) that the member states were secondarily liable for the ITC's contractual obligations; and (3) that the ITC had in fact contracted as the members' agent. The High Court dismissed the claim for not stating a valid cause of action. It held that, even if under international law the member states were secondarily liable for the organization's debts, this would not suffice, since any claim directly based upon international law would not be justiciable in the English courts. The ITC's and its member states' status therefore depended upon the domestic legislation of the UK to implement its international obligations. According to the relevant English law, the International Tin Council (Immunities and Privileges) Order 1972, the ITC was to be treated as a body corporate for whose debts its individual members were not liable.[442] Both the Court of Appeal and the House of Lords affirmed this decision.[443] The other 'direct actions', *Arbuthnot Latham Bank Ltd* v. *Commonwealth of Australia and others*,[444] *Amalgamated Metal Trading Ltd and others* v. *Department of Trade and Industry*,[445] and *Maclaine Watson & Co. Ltd* v. *Department of Trade and Industry*,[446] were decided in a similar fashion.

What these decisions have in common and what is relevant in the present context is that they were not decided on the basis of a lack-of-jurisdiction rationale but rather on the substantive ground that the complaints failed to state a valid cause of action because treaty rights were not justiciable in English courts. Lord Templeman's statement is illustrative of this fact. He contended that:

[even] if there existed a rule of international law which implied in a treaty or imposed on sovereign states which enter into a treaty an obligation (in default of a clear disclaimer in the treaty) to discharge debts of an international organisation established by that treaty, the rule of international law could only be enforced under international law. Treaty rights and obligations conferred or imposed by agreement or by international law cannot be enforced by the courts of the United Kingdom.[447]

---

[442] High Court, Queen's Bench Division (Commercial Court), 24 June 1987.
[443] Court of Appeal, 27 April 1988; House of Lords, 26 October 1989.
[444] Cited in (1990) 81 ILR 672.   [445] Cited in *ibid*.
[446] High Court, Chancery Division, 29 July 1987; Court of Appeal, 27 April 1988; House of Lords, 26 October 1989.
[447] *J. H. Rayner (Mincing Lane) Ltd* v. *Department of Trade and Industry and others, and Related Appeals*, House of Lords, 26 October 1989, (1990) 81 ILR 670 at 680.

As a consequence these cases have to be qualified as 'abstention' cases only in a rather indirect way. They relied on the broad abstention rationale of not applying or enforcing treaty provisions but they did not show any hesitation to adjudicate against an organization or its member states in principle. Quite on the contrary, the receivership action, *Maclaine Watson & Co. Ltd* v. *International Tin Council*,[448] demonstrates that the English courts did not grant immunity or consider themselves otherwise lacking adjudicative power over disputes involving an international organization.

   This line of cases was broadly followed in *Westland Helicopters Ltd* v. *Arab Organisation for Industrialisation*[449] – an English sequel to the complicated and lengthy international arbitral and judicial proceedings arising from the operational end of the Arab Organization for Industrialization (AOI). This decision differs from the *Tin Council* and the *Arab Monetary Fund* v. *Hashim* cases, however, in so far as it explicitly acknowledges that the internal affairs of an international organization are governed by public international law and not by any domestic law – notwithstanding the fact that the domestic legal personality is recognized as a result of the foreign incorporation of the AOI, treating it like a foreign corporate body. The English *Westland Helicopters* case arose from the following facts. Despite the partial annulment of the arbitral decision in *Westland Helicopters Ltd* v. *Arab Organization for Industrialization, United Arab Emirates, Kingdom of Saudi Arabia, State of Qatar, Arab Republic of Egypt and Arab British Helicopter Company*[450] by the Swiss Federal Tribunal in *Arab Organization for Industrialization, Arab British Helicopter Company and Arab Republic of Egypt* v. *Westland Helicopters Ltd, United Arab Emirates, Kingdom of Saudi Arabia and State of Qatar*,[451] Westland finally obtained a damages award from the international arbitrators in 1993 which it sought to enforce in the UK. English courts granted garnishee orders against various banks in London for the attachment of debts due from them to the AOI. These orders were challenged by the 'Egyptian AOI', the entity claiming to continue the organization after three of the four member states had withdrawn and purported to end the existence of the AOI. This claim was based on Egyptian legislation which repudiated the announcement made by the three other member states that the AOI would be liquidated and which provided that the AOI would continue to be governed not only by its basic statute but

---

[448] High Court, Chancery Division, 13 May 1987.
[449] High Court, Queen's Bench Division, 3 August 1994.
[450] Arbitration Award, 8 June 1982, 5 March 1984, 25 July 1985.
[451] Court of Justice of Geneva, 23 October 1987; Federal Supreme Court, 19 July 1988.

also by the law of its seat of management and centre of activities, Egypt, and that its affairs would be conducted exclusively by Egyptian officials. The High Court considered itself not competent to decide the issue of whether the Egyptian AOI was entitled to represent the AOI proper:

Having concluded that the proper law governing the constitution of the AOI is public international law and further that the intervener is unable to prove in the English courts that under that body of law it is the same entity as the AOI, I reject the intervenor's submission that in these courts it has standing to set aside the order . . . giving leave to enforce the award against the AOI as a judgment[452] [since that] entitlement depends upon the non-justiciable issue whether [the Egyptian law] was a justifiable countermeasure in public international law which in turn depends on the further non-justiciable issue whether the three Gulf states acted in breach of the treaty.[453]

The other side of the coin resulting from the particularly English approach of abstaining from deciding cases involving subjects of international law and matters of international law can be seen in *Reel* v. *Holder and another*.[454] This case involved a non-governmental organization, the International Amateur Athletic Federation (IAAF), and the question of whether Taiwan had been rightfully expelled from it in view of the single representation claim by mainland China. Since the courts did not regard the issue one of public international law concerning an international organization it could treat the IAAF, which enjoyed the status of an unincorporated association under English law, like any other domestic federation. Lord Denning in the Court of Appeal agreed with the decision in the court of first instance that:

we are not concerned with international law or with sovereignty. We are simply concerned with the interpretation of the rules of the federation. The rules are in English. The head office of the federation is in England. It is right that, if the rules need to be construed, the matter should come to the English courts to be decided.[455]

In a chapter of the *Arab Monetary Fund* v. *Hashim* litigation the Court of Appeal recently came to a similar conclusion. In *Arab Monetary Fund* v. *Hashim and others*,[456] an action involving the alleged acceptance of a bribe by the defendant while he was acting as the plaintiff's director general, the court rejected Hashim's non-justiciability argument based on the fact

---

[452] *Westland Helicopters Ltd* v. *Arab Organisation for Industrialisation*, [1995] 2 All ER 387 at 416.
[453] [1995] 2 All ER 387 at 415*ff.*
[454] High Court, Queen's Bench Division, 2 April 1979; Court of Appeal, 30 June 1981.
[455] [1981] 3 All ER 321.   [456] Court of Appeal (Civil Division), 1 February 1996.

that his appointment was made pursuant to public international law. In the court's view the relationship between Dr Hashim and the AMF created private contractual rights and obligations on both sides. It thus followed that:

the existence of such private rights and obligations militates conclusively against the further suggestion that the Court lacked subject matter jurisdiction of the kind described by Lord Wilberforce in *Buttes Gas & Oil Co. Ltd* v. *Hammer* [1982] AC 888 at 937. The claims are in no way concerned with the relationship between states created by the AMF treaty or any other matter of public international law.[457]

The court thus upheld the jurisdiction of English courts.

Other reasons to deny jurisdiction: refusals to exercise implicit judicial review of decisions of international organizations

In *Popineau* v. *Office Européen des Brevets*,[458] the French Conseil d'Etat took an interesting 'reverse' approach to jurisdiction. Instead of finding a particular reason to renounce its 'adjudicative power', it denied its jurisdiction by stating that no applicable norm gave it 'competence' over the kind of relief sought by the plaintiff against the European Patent Office. By a decision of the ILO Administrative Tribunal of 13 July 1994, a former employee of the European Patent Office, Mr Popineau, lost an action to annul the termination of his employment. He then tried to appeal this decision to the French Conseil d'Etat which in turn quite laconically rejected his claim by stating that no international convention nor any domestic legislation or regulation gave it competence to render a judgment of that kind.[459]

For a similar reason, a parent's attempt to challenge the decision of the European School that his daughter had to repeat a school year was unsuccessful in *Dalfino* v. *Governing Council of European Schools and European School of Brussels I*.[460] The Belgian Conseil d'Etat held that neither the Governing Council nor the European School were administrative bodies created and organized by a Belgian public authority over which it was competent to exercise powers of judicial review.

In a recent patent case not brought against but involving a decision of the European Patent Office, an English court dismissed an action seeking

---

[457] [1996] 1 *Lloyd's Reports* 589 at 596.   [458] Conseil d'Etat, 15 February 1995.
[459] '[A]ucune stipulation d'une convention internationale, ni aucune disposition legislative ou réglementaire ne donne competence au Conseil d'Etat pour connaître d'un tel jugement.' Conseil d'Etat, 15 February 1995, No. 161.784; Lexis file.
[460] Conseil d'Etat, 17 November 1982.

judicial review of a patent determination by the EPO. The case arose from a decision by the Board of Appeal of the European Patent Office to revoke a patent that had been granted to Lenzing AG. This decision was communicated to the United Kingdom Patent Office which made a corresponding entry in the UK patent register. In the course of infringement proceedings brought against a competitor, Lenzing sought judicial review of the decision of the United Kingdom Patent Office to record the revocation of its patent, arguing that only revocations 'in accordance with' the European Patent Convention should be recorded. The applicant alleged a serious procedural injustice on the part of the EPO in deciding on the revocation. In *Re Lenzing AG's European Patent*[461] the court – expressly relying on *Re International Tin Council*[462] – rejected this 'collateral attack' on the independent decision-making of an international organization, arguing that the United Kingdom:

has agreed with the other States members of the European Patent Convention that the final arbiter of revocation under the new legal system is to be the Board of Appeal of the EPO . . . It is the agreed EPO equivalent of the House of Lords, Cour de Cassation, or Bundesgerichtshof. It is not for national courts to query its doings, whether in a direct or collateral attack.[463]

No case or controversy

The power of national courts to adjudicate is frequently limited by a domestic law requirement as to the contentiousness of the issue brought before them or the existence of a genuine dispute. Examples are the US constitutional requirement of a 'case' or 'controversy' for the exercise of judicial power.[464] In elaborating on this procedural precondition, US courts have limited their adjudicative power to 'actual cases'.[465] Thus, they excluded not only the possibility to give advisory opinions,[466] but also to decide issues that lack 'ripeness' or are 'moot'.

It is likely that a number of foreign affairs cases that might have foreign policy implications would also be excluded by reason of the case

---

[461] Queen's Bench Division (Crown Office List), 20 December 1996.
[462] High Court, Chancery Division, 22 January 1987.
[463] [1997] *Reports of Patent, Design and Trademark Cases* 245.
[464] According to Article III(2) of the US Constitution '[t]he Judicial Power shall extend to all Cases . . . [and] to Controversies'.
[465] Henkin, *Foreign Affairs*, 142.
[466] *Cf. Matter of State Industrial Commission*, Court of Appeals of New York, 224 NY 13, 119 NE 1027 (1918), *per* Cardozo J: 'The function of the courts is to determine controversies between litigants . . . They do not give advisory opinions.'

or controversy requirement. This is not necessarily the case with lawsuits involving international organizations as plaintiffs or defendants. On the contrary, in most situations, an individual will be aggrieved in person or property by the conduct of an international organization. In seeking judicial redress a claimant usually raises an actual case.

One of the few instances where the case or controversy requirement might become relevant in a suit involving an international organization is a so-called taxpayer suit. These are actions alleging the unlawfulness (regularly referred to as 'unconstitutionality') of a public spending decision brought by individuals whose interest or standing solely rests on the fact that they might be financially hurt by the share of taxes they have to contribute to the controversial expenditure.

The *Curran* v. *City of New York et al.*[467] case was such a taxpayer suit. There an individual New York taxpayer brought suit against, *inter alia*, the UN and its Secretary-General, Trygve Lie, seeking to enjoin the establishment of UN headquarters in New York. As far as the organization and its Secretary-General were concerned, the suit was dismissed for lack of jurisdiction upholding the 'suggestion of immunity presented by the Department of State'.[468] The characteristic feature of the taxpayer suit was the plaintiff's attack on the grants of land and easements by the City of New York to the UN, the exemption from taxation and the allocation of additional funds for the improvement of the surrounding area as well as the city's licence to the UN for the use of a city building as a temporary meeting place for the UN General Assembly as a 'waste of public property'. Rejecting the plaintiff's arguments, the court upheld the validity of the New York statutes authorizing the benefits in question. In passing, the court also clarified that it considered the judicial remedy sought by the dissatisfied taxpayer an inappropriate one:

The remainder of the allegations . . . represent the plaintiff's personal, political opinion, in respect of which this Court makes no comment except to say that they should be addressed to the political branch of the government not the judicial. This Court is concerned with the legality rather than with the wisdom of the acts of which the plaintiff complains.[469]

This remark is, of course, also reminiscent of the underlying rationale for abstention under the political questions doctrine.[470]

A similar grievance was raised before the Swiss Supreme Court in *Jenni, Mouvement Vigilance et Groupe Vigilant du Grand Conseil Genevois* v. *Conseil*

---

[467] Supreme Court, Special Term, Queens County, 29 December 1947.
[468] 77 NYS 2d 206 at 209 (S. Ct 1947).   [469] *Ibid.*, 213.   [470] *Cf.* pp. 92*ff* above.

d'Etat du canton de Gèneve,[471] where a group of citizens of the Swiss canton of Geneva tried to challenge the grant of fiscal privileges to officials of the IATA. The Swiss Federal Tribunal dismissed on the ground of the lack of standing of the complainants. The court held that Swiss law did not provide for an *actio popularis* in such situations and that the assent of the Conseil d'Etat of Geneva to the grant of privileges and immunities to international organizations – even if their status as public international organizations was uncertain[472] – did not require a referendum and thus was not in violation of the voting rights of Geneva's citizens.

Judicial discretion to prevent harassing lawsuits and mock trials

Domestic courts might sometimes use discretionary powers to avoid adjudication, and frequently do so at the start of legal proceedings, when they consider the complaint filed to be frivolous, insincere or a mere sham. Two US cases which were brought against the UN and which had no merit show that an over-litigious society can pose a threat to the independent functioning of international organizations and potentially burden them with the unwarranted costs of defending themselves in court.[473] They also evidence, however, that courts are very well able to dispose of such harassing suits, such 'meritless, fanciful claims'[474] in an expeditious fashion.

In *Urban* v. *United Nations*[475] the District of Columbia Court of Appeals issued an injunction 'enjoin[ing] [the plaintiff] from filing any civil action in this or any other federal court of the United States without first obtaining leave of that court'.[476] The lawsuits filed by the plaintiff were characterized as 'irrational, incoheren[t] and complete[ly] lack[ing] any substantive allegations over which this court might maintain jurisdiction'.[477] While the court recognized that a 'court must take great care not to unduly impair [a litigant's] constitutional right of access to the courts . . . it is now also well settled that a court may employ injunctive remedies to protect the integrity of the courts and the orderly and expeditious administration of justice'.[478]

In *Miller* v. *United Nations and Indian Tribes*,[479] a consolidated action brought by the plaintiff against the UN and various other entities 'for unidentified legal violations' in a 'barely decipherable' way, the DC District Court did not hesitate to dispose of the claims without even

---

[471] Federal Tribunal, 4 October 1978.   [472] See p. 11 above.
[473] See pp. 237f below.   [474] *Urban* v. *United Nations*, 768 F. 2d 1497 at 1499.
[475] US Court of Appeals DC Cir., 2 August 1985.   [476] 768 F. 2d 1497 at 1500 (DC Cir. 1985).
[477] *Ibid.*, 1499.   [478] *Ibid.*, 1500.   [479] US District Court DC, 26 August 1991.

requesting a motion from the defendants invoking immunity or the total unfoundedness of the complaints. Qualifying the actions as 'clearly frivolous' the court dismissed them *sua sponte*.

An even more recent case in a similar vein is *William J. Alexander* v. *Agents for International Monetary Fund; Internal Revenue Service et al.*[480] where a harassing lawsuit was dismissed 'for lack of legal or factual sufficiency'.

According immunity to international organizations

Statistically the most frequently used avoidance technique of national courts regarding lawsuits against international organizations lies in according immunity to them. Where domestic courts consider an international organization immune from 'legal process', 'suit' or 'jurisdiction' such organization is not amenable to suit at all.

The dual, international and domestic nature of immunity

Immunity from jurisdiction possesses a dual, international and domestic, nature. As applied by a specific court, it is normally a rule of domestic law in the respective forum state; and at the same time it is usually a rule of international law giving rights to the international organization and obligations to the forum state. This dual nature of immunity is most evident when looking at the sources of immunity. It becomes apparent as well when one contemplates the potential consequences of disregarding an international organization's immunity. It might give rise to allegations of international responsibility on the part of the forum state wrongly asserting jurisdiction over an international organization and – if legal means in domestic law are exhausted – it might lead to dispute settlement on the international level.

Immunity as a public international law question

Domestic law rules on the immunity of international organizations are determined by rules of public international law and should thus conform to those rules.[481] If domestic law does not conform or if courts in applying

---

[480] US District Court NDNY, 30 December 1996.

[481] *Cf.* the *amicus curiae* brief of the UN in the *Broadbent* case, reprinted in (1980) *United Nations Juridical Yearbook* 224 at 228, stressing that, when considering the interpretation of domestic law, the US IOIA cannot alter the international obligations of the US. The view that issues of an international organization's immunity from suit are primarily matters of international law has been firmly asserted by the UN Office of Legal Affairs. In a memorandum concerning UNRWA's immunity from jurisdiction it stated: 'For reasons of principle, as well as on sound practical grounds, we are strongly of the opinion that this matter should not be judged by domestic law except to the extent, of course, that it

international rules interpret them in a fashion that unduly restricts the entitlement of international organizations, state responsibility of the forum state will follow. As a consequence, disregarding an international law duty to grant jurisdictional immunity to an international organization constitutes a clear example of a state's responsibility for the acts of its judiciary.[482] Although courts are – or at least are supposed to be – by definition independent decision-making organs, i.e. organs that do not receive any orders from the executive, it is generally accepted that their actions are directly attributable to the state and can thus give rise to state responsibility.[483]

The potential for controversies

It is not unlikely – though rare in practice – that the accordance and scope of immunity may lead to controversy. If so, disputes concerning immunities of international organizations will normally arise between an international organization claiming immunity and a state claiming to exercise jurisdiction over it. Sometimes, however, such disputes could also be inter-state controversies. For instance, a dispute concerning the immunity of an international organization could arise if a party to a treaty granting immunity to an international organization considers the actual treatment of such international organization, e.g. the disregard of its immunity by the domestic courts of another contracting state, a violation of the treaty.[484]

incorporates relevant international obligations.' UN Office of Legal Affairs, Memorandum to the Legal Adviser, UNRWA, (1984) *United Nations Juridical Yearbook* 188. Accordingly, domestic law could be considered only as a secondary source of evidence of the law, whereas public international law governs the issue of status, privileges and immunities of international organizations.

[482] See also Eduardo Jiménez de Aréchaga, 'International Responsibility of States for Acts of the Judiciary' in Wolfgang Friedmann, Louis Henkin and Oliver Lissitzyn (eds.), *Transnational Law in a Changing Society. Essays in Honor of Philip Jessup* (New York and London, 1972), 171–87 at 176, who regards judicial decisions violating the immunities and privileges of a diplomat or a foreign state the most obvious cases where state responsibility arises *ipso facto*.

[483] Ago-Report on State Responsibility 1971, *Yearbook of the International Law Commission* (1971), vol. II, Part One, 246*ff*; Brownlie, *Principles*, 449; Ipsen, *Völkerrecht*, 510; *Oppenheim's International Law*, 543.

[484] Although the 'standing' of a state party to such a treaty to claim an international organization's rights as well as the existence of a dispute between the states involved (as opposed to the relation between the international organization and the state exercising jurisdiction) might pose a problem, the general dispute settlement mechanism contained in most treaties regulating questions of personality and immunity appears to provide a proper forum for such inter-state disputes concerning immunity of international organizations. The General Convention, for instance, provides for the ICJ's jurisdiction in such situations. Its Article VII(30) states: 'All differences arising out of the

The more probable disputes, between an international organization affected and a state claiming to exercise jurisdiction, could be avoided at a preliminary stage if international organizations were given a voice in determining and possibly waiving their immunity or the scope of that immunity. Normally, however, decisions on the scope of immunity rest solely with the forum state, and the question is merely whether the courts should decide on their own or whether the executive should have a say as well. This issue clearly depends upon the domestic law of the forum state. In many countries, courts were traditionally bound by decisions of the executive branch whether or not to grant immunity. In most of them, however, one can observe a trend during the last decades from strict adherence to the executive's opinion towards a free evaluation of immunity issues by the courts themselves.[485] The rationale for deference to the executive stemmed from the apprehension that the issue of the amenability of states or international organizations to suit fell within the ambit of the state's foreign affairs policy and should therefore be left to the governmental branch conducting foreign affairs to be decided. This policy reason was largely adhered to in the context of sovereign immunity, but was certainly also valid as far as the immunity of international organizations was involved.[486]

interpretation or application of the present convention shall be referred to the International Court of Justice, unless in any case it is agreed by the parties to have recourse to another mode of settlement.'

[485] In the US the practice of 'binding' State Department 'suggestions' of immunity has been criticized for a long time. Cf. Restatement (Third), Introductory Note to § 451. The FSIA has expressly transformed the issue into a justiciable one. Its § 1602 provides: 'Claims of foreign states to immunity should henceforth be decided by courts of the United States and the States in conformity with the principles set forth in this chapter.' In Austria, Article IX(3) of the Introductory Law to the Norms on Jurisdiction provided that in cases of doubt the courts had to ask for a declaration from the Ministry of Justice as to whether a particular person enjoyed immunity from suit. Since 1970 courts are no longer legally bound by such a declaration. Verfassungsgerichtshof, 14 October 1970, Sammlung 6278; (1972) Journal de droit international (Clunet) 650; (1972) Juristische Blätter 37. In practice, however, courts are relying heavily on such authority. See Ignaz Seidl-Hohenveldern, 'Die internationalen Beamten und ihr Recht auf den gesetzlichen Richter' in Ballon and Hagen (eds.), Verfahrensgarantien im nationalen und internationalen Prozeßrecht, Festschrift für Franz Matscher (Vienna, 1993), 441–7 at 443.

[486] Cf. Curran v. City of New York et al, Supreme Court, Special Term, Queens County, 29 December 1947 (see pp. 94 and 125 above); and World Health Organization and Dr Leonce Verstuyft v. Hon. Benjamin Aquino et al., Philippine Supreme Court, 1972, (1991) 1 Asian Yearbook of International Law 169, holding that 'a categorical recognition made by the Executive Branch of the Government that certain entities should enjoy immunities accorded to international organizations is a determination that has been held to be a political question conclusive upon the courts in order not to embarrass a political department of Government'. Followed in Cohen v. Presiding Judge, Pedro C. Navarro et al., Philippine Supreme Court, 19 January 1976.

States usually show less enthusiasm about the suggestion that international organizations themselves should have a say in deciding the scope of immunity enjoyed by them.[487] The court practice of accepting or rejecting such immunity 'suggestions' or 'claims' is divided. While there are many instances where judges have actually followed the view of representatives of international organizations, it generally appears that – contrary to the practice in some states regarding executive 'suggestions' – they do not feel bound to do so. And, of course, there is contrary court practice in some states when judges reject the claims to immunity made by international organizations.[488]

Dispute settlement mechanisms

The methods of dispute settlement to be followed in cases where immunity from suit is in issue largely depend upon treaty provisions. Of course, there is always the option of diplomatic protests. However, most instruments dealing with privileges and immunities contain specific rules pertaining to dispute settlement. For instance, in headquarters agreements, arbitration is usually provided for as the mode of settling disputes between states and international organizations,[489] including disputes involving the proper scope of the immunities to be accorded to an international organization.[490] Less frequently used, but also typical for settling disputes between international organizations and states, is the method contained in the General Convention according to which a request for an advisory opinion from the ICJ has to be made which is accepted in advance as binding upon both parties.[491]

If a dispute arises with a non-member state and if there are no applicable treaty provisions, then negotiations or institutionalized forms of *ad hoc* dispute settlement, etc., remain available as remedies. Political

---

[487] Referring to the UN context, Seidl-Hohenveldern is of the opinion 'that the [Secretary-General's] certificate should be binding on domestic courts'. Letter from Ignaz Seidl-Hohenveldern to Peter H. F. Bekker of 8 February 1993, quoted in Bekker, *The Legal Position*, 174, note 768.

[488] For instance, in the well-known *Ranollo* case, a US court did not feel bound by a certificate of the UN Secretary-General that his driver was on official business and should thus be immune from suit. *Westchester County* v. *Ranollo*, City Court of New Rochelle, 8 November 1946.

[489] For example, Article 35 of the UNIDO Headquarters Agreement.

[490] Dominicé, 'L'immunité de juridiction', 158.

[491] Article VII section 30 of the General Convention states, *inter alia*: 'If a difference arises between the United Nations on the one hand and a member on the other hand, a request shall be made for an advisory opinion on any legal question involved in accordance with Article 96 of the Charter and Article 65 of the statute of the Court. The opinion given by the court shall be accepted as decisive by the parties.'

measures of last resort, such as ceasing or restricting operations in the state concerned or even the possibility that a state may be expelled from the organization, are open to international organizations whose international right to immunity has been disregarded.[492] Although this appears to be quite a harsh, and in most respects unreasonable, step, it might serve as an ultimate option.

As an illustration of this, the dispute between the FAO and Italy over the FAO's immunity before the Italian courts can be considered. The lengthy postludium to the *INPDAI* case[493] – a lease dispute where the Italian Corte di Cassazione decided that the FAO did not enjoy immunity from suit in an action brought by the landlord of one of the buildings occupied by FAO – underlines the fact that immunity issues are questions of international law, although in practice they are infrequently raised on the level of international legal persons *inter se.*

Immediately after the Italian Supreme Court's decision was rendered, the issue of the immunity of the FAO from legal process in Italy became one of the major substantive questions to be discussed by the FAO Council at its 82nd session.[494] The Council reiterated the traditional FAO view that the relevant provision in the headquarters agreement was clear and unambiguous and accorded absolute immunity from suit except where the FAO had expressly waived such immunity.[495] With respect to the Corte di Cassazione's restrictive immunity standard, the Council 'decided to place on record its serious concern at both the immediate and the long term consequences of the situation that has arisen'.[496]

However, the FAO was not only concerned by these developments, but rather insisted on its international rights under the headquarters agreement *vis-à-vis* the Italian host government. In its deliberations the FAO Council concluded that even if the government could not guarantee respect for the FAO's immunity because of the courts' constitutional independence, 'it should take the necessary action, for example through the enactment of appropriate legislation, to ensure that the immunity of

---

[492] Kathleen Cully, 'Jurisdictional Immunities of Intergovernmental Organizations' (1982) 91 *Yale Law Journal* 1167–95 at 1184*ff.*

[493] *Food and Agriculture Organization* v. *Istituto Nazionale di Previdenze per i Dirigenti di Aziende Industriali (INPDAI)*, Supreme Court of Cassation, 18 October 1982. For more detail, see pp. 187*f* below.

[494] See FAO, Office of the Legal Counsel, Constitutional Matters. (1982) *United Nations Juridical Yearbook* 113.

[495] Article VII section 16 of the FAO Headquarters Agreement, Washington, 31 October 1950.

[496] FAO, Office of the Legal Counsel, 'Constitutional Matters' (1982) *United Nations Juridical Yearbook* 114.

FAO from legal process was fully respected in the future'.[497] Thus, in its Resolution 1/82 the Council 'requested the host Government to find a suitable method of solving the problem, in consultation with the landlords of the building, with a view to the settlement of the dispute out of court'.[498]

In spite of this request, the proceedings were resumed by INPDAI and a judgment was rendered in the plaintiff's favour in 1984.[499] Again, the matter became an important issue at the 86th FAO Council session.[500] The Committee on Constitutional and Legal Matters had already reported on the further options of the FAO to deal with the matter. The Committee drew the Council's attention to two remedies available under international law. The FAO could, on the one hand, request an advisory opinion from the International Court of Justice on the relevant provisions of the headquarters agreement 'considering that the International Court of Justice would be the appropriate forum for interpreting the host Government's treaty obligations under international law'.[501] On the other hand, the FAO could invoke the arbitration clause of the headquarters agreement 'which is applicable to disputes between the host Government and the organization which arise out of the interpretation of that Agreement'.[502]

Apparently, the Italian Government was eager to avoid the embarrassment of having the ICJ determine that Italy did not live up to its obligations under international law. The Italian permanent representative to the FAO offered his good offices to negotiate an out-of-court settlement of the dispute with INPDAI, and by 1985 the execution of the judgment was effectively prevented. Italy also drafted a law concerning measures of execution against the property of foreign states or international organizations securing that no measures of restraint could be levied against the FAO.[503] Italy further offered to defend the FAO's immunity in Italian courts without cost to the organization.[504]

These proposals were not completely satisfactory to the FAO. At its 86th session the FAO Council – while trying to pursue a dialogue with the host government – went as far as to prepare the questions to be submitted to the International Court of Justice in case such recourse became necessary. They ran as follows:

---

[497] Ibid.   [498] Ibid.
[499] Istituto Nazionale di Previdenze per i Dirigenti di Aziende Industriali (INPDAI) v. Food and Agriculture Organization, Pretore di Roma, 4 April 1984.
[500] FAO, 'Constitutional and General Legal Matters' (1984) United Nations Juridical Yearbook 101ff.   [501] Ibid., 102.   [502] Ibid.
[503] FAO, 'Constitutional and General Legal Matters' (1985) United Nations Juridical Yearbook 81.
[504] Ibid., 82.

(a) Does section 16 of the Headquarters Agreement concluded between FAO and the Italian Republic mean that in Italy FAO is immune from every form of legal process in all cases in which it has not expressly waived its immunity?
(b) If the answer to (a) is negative, what are the specific exceptions to FAO's immunity from every form of legal process under section 16?[505]

When the INPDAI affair and other proceedings against the FAO were finally settled out of court in 1985 the matter seemed to have lost some of its urgency. Still, the principal issue of securing the FAO's immunity in the future remained open. A mutually acceptable solution was found in Italy's accession to the Special Convention in 1985.[506] While this treaty contains an immunity provision identical to the one found in the existing head-quarters agreement, it also obliges the organization to provide for appropriate modes of settlement of disputes arising out of contracts or other duties of a private character to which the organization may be a party[507] – a duty which was not contained in the headquarters agreement. In an exchange of notes between Italy and the FAO,[508] the two sides agreed on 'Modes of Settlement of Disputes' in accordance with the Special Convention. Since this obligation is seen as a 'natural corollary'[509] to the organization's right to immunity, the assumption obviously was that the courts would in the future respect the mandatory alternative dispute settlement procedures provided for in the FAO's contracts.[510] Furthermore, in *FAO* v. *Colagrossi*[511] the Italian Supreme Court seems to have changed its former jurisprudence in line with the requirements in the exchange of notes.

The result arrived at in the exchange of notes certainly invites criticism considering that alternative dispute settlement procedures were already provided for in the FAO's practice for years. The FAO's contracts regularly included arbitration clauses and, significantly, in the *INPDAI* case such an arbitration clause was disregarded by the Italian courts. However, the important conclusion one can draw from this controversy is that it

---

[505] *Ibid.*, 82*ff.*
[506] FAO, 'Constitutional and General Legal Matters' (1986) *United Nations Juridical Yearbook* 147.
[507] Article IX section 31 of the Special Convention.
[508] Reprinted in FAO, 'Constitutional and General Legal Matters', Annex I, (1986) *United Nations Juridical Yearbook* 156.
[509] *Ibid.*, 148.   [510] For more detail, see pp. 266*f* below.
[511] Corte di Cassazione, 18 May 1992. The Court of Cassation explicitly overruled its former case law restricting the FAO's immunity from suit as expressed most clearly in *Food and Agriculture Organization* v. *Istituto Nazionale di Previdenze per i Dirigenti di Aziende Industriali (INPDAI)*, Supreme Court of Cassation, 18 October 1982. The Supreme Court specifically referred to the diplomatically agreed upon mode of dispute settlement by exchange of notes between Italy and FAO in 1986 as a result of the *INPDAI* decision which it regarded as relevant 'subsequent practice' to the Headquarters Agreement in the sense of Article 31(3) of the Vienna Convention on the Law of Treaties.

clearly shows that disputes concerning the scope of jurisdictional immunity of an international organization are regarded as issues of public international law.

Immunity as a domestic legal question

For any national court the question of immunity from legal proceedings is an issue of domestic jurisdictional rules. Granting immunity is primarily decided as a matter of the forum state's law. In principle, there is also no reference or *renvoi* to other domestic laws in order to determine the scope of immunity to apply as opposed to issues of personality where such a reference might take place.[512] Thus, questions of immunity do not fall within the reach of ordinary private international law/conflict of laws problems. The sparse case law seems to affirm this view. For instance, in *International Tin Council* v. *Amalgamet Inc.*[513] the ITC sought to stay arbitration proceedings brought against it in the US by invoking its immunity. It expressly asked the US court to accord it 'the same immunity from suit and legal process [in the US] as would obtain had Amalgamet sought to enforce its claim in London'.[514] Without directly addressing this argument, the US court rejected it implicitly by basing its decision on the scope of immunity to be accorded to the ITC solely on domestic US legislation, the FSIA and the IOIA.

The rules on immunity are either expressly formulated by domestic legislation or directly applicable international law, be it treaty law or unwritten international law which become part of the domestic legal order by way of adoption or general transformation, etc.

Domestic legislation

Many national legal systems contain express legislation to the effect of granting immunity from suit to international organizations either in general or to specific organizations.[515] Among the most well known are the US International Organizations Immunities Act 1945[516] and the UK

---

[512] See pp. 50*ff* above.   [513] Supreme Court, New York County, 25 January 1988.

[514] 524 NYS 2d 971 at 973 (Supp. 1988).

[515] *Cf.* the overview in United Nations, *Handbook on the Legal Status, Privileges and Immunities of the United Nations*, and in United Nations, *Legislative Texts and Treaty Provisions Concerning the Legal Status, Privileges and Immunities of International Organizations*.

[516] Title I, section 2(b) of the IOIA 1945 provides: 'International organizations, their property and their assets, wherever located, and by whomsoever held, shall enjoy the same immunity from suit and every form of judicial process as is enjoyed by foreign governments, except to the extent that such organizations may expressly waive their immunity for the purpose of any proceedings or by the terms of any contract.'

International Organisations Act 1968.[517] But in other countries also specific legislation is used to provide for immunity of suit of international organizations. In Austria and Germany domestic legislation allows the grant of immunity to international organizations, which either supplements directly applicable treaty provisions,[518] or transforms non-self-executing provisions.[519]

Frequently courts expressly rely on the relevant domestic legislation even in cases where international sources may be directly applicable in the domestic legal order.[520] In dualist systems, with a clear separation between international and national law, courts are bound to rely on the domestic implementing legislation.[521]

---

[517] International Organisations Act 1968. Its section 1(2)(b) provides that 'Her Majesty may by Order in Council . . . provide that the organisation shall, to such extent as may be specified in the order, have the privileges and immunities set out in Part I of Schedule I to this Act.' Part I of Schedule I to the International Organisations Act 1968 lists among others 'Immunity from suit and legal process'. Its predecessor legislation was the Diplomatic Privileges (Extension) Act 1944, which – despite its name – was largely devoted to international organizations. It gave the executive branch the power to grant a maximum of certain rights to international organizations of which the UK and foreign states were members. These rights would have to be fixed for each designated international organization by an Order in Council. As far as the organization itself was concerned, it could be given the legal capacity of a body corporate, i.e. the power to sue in court, to hold property and to conclude contracts, and it might be granted immunity from suit.

[518] Austrian 1977 Law on the Granting of Privileges and Immunities to International Organizations. *Cf.* Ena-Marlies Bajons *Zwischenstaatliches Justizrecht* (Vienna, 1989), A2, for a list of international organizations that have been expressly granted privileges and immunities by regulations on the basis of this Act.

[519] Article 3 of the Law on the Accession of the Federal Republic of Germany to the Special Convention and on the Granting of Privileges and Immunities to other International Organizations, as amended by the Law on the General Convention, enables the Federal Government to issue regulations concerning the application of the General and Special Conventions to and the granting of privileges and immunities upon international organizations other than specialized agencies of the UN. See also Enno J. Harders, 'Haftung und Verantwortlichkeit Internationaler Organisationen' in Rüdiger Wolfrum (ed.), *Handbuch Vereinte Nationen* (2nd edn, Munich, 1991), 248–58 at 250; Kunz-Hallstein, 'Privilegien und Immunitäten internationaler Organisationen', 3071.

[520] See p. 136 below.

[521] For instance, the two Indian cases, *Mathew* v. *International Crops Research Institute for the Semi-Arid Tropics (ICRISAT) and the Government of India*, High Court of Andra Pradesh, 18 August 1982, an employment dispute dismissed by an Indian court; and *Sharma* v. *UNDP Regional Manager, South Asia*, Office of the Labour Commissioner, Delhi Administration, 10 October 1983, administrative labour proceedings dismissed by the Indian Labour Department. Both cases were decided on the basis of Indian immunity legislation, the United Nations (Privileges and Immunities) Act 1947.

International law directly applicable in the domestic legal order

In many legal systems the international sources providing for immunity from legal process – primarily treaty or customary rules – will be directly applicable. As far as treaties are concerned this is clear, for instance, in the case of the US,[522] the Netherlands,[523] etc. and can also be corroborated by the relevant case law concerning international organizations.[524] The existence of specific domestic legislation usually does not exclude this option. As far as customary international rules[525] are concerned, even countries following a dualist approach towards treaty incorporation like the UK may allow the direct application of international immunity norms by its national courts.[526]

A large number of cases show that national courts will directly apply immunity provisions contained in treaties[527] and in international custom[528] – if they find that such rules exist.[529]

---

[522] According to the *Restatement (Third)*, the immunities provisions in the General Convention, the US–UN Headquarters Agreement and the privileges and immunities agreement between the US and OAS are 'probably [*sic!*] self-executing and consequently to be given effect even without legislative implementation'. *Restatement (Third)*, § 467, Comment f.

[523] '[I]nternational agreements, also those containing provisions regarding privileges and immunities, acquire force of law as soon as they have been ratified or otherwise accepted by the Netherlands.' Note of 20 August 1959 from the Acting Permanent Representative of the Netherlands to the United Nations, reprinted in UN Doc. ST/LEG/SER.B/10 (1959), 55.

[524] In *Curran* v. *City of New York et al*, Supreme Court, Special Term, Queens County, 29 December 1947, a New York court held that, since the US was a party to the UN Charter, the provision of Article 105 'in a Treaty made under the authority of the United States, [is] the law of the land' (77 NYS 2d 206 at 212 (S. Ct 1947)) and that, also without further action by Congress or the state, immunity from taxation was included in the immunities necessary for the fulfillment of the UN's purposes. In the *Gubitchev* case, *United States* v. *Coplon et al.*, US District Court SDNY, 10 May 1949, a federal court relied both on the IOIA and Article 105 of the UN Charter in holding that espionage does not fall within the category of acts performed in the official capacity of UN officers and employees. As to Article 105 of the UN Charter, the court expressly 'assum[ed] it to be self-executing' (84 F. Supp. 472 at 474 (SDNY 1949)).

[525] See pp. 145*ff* below.

[526] *Cf. Trendtex Trading Corp.* v. *Central Bank of Nigeria*, [1977] 2 WLR 356.

[527] E.g., an Argentine decision based on a direct application of the relevant provisions of the Special Convention. *Dutto* v. *United Nations High Commissioner for Refugees*, National Labour Court of Appeal, 31 May 1989.

[528] E.g., *Mendaro* v. *World Bank*, US Court of Appeals, 27 September 1983; *WEU* case, Amtsgericht Bonn, 23 August 1961; or a number of Italian cases like *ICEM* v. *Di Banella Schirone*, Corte di Cassazione, 8 April 1975; *Cristiani* v. *Istituto italo-latino-americano*, Corte di Cassazione, 23 November 1985; or *Galasso* v. *Istituto italo-latinoamericano*, Corte di Cassazione, 3 February 1986.

[529] See pp. 149*ff* below.

Immunity and domestic procedural law

The precise legal consequences of a finding of immunity are determined by the specific applicable domestic procedural law. They are largely beyond the scope of this study, since they would involve too detailed an analysis of the relevant national procedural law framework. What interests the international lawyer here are issues closer to international law, such as the question of whether there is a need to invoke immunity on the part of the organization involved in legal proceedings or whether immunity has to be respected by national courts *ex officio*.

This issue is again primarily a question of domestic law. Under many national legal systems, it is clear that immunity from suit has to be respected by the courts *ex officio* and at any stage of judicial proceedings.[530] There are exceptions, for example national rules requiring the party intending to rely upon immunity to specifically raise it as a defence.[531] However, the question of interest in the present context is whether there are any *international* rules on this question as well.

That the respect for an organization's immunity is a matter for the courts to decide even without any insistence on it by the defendant is clearly the view of the UN Office of Legal Affairs: 'It is not necessary for international organizations to claim the immunities to which they are entitled since such immunity exists as a matter of law and is a fact of which judicial notice must be taken.'[532] While this is understandably in the interest of international organizations, it seems hard to ascertain how such a procedural issue can be regarded as uniform in all jurisdictions and not as a matter for the respective domestic procedural law. The

---

[530] For Germany, section 20 of the Gerichtsverfassungsgesetz. *Cf.* Gerhard Lüke and Alfred Walchshöfer (eds.), *Münchner Kommentar zur Zivilprozeßordnung* (Munich, 1992), vol. III, 1172; and Kunz-Hallstein, 'Die Beteiligung', 821. For Austria, Article IX of the Introductory Law to the Norms on Jurisdiction. *Cf.* Mayr in Walter Rechberger (ed.), *Kommentar zur ZPO* (Vienna and New York, 1994), 15. See also the Austrian Supreme Court decision in *Y GmbH v. X*, Supreme Court, 6 March 1990, declaring enforcement proceedings against a UNIDO senior official void when it was discovered that the defendant enjoyed immunity from Austrian jurisdiction.

[531] In the Argentine case of *Araya v. Institute for Latin-American Integration/Inter-American Development Bank*, Labor Court, 1974, a mere letter of the IDB claiming its immunity from suit in an employment dispute would not have sufficed to prevent an Argentine court from adjudicating. Under Argentine civil procedure law, a failure to appear in court in order to claim immunity or any other defence resulted in the loss of such defence. The case was subsequently settled out of court. Vorkink and Hakuta, *Lawsuits Against International Organizations*, 26.

[532] Office of Legal Affairs of the United Nations, *Memorandum to the Legal Adviser, UNRWA*, (1984) *United Nations Juridical Yearbook* 189.

reason might be that domestic law is required by international law to make it a question of judicial notice.[533]

Most relevant treaty provisions are silent on this question. However, since one can regard the obligation to grant immunity to international organizations as an obligation of result,[534] one may conclude that states are free to decide how to ensure that this immunity is respected even in the absence of a particular invocation on the part of the international organization benefiting from it. Thus, it could be provided that an independent external organ, a state attorney or advocate general, etc., is domestically entrusted with the tasks of watching over such issues. In most circumstances, however, the best solution will be to ensure that immunity questions are raised *ex officio*.

As a matter of practice, most international organizations find ways to communicate their legal point of view to courts either by the official way of informing the forum state's foreign ministry[535] or by directly communicating with the courts,[536] since – even if immunity does not have to

---

[533] The quoted legal opinion seems to hint at this possibility stating that '[s]ince international organizations are recognized entities in international law, courts are required to recognize their immunities'. *Ibid.*, 189.

[534] In the sense of Article 21 of the ILC Draft Articles on State Responsibility. *Cf.* also Ian Brownlie, *System of the Law of Nations. State Responsibility: Part I* (Oxford, 1983), 241*ff*.

[535] In a paper presented by the Office of Legal Affairs of the United Nations for a Meeting of United Nations System Legal Advisers in 1983 the following practice concerning the method of invoking UN immunity was summarized: 'In the first years of the Organization's history the United Nations entered *amicus curiae* briefs in cases which challenged United Nations immunities. The practice at the present time is to assert immunity from suit of the Organization in a written communication to the Ministry of Foreign Affairs of the State concerned, accompanied by the summons or other judicial notification. The Ministry is requested to take the necessary steps to inform the appropriate authority (Ministry of Justice, Attorney-General's Office) to appear or otherwise to move the court to dismiss the suit on the ground of the organization's immunities'. Office of Legal Affairs of the United Nations, 'Procedures Followed by the United Nations when Confronted with an Attempt to Serve Process' (1983) *United Nations Juridical Yearbook* 213. In *Barreneche* v. *CIPE/General Secretariat of the OAS*, Superior Court Bogota, 1971, and *Barrios* v. *CIPE/General Secretariat of the OAS*, Superior Court Bogota, 1973, Colombian courts accepted certificates of the Colombian Ministry of Foreign Affairs that, according to the applicable bilateral agreement, the OAS and its organs enjoyed immunity from all types of intervention, whether executive, administrative, judicial or legislative and dismissed suit brought by former employees of the OAS. Vorkink and Hakuta, *Lawsuits Against International Organizations*, 23*ff*.

[536] In the course of proceedings to stay arbitration, the Office of Legal Affairs of the United Nations sent a letter to a US judge informing him that the UN was immune from suit according to the General Convention as well as to the IOIA and that the party bringing suit had acknowledged this fact in its contract with the UN: 'Without prejudice to or in any way waiving the immunity from legal process of the United Nations, which immunity is hereby expressly reserved, I should like to bring to Your Honor's attention

be claimed by the defendant – it is frequently useful to communicate the organization's legal opinion on the matter.[537]

The procedural effect of respecting immunity normally lies in the termination of legal proceedings against an international organization. Since immunity is a question of procedural law it applies if provided for at the time proceedings are brought[538] regardless of whether it was already provided for at the time the dispute arose. Thus, any discussion concerning a retroactive application of immunity appears to be misleading.[539]

International sources of jurisdictional immunity of international organizations

The applicable public international law rules determining the extent of immunity to be granted to international organizations are normally found in treaties or might be contained in customary law.

---

the fact that the arbitral tribunal to be constituted under the auspices of the Arbitration Association of the United States in the arbitral proceedings instituted by the United Nations is the forum to deal with the issues raised by the company, and that the United Nations has agreed in the contract to be bound by any determination of the arbitral tribunal on those issues. Providing for arbitration of disputes thus fulfills the obligation placed on the United Nations by Article VIII, section 29 of the Convention to "make provisions for appropriate modes of settlement of: (a) disputes arising out of contracts or other disputes of a private law character to which the United Nations is a party . . ." Office of Legal Affairs of the United Nations, Letter to a Justice of the Supreme Court of New York, 12 December 1990, reprinted in (1990) *United Nations Juridical Yearbook* 287ff.

[537] This rather informal procedure was largely followed in the recent US case of *Abdi Hosh Askir* v. *Boutros Boutros-Ghali, Joseph E. Connor et al.*, US District Court SDNY, 29 July 1996 (see pp. 201f below) where the defendant UN officials had not been served with the summons and complaint. The Legal Counsel for the UN submitted papers asserting absolute immunity for the defendants and the United States supported these suggestions of immunity. The court dismissed the claims *sua sponte.*

[538] *Cf.* Lüke and Walchshöfer, *Münchner Kommentar*, vol. III, 1173.

[539] In the Argentine case, *Bergaveche* v. *United Nations Information Centre*, Camara Nacional de Apelaciones del Trabajo de la Capital Federal, 19 March 1958, the issue was raised of whether immunity would apply 'retroactively' – whether the UN could enjoy immunity from suit in a labour dispute with one of its employees where the subject matter of the controversy arose from the non-renewal of a fixed-term contract in 1954, when Argentine acceded to the General Convention providing for immunity for the UN only in 1956. The Argentine court correctly rejected the appellant's claim that the Convention should not be applied retroactively, 'since the statute [implementing the Convention] was a procedural one which was immediately applicable in the case of both pending and future proceedings'. *Yearbook of the International Law Commission* (1967), vol. II, 224.

Treaty law

Constituent instruments

Most instruments setting up international organizations contain at least some rules on their respective immunity from suit. The clauses actually used vary in form. These variations are similar to the different personality clauses described above.[540]

The majority of immunity clauses expressly provide for a 'functional' scope of immunities, along the standard of the UN Charter, for immunity 'necessary for the fulfilment of [the organization's] purposes'.[541] Most constituent agreements of UN specialized agencies as well as many other founding treaties of international organizations contain similar provisions.[542]

Many others contain immunity clauses that are not further qualified or suggest an absolute immunity protection by merely providing that the organization 'shall enjoy immunity from every form of judicial process'.[543] In the case of some more recently established organizations such unqualified absolute immunity clauses may be specifically restricted in respect of non-functional activities such as tort claims arising from car accidents.[544]

Some constituent agreements, in particular those of international banks, contain more restrictive immunity clauses allowing suit against the organization in principle and codifying certain exceptions where

---

[540] See pp. 43 and 72f above.

[541] Article 105 of the UN Charter states: 'The Organization shall enjoy in the territory of each of its Members such privileges and immunities as are necessary for the fulfilment of its purposes.' On a closer look, there is a slight difference to the Charter's grant of personality in Article 104 which aims not only at the 'fulfilment of its purposes', but also at the 'exercise of its functions'. There was no comparable provision in the League of Nations Covenant. Article 7(4) and (5) of the Covenant only provided for 'diplomatic immunities' for League officials 'engaged on the business of the League' and that League property was to be 'inviolable'. Jurisdictional immunity for the League itself was granted by the *modus vivendi* entered into by the League of Nations and the Swiss Government on 18 September 1926, whereby Switzerland recognized that the League possessed international personality and capacity and that it could not 'in principle, according to the rules of international law, be sued before the Swiss Courts without its consent'. Quoted in Louis Henkin, Richard C. Pugh, Oscar Schachter and Hans Smit, *International Law* (2nd edn, St Paul, MN, 1987), 964. A detailed history of League of Nations immunities with reprint of the exchanges of notes, including the *modus vivendi* of 1926, can be found in Martin Hill, *Immunities and Privileges of International Officials, The Experience of the League of Nations* (Washington DC, 1947), 138ff.

[542] E.g., Article 40(1) of the ILO Constitution; Article 67(a) of the WHO Constitution; Article XV of the IAEA Statute; Article 139 of the OAS Charter; and Article VIII(1) of the Agreement Establishing the WTO. For further examples, see *Yearbook of the International Law Commission* (1977), vol. II, Part One, 143.

[543] Article IX(3) of the IMF Articles of Agreement.

[544] E.g., Article XV(2) (Article IV, Annex I) of the ESA Convention.

immunity would be enjoyed.[545] A few such treaties do not contain their own immunity standard, but instead refer to other regimes by incorporating, e.g. a standard of 'diplomatic' immunity,[546] whereas other founding treaties contain clearer and more easily accessible references to external immunity standards.[547]

The constitutional charters of international organizations sometimes even exclude immunity from jurisdiction as is the case with the European Communities.[548]

Finally, in very rare cases and in a number of older organizations, constituent documents of international organizations may not contain any express reference to immunities.[549] In such cases the question arises whether immunity could be viewed as implied in functional capacity, whether it might be a consequence of the international legal personality of an international organization, or whether it could be enjoyed as a result of customary rules.[550]

General privileges and immunities treaties

In addition to the constituent documents of international organizations, a number of multilateral general privileges and immunities treaties

---

[545] E.g., Article VII(3) of the IBRD Articles of Agreement: 'Actions may be brought against the Bank only in a court of competent jurisdiction in the territories of a member in which the Bank has an office, has appointed an agent for the purpose of accepting service or notice of process, or has issued or guaranteed securities. No actions shall, however, be brought by members or persons acting for or deriving claims from members. The property and assets of the Bank shall, wheresoever located and by whomsoever held, be immune from all forms of seizure, attachment or execution before the delivery of final judgment against the Bank.'

[546] E.g., Article XVI(2) of the FAO Constitution.

[547] Article XII of the UNESCO Convention linking the immunity status of UNESCO to that of the UN. See also the similar provision in Article 64 of the IMO Convention.

[548] Article 183 of the EC Treaty; Article 155 of the Euratom Treaty; and Article 40(3) of the ECSC Treaty. This is not contradicted by Article 28 of the Merger Treaty which – with minor alterations – replaced Article 218 of the EC Treaty, Article 76 of the ECSC Treaty and Article 191 of the Euratom Treaty. Article 28 provides for a functional immunity standard by stating that: 'The European Communities shall enjoy in the territories of the Member States such privileges and immunities as are necessary for the performance of their tasks, under the conditions laid down in the Protocol annexed to this Treaty.' The 1965 EC Privileges and Immunities Protocol does not provide for the jurisdictional immunity of the Communities themselves.

[549] *Cf.* the legal capacity clause of Article 47 of the ICAO Convention. See also the Convention for the Creation of an International Institute of Agriculture; the Convention for the Creation of an International Institute of Refrigeration; the Agreement for the Creation of an International Office for Dealing with Contagious Diseases of Animals; and the Agreement for the Creation of an International Wine Office.

[550] See pp. 145*ff* below.

contain provisions on immunity from adjudicative jurisdiction. The most prominent among them are the General Convention,[551] which applies to the UN itself, and the Special Convention,[552] which concerns the Specialized Agencies of the UN. Since the IAEA is not a specialized agency *stricto sensu*[553] a separate agreement was concluded in respect of that organization.[554] They all provide for immunity 'from every form of legal process' with the exception of a waiver in particular cases.

For a number of other international organizations, specific multilateral treaties on their privileges and immunities also supplement the short immunity provisions of their constituent agreements. The privileges and immunities agreement of the Council of Europe, for instance, contains the same immunity standard as the two UN Conventions.[555] A Protocol on Privileges and Immunities of the European Patent Organization, on the other hand, provides for a more restrictive functional immunity standard.[556]

Since such general multilateral treaties are regularly concluded between the member states of an international organization without the direct participation of the international organization itself, the legal position of the latter and the assessment of its rights *vis-à-vis* the member states is not free from ambiguity. It is clear that as multilateral treaties they create binding rights and obligations between the contracting parties, i.e. the members of the international organizations. Their binding

---

[551] Article II section 2 of the General Convention states: 'The United Nations, its property and assets wherever located and by whomsoever held, shall enjoy immunity from every form of legal process except insofar as in any particular case it has expressly waived its immunity. It is, however, understood that no waiver of immunity shall extend to any measure of execution.'

[552] It is divided into two parts: a general part applicable to all specialized agencies providing for standard privileges and immunities and several annexes setting out modifications for each specialized agency. Article III section 4 of the Special Convention provides: 'The specialized agencies, their property and assets, wherever located and by whomsoever held, shall enjoy immunity from every form of legal process except in so far as in any particular case they have expressly waived their immunity. It is, however, understood that no waiver of immunity shall extend to any measure of execution.'

[553] Paul C. Szasz, 'International Atomic Energy Agency' in Rudolf Bernhardt (ed.), *Encyclopedia of Public International Law* (2nd edn, 1995), vol. II, 1051–7 at 1053.

[554] IAEA Privileges and Immunities Agreement.

[555] Article 3 of the General Agreement on Privileges and Immunities of the Council of Europe.

[556] 'Within the scope of its official activities the Organisation shall have immunity from jurisdiction and execution.' 'Official activities' are those which 'are strictly necessary for its administrative and technical operation, as set out in the Convention'. Article 3(1) and 4 of the Protocol on Privileges and Immunities of the European Patent Organization.

nature for states *vis-à-vis* the organization, however, is sometimes questioned.

In particular, it raises the issue of whether international organizations can be viewed as parties or merely as beneficiaries of such treaties. Most of the discussion revolves around the UN and its status under the General Convention. In the *Reparations* case the ICJ set the boundaries for the future debate by stating that the General Convention 'creates rights and duties between each of the signatories and the Organization'.[557] It left open, however, whether this was to be regarded as a consequence of the UN's status as a party or as a beneficiary. The majority of authors seemed to support the view that the UN somehow gained party status to the General Convention.

One piece of evidence in favour of this view results from the UN Secretariat's treatment of the General Convention. The fact that the Secretary-General registered it *ex officio* might indicate that he views the UN as a party to the Convention.[558] The Convention can be regarded not only as a 'multilateral inter-State agreement, but also a series of bilateral agreements between the UN and each State party to the Convention, defining rights and obligations for both parties', thus considering the UN itself to be a party to the General Convention.[559] Strong support for this view also stems from the text of the General Convention: section 35 provides that the Convention 'shall be in force as between the United Nations and every Member'. Since treaties are normally 'in force' between their parties, the UN's position considering itself as a party seems to be a logical conclusion.[560] Others emphasize the peculiar rules concerning the conclusion and entry into force of the General Convention. An important characteristic of the General Convention is that Article 105(3) of the UN Charter requires approval by the UN General Assembly. One could argue that 'the vote of approval by the General Assembly was equivalent to ratification by the UN. The Contracting Parties are, on the one hand, each Member State and, on the other, the UN as such.'[561] The dispute settlement provisions of the General Convention could also give rise to such a conclusion. It provides that '[i]f a difference arises between the United Nations . . . and a Member . . . a request shall be made for an advisory

---

[557] *Reparation for Injuries Suffered in the Service of the United Nations*, Advisory Opinion, (1949) *ICJ Reports* 174 at 179.

[558] Bowett, *The Law of International Institutions*, 344.

[559] Paul C. Szasz, 'International Organizations, Privileges and Immunities' in Rudolf Bernhardt (ed.), *Encyclopedia of Public International Law* (2nd edn, 1995), vol. II, 1325–33 at 1327.

[560] Bekker, *The Legal Position*, 130*ff*, note 572.   [561] Kunz, 'Privileges and Immunities', 848.

opinion ... The opinion given by the Court shall be accepted as decisive by the *parties*'.[562] One could indeed infer from this wording that the UN may be one of the 'parties' as this term is used in section 30.[563]

Other authors, however, maintain that international organizations are merely chief beneficiaries and guardians of multilateral immunity instruments.[564] The 'beneficiary' approach – as opposed to the 'party' approach – seems to be more compatible with principles of treaty law than the sometimes rather far-fetched interpretations given above. To regard the UN a beneficiary of the General Convention rather than a party seems to be a 'safe track' argument that can be easily accepted. The statement on behalf of the Secretary-General in the *Mazilu* case[565] before the ICJ contains this reasoning in an *in eventu* argument. He elaborates that, if the UN were not recognized as a party to the General Convention:

> it is clearly a third organization that can derive obligations and rights under that instrument pursuant to the principles codified in Articles 35 and 36 of the 1986 Vienna Convention on the Law of Treaties between States and International Organizations or between International Organizations. The acceptance or assent of the organization to such obligations and rights is evidently that given by the General Assembly in adopting the Convention and proposing it to Member States, an action taken pursuant to the explicit authorization of paragraph 3 of the Article 105 of the Charter.[566]

The ICJ, in its advisory opinion, did not solve the issue, probably because it could render its affirmative opinion on the applicability of the Convention on the basis of either theory.

Bilateral headquarters and host agreements

Apart from the multilateral treaties mentioned above, a large number of bilateral agreements regulate the issue of immunity from suit – as part of general immunities – in a rather detailed fashion. Such bilateral treaties are usually termed 'headquarters agreements' or 'seat agreements', if they are concluded between the international organization and the coun-

---

[562] Article VII section 30 of the General Convention.

[563] *Statement Made by the Legal Counsel at the 1016th meeting of the Sixth Committee of the General Assembly on 6 December 1967*, reprinted in (1967) *United Nations Juridical Yearbook* 311 at 312.

[564] Ralph Zacklin, 'Diplomatic Relations: Status, Privileges and Immunities' in Dupuy, R.-J. (ed.), *Manuel sur les organisations internationales, A Handbook on International Organizations* (1988), 179–98 at 183.

[565] *Applicability of Article VI, Section 22, of the Convention on the Privileges and Immunities of the United Nations*, Advisory Opinion, (1989) *ICJ Reports* 177.

[566] 'Applicability of Article VI, Section 22, of the Convention on the Privileges and Immunities of the United Nations', Statement of the Secretary-General, (1992) *ICJ Pleadings* 185.

try where it has its seat or one of its seats. If these special agreements are concluded with non-seat states, they may be called 'host agreements', 'technical assistance and supply agreements', etc.[567]

Frequently, such bilateral agreements are considered merely supplementary to constitutive instruments or general immunities and privileges treaties and, thus, do not contain any express provisions on immunity from suit.[568]

Unwritten immunity rules

The jurisdictional immunity of international organizations is primarily regulated by international agreements. Because of the rather dense web of existing treaty relations concerning this subject, the importance of customary law on this matter has been characterized as and probably is 'marginal'.[569] Still, there are a number of possible instances where general international law becomes relevant.

Custom might legitimately serve as a 'gap-filler'[570] in situations where applicable international agreements contain no immunity provisions or where no treaty relations exist, e.g. because of the non-ratification of a specific immunity instrument by a member state of an international organization,[571] before such an instrument is negotiated or before its entry into force, or in the case of an international organization *vis-à-vis* non-member states.[572]

Custom as a source of immunities

The existence of customary rules as a potential source of immunities, and in particular of jurisdictional immunity, is generally acknowledged in

---

[567] Abdullah El-Erian (Special Rapporteur), 'Preliminary Report on the Second Part of the Topic of Relations Between States and International Organizations' (UN Doc. A/CN.4/304) *Yearbook of the International Law Commission* (1977), vol. II, Part One, 140–55 at 145.

[568] *Cf.* third preambular paragraph of the Austria–UNIDO Headquarters Agreement: 'Considering that it is desirable to conclude an agreement, *complementary* to the Convention on the Privileges and Immunities of the United Nations, to regulate *questions not envisaged in that Convention* arising as a result of the establishment of the headquarters of [UNIDO] at Vienna . . .' (emphasis added). See also section 26 of the US–UN Headquarters Agreement 1947: 'The provisions of this agreement shall be complementary to the provisions of the General Convention.'

[569] Felice Morgenstern, *Legal Problems of International Organizations* (Cambridge, 1986), 5.

[570] *Restatement (Third)*, § 467, Comment f.

[571] *Cf. Galasso* v. *Istituto italo-latinoamericano*, Corte di Cassazione, 3 February 1986; and *Cristiani* v. *Istituto italo-latino-americano*, Corte di Cassazione, 23 November 1985. See pp. 194*ff* below.

[572] See pp. 152*ff* below.

legal writing.[573] There is, however, an almost infinite variety of opinion as far as the specific consequences are concerned. Sometimes, the methodology of inquiring into customary rules might prejudge the answers. It has been pointed out that the question of the existence of a customary law of immunity of international organizations can be asked in two very different ways. On the one hand, one could question whether there are customary rules granting immunity to international organizations and, if so, what their scope is. On the other hand, one could ask whether the general customary rules concerning immunity from jurisdiction (as they are valid between states) are applicable to international organizations.[574]

According to what probably remains the majority view, international organizations enjoy absolute immunity from legal proceedings even if no express treaty provision is applicable.[575] One opinion holds that a customary rule mandates absolute immunity for the organization, but only in the member states.[576] Others, who would agree with the presumption of a customary law governing the immunities to be accorded to the UN,[577] are more cautious, however, concerning other international organizations.[578] Yet others remain sceptical concerning the existence of non-treaty-based judicial immunity of international organizations at all.[579]

[573] Bettati, Le droit des organisations internationales, 106; Bekker, The Legal Position, 122 at 147; Harders, 'Haftung und Verantwortlichkeit Internationaler Organisationen', 249; Lalive, 'L'immunité de juridiction', 304; Morgenstern, Legal Problems, 5; Hans-Joachim Priess, Internationale Verwaltungsgerichte und Beschwerdeausschüsse, Eine Studie zum gerichtlichen Rechtsschutz für Beamte internationaler Organisationen (Berlin, 1989), 61; Restatement (Third), § 467(1) and Introductory Note to § 467, Reporters' Note 1; and Schermers, International Institutional Law, 795.

[574] Friedrich Schröer, 'De l'application de l'immunité jurisdictionnelle des états étrangers aux organisations internationales' (1971) 75 Revue générale de droit international public 712–41 at 713.

[575] Werner Gloor, 'Employeurs titulaires de l'immunité de juridiction' in Universités de Berne, Fribourg, Geneva, Lausanne et Neuchatel, Ensèignement de 3e cycle de droit 1987 (eds.), Le juriste suisse face au droit et aux jugements étrangers, ouverture ou repli? (1988), 263–89 at 278; Harders, 'Haftung und Verantwortlichkeit Internationaler Organisationen', 250; and Ignaz Seidl-Hohenveldern, 'L'immunité de juridiction des Communautés européennes' (1990) Revue du Marché Commun No. 338, 475–9 at 479.

[576] Seidl-Hohenveldern, 'L'immunité', 475; and Ignaz Seidl-Hohenveldern, 'Dienstrechtliche Klagen gegen Internationale Organisationen' in von Münch (ed.), Staatsrecht – Völkerrecht – Europarecht. Festschift für Hans-Jürgen Schlochauer (Berlin and New York, 1981), 615–34 at 628.

[577] Cf. United Nations Secretariat, 'The Practice of the United Nations, the Specialized Agencies and the International Atomic Energy Agency Concerning Their Status, Privileges and Immunities, 1967' in Yearbook of the International Law Commission (1967), vol. II, 222, note 49.

[578] Bekker, The Legal Position, 147.

[579] Beitzke, 'Zivilrechtsfähigkeit', 115; Reuter in Yearbook of the International Law Commission (1985), vol. I, 288. Similarly sceptical is Ress in ILA, Report of the 66th Conference, Buenos Aires (1994), 474.

There are various types of evidence for the customary quality of immunity from suit of international organizations. Most prominently, the near-uniformity of treaty provisions granting immunity appears to evidence a customary principle. This argument is supported by the widespread accession to the relevant treaties, i.e. near universal accession in the case of the UN (the General Convention) and broad adherence in the case of other UN organizations (the Special Convention). The treaty/custom relationship might also become pertinent in so far as treaty provisions sometimes seem to affirm the existence of customary principles.[580]

This discussion is part of the more general debate about treaties as evidence of custom.[581] The uniformity or near uniformity of treaty provisions concerning immunity from suit is the primary argument advanced by those in favour of a customary immunity rule.[582] The widespread ratification of treaty law leading to an almost universal accession to the standards contained therein might also be evidence that its provisions have gained customary status. This seems to be a rather firmly held opinion at least within the UN system.[583] However, it is well known from other areas that the same fact of a broad and uniform adherence to treaty norms may lead to an opposite conclusion, regarding the need for treaty provisions as evidence of a lack of customary rules.[584]

---

[580] See p. 148 below.

[581] Richard R. Baxter, 'Multilateral Treaties as Evidence of Customary International Law' (1965–6) 41 *British Yearbook of International Law* 275–300 at 277*ff*; Karl Doehring, 'Gewohnheitsrecht aus Verträgen' (1976) 36 *Zeitschrift für ausländisches öffentliches Recht und Völkerrecht* 77–95 at 77*ff*; Ulrich Scheuner, 'Internationale Verträge als Elemente der Bildung von völkerrechtlichem Gewohnheitsrecht' in Flume, Hahn, Kegel and Simmonds (eds.), *Internationales Recht und Wirtschaftsordnung. Festschrift für F. A. Mann* (Munich, 1977), 410–38 at 420*ff*.

[582] Lalive, 'L'immunité de juridiction', 305.

[583] For instance, the UN Secretary-General reasoned that the ratification of the General Convention by an overwhelming majority of ninety-six states after almost twenty-two years might be interpreted in a way that 'the standards and principles of the Convention had been so widely accepted that they had now become a part of the general international law governing the relations of states and the United Nations'. *Annual Report of the Secretary-General*, 23 GAOR, Supp. 1 (A/7201), 209. Almost identical language can be found in the 'Statement Made by the Legal Counsel at the 1016th meeting of the Sixth Committee of the General Assembly on 6 December 1967', reprinted in (1967) *United Nations Juridical Yearbook* 311 at 314. See also UN General Assembly Resolution 2328 (XXII) of 18 December 1967, operative para. 3 '[u]rging member states of the United Nations, whether or not they have acceded to the Convention on the Privileges and Immunities of the United Nations, to take every measure necessary to secure the implementation of the privileges and immunities accorded under Article 105 of the Charter of the Organization . . .'.

[584] *Cf.* Doehring, 'Gewohnheitsrecht aus Verträgen', 81.

The content of treaty law itself could also be regarded as evidencing custom. Sometimes, it is less the uniformity of treaty provisions or the common adherence to them, but rather their wording that seems to support the existence of customary principles or at least underlines the contracting parties' belief in their existence. A good example of this phenomenon is contained in the Agreement between Egypt and WHO which provides that '[t]he Organization and its principal or subsidiary organs shall have in Egypt the independence and freedom of action belonging to an international organization according to international practice'.[585] This treaty provision has been interpreted as an acknowledgment of the existence of customary law on the subject.[586] It seems that the Interim Arrangement on Privileges and Immunities of the United Nations concluded between the Secretary-General of the UN and the Swiss Federal Council would be open to a similar interpretation. It provides, inter alia, that '[t]he Swiss Federal Council recognizes the international personality and legal capacity of the United Nations. Consequently, according to the rules of international law, the organization cannot be sued before the Swiss Courts without its express consent.'[587] Here immunity from legal process seems to flow from an unidentified source of international law ('according to the rules of international law') and appears as a consequence of the international organization's legal personality.[588]

Sometimes the applicable treaties do not contain specific rules on the question of immunity, but rather refer to customary principles. Inspired by a comparable phenomenon in private international law this kind of reference has been called renvoi.[589] These renvoi, or 'reference' or 'incorporation' clauses, might directly refer to custom, like the 1965 Protocol on the Privileges and Immunities of the European Communities which accords to the representatives of the Communities the 'customary privileges, immunities and facilities'.[590] They may also refer to state immunity or even

---

[585] Article II(3) of the WHO–Egypt Agreement 1951.

[586] Abdullah El-Erian (Special Rapporteur), 'Preliminary Report on the Second Part of the Topic of Relations Between States and International Organizations' (UN Doc. A/CN.4/304) Yearbook of the International Law Commission (1977), vol. II, Part One, 140–55 at 152.

[587] Article I(1) of the UN–Swiss Interim Arrangement 1946.

[588] The UN Secretariat interprets this immunity provision as one 'derived from international law' thereby suggesting that it is not a legal consequence of the treaty itself, but rather of a pre-existing general international law principle. United Nations Secretariat, 'The Practice of the United Nations, the Specialized Agencies and the International Atomic Energy Agency Concerning Their Status, Privileges and Immunities' Yearbook of the International Law Commission (1967), vol. II, 222.

[589] Pierre Freymond, 'Remarques sur l'immunité de juridiction des organisations internationales en matière immobilière' (1955–6) 53 Friedens-Warte 365–79 at 369.

[590] Article 11 of the EC Privileges and Immunities Protocol.

to diplomatic law, like the FAO Constitution obliging member states to 'accord to the Organization all the immunities and facilities which it accords to diplomatic missions'.[591] Such treaties conferring 'customary privileges and immunities'[592] might indeed be interpreted as referring to customary law governing the subject. However, this conclusion is far from compelling. The term 'customary' could also be interpreted with a less technical and more literal meaning. One could regard the reference to 'customary privileges and immunities' to be a convenient shorthand of the drafters referring to the 'usual' grant of privileges and immunities. Thus, 'customary' would rather be synonymous to 'traditional' than meant to imply a customary law rule on the subject.[593]

Next to treaty provisions, domestic legislation could also serve to evidence state practice of according immunity from suit to international organizations. The domestic grant of immunity might gain evidentiary value for a customary principle where it does not merely implement a treaty obligation or where it refers to immunity provided for 'under international law'.[594] However, the grant of a broader range of immunities or a wider scope of jurisdictional immunity than mandated by treaty obligations can also be a mere unilateral decision of a host state.

According to many authors, national court decisions seem to favour immunities of international organizations even in the absence of treaty provisions.[595] A closer look, however, reveals that this claim cannot be regarded as universally confirmed by judicial practice.

A 1961 German case involving the WEU[596] holds that a rule of customary international law obliges member states to accord immunity to the international organization that they have formed. In the employment dispute of *Hetzel* v. *Eurocontrol*,[597] another German case, an administrative court of first instance seemed to have relied on similar grounds. The tribunal expressly held that, with the grant of legal personality to the organization and its capacity to regulate its internal staff affairs, Euro-

---

[591] Article XVI(2) of the FAO Constitution.

[592] *Cf.* the further examples given by Bekker, *The Legal Position*, 148.

[593] Reuter, in *Yearbook of the International Law Commission* (1977), vol. I, 209, para. 12.

[594] E.g., Article 1(2) of the Austrian 1977 Law on the Granting of Privileges and Immunities to International Organizations provides that, in addition to the privileges and immunities contained in the Act, such rights might be conferred upon international organizations according to treaties or 'as provided, for the fulfilment of its functions, by the generally recognized rules of international law'.

[595] Schröer, 'De l'application de l'immunité juridictionnelle', 712; and Morgenstern, *Legal Problems*, 5.

[596] Amtsgericht Bonn, 13 August 1961. For more detail, see pp. 67f and 248 below.

[597] Administrative Court Karlsruhe, 5 July 1979, Appellate Administrative Court Baden-Württemberg, 7 August 1979.

control was formed as an international organization which enjoyed immunity from the jurisdiction of the courts of the member states with regard to employment disputes even without an express grant of such immunity.[598] The appellate administrative court upheld the lack-of-German-jurisdiction decision based on the grant of exclusive competence over employment disputes to the ILO Administrative Tribunal. It doubted, however, the existence of a customary rule conferring immunity upon international organizations.[599]

Whether international organizations enjoyed immunity from German jurisdiction as a matter of customary international law was also at issue in a lengthy and complex litigation concerning the power of the European School in Munich to determine the tuition charged to its students. Significantly, the deciding courts were split over this question and the Bavarian appellate Administrative Court even overruled its own previous decision. A group of parents complained against the raising of school fees and brought suit before German administrative courts. In *X et al. v. European School Munich I*,[600] they sought a preliminary injunction against the school's 1988/89 'administrative' tuition decisions which was denied by a German administrative court. On appeal, the Bavarian Administrative Court upheld the jurisdiction of the German courts, reasoning that the school's personality clause conferred capacity to sue and to be sued and that no express exemption from German adjudicative jurisdiction was provided for.[601] It rejected, however, the claim on the merits. In *X et al. v. European School Munich II*,[602] the same plaintiffs sought the annulment of the school's 1989/90 tuition decisions. The lower administrative court in Munich rejected this application on the merits. With

---

[598] '... ist die Antragsgegnerin als eine internationale Organisation gebildet worden, die im Streit mit ihren Bediensteten Immunität vor den nationalen Gerichten der Vertragstaaten genießt, ohne daß es hierzu einer ausdrücklichen Verleihung bedurft hätte'. Administrative Court Karlsruhe, 5 July 1979 (VIII 61/79).

[599] 'Ob man von einem (gewohnheitsrechtlichen) Satz des allgemeinen Völkerrecht sprechen kann, demzufolge internationale Organisationen der staatlichen Gerichtsbarkeit entzogen sind, ist zweifelhaft.' Administrative Court Baden-Württemberg, 7 August 1979 (IV 1355/79).

[600] Bavarian Administrative Court Munich, 23 August 1989.

[601] 'Gemäß ... Art. 6 Satz 3 der Satzung der Europäischen Schule kann die ESM vor Gericht klagen und verklagt werden. Da hierbei nicht auf eine europäische Gerichtsbarkeit Bezug genommen wird, insbesondere die Europäischen Schulen nicht der Zuständigkeit des Gerichtshofs der Europäischen Gemeinschaften unterstellt werden, ist diese Aussage dahin zu verstehen, daß die Europäischen Schulen sich der Gerichtsbarkeit des Landes ihres jeweiligen Sitzes unterwerfen.' Bayerischer Verwaltungsgerichtshof Munich, 23 August 1989; (1989) 24 *EuropaRecht* 359 at 361.

[602] Administrative Court Munich, 29 June 1992, Bavarian Administrative Court Munich, 15 March 1995, Federal Administrative Court, 9 October 1995.

similar reasons as the appellate administrative decision in *X et al. v. European School Munich I*,[603] it upheld its jurisdiction over the defendant institution. In addition, it found that no treaty provision provided for the school's immunity from jurisdiction and expressly ruled out the possibility of a customary rule of immunity for an international organization.[604] This denial of immunity was reversed by the Bavarian appellate Administrative Court which held that the European School's personality clause providing for its capacity to sue and to be sued did not imply a renunciation of immunity. The court extensively addressed the issue of the school's immunity from jurisdiction in the absence of an express treaty or domestic law provision. It relied on scholarly opinion supporting a customary immunity for international organizations and reasoned that such immunity resulted, *inter alia*, 'from the almost identical provisions contained in the existing agreements and from the analogous interests involved'.[605] It found, however, that such immunity was not absolute. Rather, it was considered to be functionally limited. In particular, the court established that such immunity did not cover acts *ultra vires* the school's capacity to act. The court held that the European School did not have the capacity to issue administrative tuition decisions and that the German courts had jurisdiction to identify such a transgression of an international organization's powers where its *ultra vires* character was manifest.[606] It thus gave judgment for the plaintiffs.[607]

[603] Bavarian Administrative Court Munich, 23 August 1989.

[604] 'Eine Befreiung nach den allgemein anerkannten Regeln des Völkerrechts (Art. 25 GG) scheidet aus, denn diese kommt nur in Betracht im Verhältnis zu ausländischen Staaten und den für sie handelnden Organen bzw. Repräsentanten, nicht aber kommt sie zwischenstaatlichen Organisationen und deren Angehörigen zugute.' *X et al. v. European School Munich II*, Bavarian Administrative Court Munich, 29 June 1992, (unpublished).

[605] '[Immunität kraft Gewohnheitsrecht] ergibt sich aus . . . dem nahezu identischen Regelungsgehalt der jeweils bestehenden ausdrücklichen Abkommen und der dazu analogen Interessenlage.' Administrative Court, 7th Chamber, Munich, 15 March 1995, (1996) *Deutsches Verwaltungsblatt* 448.

[606] 'Mit dem Erlaß von als Verwaltungsakte zu verstehenden Bescheiden über die Erhebung von Schulgeld gegenüber den Eltern 'anderer Kinder', die nicht Angehörige der Europäischen Patentorganisation sind, überschreitet die Europäische Schule München offenkundig die ihr nach den ihr zugrundeliegenden völkerrechtlichen Verträgen zustehende Rechtsmacht (Handeln 'ultra vires'); sie unterliegt insoweit der deutschen Gerichtsbarkeit; die Offenkundigkeit dieser Befugnisüberschreitung kann jedenfalls dann von den nationalen Gerichten festgestellt werden, wenn sie sich aus dem eigenen Vortrag der internationalen Organisation ergibt.' Bavarian Administrative Court, 7th Chamber, Munich, 15 March 1995, (1996) *Deutsches Verwaltungsblatt* 448.

[607] The German Federal Administrative Court did not allow the school's appeal because it did not consider that a legal issue was of basic importance merely by the fact that it involved the law of international organizations and that an international organization regarded a national court decision as wrongly decided. Federal Administrative Court, 9 October 1995.

In *Mendaro* v. *World Bank*[608] the Court of Appeals of the District of Columbia upheld the view that immunity from suit by employees of the organization was one of the most important protections granted to international organizations and that this immunity 'is now an accepted doctrine of customary international law'.[609] One is, however, well advised to use a certain caution with US decisions affirming a particular rule as customary international law. A good example is the numerous human rights cases affirming customary international standards. Many of them show a notorious absence of state practice and *opinio iuris* analysis.[610] Other US cases do not discuss the existence of customary immunity at all. In *Steinberg* v. *International Criminal Police Organization*[611] a District of Columbia court thought that Interpol – which at that time was not designated under the IOIA[612] as enjoying immunity – could be sued for libel without any restriction. In the event, customary jurisdictional immunity was not even considered.

In a number of cases Italian courts have relied on a customary immunity standard. For instance, in *ICEM* v. *Di Banella Schirone*[613] the Italian Supreme Court, the Corte di Cassazione, considered the restrictive immunity standard in the headquarters agreement[614] to be identical with one under customary law. In *Cristiani* v. *Istituto italo-latino-americano*[615] and *Galasso* v. *Istituto italo-latinoamericano*,[616] two employment disputes involving the Italo-Latin-American Institute, the Italian Supreme Court confirmed that international organizations enjoyed restrictive immunity as a matter of customary law.[617]

Customary immunity from suit of international organizations in non-member countries

The problem of customary immunities of international organizations is most important before domestic courts in non-member states where no seat or headquarters or other bilateral agreement regulates the issue. In practice, however, courts face this kind of situation relatively infrequently. This may account for the few and inconsistent views on the matter. In

---

[608] US Court of Appeals, 27 September 1983.   [609] 717 F. 2d 610 at 615 (DC Cir. 1983).

[610] The willingness of US courts to accept a certain rule as customary – in particular in the human rights context – frequently stems from the lack of binding treaty obligations. Bruno Simma and Philip Alston, 'The Sources of Human Rights Law: Custom, *Jus Cogens*, and General Principles' (1992) 12 *Australian Yearbook of International Law* 82–108 at 84*ff*.

[611] US Court of Appeals DC Cir., 23 October 1981.

[612] *Restatement (Third)*, § 467, Reporters' Note 1.   [613] Corte di Cassazione, 8 April 1975.

[614] See p. 190 below.

[615] Tribunale Roma, 17 September 1981; Corte di Cassazione, 23 November 1985.

[616] Corte di Cassazione, 3 February 1986.   [617] For more detail, see pp. 194*ff* below.

general, where national courts have to decide upon customary immunity of 'foreign' organizations, they seem to be rather reluctant to acknowledge a customary immunity from suit enjoyed by international organizations where the forum state does not participate. This clearly contrasts with the tendency to accept the domestic legal personality of such an international organization.[618] A reason for this divergence might lie in the fact that, while courts can rely upon principles of private international law in recognizing the legal personality of a 'foreign' international organization, they would have to apply a very uncertain customary rule when they would accord immunity.

Also, legal doctrine has not formed a consensus. Frequently, the UN, its specialized agencies and regional and other major organizations are deemed to enjoy privileges and immunities also in relation to non-member states as a matter of customary law.[619] Although few authorities give reasons for their opinions, the assumption that the UN (and probably its specialized agencies) are a special case for the purposes of customary immunity seems to result from the concept of the UN's 'objective' international legal personality vis-à-vis all states including non-members.[620] For other organizations, the existence of a customary basis upon which they could claim immunity from suit in a non-member state is less clear. It would be far more relevant to establish it, however, since membership in the UN is almost universal and the practical issues that may arise between the UN and Switzerland as one of the few non-member states are regulated by bilateral agreement.[621]

In a situation where no written law governs, national courts might rely upon customary immunity in legal systems where customary law is directly applicable as, for instance, in the US where customary international law is regarded the 'law of the land'. However, despite the *Restatement*'s general endorsement of the possibility of a customary immunity from suit of international organizations of which the US is not a member,[622] US courts have predominantly denied this option. In *Steinberg v. International Criminal Police Organization*,[623] – in addition to

---

[618] *Cf.* pp. 50*ff* above.

[619] Bettati, *Le droit des organisations internationales*, 106; *Restatement (Third)*, § 467, Comment a, Reporters' Note 1; and Harders, 'Haftung und Verantwortlichkeit Internationaler Organisationen', 249.

[620] See pp. 56 note 106, 57 and 71 note 170 above.

[621] *Cf.* Article I(1) of the Interim Arrangement 1946 providing that '[t]he Swiss Federal Council recognizes the international personality and legal capacity of the United Nations. Consequently, according to the rules of international law, the organization cannot be sued before the Swiss Courts without its express consent.'

[622] *Cf. Restatement (Third)*, § 467, Comment a.   [623] 672 F. 2d 927 (DC Cir. 1981).

doubts as to the international organization status of Interpol[624] – the District of Columbia federal appellate court upheld its jurisdiction over Interpol because Interpol was a 'foreign' organization upon which no immunities had been conferred by the IOIA.[625] It did not consider the possibility of customary immunity. A similar decision was rendered in *International Tin Council* v. *Amalgamet Inc.*[626] where the court rejected the Tin Council's claim to immunity solely on the basis of domestic US law[627] and did not discuss a possible customary law standard of immunity. In the famous *International Association of Machinists* v. *OPEC*,[628] the issue of OPEC's immunity was not even reached. The courts held that this 'foreign' organization could not be legally served with process because 'FSIA applies only to foreign sovereigns, which OPEC is not; and, IOIA applies only to those international organizations in which the United States participates and the United States does not participate in OPEC'.[629]

With the exception of an administrative tax ruling concerning the European Communities,[630] the alternative strategy to treat international organizations as a group of states which according to customary law enjoy immunities has also not been pursued frequently by US courts in the past.[631] In general, the US practice of specifically designating 'foreign' organizations under the IOIA in order to ensure that they may enjoy

---

[624] See p. 170 below.

[625] Although the US participated in the work of Interpol, the court expressly noted that the 'United States is not a party to any international agreement or treaty defining Interpol's status'. 672 F. 2d 927, note 1 (DC Cir. 1981).

[626] Supreme Court, New York County, 25 January 1988.

[627] Since the US did not participate in the ITC and since the organization was not specifically designated by the President under the IOIA, this legislation did not apply.

[628] (1980) 477 F. Supp. 553 (CD Cal. 1979), *affirmed on other grounds*, 649 F. 2d 1354 (9th Cir. 1981), *cert. denied*, 454 US 1163, 102 S. Ct 1036, 71 L. Ed. 2d 319 (1982); *cf.* 'Contemporary Practice of the US' (1980) 74 *American Journal of International Law* 917; Leigh, (1982) 76 *American Journal of International Law* 162ff.

[629] (1980) 477 F. Supp. 553 (CD Cal. 1979).

[630] *Restatement (Third)*, § 467, Reporters' Note 4, quoting Revenue Ruling 68–309, (1968–1) CB 338 concerning the tax status of the EEC. In 1972 the EC Commission was designated under the IOIA. 22 USCA § 288h.

[631] *John H. Chapman* v. *Commissioner of Internal Revenue*, US Tax Court, 9 October 1947. No tax exemption was given to a League of Nations official arguing that his income should be treated as 'salary of an alien employee of a foreign government'. See p. 246 below. This accords with the official attitude of the US – certainly in the 1940s at the time before the passing of the IOIA – to deny any customary international law duty to extend any privileges and immunities to international organizations. Lawrence Preuss, 'The International Organizations Immunities Act' (1946) 40 *American Journal of International Law* 332–45 at 333.

immunities in the US,[632] coupled with the reluctance of the US courts to recognize immunity in the absence of such a statutory basis or a clear treaty provision, indicates that the US does not feel bound by a customary obligation.

Two recent US decisions may, however, change this assessment. *Re Jawad Mahmoud Hashim et al.*[633] involved the issue of whether the Arab Monetary Fund (AMF) had the legal capacity to bring legal proceedings in the US which could not be based upon the IOIA. Although this decision literally held that the AMF enjoyed such capacity – one of the privileges of an international organization – as a matter of 'customary law',[634] the court's reasoning was mainly based on the private international law rule of recognizing the 'foreign' incorporation of the AMF.[635] The court held that 'immunity and similar matters are privileges of a governmental character, but legal capacity to sue is certainly not unique to governmental entities'.[636]

The second case, also involving insolvency proceedings, relied on the premise to treat international organizations as a group of states each of which enjoyed sovereign immunity in the US. In *Re EAL (Delaware) Corp., Electra Aviation Inc. et al., Debtors; EAL (Delaware) Corp., Electra Aviation Inc. et al., Debtors in Possession* v. *European Organization for the Safety of Air Navigation and English Civil Aviation Authority*,[637] a number of aircraft leasing firms which had voluntarily filed for bankruptcy brought suit against Eurocontrol and the UK Civil Aviation Authority. Previously, Eurocontrol had obtained a seizure and detention in the UK of an aircraft owned by the plaintiffs for unpaid flight charges.[638] In the US action the plaintiffs maintained that this interfered with the US bankruptcy proceedings and violated certain court orders. The case was dismissed for lack of jurisdiction because the US court regarded Eurocontrol, an entity 'majority-held by a group of foreign states'[639] as an agency or instrumentality of a foreign state entitled to sovereign immunity under the FSIA.[640] The court expressly rejected the plaintiff's view that the FSIA did not apply unless

---

[632]   *Cf.* 22 USCA § 288f-1, § 288f-2, § 288f-3 and § 288h relating to the ESA, the Organization of Eastern Caribbean States, the OAU, the ICRC and the Commission of the European Communities.
[633]   US Bankruptcy Court D. Arizona, 15 August 1995.
[634]   188 Bankr. 633 at 649 (D. Arizona 1995).   [635]   See pp. 68*f* above.
[636]   188 Bankr. 633 at 645 (D. Arizona 1995).
[637]   US District Court D. Delaware, 3 August 1994.
[638]   *Cf.* the ensuing litigation in *Internationale Nederlanden Aviation Lease BV and others* v. *Aviation Authority and the European Organisation for the Safety of Air Navigation (Eurocontrol)*, Queen's Bench Division (Commercial Court), 11 June 1996 (see p. 184 below).
[639]   1994 US Dist. Lexis 20528, 10 (D. Delaware).   [640]   *Ibid.*

majority ownership of an agency or instrumentality vested in a single foreign state. In the court's view this was:

an unnecessary literalism that runs counter to the Act's purpose and ignores the well-established international practice of states acting jointly through treaty-created entities for public or sovereign purposes. If the policies that animate the FSIA are to be given their full range, it must, therefore, apply to treaty-created instrumentalities jointly-owned by foreign states.[641]

The court held that the acts of Eurocontrol complained of, the detention and refusal to return an aircraft belonging to the plaintiff, were performed in connection with Eurocontrol's exercise of its regulatory activities, namely imposition and collection of navigation charges levied on users of air navigation services in accordance with international agreements. It concluded that they were accordingly 'sovereign, rather than commercial, in nature because such conduct represents an exercise of powers peculiar to sovereigns that can not also be exercised by private citizens'.[642]

In *Godman* v. *Winterton*,[643] an English court took the same detour *via* the customary immunity of an organization's member states to deny its jurisdiction holding that 'in so far as the agreement was alleged to have been made with the Inter-Governmental Committee, which would naturally be taken to be a committee of representatives of sovereign States, it was an action against sovereign States and was bound to fail'.[644] The precedent value of this decision from the 1940s, however, does not appear to be very high. The court's customary law reasoning may have had to do with the doctrine of incorporation which merely prevents the direct application of treaty law; it does not prevent the reliance upon customary rules requiring immunity. Thus, despite the dualist characteristics of English law, a recognition of jurisdictional immunity of an international organizations as a matter of customary law would not be excluded.[645] An *obiter dictum* in the course of the Tin Council proceedings, however, strongly suggests that the English courts today would not even recognize the existence of a customary immunity of international organizations of which the UK is a member and *a fortiori* even less of organizations of which it is not a member. In *Standard Chartered Bank* v. *International Tin Council and others*,[646] the English High Court observed that:

---

[641] *Ibid.*, 12.   [642] *Ibid.*   [643] Court of Appeal, 12 March 1940.

[644] (1939–42) 11 *Annual Digest of Public International Law Cases* 205 at 206.

[645] *Cf. Trendtex Trading Corp.* v. *Central Bank of Nigeria*, [1977] 2 WLR 356 at 386.

[646] High Court, Queen's Bench Division (Commercial Court), 17 April 1986.

international organisations such as the ITC have never so far . . . been recognised at common law as entitled to sovereign status. They are accordingly entitled to no sovereign or diplomatic immunity in this country save where such immunity is granted by legislative instrument, and then only to the extent of such grant.[647]

A different and more customary-law-friendly jurisprudence can be found in the Netherlands. In *AS* v. *Iran–United States Claims Tribunal*,[648] the Dutch Supreme Court held with regard to a tribunal of which it was not a member state, albeit the host state, that:

it must be assumed that even in cases were there is no treaty . . . it follows from unwritten international law that an international organization is entitled to the privilege of immunity from jurisdiction on the same footing as generally provided for in [privileges and immunities] treaties . . . [A]ccording to unwritten international law as it stands at present, an international organization is in principle not subject to the jurisdiction of the courts of the host State in respect of all disputes which are immediately connected with the performance of the tasks entrusted to the organization in question.[649]

These few and partly contradictory decisions addressing the issue of whether non-universal organizations enjoy immunity from suit in non-member states are hardly sufficient to draw any conclusions concerning the scope and content of a potential customary rule. *A contrario*, however, one may conclude that in the absence of a clear court practice to respect such immunity no customary obligation of states to accord immunity to organizations of which they are not members has emerged.

Immunity as a tool to deny jurisdiction in judicial practice

Absolute immunity

Many international organizations enjoy absolute immunity according to the applicable treaty provisions.[650] In fact, it is probably most common for constitutional documents of international organizations as well as for conventions on privileges and immunities of international organizations to speak of 'immunity from every form of legal process'[651] which has traditionally been regarded as a standard of 'absolute' immunity. Frequently, an attempt seems to be made to base this absolute character of the immunity of international organizations – as opposed to the restrictive immunity regularly enjoyed by states – on

---

[647] (1988) 77 ILR 8 at 17.   [648] Supreme Court, 20 December 1985.
[649] (1987) 18 *Netherlands Yearbook of International Law* 357 at 360.   [650] See pp. 140*ff* above.
[651] See Article IX(3) of the IMF Articles of Agreement; and Article II section 2 of the General Convention.

their different nature,[652] although most of these assertions fail to give reasons for such an inherent difference.[653]

The formulation 'immunity from every form of legal process' has generally been interpreted broadly in the sense that 'legal process' includes every type of legal proceedings before national authorities, regardless of whether they are qualified as judicial, administrative or executive.[654] It also broadly encompasses the various potential roles of an international organization in domestic legal proceedings. Thus, 'immunity from every form of legal process' implies that an organization enjoys such immunity not only as defendant, but also as a potential source of information, or from the performance of some ancillary duties: accordingly, courts have concluded that international organizations are exempted from a duty to produce evidence that may be in their possession.[655]

---

[652] In a memorandum concerning UNRWA's immunity from jurisdiction, the UN Office of Legal Affairs added '[a] word about the nature of international organization immunity' and stated that '[t]he immunity accorded international organizations under this system of law [i.e., under public international law as opposed to domestic law] is an absolute immunity and must be distinguished from sovereign immunity which in some contemporary manifestations, at least, is more restrictive'. UN Office of Legal Affairs, 'Memorandum to the Legal Adviser, UNRWA' (1984) *United Nations Juridical Yearbook* 188.

[653] See pp. 348ff below.

[654] *Yearbook of the International Law Commission* (1967), vol. II, 224.

[655] *Mary O'Brien* v. *Ireland*, High Court, 26 August 1994. In a negligence action of the wife of an Irish soldier killed while serving in the UN peacekeeping force in Lebanon, the court confirmed the UN's exemption from a duty to produce certain relevant documents as a matter of Irish law which generally endorsed the prerogatives contained in the General Convention. In the court's view the Convention's inviolability provisions regarding the archives and documents of the UN precluded an order to produce evidence. The same rationale used to be applied to employees of an international organization. *Cf. Keeney* v. *United States*, US Court of Appeals DC Cir., 26 August 1954, where a UN employed US citizen was held not in contempt of Congress for refusing to answer questions of the House Committee on Un-American Activities. It is interesting to note a recent change in this regard at least in some national jurisdictions. For instance, the Court of Appeal of The Hague in a case related to the English Tin Council litigations, in *Algemene Bank Nederland* v. *KF and others*, Court of Appeal of The Hague, 26 January 1989; Supreme Court, 22 December 1989, observed that '[i]nternationally too, there is a trend towards greater openness and greater responsibility regarding the actions and conduct of States', which led it to conclude that confidentiality requirements under the Tin Council agreements had to be overridden. In this case Algemene Bank Nederland brought suit against Dutch officials requesting the release of confidential information relating to the operation of the Tin Council. While the Court of Appeal rejected this request, balancing the interest in obtaining evidence against the 'reliability of the Netherlands as a partner in international relations', the Supreme Court allowed it, holding that 'society's interest in ensuring that the truth comes to light in legal proceedings is so strong that it is impossible to accept so broad and far-reaching an exception' (1994) 96 ILR 353 at 355. This lawsuit was preceded by a decision of the Dutch Council of State in *Algemene Bank Nederland* v. *Minister for Economic Affairs*, Council of State, 11 June 1987. In order to secure

Only recently, the notion that an organization's broad 'immunity from every form of legal process' should protect it against the disclosure of evidence in its possession has been eroded.[656]

Courts have also interpreted absolute immunity to prevent the service of garnishee orders upon international organizations in salary or pension sequestration proceedings involving their officials.[657] Thus, in garnishee

its legal position against the defendant organization, the plaintiff bank requested information from the Dutch Government relating to the activities of the Tin Council. The Council of State dismissed this application on the merits because it thought that the principle of confidentiality would outweigh any requirement to publish the information sought. Interestingly, the Council of State rejected the applicant's argument that the internal rules of the ITC protecting confidentiality should apply. It conceded that these were drawn up in the interest of the functioning of the ITC. However, since the ITC had ceased to be active, there was no longer any reason for the rules to apply. (1994) 96 ILR 348.

[656] In *Maclaine Watson & Co. Ltd* v. *International Tin Council (No. 2)*, High Court, Chancery Division, 9 July 1987, the High Court ordered an organization to disclose its assets for the purpose of enforcing an arbitral award rendered against it. After the plaintiff's motion to appoint a receiver was denied (*cf. Maclaine Watson & Co. Ltd* v. *International Tin Council*, High Court, Chancery Division, 13 May 1987) it sought to enforce its arbitral award against the ITC by executing directly against the ITC's assets. Since the ITC refused to provide information on the amount and location of such assets, the plaintiff applied for an order of court requiring an officer of the ITC to be examined. The court held that it lacked jurisdiction to grant such relief which was available only against an individual or a body corporate, because the ITC was strictly speaking neither; it only had the capacities of a body corporate conferred upon it by the International Tin Council (Privileges and Immunities) Order 1972. Nevertheless, it granted the relief sought by the applicants under the court's inherent powers and ordered the ITC to disclose full particulars of the nature, value and location of all its assets within the UK. This decision was affirmed in *Maclaine Watson & Co. Ltd* v. *International Tin Council (No. 2)*, Court of Appeal, 27 April 1988. Also the decision in *Shearson Lehman Brothers Inc. and another* v. *Maclaine Watson & Co. Ltd and another and International Tin Council (Intervener)*, High Court, Queen's Bench Division, 29 June 1987; Court of Appeal, Civil Division, 31 July 1987; House of Lords, 3 December 1987, related to the issue of the disclosure of evidence. Following the ITC's insolvency, the Committee of the London Metal Exchange suspended all trading in tin and ruled that tin sales had to be repurchased at a fixed price. The plaintiffs claimed the invalidity of this ruling and brought suit against their buyers and against the Committee. Both parties intended to produce evidence *inter alia* from ITC documents relating to tin trading. These documents originally were disclosed either by ITC staff or member states. The ITC intervened, claiming the inadmissibility of such documents based on the International Tin Council (Immunities and Privileges) Order 1972 which provided for the same inviolability of official archives as that accorded to a diplomatic mission. On a preliminary appeal, the House of Lords ruled that the inviolability accorded to 'archives' in the 1972 Order referred to all documents belonging to or held by the ITC. Once such documents had been transmitted to member states or their representatives, they are no longer protected under the 1972 Order.

[657] In *Means* v. *Means*, 60 Misc. 2d 538 (NY Fam. Ct 1969), the attempted garnishment of employees' wages for the support of estranged wives and their children brought against the UN was dismissed for immunity reasons. Similarly, in *Shamsee* v. *Shamsee*, New York Supreme Court, Appellate Division, 2nd Dept, 19 May 1980, an attempt to sequester a

former UN employee's pension benefits was dismissed because of the UN's immunity from legal process. The result in *Shamsee* was not easily reached, however. The estranged wife of a UN employee was awarded a weekly support payment order against her husband by a New York court in 1975. After his retirement Mr Shamsee returned to his home country, Pakistan, taking with him all the family assets. Since he received a pension from the UN Joint Staff Pension Fund in New York, his wife tried to proceed directly against this asset. In 1976 she obtained a sequestration order against her husband under which the Fund would have had to pay Mrs Shamsee directly. When the Fund's Secretary – relying on his personal as well as the Fund's immunity from suit – refused to comply, the New York court held them both in contempt of court for failure to comply with a court order. In a letter to the US UN mission, the UN requested the State Department 'to issue a suggestion of immunity from legal process for the [Fund] and its Secretary to the appropriate officials of the [New York] court'. UN Office of Legal Affairs, 'Letter to the Permanent Representative of the United States to the United Nations' (1978) *United Nations Juridical Yearbook* 186*ff*. The Appellate Division reversed the sequestration order and vacated the contempt orders. It specifically recognized the Fund and its Secretary as immune from the sequestration under 'under the applicable Federal law', i.e. under the General Convention as 'the supreme law of the land' and under the IOIA. In *Shamsee*, the issue was discussed solely as a matter of 'immunity from legal process' in general and did not specify that a sequestration order and the court's contempt order even threatening the arrest of the Secretary could be qualified as a measure of execution. This qualification was correctly made in the UN Administrative Tribunal's judgment in *Shamsee* v. *United Nations Joint Staff Pension Board*, Judgment No. 245, 25 May 1979, wherein Mrs Shamsee sought to have the pension fund ordered to comply with the sequestration order. The tribunal, however, rejected the application which ran counter to the fund's immunity from suit. It critically observed that under the applicable legal regime former UN employees could 'indirectly benefit unduly' from the fund's immunity and from the lack of a provision similar to the staff rules which expressly permitted deductions from salaries, wages and other emoluments for the purpose of indebtedness to third parties. It remarked, however, that it was for the General Assembly to consider whether the pension fund regulations should be amended and that it lacked authority to comply with the application. In *Menon* v. *Weil*, Civil Court of the City of NY, New York County, 26 March 1971, the estranged wife of a UN field worker stationed in South Korea brought a number of actions for support and maintenance against various UN officials as 'agents' of the absent Mr Menon. Default judgments and a garnishment order of the personal bank account of a UN under-secretary were vacated as a result of the State Department's 'suggestion' of immunity. The court thought that even without this 'executive intervention' the General Convention as a treaty forming the 'supreme law of the land' requiring immunity of UN officials for their 'official acts' would mandate dismissal of plaintiff's actions. 320 NYS 2d 405 at 407 (NY City Civ. Ct 1971). In the case of *R. Peter Panuschka* v. *Peter Schaufler*, Commercial Court of Vienna, 29 November 1965, an Austrian court did not allow an attempted garnishee order to be served on the IAEA. It qualified such an order as service of legal process which – according to the applicable headquarters agreement – could not take place within the headquarters seat of the organization. It further reasoned that the issuance of such an order would be prevented by the organization's immunity from legal process. The Commercial Court thought that, although this last provision related first and foremost to measures of execution against the IAEA, its wording also covered measures of execution which were directed primarily against other persons but in which the IAEA was in some way involved. (1965) *United Nations Juridical Yearbook* 246. In the *WEU* case, Amtsgericht Bonn, 23 August 1961, a German court refused to issue an injunction ordering the organization not to make payments to the applicant's judgment debtor on

attempts, immunity is still a valid and generally accepted defence. Exceptions are rare; they relate either to some of the more recent immunity instruments expressly exempting court orders against organizations in execution of a judgment against their employees[658] or to sparse examples in the older case law like the frequently cited Swiss *Re Poncet* case.[659] Only in the context of the European Communities – based on their special immunity regime – has a different practice evolved. Whereas Community law does not provide for the Communities' immunity from suit in the courts of its members states, the Protocol on the Privileges and Immunities of the European Communities expressly grants them immunity from execution which can be waived by the ECJ.[660] Originally, the ECJ routinely authorized garnishee requests in the contexts of suits brought against Community officials.[661] After some time, however, the ICJ no longer thought that such requests would require its consent unless the Commu-

the basis of a treaty provision granting the WEU immunity from enforcement measures because it qualified the payment prohibition inherent in an attachment order as a measure of constraint. 'Der Pfändungs- und Überweisungsbeschluß ist aber des in ihm enthaltenen Zahlungsverbots wegen als Zwangsmaßnahme auch gegen die Drittschuldnerin anzusehen.' (1962) *Monatsschrift für deutsches Recht* 315. See also *Yearbook of the International Law Commission* (1967), vol. II, 224; (1983) *United Nations Juridical Yearbook* 213*ff*, stressing that '[s]ervice of a garnishment or attachment order upon the Organization is a form of legal process from which the Organization is immune'; and (1968) *United Nations Juridical Yearbook* 216, maintaining that a court order to make UNIDO directly pay debts of one of its employees in execution of a judgment against such employee would violate UNIDO's immunity from legal process.

[658] E.g., ESA's immunity from jurisdiction and execution is excluded 'in the event of the attachment, pursuant to a decision by the judicial authorities, of the salaries and emoluments owed by the Agency to a staff member'. Article XV(2) (Article IV, Annex I) of the ESA Convention.

[659] In the Swiss *Re Poncet* case, Federal Tribunal, 12 January 1948, local proceedings were instituted in Geneva in order to attach the salary of a UN staff member to satisfy debts incurred by her. The lower level authorities declined the request, considering the garnishee, the UN, outside local jurisdiction. The Swiss Federal Tribunal, however, returned the case to the local authorities for a determination whether the judgment debtor was immune. It considered the immunity of the garnishee not a bar to proceedings for attachment of the debts of its employees in principle. What is not reported in the United Nations practice summary, however, is the fact that the Federal Tribunal based its decision on a *modus vivendi* of 7 February 1947 between the United Nations and the financial departments of Geneva 'au sujet précisément de la saisie des salaires des employés'. *Yearbook of the International Law Commission* (1967), vol. II, 224.

[660] According to its Article 1 '[t]he property and assets of the Communities shall not be the subject of any administrative or legal measure of constraint without the authorisation of the Court of Justice'.

[661] *Application for Authorization to Enforce a Garnishee Order Against the High Authority of the European Coal and Steel Community (Hübner)*, Case 4/62, ECJ, 13 March 1962; *Potvin v. van de Velde (Authorization to Serve a Garnishee Order on the European Economic Community)*, Case 64/63, ECJ, 1 July 1963.

nity organ concerned opposed them.[662] If there is such opposition, however, national courts are reluctant to question this broad immunity. The Belgian proceedings in the *Universe Tankship* case illustrate this fact. After the ECJ had declared it unnecessary to apply for authorization to serve a garnishee order on the Commission of the EC in *Universe Tankship Company Incorporated* v. *Commission of the European Communities*,[663] the plaintiff company, which had obtained a judgment against the Belgian state, sought to enforce that judgment by collecting moneys owed by the Community to the Belgian state. In *Etat belge, min. Communications* v. *Tankship Cy. Inc.* v. *Commission*,[664] however, the Cour d'Appel de Bruxelles quashed the garnishee order of the court of first instance apparently because the Commission voiced its concern that the functioning and independence of the Communities might be put at risk by such a court decision.

As far as 'regular' contentious proceedings are concerned, courts appear to interpret 'immunity from every form of legal process' generally as absolute immunity. For instance, in the *Boimah* v. *United Nations General Assembly*[665] case a US court held that '[u]nder the [General] Convention the United Nations' immunity is absolute, subject only to the organization's express waiver thereof in particular cases'.[666] The same interpretation was used in *Mark Klyumel* v. *United Nations*.[667] In *Loughran et al.* v. *United States*,[668] the absolute immunity from suit of the IMF was also implicitly recognized.

In *FAO* v. *Colagrossi*,[669] the Italian Supreme Court affirmed the dismissal of an employment suit brought against the FAO on the ground of the

---

[662] *Application for Authorization to Enforce a Garnishee Order*, Case SA 1/71, ECJ, 11 May 1971. *Cf.* the earlier case of *Application for Authorization to Serve a Garnishee Order (Grands Magasins de l'Innovation)*, Case 85/63, ECJ, 25 September 1963. See also the more recent cases of *Universe Tankship Company Incorporated* v. *Commission of the European Communities*, Case 1/87, ECJ, 17 June 1987; and *SA Générale de Banque* v. *Commission of the European Communities (Application for Authorization to Serve an Attachment Order on the Commission of the European Communities)*, Case 1/88, ECJ, 11 April 1989.

[663] Case 1/87, ECJ, 17 June 1987.   [664] Cour d'appel de Bruxelles, 1 June 1989.

[665] US District Court EDNY, 24 July 1987.   [666] 664 F. Supp. 69 at 71 (EDNY 1987).

[667] US District Court SDNY, 4 December 1992.

[668] US Court of Appeals DC Cir., 18 April 1963. In this case the owners of real property expropriated by the US to allow construction of additional buildings for the IMF challenged this taking. In order to decide an interlocutory appeal the District of Columbia Court of Appeals had to pass on the finality of the district court's taking judgments. It held that the intended immediate transfer of title to the IMF after the US had validly acquired title as a result of the district court's judgment made this judgment a final one which could not be appealed, because the IMF was 'an entity which [was] immune from all judicial process of the United States'. 317 F. 2d 896 at 898 (DC Cir. 1963).

[669] Corte di Cassazione, 18 May 1992.

FAO's 'immunity from every form of legal process'. This case appears particularly important in so far as it explicitly abandons the Supreme Court's former jurisprudence restricting the FAO's immunity from suit as expressed most clearly in the FAO *cause célèbre*, *FAO* v. *INPDAI*.[670]

In *Groupement d'entreprises Fougerolle & consorts* v. *CERN*,[671] the Swiss Federal Tribunal dismissed an action for annulment of an arbitral award on the ground of CERN's 'absolute immunity' from suit.[672]

Frequently, courts do not even qualify an immunity provision, but merely state that because of the immunity an international organization enjoys they will not exercise their adjudicative authority.[673]

Applying restrictive immunity concepts widely

While most absolute immunity provisions will lead to the unequivocal result of immunity from suit in particular circumstances, more genuine avoidance cases arise in situations where the lack of adjudicative power of domestic courts is less a consequence of clear-cut rules than of judicial interpretation of the existing norms. Among the preferred techniques to avoid lawsuits is the wide interpretation of the normative framework to be applied. For instance, courts sometimes choose to interpret immunity concepts that have a limited, less than absolute scope, such as restrictive or functional immunity,[674] in a very wide fashion.

---

[670] *Food and Agriculture Organization* v. *Istituto Nazionale di Previdenze per i Dirigenti di Aziende Industriali (INPDAI)*, Supreme Court of Cassation, 18 October 1982. See pp. 131*ff* above and 187*ff* below for details of the case.

[671] Swiss Federal Tribunal, 21 December 1992.

[672] A private construction company sought to annul an arbitral award rendered in its favour against CERN before the Swiss Federal Tribunal. In the arbitral procedure, which was carried out according to a specific arbitration clause in CERN's contract with the company which had constructed a large circular tunnel for CERN's research purposes, the private party was awarded far less additional costs than it had originally claimed.

[673] In *Bellaton* v. *Agence spatiale européenne*, Cour de Cassation, 24 May 1978, the Cour de Cassation affirmed the dismissal of the Paris Court of Appeal of a suit brought by a former employee against the European Space Agency. The organization had not expressly waived its immunity, and the termination of Mr Bellaton's employment contract was already the subject of administrative proceedings within ESA's Appeals Commission. In another employment dispute brought against the same organization, *Van Knijff* v. *European Space Agency*, Labour Court Darmstadt, 27 November 1980, a German court declined jurisdiction in an action seeking a declaration that the plaintiff was in fact – according to the German Provision of Labour Act – an employee of the defendant organization. Similarly, in the Argentine case of *Dutto* v. *United Nations High Commissioner for Refugees*, National Labour Court of Appeal, 31 May 1989, an employment claim brought against the UNHCR was dismissed on the ground of immunity.

[674] As to the scope and meaning of these concepts, see pp. 185 *ff*, 205 *ff* and 331 *ff* below.

For instance, in *E GmbH* v. *European Patent Organization*,[675] the Austrian Supreme Court regarded the 'functional immunity' of the European Patent Organization as in principle absolute within the framework of its functional limitation.[676]

In *Mininni* v. *Bari Institute*,[677] the Italian Supreme Court had an opportunity to rule on the functionally limited scope of immunity from execution of international organizations. It affirmed the lower courts' decisions denying the attachment of bank deposits of the Bari Institute holding that all properties of the Institute which serve the institutional functions of the organization – including bank deposits – are covered by immunity from execution.

Cases involving international lending institutions such as the World Bank and various regional development banks which regularly, as a matter of treaty law, enjoy immunity from suit only to a very limited extent[678] provide another possibility for domestic courts to interpret the remaining immunity provisions very broadly in order to abstain from adjudicating such disputes. According to their constituent agreements most of these international banks can be sued before domestic courts by private parties but not by member states.[679] As a result a US court was prepared to allow a suit brought by a borrower against the Inter-American Development Bank. In *Lutcher SA Celulose e Papel* v. *Inter-American Development Bank*[680] the District of Columbia Circuit Court interpreted Article XI(3) of the Bank's Articles of Agreement – which is identical to Article VII(3) of the IBRD Articles of Agreement – as a broad 'waiver of immunity'[681] the Bank would otherwise enjoy under the IOIA.[682]

---

[675] Austrian Supreme Court, 11 June 1992.   [676] For more detail, see pp. 211 f below.

[677] Pretore di Bari, 29 November 1980, Tribunale Bari, 20 June 1981, Corte di Cassazione, 4 April 1986.   [678] *Cf.* p. 141 note 545 above.   [679] See p. 141 above.

[680] US Court of Appeals DC Cir., 13 July 1967. A Brazilian corporation brought suit for damages and sought an injunction against the Inter-American Development Bank. They argued that loans made or about to be made to the plaintiff's competitors violated an 'implied obligation' of its own loan agreement with the Bank to act prudently in considering loan applications from competitors. Although the federal appeals court affirmed the district court's dismissal for failure to state a claim, it disagreed with its alternative reason that the Bank enjoyed immunity from suit.

[681] See pp. 215 *ff* below as to the 'waiver' quality of such an exception.

[682] The Bank had argued that the provision allowing suit in competent courts of the member states allowed only actions brought by 'bondholders, creditors, and beneficiaries of its guarantees' which would contribute to the effectiveness of the Bank's operation. The court disagreed on the basis of the text of Article XI(3) which only excluded suits by member states and contemplated suits brought 'in *any* member country where the Bank has an office'. This was interpreted to 'facilitate suit for . . . borrowers'. 382 F. 2d 454 at 458 (DC Cir. 1967).

Subsequent cases, however, curtailed the broad implications of this rationale and excluded 'internal' administrative disputes from the jurisdiction of US courts. In *Mendaro* v. *World Bank*,[683] Article VII(3) of the IBRD Articles of Agreement was interpreted to permit only suits in respect of external affairs of the Bank, thus holding the Bank immune from suits in employment disputes.[684] *Morgan* v. *IBRD*[685] expanded this employment immunity to a person working at the Bank on placement from a temporary employment agency[686] who brought a tort action not directly connected with the employment relationship.[687]

In *Chiriboga* v. *IBRD*,[688] a personal representative of a deceased World

---

[683] 717 F. 2d 610 (DC Cir. 1983). The Argentine plaintiff's appointment, formerly employed by the World Bank as a researcher, came to an end in 1979. Claiming that she was the victim of sexual discrimination and harassment, she filed a complaint with the US Equal Employment Opportunity Commission alleging that her rights under Title VII of the US Civil Rights Act of 1964 had been violated. The Commission dismissed for lack of jurisdiction. The DC District Court and, on appeal, the DC Court of Appeals affirmed the dismissal.

[684] Although the pertinent provision uses very broad language according to which '[a]ctions may be brought against the Bank only in a court of competent jurisdiction in the territories of a member in which the Bank has an office, has appointed an agent for the purpose of accepting service or notice of process, or has issued or guaranteed securities. No actions shall, however, be brought by members or persons acting for or deriving claims from members', the court refused to read this as a blanket 'waiver of immunity' from every type of suit not expressly prohibited by reservations in Article VII(3). According to a systematic reading of the cited provision taking into account the 'functions of the Bank' and the 'underlying purposes of international immunities' it was evident, in the court's opinion, that the Bank's members only intended to waive the organization's immunity from suit by its 'debtors, creditors, bondholders, and those other potential plaintiffs to whom the Bank would have subject itself to suit in order to achieve its chartered objectives. Since a waiver of immunity from employees' suits arising out of internal administrative grievances is not necessary for the Bank to perform its functions, this immunity is preserved by the members' failure expressly to waive it.' 717 F. 2d 610 at 615 (DC Cir. 1983).

[685] US District Court DC, 13 September 1990.

[686] Although the plaintiff was not technically an employee of the Bank, the court resorted to a 'narrow' interpretation of the exceptions of immunity according to Article VII(3) of the Bank's Articles of Agreement and concluded that consequently 'employee relations of any kind cannot be the subject of litigation against the Bank'. 752 F. Supp. 492 at 494 (DDC 1990).

[687] The plaintiff, an employee of a temporary employment agency placed in a position at the World Bank, alleged that he had been forcibly detained by Bank's security guards, accused of stealing money and exposed to subsequent acts of harassment. His tort action against the Bank for libel, slander, infliction of emotional distress and false imprisonment was dismissed for immunity reasons. The court found '[p]ursuant to applicable provisions [IOIA] and principles of international law, international organizations such as the World Bank are, absent waiver, absolutely immune from suits arising out [of] their internal operations'. 752 F. Supp. 492 at 493 (DDC 1990).

[688] US District Court DC, 29 March 1985.

Bank employee, who died in a plane crash while on home leave, and beneficiaries under her World Bank employees' benefits plan, brought proceedings against the Bank and her insurer to recover under her travel accident policy. Without any in-depth analysis the court qualified the dispute as an employment dispute for which the Bank was immune under the *Mendaro* and *Broadbent* precedents.[689]

A similar result upholding immunity was reached in the Nigerian case of *African Reinsurance Corporation* v. *Abate Fantaye*.[690] In that case, however, a provision in the headquarters agreement allowing suit against the organization in general was held not to qualify as an express waiver under the applicable domestic law.[691]

In the Argentine case of *Ezcurra de Mann* v. *Inter-American Development Bank*,[692] the deciding courts interpreted the restricted immunity of an international lending institution broadly.[693]

---

[689] 'The dispute focuses on what the Bank did or did not contract to provide to its employees. It is difficult to imagine a suit that touches more closely on the internal operations of an international organization.' 616 F. Supp. 963 at 967 (DDC 1985).

[690] Supreme Court, 20 June 1986.

[691] A former employee of the African Reinsurance Corporation, an international organization set up between the member states of the OAU and the African Development Bank with its headquarters in Nigeria, claimed damages for wrongful termination of his employment contract. The defendant organization's plea of immunity was rejected by the High Court at Lagos and by the appellate court interpreting a provision in the headquarters agreement as a waiver of immunity. The provision in question – typical for international financial organizations – stated that: 'Legal actions may be brought against the Corporation in a court of competent jurisdiction in the territory of a country in which the Corporation has its Headquarters, or has appointed an agent for the purpose of accepting service of process, or has otherwise agreed to be sued'. The Supreme Court reversed the decision, holding that the Nigerian Government had conferred upon the Corporation the status of a recognized international organization and that as such it enjoyed diplomatic immunity and had immunity from suit and legal process. Although the treaty establishing the Corporation did not contain an express immunity from suit provision, Nigerian domestic legislation (which in structure and content was close to the English one) provided for its immunity from suit and legal process. It further stated that the headquarters provision in question was no waiver of immunity which – according to domestic legislation – had to be express and positive.

[692] National Labour Court, 1978, Court of Appeals, 1979.

[693] In an employment termination suit brought against the Inter-American Development Bank, the Argentine courts decided that they lacked jurisdiction since the Bank enjoyed diplomatic immunity which could only be waived by the express consent of the defendant. The Bank's statute foresaw, *inter alia*, that 'actions may be brought against the Bank only in a court of competent jurisdiction in the territories of a member in which the Bank has an office [or] has appointed an agent for the purpose of accepting service or notification of process'. (Article XI(3) of the IDB Articles of Agreement). The Court of Appeals concluded that this did not constitute a 'waiver of immunity' (*cf*. pp. 164 f above as to the US so-called waiver of immunity cases *Lutcher* and *Mendaro*) but rather that the Bank 'may or may not accept such service or notice' and affirmed the lower court's

Sometimes courts may also infer immunity from suit *per analogiam*. In the French case of *International Institute of Refrigeration* v. *Elkaim*,[694] the applicable headquarters agreement between France and the International Institute of Refrigeration only provided for the Institute's immunity from execution, not mentioning immunity from suit. The highest French court, nevertheless, dismissed an employment suit brought against the organization ruling that one could infer from the organization's employees' treaty-based grant of immunity from suit that the organization itself also enjoyed such immunity.[695]

Assuming a customary rule of immunity

In most cases, the jurisdictional immunity of international organizations is expressly provided for in applicable treaties or domestic legislation. Where it is not, courts sometimes assume a customary rule of immunity in order to avoid adjudicating a dispute involving an international organization as defendant.

The Dutch Supreme Court in *AS* v. *Iran–United States Claims Tribunal*[696] was very explicit in this regard and based its lack of jurisdiction decision on an unwritten rule of international law.[697]

In the *WEU* case,[698] a German court refused to issue an injunction ordering the organization not to make payments to the applicant's judgment debtor. It did so on the basis of a treaty provision granting the WEU immunity from enforcement measures and because it qualified the payment prohibition inherent in an attachment order as a measure of

decision holding that the appointment of an agent alone would not suffice to subject the Bank to the jurisdiction of Argentine courts but rather that such agent 'is empowered to accept service or notification of process or, conversely, not to accept same'. Vorkink and Hakuta, *Lawsuits Against International Organizations*, 36.

[694] Court of Appeal of Paris, 7 February 1984, Cour de Cassation, 8 November 1988.

[695] In the lower courts, the defendant was held to be subject to the jurisdiction of the French courts in an action for wrongful dismissal by a former secretary. The applicability of French labour law was warranted by the Institute's own staff regulations adopted in pursuance of the headquarters agreement ('for all matters not specified in these rules, reference is to be made to the provisions of the French Employment Code'). Since they did not regulate questions of wrongful repudiation of employment contracts, the subject matter of Mrs Elkaim's suit, French law was held to be governing. The Cour de Cassation overturned this decision: 'Attendu que ce texte n'a pu vouloir conférer aux agents de cette organisation internationale une immunité dont l'organisation ne bénéficierait pas elle-même; que l'[Institute] peut donc s'en prévaloir à l'égard des poursuites dirigées contre lui a l'occasion d'actes accomplis en son nom par ses représentants;' Cour de Cassation, 8 November 1988, (1989) 35 *Annuaire français de droit international* 875*ff*.

[696] Supreme Court, 20 December 1985.   [697] See p. 157 above.

[698] Amtsgericht Bonn, 23 August 1961.

constraint. Since it considered the treaty provision granting immunity to the WEU not yet in force, and while it overlooked that German domestic law provided already for immunity,[699] the court also based its decision presumably on a customary principle.[700]

In a Philippine employment case, *Southeast Asian Fisheries Development Center-Aquaculture Department v. National Labor Relations Commission*,[701] the Philippine Supreme Court also apparently relied on an unwritten rule of functional immunity in order to deny the jurisdiction of the domestic courts. In the court's view the applicant, 'being an intergovernmental organization, enjoy[ed] functional independence and freedom from control of the state in whose territory its office is located'.[702]

---

[699] Seidl-Hohenveldern, *Die Immunität internationaler Organisationen*, 48.

[700] *Cf.* Seidl-Hohenveldern, 'L'immunité', 475.

[701] Philippine Supreme Court, 14 February 1992, reversing a ruling of the National Labor Relations Commission which had ordered the applicant organization to pay severance payments to a former employee.

[702] *Ibid.*, 214.

3   Strategies of judicial involvement

While the majority of cases involving international organizations before national courts certainly provoke the various avoidance techniques as outlined in chapter 2, judges might also actively seek to uphold jurisdiction over such disputes. In most cases, this will not be any purposeful assertion of jurisdiction, but rather a result of the clear inapplicability of a norm excluding international organizations from their jurisdiction, i.e. the absence of an applicable treaty norm requiring immunity, etc. Sometimes, however, denying immunity and upholding jurisdiction necessitates a more sophisticated reasoning. The organization affected could be 'disqualified' as an international organization which potentially enjoys immunity; an international rule requiring judicial abstention could be held to be inapplicable in the domestic realm; in the case of direct applicability of customary international law in the domestic legal order as a matter of principle, the existence of such a rule requiring the granting of immunity to international organizations might be denied; or an applicable rule providing for immunity might be limited in its scope, etc.

Most of the cases where national courts actively seek to exercise jurisdiction over disputes involving international organizations concern organizations as defendants whose potential immunity may deprive domestic tribunals of their adjudicative competence. Where international organizations appear as plaintiffs, national courts regularly have to address only the issue of whether to treat them like other persons under domestic law who are in a position to have recourse to judicial dispute settlement. This seemingly simple problem has proven thorny from time to time.

Non-qualification as international organization

Under certain circumstances, the legal quality or correct qualification of an entity involved in a dispute brought before a national court might be in doubt. In particular, the question of whether a specific organization can be qualified as a public international organization might be unclear. If a court denies this quality to an entity, it is relieved from any potential immunity considerations and can thereby uphold its jurisdiction. The most clear-cut cases will be those where an entity can be characterized as a non-governmental, or other 'private' international organization or association.

National courts have – albeit not very frequently – resorted to this avenue providing ground for their assertion of jurisdiction over such entities. In *Steinberg* v. *International Criminal Police Organization*,[1] the District of Columbia federal appellate court upheld its jurisdiction over Interpol not only because Interpol was not considered an organization in which the US participated, upon which immunities could have been conferred according to the IOIA,[2] but apparently also because it had some doubts as to the status of Interpol as an international organization. The court noted the divergent characterizations of Interpol as an 'intergovernmental' or 'private' or 'non-governmental' organization and concluded that:

Interpol appears to occupy a rather ambiguous and shadowy existence in this country. It claims not to exist in the United States, yet it disseminates information here, maintains close liaison with United States law enforcement authorities, is in effect represented in court by the US Department of Justice and, if the complaint is to be believed ... defames American citizens in the United States as well as elsewhere.[3]

After this decision, Interpol was expressly designated as an international organization according to the IOIA.[4]

An even more obvious example of a court not paying regard to the specific quality of a defendant as an international organization can be found in the Egyptian case of *YY* v. *UNRWA*.[5] There a Gaza court decided 'that UNRWA was not an organ of the United Nations; that under the Agreement of 1950 it did not enjoy jurisdictional immunity; and that,

---

[1] US Court of Appeals DC Cir., 23 October 1981.   [2] See pp. 152*ff* above.

[3] (1985) 672 F. 2d 927 at 928 (DC Cir. 1981).

[4] *Cf.* the 1983 designation of Interpol as an organization entitled to enjoy the privileges (including domestic legal personality), exemptions and immunities conferred by the IOIA by Presidential Executive Order No. 12425, 48 *Federal Register* 28069.

[5] Court in Gaza, 17 August 1957.

therefore, the court was competent to hear a claim lodged against [UNRWA] by a former staff member'.[6] Since UNRWA was in fact a subsidiary organ of the United Nations,[7] this clearly amounted to a case of a judicial de-recognition of the UN's status as an international organization.

In general, however, most national courts seem to be very ready to qualify an entity as a public international organization where this characterization might be at least doubtful as a matter of international law (this tendency probably reflects an inclination of domestic courts to lay a foundation to accord immunity which enables them to subsequently avoid decision-making). In most cases the qualification as international organizations of entities which would not or would not exactly qualify as international organizations under general international law will result from an explicit provision of domestic law, recognizing such entities as international organizations[8] or at least granting them the same or similar privileges and immunities as enjoyed by international organizations.[9]

[6] *Annual Report of the Director of UNRWA*, 12 UN GAOR, Supp. (No. 14) 47, note 34, UN Doc. A/3686 (1957).

[7] William Dale, 'UNRWA – A Subsidiary Organ of the United Nations' (1974) 23 *International and Comparative Law Quarterly* 576–609; Peter Macalister-Smith, 'United Nations Relief and Works Agency for Palestine Refugees in the Near East' in Rudolf Bernhardt (ed.), *Encyclopedia of Public International Law* (1985), vol. VIII, 519–22 at 520; and Henry G. Schermers, *International Institutional Law* (Alphen aan den Rijn and Rockville, 2nd edn, 1980), 840. *Radicopoulos v. UNRWA*, UN Administrative Tribunal, 23 August 1957, Judgment No. 70, (1957) 24 ILR 683 at 684. See also the cases concerning UNRWA at pp. 172f below.

[8] *Cf.* the Dutch cases concerning the Iran–US Claims Tribunal, *AS v. Iran–United States Claims Tribunal*, Local Court of The Hague, 8 June 1983, District Court of The Hague, 9 July 1984, Supreme Court, 20 December 1985; see pp. 195f below.

[9] *Cf. Jenni, Mouvement Vigilance et Groupe Vigilant du Grand Conseil Genevois v. Conseil d'Etat du canton de Genève*, Federal Tribunal, 4 October 1978, where the Swiss Federal Tribunal qualified IATA as a 'non-governmental' or 'quasi-governmental' international organization the recognition of which as a 'public' international organization by the Swiss government in conferring certain privileges and immunities upon it was not deemed unreasonable. This practice has been followed in Switzerland where the Federal Department of Foreign Affairs considered it feasible to conclude a fiscal agreement with the Union internationale pour la conservation de la nature et de ses ressources, an NGO, which the Department regarded as a 'quasi-governmental' international organization. reprinted in (1986) 42 *Annuaire suisse de droit international* 72*ff*. Two relatively recent Philippine cases also demonstrate how NGOs can be treated as international organizations by legislative fiat. First, was the case of *International Catholic Migration Commission v. Pura Calleja*, Philippine Supreme Court, 28 September 1990. Philippine law granted privileges and immunities to the International Catholic Migration Commission, a non-profit-making, private agency, in accordance with an agreement entered into between the Commission and the Philippine Government which provided that the Commission shall have a status 'similar to that of a specialized agency' of the UN. Since the Special Convention provided for 'immunity from every form of legal process', the Philippine

No delegation of immunity

While cases where the specific legal quality of an international organization was not recognized by domestic courts – and thus led to adjudication – are rare, attempts to broaden the personal scope of immunity, for instance through concepts of delegation, etc., were generally not accepted by the judiciary. This does not alter the fact that subsidiary organs, if directly sued instead of the organization to which they belong, are regularly accorded the immunity due to the organization. In a number of employment-related cases brought against UNRWA in local courts in the Middle East as well as in suits against UN economic subsidiary organs before Latin American courts, the UN's immunity shielded such organs against adjudication. Of course, these cases do not really present issues of delegation, since they only involve an organization and its sub-units:

For instance, in *Giurgis* v. *UNRWA*,[10] a claim for compensation for alleged wrongful termination of an employment contract was dismissed since immunity from suit had not been waived. The Cairo court held that 'UNRWA, as a subsidiary organ of the United Nations, enjoyed the privileges and immunities of the General Convention'.[11] In a similar case, in *Hilpern* v. *UNRWA*,[12] an employment-related suit for termination payments brought by a former UNRWA employee was withdrawn after the UN Secretary-General requested the Egyptian courts to recognize UNRWA's immunity. Similarly, in *Radicopoulos* v. *UNRWA*,[13] a lawsuit in a domestic court was withdrawn after an indication by UNRWA that an internal remedy was open to plaintiff. Subsequently, both cases were decided by the UN Administrative Tribunal.[14] Thus, the

Supreme Court thought that it 'extends to immunity from the application of Philippine labor laws' and thus prevented a 'certification election' for the purpose of establishing a labour union in the Commission. Secondly, there was the case of *Kapisanan Ng Manggagawa AT Tac Sa IRRI (International Rice Research Institute)* v. *Secretary of Labor and Employment*, Philippine Supreme Court, 28 September 1990. A Philippine presidential decree granted to a private, philanthropic, non-profit-making organization, the International Rice Research Institute, privileges and immunities, including, *inter alia*, 'immunity from every form of legal process'. This was defined as 'immunity from any penal, civil and administrative proceedings' which was interpreted by the Philippine Supreme Court to include an exemption from the coverage of Philippine labour laws and thus prevented a 'certification election' for the purpose of establishing a labour union in the Institute.

[10] Labour Court Cairo, 31 December 1961.
[11] *Yearbook of the International Law Commission* (1967), vol. II, 224 at 233.
[12] Egyptian Court, 1952.   [13] Egyptian Court, 1957.
[14] *Hilpern* v. *UNRWA*, UN Administrative Tribunal, 7 December 1956, Judgment No. 65; and *Radicopoulos* v. *UNRWA*, UN Administrative Tribunal, 23 August 1957, Judgment No. 70.

above-mentioned Egyptian case *YY v. UNRWA*,[15] which decided 'that UNRWA was not an organ of the United Nations',[16] appears to be an exceptional one.

In *X v. UN Economic Commission for Latin America*,[17] an employment dispute brought against the UN Economic Commission for Latin America (ECLA) was dismissed after the Chilean Supreme Court set aside the summons served upon ECLA and one of ECLA's executive secretaries. The Chilean court regarded the immunity provisions of the headquarters agreement between Chile and the UN Economic Commission for Latin America[18] as 'merely a specific application of Article II section 2 and Article V section 18 of the [General Convention]'.[19] Similarly, in *Diaz-Diaz v. UN Economic Commission for Latin America*,[20] the Mexican Supreme Court held that domestic courts had no jurisdiction to entertain a suit brought against the UN by one of its former employees concerning termination indemnities and overtime payments. In a comparable way an Argentine court in *Schuster v. UN Information Center*[21] denied its jurisdiction to adjudicate in an employment dismissal action, reasoning that the UN was a juridical person under public international law.

The German appellate administrative decision in *X et al. v. European School Munich II*[22] confirms the principle that a dependent sub-unit of an international organization enjoys the same immunity as its principal organization. It held that the European School Munich was included in the international legal personality of the international organization, the European School, and that it therefore likewise enjoyed immunity from German jurisdiction.[23]

True problems of delegation have been raised in some lawsuits by interested parties. In a number of cases private persons tried to benefit from the special status enjoyed by international organizations (usually

---

[15] Court in Gaza, 17 August 1957.   [16] See also pp. 170f above.
[17] Supreme Court of Chile, 8 November 1969.
[18] Agreement Between Chile and the UN Economic Commission for Latin America of 16 February 1953.
[19] (1969) *United Nations Juridical Yearbook* 237.
[20] Junta de Conciliacion y Arbitraje, 7 August 1953.   [21] National Labour Court, 1952.
[22] Administrative Court Munich, 29 June 1992, Bavarian Administrative Court Munich, 15 March 1995, Federal Administrative Court, 9 October 1995.
[23] 'Die Institution "Europäische Schule" ist eine internationale Organisation mit funktionell begrenzter Völkerrechtspersönlichkeit. Die "Europäische Schule München" nimmt als deren unselbständige Untergliederung und dieser Völkerrechtspersönlichkeit teil und genießt wie diese Befreiung von der deutschen Gerichtsbarkeit (Immunität).' Bavarian Administrative Court, 7th Chamber, Munich, 15 March 1995, (1996) *Deutsches Verwaltungsblatt* 448.

immunity from suit) claiming that they acted on behalf of an international organization which would enjoy immunity if it had acted itself. These claims, however, have been regularly rejected by domestic courts.

In *Dumont & Besson* v. *Association de la Muette*,[24] the French courts exercised jurisdiction in a suit brought against building contractors erecting offices for the OECD in Paris alleging disturbances caused by the construction works. The fact that the work in question was carried out on behalf of and in the interest of an international organization did not remove the issue 'outside the appreciation of the [French] judicial tribunals'.[25]

In two US cases reported together as *Herbert Harvey Inc.* v. *National Labor Relations Board*,[26] the claim of an independent contractor engaged by the World Bank that it enjoyed an immunity derived from the Bank's immunity was rejected. The District of Columbia Circuit Court confirmed that an independent contractor providing maintenance and operating services for an international organization is subject to the US National Labor Relations Act and to the jurisdiction of the National Labor Relations Board (NLRB). The dispute arose from an order issued by the NLRB requiring Herbert Harvey Inc. to engage in collective bargaining with the representatives of its service personnel working on World Bank premises.[27] In the 1967 case the petitioner argued that the NLRB did not have jurisdiction over labour relations at the Bank. It contended that the Bank was an exempt organization and that its own operations were so intimately connected with the Bank that the Board should decline to assert its jurisdiction. Alternatively, it argued that – because of the Bank's considerable supervisory powers – the personnel affected were in fact employees of the World Bank. The court remanded the case to the NLRB to determine the jurisdictional issue.[28] In its supplemental decision the NLRB reaffirmed its previous order. It acknowledged that the Bank enjoyed immunity and that it was thus not subject to the NLRB's jurisdiction. However, it held that, even if one accepted the view that the Bank and Herbert Harvey Inc. were joint employers, Herbert Harvey Inc. had sufficient control over the working conditions of the service personnel at the World Bank as to enable it to bargain with a trade union.[29] Herbert Harvey Inc.'s second challenge to

[24] Court of Appeal of Paris, 11 June 1966.   [25] (1974) 47 ILR 346.

[26] US Court of Appeals DC Cir., 26 October 1967, US Court of Appeals DC Cir., 19 September 1969.

[27] *Herbert Harvey Inc.*, 162 NLRB 890 (1967).

[28] US Court of Appeals DC Cir., 26 October 1967.

[29] *Herbert Harvey Inc.*, 171 NLRB 1968-1 (1968).

this order was rejected in the 1969 decision of the District of Columbia appellate court. The court approvingly cited the NLRB's 'intimately connected' test in deciding on its jurisdiction over employment relationships.[30]

These cases involving claims to a 'delegated' immunity are not to be confused with the decision in *Alpha Lyracom Space Communications Inc.* v. *Communications Satellite Corp.*,[31] where a US court held that the defendant, Comsat, a private corporation created by the US Congress and designated as the US representative to Intelsat, was immune from suit brought under US antitrust law. Although it was derived from Intelsat's status, this immunity from antitrust law was in fact an exemption from the applicable US competition rules.[32] The defendant thus enjoyed a privileged position as a result of its relationship to Intelsat; it was not, however, immune from suit.[33]

Recognition of an international organization as a legal person under domestic law

In order to assert jurisdiction over a dispute involving an international organization, either as plaintiff or as defendant, national courts must be satisfied as to an international organization's capacity to bring suit or to be sued. Normally courts will discuss this precondition as an issue of 'capacity' or 'competence' to sue or as a broader 'legal personality' question. However, regardless of the terminology used, it is clear that all legal systems draw a line between entities whose ability to appear in court they recognize and those entities that are perceived to lack such an ability. In a way, this is the other side of the same coin that has been discussed above when dealing with 'non-recognition as a legal person under domestic law' as one of the possible avoidance approaches of national courts.[34]

---

[30] US Court of Appeals DC Cir., 19 September 1969.
[31] US District Court SDNY, 13 September 1990.
[32] The court held that 'the substance and chronology of the legislative history compel the conclusion dictated by the fundamental objectives of the [Satellites Communications] Act, namely, that Congress did not intend the "antitrust consistency" phrase to authorize private lawsuits against Comsat in its role as the United States representative to Intelsat.' (1990–2) *Trade Cases* 69,188 (SDNY 1990).
[33] In spite of the court's correct finding as to a substantive exemption of the law in favour of the defendant, it ruled that the 'immunity conferred on defendant under the HQ Agreement bars this suit' and therefore it need not consider all of the defendant's arguments. (1990–2) *Trade Cases* 69,188 (SDNY 1990).
[34] See pp. 37*ff* above.

Of course, in most cases this ability will not pose any serious legal issue at all. Normally, a domestically applicable legal rule will expressly provide for the 'capacity' to 'institute legal proceedings', etc.[35] and courts will be ready to accept the ability of international organizations to bring suit, like the Belgian courts in proceedings instituted by the European School in order to collect outstanding tuition fees referred to in *European School Mol* v. *Hermans-Jacobs and Heuvelmans-Van Iersel*.[36] This capacity becomes more problematic where there are no directly applicable treaty provisions or corresponding domestic rules providing for an international organization's ability to appear in domestic courts. This situation may arise where, in a member state that follows a dualist tradition, no implementing legislation has been enacted or, in the case of a non-member state, where such a state has not expressly provided for the international organization's ability to be a party to judicial proceedings under its domestic legal order.

The most prominent case, which was widely commented on by scholars, was *Arab Monetary Fund* v. *Hashim (No. 3)*[37] where the AMF's personality under English law – as a legal prerequisite in order to sue its former director-general for fraudulent acts – was fiercely contested. It was indeed the sole issue on appeal until the ability of the AMF, an international organization of which the UK was not a member state, to sue in English courts was finally accepted by the House of Lords.[38] Both the court of first instance and the House of Lords established the AMF's legal personality for similar reasons, basically recognizing the legal personality of entities created under the law of foreign states.

In some cases, even where the domestic legal personality of an international organization and its capacity to sue was beyond doubt, domestic courts had to engage in a prudent interpretation of the specific quality of the domestic legal status of an international organization in order to avoid its capacity being rendered worthless. In the Canadian case *United Nations* v. *Canada Asiatic Lines Ltd*,[39] the defendant tried to rely on the rules of domestic company law by arguing that an act necessary to institute

---

[35] As to the various domestic personality clauses, see pp. 43, 49 and 72f above.

[36] Belgian Court of Arbitration, 1994. In a preliminary question procedure from the justice of the peace for the canton of Mol, the Belgian Court of Arbitration upheld the constitutionality of the requirement to pay tuition in the European Schools because they were not (Belgian) public authorities which were bound by the guarantee of free access to education.

[37] Chancery Division, 9–12 October, 14 November 1989; Court of Appeal, 26–27 March, 9 April 1990; House of Lords, 26–28 November 1990, 21 February 1991.

[38] For more detail, see pp. 65ff above.   [39] Superior Court Montreal, 2 December 1952.

legal proceedings had been performed by the wrong organ of an international organization.[40]

Denying immunity

In most cases involving international organizations before national courts a potential threat to their jurisdiction will stem from an organization's enjoyment of immunity under international law by way of treaty provisions or a potential customary rule.

Where a relatively unambiguous international rule to this effect binding upon the forum state exists, it will be difficult for national courts to disregard it, unless it somehow manages to treat the international rule as inapplicable and unless it is confronted with a corresponding domestic rule, e.g. implementing legislation requiring it to accord immunity. Here, generally used avoidance techniques concerning the non-application of international law can operate as a tool to assert jurisdiction over international organizations by denying their (internationally owed) immunity from suit.[41]

Denying the international applicability of immunity instruments

Without (or rather before) referring to the specifics of the relationship between international law and domestic law, national courts may avoid applying a rule of international law embodied in a treaty provision – as is the rule for immunity from suit – by finding a reason to deny the applicability of the relevant treaty as international law. Lack of treaty ratification by the forum state, non-fulfilment of objective requirements to enter into force, etc., may serve this purpose to avoid an international obligation.

In *Velasquez v. Asian Development Bank*,[42] an employment dispute, a

---

[40] In an action brought by the UN for the recovery of money allegedly owed to it, the defendant moved to reject the power of attorney signed by the Secretary-General claiming that he had no authority to bind the UN, presumably because it would have required a decision of a board of directors. The Canadian court dismissed the motion, regarding the power of attorney valid as signed by the chief administrative officer of the UN. It held that under Canadian law the UN had the legal capacity of a body corporate, possessed juridical personality and had the right to institute proceedings. Since the UN affairs were administered by the secretariat and not by a board of directors, parts of the law concerning the authority to give a power of attorney were, however, inapplicable. (1954) 48 *American Journal of International Law* 668.

[41] *Cf.* Institut de droit international, 'The Activities of National Judges and the International Relations of Their State' (1993 I) 65 *Annuaire de l'Institut de Droit International* 327–448 at 342ff.

[42] Ministry of Labour, 25 November 1979.

Philippine decision rested mainly on such reasons. A domestic labour arbitrator upheld his jurisdiction holding that the defendant organization had failed to show that the Bank's constituent treaty and headquarters agreement had been ratified by the Philippines and that they had been in any way superseded by domestic labour legislation. On the basis of such law, he ordered reinstatement of the Bank's employee and the payment of back wages. After representations made by the organization, the Philippine Foreign Ministry advised the Ministry of Labor that the latter had no jurisdiction to decide on the matter. A similar claim in the Philippines was, albeit unsuccessfully, raised in *United States Lines Inc. v. World Health Organization.*[43] There, a shipping company brought suit against the WHO in order to recover a sum of money it claimed, due to the WHO's failure to remove cargo from the port after ten days following arrival. The appellate court upheld the court of first instance's dismissal of the claim. It held that the WHO was immune from all form of legal process in the Philippines as a result of its ratification of the Special Convention regardless of the status of the WHO–Philippines Host Agreement of 1951 which the plaintiff had considered invalid for lack of proper ratification requirements.

Denying the domestic direct applicability of international law

To deny the direct applicability of an international rule requiring immunity from suit, national courts will in principle have recourse to two types of avoidance techniques. They can either rely on a general dualist concept of the relationship between international and domestic law or, if such direct applicability is feasible as a matter of principle, they may claim that certain preconditions for the domestic applicability of international law are not fulfilled, such as the requirement of a clear and precise character of the international norms in question. In practice, however, this lack of a self-executing character of immunity norms is rarely claimed.

Resort to the first type of avoidance techniques in this context is far more frequent. Courts rely on the inapplicability of international rules on organizational immunity as a result of their domestic legal order's choice of a dualist system. As already mentioned the English system with its doctrine of incorporation is a clear example of this approach.[44] Consequently, English courts have reiterated the view that international organizations would enjoy immunity before English courts only in so far as

---

[43] Intermediate Appellate Court, 30 September 1983.   [44] See pp. 48*f* and 63*f* above.

they had been expressly granted such immunity by English domestic law.[45]

In such a situation the avoidance of immunity also requires, of course, a lack of domestic implementing legislation. Such legislation would force the court to do what it just avoided by disregarding international law, i.e. to deny its jurisdiction. Normally, implementing legislation will correspond to the international rule it is intended to incorporate into domestic law. It is, however, conceivable that specific implementing legislation is not wholly in conformity with the international rules it purports to incorporate.

A good example of such a possible discrepancy between international and domestic immunity standards is the US International Organizations Immunities Act 1945 (IOIA). The IOIA, for instance, on the one hand provides for presidential discretion in withholding immunity from certain organizations.[46] Such a restriction or exclusion of immunity might be decreed independently from an international arrangement limiting immunity. On the other hand and more importantly, the IOIA still contains the controversial linkage of jurisdictional immunity of international organizations to that of states. While one might argue about the policy rationales of equating the scope of immunity from suit of states and international organizations and also whether some aspects of this restrictive immunity concept have already infiltrated the immunity of organizations,[47] suffice it to say here that under many treaty provisions in force for the US the immunity granted to international organizations is an absolute one. The IOIA's standard of the 'same immunity from suit . . . as is enjoyed by foreign governments'[48] could be seen at least as an invitation to the US courts to deny immunity to international organizations in certain cases and to exercise jurisdiction over them.

[45] In *Standard Chartered Bank* v. *International Tin Council and others*, High Court, Queen's Bench Division (Commercial Court), 17 April 1986, (1988) 77 ILR 8–18 at 17, the High Court observed that 'international organisations such as the ITC have never so far . . . been recognised at common law as entitled to sovereign status. They are accordingly entitled to no sovereign or diplomatic immunity in this country save where such immunity is granted by legislative instrument, and then only to the extent of such grant.'

[46] Title 1, section 1 of the IOIA authorizes the president 'by appropriate Executive order to withhold or withdraw from any such organization . . . any of the privileges, exemptions, and immunities provided for in this title . . . or to condition or limit the enjoyment by any such organization . . . of any such privilege, exemption, or immunity. The President shall be authorized, if in his judgment such action should be justified by reason of the abuse by an international organization . . . of the privileges, exemptions, and immunities herein provided or for any other reason, at any time to revoke the designation of any international organization under this section . . .'

[47] *Cf.* pp. 185*ff* below.   [48] Title I, section 2(b) of the 101 A.

Interestingly, though, US courts have been very careful to avoid deciding this issue. Although a clear judicial pronouncement to the effect of declaring the restrictive immunity standard applicable to international organizations – as seems to be required by the wording of the IOIA – is missing,[49] courts have generally decided the cases that brought the issue up by relying on a 'safe-track' argument: they found the activity in question to be a non-commercial one, for which under a restrictive standard even states could not be sued, and granted immunity.[50]

Denying a potential customary rule in the absence of conventional immunity provisions

Where international law becomes directly relevant in the domestic legal order, courts will not evade recognition of the immunity of an international organization where it is clearly required. Thus, an applicable treaty norm or domestic legislation might leave no choice but to recognize immunity. Since the existence of a customary rule of international law mandating states to grant immunity to international organizations is, however, quite controversial,[51] a national judge might also assert jurisdiction by denying its existence.

Although the issue is similar to the problem of 'customary' personality under domestic law,[52] the outcome is diametrically opposed. If personality is denied, there will be no suit and no legal remedy available against the – at least for domestic purposes – 'non-existing' entity. If, on the other hand, immunity is denied, the defendant international organization will be amenable to suit and, thus, there will be a legal remedy for a potential plaintiff.

An analysis of the existing case law shows that courts, in fact, rarely engage in a thorough investigation as to the existence of a customary rule of immunity for international organizations. What appears more frequently to be the case is that courts do not even consider the existence of an unwritten international rule of jurisdictional immunity for an international organization. When there is no treaty provision or domestic

---

[49] There appears to be only one case denying immunity for *iure gestionis* acts. In *Dupree Associates Inc.* v. *OAS*, US District Court for the District of Columbia, 31 May 1977, 22 June 1977, the District of Columbia Federal District Court thought that since the IOIA conveyed the 'same immunity from suit' on international organizations 'as is enjoyed by foreign governments', and since states are entitled only to restrictive immunity, 'it follows that international organizations are entitled only to restricted immunity'. For more detail, see pp. 202 below.

[50] For more detail, see pp. 192*ff* below.   [51] See p. 145*ff* above.

[52] See p. 45*f* above.

legal rule applicable, courts usually do not bother even to investigate whether there might be a customary international law rule of immunity. As a consequence, it is often doubtful whether one can indeed speak of a 'strategy' of the courts in this respect.

For instance, in *Viecelli* v. *IRO*,[53] an Italian court not only disregarded the applicable conventional norms of immunity,[54] but failed to consider a possible basis in customary law as well. Assuming that only sovereign international persons could enjoy immunity, it denied such a possibility for the IRO.[55] This would not be remarkable at all, were it not for the numerous other Italian cases which considered a jurisdictional immunity standard for international persons was more or less a matter of customary law.[56]

In the French employment case *International Institute of Refrigeration* v. *Elkaim*,[57] both the Labour Tribunal and the Paris Court of Appeal upheld the jurisdiction of French courts since the applicable headquarters agreement between France and the International Institute of Refrigeration provided for immunity only from execution, with no mention of immunity from jurisdiction. This decision, however, was overturned by the Cour de Cassation[58] who regarded the missing immunity provision for the organization as implied in the agreement.[59]

The US case of *International Tin Council* v. *Amalgamet Inc.*[60] illustrates that national courts may be reluctant to assume a customary rule of immunity from suit. In this US sequel to the English ITC litigation, the Tin Council had moved to stay arbitration proceedings in New York brought against it by Amalgamet Inc. on the ground that it enjoyed immunity.[61] The court dismissed the petition finding no reason to grant immunity to the ITC. Since the ITC was not a state, it could not enjoy immunity under the FSIA and, since the US did not participate in the ITC nor was it designated by the President under the IOIA, the IOIA did not apply. The

---

[53] Tribunale Trieste, 20 July 1951.
[54] Riccardo Monaco, 'Capacités de droit privé des organisations internationales' in Ernst von Caemmerer *et al.* (eds.), *Festschrift für Pan Zepos* (Athens and Freiburg, 1973), 475–90 at 475.
[55] 'L'IRO . . . non può venire riconosciuta quale ente sovrano avendo una limitata capacità giuridica internazionale ed alla quale, pertanto, non può venire riconosciuta l'immunità giurisdizionale.' (1953) 36 *Rivista di diritto internazionale* 471. The court, however, based its case dismissal on the express choice of forum clause contained in the employment contract between Viecelli and the IRO which provided for arbitration in cases of dispute.
[56] See pp. 194*ff* below.   [57] Court of Appeal of Paris, 7 February 1984.
[58] Cour de Cassation, 8 November 1988.
[59] See p. 167 above.   [60] Supreme Court, New York County, 25 January 1988.
[61] See also p. 154 above.

ITC's argument that under rules of comity the US court should recognize its immunity granted under English law was rejected since the applicable English 1972 legislation was interpreted not to be intended to have extraterritorial effect and because even under that foreign law the ITC would not enjoy immunity. The court, thus, tested immunity only on the basis of US domestic law, and did not discuss a possible customary law standard of immunity.

Two decisions in the course of the litigation concerning the power of the European School in Munich to determine the tuition charged to its students[62] were also rendered on basis of the assumption that no customary rule of immunity prevented German courts from exercising jurisdiction. In X et al. v. *European School Munich I*[63] the Bavarian appellate Administrative Court and in X et al. v. *European School Munich II*[64] the lower administrative court of Munich upheld their jurisdiction over the defendant institution in the absence of any treaty provision calling for the school's immunity from jurisdiction. The second decision even expressly excluded the possibility of a customary rule of immunity for an international organization.[65] This ruling was reversed, however, by the appellate courts.[66]

Immunity as a non-issue

In a few cases immunity plays no role at all. For instance, in the Belgian case of *Devos* v. *Supreme Headquarters Allied Powers Europe (SHAPE) and Belgium*,[67] immunity was simply not an issue.[68] In *Beaudice* v. *ASECNA*[69] and *Kehren* v. *Institut franco-allemand de Saint-Louis*[70] French appellate courts

---

[62] For more detail, see pp. 150f above.

[63] Bavarian Administrative Court Munich, 23 August 1989.

[64] Administrative Court Munich, 29 June 1992, Bavarian Administrative Court Munich, 15 March 1995, Federal Administrative Court, 9 October 1995.

[65] 'Eine Befreiung nach den allgemein anerkannten Regeln des Völkerrechts (Art. 25 GG) scheidet aus, denn diese kommt nur in Betracht im Verhältnis zu ausländischen Staaten und den für sie handelnden Organen bzw. Repräsentanten, nicht aber kommt sie zwischenstaatlichen Organisationen und deren Angehörigen zugute.' X et al. v. *European School Munich II*, Bavarian Administrative Court Munich, 29 June 1992 (unpublished).

[66] Bavarian Administrative Court Munich, 15 March 1995, Federal Administrative Court, 9 October 1995.

[67] Belgian Cour de Cassation, 13 November 1985.

[68] The plaintiff, a Belgian national, claimed employment benefits arising under Belgian law. The Labour Court of Mons rejected this claim as 'unfounded since the relations between the parties are not subject to the application of national law'. (1993) 91 ILR 242–9 at 245. The Court of Cassation upheld this decision qualifying the plaintiff as a member of SHAPE's international civil personnel.

[69] Court of Appeal of Paris, 25 November 1977. See p. 227 below.

[70] Cour d'Appel de Colmar, 28 January 1971.

assuming jurisdiction over an employment disputes did not even deal with the issue of immunity from suit.

Similarly, in the Jordanian case of *Y* v. *UNRWA*,[71] a suit for damages by a former staff member led to a default judgment and execution against UNRWA regardless of UNRWA's claim to immunity. In two other Lebanese employment termination cases concerning UNRWA, *W* v. *UNRWA*[72] and *X* v. *UNRWA*,[73] default judgments were rendered against UNRWA for the payment of employment termination indemnities to former staff members. Apparently both were not executed following an official communication to the Lebanese Ministry of Foreign Affairs.

In 1951 the Syrian courts rendered two judgments in favour of Palestinian refugees, *WW* v. *UNRWA*[74] and *XX* v. *UNRWA*,[75] awarding them employment termination indemnities. In order to enable the plaintiffs to execute the judgments the courts also ordered the seizure of UNRWA's assets held in local banks. In 1955–6 both execution measures were terminated after settling the case 'in a manner which took [UNRWA's] legal status into account'.[76]

In some of the older cases involving organizations which had not been granted immunity it could not even be an issue. Thus, for instance, in the case of *Institut international pour l'agriculture* v. *Profili*,[77] the Court of Appeals of Rome held that there was 'nothing to prevent the Italian courts from exercising jurisdiction in regard to a relation of employment which arose and was terminated in Italy, between a private individual and the Institute'.[78] Nevertheless, the Corte di Cassazione reversed this judgment, holding that the Institute was an international entity 'autonomous and removed from the interference of any one State'.[79]

Interestingly, in some more recent cases brought in the course of the Tin Council litigation, immunity – although expressly contained in applicable instruments – did not play a decisive role. For instance, in *Maclaine Watson & Co. Ltd* v. *International Tin Council*,[80] the court did not deal with the

---

[71] Magistrate Court, January 1954.
[72] Labour tribunal attached to the Lebanese Ministry of National Economy, 1952.
[73] Lebanese Labour Arbitration Tribunal, July 1953.   [74] Syrian Court, 1951, 1955–6.
[75] Syrian Court, 1951, 1955–6.
[76] A. N. Vorkink and M. C. Hakuta, *Lawsuits Against International Organizations – Cases in National Courts Involving Staff and Employment* (Washington DC, World Bank Legal Department, 1985), 16.
[77] Tribunal of Rome, 1 February 1930; Corte di Cassazione, 26 February 1931.
[78] Tribunal of Rome, (1929–30) 5 *Annual Digest of Public International Law Cases* 413 at 414.
[79] Corte di Cassazione, (1929–30) 5 *Annual Digest of Public International Law Cases* 413 at 414. See also p. 117 above.
[80] High Court, Chancery Division, 13 May 1987. See p. 119 above for the facts of this case.

ITC's claim to immunity from suit under the International Tin Council (Immunities and Privileges) Order 1972. Rather, it dismissed the motion to appoint a receiver for lack of stating a valid cause of action. One might thus argue that, by asserting jurisdiction in principle, the English court denied immunity.

In *Lyritzis* v. *Inmarsat*,[81] an employment case instituted before an English labour court, immunity was no issue at all. Since the Inmarsat Convention only contained a personality clause enabling the organization 'to be a party to legal proceedings' and a number of fiscal privileges,[82] the Inmarsat (Privileges and Immunities) Order 1979[83] did not provide for immunity from suit.

In two tort suits brought against Eurocontrol immunity was not in issue. In both cases the UK Civil Aviation Authority had obtained detention orders against the plaintiffs' aircraft for the non-payment of flight charges. In *Internationale Nederlanden Aviation Lease BV and others* v. *Aviation Authority and the European Organization for the Safety of Air Navigation (Eurocontrol)*,[84] the plaintiffs claimed that the detention was unlawful and asked for damages; in *Irish Aerospace (Belgium) NV* v. *European Organization for the Safety of Air Navigation and Civil Aviation Authority*,[85] the plaintiffs additionally claimed that the defendants abused their dominant position which they occupied within the European Community. Since Eurocontrol did not enjoy immunity from suit either under treaty law or according to English statutory provisions, the courts heard and dismissed the claims on the merits. In the latter case, the plaintiff's claim under Article 86 of the EC Treaty failed because 'Eurocontrol's public service assignment of ensuring the safety of air navigation could not be deemed to be an economic or commercial activity'.[86]

There was also no role for immunity in *Robert A. Mitishen* v. *Otis Elevator Company and IBRD*,[87] a tort action arising from an elevator accident

---

[81] Employment Appeal Tribunal, 26 March 1996.
[82] Articles 25 and 26 of the Inmarsat Convention.
[83] (1979) 50 *British Yearbook of International Law* 307.
[84] Queen's Bench Division (Commercial Court), 11 June 1996.
[85] Queen's Bench Division (Commercial Court), 6 June 1991.
[86] [1992] 1 *Lloyd's Reports* 383. See also the similar qualification of Eurocontrol's tasks as non-commercial activities in two cases relied upon in *Irish Aerospace*: *LTU* v. *Eurocontrol*, Case 29/76, ECJ, 14 October 1976, and *Soc. dr. allem. Sat Fluggesellschaft mbH* v. *Eurocontrol*, Cour d'appel de Bruxelles, 4 October 1990. See also *Eurocontrol (Flight Charges II)*, German Federal Constitutional Court, 23 June 1981, and *Trans-Mediterranean Airways* v. *Eurocontrol*, Dutch administrative decision of the Crown, 16 January 1974, qualifying flight charge invoices as *iure imperii* acts of respectively a non-German and a non-Dutch authority not giving rise to administrative recourse in German or Dutch law.
[87] US District Court DC, 19 September 1990.

on the premises of the World Bank, probably because the defendant organization, as a matter of the applicable agreements, does not enjoy a broad immunity from suit.[88] Rather, the court held that the plaintiff, as an employee of the IBRD, could only claim workers' compensation benefits.

Restricting the scope of immunity

In most cases, international organizations will enjoy some degree of immunity as a matter of the applicable law in the forum state. Domestic courts will thus be able to assert jurisdiction over disputes involving international organizations only by qualifying a particular dispute as falling outside the protective cloak of immunity.

The judicial activism of asserting the adjudicative power of courts in such disputes is, of course, a matter of degree depending upon the specific scope of immunity provided for in the applicable regime. The law might already contain a restrictive concept, for instance calling for the application of functional immunity or of a standard equal to the relative immunity enjoyed by states. While in the latter case the restrictive parameters along the *iure imperii/iure gestionis* distinction appear to be rather precise, they are less so in the case of immunity where the exact determination of 'functional' acts, acts 'necessary for the performance of an international organization's duties', or 'official' acts poses considerable difficulties. As a consequence, courts enjoy a greater 'interpretative freedom' to read functional immunity in a more (or less) restrictive fashion than they do when applying a relative immunity standard.

The furthest-reaching examples of activist judicial engagement strategies can be found in situations where the applicable law provides for absolute immunity but courts nevertheless find reasons to restrict this unlimited immunity in various ways. In this context one can find the most articulate judicial involvement techniques. It is not surprising that these methods are frequently inspired by restrictive or functional immunity paradigms.

Restrictive immunity

In a number of cases domestic courts actually applied a standard of restrictive immunity as used in the field of state immunity.

---

[88] See p. 141 note 545 above.

Restrictive judicial interpretation of treaty provisions according immunity

The numerous Italian cases limiting the scope of immunity enjoyed by international organizations along the restrictive immunity standard valid for states are probably the best-known examples of asserting adjudicative power in a far-reaching manner.[89] The interesting feature of many of these decisions is that the Italian courts narrow down the scope of immunity although they are supposed to apply absolute immunity clauses.

In this context, however, it is important to note that a restrictive immunity standard is sometimes called for as a result of Italy's express reservations to the applicable instruments.[90] It is remarkable, however, that where no such reservation has been made Italian judges nevertheless frequently apply a restrictive immunity standard.[91]

The Italian 'reservation' to absolute immunity provisions

Examples of the application of a restrictive immunity standard to international organizations, intended to enjoy broad, either unlimited or expressly absolute, immunity, are those Italian cases resting on a legislative mandate resulting from an Italian 'reservation' to the respective 'absolute immunity' provision.

This is the case, for instance, with the jurisdictional immunity regime of the Bari Institute of the International Centre for Advanced Mediterranean Agronomic Studies, a Paris-based international organization established under the auspices of the OECD and the Council of Europe in 1962. According to the applicable international agreement setting up the Centre and the Institute, they both enjoy complete immunity from suit in the member states. Italy, however, made a reservation according to which it would accept the Institute's immunity only to the extent that immunity has to be granted to foreign States under 'general principles of international law'. Consequently, the Italian Supreme Court determines lawsuits brought against the Institute in accordance with the restrictive state immunity standard. In *Bari Institute of the International Centre for Advanced Mediterranean Agronomic Studies* v. *Jasbez*,[92] a labour dispute between an interpreter and her employer, it upheld the jurisdiction of the

---

[89] See Antonio Cassese, 'L'immunité de juridiction civile des organisations internationales dans la jurisprudence italienne' (1984) 30 *Annuaire français de droit international* 556–66 at 556*ff*.

[90] *Cf.* pp. 187*ff* below.   [91] *Cf.* pp. 189*ff* and 194*ff* below.

[92] Corte di Cassazione, 21 October 1977.

Italian courts because it thought that the dispute arose from an employment situation not sufficiently closely related to the international organization's decision-making process to be covered by immunity. It is interesting to note that this, as well as a number of other cases expressly stating that they apply a restrictive immunity standard, in fact incorporate a reasoning inspired by functional immunity considerations.[93] As a result of the Italian reservation, the court went on to determine the applicable customary international law standard – evidenced by the European Convention on State Immunity – as immunity for *iure imperii* acts only. In particular, it referred to the Convention's provision denying immunity if proccedings relate to a contract of employment between a state and an individual where the work is to be performed on the territory of the forum state unless the employee is a national of the defendant foreign state.[94]

More controversial was the legal effect of an identical Italian reservation to the Special Convention. Italy had made a reservation to its Article 3, which provides for 'immunity from every form of legal process', intending to restrict the extent of that immunity to one enjoyed by foreign states under general international law. In the context of the General Convention it has been argued that an approximation to sovereign immunity principles would be against the 'object and purpose' of the Convention; consequently comparable reservations had been rejected.[95] As far as the Special Convention was concerned, Italy has been subsequently treated as non-party to it.[96]

The Italian courts, however, did not hesitate to assume the validity of the Italian reservation to the Special Convention. A number of cases affirmed this view, among them the 1982 *cause celèbre* of *FAO* v. *INPDAI*, ultimately resulting in consultations on the international level between the Government of Italy and the FAO.[97] In *Food and Agriculture Organization of the United Nations* v. *Istituto Nazionale di Previdenze per i Dirigenti di Aziende Industriali (INPDAI)*,[98] the FAO's landlord brought suit against the organization claiming rent increases according to a contractual clause providing

---

[93] See also pp. 192*ff* below.
[94] Article 5 of the European Convention on State Immunity.
[95] *Cf.* the rejection by the UN Secretary-General of a reservation denying to any UN official of the reserving state's nationality any privilege or immunity under the General Convention, in (1963) *United Nations Juridical Yearbook* 188.
[96] Christian Dominicé, 'L'immunité de juridiction et d'exécution des organisations internationales' (1984 IV) 187 *Recueil des Cours* 145–238 at 170*ff*; Felice Morgenstern, *Legal Problems of International Organizations* (Cambridge, 1986), 6.
[97] See pp. 131*ff* above.   [98] Corte di Cassazione, 18 October 1982.

for such rent increases on the basis of the official Italian Government consumer index. The FAO moved to dismiss for lack of jurisdiction since it enjoyed immunity from suit in Italian courts.

The Italian Supreme Court, relying on Italy's reservation, applied a restrictive immunity standard and concluded that the Italian courts had jurisdiction. Concerning the extent of immunity the FAO was entitled to, the court considered that, whenever international organizations acted in the private law domain, they (like states) placed themselves on the same footing as private parties with whom they had entered into contracts, and thus forewent the right to be treated as sovereign bodies that were not subject to the sovereignty of others. In order to determine the private character of the FAO's activity, the court relied less on a strict nature test than on a determination of the aims that such activities were intended to achieve and whether or not they were directly related to the institutional aims pursued by the foreign entity. Returning to the traditional nature test and considering the private nature of the lease contract, the Corte di Cassazione had no doubt as to the jurisdiction of Italian courts.[99]

After the Corte di Cassazione's decision that the FAO was not immune from suit with respect to alleged rent increases owed to its landlords in Rome, the suspended proceedings were resumed by INPDAI. In *Istituto Nazionale di Previdenze per i Dirigenti di Aziende Industriali (INPDAI)* v. *Food and Agriculture Organization*,[100] the court of first instance gave judgment for plaintiffs awarding the rent payments sought and declared the decision to be provisionally executory.

The Corte di Cassazione's decision provoked strong protests by the FAO.[101] A request for an advisory opinion of the ICJ was already in sight when the parties to the dispute, the Italian Government and the FAO, found a diplomatic solution. Italy became a party to the Special Convention in 1985 without the previous reservation, and the issue was settled thereafter through official correspondence between Italy and FAO, finally leading to interpretation agreements in March 1991.[102]

---

[99] The court was not impressed by the fact that the contract for the lease of office space entered into by the FAO in 1969 contained, *inter alia*, a provision that stipulated that nothing in it could be construed as constituting a waiver of immunity enjoyed by the FAO and provided for International Chamber of Commerce arbitration for the settlement of any dispute.

[100] Pretore di Roma, 4 April 1984.   [101] See pp. 131*ff* above.

[102] J. P. Dobbert and Peter Rädler, 'Food and Agriculture Organization of the United Nations' in Rudolf Bernhardt (ed.), *Encyclopedia of Public International Law* (2nd edn, 1995), vol. II, 413–19 at 419.

Interpreting absolute immunity as restrictive immunity

Probably one of the most perplexing techniques of domestic courts in asserting their adjudicative power over disputes involving international organizations where they should enjoy immunity, lies in eliminating – by way of interpretation – a grant of absolute immunity and turning it into a mere restrictive one.

A number of Italian cases decided on the basis of a restrictive immunity concept without an express domestic or international norm containing such limitation, seem to rest on the assumption of an implicit limitation or a *renvoi* of such immunity clauses to state immunity. This assumption has been severely criticized by some commentators. They claim that, since conventional provisions are usually very precise and detailed, in particular as far as exceptions to immunity are concerned, one cannot infer any 'implied' restrictions to the provisions granting immunity.[103] It is, however, not quite clear when a treaty incorporates or refers to other sources. Even critics of the Italian case law acknowledge that certain implied exceptions to the broad absolute immunity of international organizations contained in many instruments exist.[104]

The appellate court in the French *Agence de Coopération Culturelle et Technique* v. *Housson*[105] case followed such an approach to read an implied restriction into an unqualified provision granting immunity. According to its headquarters agreement of 1972 and a 1980 accord with France, the defendant organization enjoyed immunity from suit with the possibility of a waiver in specific cases.[106] The Court of Appeals, however, held that it was still necessary to make – in the case of an international organization as employer – a distinction between official and private acts (*actes d'autorité* and *actes de gestion*) and between permanent agents and personnel recruited on the basis of contracts governed by French private law. In the latter case – which it saw fulfilled in Mrs Housson's employment relationship – the Agency would not enjoy immunity from suit without even having to waive it expressly.[107]

---

[103] Dominicé, 'L'immunité de juridiction', 180. Dominicé also points out that the Italian case law is 'isolated' and that other national decisions do not reflect this attitude.

[104] E.g., possibly for counterclaims. See pp. 203*ff* below.

[105] Cour d'appel de Bordeaux, 18 November 1982, Cour de Cassation, 24 October 1985. See p. 225 below for details of the case.

[106] The Agency 'jouit de l'immunité de juridiction sauf renonciation de sa part, dans un cas particulier'.

[107] The Cour de Cassation affirmed the lower court's decision, regarding a choice of forum clause in favour of French courts as a waiver of the organization's immunity. See also pp. 224*ff* below.

Similarly, a number of Italian cases involving the Intergovernmental Committee for European Migration (ICEM) interpreted an absolute immunity standard along the restrictive sovereign immunity standard. According to the applicable agreement, ICEM enjoyed the same immunity as provided for in Article 3 of the Special Convention, which in turn contained a general immunity clause 'from every form of legal process'. Since the reference was made to the Convention itself and not to the specific Italian participation, Italy's reservation to Article 3 (limiting the absolute immunity of the Convention to the extent to which it is granted to foreign States under international law)[108] was technically not relevant.[109] Thus, the applicable immunity regime was one of absolute immunity. Nevertheless, the Italian Supreme Court applied a restrictive immunity standard. On this basis, it dismissed two employment disputes between the Committee and Italian nationals who had clerical duties, not on the ground of the organization's absolute immunity, but rather because their employment relations were held to fall within the *iure imperii* category of employment relationships.

In *ICEM v. Di Banella Schirone*,[110] the Italian Court of Cassation confirmed its jurisprudence according to which international organizations – as subjects of international law – are immune from local jurisdiction only in relation to acts performed *iure imperii* and held that this perceived customary law standard was the same as the one provided for in the headquarters agreement. The court held that international organizations were immune from domestic proceedings not only in respect of employment relationships with high-level management officials but also with 'persons who permanently and continuously form part of the establishment of the body concerned'.[111] It thought that the secretarial work performed by Mrs Di Banella Schirone was – 'although instrumental in nature' – 'undoubtedly of a public character and . . . directly connected with the pursuit of [ICEM's] institutional aims'.[112] Stressing the functional relationship between her and ICEM, the court obviously regarded all employment contracts whose purpose was to further the international organization's aims to fall within the *iure imperii* category. The only type of employment contracts not covered by this broad definition in the court's view were those with persons providing 'irregular or casual services' and with 'manual workers'.[113]

The Corte di Cassazione came to the same result in *ICEM v. Chiti*,[114]

---

[108] See p. 187 above.   [109] See also (1976) 2 *Italian Yearbook of International Law* 347.
[110] Corte di Cassazione, 8 April 1975.   [111] (1988) 77 ILR 575.   [112] *Ibid.*   [113] *Ibid.*
[114] Corte di Cassazione, 7 November 1973.

which is of particular interest as far as the court's interpretation of the applicable treaty standard is concerned. The court reasoned that:

The immunity envisaged for specialized agencies by the Convention [on the Privileges and Immunities of the UN Specialized Agencies] of November 21, 1947 [providing for immunity 'from every form of legal process'] does not contain any wording which allows it to be extended to private activity; nor can this be deduced from the intention of the Contracting Parties . . . On the contrary, the contents of the individual conventions with the various specialised organizations help in defining the limits of the institutional functions of such organizations and in identifying the public character of the activity exempted from the jurisdiction of the member States.[115]

In other words, the court plainly disregarded the clear text of the treaty provision and replaced it by its own interpretation of what is appropriate for international organizations.

In a Greek case, X v. *International Centre for Superior Mediterranean Agricultural Studies*,[116] a domestic court upheld its jurisdiction over an employment dispute with an international organization based on a restriction of the expressly granted absolute immunity of the defendant organization. The Court of Appeals of Crete reversed a lower court's decision granting immunity to the International Centre for Superior Mediterranean Agricultural Studies in an employment dispute. It held that 'Greek Courts had jurisdiction to judge cases arising from labour relations directed against the respondent international organisation, since these are related to its private activity and do not result from the exercise of sovereignty'.[117] Although the court noted that in the constituent convention the Centre was granted unqualified jurisdictional immunity to ensure its functioning, it went on to interpret the true meaning of this grant of immunity as one incorporating the restrictive state immunity standard. The court considered that:

According to the real sense of the above privilege [the Centre enjoyed immunity] according to the prevailing, in international law, fundamental principle of state sovereignty . . . but only in relation to disputes arising from the exercise of *imperium* and not for its relations created by its activity in its quality of fiscus,[118] i.e. relations of private law.[119]

---

[115] (1976) 2 *Italian Yearbook of International Law* 350. The Italian Supreme Court accepted the contention of the appellant, a secretarial employee of the Committee, that 'Chiti's contract of employment . . . was the expression of the organizing power of the Institution exercised for the fulfilment of its institutional aims and hence protected by the alleged immunity'. *Ibid.*, 349.
[116] Court of Appeals of Crete, 1991.   [117] *Ibid.*
[118] 'Fiscus' refers to the state as property owner.   [119] *Ibid.*

Approximating restrictive immunity to functional immunity

National courts frequently adopt sovereign immunity concepts in a wholesale manner to resolve disputes concerning international organizations. As if to mitigate the potential immunity-limiting effect of such an approach, they are sometimes very willing to accept a *iure imperii* character of acts which might be qualified as 'commercial' if a state had undertaken them as long as those acts could be seen to be essential or at least instrumental for the functioning of an international organization. In various cases employment contracts with interpreters – frequently based on a purely private law relationship between the organization and the interpreter – were held to warrant immunity from suit because such translating and interpreting services were considered 'essential' for the organization duly to perform its tasks. Some cases, explicitly stating to apply a restrictive immunity standard as established in state immunity, in fact incorporate functional immunity considerations.

In *Iran–US Claims Tribunal v. AS*,[120] a Dutch appellate court denied the jurisdiction of Dutch courts over an employment dispute instituted by a Dutch interpreter against the tribunal. Applying a principle of restrictive immunity as a matter of customary law,[121] it qualified the translating and interpreting services provided by the plaintiff as falling 'within the category of *acta jure imperii*, since these services are essential for the Tribunal to duly perform its tasks'.[122] A remarkable aspect of this and similar cases is that, by shifting the *iure imperii* characterization to a functional criterion, the courts manage to concentrate less on the underlying legal relationship, which is frequently a contract clearly governed by private law, than on the official purpose of the services provided.

It is interesting to note that in a similar situation and by applying similar immunity standards the Italian Supreme Court reached a contrary result. In *Bari Institute of the International Centre for Advanced Mediterranean Agronomic Studies v. Jasbez*,[123] a labour dispute between an interpreter and her employer, the Corte di Cassazione upheld the jurisdiction of the Italian courts after a lengthy discussion of state immunity principles which it thought applicable. In the end, however, the court appears to have chosen a functional immunity rationale by asserting that the dispute arose from an employment situation not sufficiently closely related to the international organization's decision-making process to be covered by

---

[120] District Court of The Hague, 9 July 1984.   [121] See pp. 157 and 167 above.
[122] (1985) 16 *Netherlands Yearbook of International Law* 472.
[123] Corte di Cassazione, 21 October 1977.

immunity. It characterized the plaintiff's interpreting functions as 'un-connected with the intellectual process of taking decisions in the further-ance of the organization's aims'. Distinguishing Mrs Jasbez's tasks from an embassy interpreter's, 'whose responsibilities constitute an essential and indispensable medium for the performance of the State's public func-tions', the court qualified hers as not forming part of the international organization's public function, and thus not warranting its immunity.[124]

Adhering to the same functional test in *Bari Institute of the International Centre for Advanced Mediterranean Agronomic Studies* v. *Scivetti*,[125] the Tribu-nale di Bari, however, granted immunity to the organization because – in the court's view – the plaintiff, a principal accountant employed at the Bari Institute, had been integrated into the organization and took part in the performance of the institutional activities of the international organ-ization.

The two employment disputes involving Italian staff members of the Intergovernmental Committee for European Migration (ICEM), *ICEM* v. *Di Banella Schirone*[126] and *ICEM* v. *Chiti*,[127] evidence a similar tendency. Al-though the Corte di Cassazione expressly applied a *iure imperii* test in denying its jurisdiction over the cases, the court in effect assimilated the *iure imperii* to functional criteria.[128]

Also in *Camera confederale del lavoro and Sindicato scuola CGIL* v. *Istituto di Bari del Centro internazionale di alti studi agronomici mediterranei*,[129] the court of first instance was willing to turn to a more functional differentiation, notwithstanding the explicit relevance of the distinction between *iure imperii* and *iure gestionis* acts as a result of the Italian reservation to the Centre's immunity provision.[130] The Pretore di Bari reasoned that:

This distinction, which was applied without qualification to international organ-izations, has lately been adapted to the particular feature of such organizations as they are not sovereign bodies, and has, accordingly, been more appropriately expressed as the distinction between acts connected with the institutional func-tion of the organization and acts not directly connected therewith, and immunity is granted only in respect of the former.[131]

In *Allied Headquarters in Southern Europe (HAFSE)* v. *Capocci Belmonte*,[132] the Italian Supreme Court moved slightly away from this approximation of

---

[124] (1988) 77 ILR 609.   [125] Tribunale di Bari, 23 December 1975.
[126] Corte di Cassazione, 8 April 1975.   [127] Corte di Cassazione, 7 November 1973.
[128] See pp. 190*f* above.
[129] Pretore di Bari, 15 February 1974; Corte di Cassazione, 27 April 1979. See pp. 112*f* above as to the facts of this case and as to the lack of jurisdiction argument.
[130] See p. 186 above.   [131] (1977) 3 *Italian Yearbook of International Law* 314.
[132] Corte di Cassazione, 5 June 1976.

iure imperii to functional acts. The dispute arose from a private law contract between HAFSE and an Italian lawyer who had served as its legal advisor for a number of years and who now sued for outstanding payments. The court was aware of the fact that the legal services rendered by the plaintiff were activities incidentally necessary for the exercise of HAFSE's functions and could thus be thought covered by HAFSE's functional immunity; however, it based its affirmation of the jurisdiction of the Italian courts over the dispute on the fact that the services were solicited as a matter of a private law contract. It differentiated:

between acts of the international organization performed in the exercise of sovereign powers and including the organization of offices and the engagement of the related personnel . . . and private law acts even though they are designed to procure the means and the services necessary for the fulfilment of the tasks proper to the organization or its component bodies.[133]

Applying a state immunity standard to international organizations in the absence of any express rules: a 'customary' standard of restrictive immunity?

In the absence of an international or domestic immunity regime, courts have to decide what scope of jurisdictional immunity they might accord to international organizations. In a number of countries courts have concluded that – as a matter of general international law – international organizations should enjoy only restrictive immunity, as granted to foreign states, and thereby extended their jurisdiction over a number of disputes where they appeared as defendants.

In two employment cases brought against the Italo-Latin-American Institute, an international organization established by a 1966 treaty between twenty Latin-American countries and Italy, the Italian Supreme Court had to address the issue of a customary-law-based immunity of an international organization, since the headquarters agreement between the Institute and Italy had not been ratified and the convention establishing the Institute only granted juridical personality to the 'international organization' and was silent on the issue of immunity. *Galasso* v. *Istituto italo-latinoamericano*[134] confirmed that as a result of Article 10 of

---

[133] (1977) 3 *Italian Yearbook of International Law* 329.
[134] Corte di Cassazione, 3 February 1986. An employee assigned to the library had brought suit against the Institute demanding that her employer should 'regulate' her social security position. The Institute claimed immunity from suit which the Pretore di Roma granted. The Corte di Cassazione affirmed the decision. It held that the tasks of a librarian to be performed by Mrs Galasso were such as to fall within the functional scope of the organization wherein it enjoyed immunity.

the Italian Constitution the customary international law rule of *par in parem non habet iurisdictionem* automatically applied to the Institute, an entity enjoying international legal personality, even in the absence of any conventional norm. Although the court based its justification for the grant of immunity on an analogy between international organizations and states as subjects of international law, it refused to delimit the scope of immunity in an exactly analogous way. The applicant wanted to rely on the standard of the 1972 European Convention on State Immunity which would have provided for an exception of immunity in cases of employment contracts where the employee was a citizen or resident of the forum state. The court, however, found that international organizations enjoyed a larger immunity from suit than states in cases of employment disputes. In *Cristiani* v. *Istituto italo-latino-americano*,[135] the court recognized a *communis opinio* in the doctrine and case law of various countries of a 'necessary relationship between international personality and immunity'.[136] It thought that – by analogy with states – the principle of *par in parem non habet iurisdictionem* applied also to international organizations.

In *AS* v. *Iran–United States Claims Tribunal*,[137] the Dutch courts had to refer to a customary principle since there was no treaty in force providing for privileges and immunities of the tribunal in the Netherlands. In an employment action brought by a Dutch interpreter challenging his dismissal,[138] the court of first instance found that 'international organizations such as the Tribunal, which have been constituted by States, enjoy in principle the same immunity that is accorded to States . . . The same distinction between *acta jure imperii* and *acta jure gestionis* should therefore be made in the case of international organizations such as the Tribunal.'[139] It qualified the 'oral private agreement' to provide translat-

---

[135] Tribunale Roma, 17 September 1981; Corte di Cassazione, 23 November 1985.
[136] Corte di Cassazione, (1986) 69 *Rivista di diritto internazionale* 150.
[137] Local Court of The Hague, 8 June 1983.
[138] The plaintiff, a Dutch national, had been employed by the Iran–US Claims Tribunal as an interpreter and translator by oral contract. He instituted legal proceedings in the Dutch courts challenging his dismissal. Written employment contracts between the Tribunal and its employees usually contained a specific administrative procedure to settle employment disputes. No such written agreement was concluded between the plaintiff and the defendant in this case. There was no treaty in force providing for privileges and immunities of the Tribunal in the Netherlands. The defendant claimed that it enjoyed the 'usual immunity' from jurisdiction of international organizations necessary for the performance of the tasks for which they were established. This claim was supported by the Netherlands Government.
[139] (1984) 15 *Netherlands Yearbook of International Law* 431.

ing and interpreting services as *acta iure gestionis* on the part of the tribunal and thus found that Dutch courts had jurisdiction over a dispute relating to such employment contracts.[140]

Without expressly calling it a customary international law rule, the Malaysian case *Bank Bumiputra Malaysia Bhd* v. *International Tin Council and another*[141] restricted the jurisdictional immunity of an international organization according to the restrictive immunity standard valid for states. The Malaysian plaintiff bank was one of the Tin Council's unpaid creditors. It claimed that the ITC had deposited tin warrants issued by the second defendant as security. In the Malaysian proceedings the plaintiff not only sought to recover the outstanding loan but also asked for a declaration that it was entitled to the tin covered by the warrants, which was in the possession of the second defendant who refused to hand it over to plaintiff. The court did not allow the first claim because it considered the extrajurisdictional service of the writ in London to be an abuse of the process of the court. It did, however, admit the second claim relating to the tin and specifically denied the ITC's claim to immunity. At the outset, the Malaysian court held that the ITC did not enjoy immunity from suit in Malaysia because the applicable treaties granted such immunity only in respect of the English courts. It added, however, that since the ITC entered into a commercial transaction it could not claim sovereign immunity in any event. In relying on the 'modern rule' as embodied in the English *Trendtex* case, a leading decision on state immunity, the court apparently thought that the ITC was to be treated as a 'foreign sovereign'.[142]

In some of the Italian cases involving NATO, a restrictive immunity standard is applied. A typical case is *Branno* v. *Ministry of War*,[143] where a

---

[140] The appellate court in *Iran–US Claims Tribunal* v. *AS*, District Court of The Hague, 9 July 1984, reversed the decision, without, however, disputing the lower court's equating of states and international organizations as far as the proper standard of immunity was concerned. Rather, it chose to qualify the translating and interpreting services provided by the plaintiff as falling 'within the category of *acta jure imperii*, since these services are essential for the Tribunal to duly perform its tasks'. (1985) 16 *Netherlands Yearbook of International Law* 472. The Dutch Supreme Court in *AS* v. *Iran–United States Claims Tribunal*, Supreme Court, 20 December 1985, adopted a 'functional' standard according to which an 'international organization is in principle not subject to the jurisdiction of the courts of the host State in respect of all disputes which are immediately connected with the performance of the tasks entrusted to the organization in question'. (1987) 18 *Netherlands Yearbook of International Law* 360.

[141] Malaysian High Court, 13 January 1987.   [142] (1989) 80 ILR 24.

[143] Corte di Cassazione, 14 June 1954.

contract for the provision of canteen facilities by a private individual to the staff of NATO headquarters offices was qualified as a *iure gestionis* activity on the part of the international organization for which it enjoyed no immunity from suit. The Italian Corte di Cassazione did not discuss any treaty-based immunity. Rather, it relied on the customary principle that the NATO 'member States cannot exercise judicial functions with regard to any public activity of the North Atlantic Treaty Organization connected with its organization or with regard to acts performed on the basis of its sovereignty [*sic*]'[144] concluding that 'its private law activities were subject to the jurisdiction of the Italian courts'.[145] In *Sanità and Ferraro* v. *Command Allied Land Forces Southern Europe*,[146] a lawsuit brought against NATO headquarters in Italy by two employees working as telephone operators, the Italian court denied immunity on the ground that the plaintiffs were 'local civilian labour' whose work contracts were governed by Italian law and came under Italian jurisdiction in case of a dispute. It specifically approved the sovereign immunity standard of restrictive immunity by equalizing states to international organizations (referred to as international law bodies):

In accordance with the principle of what is called restricted immunity, which prevails in the countries of continental Europe and is followed by Italian case law, an international law body is immune from the jurisdiction of the host State only if it has acted within the scope of its particular sphere of sovereign activity and not if it has acted on a footing of equality in the exercise of its private law capacity.[147]

The IOIA: incorporating a FSIA standard of restrictive immunity?

A number of US cases decided on the basis of the International Organizations Immunities Act 1945 (IOIA) had to address the issue of whether the immunity standard provided therein, according to which international organizations 'shall enjoy the same immunity from suit and every form of judicial process as is enjoyed by foreign governments', should be regarded as a restrictive one.

It is undisputed – at least since the US Supreme Court's decision in the *Alfred Dunhill* case[148] and the enactment of the Foreign Sovereign Immunities Act 1976 (FSIA) – that the immunity accorded to foreign states in US

---

[144] (1955) 22 ILR 757.   [145] *Ibid.*, 756.   [146] Pretore di Verona, 17 May 1975.
[147] (1977) 3 *Italian Yearbook of International Law* 332.
[148] *Alfred Dunhill of London* v. *Republic of Cuba*, 425 US 682 (1976).

courts is a restrictive one.[149] However, in the 1940s when the IOIA was enacted, US courts still adhered to a standard of absolute immunity for foreign sovereign states. This fact has given rise to the argument that – although the plain wording of the IOIA's grant of immunity, as read today, seems to accord restrictive immunity to international organizations – the standard of immunity of international organizations is determined by a reference to the then prevailing absolute immunity standard. The ensuing discussion has led to a substantial confusion both in judicial opinion and scholarly literature as to whether the IOIA standard of immunity for international organizations was affected by the change of sovereign immunity or not. The court in *Boimah* v. *United Nations General Assembly*[150] clearly spelled out the issue:

It is unclear whether the [IOIA], by granting to international organizations immunity co-extensive with that of foreign governments, confers the absolute immunity foreign governments enjoyed at the time of the Act's passage, or the somewhat restrictive immunity provided for in the [FSIA].[151]

The opinion among jurists is split. Those advocating an identical standard – having the advantage of being able to rely on the clear language – contend that the 'overriding Congressional intent which springs from a reading of the immunity provisions of the [IOIA] is that international organizations and foreign sovereigns shall be treated the same'[152] and

---

[149] The doctrine of sovereign immunity under international law was recognized early by US domestic courts. Since international law forms part of the law of the land, US courts could directly apply its rules. In a long tradition of cases dating back to *The Schooner Exchange* v. *McFadden*, 11 US (7 Cranch) 116 (1812), US courts granted immunity to foreign sovereign states. The absolute immunity from suit granted for decades came under attack in the 1940s when courts began to question its appropriateness. Since the courts generally deferred to the executive's opinion whether to grant immunity or not, the State Department's 'Tate Letter' of 1952, (1952) 26 *Department of State Bulletin* 984, was of considerable influence on US immunity practice. Therein the State Department adopted the restrictive immunity theory indicating that private acts of foreign sovereigns should no longer receive immunity. In the famous *Alfred Dunhill* case, the US Supreme Court confirmed this attitude by declaring that sovereign immunity would no longer be extended to commercial acts of foreign states. Thereby it clearly followed the general practice of other Western states with regard to the extent of sovereign immunity. This practice, and in particular this restrictive immunity standard, was codified by the enactment of the FSIA in 1976.

[150] US District Court EDNY, 24 July 1987.   [151] 664 F. Supp. 69 at 71 (EDNY 1987).

[152] Thomas J. O'Toole, 'Sovereign Immunity Redivivus: Suits Against International Organizations' (1980) 4 *Suffolk Transnational Law Journal* 1–16 at 11*ff*. Significantly, the US Government in its brief as *amicus curiae* in the *Broadbent* case also argued for an analogy to state immunity.

that the IOIA standard 'should be read to incorporate foreign governmental immunity as it stands when suit is brought and not just as it was
in 1945'.[153] Most commentators, however, rely on an absolute immunity
standard. One important argument is that 'as a matter of law, the passage
of the FSIA has had no effect on the IOIA'[154] which thus continues to
accord absolute immunity. It was also emphasized that – at least as far as
the UN is concerned – the absolute immunity clause of the General
Convention, which entered into law in the US after the US accession in
1970, in any event superseded the domestic Act's questionable extent of
immunity.[155]

It is frequently asserted that US courts managed to avoid the issue of
the correct scope of immunity at all by holding that even under a
restrictive standard taken from the FSIA international organizations
would enjoy immunity.[156] Indeed, most of the cases that went to court
concerned employment issues which the judges were ready to qualify as
internal administrative matters entailing immunity from suit. The classic example is the *Broadbent* case brought against the Organization of
American States (OAS). In *Marvin R. Broadbent et al. v. OAS et al.*,[157] seven
former employees of the OAS claimed damages for breach of employment
contracts. Their employment had been terminated as a consequence of a
reduction in staffing by the OAS. An appeal before the OAS Administrative Tribunal had already failed before the proceedings were instituted in
national court. The circuit court held that '[the] relationship of an international organization with its internal administrative staff is noncom-
mercial, and, absent waiver, activities defining or arising out of that
relationship may not be the basis of an action against the organization'.[158] The district court had not followed such an avoidance strategy

[153] Frederic L. Kirgis, *Teacher's Manual to International Organizations in Their Legal Setting* (2nd
edn, St Paul, MN, 1993), 7.
[154] Kathleen Cully, 'Jurisdictional Immunities of Intergovernmental Organizations' (1982)
91 *Yale Law Journal* 1167–95 at 1179. Oparil recites, *inter alia*, a failed amendment Bill to
the IOIA introduced at the passing of the FSIA which would have expressly reduced the
immunity standard for international organizations along the lines of the FSIA as a
strong indication of the continuing absolute immunity standard for international
organizations. Richard J. Oparil, 'Immunity of International Organizations in United
States Courts: Absolute or Restrictive?' (1991) 24 *Vanderbilt Journal of Transnational Law*
689–710 at 707.
[155] Kirgis, *Teacher's Manual*, 7.
[156] E.g., *Restatement (Third) of the Law, The Foreign Relations Law of the United States* (ed. American
Law Institute, St Paul, MN, 1987), §467, Reporters' Note 4.
[157] US District Court DC, 25 January 1978, 28 March 1978; US Court of Appeals DC Cir., 8
January 1980.
[158] 628 F. 2d 27 at 35 (DC Cir. 1980).

but rather squarely addressed the issue, and had its problems with it. It first decided that the 'express language . . . and the statutory purposes underlying the [IOIA] bring international organizations within the terms of the [FSIA] and that . . . this Court has jurisdiction over the parties and controversy involved in the case'.[159] The same court, however, later reconsidered its decision and then thought that international organizations 'stand in a different position with respect to the issue of immunity than sovereign nations' which 'persuaded' the court that international organizations are immune from every form of legal process. It noted that the FSIA 'makes no mention of international organizations' and that '[n]othing in the [IOIA] provides for jurisdiction in the district courts over civil actions against international organizations'.[160] Accordingly, it dismissed the action.

A number of other decisions also avoided the issue of the scope of IOIA immunity by deciding the cases brought on the basis of restrictive immunity. In *Morgan* v. *IBRD*,[161] a tort action against the World Bank for libel, slander, infliction of emotional distress and false imprisonment which was dismissed for immunity reasons, the District of Columbia district court thought that the applicability of a relative sovereign immunity standard under the IOIA was an 'issue not resolved in this Circuit'. Nevertheless the court analyzed the complaint *in eventu* also under an FSIA standard and concluded that the plaintiff's claims arose 'directly from the World Bank's employment practices, which do not constitute "commercial activity" within the meaning of the statute'.[162] It further considered the Bank's acts to be immune under an FSIA standard exempting libel and slander as well as 'discretionary functions' from the tort exception to sovereign immunity.[163] In *Tuck* v. *Pan American Health Organization*,[164] the court held that it need not decide the notoriously open issue of whether IOIA read in the light of the FSIA granted absolute or merely restrictive immunity. It determined that even under the restrictive standard it enjoyed immunity since the action forming the basis of Tuck's complaint, i.e. PAHO's supervision of its employees, fell outside the

---

[159] 481 F. Supp. 907 at 908 (DDC 1978).   [160] *Ibid.*
[161] US District Court DC, 13 September 1990.
[162] 752 F. Supp. 492 at 494 (DDC 1990).   [163] *Cf.* FSIA, § 1605 (a)(5).
[164] US District Court DC, 17 November 1980, US Court of Appeals DC Cir., 13 November 1981. The Staff Association of the Pan American Health Organization, integrated since 1949 into the regional office of the WHO, had hired Ronald Tuck, a US lawyer, for the provision of legal services. Tuck filed suit against PAHO and its director for interference with his contract of services. The Court of Appeals dismissed the claim on the ground that both defendants enjoyed immunity from suit.

commercial activity exception of the FSIA. Similarly, in *Weidner* v. *International Telecommunications Satellite Organization*,[165] a breach of contract suit by an employee was dismissed because of the international organization's immunity under the IOIA for 'public' functions. Another recent example is *De Luca* v. *United Nations Organization, Perez de Cuellar, Gomez, Duque, Annan et al.*,[166] where a former UN employee sued the organization and a number of high-level UN officers personally for failure to reimburse him for withheld income taxes in accordance with normal reimbursement schemes. The court dismissed the action on the ground of the UN's immunity which it enjoyed both under the General Convention and under the IOIA. It noted that the IOIA referred to immunity of foreign governments as far as the scope of immunity of international organizations was concerned and thought that this immunity was 'now governed by the [FSIA]'.[167] The court realized that due to 'several exceptions' to immunity in the FSIA this would result in a limited immunity standard. Since it based its finding on the General Convention, it did not discuss the relationship between the IOIA and the FSIA any further, although the reasoning indicates that the court considered the IOIA standard limited along the FSIA lines. 'We need not consider the application of these exceptions to the instant case, for the UN Convention, which contains no such exceptions, provides sufficient ground for finding the UN immune from plaintiff's claims.'[168]

In cases not related to employment disputes US courts have managed to leave the issue of whether the IOIA confers absolute or restrictive immunity upon international organizations undecided. In *Abdi Hosh Askir* v. *Boutros Boutros-Ghali, Joseph E. Connor et al.*,[169] the plaintiff claimed US$190 millions in damages for unauthorized and unlawful possession of his property in Somalia during the UN's peacekeeping activities in 1992. The lawsuit was brought against the UN's Secretary-General[170] and its Under-Secretary-General for Administration and Management 'in their official and individual capacities'. With the plaintiff's acknowledgment, the court considered that his complaint 'may be treated as an action against the United Nations itself'.[171] The court dismissed the action and granted immunity – expressly stating that it considered it

---

[165] DC Court of Appeals, 21 September 1978.
[166] US District Court SDNY, 10 January 1994.
[167] 841 F. Supp. 531 at 533, note 1 (SDNY 1994).   [168] *Ibid.*
[169] US District Court SDNY, 29 July 1996.
[170] The plaintiff subsequently dropped his claim against Boutros Boutros-Ghali in order to avoid problems with US Federal Rules concerning diversity jurisdiction.
[171] 933 F. Supp. 368 at 370, note 3 (SDNY 1996).

'unnecessary to decide whether the restrictive immunity doctrine of the FSIA applies to the United Nations through the IOIA'.[172] The seizure and occupation of the plaintiff's property by the UN as part of its peacekeeping mission in Somalia was regarded as a non-commercial, governmental activity. In the court's words '[a] military operation, even one directed at ensuring the delivery of humanitarian relief, is not an endeavor commonly associated with private citizens – indeed, military operations are a distinctive province of sovereigns and governments'.[173] In the court's view 'even if the immunity available to the United Nations and its officials is only restrictive immunity, the immunity still applies because the nature of the acts complained of by the plaintiff are the exercise of governmental functional rather than private commercial activity'.[174]

There is, however, at least one older and one very recent case where US courts have affirmed their adjudicative power over suits bought by private parties against international organizations on the basis of reading the IOIA standard as one requiring only restrictive immunity. In *Dupree Associates Inc.* v. *OAS*[175] the District of Columbia Federal District Court upheld its jurisdiction over a suit for breach of contract – in a dispute concerning the construction of buildings for the Organization of American States (OAS) – and expressly denied the defendant's motion to dismiss the case on grounds of jurisdictional immunity it enjoyed as international organization. The court reasoned that, since the IOIA conveyed the 'same immunity from suit' on international organizations 'as is enjoyed by foreign governments' and since states are entitled only to restrictive immunity, 'it follows that international organizations are entitled only to restricted immunity. It is this court's opinion that this is the proper interpretation of the IOIA.'[176]

In *Margot Rendall-Speranza* v. *Edward A. Nassim and the International Finance Corp.*,[177] a sexual harassment action brought by an employee of the International Finance Corporation (IFC) against her superior and the organization, the District of Columbia District Court denied the IFC's claim to immunity from suit by its employees involving 'internal operations and administrative matters'. In a first decision, distinguishing *Morgan* v. *IBRD*,[178] the court held that the acts complained of did not involve a policy judgment on the part of the IFC which would confer immunity from suit under the FSIA discretionary function exception to

[172] *Ibid.*, 371.   [173] *Ibid.*, 372.   [174] *Ibid.*
[175] US District Court DC, 31 May 1977, 22 June 1977.   [176] (1982) 63 ILR 95.
[177] US District Court DC, 18 March 1996, 3 July 1996.
[178] US District Court DC, 13 September 1990. See pp. 165 and 200 above.

the tort exemption from immunity.[179] In a second order, the same court even more specifically addressed the nature of the IFC's immunity from suit under US law. The court noted that the issue of whether 'the IOIA incorporates the subsequently enacted FSIA . . . is an unsettled question' and went on to hold that it had to 'adhere to the plain language of the IOIA, which affords to international organizations only the immunity of foreign governments'.[180]

An English court came to a similar conclusion in the course of the Tin Council litigation. The International Tin Council (Immunities and Privileges) Order 1972 which implemented the relevant provisions of the UK–ITC Headquarters Agreement provided for a scope of immunity analogous to the one enjoyed by states. In *Standard Chartered Bank* v. *International Tin Council and others*,[181] an English court rejected the argument that the immunity of an international organization ought to be interpreted in accordance with the law of sovereign immunity at the time the Order was enacted which in effect meant in accordance with an absolute immunity standard.[182] The court, however, did not directly apply a restrictive immunity standard in the sense that it denied immunity by qualifying the underlying activity as a commercial one. Rather, it refused to apply the rule stemming from absolute immunity according to which a foreign 'sovereign could effectively waive his immunity not by agreeing in advance to submit to English jurisdiction but only by an actual submission to the jurisdiction in the face of the court'.[183] Consequently, it gave effect to an advance waiver in accordance with the law of sovereign immunity as applicable at the time of decision.[184]

Implicit exceptions concerning real property and counterclaims

In a fashion similar to the Italian courts' interpretation of absolute immunity as really meaning restrictive immunity,[185] it has been asked whether – in the face of seemingly clear and unequivocal treaty provisions – an implicit exception deriving from customary international law can be read into a treaty text.

It has been suggested that one such implicit exception might relate to

---

[179] 942 F. Supp. 621 at 627 (DDC 1996).   [180] 932 F. Supp. 19 at 24 (DDC 1996).
[181] High Court, Queen's Bench Division (Commercial Court), 17 April 1986.
[182] The court reasoned thus: 'Whatever the merits of this doctrine [of absolute immunity] as between personal sovereigns or sovereign states, it is not obviously apt to be applied to a body such as the ITC of which sovereign states are no more than members and whose own sovereign status is said to have a certain Cheshire cat quality.' 77 ILR (1988) at 16.
[183] *Ibid.*   [184] See pp. 217ff below as to the issue of advance waivers of immunity.
[185] *Cf.* pp. 190ff above.

actions concerning real property.[186] In *Procurateur Général près de la Cour de Cassation* v. *Société Immobilière Alfred Dehodencq*,[187] the French Supreme Court, however, clearly rejected such a suggested limitation. The Organization for European Economic Cooperation (OEEC) had started to construct office buildings in Paris. Upon the request of the owners of an adjoining piece of real property, who claimed that they were entitled to an easement precluding anyone to erect an office building on the land then owned by OEEC, the court of first instance enjoined the OEEC from continuing with the construction. The *Procurateur Général* appealed this decision, and the Cour de Cassation held that the OEEC enjoyed complete immunity from suit in France and thus set aside the court of first instance's decision. In particular, it held that the Protocol to the Convention for European Economic Co-operation of 16 April 1948 granting immunity to the OEEC had the 'definite object of conferring complete immunity from jurisdiction on OEEC and, as a necessary consequence thereof, of eliminating the distinction sometimes made between actions concerning immovable and actions concerning movable property'.[188]

A recent US case, however, denying any special exemption from local zoning law *vis-à-vis* the Pan American Health Organization indicates that international organizations may also be subject to the local jurisdiction in other matters concerning real property. In *Pan American Health Organization* v. *Montgomery County, Maryland, County Council for Montgomery County*,[189] the Court of Appeals of Maryland rejected the plaintiff's contention that the defendant's zoning regulation was invalid 'because the County lack[ed] zoning authority over public international organizations'.[190]

The possibility of being exposed to counterclaims – normally not expressly mentioned in treaty immunity provisions[191] – is sometimes re-

---

[186] Freymond investigates whether an exception of the ILO's immunity from local judicial jurisdiction can be ascertained for 'actions immobilières réelles' although the relevant headquarters agreement between Switzerland and ILO in its Article 6 provides for 'immunité à l'égard de toute forme d'action judiciaire'. Pierre Freymond, 'Remarques sur l'immunité de juridiction des organisations internationales en matière immobilière' (1955–6) 53 *Friedens-Warte* 365–79 at 365ff. He denies such a restriction, interestingly enough not because he regards the existence of an implicit limitation untenable, but rather because – after a review of the relevant case law – he concludes that general international law does not contain such an exception for 'real property actions'.

[187] Cour de Cassation, 6 July 1954.   [188] (1954) 21 ILR 280.

[189] Court of Appeals of Maryland, 11 May 1995.

[190] 228 Md 214 at 220 (Court of Appeals Md).

[191] One of the few exceptional rules relating to counterclaims is provided for in the 1990 Dutch Host State Agreement with the Iran–United States Claims Tribunal. Article 4 provides: '(1) If the Tribunal institutes or intervenes in proceedings before a court in the

garded as a customary-law-based exception to the principle of immunity.[192] Although apparently not expressly decided in the existing case law, an *obiter dictum* in *Balfour, Guthrie & Co. Ltd et al. v. United States et al.*[193] seems to indicate that a US court allowing a lawsuit brought by the UN against the US, in an action for damages concerning the shipment of goods, would not allow the plaintiff's assertion of immunity in the case of counterclaims. It rejected the US argument that, because of the UN's immunity, an equitable judicial settlement could not be had and held: 'For the United Nations submits to our courts when it urges its claim and cannot consequently shut off any proper defenses of the United States.'[194]

Functional immunity

It is widely perceived that international organizations generally enjoy or should enjoy functional immunity,[195] but the content and scope of functional immunity is far from precise.[196] While some, if not the majority of jurists, suggest that the notion of functional immunity is merely synonymous with absolute immunity,[197] others maintain that 'functional' has a genuine meaning making it discernible from 'absolute', 'relative', and other standards of immunity. Whether functional immunity should be limited to the exercise of an international organization's official functions, whether it should be understood as a *renvoi* to diplomatic or consular law, etc., there appears to be no readily ascertainable consensus

Netherlands, it submits, for the purpose of those proceedings, to the jurisdiction of the Netherlands courts. (2) In such cases the Tribunal cannot claim immunity from the jurisdiction of the courts in respect of a counterclaim if the counterclaim arises from the legal relationship or the facts on which the principal claim is based.'

[192] Dominicé, 'L'immunité de juridiction', 184. According to Schermers such a customary 'refinement of the law' is derived from diplomatic law. Schermers, *International Institutional Law*, 796. See also pp. 361f below.

[193] USDC ND Cal., 5 May 1950. See also pp. 47f above.

[194] (1950) 17 ILR 323 at 326.

[195] See *Restatement (Third)*, § 467, para. 1: 'Under international law, an international organization generally enjoys such privileges and immunities from the jurisdiction of a member state as are necessary for the fulfillment of the purposes of the organization, including immunity from legal process, and from financial controls, taxes, and duties.'

[196] Jean-Flavien Lalive, 'L'immunité de juridiction des états et des organisations internationales' (1953 III) 84 *Recueil des Cours* 205–396 at 304.

[197] *Cf.* the *amicus curiae* brief of the UN in *Marvin R. Broadbent et al. v. OAS et al.* on differentiating between sovereign and 'organizational' immunity: 'Consequently the immunities of States are those attributable to sovereigns and thus reflect those that States reserve to themselves, whether absolute or relative; those of international organizations are functional and thus reflect their needs, which require complete protection from national jurisdiction.' (1980) *United Nations Juridical Yearbook* 224 at 230.

concerning most of these important aspects.[198] Sometimes it even appears that this lack of precision is not totally unwelcome.[199]

The fundamental problem is clearly that functional immunity means different, and indeed contradictory, things to different people or rather different judges and states. The following section tries to shed light on the meaning and interpretations the notion of functional immunity has received before national courts. In a later section the potential for future developments – inherent in a functional immunity concept – will be discussed.[200]

Areas covered by functional immunity in court decisions

National courts, called upon to apply a functional immunity standard, demonstrate a certain uneasiness with this concept. In particular, they seem to have difficulties to navigate their way through the scylla of absolute and the charybdis of restrictive immunity when interpreting the meaning of functional immunity. Thus, some decisions seem to simply rely on an equalization of functional with *iure imperii* acts, while another line of cases – probably inspired by the traditional absolute immunity rationale – considerably widens the scope of functional immunity.

It is interesting to note that in a number of decisions in employment and lease disputes, which in an inter-state context would not be considered to warrant immunity, have been regarded as covered by functional immunity.

Employment disputes

Boimah v. United Nations General Assembly[201] illustrates the willingness of US courts to view staff disputes of international organizations as covered by the international organizations' immunity: '[A]n international organization's self-regulation of its employment practices is an activity essential to the "fulfillment of its purposes," and thus an area to which immunity

---

[198] See pp. 331ff below.

[199] The UN Office of Legal Affairs, for instance, when dealing with the functional immunity of one of its officials, observed that: 'There is no precise definition of the expressions "official capacity", "official duties", or "official business". These are functional expressions and must be related to a particular context. Indeed, it is doubtful whether a definition would be desirable since it would not be in the interest of the organization to be bound by a definition which may fail to take into account the many and varied activities of United Nations officials.' UN Office of Legal Affairs, 'Letter to the Legal Liaison Officer, UNIDO' (1977) *United Nations Juridical Yearbook* 247.

[200] See pp. 330ff below.   [201] US District Court EDNY, 24 July 1987.

must extend.'[202] A similar qualification of employment issues was reached in two US cases brought not against organizations directly, but rather against their highest officials. In *Donald* v. *Orfila*,[203] the former Secretary-General of the Organization of American States was sued for allegedly unlawful interference with the plaintiff's employment contract and the intentional infliction of emotional distress. The court, however, found that 'personnel management was among the functional duties of the defendant as Secretary-General'[204] for which he enjoyed immunity from suit. Similarly, in *Kissi* v. *De Larosiere*,[205] a US citizen brought an employment discrimination suit against the Managing Director of the International Monetary Fund (IMF) alleging that he had been unlawfully denied a position within the IMF. Noting the functional immunity of IMF officials with respect to acts performed in their official capacity, the court dismissed the action since the 'law could not be clearer as to the defendant's immunity from this suit, which undeniably involves action by defendant, in rejecting plaintiff's employment applications, in his official capacity'.[206]

In *Mukoro* v. *European Bank for Reconstruction and Development and another*,[207] an English court affirmed the EBRD's immunity from suit brought by a potential employee alleging unlawful racial discrimination in rejecting his application for employment.[208] Under the applicable

---

[202] 664 F. Supp. 69 at 71 (EDNY 1987). The plaintiff, who was temporarily employed by the UN, sued under the US Civil Rights Act alleging employment discrimination because he was denied a permanent position. The court held that the UN General Assembly 'as one of the six principal organs of the United Nations . . . enjoys these same immunities [as provided in the General Convention and in the IOIA]'. *Ibid.*, 71. It found that, as far as employment disputes were concerned, the UN enjoyed immunity from suit in US courts either under the 'absolute' immunity grant of the General Convention or under the IOIA, because – even if that immunity was restrictive as a result of the FSIA – an employment relationship with an organization's internal staff was not 'commercial activity'. *Ibid.*

[203] US District Court DC, 30 July 1985, *affirmed*, US Court of Appeals DC Cir., 18 April 1986.

[204] 618 F. Supp. 645 at 648 (1985).

[205] US District Court DC, 23 June 1982.

[206] US District Court DC, 23 June 1982 (unpublished).

[207] Employment Appeal Tribunal, 19 March 1994.

[208] The plaintiff appealed the industrial tribunal's decision to dismiss his complaint for lack of jurisdiction over the defendants who – in the tribunal's view – enjoyed immunity from suit and legal process according to relevant legislation. On appeal, the applicant argued that the immunity conferred upon the defendants, which covered 'official activities', did not extend to unlawful acts and that the order conferring immunity for 'official activities' was *ultra vires* the International Organisations Act 1968 which limited the potential grant of immunities contained in Orders in Council to the extent 'required to be conferred in accordance with any agreement to which the United Kingdom . . . is then a party'. At the time the order was made the only applicable agreement requiring

immunity regime the EBRD was to enjoy functional immunity for 'official acts'. The court held that the activity qualified as 'official' was the selection of staff for employment and not the alleged unlawful discrimination which concerned only 'the mode of performance of the activities and the consequences of performance'. The order expressly interpreted 'official activities of the bank' to include 'its administrative activities' which in the court's view clearly covered staff selection procedures. This precedent was recently followed in *Bertolucci v. European Bank for Reconstruction and Development and others*,[209] a sexual discrimination claim dismissed because of the EBRD's immunity from suit. The Employment Appeal Tribunal expressly held that 'staff management falls within the acts performed by managers in their official capacity, whether or not it was performed in a discriminatory manner, and the employment of staff and management of staff relations falls within the official activities of the Bank'.[210]

In *AS v. Iran–United States Claims Tribunal*,[211] the Dutch Supreme Court held that national courts lacked jurisdiction over a suit brought by an employee of an international organization for unjustified dismissal. It assumed an unwritten rule of international law providing for jurisdictional immunity of international organizations[212] according to which an 'international organization is in principle not subject to the jurisdiction of the courts of the host State in respect of all disputes which are immediately connected with the performance of the tasks entrusted to the organization in question'.[213] The court found that since the plaintiff 'belonged to the category of employees of the Tribunal who play an essential role in the performance of the tasks entrusted to the Tribunal'[214] the tribunal's functional immunity prevented the plaintiff from successfully bringing it before the Dutch courts.

immunities was the agreement establishing the Bank. This treaty included immunity provisions for Bank officials and employees, but no immunity from suit for the Bank itself. Full immunity from suit and legal process was only provided for in the headquarters agreement with the United Kingdom which was concluded after the order was made. The Employment Appeal Tribunal rejected both contentions. As far as the *ultra vires* argument was concerned, it held that the reference in the 1968 Act to 'agreement[s] to which the United Kingdom . . . is then a party' required an international obligation at the time the order takes effect, not – as the applicant contended – at the time the order is made. Since the order provided that it should enter into force on the date on which the headquarters agreement entered into force, the United Kingdom was 'then a party' to an agreement requiring such immunity. (1997) 107 ILR 604–13.

[209] Employment Appeal Tribunal, EAT/276/97, 19 August 1997.
[210] Employment Appeal Tribunal, EAT/276/97, 19 August 1997, Lexis transcript.
[211] Supreme Court, 20 December 1985.   [212] See pp. 157 and 167 above.
[213] (1987) 18 *Netherlands Yearbook of International Law* 360.   [214] *Ibid.*, 361.

The German decision in *T* v. *European Patent Organization*[215] evidences that national courts are often willing to regard employment matters to be covered even by a very strict functional immunity standard. The plaintiff worked as a patent registrar with the European Patent Agency in Munich. In his application he sought to annul the Agency's decision to transfer him to a different workplace. He argued that the organization's immunity which was limited to its 'official activities'[216] extended only to issues relating to the grant of patents for inventions and that his employment dispute was therefore not exempted from the jurisdiction of the German courts. On appeal, the Bavarian administrative court rejected this claim arguing that 'official activities' covered all activities that are strictly necessary for the organization's administrative and technical work. Accordingly, the notion of 'official activities' included the legal relationship between the EPO and its employees.[217]

In a number of cases arising from similar employment situations – although formally decided on the basis of a *iure imperii* immunity standard – Italian courts have refused to exercise jurisdiction because the employment relationship in question was considered to be closely linked to the fulfilment of the defendant organization's functions. In *ICEM* v. *Di Banella Schirone*,[218] the Italian Supreme Court held that the secretarial work performed by the plaintiff was – 'although instrumental in nature' – 'undoubtedly of a public character and ... directly connected with the pursuit of [ICEM's] institutional aims'.[219] Stressing the 'functional relationship' between her and ICEM, the court obviously regarded all employment contracts whose aim it was to further the international organization's aims to fall within the *iure imperii* category. Practically the same

---

[215] Administrative Court Munich, 19 December 1990, Bavarian Appellate Administrative Court Munich, 13 November 1991.

[216] 'Within the scope of its official activities the Organisation shall have immunity from jurisdiction and execution.' 'Official activities' are those which 'are strictly necessary for its administrative and technical operation, as set out in the Convention'. Article 3(1) and (4) of the EPO Privileges and Immunities Protocol.

[217] 'Nach Art. 3 Abs. 4 Privilegienprotokoll sind unter "amtlicher Tätigkeit" alle Tätigkeiten zu verstehen, die für ihre im Übereinkommen vorgesehene Verwaltungsarbeit und technische Arbeit unbedingt erforderlich sind. Hiervon ausgehend erfaßt der vorgenannte Begriff auch die Rechtsbeziehungen zwischen der EPO und ihren Bediensteten ... Denn zur Verwaltungsarbeit und technischen Arbeit der EPO gehört die Personalverwaltung notwendig dazu; sie könnte ohne einen entsprechenden Mitarbeiterstab, der für die Erfüllung ihrer Aufgaben im Sinne des Art. 3 Abs. 4 Privilegienprotokoll "unbedingt erforderlich" ist, die ihr zukommende Prüfertätigkeit nicht leisten.' Bavarian Appellate Administrative Court Munich, 13 November 1991, 3 B 91.1972 (unpublished).

[218] Corte di Cassazione, 8 April 1975. See also p. 190 above.

[219] (1988) 77 ILR 575.

result was reached in *ICEM* v. *Chiti*.[220] Similarly, in *Giovanni Porru* v. *FAO*,[221] an employment suit by a former FAO employee, a court in Rome held that 'acts by which an international organization arranges its internal structure fall undoubtedly in the category of acts performed in the exercise of its established function and that in this respect therefore the organizations enjoys immunity from jurisdiction'.[222]

Probably the most far-reaching decision in this context was rendered by a Berlin labour court in *X* v. *European Patent Organization*.[223] When construing the scope of the EPO's functional immunity, the German court held that such immunity also covered the temporary employment of local workers. In its view:

the employment of personnel in order to fulfil its official functions . . . is part of the official activities of an organization which are strictly necessary in order to perform the administrative tasks provided for in the [European Patent] agreement. Without personnel [the] defendant cannot fulfil its administrative duties. In this respect one cannot differentiate whether the respective employee himself performs an official task, fulfills any other externally visible function and whether he ranks high in the hierarchy of the organization or whether he is entrusted with inferior auxiliary duties which are not directly perceived by the public or by contractual partners of the organization. Also the latter type of activities are indispensable for the administrative work.[224]

In *Maida* v. *Administration for International Assistance*,[225] the Italian Supreme Court considered a dispute arising from a contract for the provi-

---

[220] Corte di Cassazione, 7 November 1973. See also pp. 190f above.

[221] Rome Court of First Instance, 25 June 1969.

[222] (1969) *United Nations Juridical Yearbook* 238 at 239. First, the Court reaffirmed the Italian view that 'immunity could only be recognized with regard to public law activities, i.e. in the *case of an international organization with regard to activities by which it pursues its specific purpose* (iure imperii) but not with regard to private law activities where the organization acts on an equal footing with individuals (uti privatus)'. *Ibid.*

[223] Labour Court Berlin-Charlottenburg, 22 February 1994; State Labour Court Berlin, 12 September 1994.

[224] 'Die Einstellung von Personal zur Erfüllung ihrer amtlichen Aufgaben . . . gehört zur "amtlichen Tätigkeit" der Organisation, die für ihre im Übereinkommen vorgesehenen Verwaltungsarbeit "unbedingt erforderlich" ist. Ohne Personal kann die Beklagte ihre Verwaltungsaufgaben nicht erfüllen. Dabei kann nicht danach unterschieden werden, ob der betreffende Bedienstete eine hoheitliche Aufgabe, eine sonst nach außen in Erscheinung tretende Arbeitsaufgabe unmittelbar selbst wahrnimmt und ob er in der Unternehmenshierarchie hoch angesiedelt ist, oder ob er mit subalternen Hilfsaufgaben betraut ist, die vom Publikum oder von Vertragspartner der Organisation nicht unmittelbar wahrgenommen werden. Auch letztere Tätigkeiten sind für die Verwaltungsarbeit unverzichtbar.' State Labour Court Berlin, 12 September 1994, 16 Sa 58/94 (unpublished).

[225] Corte di Cassazione, 27 May 1955. See also pp. 224f below.

sion of medical expertise by an Italian doctor, concluded outside the institutional framework of an organization (who was thus employed on the basis of a private contract, and not appointed as an official), to be covered by functional immunity. In the court's view, employment contracts of doctors like the plaintiff were:

directly linked with the institutional purposes of the IRO, the doctor being appointed for the performance of tasks [sanitary services] within the specific scope for which the Organization has been established. The transaction [contract of employment between the plaintiff and the IRO], therefore, of which the contract to perform professional work forms part, is – so to speak – merged in the public purposes of the international organization, and the rule of exemption from the jurisdiction should accordingly apply unless the IRO has waived its immunity.[226]

Lease contracts

The Austrian *E GmbH* v. *European Patent Organization*[227] case quite aptly illustrates the difficulties courts frequently have in applying a standard of functional or official immunity for international organizations. The plaintiff, an Austrian corporation owning buildings in Vienna, brought suit to recover rent arrears from its tenant, the European Patent Organization, and sought to evict it from the premises. While the lower court had rejected the claim for lack of jurisdiction, since it considered the lease of business space to be part of defendant's official activities, the Court of Appeals reversed and admitted the plaintiff's claim. It was clear from the seat agreement between the EPO and Austria that the organization should enjoy immunity from suit before the Austrian courts only for its 'official activities'.[228] In interpreting this agreement, the appellate court thought that only those administrative and technical activities strictly necessary for the granting of European patents could be considered 'official activities'[229] while all other acts of a private law nature were subject to Austrian jurisdiction. In order to differentiate between official and private acts, the court referred to the generally accepted distinction in the field of sovereign immunity between acts *iure imperii* and acts *iure*

---

[226] (1965) 23 ILR 512.   [227] Austrian Supreme Court, 11 June 1992.

[228] Article 4 of the EPO Vienna Sub-Office Headquarters Agreement with Austria.

[229] This interpretation could be supported by the definition of the term 'official activities' in the headquarters agreement. Article 1(f) defines them as 'any activities strictly necessary for the administrative and technical work which the European Patent Organization is required to perform by the Convention on the Grant of European Patents of 5 October 1973'. EPO Vienna Sub-Office Headpuorteo Agreement with Austria. See also the similar definition in Article 3 of the EPO Privileges and Immunities Protocol. *Cf.* p. 209 note 216 above.

gestionis which would lie in the nature of the act concerned. If an activity could be exercised by a private individual, it would have to be qualified as *iure gestionis* act. Since this was the case with a lease agreement, the claim was amenable to suit.

The Supreme Court reversed and reinstated the dismissal order of the court of first instance. It reiterated the difference between the restrictive immunity of states and the further-reaching privileges of international organizations, expressly adopting Seidl-Hohenveldern's view that the immunity of international organizations – contrary to that of states – had to be regarded in principle absolute within the framework of its functional limitation (which coincided with the true sovereign purpose of the organization).[230] The court concluded that, as a result of a grammatical and teleological interpretation of the term 'official activity', the defendant exercised its functions according to the seat agreement at the premises in question, that for the administrative and technical activities performed in the exercise of these functions it was necessary to use adequate premises, and that, accordingly, the lease of such premises fell under 'official activity'. As a consequence, the defendant organization enjoyed immunity from suit.

Assertion of jurisdiction by qualifying activities outside the scope of functional immunity

In *Camera confederale del lavoro and Sindicato scuola CGIL v. Istituto di Bari del Centro internazionale di alti studi agronomici mediterranei*,[231] the Italian court of first instance applied a very strict standard of functional immunity demanding that actions, to be covered by immunity, must be such as could be held 'to be inherent in, or essential for, the institutional purposes of the Centre [constituting] the means which are necessary or appropriate for the attainment of those objectives'.[232] Since the court viewed the purpose of the Centre to lie in providing instruction in agricultural economics and technology and encouraging international cooperation in this field, it freely concluded that the anti-union acts complained of[233] were 'necessary neither in reason nor in law to ensure the achievement of the said aims'. As a consequence, it found that it had jurisdiction to entertain the complaint brought.[234]

---

[230] *Cf* p. 343 below.
[231] Pretore di Bari, 15 February 1974; Corte di Cassazione, 27 April 1979.
[232] (1977) 3 *Italian Yearbook of International Law* 315.   [233] See pp. 112f above.
[234] The decisions were, however, reversed by the Corte di Cassazione which granted immunity arguing, *inter alia*, that trade union labour relations fell outside the scope of Italian jurisdiction in a way similar to the law of foreign public officials and thus could not be adjudicated by the Italian courts. See p. 118 above.

A similar test was applied by the District of Columbia Court of Appeals in *Herbert Harvey Inc.* v. *National Labor Relations Board*.[235] Although not directly relating to the issue of the World Bank's own immunity from jurisdiction, but rather to the question of whether a contractor providing maintenance services for the Bank could enjoy immunity from the National Labor Relations Board's jurisdiction,[236] the court's reasoning also related to the World Bank. In the appellate court's view:

The World Bank is an international investment institution engaged in making or guaranteeing loans for productive reconstruction and development projects in the territories of its members. The Bank supplements its investment activities by providing technical assistance of various kinds to underdeveloped member countries. [Herbert Harvey Inc.'s] employees are engaged exclusively in the operation and maintenance of the buildings in which the World Bank is located. These housekeeping duties performed by [Herbert Harvey Inc.'s] employees have no connection with the functions of the World Bank as an investment institution.[237]

Accordingly, the petitioner's claim to enjoy a 'delegated' immunity was rejected. It seems, however, that under this rationale the World Bank's own employees of this rank would also not have been covered by the Bank's immunity.

To a certain extent – in addition to the Austrian decision of the appellate court in *E GmbH* v. *European Patent Organization*[238] which allowed a lawsuit brought by an international organization's landlord for rent arrears because it qualified such acts as concluding a lease agreement as outside the scope of an organization's official activities[239] – the Italian *cause célèbre* of *Food and Agriculture Organization* v. *Istituto Nazionale di Previdenze per i Dirigenti di Aziende Industriali (INPDAI)*[240] could also be interpreted as an assertion of jurisdiction over disputes involving international organizations by qualifying lease contracts to fall outside the scope of acts for which international organizations enjoy immunity. The case was mainly decided on state immunity principles which the Corte di Cassazione thought applicable. In order to determine the private domain character, however, the court relied less on a strict nature test than on a determination of the aims that such activities were intended to achieve and whether or not they were directly related to the institutional aims pursued by the foreign entity.

[235] US Court of Appeals DC Cir., 19 September 1969.
[236] *Cf.* pp. 174f above as to the facts of this case.   [237] 424 F. 2d 770 at 782 (DC Cir. 1969).
[238] Austrian Supreme Court, 11 June 1992.   [239] See pp. 221f above.
[240] Tribunale Roma, 24 January 1981; Corte di Cassazione, 18 October 1982. For more detail, see pp. 187f above.

The German appellate decision in *X et al.* v. *European School Munich II*[241] – upheld by the Federal Administrative Court – is also an example for a decision in which a national court asserted jurisdiction over activities of an international organization that went beyond its functional limits. The court held that the European School did not have the capacity to issue administrative tuition decisions and that German courts had jurisdiction to identify such a transgression of an international organization's powers where its *ultra vires* character was manifest.[242]

The *Manderlier* v. *Organisation des Nations Unies and Etat Belge (Ministre des Affaires Etrangères)*[243] case did not decide the issue of immunity from suit on the basis of Article 105 of the UN Charter because it dismissed the claim brought against the UN on the basis of the 'general and absolute' immunity from jurisdiction accorded to it in the General Convention. In an interesting *obiter dictum*, however, the Civil Tribunal of Brussels elaborated on its understanding of functional acts of international organizations. Regarding the allegedly tortious interference and destruction of the claimant's property by UN forces, the court – in assessing the scope of immunities and privileges under Article 105 of the UN Charter as those 'necessary to [the UN] for the fulfilment of its purposes' – held that '[t]hose purposes, as enumerated in Article I of the Charter, do not include acts against private citizens such as are the subject of the plaintiff's complaints'.[244] It seems to follow that tortious acts qualified as non-functional would thus not be considered to merit immunity.

Broad waiver interpretation

Even if international organizations enjoyed immunity from suit according to specific applicable rules, courts could assert jurisdiction over lawsuits involving them as defendants where this immunity has been waived. Normally the existence of a waiver of immunity by an interna-

---

[241] Administrative Court Munich, 29 June 1992; Bavarian Administrative Court Munich, 15 March 1995; Federal Administrative Court, 9 October 1995.

[242] 'Mit dem Erlaß von als Verwaltungsakte zu verstehenden Bescheiden über die Erhebung von Schulgeld gegenüber den Eltern "anderer Kinder", die nicht Angehörige der Europäischen Patentorganisation sind, überschreitet die Europäische Schule München offenkundig die ihr nach den ihr zugrundeliegenden völkerrechtlichen Verträgen zustehende Rechtsmacht (Handeln '*ultra vires*'); sie unterliegt insoweit der deutschen Gerichtsbarkeit; die Offenkundigkeit dieser Befugnisüberschreitung kann jedenfalls dann von den nationalen Gerichten festgestellt werden, wenn sie sich aus dem eigenen Vortrag der internationalen Organisation ergibt.' Bavarian Administrative Court, 7th Chamber, Munich, 15 March 1995, (1996) *Deutsches Verwaltungsblatt* 448.

[243] Civil Tribunal of Brussels, 11 May 1966; Brussels Appeals Court, 15 September 1969.

[244] (1972) 45 ILR 446 at 453.

tional organization is an issue of assessing a legally relevant act performed by someone empowered to act for an international organization.
This usually does not leave much discretion to domestic courts. Since a
number of questions concerning the law and practice of waivers of
immunity remain unsettled or unclear as a matter of the applicable
provisions, courts might sometimes engage in judicial 'activism' in order
to decide a specific case.

Most relevant treaties and domestic legal instruments contain express
waiver provisions. The availability and exact scope of the possibility of a
waiver, however, varies – a fact that, in turn, might give rise to a number
of different interpretations by courts. The broadest waiver regimes provide a possibility to waive immunity both *ad hoc* and in advance by
contractual stipulation; the respective waiver regimes usually provide for
immunity 'except to the extent that [the organization] expressly waives
its immunity for the purpose of any proceedings or by the terms of any
contract'.[245] In other instruments, waivers are foreseen 'only for particular cases',[246] while some even provide for an organization's duty to waive
its immunity.[247] Other applicable immunity rules do not contain any
language indicating the possibility of waiver of immunity at all. These
two situations have given rise to a considerable degree of disagreement
whether advance waivers or waivers in general are legally effective if not
contemplated in the basic immunity regime.

A waiver of immunity is a renunciation of a particular right a person
would otherwise enjoy.[248] To 'waive' one's immunity presupposes that
one enjoys immunity as a matter of international or domestic law. Where
immunity is not granted as a matter of law one cannot properly speak of a
waiver. Thus, in a number of the probably best-known 'waiver of immunity' cases involving international organizations, such waiver should be
understood metaphorically and not in a technical sense. In these cases,
the US courts have developed a jurisprudence of delimiting the scope of
the immunity of international lending institutions such as the World
Bank and various regional development banks by discussing a 'waiver of
immunity' contained in their constituent texts. However, such waiver

---

[245] E.g., Article IX(3) of the IMF Articles of Agreement; Title I, section 2(b) of the IOIA.

[246] E.g., Article II(2) of the General Convention.

[247] E.g., Article XV(2) (Article IV(1)(a), Annex I) of the ESA Convention providing that 'the
Council has the duty to waive this immunity in all cases where reliance upon it would
impede the course of justice and it can be waived without prejudicing the interests of
the Agency'.

[248] *Cf.* Michael Singer, 'Jurisdictional Immunity of International Organizations: Human
Rights and Functional Necessity Concerns' (1995) 36 *Virginia Journal of International Law*
53–165 at 73.

was not performed as a unilateral act renouncing a prerogative the organizations would have otherwise enjoyed, but rather was the result of an interpretation of the applicable treaty law. Thus, the term 'waiver' is technically inaccurate.[249] The reason why US courts use the expression 'waiver' in such situations probably has to do with domestic law. The applicable statute, the IOIA, provides for 'absolute' immunity except if 'waived' by the organization.[250] Thus, from the perspective of US law, any restriction of an international organization's immunity has to be interpreted as a 'waiver' of immunity.

The leading case is *Lutcher SA Celulose e Papel* v. *Inter-American Development Bank*,[251] where a Brazilian corporation brought suit for damages and sought an injunction against the Inter-American Development Bank (IDB). The plaintiff argued that loans made or about to be made to the plaintiff's competitors violated an 'implied obligation' of its own loan agreement with the Bank to act prudently in considering loan applications from competitors. Although the federal appellate court affirmed the district court's dismissal for failure to state a claim, it disagreed with the lower court's alternative reasoning that the Bank enjoyed immunity from suit. The District of Columbia Circuit Court interpreted Article XI(3) of the IDB Articles of Agreement[252] as a broad 'waiver of immunity' of the Bank which would, thus, in general allow a suit brought by a borrower against the Bank.

The second famous waiver case restricted the scope of *Lutcher's* potential reach. In *Mendaro* v. *World Bank*,[253] the same court held that the waiver of Article VII(3) of the Articles of Agreement of the IBRD[254] – a provision worded identically to Article XI(3) of the IDB Articles of Agreement – related only to suits in respect of external affairs of the Bank, not to employment suits for which domestic courts lacked jurisdiction. The Argentine plaintiff's appointment, employed by the World Bank as a researcher, came to an end in 1979. Claiming that she was the victim of

---

[249] The court in *Mendaro* realized that the provision of the Articles of Agreement could not be read as an 'express waiver by the Bank of its immunity to [a] particular suit', but might rather be seen as a 'functional waiver'. 717 F. 2d 610 at 614 (DC Cir. 1983). It has also been termed 'constitutive waiver'. Singer, 'Jurisdictional Immunity of International Organizations', 80.

[250] Title I, section 2(b) of the IOIA provides: 'International organizations, their property and their assets, wherever located, and by whomsoever held, shall enjoy the same immunity from suit and every form of judicial process as is enjoyed by foreign governments, except to the extent that such organizations may expressly waive their immunity for the purpose of any proceedings or by the terms of any contract.'

[251] US Court of Appeals DC Cir., 13 July 1967.   [252] See pp. 141 and 164 above.

[253] US Court of Appeals DC Cir., 27 September 1983.

[254] See p. 141 note 545 above.

sexual discrimination and harassment, she filed a complaint with the US Equal Employment Opportunity Commission alleging that her rights under Title VII of the US Civil Rights Act of 1964 had been violated. In *Mendaro v. McNamara*,[255] the Commission dismissed for lack of jurisdiction. The District of Columbia District Court and, on appeal, the District of Columbia Court of Appeals affirmed the dismissal.

In Germany a number of more recent decisions rendered in the course of proceedings brought against the European School Munich were also decided on the basis of a perceived waiver of immunity (*Immunitätsverzicht*) resulting from an organization's statute. In *X et al. v. European School Munich I*[256] as well as in *X et al. v. European School Munich II*,[257] the German courts construed the school's personality clause conferring capacity to sue and to be sued as an implied waiver of the organization's immunity.[258] This interpretation was corrected by the German appellate court in *X et al. v. European School Munich II*,[259] clarifying that the personality clause in question related only to the legal status of the European School under domestic law and did not intend to waive its immunity. It further reaffirmed that any waiver of immunity had to be express.[260]

The possibility of an advance waiver in the absence of a provision contemplating it in the relevant immunity regime

The General Convention's grant of immunity 'except insofar as in any particular case it [the UN] has expressly waived its immunity'[261] is a typical case of a waiver provision that appears to accept only *ad hoc*

---

[255] Equal Employment Opportunity Commission, 12 February 1980.

[256] Bavarian Administrative Court Munich, 23 August 1989.

[257] Administrative Court Munich, 29 June 1992; Bavarian Administrative Court Munich, 15 March 1995; Federal Administrative Court, 9 October 1995.

[258] 'Gemäß ... Art. 6 Satz 3 der Satzung der Europäischen Schule kann die ESM vor Gericht klagen und verklagt werden. Da hierbei nicht auf eine europäische Gerichtsbarkeit Bezug genommen wird, insbesondere die Europäischen Schulen nicht der Zuständigkeit des Gerichtshofs der Europäischen Gemeinschaften unterstellt werden, ist diese Aussage dahin zu verstehen, daß die Europäischen Schulen sich der Gerichtsbarkeit des Landes ihres jeweiligen Sitzes unterwerfen.' Bavarian Administrative Court Munich, 7th Chamber, Munich, 23 August 1989, (1989) 24 *EuropaRecht* 359 at 361. 'Dies kann nach dem Beschluß des BayVGH ... nur so verstanden werden, daß sich die Europäischen Schulen der Gerichtsbarkeit des Landes ihres jeweiligen Sitzes unterwerfen.' Bavarian Administrative Court Munich, 29 June 1992 (unpublished).

[259] Bavarian Administrative Court Munich, 15 March 1995.

[260] 'Auch der Wortlaut der Regelung im Sinne einer Statusgewährung spricht nicht für eine Unterwerfungsklausel, zumal nach einer verbreiteten Ansicht stets eine ausdrückliche Unterwerfung unter die innerstaatliche Gerichtsbarkeit erforderlich ist.' Bavarian Administrative Court, 7th Chamber, Munich, 15 March 1995, (1996) *Deutsches Verwaltungsblatt* 448.

[261] Article II(2) of the General Convention.

waivers of immunity. Such waiver clauses are normally silent on the availability of an advance waiver, for instance, in a contract with a private party, although the required 'particularity' is probably broad enough to cover an advance waiver for particular kinds of disputes.

Ad hoc waiver provisions

The question of whether an advance waiver of immunity is legally possible at all has turned out to be rather controversial. The prevailing opinion among jurists seems to deny such a possibility.[262] In line with this view the UN has adhered to a practice of deciding whether to waive immunity or not in an *ad hoc* fashion.[263] In the case of the General Convention this assumption is supported by the peculiarities of its drafting history. An original proposal containing the wider phrase 'except to the extent that it expressly waives its immunity for the purpose of any proceedings or by the terms of a contract' was later dropped. It thus appears plausible to conclude that it was not the intention of the drafters of the General Convention 'to extend the right of waiver to waiver in future by the terms of a contract'.[264] This *a contrario* argument is bolstered by the fact that other instruments expressly provide for the possibility of an advance waiver in contracts. One can thus conclude that if such possibility is not contained in the relevant instrument it is excluded. General policy considerations demanding a high level of protection for international organizations might also support such a – for international organizations very advantageous – conclusion.

On the other hand, reflections on the policy justifications for allowing or excluding advance waivers where the controlling texts do not expressly address the issue might as well go the other way. Treaty provisions on immunity protect international organizations against intervention by state organs. Where they renounce such protection in a contract, international organizations do not violate any right of the state but merely abandon their own rights. Moreover, the language of waiver provisions as

---

[262] Without giving reasons, the *Restatement (Third)* denies that this is an option for the UN under the General Convention. *Restatement (Third)*, § 467, Reporters' Note 7. Equally, in an internal legal memorandum prepared by the Office of Legal Affairs of the UN in 1948, the possibility of an anticipated waiver of immunity in a contractual clause is rejected. Reprinted in part in *Yearbook of the International Law Commission* (1967), vol. II, 225.

[263] (1975) *United Nations Juridical Yearbook* 160ff.

[264] Opinion of the UN Office of Legal Affairs, in United Nations Secretariat, 'The Practice of the United Nations, the Specialized Agencies and the International Atomic Energy Agency Concerning Their Status, Privileges and Immunities', *Yearbook of the International Law Commission* (1967), vol. II, 225.

the one contained in the General Convention is far from clear. Why should an advance contractual waiver of immunity concerning disputes arising out of a certain contract not be regarded a waiver 'in a particular case'? Certainly, a contractual waiver usually contemplates particular types of controversies that may arise. Sometimes domestic courts have been quite unimpressed by this discussion and simply upheld their jurisdiction by regarding an advance waiver as one made 'in a particular case'.

In *Standard Chartered Bank* v. *International Tin Council and others*,[265] an English court rejected the argument that an advance waiver[266] should be invalid because the applicable immunity regime required waivers to be 'in a particular case'.[267] The judge said that '[t]he waiver must be in a particular case, but that in my view means no more than that it must relate to a specific transaction. I find no warrant in the language for reading the phrase "in a particular case" as if it meant "a particular dispute" or "a particular legal proceeding".'[268] Accordingly, he upheld his jurisdiction and gave judgment on the merits.

In *Arab Banking Corporation* v. *International Tin Council and Algemene Bank Nederland and others (Interveners) and Holco Trading Company Ltd (Interveners)*,[269] another sequel to the ITC litigation, the English High Court interpreted a choice of forum clause in favour of English courts[270] as a waiver of immunity from suit that could be effectively performed in advance. Although the court rejected the relief sought,[271] it implicitly held that an advance waiver contained in a contract could be valid where the applicable international and domestic waiver provision required that the organization 'shall have expressly waived its immunity in a particular case'.

---

[265] High Court, Queen's Bench Division (Commercial Court), 17 April 1986.

[266] Standard Chartered Bank brought suit against the ITC for default in repayment of a UK£10 million loan after the ITC's inability to meet its financial obligations in late 1985. The bank relied on a choice of law and a choice of forum clause in the credit agreement as follows: 'This facility letter shall be governed by and interpreted in accordance with English law and you hereby irrevocably submit to the non-exclusive jurisdiction of the High Court of Justice in England and consent to the giving of any relief and/or the issue of any process for enforcement or otherwise against you.'

[267] The ITC disputed the court's jurisdiction, contending that waivers of immunity could not extend to contractual undertakings because the Headquarters Agreement required waivers 'in a particular case' and thus they could not be made in advance.

[268] (1988) 77 ILR 16.   [269] High Court, Queen's Bench Division, 15 January 1986.

[270] The ITC had consented to a provision in a loan agreement according to which the contract should be subject to the non-exclusive 'jurisdiction of the English courts'.

[271] *Cf.* pp. 220f below for the detailed facts.

Provisions that are silent on the question of waivers

Similarly, if the possibility of a waiver of immunity is not directly contemplated in the applicable immunity clause at all,[272] one might raise the question of whether the option of a waiver is still available. This could be denied on the ground that the possibility to waive its immunity forms part of the internal law of an organization, an internal law that cannot be transgressed to the detriment of its members.

The contrary view, however, regards the ability to waive its immunity either as an organization's 'inherent power'[273] or as an option that is always available because it does not infringe upon any obligation *vis-à-vis* another subject of international law, but merely renounces its own right to increased protection.[274]

Waiver of immunity from enforcement measures

Some immunity regimes appear to exclude the possibility to waive immunity from execution at all.[275] One could, however, interpret such clauses as mere precautionary rules providing that waivers of immunity from suit as such should not be construed as waivers of immunity from execution.[276] In other words, immunity from execution would still be regarded as legally possible but would require an additional act.

What seems to be frequently in issue is the question of whether a waiver performed by an international organization relates to its immunity from suit only or encompasses immunity from enforcement measures as well. In *Arab Banking Corporation* v. *International Tin Council and Algemene Bank Nederland and others (Interveners) and Holco Trading Company Ltd (Interveners)*,[277] the English High Court refused to regard a choice of forum clause in favour of English courts as a waiver of the ITC's immunity from

---

[272] This is the case in the constitutive texts of the World Bank and the International Development Association (IDA), *cf.* Article VII(3), (4) and (5) of the IBRD Articles of Agreement, 22 July 1944; and Article VIII(3), (4) and (5) of the IDA Articles of Agreement, 26 January 1960. See also Manfred Wenckstern, *Die Immunität internationaler Organisationen. Handbuch des Internationalen Zivilverfahrensrechts* (Tübingen, 1994), vol. II/1, 132.

[273] Ludwig Gramlich, 'Diplomatic Protection Against Acts of Intergovernmental Organs' (1984) 27 *German Yearbook of International Law* 386–428 at 394.

[274] Dominicé, 'L'immunité de juridiction', 183.

[275] *Cf.* the General Convention's provision concerning 'immunity from every form of legal process except insofar as in any particular case [the UN] has expressly waived its immunity. It is, however, understood that no waiver of immunity shall extend to any measure of execution.' Article II(2) of the General Convention.

[276] *Cf.* Kirgis, *Teacher's Manual*, 7.

[277] High Court, Queen's Bench Division, 15 January 1986.

execution. The plaintiff bank sought recovery of a UK£15 million loan made to the ITC and moved for a *Mareva* injunction[278] to restrain the defendant organization from removing funds from England.[279] The court denied this enforcement remedy. It found that the ITC, by consenting to a provision in the loan agreement according to which the contract would be subject to the non-exclusive 'jurisdiction of the English courts' had waived only its immunity from suit; in the court's view, however, it had not done so with respect to its immunity from enforcement actions.

The High Court held that immunity from legal process had to be equated with immunity from execution and that it was a wholly different concept than immunity from suit. Although the term 'jurisdiction' was ambiguous and could encompass both the adjudicative and the enforcement powers of a court, the High Court viewed it as relating to 'immunity from suit' only, since – as a general rule – waivers of immunity had to be interpreted restrictively. It was probably also decisive and, in fact, expressly noted by the court that in English legal practice the phrase 'immunity from suit' is used interchangeably with the phrase 'immunity from jurisdiction', in the same way as 'immunity from legal process' is considered to have the same meaning as the phrase 'immunity from execution'.[280]

Competent organ

Sometimes the provisions of waivers of immunity provide for which particular organ is competent to waive an international organization's immunity.[281] However, if this is not expressly provided for – as is true for

---

[278] Named after the decision in *Mareva Cia Naviera SA* v. *International Bulk Carriers SA*, Court of Appeal, 1980, this is an interlocutory injunction to restrain a defendant from removing his or her assets from the jurisdiction pending the trial of an action against him or her. *Cf.* Cheshire and North, *Private International Law* (ed. by P. M. North and J. J. Fawcett, 11th edn, London, 1987), 195.

[279] The plaintiff sought to prevent the anticipated negative effects of plans to transform the Tin Council into a new company which would have changed the bank's position from that of a lending bank into a trader of tin with no prospect of repayment if the market were to move against it.

[280] (1988) 77 ILR 6. Article 6 of the International Tin Council (Immunities and Privileges) Order 1972, the provision granting 'immunity from suit and legal process', corresponded to Article 8 of the Headquarters Agreement providing for 'immunity from jurisdiction and execution'.

[281] E.g., Article 3 of the General Agreement on Privileges and Immunities of the Council of Europe providing that the Committee of Ministers should expressly authorize waivers of immunity. See also Article XV(2) (Article IV(1)(a), Annex I) of the ESA Convention providing for the ESA Council to waive the Agency's immunity. See the further references in Wenckstern, *Die Immunität internationaler Organisationen*, 134, note 846.

the majority of organizations – the question of who is to be considered the 'appropriate organ of the international organization' by which a waiver is to be performed becomes pertinent. As far as the UN is concerned, it appears to be common agreement that this is only the Secretary-General in his capacity as chief administrative officer of the UN,[282] not executive directors of semi-independent programs, or others.[283]

The *Manderlier* v. *Organisation des Nations Unies and Etat Belge (Ministre des Affaires Etrangères)*[284] case aptly illustrated that courts are ready to accept waivers of immunity by an international organization only if made by the competent organ and expressly. In that case, the plaintiff had argued that the Belgian Minister of Foreign Affairs had stated publicly in the Belgian Senate that the UN had waived its immunity. The court, however, rejected this contention, holding that the Belgian minister 'cannot bind the United Nations, nor its Secretary-General, through declarations he makes in the Belgian Legislative Chamber'.[285]

Implicit waivers

Apart from express waivers of immunity, the law of jurisdictional immunity in general recognizes the possibility that a person enjoying such immunity might implicitly renounce it by certain acts. The most prominent of such implicit waivers is the provision for arbitration which is frequently also considered a renunciation of immunity from suit as far as actions relating to arbitration are concerned (i.e., the supervision of proceedings and/or enforcement of awards).[286] Choice of forum clauses,

---

[282] Article 97 of the UN Charter.

[283] Schermers, *International Institutional Law*, 796, quoting (1969) *United Nations Juridical Yearbook* 224ff. See also *Restatement (Third)*, § 467, Comment d. According to an internal legal memorandum prepared by the Office of Legal Affairs of the UN in 1948, a clarification of this competence in the General Convention – as in the case of waiver of UN officials' immunities by the Secretary-General and not the officials themselves – was not deemed necessary since this authority fell within the agenda of the Secretary-General as chief administrative officer. Reprinted in part in *Yearbook of the International Law Commission* (1967), vol. II, 225. In *Effect of Awards of Compensation Made by the United Nations Administrative Tribunal*, (1954) *ICJ Reports* 47 at 53, the ICJ held that 'the Secretary-General in his capacity as the chief administrative officer of the United Nations Organization, act[s] on behalf of that Organization as its representative'.

[284] Civil Tribunal of Brussels, 11 May 1966.   [285] (1972) 45 ILR 446 at 452.

[286] *Cf.* Draft Article 17 on 'Jurisdictional immunities of states and their property' and commentary thereto, *Yearbook of the International Law Commission* (1991), vol. II, Part Two, 12 at 54, precluding a state which consented to arbitration from invoking immunity in a 'proceeding which relates to: (a) the validity or interpretation of the arbitration agreement; (b) the arbitration procedure; or (c) the setting aside of the award; unless the arbitration agreement otherwise provides'. See also *Restatement (Third)*, § 456(2)(b) characterizing as a rule of US law that 'an agreement to arbitrate is a waiver of immunity from

specifically providing for the jurisdiction of a domestic court, can also be regarded as waivers of immunity. Similarly, although less clear and often more controversial, the choice of domestic law is sometimes considered as an implied waiver of immunity. On the other hand, in order to avoid the possibility that national courts might interpret certain choice of law or choice of forum clauses as implicit waivers of immunity, organizations frequently insert express disclaimers into their contracts with private parties[287] or stress that any waiver they made related to a particular case only and cannot be extended.[288]

Of course, appearance in court specifically to claim immunity cannot be interpreted as an implicit waiver, while activities undertaken to defend oneself may well be regarded an implicit submission to a court's jurisdiction. Accordingly, in *United States Lines Inc.* v. *World Health Organization*,[289] the plaintiff's assertion that the WHO had waived its immunity by appearing voluntarily in court in order to plead its immunity was rejected. In *African Reinsurance Corporation* v. *Abate Fantaye*,[290] however, a Nigerian appellate court found an implicit waiver by the following acts: '[The organization] appeared without protest before the learned trial

jurisdiction in (i) an action or other proceeding to compel arbitration pursuant to the agreement; and (ii) an action to enforce an arbitral award rendered pursuant to the agreement'.

[287] For instance, the FAO's 'Requests for Bids and Purchase Orders, General Conditions' contains the following paragraph VIII: 'Nothing contained in this agreement shall be deemed a waiver, express or implied, of any privilege of immunity which the Food and Agriculture Organization may enjoy, whether pursuant to the Convention on Privileges and Immunities of the Specialized Agencies or any other convention or agreement, law, order or decree of an international or national character or otherwise.' *Food and Agriculture Organization of the United Nations* v. *BEVAC Company*, ICC Arbitral Award, 29 July 1986, (1986) *United Nations Juridical Yearbook* 347. See also Mahnoush H. Arsanjani, 'Claims Against International Organizations – *Quis Custodiet Ipsos Custodes*' (1980–1) 7 *Yale Journal of World Public Order* 131–76 at 137ff, note 20. Against this *de facto* no-waiver practice, the assessment of Schütz appears to be too optimistic. He thinks that '[a]s a rule, an organization will [waive its claim to jurisdictional immunity] if an opponent in a civil law suit – for example in a case on damages – would otherwise sustain unfair disadvantages'. Hans-Joachim Schütz, 'Host State Agreements' in Rüdiger Wolfrum (ed.), *United Nations: Law, Policies and Practice* (Dordrecht, London and Boston, 1995), vol. 1, 581–90 at 585.

[288] In *Hénaut* v. *Etat-Major des Forces alliées Centre-Europe*, Tribunal de Paix de Fontainebleau, 5 December 1955, a French court upheld its jurisdiction over an employment dispute within NATO – apparently because it considered the defendant's decision not to raise its objection to the court's jurisdiction an implicit waiver of immunity. The court, however, stressed that NATO's acceptance of jurisdiction related only to the particular case and could not be interpreted as general and in principle. (1956) 2 *Annuaire français de droit international* 764.

[289] Intermediate Appellate Court, Philippines, 30 September 1983. See p. 178 above.

[290] Supreme Court, 20 June 1986.

Judge and opposed a motion for an interim injunction [and] was granted leave to file statement of defence . . . This to my mind amounts to submission to the jurisdiction of the trial court.'[291] The Supreme Court, however, only found a conditional appearance to set aside the writ on the ground of immunity. It therefore saw no waiver of immunity and reversed the decision.[292]

Choice of law and choice of forum clauses

In general domestic courts seem to be ready to accept an implicit waiver of immunity. Thus, they have interpreted, for instance, choice of law and choice of forum clauses as implicit renunciations of immunity.

In *Branno* v. *Ministry of War*,[293] the Italian Corte di Cassazione held that:

Subjects of international law and public bodies alike . . . may perform acts of a private law nature, including entering into contracts which are regulated by rules of private law. In such a case, there is a waiver by the subject of international law of its jurisdictional immunity: when it enters into contracts with private individuals it thereby agrees to be subject to the laws of Italian civil law which regulate such contracts, and therefore, it agrees also to submit to the jurisdiction of the courts.[294]

In *Maida* v. *Administration for International Assistance*,[295] the Italian Supreme Court – although it did not expressly say so – appears to have relied on a waiver of immunity argument when upholding the jurisdiction of Italian courts over a dispute concerning the provision of services by an Italian doctor to the defendant organization. The plaintiff, an Italian doctor, brought suit in a domestic court against his employer, the International Refugee Organization (IRO). Since the IRO had ceased to exist in 1952[296] it was replaced by the Administration for International Assistance for the purpose of defending the action instituted by Maida. The Civil Labour Court of Naples dismissed the action for lack of jurisdiction since it regarded the case as falling within the competence of the Italian administrative courts. On appeal the Italian Supreme Court disagreed and held that the competent Civil Labour Court had jurisdiction over the action brought by the plaintiff. After first establishing at length the IRO's functional immunity from the Italian courts,[297] the Supreme Court concluded

---

[291] (1991) 86 ILR 655 at 663.   [292] For details of the case, see p. 166 above.
[293] Corte di Cassazione, 14 June 1954.
[294] (1955) 22 ILR 757.   [295] Corte di Cassazione, 27 May 1955.
[296] Eberhard Jahn, 'International Refugee Organization' in Rudolf Bernhardt (ed.), *Encyclopedia of Public International Law* (2nd edn, 1995), vol. II, 1351–4 at 1352.
[297] See pp. 210f above.

from the reference in the Staff Regulations to the relevant Italian legislation on private employment as subsidiarily applicable law that this
would also lead to the competence of Italian courts:

It accordingly follows that the IRO, notwithstanding that it is a subject of international law, places itself indirectly and in a subsidiary manner under Italian law in
certain respects. This fact must serve as a guide in the present case to determine the
competent body which can decide the dispute between the IRO and the plaintiff.[298]

Thereby the court seems to have interpreted the reference to Italian
legislation on private employment as an implicit waiver.[299]

In *Agence de Cooperation Culturelle et Technique* v. *Housson*,[300] a choice of
forum clause in favour of the French courts was held to constitute a
waiver of immunity on the part of an international organization.[301] The
French Cour de Cassation considered a clause in the employment contract between a French citizen and an international organization providing that any dispute concerning the interpretation or execution of it
would be referred to the competent court at the place of employment to
be a specific renunciation of the organization's immunity.

The already mentioned English *Arab Banking Corporation* v. *International
Tin Council and Algemene Bank Nederland and others (Interveners) and Holco
Trading Company Ltd (Interveners)*[302] decision also affirms the principle that

---

[298] (1956) 23 ILR 513.
[299] It rejected the defendant organization's claim that Italian courts were in general not
competent to adjudicate such disputes which could only be determined by arbitration as
provided for in the Staff Regulations of the IRO. In the court's view, the arbitration
clause was defective because it did not provide for an enforceable appointment procedure for arbitrators.
[300] Cour d'appel de Bordeaux, 18 November 1982, Cour de Cassation, 24 October 1985.
[301] Mrs Housson was hired in 1974 as a receptionist at the International School at Bordeaux,
an 'organisme' of the Agence de Cooperation Culturelle et Technique, an international
organization having its seat in Paris. When in 1981 her employment was unilaterally
terminated for reasons of 'irregularities' on her side, she brought suit in French courts
alleging the illegality of her job termination while she was pregnant and asking for
damages. The Agency appealed against the Bordeaux Court of Appeals judgment in
favour of Mrs Housson. It invoked, *inter alia*, its immunity from French jurisdiction based
on its headquarters agreement of 1972 and a 1980 accord with the French Republic.
Under these treaties, the Agency enjoyed immunity from suit with the possibility of a
waiver in specific cases ('jouit de l'immunité de juridiction sauf renonciation de sa part,
dans un cas particulier'). The Cour de Cassation found that the Agency's consent to the
employment contract with Mrs Housson which contained a clause providing that any
dispute concerning the interpretation or execution of it will be referred to the competent court at the place of employment ('toute contestation née de l'interprétation ou à
l'occasion de l'exécution du present contrat serait soumise à la juridiction compétente
du lieu d'emploi') in itself constituted a specific renunciation of the Agency's immunity
in the sense of the headquarters agreement. Accordingly, it rejected the Agency's claim
of immunity.   [302] High Court, Queen's Bench Division, 15 January 1986.

an international organization may implicitly waive its immunity by agreeing on (the laws of England and) the jurisdiction of English courts. There the High Court held that the International Tin Council had waived its immunity by consenting to a provision in the loan agreement according to which the contract should be subject to the non-exclusive 'jurisdiction of the English courts'.[303]

A very different result was reached by a German labour court. In *X v. European Patent Organization*,[304] an employment dispute concerning the non-renewal of a contract of a *sur place* employee, the plaintiff tried to interpret the provision that '[i]n addition, the employment relation is governed by the national labour and social security provisions in force at the place of work; this also applies with respect to access to national courts',[305] contained in the relevant staff rules as a waiver of the EPO's immunity from suit. The court disagreed and held that the phrase 'In addition' indicated both that substantive national law should only apply and that access to national courts should only be granted where the staff rules did not contain provisions on their own. Since they did in fact regulate the issue of the duration of employment relations the German courts lacked jurisdiction to address this issue.

Arbitration clauses

Whether an arbitration clause by itself constitutes an implicit waiver of an organization's immunity, and if so to what extent, is not uncontroversial. Sometimes the applicable domestic or international immunity rules expressly contemplate arbitration and regulate its effect on immunity.[306] In most cases, however, they are silent on the issue. Thus, it becomes necessary to ascertain whether an agreement to arbitrate entered into by an international organization can be interpreted to imply that domestic courts are competent to exercise the usual control or supervision over such arbitral proceedings and/or to order the enforcement of final awards.

---

[303] See pp. 210*f* above for the details of the case.

[304] Labour Court Berlin-Charlottenburg, 22 February 1994; State Labour Court Berlin, 12 September 1994.

[305] 'Das Dienstverhältnis bestimmt sich im übrigen nach den am Dienstort geltenden nationalen arbeits- und sozialrechtlichen Bestimmungen, dies gilt auch für den Rechtsweg zu den nationalen Gerichten.' State Labour Court Berlin, 12 September 1994, 16 Sa 58/94 (unpublished).

[306] For instance, Article 6(1) of the International Tin Council (Privileges and Immunities) Order 1972 giving effect to a provision of the ITC–United Kingdom headquarters agreement provided for the ITC's immunity from suit and legal process 'except: (a) to the extent that [the ITC] shall have expressly waived such immunity in a particular case . . . and (c) in respect of the enforcement of an arbitration award'.

Some scholars are of the opinion that an international organization's agreement to arbitrate as such does not imply a waiver of its immunity from legal proceedings.[307] Only an express stipulation that the arbitration procedure itself should be governed by a certain domestic law could be interpreted as an implicit waiver of an organization's immunity from suit as far as the supervisory judicial powers of national courts are concerned.[308] This opinion heavily relies on the French case of *Beaudice* v. *ASECNA*,[309] where an appellate court held that a choice of a domestic law to govern arbitral proceedings gave domestic courts adjudicative power to exercise judicial control over the arbitration. The case arose from an employment dispute between a technician and the Agence pour la sécurité de la navigation aérienne en Afrique et à Madagascar (ASECNA), an organization with tasks similar to those of Eurocontrol. The employment contract called for arbitration in such situations under the auspices of an arbitrator nominated by the President of the Administrative Tribunal of Paris. Unsatisfied with the final award, the plaintiff brought proceedings in the French courts to appeal the arbitral decision. Without expressly mentioning the organization's immunity the court upheld its jurisdiction because it thought that the contract's nomination rule for an arbitrator implicitly opted for French law to govern the arbitral procedure. According to French arbitral law, recourse to domestic courts to appeal an arbitral award was possible. The court, however, denied the plaintiff's claim on the merits. The reliance on *Beaudice* v. *ASECNA* for the proposition that a choice of a specific law to govern arbitration could be interpreted as an implicit waiver of immunity, however, is somewhat problematic considering that the French court did not explicitly deal with the issue of immunity and its potential implicit waiver by the specific arbitration clause.[310]

The view that only an express choice of a certain domestic law to govern the arbitration procedure itself could be interpreted as an implicit waiver of an organization's immunity might find stronger support by an arbitral decision involving UNRWA. In *UNRWA* v. *General Trading and*

---

[307] Panayotis Glavinis, *Les litiges relatifs aux contrats passés entre organisations internationales et personnes privées*, Travaux et recherches Panthéon-Assas, Paris II (Paris, 1990), 132.

[308] Christian Dominicé, 'L'arbitrage et les immunités des organisations internationales' in Christian Dominicé, Robert Patry and Claude Reymond (eds.), *Etudes de droit international en l'honneur de Pierre Lalive* (Basel and Frankfurt am Main, 1993), 483–97 at 492.

[309] Cour d'appel de Paris, 25 November 1977.

[310] Loquin, (1979) 106 *Journal de droit international* (Clunet) 131 at 135. Loquin criticizes this decision, questioning whether a choice of (a domestic) law to govern arbitral proceedings could be interpreted to be an implicit waiver of an international organization's immunity as regards the judicial control of the arbitration.

Transport Co. (the *Rice Case*),[311] the arbitrator concluded from the fact that the arbitration clause between UNRWA and a private party was based on and thus governed by international law and not a national system of law that recourse to a domestic judge to supervise the arbitral proceedings was excluded.[312]

In the *Centre pour le développement industriel (CDI)* v. *X*[313] case, a Belgian court found that by agreeing to arbitration the international organization involved had in fact waived its immunity from Belgian jurisdiction. Thus it could not ask for an annulment of a lower court's *exequatur* order allowing the enforcement of an arbitral award rendered against the organization. In trying to attack the validity of the award, the CDI argued, *inter alia*, that its immunity from jurisdiction impeded the arbitrability of the dispute it had with its employee. The court, however, rejected this argument, considering that the internal law of the CDI foresaw arbitration as the exclusive mode of dispute settlement for its contractual relationships and that by agreeing upon arbitration the CDI had anyhow waived its immunity from jurisdiction.[314]

The issue of the effect of an arbitration agreement was not reached in

---

[311] Arbitration Award, 1958.

[312] 'Attendu que si certaines systèmes juridiques permettent au signataire d'une clause compromissoire de saisir le juge de droit commun soit pour surveiller la procédure arbitrale, soit même, si ce juge l'estime opportun, pour le substituer à l'arbitre, une telle substitution suppose que la cause relève d'un système national ayant prévu cette possibilité, réglé ses conséquences; que s'agissant en l'espèce d'une cause qui ne relève d'un système juridique national, mais du droit international public lequel n'a pas prévu une telle possibilité, sans posséder d'ailleurs d'organisation propre à en régler les conséquences, il y a lieu d'entendre la clause compromissoire stipulée selon ses termes, lesquels excluent le recours au juge de droit commun sur les différends qu'elle vise, la solution étant d'ailleurs seule compatible avec l'immunité de juridiction des organismes internationaux.' *Yearbook of the International Law Commission* (1967), vol. II, 208.

[313] Tribunal Civil de Bruxelles, 13 March 1992. See pp. 39f above.

[314] The court's reasoning here seems to be not entirely free from misunderstandings. The court also complained of the CDI's lengthy pleadings 'sans préciser claiment l'argument qu'il entend de tirer'. (1992) *Actualités du droit* 1377 at 1382. Normally, an organization's arbitration agreement might be interpreted as an implicit waiver of immunity where court proceedings relating to that arbitration are brought against an international organization. In the Belgian case, however, the CDI brought suit clearly relying on the Belgian court's jurisdiction for the subject matter of its claim. The assertion that the underlying employment dispute could not be arbitrated – allegedly as a result of its immunity – seems to rest more on the concept of certain types of disputes (with international organizations) which should be excluded from settlement either by domestic courts or by private arbitration. A valid argument can be made that – under the condition that an effective system of legal recourse, e.g. in the form of an administrative tribunal, exists – employment disputes might be excluded from the jurisdiction of domestic courts (and one might add of arbitral tribunals). The Belgian court, however, did not consider this point.

International Civil Aviation Organization v. *Tripal Systems Pty Ltd et al.*[315] where a Canadian court refused to render a declaratory judgment confirming that the ICAO enjoyed 'absolute immunity from judicial process of every kind' which probably included arbitration. The court did not grant the relief sought because it considered it to fall outside the supervisory powers of a national court legitimately exercised over arbitral proceedings.

Part II
Policy issues

4   Rationales for judicial abstention

This chapter focuses on the rationales of the approaches of domestic courts when they are confronted with disputes to which international organizations are parties. It aims to clarify the underlying policy reasons for abstention on the one hand and involvement on the other hand which are sometimes very expressly advanced, and sometimes only implicit, in the court decisions analyzed. The major part of this discussion of judges and scholars arises from a context of immunity cases. Nevertheless, most rationales are valid beyond the narrow framework of immunity in a technical sense. Thus, they will be discussed here in a broader context, resulting from the use of various abstention and involvement techniques as outlined in Part I.

A number of reasons have been put forward to justify immunity for international organizations. Normally they are not expressly limited to immunity from suit, but form part and parcel of a wholesale grant of privileges and immunities to international organizations. It is also useful to analyze the case law and to inquire into the reasons why immunities and privileges should not be granted to international organizations. Balancing those competing rationales might ultimately form the basis for an appropriate solution to decide actual immunity issues as will be undertaken in Part III.

The protection of the functioning and independence of an international organization

The paramount rationale for granting immunities to international organizations in general and immunity from legal process in particular lies in securing their independence and guaranteeing their functioning. Most legal writers will agree with the explanation that:

The privileges and immunities of international organizations are designed mainly to protect the *independence* of organizations from undue outside influence and otherwise to ensure that they are able to carry out their missions.[1]

According to the ILC special rapporteur on relations between states and international organizations, the justification for organizational privileges and immunities lies in their aim 'to guarantee the autonomy, independence and functional effectiveness of international organizations and protect them against abuse of any kind'.[2] In the Council of Europe report on the same subject, the independence of the organization is considered one of the principal reasons for according privileges and immunities.[3] In the course of its legal quarrel with Italy over its immunity from suit,[4] the FAO insisted on the 'fundamental purposes for which immunity from legal processes was accorded to intergovernmental organizations' which it identified at 'ensur[ing] that the intergovernmental organizations concerned could carry out their aims smoothly and independently'.[5]

Domestic legislation sometimes reflects this functional necessity rationale. For instance, Article 1(2) of the Austrian 1977 Law on the Granting of Privileges and Immunities to International Organizations[6] provides that, in addition to the privileges and immunities contained in the Act, such rights might be conferred upon an international organization according to treaties or 'as provided, *for the fulfilment of its functions, by the generally recognized rules of international law*'.[7]

Many court decisions involving the immunity from suit of international organizations incorporate the independent functioning argument. They speak of the grant of immunity 'in order to facilitate the working of an international body',[8] to 'ensure its functioning',[9] 'to avoid

---

[1] C. T. Oliver, E. B. Firmage, C. L. Blakesley, R. F. Scott and S. A. Williams, *The International Legal System: Cases and Materials* (4th edn, Westbury, NY, 1995), 613. See also Gordon H. Glenn, Mary M. Kearney and David J. Padilla, 'Immunities of International Organizations' (1982) 22 *Virginia Journal of International Law* 247–90 at 276, speaking of the 'indispensability of jurisdictional immunity to the effective functioning of international organizations'.

[2] Leonardo Díaz-González (Special Rapporteur), 'Fourth Report on Relations Between States and International Organizations (Second Part of the Topic)' (UN Doc. A/CN.4/424) *Yearbook of the International Law Commission* (1989), vol. II, Part One, 153–68 at 157.

[3] Conseil de l'Europe (ed.), *Privilèges et immunités des organisations internationales, Resolution (69) 29 adoptée par le Comité des Ministres du Conseil de l'Europe le 26 septembre 1969 et rapport explicatif* (Strasbourg, 1970), 12.

[4] For more detail, see pp. 131*ff* above.

[5] See FAO, Office of the Legal Counsel, 'Constitutional Matters' (1982) *United Nations Juridical Yearbook* 113.

[6] (1977) *United Nations Juridical Yearbook* 3.   [7] Emphasis added.

[8] *Ary Spaans* v. *The Netherlands*, European Commission of Human Rights, Application No. 12516/86, 12 December 1988, (1988) 58 *Decisions and Reports* 119 at 122.

hindrances to the independent functioning',[10] etc. It is certainly the most frequently used argument, if policy considerations are made explicit in the decisions at all. A number of cases are content to apply the legal rules without reflecting on their justifications.[11]

It seems that the almost universally shared opinion that it would be necessary to grant international organizations immunity from suit in order to protect their independent functioning remains largely unchallenged. It might nevertheless be worthwhile to question this generally shared belief. Paraphrasing a famous critique of traditional rationales for sovereign immunity, one might share the opinion that:

In fact it is not easy to see why the principle of independence and equality should preclude the courts of a state from exercising jurisdiction over [an international organization] and its property so long as the state exercising jurisdiction merely applies its ordinary law, including its rules of private international law, and so long as it applies it in an unobjectionable manner not open to the reproach of a denial of justice.[12]

Hostile domestic environment: prejudices

Some authors argue that immunity from suit is necessary to protect international organizations against a potentially hostile environment (primarily of the seat state),[13] against 'unilateral and sometimes irresponsible interference by individual governments',[14] while others see a

---

9 *X* v. *International Centre for Superior Mediterranean Agricultural Studies*, Court of Appeals of Crete, 1991.

10 *Application for Authorization to Enforce a Garnishee Order Against the High Authority of the European Coal and Steel Community*, Case 4/62, ECJ, 13 March 1962. Here, the ECJ justified the need for its authorization of enforcement measures against the ECSC by national courts in accordance with Article 1 of the Protocol on the Privileges and Immunities of the European Coal and Steel Community on functional reasons. It thought that such authorization was necessary 'in order to avoid untimely and inappropriate hindrances to the independent functioning of the Community on behalf of private interests'. [1962] ECR 41 at 43.

11 The Austrian *X* v. *Country Y* case, Supreme Court, 21 November 1990, is a good example for its close adherence to legal doctrine. Although this case does not directly involve an international organization or its privileges and immunities, it is interesting in so far as the defendant state tried to invoke a privileged position expressly granted to international organizations by Austrian legislation by way of analogy. The court, however, considered the difference justified. It remarked that – whereas states enjoyed only relative immunity – international organizations were regularly granted (unqualified) immunity in order to protect them against interferences and influences of the organs of single states.

12 Sir Hersch Lauterpacht, 'The Problem of Jurisdictional Immunities of Foreign States' (1951) 28 *British Yearbook of International Law* 220–72 at 229.

13 Jean-Flavien Lalive, 'L'immunité de juridiction des états et des organisations internationales' (1953 III) 84 *Recueil des Cours* 205–396 at 298*ff*.

general danger of prejudice against international organizations among judges.[15] The hostile domestic environment might find its expression in prejudices among individuals against which the forum state should guard. This concern has been formulated most succinctly in the famous phrase of McKinnon Wood that international organizations need protection against 'baseless actions brought from improper motives or by the numerous cranks, fanatics or cantankerous persons who may conceive that they have a duty to compel the organization to take some particular step or that they have suffered wrong at its hands'.[16]

It still remains doubtful whether the threat of unwarranted lawsuits alone is a proper reason to deny the possibility of bringing any suits. In particular, the right of access to court[17] might weigh heavier than the 'speedy administration of justice'.

Lack of familiarity with the issues

In support of the immunity of international organizations, it is sometimes argued that domestic judges may not be trained well enough in international matters in order to decide issues concerning international organizations. This assertion, however, is overly broad. In order to present a valid argument one needs to differentiate between different issues of substance arising in disputes involving international organizations.

As far as internal disputes of a 'constitutional' character are concerned,[18] and possibly disputes concerning the staff of an international organization, this argument has its merits.[19] In such 'internal' dis-

---

[14] Paul C. Szasz, 'International Organizations, Privileges and Immunities', in Rudolf Bernhardt (ed.), *Encyclopedia of Public International Law* (2nd edn, 1995), vol. II, 1325–33 at 1326.

[15] Kuljit Ahluwalia, *The Legal Status, Privileges and Immunities of the Specialized Agencies of the United Nations and Certain Other International Organizations* (The Hague, 1964), 200; Derek W. Bowett, *The Law of International Institutions* (4th edn, London, 1982), 349; Peter H. F. Bekker, *The Legal Position of Intergovernmental Organizations. A Functional Necessity Analysis of Their Legal Status and Immunities* (Dordrecht, Boston and London, 1994), 101; Christian Dominicé, 'L'immunité de juridiction et d'exécution des organisations internationales' (1984 IV) 187 *Recueil des Cours* 145–238 at 159; and Henry G. Schermers, *International Institutional Law* (Alphen aan den Rijn and Rockville, 2nd edn, 1980), 796.

[16] Hugh McKinnon Wood, 'Legal Relations Between Individuals and a World Organization of States' (1944) 30 *Transactions of the Grotius Society* 141–64 at 144; frequently cited, *inter alia*, by Bekker, *The Legal Position*, 102; and Schermers, *International Institutional Law*, 796.

[17] See pp. 280ff below.   [18] See pp. 374ff below.

[19] Michael Akehurst, *The Law Governing Employment in International Organizations* (Cambridge, 1967), 12; and Hans-Joachim Priess, *Internationale Verwaltungsgerichte und Beschwerdeausschüsse, Eine Studie zum gerichtlichen Rechtsschutz für Beamte internationaler Organisationen* (Berlin, 1989), 53.

putes, where the familiarity of domestic judges with the issues involved may be justly doubted, their removal from national courts makes sense as a practical matter. It is not surprising that such disputes are often treated as 'lack of competence' cases.[20] Where it is in fact the internal constitutional order of the international organization that is the subject of a claim before a domestic court, it might well be that this matter is removed from the competence of a national court. A similar 'lack of jurisdiction' argument can be made in regard to the internal administrative law of an international organization which should be properly adjudicated and administered by the competent internal tribunals.[21]

However, the argument of a possible lack of familiarity with the issues involved seems to be unfounded in the context of ordinary private law disputes resulting from an organization's activities governed by the domestic law of a particular country. Where a contractual dispute or a question resulting from damages caused by an international organization to an individual arises, domestic judges are likely to be the best arbiters and to be the most familiar with the legal issues involved.

Harassment aspect: costs of lawsuits

An argument sometimes raised although interestingly almost exclusively by US lawyers is the harassment effect of the frequently enormous costs of litigation that have to be borne by an international organization even if it successfully defends itself against unjustified claims.[22]

One has to put this argument into perspective, however. It seems to be valid only in jurisdictions which do not allow for the recovery of legal costs from the party losing a lawsuit[23] and where these costs are so substantial as to inflict serious damage upon innocent defendants. However, extremely high legal fees in litigation are not a general phenomenon, common to all legal systems, but seem to be characteristic of having recourse to courts in the US. Thus, the potential of being exposed to substantial legal costs does not appear to be a specific ground for denying jurisdiction in cases involving international organizations, but

---

[20] See pp. 99ff above.   [21] See pp. 377ff below.

[22] This concern was raised by various US attorneys during the discussion following the author's presentation of parts of this book in spring 1996 at the law firm of Arent Fox & Partners in Washington DC.

[23] This is the case, in particular, in the US and Japanese legal systems. Cf. Mauro Cappelletti and Bryant Garth, 'Access to Justice: The Worldwide Movement to Make Rights Effective' in Mauro Cappelletti and Bryant Garth (eds.), Access to Justice (Alphen aan den Rijn, 1978), vol I, book II, 5–124 at 11.

rather appears to be a common problem affecting all innocent defendants in certain legal systems.[24]

However, even under US civil procedure rules, the compensation of legal costs may be ordered as an exceptional measure. For instance, in *Adiren* v. *Camarena et al.*,[25] an employment dispute brought by a staff member of the Inter-American Development Bank against three of his supervisors, which was dismissed on the ground of immunity, the plaintiff was ordered to pay the defendants' costs and legal fees.

A counterbalance to the relative weakness of international organizations

In connection with the independence argument, the relative 'weakness'[26] of international organizations (compared to states) is sometimes cited in order to justify their immunities and, in particular, to justify a wider scope of such immunities which should not therefore be affected by restrictions accepted in the field of sovereign immunity. In this manner, some authors try to justify an absolute immunity for international organizations because of their vulnerability since they have no territory of their own[27] and thus 'necessarily operate within the jurisdiction of other legal systems'.[28]

It is hard to take this weakness argument seriously. Of course, many international organizations exist basically at the mercy of their member states who remain the absolute 'masters of the treaties' setting up those international organizations. However, even their relative weakness, compared to the power of states which is of course also relative and differs from state to state appears as strength in comparison to their potential opponents when immunity issues arise. Compared to an individual person or company trying to pursue a contractual or delictual claim against an international organization, even the weakest among them hardly merit the additional protection of jurisdictional immunity.

---

[24] Earl Johnson *et al.*, 'Access to Justice in the United States: The Economic Barriers and Some Promising Solutions' in Cappelletti and Garth (eds.), *Access to Justice*, vol. 1, book II, 915–1023 at 915*ff*.

[25] Superior Court DC Civil Division, 8 May 1984.

[26] Nicolas Valticos, 'Les contrats conclus par les organisations internationales avec des personnes privées, Rapport provisoire et projet de résolution – Rapport définitif et projet de résolution' (1977) *Annuaire de l'Institut de Droit International* 1–191 at 3; see also Michael Singer, 'Jurisdictional Immunity of International Organizations: Human Rights and Functional Necessity Concerns' (1995) 36 *Virginia Journal of International Law* 53–165 at 67.

[27] For the 'lack of territory' argument in favour of granting immunity, see pp. 248*f* below.

[28] Felice Morgenstern, *Legal Problems of International Organizations* (Cambridge, 1986), 6.

The influence of states on an international organization should be channelled through its 'internal law'

A more sophisticated argument related to the independence rationale relies on the proper modes of influence that member states should be able to exert on the activities of an international organization. This influence of individual states on international organizations is laid down in the constitutional or internal law of the organization, its founding treaties, its organizational practice, rules emanating from organs of the organization, etc.[29] It is usually clearly defined in the decision-making process, but also budgetary procedures lay down the options available to states to exercise influence within an international organization. The argument for the protection of international organizations from the adjudicative power of national courts maintains that this proper process must not be circumvented by any forms of additional and external 'commands' addressed to international organizations or their officials through any state organ, in particular, through courts.[30]

This consideration was one of the main arguments raised in the UN *amicus curiae* brief in the *Broadbent v. OAS* case.[31] To justify a scope of immunity for international organizations different from that of states, the UN reasoned, *inter alia*, that:

Intergovernmental organizations may be considered as collective enterprises of their member States. Their constituent treaties define precisely the influence each member is to have on the operations of the organizations, and how that influence is to be exercised generally through collective organs. If individual members could then exert additional influence on those organizations, largely through the fortuitous circumstance of where their headquarters, or the offices or officials or assets, happen to be located this could drastically change the constitutionally agreed sharing of power within the organizations. Thus the immunity granted by states to an intergovernmental organization is really their reciprocal pledge that none will attempt to garner unilaterally an undue share of influence over its affairs.[32]

This language is almost exactly echoed by the European Commission of Human Rights's recent decision in *Richard Waite and Terry Kennedy* v.

---

[29] See in general Rudolph Bernhardt, 'Qualifikation und Anwendungsbereich des internen Rechts internationaler Organisationen' (1973) 12 *Berichte der Deutschen Gesellschaft für Volkerrecht* 7–46 at 7*ff.*

[30] Szasz, 'International Organizations, Privileges and Immunities', 1326.

[31] US District Court DC, 28 March 1978; US Court of Appeals DC Cir., 8 January 1980.

[32] Reprinted in (1980) *United Nations Juridical Yearbook* 229.

Germany[33] where it accepted the protection from unilateral interference by individual governments as the main rationale for privileges and immunities. In the Commission's view:

The constitutional instruments of inter-governmental organisations elaborately define their decision-making processes, and in particular the type and degree of influence each government is to have in respect of the organisation. It is therefore considered unacceptable for individual governments to be able, whether through their executive, legislative or judicial organs, to require an international organisation to take certain actions by commands addressed to the organisation itself or to any of its officials.[34]

Although the basis for this argument is certainly legitimate, it seems that it should be applied more restrictively than it was in *Broadbent* v. *OAS* and *Waite and Kennedy* v. *Germany* where it led to denials of jurisdiction in employment-related claims brought by international officials and by persons outside the staff of an organization rendering services to it. It cannot justly serve as a complete shield from domestic adjudication. In its legitimate scope, however, trying to prevent the litigation of constitutional or other internal disputes before national courts, one might ask whether a lack of jurisdiction mechanism could not adequately substitute for immunity.[35]

Such a more limited rationale was taken up in *Re International Tin Council*[36] where the English High Court denied a petition to grant a winding-up order against the ITC. The court thought that it lacked jurisdiction to do so and justified its decision, *inter alia*, by arguing that through a forced liquidation the Tin Council:

would be compelled, by the decision of the court of a single member state, to remove its headquarters from the United Kingdom, a matter which under the terms of the Agreement is for the members by a prescribed majority to decide . . . the making of a winding up order would be inconsistent with the Agreement and would interfere with the continued activities of the ITC . . . and whatever arrangements the members states may make to deal with the unforeseen situation which has arisen and to contribute to or make good the shortfall.[37]

---

[33] European Commission of Human Rights, Application No. 26083/94; 24 February 1997. See pp. 304f below.

[34] Application No. 26083/94; 24 February 1997, para. 70.   [35] See pp. 372ff below.

[36] High Court, Chancery Division, 22 January 1987. See p. 118 above for details of this decision.

[37] (1988) 77 ILR 18 at 32.

Equality of the member states of an international organization

Sometimes the principle of equality among an international organization's member states is put forward as a justification for the privileges and immunities of an international organization.[38]

However, it is generally felt that this rationale probably only applies to the grant of fiscal privileges.[39] Host states or other states where international organizations operate should not gain a disproportionate (and thus unequal) financial advantage resulting from the application of their tax laws to such international organizations. This was one of the major arguments put forward by the European Molecular Biology Laboratory (EMBL) in the course of arbitral proceedings against Germany in order to prevent the host state from taxing the Laboratory's income derived from and the goods required for the operation of a guest-house and canteen used by staff members and visiting scientists. In *European Molecular Biology Laboratory* v. *Germany*,[40] the organization tried to rely on a customary principle 'that a host state must not draw financial advantages from the official activities of an international organization. Otherwise it would adversely affect the financial resources of the organization at the expense of the financial contribution of the other member States.'[41] The arbitral tribunal, however, did not consider it necessary to refer to any customary rules. Rather, it held that on the basis of specific Articles of the EMBL headquarters agreement providing for fiscal exemptions only in respect of official activities of the Laboratory the organization did not enjoy the fiscal privileges claimed where meals and accommodation were supplied against payment.[42]

It is worth noting that the argument that equality mandates tax 'immunity'[43] has not been left unchallenged. It has been said that host states generally have to bear larger costs than those which might be offset by the spending of the organizations and missions in their territory.[44]

---

[38] Ahluwalia, *The Legal Status*, 89ff; Bekker, *The Legal Position*, 104; Alice Ehrenfeld, United Nations Immunity Distinguished from Sovereign Immunity' (1958) 52 *Proceedings of the American Society of International Law* 88–94 at 90; and Josef L. Kunz, 'Privileges and Immunities of International Organizations' (1947) 41 *American Journal of International Law* 828–62 at 847.

[39] Conseil de l'Europe, 12ff; ILC Special Rapporteur in *Yearbook of the International Law Commission* (1989), vol. II, Part One, 153–68 at 158.

[40] Arbitration Award, 29 June 1990.   [41] (1997) 105 ILR 1 at 20.   [42] *Ibid.*, 68.

[43] More correctly, one should speak of a tax privilege. See pp. 13ff above.

[44] Heribert Franz Köck, 'Multinational Diplomacy and Progressive Development of International Law' (1977) 28 *Österreichische Zeitschrift für öffentliches Recht* 51–105 at 63, quoting Zemanek at the 1975 conference adopting the Vienna Convention on the Representation of States in Their Relations with International Organizations of a Universal Character.

Thus, an 'additional' fiscal advantage would in effect only put the host state on an equal footing with the other members.

In a more indirect way, however, the equality argument could also be valid for immunity from legal process. Even if a state asserting jurisdiction over an international organization would not directly interfere with an organization's own affairs through its judiciary in most cases and although it might well be that in the long run a legal dispute is decided in favour of the international organization, the potential of harassment and interference with the international organization's work would definitely give the member state denying immunity to the international organization a more influential position. This view was expressly asserted in *Mendaro* v. *World Bank*,[45] where the court found that the purpose of immunity from employees' actions was rooted 'in the need to protect international organizations from unilateral control by a member nation over the activities of the international organization within its territory'.[46] According to the US court, 'the very structure of an international organization . . . requires that the organization remain independent from the intra-national policies of its individual members'.[47] The example demonstrates quite clearly, however, that the argument can be reduced to a non-interference rationale. International organizations should remain independent from the influence of all states, not only host states. The factual circumstances may make it more likely that host states will have an opportunity to interfere in an international organization's affairs by means of their judiciary, but the fact remains that all kinds of interference by all states are unwelcome.

This principle of equality of member states is even more in danger of being infringed in situations where the judicial action of a single member would threaten the very existence of an international organization. Where suit is brought with the aim of achieving the liquidation of an organization such considerations are particularly relevant. Thus, the English High Court's judgment in *Re International Tin Council* noted above,[48] denying a petition to grant a winding-up order against the ITC, referred to the equality argument, not, however, to grant immunity but rather to deny the remedy sought. The court reasoned that if an organization's member states:

---

[45] US Court of Appeals, 27 September 1983.   [46] 717 F. 2d 610 at 615 (DC Cir. 1983).
[47] *Ibid.*, 616.
[48] High Court, Chancery Division, 22 January 1987. See pp. 99, 108 and 124 above.

choose instead to carry on [a collective enterprise] through the medium of an international organisation, no one member state, by executive, legislative or judicial action, can assume the management of the enterprise and subject it to its own domestic law. For if one could, all could; and the independence and international character of the organisation would be fragmented and destroyed.[49]

Securing uniformity in dispute settlement

Though frequently dealt with as an aspect of the attempt to secure the organization's independence,[50] the negative effect of inconsistent judgments by various national courts and the lack of any harmonization mechanism are also brought forward to support the grant of immunity from domestic lawsuits.[51] It has been argued that an organization created for the common interest of its member states 'must therefore speak with *one* voice and can only regulate its legal relations through one *uniform* body of law'.[52]

It is true that judicial interpretations of the law, and in particular when made by the courts of different countries, may, in effect, change the actual content of the legal rules applied. However, this general problem, concerning the uniformity of interpreting and applying the law, arises in the same way within a single domestic legal system. Further, the issue of securing uniformity of interpretation and application of the law is particularly acute in private international law/conflict of laws situations where the quest for coherent decisions (*internationaler Entscheidungseinklang*)[53] remains a goal that cannot always be attained. However difficult it may be to ensure the harmonious and coherent interpretation of the law of international organizations, methods other than ousting the jurisdiction of domestic courts should be found. Using the argument of potentially divergent judicial results, all issues of international law would escape judicial appraisal by domestic courts.

The most visible example where coherent decisions are of crucial importance are employment disputes. In order to justify immunity from suit by former employees of international organizations, it is frequently argued that the independence of the international civil service can only

---

[49] (1988) 77 ILR 18 at 36.   [50] E.g., by Bekker, *The Legal Position*, 102*ff.*

[51] Ahluwalia, *The Legal Status*, 200; Bowett, *The Law of International Institutions*, 349; Priess, *Internationale Verwaltungsgerichte*, 53; Schermers, *International Institutional Law*, 796; and Seidl-Hohenveldern, *Die Immunität internationaler Organisationen*, 13; Wood, 'Legal Relations', 144.

[52] Bekker, *The Legal Position*, 103.

[53] Gerhard Kegel, *Internationales Privatrecht* (5th edn, Munich, 1985), 77*ff.*

be guaranteed if the law governing this field is unaffected by competing national policies as expressed by competing national legislation.[54] This is, however, a choice of law question which must be separated from the issue of immunity. It is certainly true that the simultaneous application of different and potentially incongruent national legal rules concerning employment relations to international organizations and their staff might lead to unacceptable results. However, as far as employment relations within international organizations are concerned, it is generally acknowledged and well established that these issues are not governed 'by any municipal labour law but by the organization's regulations supplemented where necessary by general principles of labour law'.[55] This

[54] Cf., inter alia, Broadbent et al. v. OAS et al., US Court of Appeals DC Cir., 8 January 1980: 'An attempt by the courts of one nation to adjudicate the personnel claims of international civil servants would entangle those courts in the internal administration of those organizations. Denial of immunity opens the door to divided decisions of the courts of different member states passing judgment on the rules, regulations, and decisions of the international bodies. Undercutting uniformity in the application of staff rules or regulations would undermine the ability or the organization to function effectively.' 628 F. 2d 27 at 35 (1980) See also Frances W. Henderson, 'How Much Immunity for International Organizations?: Mendaro v. World Bank' (1985) 10 North Carolina Journal of International Law and Commercial Regulation 487–97 at 493. Cf. the similar reasoning by a Berlin labour court in X v. European Patent Organization, State Labour Court Berlin, 12 September 1994 (unpublished), arguing that the object and purpose of immunity in staff disputes lies in the ability of an organization to regulate its staff and employment relations in an autonomous fashion without being compelled to deal with different legal systems and, in particular, with different and potentially contradictory views of national courts. 'Sinn und Zweck der Immunität im Personalbereich bestehen darin, daß die Organisation ihre beamten- und arbeitsrechtlichen Beziehungen autonom soll gestalten können und dabei nicht gezwungen sein soll, sich mit unterschiedlichen, womöglich gegensätzlichen Auffassungen der nationalen Gerichte auseinanderzusetzen.' See also the German decision in X et al. v. European School Karlsruhe, Federal Administrative Court, 29 October 1992, where the court held that the lack of jurisdiction of German courts over staff employment issues directly flowed from the exclusive jurisdiction of international organizations to regulate their staff relations including the ways of redress. It thought that such exclusivity was necessary 'in order to safeguard coherent legal and factual situations in internal organizational matters' of an international organization. 'Diese Regelungsbefugnis [die Bestimmung des Rechtsschutzes und der Rechtsschutzgewährung bei Streitigkeiten dienstrechtlicher Art] entspricht einer weitverbreiteten Praxis der Staaten, von ihnen geschaffenen internationalen Organisationen zur Gewährleistung einheitlicher Rechts- und Lebensverhältnisse im innerorganisatorischen Bereich die autonome Regelungs- und Entscheidungsbefugnis hinsichtlich ihrer Bediensteten einzuräumen, die namentlich auch die Einrichtung eines den nationalen Rechtsweg ausschließenden besonderen Rechtsschutzsystems umfaßt.' (references omitted; emphasis added) BVerwGE 91, 126 at 129.

[55] Georges van Hecke, 'Contracts Between International Organizations and Private Law Persons' in Rudolf Bernhardt (ed.), Encyclopedia of Public International Law (2nd edn, 1992), vol. I, 812–14 at 813.

choice-of-law result in favour of an autonomous internal law of staff rules is independent of the question of who should apply such law. In other words, the choice-of-forum result determining which courts decide a particular dispute, whether a domestic court or an internal administrative tribunal, does not (or rather should not) affect the applicable substantive law. Furthermore, there is no intrinsic reason why different (national) courts should not be able to apply identical legal rules. As a matter of fact, the viability of this option clearly forms the working premise of private international law/conflict of laws.

Derived or delegated state sovereignty

Despite a general refutation of the relevance of state immunity principles for international organizations,[56] the grant of immunities to international organizations is sometimes considered to be justified 'on the ground of transfer of portions of State sovereignty or of State functions'.[57] It seems that the concept of a delegation or transfer of sovereign powers, which is probably most explicit in the notion of international organizations as 'derived' or 'derivative' persons or subjects of international law,[58] contributed strongly to this idea of 'derived immunities'. Some courts have expressly deduced the immunity of international organizations from the fact that their members enjoy such immunity. In X v. NATO,[59] a German labour court dismissed an employment dispute brought against the organization reasoning that NATO as 'holder of foreign sovereign rights is not subject to the jurisdiction of German courts'.[60] Similarly, in Godman v. Winterton[61] where the plaintiff sued the chairman and other individual members of the Inter-Governmental Committee, a committee whose purpose it was to secure the emigration of

---

[56] See pp. 347ff below.
[57] Morgenstern, Legal Problems, 6. When introducing the UK Diplomatic (Extension) Act 1944, the Minister of State explained to Parliament that 'where a number of Governments joined together to create an international organization to fulfil some public purpose, the organization should have the same status, immunities and privileges as the foreign Government members thereof enjoyed under ordinary law'; quoted in Yearbook of the International Law Commission (1977), vol. II, Part One, 152.
[58] See p. 57 note 109 above.   [59] Landesarbeitsgericht Rheinland-Pfalz, 23 February 1960.
[60] 'Die einzelnen Mitgliedstaaaten der NATO haben . . . dieser Teilausschnitte ihrer Souveränitätsrechte übertragen. Die NATO muß insoweit als Träger der ausländischen Souveränitätsrechte als von der deutschen Gerichtsbarkeit ausgenommen angesehen werden.' Cited by Friedrich, Schröer, 'De l'application de l'immunité juridictionnelle des états étrangers aux organisations internationales' (1971) 75 Revue générale de droit international public 712–41 at 723, note 31.
[61] Court of Appeal, 12 March 1940.

Jewish people from Nazi Germany, to recover expenses and to secure reasonable remuneration for services rendered to the Committee on the basis of an oral agreement, the appellate court affirmed the lower court's dismissal of the claim on the ground that 'in so far as the agreement was alleged to have been made with the Inter-Governmental Committee, which would naturally be taken to be a committee of representatives of sovereign States, it was an action against sovereign States and was bound to fail'.[62]

In some cases, the concept of an organization's immunity as one derived from its member states may also result from specific national legal requirements. In many legal systems, to accord immunities to an international organization may require a specific legal basis and such a basis may not be available or may be available only uncertainly if the domestic legal instrument providing for organizational immunity does so in respect only of international organizations of which the forum state is a member. Thus, it was argued in a US tax ruling concerning the status of the EEC that in special cases international organizations might be treated as a 'group of states enjoying the immunities of the constituent members'.[63] An older US precedent, *John H. Chapman* v. *Commissioner of Internal Revenue*,[64] clearly contradicts this reasoning. In this decision, rendered before the enactment of the International Organizations Immunities Act 1945, the claim of a League of Nations official that his income should be tax-exempt under US revenue provisions as 'salary of an alien employee of a foreign government' was rejected on the ground that the League was not a foreign government. Consequently, the court denied the applicability of immunities enjoyed by foreign states to the League of Nations.

Immunity as an inherent quality of international legal personality

The view that a subject of international law is automatically or inherently exempted from the jurisdiction of national courts is frequently put forward both in scholarly writing and in judicial decisions. It seems to

---

[62] (1939–42) 11 *Annual Digest of Public International Law Cases* 205 at 206*ff.*

[63] Revenue Ruling 68–309, (1968–1) CB 338 concerning the tax status of the EEC, quoted in *Restatement (Third) of the Law, The Foreign Relations Law of the United States* (ed. American Law Institute, St Paul, MN, 1987), §467, Reporters' Note 4. The 'special case' might lie in the fact that the US is, of course, not a member state of the EEC and that under the IOIA privileges and immunities are granted only to international organizations in which the US participates.

[64] US Tax Court, 9 October 1947.

rest mainly on the perceived applicability of the traditional state immunity rationale *par in parem non habet imperium*. A number of authorities suggest that the enjoyment of immunities is a consequence of the international legal personality of an international organization.[65] They portray immunity as one of the rights automatically enjoyed by international legal persons. Some state practice seem to confirm the view of an inherent or automatic right to privileges and immunities flowing from the international legal personality of international organizations.[66] Other scholars seem to follow similar views on 'immunity as an inherent quality of international legal personality' when they state that 'privileges and immunities arc granted as a result of the recognition of [the international organization's] international personality'[67] or that '[p]ossession of such international personality will normally involve, as a consequence, the attribution . . . of privileges and immunities'.[68]

The concept that international organizations are immune because they are international organizations, because they are subjects of international law, has been repeatedly affirmed by Italian courts.[69] In *Galasso* v. *Istituto italo-latinoamericano*,[70] the Italian Supreme Court found that as a

---

[65] *Cf. Restatement (Third)*, § 467, Comment a; Lalive, 'L'immunité de juridiction', 314, referring to the privileges and immunities as an 'attribute' of the international organization's legal personality. Georges Vandersanden, 'Administrative Tribunals, Boards and Commissions in International Organizations' in Rudolf Bernhardt (ed.), *Encyclopedia of Public International Law* (2nd edn, 1992), vol. I, 27–31 at 26, speaks of '[o]ne of the attributes generally ascribed to international organizations as a result of their legal personality under international law [is] the right to jurisdictional immunity'. Enno J. Harders, 'Haftung und Verantwortlichkeit Internationaler Organisationen' in Rüdiger Wolfrum (ed.), *Handbuch Vereinte Nationen* (2nd edn, Munich, 1991), 248–58 at 249, thinks that because of their international legal personality international organizations have international legal rights and duties. Thus, they are able to conclude treaties and to enjoy privileges and immunities. Without further elaboration, Morgenstern recites the justification for granting immunities to international organizations on the ground 'that an international body is by its nature, or the nature of its acts, not subject to national law'. Morgenstern, *Legal Problems*, 6. One might wonder, however, whether she is talking about immunity issues at all, since immunity is not a question of 'choice of law'; it is rather a limited exception from a state's (national) jurisdiction to adjudicate or to enforce. Morgenstern's reasoning becomes even more difficult to follow when she justifies an 'absolute immunity' for international organizations by their 'vulnerability' because they had no territory of their own and thus 'necessarily operate within the jurisdiction of other legal systems'. *Ibid.*

[66] E.g., the Interim Arrangement 1946 which provides: 'The Swiss Federal Council recognizes the international personality and legal capacity of the United Nations. *Consequently, according to the rules of international law*, the organization cannot be sued before the Swiss Courts without its express consent.' (emphasis added).

[67] Ahluwalia, *The Legal Status*, 208.   [68] Bowett, *The Law of International Institutions*, 339.

[69] Dominicé, 'L'immunité de juridiction', 167.   [70] Corte di Cassazione, 3 February 1986.

result of Article 10 of the Italian Constitution the customary international law norm of *par in parem non habet iurisdictionem* automatically
applied to the Institute, an entity enjoying international legal personality, even in the absence of any conventional norm.[71] A similar reasoning
was used shortly before *Galasso* in a similar case, *Cristiani v. Istituto italo-
latino-americano*,[72] where the Italian Supreme Court recognized a *communis opinio* in the doctrine and case law of various countries of a 'necessary
relationship between international personality and immunity'.[73] It
thought that in analogy to states the principle of *par in parem non habet
iurisdictionem* also applied to international organizations.

In the German *WEU* case,[74] a lower German court thought that it would
follow from the nature of the WEU as an international organization that
it was not subject to German adjudicative jurisdiction and that it could
not subject itself to the enforcement jurisdiction of Germany in the
future.[75]

The view that the immunity of international organizations is one of
their inherent qualities has not been left unchallenged. Critics maintain
that immunity rather depends upon a specific legal source. Consequently, international organizations only enjoy immunities in so far as these
are attributed to them by a rule of international law.[76] As a result, if no
specific rule of international law according immunity to an international
organization can be ascertained, it will enjoy no immunity from suit.
Frequently, this discussion lacks a clear distinction between the concept
of immunity as an aspect inherent in an international organization's
legal personality and customary immunity.[77]

Lack of territory

A rather curious argument in favour of granting immunities to international organizations is based on their specific nature: international organizations should enjoy absolute immunity from suit because they have

---

[71] See pp. 194*f* above for the details of this case.
[72] Tribunale Roma, 17 September 1981; Corte di Cassazione, 23 November 1985. See pp. 152
and 195 above.
[73] (1986) 69 *Rivista di diritto internazionale* 150.
[74] Amtsgericht Bonn, 23 August 1961. See pp. 149 and 167*f* above.
[75] '[Es] folgt aber bereits aus dem Wesen der WEU als überstaatlicher Organisation, daß sie
weder im gegenwärtigen Zeitpunkt der deutschen Gerichtsbarkeit unterliegt noch sich
für die Zukunft der Zwangsgewalt der Bundesrepublik unterwerfen kann'. (1962) *Monatsschrift für deutsches Recht* 315.
[76] Dominicé, 'L'immunité de juridiction', 167.   [77] *Cf.* pp. 145*ff* above.

no territory of their own.[78] The authors proposing this argument usually do not elaborate or explain it in more detail. Thus, it remains unclear what the underlying rationale is.

It is not disputed that international organizations have no territory and that they consequently do not enact their own private law (contracts, torts, etc.) apart from administrative rules and organizational law. However, this merely seems to exclude a potential choice of law (as a result of rules of private international law). There simply is no tort law or contracts law of international organizations. Thus, it will be the law of the commission of the act or of an international organization's seat or of the other contracting party which will govern.[79] However, this has nothing to do with the procedural issue of jurisdiction over international organizations. A limitation based on governing laws seems to be no reason for denying jurisdiction over a suit against an international organization which is clearly subject to a certain legal order.

One author develops the argument somewhat further by explaining that states could regulate by their internal law the possible legal recourses of private persons against them, e.g. whether by administrative or judicial procedure, and thereby influence their accountability and protect themselves. Because they have no comparable legal order of their own this option would not be open to international organizations.[80] This reasoning based on a comparison with the situation of states operating on foreign soil or with another jurisdictional link to a foreign sovereign is, however, not fully convincing. It is precisely in such situations that the

---

[78] Morgenstern is of the opinion that international organizations having no territory of their own and 'thus necessarily operating within the jurisdiction of other legal systems' should receive different treatment from states and consequently enjoy 'absolute immunity'. Morgenstern, *Legal Problems*, 6. A similar argument is made by Lalive, who holds the distinction between *iure imperii* and *iure gestionis* acts to be inapplicable in the case of international organizations because they have no territory of their own and thus necessarily have to contract under a 'foreign' private law. Lalive, 'L'immunité de juridiction', 296*ff*. The 'lack of territory' argument also appears in the ILC Special Rapporteur's report, but not as a separate justification for granting immunity to international organizations, but rather as a subsidiary rationale. Noting that international organizations have to be based in the territory of a state, he recounts the need to afford them some protection against local judicial or administrative interference by granting immunity. *Yearbook of the International Law Commission* (1989), vol. II, Part One, 153 at 158.

[79] A rare exemption to this generally acknowledged fact – and again very limited in its scope – is the UN's 1986 legislation limiting its liability for tortious acts occurring within the headquarters premises. This UN-created law partly derogates from the otherwise applicable US law. *Cf.* Regulation No. 4, General Assembly Resolution 41/210. See also pp. 15*f* above.

[80] Lalive, 'L'immunité de juridiction', 298.

issue of their immunity is raised. Whether they will enjoy it or not depends upon the qualification of their acts, but it is undisputed that they are subject to the foreign law and to foreign procedural rules although they had no opportunity to influence them in order to 'protect' themselves.

In fact, the 'lack of territory' argument could be reversed and used against granting immunity to international organizations. While the respect of immunity from suit of states might be justified, because possessing territory they can be regularly sued in their own courts, these alternative fora are usually not available in respect of international organizations. Thus, it is not the absence of territory, but the concomitant lack of courts of international organizations which might militate against their immunity. It seems that in the Greek decision of X v. *International Centre for Superior Mediterranean Agricultural Studies*,[81] the Court of Appeals of Crete might have been aware of this relationship. It thought its denial of the Centre's immunity from suit in an employment dispute was 'reinforced' by the fact that otherwise there would have been no alternative forum for claims against the organization, 'since [it] enjoys jurisdictional immunity within all member states, does not possess its own territory' and could hardly be brought before courts in third countries.

It might be that the true, but unexpressed, reason for granting immunity to international organizations as a consequence of their lack of territory is in fact 'compensatory' in nature. Since international organizations have the disadvantage of lacking territory they should benefit from immunity. While states could protect themselves against unwarranted legal recourse against them under foreign laws by simply avoiding any contacts with foreign countries, international organizations by definition can only operate on the territory of a state. To compensate for this structural weakness immunity from suit might be justified.[82]

Precedent and prestige

Among other reasons to grant special rights to international organizations, the existence of precedents, the principle of reciprocity and the

---

[81] Court of Appeals of Crete, 1991 (unpublished).
[82] *Cf.* the argument made by Morgenstern, *Legal Problems*, 6, about the 'vulnerability' of international organizations lacking territory and thus necessarily operating within the jurisdiction of other legal systems. See also p. 238 above.

prestige of an international organization are sometimes discussed.[83] A wide variety of such prerogatives is likely to underline the importance of an international organization. Although frequently considered not to legitimately deserve consideration,[84] it seems that, in practice, prestige and precedent are among the dominant purposes of according privileges and immunities to international organizations.[85] The reasons for these privileges and immunities may not lie solely in a organization's self-interest in special and preferential treatment. As an indication of an international organization's international legal personality,[86] a certain range of privileges and immunities may be important for it to attain.

Nevertheless, prestige and precedent are hardly reasons to be taken seriously in an inquiry of legitimate grounds warranting the exemption of international organizations from the jurisdiction of national courts.

[83] Conseil de l'Europe, 13*ff*; Bekker, *The Legal Position*, 107*ff*.
[84] Conseil de l'Europe, 13*ff*.
[85] See the Memorandum of the UK on the privileges and immunities of international organizations, in Conseil de l'Europe, 75, appendix.
[86] See pp. 141 and 247 above.

5   Reasons for asserting jurisdiction

The following discussion looks at the rationales that are or should be used by courts in asserting jurisdiction over international organizations. It will focus on the reasons for denying or at least restricting the jurisdictional immunity of international organizations as the major abstention rationale.

It starts with a contextual argument,[1] and progresses *via* systematic reasoning[2] to material policy grounds addressing the interests of international organizations[3] and of third parties potentially affected by an organizations' immunity.[4]

Judicial protection as a public good sought by and against international organizations

The availability of judicial assistance to safeguard one's rights can be viewed as a 'public good' sought not only by individuals against international organizations,[5] but also by international organizations in asserting their rights against individuals. Further, the jurisdiction of domestic courts is in the interest not only of an individual or organization seeking their assistance but may also be in the broader interest of the forum state in exercising jurisdiction as a manifestation of public authority.

In *Arab Monetary Fund* v. *Hashim (No. 3)*,[6] where the judicial protection of

---

[1] Making sense of immunity qualifications. See pp. 253*ff* below.
[2] Encroachment on territorial sovereignty and higher degree of integration. See pp. 254*f* below.
[3] Enhancing the creditworthiness of international organizations. See pp. 255*ff* below.
[4] Fairness to third parties and human rights – constitutional limits. See pp. 262*ff* below.
[5] See pp. 280*ff* below as to a potential right of access to courts.
[6] Chancery Division, 9–12 October, 14 November 1989; Court of Appeal, 26–27 March, 9 April 1990; House of Lords, 26–28 November 1990, 21 February 1991.

an international organization was almost denied on the technical reason of the perceived lack of its domestic legal personality,[7] this interest was clearly spelled out. Closing the door of justice to 'foreign' international organizations would not only have caused embarrassment to the foreign ministry of the UK, which had apparently assumed that courts would implicitly recognize the AMF's legal personality, but would also lead to a 'potential loss of commercial dealings in London'[8] if international organizations felt that they would be denied judicial protection in England when they sought it.[9]

On a more general level, the existence of an advanced legal system, frequently advertised as an important element for the use of New York and London for international commercial litigation, might certainly also be a consideration for international organizations in choosing a particular seat state.

Making sense of immunity qualifications

Whenever a customary or conventional rule is applicable that prescribes a standard of 'necessary' or 'functional', or in some other way qualifies immunity, there are strong arguments to conclude that these qualifications signify a different and consequently lower degree of immunity than an unqualified 'immunity from suit' or an express 'absolute immunity'.[10] It is submitted that the view that these qualified immunities in fact embody the same standard as absolute immunity[11] ignores the relevance of the qualifications.

In particular, the term 'necessary' signifies a restrictive concept. Its connotations with 'essential', 'key', 'indispensable', 'urgent', 'needed', etc., imply that not everything is 'necessary'. Rather only a limited number of things might be. Referring to the classic functional immunity standard, as expressed, for instance, in Article 105 of the UN Charter speaking of the organization's immunity 'necessary for the fulfilment of its purposes', such a literal reading has led commentators to argue that, since the activities of an international organization are prescribed by its

---

[7] See pp. 65ff above.

[8] Ilona Cheyne, 'Status of International Organisations in English Law' (1991) 40 *International and Comparative Law Quarterly* 981–4 at 982.

[9] See also Jeremy P. Carver, 'International Organisations After Arab Monetary Fund' (1991) 6 *Butterworths Journal of International Banking and Financial Law* 215–18 at 217.

[10] See, however, p. 334 below as to the potential meaning of 'functional' or 'necessary' as characterizing only the rationale for immunity and not qualifying its scope.

[11] See pp. 332ff below.

constituent document, 'it is open to question whether absolute immunity is required to that end'.[12]

In general courts have also recognized that functional immunity is a restrictive concept. For instance, in *United States ex relatione Casanova* v. *Fitzpatrick*,[13] a US District Court in a case involving alleged espionage by a member of the Cuban Mission to the UN qualified the functional immunity standard of Article 105 of the UN Charter as 'limited immunity'.[14] In the *People* v. *Mark S. Weiner*[15] case, the Criminal Court of the City of New York saw in the 'privileges and immunities granted to the organization by article 104 and subdivision 1 of article 105 of the Charter of the United Nations' an 'intentional limitation of immunity'.[16]

Encroachment on the territorial sovereignty of the forum state

The technical legal issue of the proper qualification of the relationship between a state's jurisdiction to adjudicate and the immunity from suit of another subject of international law can be used to argue for a general restriction of immunity because any exemption from a state's jurisdiction could be viewed as an encroachment on its full territorial sovereignty. The issue is, of course, a double-edged sword, because – depending on the particular view – it could also be used to argue for a broader immunity. Based on the *Lotus* decision of the Permanent Court of International Justice[17] – frequently cited whenever a point is made for state freedom of action[18] – it has been argued that states are generally free to exercise adjudicative jurisdiction and that exceptions to this rule have to be proven by specific norms of international law (customary or conventional) evident beyond doubt.[19] Following this line, some courts have confirmed that

---

[12] *Restatement (Third)*, §467, Reporters' Note 4. See also the critique of the Austrian delegate to the 44th UN General Assembly concerning Draft Article 7 submitted by the Special Rapporteur on 'Relations between states and international organizations (second part of the topic)', providing for an unqualified (absolute) immunity from suit: '[T]he Austrian delegation is of the opinion that the realisation of the principle ne impediatur officia does not necessarily imply that international organizations have in every case to be granted total immunity from legal process.' It thought that 'further considerations on possible exceptions from this immunity are necessary', mentioning as an example car-accident claims brought against an international organization; reprinted in (1991) 42 *Austrian Journal of Public and International Law* 542.

[13] US District Court SDNY, 16 January 1963.   [14] 214 F. Supp. 425 at 429 (SDNY 1963).

[15] Criminal Court of the City of New York, New York County, 19 January 1976.

[16] 378 NYS 2d 966.   [17] PCIJ, Judgment No. 9, 1927, Series A, No. 10.

[18] *Cf.* Martti Koskenniemi, *From Apology to Utopia* (Helsinki, 1989), 221.

[19] Albert Bleckmann, *Internationale Beamtenstreitigkeiten vor nationalen Gerichten, Materialien zum Recht der internationalen Organisationen und zur Immunität, Rechtsgutachten für die Union*

the exercise of jurisdiction is the rule and that exemptions from jurisdiction are exceptions that have to be specifically justified.[20]

Similarly, the 'jurisdiction and security needs' of host states have been mentioned as legitimate interests which should be balanced against the interests of international organizations needing privileges and immunities for the efficient fulfilment of their functions.[21] It is, however, hard to see how the assertion of jurisdiction could be viewed as a security measure.

Higher degree of integration: the federal state analogy

International organizations achieving a high degree of integration, which places them into a category close to a federal state, might have no, or only a lesser, need to protect themselves against interference by member states that are no longer wholly independent states themselves, but are in turn closely integrated entities within such organizations.

It has been said that one of the reasons why the European Community does not enjoy immunity in its member states' courts is that the Community was originally conceived as an entity developing towards a federal state and that in such federal states the federation usually does not enjoy immunity before state courts.[22]

Enhancing the creditworthiness of international organizations as a functional reason to limit immunity

It is an obvious and perfectly rational reason that restricting an international organization's immunity from suit will enhance its credit-

---

Syndicale, Section Eurocontrol (Berlin, 1981), 18. Similarly, Sir Hersch Lauterpacht, 'The Problem of Jurisdictional Immunities of Foreign States' (1951) 28 *British Yearbook of International Law* 220–72 at 229, reminds the reader of the general premise formulated in the context of sovereign immunity, but valid also with regard to the immunity of international organizations, that '[a]ny derogation from [that] jurisdiction is an impairment of the sovereignty of the territorial state and must not be readily assumed'.

[20] 'Dem Grundsatz nach ist die Gerichtsbarkeit eines Staates innerhalb seines Staatsgebietes immer gegeben, falls nicht eine besondere Rechtsnorm dem entgegensteht.' S v. S, Bavarian High Court of Appeals, 30 September 1971; (1971) *Entscheidungen des Bayerischen Obersten Landesgerichts in Zivilsachen, Neue Folge* 303 at 304.

[21] Peter H. F. Bekker, *The Legal Position of Intergovernmental Organizations. A Functional Necessity Analysis of Their Legal Status and Immunities* (Dordrecht, Boston and London, 1994), 182. He cites Article 17 of the ILC Draft as 'on this point'. Article 17 reads: 'None of the provisions of this chapter shall affect the right of each State party [to this Convention] to adopt the necessary precautions and appropriate measures in the interest of its security.'

[22] Ignaz Seidl-Hohenveldern, 'L'immunité de juridiction des Communautés européennes' (1990) *Revue du Marché Commun* No. 338, 475–9 at 476.

worthiness and will increase the willingness of private parties to do business with it. Interestingly, this consideration, which is definitely in the 'enlightened' self-interest of the respective international organization concerned, has rarely been addressed outside the field of international financial organizations. There, however, its adoption even led to an express restriction of immunity. The best-known example is the formulation contained in Article VII(3) of the IBRD Articles of Agreement providing that '[a]ctions may be brought against the Bank [only] in a court of competent jurisdiction in the territories of a member in which the Bank has an office, has appointed an agent for the purpose of accepting service or notice of process, or has issued or guaranteed securities'.

The example of international lending institutions demonstrates the economic rationale behind a limitation of immunity very clearly. To make them subject to the adjudicative power of domestic courts facilitates the market access of these international organizations. Thus, the World Bank's restricted immunity has been regarded as instrumental in reassuring the financial community and encouraging potential lenders to do business with the Bank.[23] Its amenability to suit by private persons in claims which are not derived from member states, usually arising from financing agreements of the Bank, has even been characterized as resting on a 'functional basis'.[24] Indeed, the limitation of immunity from suit allows international organizations to function better on the international capital markets.

It is certainly true that this rationale is mainly applicable to international banks which rely heavily on private financing in their operation. Its importance will depend upon the ratio of capital raised by refinancing on the private capital market to the contributions of member states. To a lesser degree, however, all international organizations have some outside business contacts in their day-to-day operation which are simply necessary for their practical functioning. It seems that in this context also the notion of confidence creation should not be completely overlooked.[25] Office leases, procurement contracts, etc. are important aspects of run-

---

[23] Arghyrios A. Fatouros, 'The World Bank's Impact on International Law – A Case Study in the International Law of Cooperation' in Gabriel M. Wilner (ed.), *Jus et Societas. Essays in Tribute to Wolfgang Friedmann* (The Hague, Boston and London, 1979), 62–95 at 65.

[24] Aron Broches, 'International Legal Aspects of the Operations of the World Bank' (1959 III) 98 *Recueil des Cours* 296–409 at 309.

[25] E.g., Eurocontrol, which voluntarily submitted part of its primary activity (in carrying out its functions) to the jurisdiction of domestic courts in order to give an additional guarantee to the users of its services. Ignaz Seidl-Hohenveldern, *Die Immunität internationaler Organisationen in Dienstrechtsstreitfällen, Rechtsgutachten für Eurocontrol. Schriften zum Völkerrecht* (Berlin, 1981), vol. 71, 36.

ning an international organization. In this respect, only a creditworthy entity, an institution with which private contractors, suppliers of goods and services, etc. are willing to contract, will be able to function well.

Traditionally, it was argued that, since these private law activities are at least incidental to the fulfilment of an international organization's functions, they may be regarded as functionally necessary and should thus fall under immunity protection. However, one could equally well reverse the argument and ask whether the functional argument would not – as demonstrated in the World Bank context – find a more appropriate usage in justifying a restriction of the immunity shield.

It is true that so far in most cases all works well without adapting or restricting the traditional immunity standard. However, it probably worked well only at higher cost since prudent businesspersons certainly deal with international organizations only by adding risk premiums. If one's business partner might refuse performance of the contract and might escape liability on account of his or her immunity, it is only rational to include such potential costs in the final price charged to that partner. In order to reduce these additional costs, amenability to suit before national courts that are easily accessible would certainly be in the long-term interest of the international organization. In general, this long-term interest might be far better served if one allowed claims brought against international organizations to be litigated and, if lost, the judgments to be enforced. It would not only enhance the business-oriented creditworthiness of the international organization,[26] but would also enhance an international organization's general credibility as far as compliance with the law is concerned.[27] It is apparent that for some international organizations their insistence on their jurisdictional immunity, as a shield against justified claims brought against it, might even result in a poor public perception of the organization.[28]

Courts only rarely show interest in such policy considerations. An

---

[26] Ignaz Seidl-Hohenveldern, 'Le droit applicable aux entreprises internationales communes, étatiques ou paraétatiques' (1983 I) 60 *Annuaire de l'Institut de Droit International* 1–37 and 97–102 at 35.

[27] In this context, it is interesting to note the IDI's resolution on 'Contracts Concluded by International Organizations with Private Persons'. It addresses not only the issue of applicable law but also the problem of dispute settlement and considers the 'respect du droit et sécurité des transactions et des relations juridiques' highly desirable. (1977 II) 57 *Annuaire de l'Institut de Droit International* 332.

[28] In a memorandum dealing with the immunity from suit of its officials, the UN Office of Legal Affairs advised against an automatic invocation of such immunity in traffic cases which would give rise to considerable difficulties, 'not to mention the political consequences at a time when the general public and legislative bodies are opposed to privileges and immunities'. (1977) *United Nations Juridical Yearbook* 248.

exception is *Safehaven Investments Inc.* v. *Springbok Ltd*,[29] where an English court expressly took notice of the fact that a prospective buyer of real property and landlord of the International Coffee Organization encountered difficulties in raising bank financing for such acquisition because of 'misgivings which their bankers had expressed about the status of the [International Coffee Organization]' since this organization might not be amenable to suit in English courts. In addition to the economic self-interest of international organizations there may as well be a valid economic argument for the forum state to provide access to its courts against international organizations in order to attract and keep international business.[30] The fear expressed in the context of the *Arab Monetary Fund* v. *Hashim (No. 3)*[31] decision that not providing access to English courts in a case involving an international organization doing business in England could lead to a 'potential loss of commercial dealings in London'[32] evidences similar considerations.

No immunity for *iure gestionis* activities: the same immunity standard as the one used for states

Equalization with states

Historically, international organizations were regarded as comparable to states in so far as a grant of immunity was concerned. In particular, some older immunity legislation seems to reflect this equalization with states as a rationale to accord them immunity from suit.[33] The fact that, at the time of enactment, it was probably absolute immunity which was meant,[34] does not affect the equalization in principle.

[29] Chancery Division, 18 May 1995.
[30] See Georg Ress, 'Ex Ante Safeguards Against Ex Post Opportunism in International Treaties: Theory and Practice of International Public Law' (1994) 150 *Journal of Institutional and Theoretical Economics* (formerly *Zeitschrift für die gesamte Staatswissenschaft*) 279–303 at 281, raising this argument in the context of state immunity.
[31] See pp. 65*ff* above.   [32] Cheyne, *Status of International Organisations*, 982.
[33] The UK Diplomatic Privileges (Extension) Act 1944, for instance, provides for immunity to be accorded to international organizations to the same extent as to states. *Yearbook of the International Law Commission* (1977), vol. II, Part One, 152. In its message of 4 August 1919 concerning the League of Nations, the Swiss Federal Council declared it 'natural that the League of Nations should enjoy the same privileges and immunities as any state with which [Switzerland] maintained diplomatic relations'. Cited in Pierre Freymond, 'Remarques sur l'immunité de juridiction des organisations internationales en matière immobilière' (1955–6) 53 *Friedens-Warte* 365–79 at 366.
[34] In the case of the League of Nations, this might also be evidenced in the subsequent development leading to the *modus vivendi* incorporating 'absolute immunity'. *Cf.* p. 140 note 541 above.

A potential reason for this traditional equalization of international organizations with states might lie in the fact that international organizations were originally not seen as separate legal persons, but rather as collective entities representing their member states.[35] Thus, it was only logical to extend state or diplomatic immunity to those organizations and their officials. A number of older immunity cases are also based on the premise that international organizations are collective undertakings of states that should be treated like states.[36]

International organizations as subjects of international law

The possibility of equating international organizations with states is nowadays largely dismissed. However, there remain two arguments for applying a sovereign immunity concept to international organizations. One argument would regard international organizations as sovereign in a sufficiently similar way to states in order to apply immunity principles; the other argument would view international legal personality as the term of reference for immunity.

The definition of 'sovereignty' and, in particular, its crucial constitutive criteria are far from clear. Thus, the question of whether international organizations could qualify as sovereign entities depends very much upon a terminological clarification. As a matter of common consensus, most authors would agree that international organizations are not 'sovereign'. However, if one stresses – as the defining element of sovereignty – independence from the will of others, one may argue that international organizations can be regarded as 'sovereign' in a certain sense.[37] Similarly, one might view subjectivity under international law or international legal personality, and not exclusively sovereignty, as proper terms of reference for the rule of *par in parem non habet imperium*.[38]

Commercial activity exception regardless of trading person

Traditionally, the argument that international organizations are not sovereign is followed by underlining that the distinction between acts *iure imperii* and acts *iure gestionis*, common in the field of state activities,

---

[35] *Cf.* Bardo Faßbender, 'Die Völkerrechtssubjektivität internationaler Organisationen' (1986) 37 *Österreichische Zeitschrift für öffentliches Recht und Völkerrecht* 17–47 at 20, dealing with the doctrine of 'common organs'.

[36] See pp. 245*f* above.

[37] *Cf.* sovereignty as in Seyersted's articles on objective international personality. See p. 59 below.

[38] See pp. 246*f* above. See also the detailed discussion on traditional reasons for differentiating from states at pp. 348*ff* below.

cannot be transferred to international organizations. As a consequence, the restrictive immunity standard which in its practical application largely depends upon this distinction seems inoperative in the context of international organizations.

Many commentators, however, pursue a more cautious approach, leaving open the possibility of talking of commercial and public acts of international organizations at least in an analogous way.[39] Thus, a 'commercial activity exception' appears to be more and more acceptable to many scholars, leading some of them to the conclusion that 'an organization which performs purely commercial functions, entering the marketplace seeking customers for its industrial goods and services . . . has no justified need for any privileges and immunities at all'.[40]

[39] *Cf.*, e.g., Nicolas Valticos, 'Les contrats conclus par les organisations internationales avec des personnes privées, Rapport provisoire et projet de résolution – Rapport définitif et projet de résolution' (1977) *Annuaire de l'Institut de Droit International* 1–191 at 3, who states that the distinction 'entre actes de puissance publique et actes de gestion ne saurait se retrouver – du moins dans la même signification – dans le cas des organisations internationales encore que . . . une distinction un peu analogue puisse être esquissée à certains égards'. Even Seidl-Hohenveldern, an outspoken defender of the classic rule of absolute immunity *ratione personae* of international organizations, acknowledges that, if situations like the one involving the Tin Council collapse occurred more frequently, the socio-economic justification of treating states and international organizations differently – as far as immunity from suit is concerned – would disappear. In this case he seems to support an 'assimilation' of the treatment of international organizations to that of states. Seidl-Hohenveldern, 'L'immunité', 479. Similar arguments can be found in C. Wilfred Jenks, *International Immunities* (London and New York, 1961), 151*ff*, (restricted immunity might become appropriate if international organizations engage in commercial activity); Henry G. Schermers, 'International Organizations, Legal Remedies Against Acts of Organs' in Rudolf Bernhardt (ed.), *Encyclopedia of Public International Law* (2nd edn, 1995), vol. II, 1318–20 at 1318 ('Governmental organizations may take actions which are so much of a private law nature that the organization does not object to those acts being subjected to the legal control of a national court. For its operations under private law, it is possible, therefore, to serve process on a public international organization before a national court.'); and legislative materials to the IOIA in the 1945 Senate Report (commercial activity as ground for revoking an international organization's immunity), cited in Kathleen Cully, 'Jurisdictional Immunities of Intergovernmental Organizations' (1982) 91 *Yale Law Journal* 1167–95 at 1187.

[40] Bekker, *The Legal Position*, 114. This general statement is subsequently qualified when he dismisses the adaptability of the sovereign immunity concept of commercial activity and proposes an official/non-official acts differentiation as determinative for deciding immunity questions. Noting the difficulty in deciding on the official or non-official character of an act in a given case, Bekker proposes that '[a] way out of this controversy relating to the proper boundaries of the suggested criterion might be to use as a test whether the organization concerned not only participates on the market by concluding agreements with private contractors, but enters the marketplace seeking customers as a supplier and trader of goods or services for profit, thereby exposing itself to the ordinary forces of market competition'. As a result he re-introduces the commercial activity standard with the additional proviso of a profit-making requirement (actual or at least sought).

It has been argued that 'the very fact that States have grouped together to fulfil certain objectives bestows a public characterization'.[41] Such an argument would, of course, render any discussion about a *iure gestionis* character of any international organization superfluous, since all international organizations are groupings of states to fulfil certain objectives. This assertion stresses the 'public' character of forming an international organization by concluding an international agreement, which is certainly a public act; but so is the structure and existence of a state a matter of public law. The characterization of an activity as commercial or public, however, should correctly depend upon the activity itself and not on the fact that the activity is commonly undertaken in the form of an international organization or on the fact that it was a treaty, being of a public character, that led to the formation of such a common undertaking. This view has been strongly expressed by the reasoning of the court in *International Association of Machinists* v. *OPEC*[42] that '[i]t is ridiculous to suggest that the essentially governmental nature of an activity changes merely by the act of two or more countries coming together to agree upon how they will carry out that activity'.[43] It is important to note, however, that in this case the Californian district court argued in a reverse fashion that a public activity cannot become a private one merely because the method of agreeing upon its joint execution might be considered private.

Enhanced judicial protection of private parties: commercial activities of international organizations

The main underlying policy reasons that have led to a restrictive immunity standard valid for states, i.e. an expression of fairness to parties dealing with them and to other third parties affected by their activities as well as a growing concern over the private parties' rights of access to judicial determination of their rights,[44] are probably equally valid for relations between international organizations and private parties. This suggests that a similar limitation of the immunity of international organizations would be appropriate.

Such a development could be supported probably less by the fact that the position of international organizations may be equal or analogous to

---

[41] Romana Sadurska and Christine M. Chinkin, 'The Collapse of the International Tin Council: A Case of State Responsibility?' (1990) 30 *Virginia Journal of International Law* 845–90 at 854.

[42] US District Court CD Cal., 18 September 1979, *affirmed on other grounds*, US Court of Appeals 9th Cir., 6 July–24 August 1981.

[43] 477 F. Supp. 553 at 569 (CD Cal. 1979).   [44] See p. 198 above.

that of states, than by the same reason which led to a restriction of state immunity that is valid also for international organizations. If one concedes that the abandonment of the absolute immunity standard for states primarily 'stemmed from [a] growing concern for individual rights and public morality, coupled with an increasing entry of governments into what had previously been regarded as private pursuits',[45] then there should be no reason to deny that similar considerations might lead to similar conclusions in the case of international organizations.[46]

A number of court decisions follow this rationale. In *African Reinsurance Corporation* v. *Abate Fantaye*,[47] for instance, reflecting on the rationale of immunity provisions for an international financial organization, a Nigerian judge of the Court of Appeal – subsequently reversed by the Supreme Court – stated: 'It is my respectful view that the framers of [the Headquarters] Agreement did not intend to protect the appellant from being sued once its main object was to undertake mercantile transactions'.[48] In *SAT Fluggesellschaft mbH* v. *Eurocontrol*,[49] Advocate-General Tesauro also pointed towards the:

inadequacy of the proposition that ascribes absolute immunity to such organizations ... taking into account, moreover, the need not to deprive individuals of the protection afforded to subjective rights that might be impaired by the activities of international organizations, also in view of the growing number of organizations carrying on economic activities.[50]

Fairness to third parties

Immunity from suit of international organizations has given rise to a number of concerns as to its negative effect concerning the enforcement of legal obligations. It is widely perceived that international organizations would gain an 'unfair'[51] procedural advantage in their dealings with third parties, i.e. private individuals and non-member states, if they

---

[45] Mark Gordon, 'Recent Developments: International Organizations: Immunity – *Broadbent* v. *Organization of American States*' (1980) 21 *Harvard International Law Journal* 552–61 at 555, relying on *Victory Transport* v. *Comisaria General de Abastecimientios y Transportes*, 336 F. 2d 354 at 357 (2d Cir. 1964), *cert. denied*, 381 US 934 (1965).

[46] *Cf.* Ignaz Seidl-Hohenveldern, 'Eurocontrol und EWG-Wettbewerbsrecht' in Konrad Ginther, Gerhard Hafner, Winfried Lang, Hanspeter Neuhold and Lilly Sucharipa-Beermann (eds.), *Völkerrecht zwischen normativem Anspruch und politischer Realität. Festschrift für Karl Zemanek* (Berlin, 1994), 251–73 at 263, supporting a restriction of the immunity protection of international organizations concerning their commercial activities even if they ultimately serve a public purpose in order to protect (private) third parties.

[47] Supreme Court, 20 June 1986.   [48] (1991) 86 ILR 655 at 673.

[49] Case 364/92, ECJ, 19 January 1994.   [50] [1994] ECR I-43 at 48.

[51] *Cf.* C. Byk, 'Case Note to *Hintermann* v. *Union de l'Europe occidental*' (1997) 124 *Journal de droit international* 142–51 at 143, speaking of a 'situation inéquitable'.

were not amenable to suit in legal disputes arising from such dealings or other contacts. The widely repeated assertion that international organizations on the whole tend to fulfil their obligations diligently and in case of disputes agree to waive their immunity or to alternative dispute settlement[52] is of little help to the unsatisfied creditor's claim against a recalcitrant organization.[53]

Thus, in the case of international organizations policy considerations similar to those resulting in a restriction of sovereign or other forms of immunity are also very likely to apply.

Immunity as unjustifiable privilege potentially leading to a denial of justice

While the privileged position enjoyed by states in the procedural sphere as a result of their jurisdictional immunity has been on the whole successfully challenged in most domestic courts as a matter of 'fairness to plaintiffs'[54] and 'under the rule of law'[55] and – as a consequence – was reduced to a restrictive immunity scope, the same privileged position of international organizations under the dominant absolute immunity standard is still considered valid and justified. Judicial criticism is only sparingly mounted against this archaic preferential treatment of a specific group of actors. In a few decisions, however, judges have chosen quite strong words to characterize what they thought an indefensible privilege.

In the *People* v. *Mark S. Weiner* case,[56] the Criminal Court of the City of New York reasoned that to uphold a UN security officer's immunity from suit would be 'so unconscionable that it violates on its face the concepts of fundamental fairness and equal treatment of all persons who seek judicial determination of a dispute'.[57] Similarly critical words were employed in an early French decision, *Avenol* v. *Avenol*,[58] concerning the

---

[52] See Hans-Joachim Schütz, 'Host State Agreements' in Rüdiger Wolfrum (ed.), *United Nations: Law, Policies and Practice* (Dordrecht, London and Boston, 1995), vol.1, 581–90 at 585, who thinks that '[a]s a rule, an organization will [waive its claim to jurisdictional immunity] if an opponent in a civil law suit – for example in a case on damages – would otherwise sustain unfair disadvantages'.

[53] *Cf.* the High Court's assessment of the behaviour of the Tin Council in *Maclaine Watson & Co. Ltd* v. *International Tin Council (No. 2)*, High Court, Chancery Division, 9 July 1987: 'The ITC, it must be said, has behaved more like a disreputable private creditor than the responsible international organisation that it claims to be'. (1988) 77 ILR 160 at 162.

[54] James Crawford, 'International Law and Foreign Sovereigns: Distinguishing Immune Transactions' (1983) 54 *British Yearbook of International Law* 75–118 at 77.

[55] Lauterpacht, 'The Problem', 220.

[56] Criminal Court of the City of New York, New York County, 19 January 1976.

[57] 378 NYS 2d 966 at 975*ff*.   [58] Juge de Paix Paris, 8 March 1935.

Secretary-General of the League of Nations. In an action for maintenance payment brought by his separated wife the Secretary-General's claim to absolute diplomatic immunity from the jurisdiction of French courts was rejected with the following strong words:

> If we were to decide that Avenol is covered by diplomatic immunity before the courts of the sixty States, Members of the League, we should have reached a decision which is . . . palpably contrary to all notions of law which have been gradually imposed on the human conscience since the ages of barbarism . . . It is not possible that the Covenant of the League of Nations, which Avenol summons to aid his contention, the Covenant which governs the highest moral and judicial authority in the world, entrusted with the establishment of the law of nations, should provide the world with an astonishing example of a provision which is in such flagrant contradiction to the sacred and profound sentiment of justice.[59]

In the French court's view the immunity of League officials was functionally and territorially limited and thus applied only to acts 'in the exercise of their functions at Geneva and in Switzerland'.[60]

Academic writers trying to restrict the immunities of international organizations frequently argue with the unjustifiably 'privileged' position otherwise enjoyed by international organizations.[61] In their view, this position might even lead to a denial of justice where there is no alternative dispute settlement provided for.[62] The fact that the immunity

---

[59] (1935–7) 8 *Annual Digest of Public International Law Cases* 395 at 396.   [60] *Ibid.*

[61] For instance, Cully, while acknowledging that the US IOIA cannot be read to incorporate the restricted FSIA standard, argues that '[intergovernmental organizations] may have no need of an absolute immunity that in itself is undesirable'. Cully, 'Jurisdictional Immunities', 1179. This 'undesirability' becomes evident from the fact that it confers a privileged status 'which subverts the principle that legal rights entail legal responsibility . . . and allows the immune person to harm others with impunity'. *Ibid*, 1179, note 101. As a minor criticism, one might mention that it is rather the principle that legal duties entail legal responsibility and answerability which is violated. It is not doubted at all that international organizations can legally obligate themselves; rather it may be questionable whether such legal duties can be procedurally enforced.

[62] *Cf.* Jean-Flavien Lalive, 'L'immunité de juridiction des états et des organisations internationales' (1953 III) 84 *Recueil des Cours* 205–396 at 302; David Ruzié, 'Diversité des juridictions administratives internationales et finalité commune. Rapport général' in Société Française pour le Droit International (ed.), *Le Contentieux de la fonction publique international* (Paris, 1996), 11–65 at 13; and Ignaz Seidl-Hohenveldern, 'Jurisdiction over Employment Disputes in International Organizations' in University of Oviedo (ed.), *Colección de Estudios Jurídicos en Homenaje al Prof. Dr D. José Pérez Montero* (1988), vol. III, Oviedo, 359–72 at 368. See also the French Cour de Cassation's opinion in its annual report of 1995: 'Les immunités de juridiction des organisations internationales . . . ont, pour conséquence, lorsque n'est pas organisé au sein de chaque organisation un mode de règlement arbitral ou juridictionnel des litiges, de créer un déni de justice.' Cour de Cassation, *Rapport annuel* (1995),

of international organizations before domestic courts deprives individuals of their legal remedies against such organizations is a grave concern for some commentators who have developed various strategies to cope with these irritations ranging from denouncing immunity as such to satisfying themselves with the availability of alternative ways to seek procedural redress. Thus, it is frequently asserted that the principle of legality/rule of law and the necessity to avoid abuses by international organizations calls for an impartial system of dispute settlement.[63]

Alternative dispute settlement in the case of immunity

Jurisdictional immunity of international organizations cannot release them from their substantive legal obligations under domestic law. It is clear that immunity is only a procedural barrier to the adjudication and/or enforcement of legal obligations which in themselves remain unaffected. Immunity does not alter any substantive rights and obligations.[64] It is clear, however, that immunity may frustrate the effective implementation of the law. In particular, disputes concerning contractual or non-contractual relations with private persons need to be settled. In order to avoid or at least to mitigate the injurious effect of immunity on private parties, two practical options are always available: international organizations may waive their immunity and thereby consent to the adjudicative power of domestic courts[65] or they may have consented to alternative ways of dispute settlement, in particular to arbitration or to the jurisdiction of international courts or tribunals. Because international organizations rarely waive their immunity in

418, cited by Byk, 'Case Note', 142. See also the European Court of Human Rights in the *Golder* case: 'The principle whereby a civil claim must be capable of being submitted to a judge ranks as one of the universally recognised fundamental principles of law; the same is true of the principle of international law which forbids the denial of justice.' *Golder*, European Court of Human Rights, 21 February 1975, Series A, No. 18, para. 35.

[63] Valticos, 'Les contrats conclus', 65. *Cf.* also the recent decision of the European Court of Human Rights in *Stran Greek Refineries and Stratis Andreadis* v. *Greece*, European Court of Human Rights, 9 December 1994, Series A, No. 301-B, para. 46, stating that 'the principle of the rule of law . . . finds expression, *inter alia*, in Article 6 of the [European] Convention [on Human Rights and Fundamental Freedoms] [securing] in particular the right to a fair trial and . . . the requirement of equality of arms in the sense of a fair balance between the parties'.

[64] Henry G. Schermers, *International Institutional Law* (Alphen aan den Rijn and Rockville, 2nd edn, 1980), 796.

[65] The clause on the immunity from jurisdiction of the ESA appears to acknowledge this necessity by providing: 'the Council has the duty to waive this immunity in all cases where reliance upon it would impede the course of justice and it can be waived without prejudicing the interests of the Agency.' Article XV(2) of the ESA Convention.

practice,[66] it is primarily the second option, recourse to alternative methods of dispute settlement, which is of factual relevance.

Of course, there is always the ultimate possibility of elevating a dispute between an organization and a private party to the international level between the individual's home state and the international organization. According to the Institut de Droit International, negotiations and diplomatic protection should precede a possible waiver of immunity or arbitration.[67] However, while direct negotiations between the private party and the international organization attempting to settle any differences between them will certainly precede any institutionalized dispute settlement procedure, international responsibility is usually perceived as a measure of last resort.[68]

Apart from the proper sequencing of different ways of redress, for the individuals concerned 'judicial' methods of dispute settlement are also clearly preferable to the discretionary exercise of diplomatic protection. In a proper adjudicative process it is less likely that their rights and claims will be compromised in a settlement with an international organization.

An alternative method: arbitration

In practice, the most frequently used method of securing dispute settlement with private parties lies in providing for arbitration. International organizations regularly include arbitration clauses in their contracts with private persons.[69] They do so not only on the basis of practical

[66] See p. 223 note 287 above.

[67] The IDI draft resolution on contracts between international organizations and private parties speaks of disputes which cannot be 'résolu à l'amiable à la suite, soit de négociation entre les parties, soit de l'intervention diplomatique d'un Etat'. (1977 I) 57 *Annuaire de l'Institut de Droit International* 109.

[68] See also Sadurska and Chinkin, 'The Collapse of the International Tin Council', 856, reasoning that, after the dismissal of the claims against the ITC and its member states in the courts, the 'only remaining avenue of legal redress ... would be through claims made under international law'. Delictual capacity of international organizations is generally accepted although it has been stressed that organizational liability differs from state responsibility. ILC Report on State Responsibility, *Yearbook of the International Law Commission* (1975), vol. II, 87*ff*; Konrad Ginther, *Die völkerrechtliche Verantwortlichkeit internationaler Organisationen gegenüber Drittstaaten* (Vienna and New York, 1969). Byk considers the possibility of the home state of an organization's employee who has not been granted access to domestic courts, internal grievance procedures or other dispute settlement mechanisms having 'recours à une démarche d'ordre diplomatique'. Byk, 'Case Note', 144.

[69] *Cf.* the overview given by Valticos, 'Les contrats conclus', 66*ff*. When ILO decided to build a new headquarters office in Geneva all agreements with construction companies taking part contained arbitration clauses. Blaise Knapp, 'Questions juridiques relatives à la construction d'immeubles par les organisations internationales' (1977) 33 *Schweizerisches Jahrbuch für Internationales Recht* 51–80 at 75.

expedience but also because in many cases they are required to provide for arbitration by the applicable immunity regime.[70] Given the frequency of arbitration clauses included in contracts of international organizations with private third parties it is surprising that arbitral decisions involving international organizations are very rarely rendered in practice.[71]

Alternative fora: administrative tribunals

Many international organizations established administrative tribunals competent to adjudicate disputes between themselves and their employees or other persons.[72] The most important of these tribunals are the UN Administrative Tribunal,[73] the ILO Administrative Tribunal[74] and the

---

[70] E.g., Article 21 of the General Agreement on Privileges and Immunities of the Council of Europe: 'Any dispute between the Council and private persons regarding supplies furnished, services rendered or immovable property purchased on behalf of the Council, shall be submitted to arbitration, as provided in an administrative order issued by the Secretary-General with the approval of the Committee of Ministers.' The General Convention and the Special Convention leave it to the discretion of the organization concerned as to which particular kind of alternative dispute settlement procedure it will choose. Article 29 of the General Convention and Article 31(a) of the Special Convention provide that the organizations shall make provision for 'appropriate modes of settlement of disputes' arising out of 'contracts or other disputes of a private law character to which the [United Nations/specialized agency] is a party'. In practice, it is mainly arbitration that is chosen.

[71] In his study on the settlement of disputes arising from contracts between international organizations and private parties, Glavinis discusses only seven arbitral awards and thus rightly speaks of a 'jurisprudence quasi-inexistante'. Panayotis Glavinis, *Les litiges relatifs aux contrats passés entre organisations internationales et personnes privées*, *Travaux et recherches Panthéon-Assas, Paris II* (Paris, 1990), 15. A few other arbitral proceedings are mentioned in Valticos, 'Les contrats conclus', 88ff. Even if one takes into consideration the fact that arbitral awards are frequently treated confidentially and thus not published, this apparently extremely low number of arbitrations is surprising.

[72] See in general Hans-Joachim Priess, *Internationale Verwaltungsgerichte und Beschwerdeausschüsse, Eine Studie zum gerichtlichen Rechtsschutz für Beamte internationaler Organisationen* (Berlin, 1989); and Société Française pour le Droit International (ed.), *Le Contentieux de la Fonction Publique International* (Paris, 1996).

[73] Adopted by General Assembly Resolution 351 A (IV), 24 November 1949, amended by General Assembly Resolution 782 B (VIII), 9 December 1953 and General Assembly Resolution 957 (X), 8 November 1955.

[74] Adopted by the International Labour Conference, 9 October 1946, amended on 29 June 1949 and 17 June 1986. See Frank Gutteridge, 'The ILO Administrative Tribunal' in C. de Cooker (ed.), *International Administration* (looseleaf, The Hague, Boston and London, 1989–), V.2/1; and Blaise Knapp, 'International Labour Organisation Administrative Tribunal' in Rudolf Bernhardt (ed.), *Encyclopedia of Public International Law* (2nd edn, 1995), vol. II, 1156–9 at 1156.

World Bank Administrative Tribunal.[75] The ECJ,[76] and since 1988 the Court of First Instance,[77] serve as administrative tribunals for staff disputes of the European Communities.[78] Where international organizations do not establish their own tribunals, they may declare other tribunals competent for such disputes. As a consequence of such references, the ILO Administrative Tribunal has jurisdiction over complaints brought by the staff of several other UN organizations.[79] As a rule administrative recourse procedures precede access to judicial organs.[80] However, these internal grievance procedures usually do not have the character of true judicial proceedings.[81]

As already mentioned, the jurisdiction of administrative tribunals may sometimes be extended to non-staff disputes. For instance, the Statute of the ILO Administrative Tribunal provides that '[t]he Tribunal shall be

[75] Adopted by the Boards of Governors of the IBRD, the IDA and the IFC on 30 April 1980. See C. F. Amerasinghe, 'The World Bank Administrative Tribunal' (1982) 31 *International and Comparative Law Quarterly* 748–64 at 748; Eduardo Jiménez de Aréchaga, 'The World Bank Administrative Tribunal' (1982) 14 *New York University Journal of International Law and Politics* 895–909 at 895*ff*; and Theodor Meron and Betty Elder, 'The New Administrative Tribunal of the World Bank' (1982) 14 *New York University Journal of International Law and Politics* 1*ff*.

[76] According to Article 179 of the EC Treaty, the ECJ 'shall have jurisdiction in any dispute between the Community and its servants within the limits and under the conditions laid down in the Staff Regulations or the Conditions of Employment'.

[77] The Court of First Instance was 'attached' to the ECJ pursuant to the authorization contained in Article 168a of the EC Treaty by Decision 88/591, OJ C215/1, 21 August 1989. Its jurisdiction covers primarily staff and competition cases. *Cf.* Henry G. Schermers, 'The European Court of First Instance' (1988) 25 *Common Market Law Review* 541 at 541*ff*.

[78] See Jacques Biancarelli, 'Le Juge communautaire et le contentieux de la fonction publique communautaire' in Société Française pour le Droit International (ed.), *Le Contentieux de la fonction publique international* (Paris, 1996), 193–207 at 193*ff*.

[79] Article II(5) of the ILO Administrative Tribunal Statute provides that '[t]he Tribunal shall also be competent to hear complaints . . . of officials . . . of any other intergovernmental organisation approved by the Governing Body which has addressed to the Director-General a declaration recognising, in accordance with its Constitution or internal administrative rules, the jurisdiction of the tribunal for this purpose, as well as its Rules of Procedure'. Among others, the WHO, UNESCO, the FAO, the WMO, the IAEA and GATT have made such declarations. Georges Vandersanden, 'Administrative Tribunals, Boards and Commissions in International Organizations' in Rudolf Bernhardt (ed.), *Encyclopedia of Public International Law* (2nd edn, 1992), vol. I, 27–31 at 27.

[80] Gordon W. Wattles, 'Internal Recourse Procedures of International Organizations' (1982) 14 *New York University Journal of International Law and Politics* 871–94 at 871*ff*.

[81] See Jiménez de Aréchaga, 'The World Bank Administrative Tribunal', 896. Sometimes the fairness of such internal administrative procedures is challenged. *Cf.* the complaint in *HvdP v. The Netherlands*, UN Human Rights Committee, Communication No. 217/1986, 8 April 1987, calling the Internal Appeals Committee of the European Patent Office a 'travesty of competence, independence and impartiality as required by Article 14 [of the International Covenant on Civil and Political Rights]'. The application was not heard on jurisdictional grounds. See also p. 302 below.

competent to hear disputes arising out of contracts to which the International Labour Organisation is a party and which provide for the competence of the Tribunal in any case of dispute with regard to their execution'[82] and according to Article 181 of the EC Treaty, the EC's 'administrative tribunal', the ECJ, 'shall have jurisdiction to give judgment pursuant to any arbitration clause contained in a contract concluded by or on behalf of the Community, whether that contract be governed by public or private law'. However, this legal option that administrative tribunals are also open to private third parties to bring their complaints against the organization[83] – although frequently contractually provided for[84] – has not resulted in a large body of case law.[85]

The danger that through their administrative tribunals international organizations might actually be 'judges in their own matter' and the risk of bias or even denial of justice[86] seem to be unfounded in practice.[87]

---

[82] Article II(4) of the ILO Administrative Tribunal Statute.

[83] The Oslo Resolution of the IDI expressly mentions 'une juridiction établie par une organisation internationale, si l'attribution de cette compétence est compatible avec des règles de l'organisation' as an appropriate independent body for the settlement of disputes in cases where international organizations enjoy immunity from suit. (1977 II) 57 Annuaire de l'Institut de Droit International 336.

[84] The ILO regularly includes the following clause in contracts concerning insurance policies, the provision of office material and in other contracts with external collaborators: 'Si un litige survient entre les parties et qu'elles ne puissent le régler par voie de consultation, il sera soumis au Tribunal administratif de l'OIT, conformément aux dispositions du statut du Tribunal. La décision du Tribunal est définitive et aura force obligatoire pour les parties.' Cited by Valticos, 'Les contrats conclus', 84, note 164. Article 10 of the Conditions générales applicables aux contrats d'études de la Commission des Communautés européennes and Article 17 of the Cahier des conditions générales applicables aux marchés de fournitures courantes contain the following stipulation: 'Au cas où la procédure prévue à l'article 16 [involving a proposal by an expert for an amicable settlement] n'aboutit pas à un règlement amiable du différend, chaque partie contractante peut porter le litige devant la Cour de Justice des Communautés européennes. La compétence de tout autre tribunal est exclue.' Cited by Valticos, 'Les contrats conclus', 86, note 170.

[85] According to Knapp, as of 1983, no dispute between a private party and an international organization has been referred to the ILO Administrative Tribunal. Knapp, 'International Labour Organisation Administrative Tribunal', 1157. Glavinis recounts only one case where the ILO Administrative Tribunal rendered a decision as an arbitral tribunal in a dispute between a doctor and the WHO to which he had provided medical services. Rebeck v. World Health Organization, Arbitration Award of the ILO Administrative Tribunal, Judgment No. 77, 1 December 1964. Also the ECJ's jurisprudence as elected arbitral forum in disputes between the Community and private persons is meagre. A recent study on this point reports only one case, Pellegrini & CS v. Commission and Flexon Italia SpA, Arbitral Award of the ECJ, Case 23/76, 7 December 1976.

[86] Cully, 'Jurisdictional Immunities', 1182.

[87] C. F. Amerasinghe, The Law of the International Civil Service (As Applied by International Administrative Tribunals) (2nd edn, Oxford, 1994), vol. I, 68ff.

An international duty to establish administrative tribunals?

International lawyers are familiar with the question of whether international organizations are competent to establish administrative tribunals even if their constituent treaties do not contain any express authorization to do so.[88] The *Effect of Awards* advisory opinion of the ICJ,[89] where the ICJ contributed considerably to the jurisprudence of the implied powers of international organizations,[90] answered this question in the affirmative. The ICJ held that the UN had the legal power to establish an administrative tribunal – a capacity which arises by 'necessary intendment out of the Charter'.[91] At first sight, the issue of whether international organizations are also under a *duty* to establish administrative tribunals or at least to submit their employment disputes to the jurisdiction of a tribunal already established appears very academic. However, it might as well have direct relevance for the immunity problem, since in both areas the problem of the availability of means of legal recourse is central.

The ILC special rapporteur on relations between states and international organizations – in the course of justifying absolute immunity from suit of international organizations – generally speaks of an 'obligation imposed on international organizations to institute a judicial system for the settlement of conflicts or disputes in which they may become involved'.[92] It has also been cautiously suggested that organizations might be bound to establish administrative tribunals by virtue of the dispute settlement obligations contained in the General and Special Conventions and similar treaties.[93] The wording of these obligations 'to make provisions for appropriate modes of settlement', however, strictly relates only to disputes arising out of private law contracts with the UN and to disputes involving UN officials whose immunity has not been waived.[94] They do not refer to employment disputes. Nevertheless, they can be regarded as an acknowledgment of a need to settle disputes in cases

---

[88] Finn Seyersted, 'Settlement of Judicial Disputes of Intergovernmental Organizations by Internal and External Courts' (1963) 24 *Zeitschrift für ausländisches öffentliches Recht und Völkerrecht* 1–121 at 15*ff*.

[89] *Effect of Awards of Compensation Made by the United Nations Administrative Tribunal*, (1954) *ICJ Reports* 47.

[90] See pp. 56*ff* and 76*f* above.

[91] *Effect of Awards of Compensation Made by the United Nations Administrative Tribunal*, (1954) *ICJ Reports* 47 at 57.

[92] Leonardo Díaz-González (Special Rapporteur), 'Fourth Report on Relations Between States and International Organizations (Second Part of the Topic)' (UN Doc. A/CN.4/424) *Yearbook of the International Law Commission* (1989), vol. II, Part One, 153–68 at 161.

[93] Seidl-Hohenveldern, 'Jurisdiction over Employment Disputes', 360.

[94] *Cf*. Article VIII section 29 (a) and (b) of the General Convention.

where the organization or its officials enjoy immunity from suit before domestic courts.

Another possible argument in favour of such a duty can be derived from the *Effect of Awards* advisory opinion where the ICJ not only regarded the UN as competent to establish an administrative tribunal, but also hinted that there might be an obligation to do so when arguing that it would 'hardly be consistent with the expressed aim of the Charter to promote freedom and justice for individuals ... that [the United Nations] should afford no judicial or arbitral remedy to its own staff for the settlement of any disputes which may arise between it and them'.[95]

It has also been suggested that:

[the] availability of a legal remedy – as a guarantee of respect for the law – may now be considered a general principle of law in the sense of Article 38 of the Statute of the International Court. This is so by virtue of a customary international rule that is tending to assert itself more and more, that international organizations today appear bound to establish legal remedies for the good of all their personnel and to those who may invoke statutory rules.[96]

This assertion raises, of course, interesting and still largely unresolved questions concerning the binding character of general principles or customary rules of international law for international organizations.[97] It also touches upon important aspects of the existence of and evidence for a perceived customary rule. Whether the establishment of numerous administrative tribunals by international organizations is relevant practice,[98] whether they have been established with a belief that they are necessary to fulfil a duty under international law, etc., is not easy to ascertain.[99]

---

[95] *Effect of Awards of Compensation Made by the United Nations Administrative Tribunal*, (1954) *ICJ Reports* 47 at 57.

[96] Suzanne Bastid, 'Have the UN Administrative Tribunals Contributed to the Development of International Law' in Wolfgang Friedmann, Louis Henkin and Oliver Lissitzyn (eds.), *Transnational Law in a Changing Society: Essays in Honor of Philip C. Jessup* (New York and London, 1972), 298–312 at 309.

[97] See Albert Bleckmann, 'Zur Verbindlichkeit des allgemeinen Völkerrechts für Internationale Organisationen' (1977) 37 *Zeitschrift für ausländisches öffentliches Recht und Völkerrecht* 107ff; August Reinisch, 'Das Jugoslawientribunal der Vereinten Nationen und die Verfahrensgarantien des II. VN-Menschenrechtspaktes. Ein Beitrag zur Frage der Bindung der Vereinten Nationen an nicht-ratifiziertes Vertragsrecht' (1995) 47 *Austrian Journal of Public and International Law* 173ff.

[98] Suggested by Priess, *Internationale Verwaltungsgerichte*, 73.

[99] One further piece of evidence demonstrating an *opinio iuris* of being obligated to establish an intra-organizational recourse procedure is the explanation given by the IBRD President for establishing the World Bank Administrative Tribunal. He referred to a principle accepted in many national legal systems and reaffirmed in the Universal Declaration of

Administrative tribunals extending their jurisdiction in order to avoid a denial of justice

In this context it is interesting to note that some administrative tribunals interpreted their jurisdictional competence in a very broad fashion so as to avoid a denial of justice of an aggrieved employee who would have no other recourse against his or her employer organization.

The ILO Administrative Tribunal, followed by the UN Administrative Tribunal, started to declare itself competent to hear claims brought by persons who did not strictly qualify as staff members under the relevant staff rules and regulations. In *Chadsey v. Universal Postal Union*,[100] the ILO Administrative Tribunal held that:

> While the Staff Regulations of an organization were as a whole applicable only to those categories of employees expressly specified therein, some of their provisions were merely the translation into written form of general principles of civil service law; those principles must be considered applicable to any employees having a link other than a purely casual one with an organization and consequently could not lawfully be ignored in individual contracts. That applied in particular to the principle that such employees were entitled, in the event of a dispute with their employers, to the safeguard of some appeals procedure.[101]

The UN Administrative Tribunal expressly relied on this holding in *Teixera v. Secretary-General of the United Nations*.[102] Mindful of the UN's duty to provide for appropriate modes of dispute settlement contained in Article VIII section 29 of the General Convention, it awarded damages to the applicant for the delay caused by the UN which did not agree upon arbitration immediately when a dispute with a non-staff member arose but only three years later. In *Irani v. Secretary-General of the United Nations*,[103] the UN Administrative Tribunal had already extended its jurisdiction to a dispute involving a non-staff member. It noted that:

> unless the tribunal was competent in the case before it, the safeguard of some appeals procedure for the benefit of the applicant [as called for in *Chadsey v. Universal Postal Union*] would not exist, and article V of the contract between the

Human Rights which required that, wherever administrative power was exercised, a machinery should be available to accord a fair hearing and due process to an aggrieved party in cases of disputes. *Cf.* Memorandum to the Executive Directors from the President of the World Bank, 14 January 1980, Doc. R80-8, 1*ff*, cited in Amerasinghe, *The Law of the International Civil Service*, vol. II, 41.

[100] ILO Administrative Tribunal, 15 October 1968, Judgment No. 122.
[101] (1968) *United Nations Juridical Yearbook* 176.
[102] UN Administrative Tribunal, 14 October 1977, Judgment No. 230.
[103] UN Administrative Tribunal, 6 October 1971, Judgment No. 150.

applicant and the Organization [providing for the establishment of appropriate machinery to hear and to decide disputes] would not be respected.[104]

In *Zafari v. UNRWA*[105] and in *Salaymeh v. UNRWA*,[106] the UN Administrative Tribunal extended its jurisdiction to claims brought by local UNRWA staff for whose complaints, in general, a Special Panel of Adjudicators and not the UN Administrative Tribunal was competent.[107] The jurisdiction of this Special Panel was, however, very limited; it was basically restricted to scrutinizing the legality of an employment termination. In *Zafari v. UNRWA*, the applicant disputed the qualification of the end of his employment as an early voluntary retirement, whereas in *Salaymeh v. UNRWA*, the applicant complained that the calculation of his contribution to UNRWA's pension fund was incorrect. In both cases the UN Administrative Tribunal thought that the Special Panel of Adjudicators would not have jurisdiction.[108] In the Tribunal's view, the applicant Zafari was 'thus deprived of any recourse against the decision of the Commissioner-General of UNRWA' and 'has truly been denied justice'.[109] Relying on the above-quoted passage from the ICJ's *Effect of Awards* opinion[110] as well as on the World Court's view in *Judgments of the Administrative Tribunal of the International Labour Organisation upon Complaints Made Against the United Nations Educational, Scientific and Cultural Organization*,[111] according to which 'arguments, deduced from the sovereignty of States, which might have been invoked in favour of a restrictive interpretation of provisions governing the jurisdiction of a tribunal adjudicating between States are not relevant to a situation in which a tribunal is called upon to adjudicate upon a complaint of an official against an international organization',[112] the UN Administrative Tribunal decided to fill the legal vac-

---

[104] (1971) *United Nations Juridical Yearbook* 164.

[105] UN Administrative Tribunal, 10 November 1990, Judgment No. 461.

[106] UN Administrative Tribunal, 17 November 1990, Judgment No. 469.

[107] *Cf.* David Ruzié, 'Le recours à l'arbitrage dans le contentieux de la fonction publique internationale: L'exemple du personnel local de l'UNRWA' (1986) 113 *Journal de droit international* 109–21 at 109ff; and Ignaz Seidl-Hohenveldern, 'Die internationalen Beamten und ihr Recht auf den gesetzlichen Richter' in Ballon and Hagen (eds.), *Verfahrensgarantien im nationalen und internationalen Prozeßrecht, Festschrift für Franz Matscher* (Vienna, 1993), 441–7 at 441ff.

[108] Seidl-Hohenveldern criticizes that in the first case the applicant in fact argued that his employment had been unilaterally terminated and that for such a complaint the Special Panel of Adjudicators would have been competent. Seidl-Hohenveldern, 'Die internationalen Beamten', 446.

[109] *Zafari v. UNRWA*, UN Administrative Tribunal, 10 November 1990, Judgment No. 461 (unpublished), para. VII.

[110] *Cf.* p. 271 above.   [111] ICJ, 23 October 1956, Advisory Opinion, (1956) *ICJ Reports* 77.

[112] *Ibid.*, 97.

uum which the existing staff regulations and staff rules had left. It considered 'that in the absence of any judicial procedure established by the area Staff Regulations and Staff Rules . . . the competence of the Tribunal as stated in its earlier judgements remains'.[113] In *Salaymeh*, the UN Administrative Tribunal relied on *Zafari* and held that 'the Tribunal's competence is derived from the lack of any jurisdictional procedure laid down by the UNRWA Staff Regulations and Staff Rules applicable to the Applicant'.[114]

Do administrative tribunals protect fundamental or constitutional rights?

The question of whether administrative tribunals protect fundamental or constitutional rights of individuals in a way comparable to national courts might become directly relevant for the issue of the jurisdictional immunity of the organization. If one accepts that domestic courts are under a human rights obligation and frequently under an additional domestic constitutional law obligation to afford certain minimum procedural rights and, most importantly, are under a duty to grant access to the judicial determination of one's civil rights,[115] the question will arise whether, in case they grant immunity, an alternative tribunal would adequately protect these fundamental rights.

Evaluating the practice of existing administrative tribunals, it has been concluded that they generally satisfy the requirements imposed by due process, the rule of law and similar principles.[116] It is interesting to note that some administrative tribunal decisions even expressly rely on international human rights instruments. These tribunals are acting as organs of organizations that are usually not formally bound by such instruments. Apparently they consider some principles and rules contained therein (and relevant for procedures before them) to be general principles of law which they have to respect.[117] This solution resembles the funda-

---

[113] *Zafari v. UNRWA*, UN Administrative Tribunal, 10 November 1990, Judgment No. 461 (unpublished), para. X.

[114] *Salaymeh v. UNRWA*, UN Administrative Tribunal, 17 November 1990, Judgment No. 469 (unpublished), para. III.

[115] See pp. 280*ff* below.

[116] *Cf.* the ICJ in *Judgments of the Administrative Tribunal of the International Labour Organisation upon Complaints Made Against the United Nations Educational, Scientific and Cultural Organization*, 23 October 1956, Advisory Opinion, (1956) *ICJ Reports* 77 at 85*ff*, holding that the principle of equality of the parties, following from the 'requirements of good administration of justice', has not been impaired by certain procedural rules applying to the ILO Administrative Tribunal. See also Amerasinghe, *The Law of the International Civil Service*, vol. I, 68*ff*; and Seidl-Hohenveldern, *Die Immunität internationaler Organisationen*, 89*ff* affirming that administrative tribunals in general adhere to principles of the rule of law.

[117] *Cf. de Merode*, (1981) *World Bank Administrative Tribunal Reports*, Decision No. 1, stating that 'the internal law of the Bank as the law governing the conditions of employment'

mental rights jurisprudence of the ECJ. This court regularly holds that institutions of the European Communities have to respect the provisions of the European Convention on Human Rights although the European Communities themselves are not parties to it. In the ECJ's opinion, the rules of the European Convention on Human Rights reflect general principles of law – principles which it is called upon to apply.[118]

The fact that some tribunals regard fundamental rights as general principles of law applicable within their jurisdiction does not imply, however, that comparable domestic or even constitutional law will also be applied.[119]

Is the rule of law sufficiently guaranteed by the availability of alternative dispute settlement mechanisms?

Most commentators and many courts seem to be satisfied with recognizing that international instruments conferring jurisdictional immunity usually prescribe some kind of alternative dispute settlement procedure for the international organization in order to guarantee a fair legal protection to the third parties affected.[120] For instance, Article 7 of the

contains 'certain general principles of law'; see also the *Artzet* case, Council of Europe Appeals Board, Appeal No. 8, 1973, describing the non-discrimination principle as contained in the European Convention on Human Rights and other international instruments as a general principle of law which had to be applied in an employment dispute. See Amerasinghe, *The Law of the International Civil Service*, vol. I, 172; and Priess, *Internationale Verwaltungsgerichte*, 74*ff*, for further cases.

[118] *Cf.* the line of ECJ decisions starting with *Nold* v. *Commission*, Case 4/73, ECJ, 14 May 1974. The ECJ bases its jurisdiction to review the human rights conformity of Community acts on, *inter alia*, its general competence, according to Article 164 of the EC Treaty, to ensure that 'the law' is observed when interpreting and applying the Treaty. See also Ralph H. Folsom, *European Union Law* (St Paul, MN, 1995), 71; and George A. Bermann, Roger J. Goebel, William J. Davey and Eleanor M. Fox, *European Community Law* (St Paul, MN, 1993), 145*ff*.

[119] In *Hebblethwaite et al.* v. *Secretary-General of the OAS*, 1 June 1977, Judgment No. 30, the OAS Administrative Tribunal expressly held that it was not competent to hear alleged violations of the laws of the member states, in the particular case, of US constitutional rights and guarantees.

[120] Bekker, *The Legal Position*, 182; and Georges van Hecke, 'Contracts Between International Organizations and Private Law Persons' in Rudolf Bernhardt (ed.), *Encyclopedia of Public International Law* (2nd edn, 1992), vol. I, 812–14 at 814. In *X* v. *Country Y*, Austrian Supreme Court, 21 November 1990, the highest Austrian court reasoned that a privileged position for international organizations in the area of employment relations could also be justified by the existence of their own administrative tribunals. *Cf.* also *Marré* v. *Istituto internazionale per l'unificazione del diritto privato (Unidroit)*, Tribunale Roma, 12 June 1965, (see p. 103 above) as well as the opinion of an arbitrator in a dispute between an international organization and a French company holding that organizations enjoying immunity have a duty to arbitrate: 'L'immunité de juridiction accordée à un organisme international qui n'a pas de juridictions propres oblige celui-ci à recourir à un arbitrage pour le litiges soulevés par son activité.' *A (organisation internationale)* v. *B (société)*, Arbitration Award, 14 May 1972.

1977 Oslo Resolution of the Institut de Droit International provides that:

Contracts concluded with private persons by international organizations should, in cases where the latter enjoy immunity from jurisdiction, provide for the settlement of disputes arising out of such contracts by an independent body.[121]

and counts among the independent dispute settlement organs in Article 8:

(a) an arbitration body set up in accordance with the rules of a permanent institution or in pursuance of *ad hoc* clauses; (b) a tribunal set up by an international organization, if conferring such jurisdiction is compatible with the rules of the organization; or (c) a national judicial body, if this is not incompatible with the status and functions of the organization.[122]

Sometimes, however, courts may be very well aware of the fact that no alternative forum is available, as was the Belgian court in *Manderlier v. Organisation des Nations Unies and Etat Belge (Ministre des Affaires Etrangères)*,[123] and they may even expressly assert that the immunity of an organization does not depend upon the creation of an internal employment jurisdiction, as a German court held in *X* v. *Y* (the *ESRO* case).[124] On the other hand, courts may also positively take into account that – in the absence of their own jurisdiction – plaintiffs would have no other forum to decide their disputes with an international organization, as a German administrative court did in *X et al.* v. *European School Munich II*.[125]

---

[121] (197711) 57 *Annuaire de l'Institut de Droit Internationale* 336.

[122] *Ibid.* From a systematic point of view, it seems rather unfortunate to call the last option, a national judicial body, an 'alternative' in cases where an international organization enjoys immunity from jurisdiction. See also the criticism of Rigaux during the Tenth Plenary Session of the IDI, in (1977 II) 57 *Annuaire de l'Institut de Droit International* 311. The importance of offering some kind of legal recourse against acts of international organizations which affect private persons was already recognized in the IDI's Amsterdam Resolution of 1957 where the Institute, as a result of the 'duty [of every international organization] to respect the law', demanded that 'for every particular decision of an international organ or organization which involves private rights or interests, there be provided appropriate procedures for settling by judicial or arbitral methods juridical differences which might arise from such a decision'. (1957 II) 47 *Annuaire de l'Institut de Droit International* 488.

[123] Civil Tribunal of Brussels, 11 May 1966; Brussels Appeals Court, 15 September 1969.

[124] Federal Labour Court, 25 January 1973.

[125] 'Will man nicht unterstellen, daß der Satzungs- bzw. der Gesetzgeber, der diese Satzung ratifiziert hat, das Problem, ob und welcher Gerichtsbareit die Beklagte unterworfen ist, ungelöst sein lassen wollte oder nicht gesehen haben sollte, so verbleibt nur die einzig mögliche Auslegung, daß die Europäischen Schulen sich der Gerichtsbarkeit des Landes ihres jeweiligen Sitzes unterworfen haben'. Bayerisches Verwaltungsgericht (Administrative Court) Munich, 29 June 1992, (unpublished). See also pp. 150f above. *Cf.* also the Greek *X* v. *International Centre for Superior Mediterranean Agricultural Studies* case, Court of Appeals of Crete, 1991, considering the denial of immunity 'reinforced by the fact that in the opposite case, for the largest part of disputes of private law concerning the interna-

It seems important, however, to make a distinction between the mere existence of an international organization's obligation to provide for alternative dispute settlement procedures and their actual availability. Since obligations to submit private law disputes to arbitration or other dispute settlement procedures are usually contained in headquarters agreements or similar treaties,[126] individuals normally cannot rely on such provisions in cases where an organization has failed to comply with these obligations. This has obviously been overlooked by an Argentine court in *Dutto* v. *United Nations High Commissioner for Refugees*,[127] which thought that the interests of third parties are not deprived of all protection. In the court's view '[s]uch persons are entitled to have recourse to the procedures under Section 31 [of the Special Convention]' which provides that each specialized agency shall make provision for 'appropriate modes of settlement of disputes' arising out of 'contracts or other disputes of a private law character to which the specialized agency is a party'. In practice, this is mainly arbitration. The Argentine court, however, did not pay heed to the fact that this provision is generally not considered to confer rights directly upon individuals. It is thus crucial that alternative dispute settlement methods are not only legally called for, but that they are actually available.[128]

Even in the absence of arbitral or other dispute settlement mechanisms – directly accessible to individuals – one might argue that the option of diplomatic protection for an injured individual by his or her home state might sufficiently guarantee the fairness in dealings of international organizations with private parties. While this might be correct on an abstract theoretical level, actual practice, in particular the frequent reluctance of states to espouse the claims of their nationals for political reasons, makes this mode of last resort a rather questionable guarantee of fairness to individuals.

From a policy-oriented point of view, it is indeed more desirable to avoid

tional organisations, nowhere on earth would there be jurisdiction'. An arbitral decision rendered in a dispute between an international organization and a French company argued to the contrary. It deduced a duty to arbitrate where an organization enjoys immunity: 'L'immunité de juridiction accordée à un organisme international qui n'a pas de juridictions propres oblige celui-ci à recourir à un arbitrage pour les litiges soulevés par son activité'. *A (organisation internationale)* v. *B (société)*, Arbitration Award, 14 May 1972.

[126] See p. 270 above.   [127] National Labour Court of Appeal, 1989.

[128] Thus, the FAO – in its insistence on immunity from suit in Italy (see pp. 131*ff* above) – stressed that such immunity did not result in a denial of justice, 'since (as in the case under consideration) alternative methods of settling disputes were provided for'. See FAO, Office of the Legal Counsel, 'Constitutional Matters' (1982) *United Nations Juridical Yearbook* 113.

the detour *via* international law and political considerations, and to clearly subject international organizations not only to the substantive domestic law when dealing with individuals on an equal footing, but also to the normal legal consequences for non-compliance with legal obligations, i.e. answerability before national courts.[129]

It is interesting to note that few authors draw conclusions from the absence of an alternative dispute settlement mechanism and even fewer seem prepared to take this into account when measuring the scope of immunity to be accorded to an international organization.[130]

However, the importance of assuring substantive rights and obligations through procedural means in order to satisfy basic considerations of fairness should not be overlooked. Indeed:

One always returns to the fundamental problem of assuring a guarantee in the application of the law while maintaining the immunity of jurisdiction of the international organization. This last principle obviously depends on the international juridical order, as does also the obligation of the organizations to ensure respect for the law established by their organs in accordance with their constitutions.[131]

To provide a competent forum for the respective fields of exercising power of international organizations is indeed most important. It is not limited to constitutional disputes between organs of international organizations or with members, etc., but includes external affairs on a private law level as well.[132]

Human rights and constitutional limits

The reflections above on fairness receive additional relevance if one considers that they may be supported by human rights concerns and, in many countries, by constitutional guarantees.

[129] While the theoretical distinction between the choice of law question and the jurisdictional issue is certainly important, it seems that the practical danger of an immunity 'privilege' rendering an international organization's subjection to substantial rules of law inoperative is too great in order to attach so much importance to it.

[130] See p. 366 below.

[131] Bastid, 'Have the UN Administrative Tribunals Contributed', 309, makes this observation with particular regard to employment disputes.

[132] In light of these considerations, Jenks' reminder, when considering 'multinational entities', among which most prominently he counts traditional international organizations, seems of particular importance: 'Every legal system as it develops must grapple with the problem of placing an effective restraint upon power and ensuring responsibility; this is the essence of the whole concept of due process of law.' C. Wilfred Jenks, 'Multinational Entities in the Law of Nations' in Wolfgang Friedmann, Louis Henkin and Oliver Lissitzyn (eds.), *Transnational Law in a Changing Society: Essays in Honor of Philip Jessup* (New York and London, 1972), 70–83 at 71.

The grant of immunity to international organizations when sued by private parties in domestic courts effectively deprives these parties of their primary judicial remedy. When a national court grants sovereign immunity or diplomatic or consular immunity, there is regularly a home state judiciary of the state, diplomatic or consular officer sued where the plaintiff might bring his or her claim. Since international organizations – although they regularly have a seat in a state – have no home state in a comparable sense, this option of other national courts is clearly not available to potential plaintiffs. They would rather have to rely on alternative dispute settlement procedures like arbitration or access to administrative courts. In many cases it is doubtful, however, whether any of these are available at all.[133]

The fundamental rights dimension of immunity from suit of international organizations is aptly illustrated by *Manderlier* v. *Organisation des Nations Unies and Etat Belge (Ministre des Affaires Etrangères)*,[134] one of the leading cases on the immunity of international organizations dealing, *inter alia*, with the nature and justification of immunity from suit of international organizations.[135] It is also of particular interest in the context of a possible human rights argument limiting the scope of immunity, since this argument was expressly raised during the proceedings.

The plaintiff, a Belgian citizen, owned property in the Congo, which in 1962 during hostilities involving the UN operation in Congo was burnt and looted by members of UN forces. The UN at first rejected his direct claim for compensation, and only after intervention of the Belgian government did it agree to accept financial liability where the damage was the result of action taken by agents of the UN in violation of the laws of war and the rules of international law. On 20 February 1965, the UN and Belgium entered into a global settlement agreement providing for the payment of US$1.5 million as compensation for all claims brought by Belgian nationals as a result of UN operations in the Congo.[136] As a consequence of the national implementing legislation, Manderlier would have received a sum far below what he had originally claimed. Belgian law further stated that acceptance of any payments under this compensation scheme constituted a waiver of any further claims against the UN.

---

[133] See pp. 265*ff* above.   [134] Civil Tribunal of Brussels, 11 May 1966.
[135] See pp. 214 and 222 above.
[136] Exchange of Letters Constituting an Agreement Between the United Nations and Belgium Relating to the Settlement of Claims Filed Against the United Nations in the Congo by Belgian Nationals, New York, 20 February 1965, (1965) *United Nations Juridical Yearbook* 39*ff*.

Manderlier rejected these terms and brought suit in Belgian courts jointly against the UN and the Belgian state.

The Brussels Civil Tribunal granted the UN's plea of immunity from suit based on the absolute immunity clause of the General Convention. It held that the UN was competent to appear in legal proceedings in Belgium as a result of its legal personality according to Article 104 of the UN Charter, but that as a consequence of the general and absolute wording of the immunity provision contained in the General Convention the organization could not be sued before Belgian courts without a waiver. The court recognized that in the absence of provisions made by the UN to set up an appropriate mode of settlement of disputes between itself and private parties in such situations, the plaintiff actually had no available means of legal recourse. Nevertheless, the court expressly rejected the plaintiff's argument that as a consequence of his fundamental right 'to a public hearing by an independent and impartial tribunal in the determination of his rights and obligations' as embodied in Article 10 of the Universal Declaration of Human Rights, Belgian courts should exercise jurisdiction over the dispute. The court had no difficulty in disposing of this claim by qualifying the Universal Declaration as a non-binding 'mere . . . collection of recommendations' without the force of law.[137] While it could not do the same with the European Convention on Human Rights which had been ratified by Belgium and incorporated into Belgian law, it simply stated that this Convention 'was concluded between fourteen European States only, and cannot be applied to and imposed upon the United Nations'.[138] Thus, 'however inconvenient may be its results for litigants', the immunity granted to the UN by the General Convention was held to be 'unconditional' and unaffected by human rights concerns.

This decision was affirmed by the Brussels Appeals Court in *Manderlier v. Organisation des Nations Unies and Etat Belge*.[139] In affirming the correctness of the legal reasoning of the court of first instance, the appellate court, however, 'admitted that in the present state of international institutions there is no court to which the appellant can submit his dispute with the United Nations' and that this situation 'does not seem to be in keeping with the principles proclaimed in the Universal Declaration of Human Rights'.[140]

---

[137] (1972) 45 ILR 446 at 451.   [138] *Ibid.*, 452.
[139] Brussels Appeals Court, 15 September 1969.
[140] (1969) *United Nations Juridical Yearbook* 237.

The emerging international standard of a human right of access to court

A deprivation of access to the regular courts in order to determine civil rights (and obligations) of individuals will pose serious constitutional problems in many legal systems[141] and – from an international law point of view even more alarmingly – important human rights questions.

International human rights texts reflect an emerging consensus that access to court in order to have one's rights and duties determined can be regarded a fundamental right. According to Article 10 of the Universal Declaration of Human Rights:

Everyone is entitled in full equality to a fair and public hearing by an independent and impartial tribunal, in the determination of his rights and obligations and of any criminal charge against him.

Article 14(1) of the International Covenant on Civil and Political Rights provides, *inter alia*, that:

All persons are equal before the courts and tribunals. In the determination of any criminal charge against him, or of his rights and obligations in a suit at law, everyone shall be entitled to a fair and public hearing by a competent, independent and impartial tribunal established by law.

Article 6(1) of the European Convention on Human Rights states that:

In the determination of his civil rights and obligations or of any criminal charge against him, everyone is entitled to a fair and public hearing within a reasonable time by an independent and impartial tribunal established by law.

The wording of these provisions, in particular of Article 6(1) of the European Convention on Human Rights might leave some doubt as to whether it merely entitles a person to a fair and public trial in pending proceedings or whether it also confers an entitlement to such proceedings. Since its judgment in *Golder*,[142] however, the European Court of Human Rights has repeatedly held that 'the right of access [to court] constitutes an element which is inherent in the right stated by Article 6 § 1'[143] – an element without which the scrupulously enumerated characteristics of 'fair, public and expeditious . . . proceedings' were 'of no value at all'.[144] In *Golder*, the court concluded that:

---

[141] See pp. 290*ff* below.
[142] European Court of Human Rights, 21 February 1975.
[143] *Golder*, European Court of Human Rights, 21 February 1975, Series A, No. 18, para. 36.
[144] *Ibid.*, para. 35.

Article 6 § 1 secures to everyone the right to have any claim relating to his civil rights and obligations brought before a court or tribunal. In this way the Article embodies the 'right to a court', of which the rights of access, that is the right to institute proceedings before courts in civil matters, constitutes one aspect only.[145]

This is also in conformity with the draft language used for Article 10 of the Universal Declaration of Human Rights which originally provided that:

Every one *shall have access* to independent and impartial tribunals in the determination of any criminal charge against him, and of his rights and obligations.[146]

The right of access to court and jurisdictional immunity

It is surprising to note that the apparent contradiction between an international-law-based human right of access to court and the restriction of such access by the concept of immunity has rarely been discussed.[147] The controlling instruments state that 'in the determination of his (civil) rights and obligations' 'everyone' shall have recourse to a fair judicial proceeding – a language that does not contain any restrictive wording implying limits *vis-à-vis* a certain class of persons. This broad and unqualified language indeed does not suggest any exceptions necessary for immunity reasons.[148] Nevertheless, the idea that a wholesale exclusion of foreign states from the jurisdiction of domestic courts might contravene human rights requirements has been advanced only very occasionally.[149]

[145] *Ibid.*, para. 36. Reaffirmed and quoted in *Ashingdane*, European Court of Human Rights, 28 May 1985, Series A, No. 93, para. 55; *Philis*, European Court of Human Rights, 27 August 1991, Series A, No. 209, para. 59; *Fayed*, European Court of Human Rights, 21 September 1994, Series A, No. 294-B, para. 65, *The Holy Monasteries*, European Court of Human Rights, 9 December 1994, Series A, No. 301-A, para. 80.

[146] Report of the UN Human Rights Commission, (ECOSOC) Official Records, 3rd year, 6th Session, E/600, Annex A (emphasis added).

[147] See, however, Lauterpacht, 'The Problem', 2, who had argued in 1951 that, with 'the recognition of human freedoms as part of international law . . . it may be opportune to re-examine the problem of jurisdictional immunities of foreign states'.

[148] The European Court of Human Rights, however, acknowledged that the right of access to court resulting from Article 6(1) of the European Convention on Human Rights was 'not absolute' and contained 'implicit limitations'. *Cf. Ashingdane*, European Court of Human Rights, 28 May 1985, Series A, No. 93, 24; *Fayed*, European Court of Human Rights, 21 September 1994, Series A, No. 294-B; *Golder*, European Court of Human Rights, 21 February 1975, Series A, No. 18, 37; *Lithgow and others*, European Court of Human Rights, 8 July 1986, Series A, No. 102, 71; see also pp. 284f and 307 below.

[149] The contribution of Pahr to the *Festschrift Modinos* which expressly addresses state immunity and Article 6(1) of the European Convention on Human Rights is such a rare exception. Pahr argues that, since the European Convention on Human Rights's Article 6(1) contains no restrictions, it is in principle applicable to legal disputes of a civil

For the silent majority, sovereign immunity and other jurisdictional immunities are obviously taken for granted and considered unaffected by the adoption of Article 6(1) of the European Convention on Human Rights. One of the main arguments for harmonizing the apparent contradiction between Article 6(1) and state immunity might be found in a historic interpretation of the European Convention on Human Rights provisions. The rules on state immunity could be regarded as pre-existing norms of international law which were not intended to be affected by Article 6(1). Thus, the further validity of state immunity might be seen as an implicit exception to Article 6(1).[150]

Although there appear to be no authoritative statements of organs applying human rights guarantees which would expressly confirm this view – regarding state immunity, diplomatic immunity or the immunity of international organizations – there are decisions of such bodies that seem to support the view that the 'enactment' of rights of access to court did not intend to abrogate existing international law principles. For

character between states and private parties. Willibald P. Pahr, 'Die Staatenimmunität und Artikel 6 Absatz 1 der Europäischen Menschenrechtskonvention', in *Mélanges offerts à Polys Modinos. Problèmes des droits de l'homme et de l'unification Européenne* (Paris, 1968), 222–32 at 223. Although a clear delimitation of what constitutes 'civil rights and obligations' does not appear feasible to him, Article 6(1) guarantees in a certain core area of law – which is at least roughly ascertainable – a fair trial without any restriction or regard to who is a party to such proceedings. In this respect he considers state immunity incompatible with Article 6(1) (Pahr, 'Die Staatenimmunität', 231: 'In diesem Rechtsbereich ist daher für eine Staatenimmunität im oben dargelegten Sinn kein Raum.'). While he deals at length with the difficulty of defining 'civil rights and obligations' in order to determine the scope of application of Article 6(1), he does not elaborate on the potential justification for a further existence of the rule of state immunity also within the framework of the European Convention on Human Rights. Without further reasoning, he dismisses the argument that states would continue to be amenable to suit in their own courts as insufficient to guarantee a fair trial and to uphold the principle of equality of arms before the courts (*Waffengleichheit*). Pahr, 'Die Staatenimmunität', 231. This statement is even more surprising considering the fact that, after the 1950s, state immunity remained part of the accepted rules of international law applied by domestic courts in Europe.

[150] *Cf.* Helmut Damian, *Staatenimmunität und Gerichtszwang. Grundlagen und Grenzen der völkerrechtlichen Freiheit fremder Staaten von inländischer Gerichtsbarkeit in Verfahren der Zwangsvollstreckung oder Anspruchssicherung* (Berlin, Heidelberg, New York and Tokyo, 1985), 17, arguing that the right of access to court has its effect *de lege lata* only within the scope of a state's jurisdiction which means beyond the limits of the international rules on immunity: 'Die Rechtsschutzgarantie entfaltet ihre Wirkung *de lege lata* innerhalb des staatlichen Zuständigkeitsbereichs, also jenseits der überkommenen völkerrechtlichen Grenzen des Immunitätsrechts'. See also Michael Bothe, 'Die strafrechtliche Immunität fremder Staatsorgane' (1971) 31 *Zeitschrift für ausländisches öffentliches Recht und Völkerrecht* 246–70 at 256; and Wolfgang Heidelmeyer, 'Immunität und Rechtsschutz gegen Akte der Besatzungshoheit in Berlin' (1986) 46 *Zeitschrift für ausländisches öffentliches Recht und Völkerrecht* 519–38 at 520, note 2.

instance, in *Lingens and Leitgeb* v. *Austria*,[151] the European Commission of Human Rights thought that:

The fact that certain crucial evidence . . . remained outside the reach of the court due to the witness' parliamentary immunity cannot, however, be regarded as an unfair element in the proceedings because it cannot be assumed that the States parties to the Convention wished, in undertaking to recognise the right set forth in Article 6, to make any derogation from the fundamental principle of parliamentary immunity which is embodied in the Constitutions of most States with a parliamentary system.[152]

Similarly in *Re a Solicitor, H* v. *United Kingdom*,[153] the European Commission of Human Rights found that 'it is not a denial of a fair hearing under Article 6 . . . if [the applicant's] claim against the trial judge is struck out on the ground that the trial judge enjoys immunity from suit while acting in his judicial capacity'. If this argument is correct concerning domestic immunity principles, it may be all the more pertinent where international law principles mandating immunity are concerned. In a number of judgments[154] the European Court of Human Rights explicitly stated that the right of access to court as guaranteed by Article 6(1) is 'not absolute' and acknowledged 'implicit limitations' of this right. Although it has not been expressly decided that way, it may well be that immunity ought to be considered one of these implicit limitations.[155]

Acceptance of the traditional practice of granting immunity to international organizations might have been also a decisive factor for the European Commission of Human Rights to see no human rights concerns

---

[151] European Commission of Human Rights, Application No. 8803/79, 11 December 1981.

[152] *Lingens and Leitgeb* v. *Austria*, European Commission of Human Rights, Application No. 8803/79, 11 December 1981, (1983) 34 *Decisions and Reports* 171 at 179. See already *Agee* v. *United Kingdom*, European Commission of Human Rights, Application No. 7729/76, 17 December 1976, (1977) 7 *Decisions and Reports* 164 at 175, holding that 'Article 6(1) must be interpreted with due regard to parliamentary immunity as traditionally recognised in the States parties to the Convention. The principle of immunity in respect of such statements is generally recognised as a consequence of an effective political democracy within the meaning of the preamble to the Convention.'

[153] European Commission of Human Rights, Application No. 8083/77, 13 March 1980.

[154] *Ashingdane*, European Court of Human Rights, 28 May 1985, Series A, No. 93, 24; *Fayed*, European Court of Human Rights, 21 September 1994, Series A, No. 294-B; *Golder*, European Court of Human Rights, 21 February 1975, Series A, No. 18, 37; *Lithgow and others*, European Court of Human Rights, 8 July 1986, Series A No. 102, 71.

[155] *Cf.* Jochen A. Frowein and Wolfgang Peukert, *Europäische MenschenRechtsKonvention. EMRK-Kommentar* (2nd edn, Kehl, Strasbourg and Arlington, 1996), 205, who argue that according to the European Commission of Human Rights Article 6 has to be interpreted in light of the reservation of the traditional and generally recognized principle of parliamentary and diplomatic immunity.

involving Article 6(1). In *Ary Spaans* v. *The Netherlands*,[156] a case involving the immunity from suit of an international organization,[157] the Commission laconically remarked:

The Commission notes that it is in accordance with international law that States confer immunities and privileges to international bodies like the Iran–United States Claims Tribunal which are situated in their territory. The Commission does not consider that such a restriction of national sovereignty in order to facilitate the working of an international body gives rise to an issue under the Convention.[158]

In two recently decided cases before the European Commission on Human Rights, in *Karlheinz Beer and Philip Regan* v. *Germany*[159] and *Richard Waite and Terry Kennedy* v. *Germany*,[160] the defendant government tried to rely on this jurisprudence. Germany maintained that 'the right of access to court is subject to inherent limitations which include the traditional and generally recognised principle of parliamentary and diplomatic immunity and also the immunity of international organisations'.[161] Despite earlier decisions on the admissibility of the complaints[162] the Commission did not substantively change its previous case law. Rather, it found no violation of Article 6(1) as long as an 'equivalent legal protection' was available.[163]

Nevertheless, even if the historical acceptance of state and organizational immunity as a limitation of the scope of Article 6(1) may be plausible and currently predominant, it seems that a dynamic interpretation of human rights texts – demanding constant revision of hitherto accepted standards[164] – could have rendered this traditional approach invalid. The 'European consensus' relating to the material content of the rights contained in the European Convention on Human Rights is clearly something

---

[156] European Commission of Human Rights, Application No. 12516/86, 12 December 1988 (admissibility).

[157] See pp. 299f below in more detail.

[158] (1988) 58 *Decisions and Reports* 119 at 122.

[159] European Commission of Human Rights, Application No. 28934/95; 2 December 1997.

[160] European Commission of Human Rights, Application No. 26083/94; 2 December 1997.

[161] European Commission of Human Rights, Application No. 28934/95; 2 December 1997, para. 54.

[162] European Commission of Human Rights, Application Nos. 28934/95 and 26083/94; 24 February 1997.

[163] See pp. 304f below.

[164] *Cf.* the Court's judgment in *Tyrer*, European Court of Human Rights, 25 February 1978, Series A No. 26, para. 31, stating that '[t]he Convention is a living instrument which . . . must be interpreted in the light of present-day conditions'. See also Franz Matscher, 'Methods of Interpretation of the Convention' in R. St. J. Macdonald, F. Matscher and H. Petzold (eds.), *The European System for the Protection of Human Rights* (Dordrecht, Boston and London, 1993), 63–81 at 68, on the 'evolutive and dynamic method' of interpretation used by the Strasbourg organs.

that is not unchangeable. It may well be that the exclusion of a certain class of potential defendants (international organizations and sovereign states under an absolute immunity standard) was acceptable in the 1950s; this concept, however, may have changed. The expansive interpretation of the rights protected under the European Convention of Human Rights in general is a clear evidence for this trend. The European Commission of Human Rights seems to be well aware of the potential friction between access to court and immunity demands. In *Graham Dyer* v. *United Kingdom*,[165] relying on the Court's judgment in the *Golder*[166] case, it reasoned:

Were Article 6(1) to be interpreted as enabling a State Party to remove the jurisdiction of the courts to determine certain classes of civil claim [*sic!*] or to confer immunities from liability on certain groups in respect of their actions, without any possibility of control by the Convention organs, there would exist no protection against the danger of arbitrary power.[167]

As far as access to court as an element of the vindication of individual rights is concerned, an interesting parallel can be derived from the developments in the context of human rights violations and amnesty laws both on the inter-American and the universal International Covenant on Civil and Political Rights (ICCPR) level. Stopping short of giving individual victims a right to see their aggressors punished, authoritative interpretations of the relevant human rights instruments by the Inter-American Commission on Human Rights and the United Nations Human Rights Committee concluded that general amnesty laws are, as a matter of principle, incompatible with the duties of states parties to the Inter-American Convention on Human Rights and the ICCPR. In particular, as far as grave violations of human rights are concerned, such as torture, disappearance, etc., national legislative acts leading to the impunity of those having committed such human rights violations were considered to be contrary to the general obligation of states to 'respect and ensure' specific human rights.[168]

---

[165] European Commission of Human Rights, Application No. 10475/83, 9 October 1984.

[166] European Court of Human Rights, 21 February 1975, Series A, No. 18, para. 35.

[167] *Graham Dyer* v. *United Kingdom*, European Commission of Human Rights, Application No. 10475/83, 9 October 1984, (1984) 39 *Decisions and Reports* 246 at 252.

[168] *Cf.* General Comment Nos. 7 and 20, 'Article 7', adopted by the Human Rights Committee under Article 40(4) of the International Covenant on Civil and Political Rights. See also the Reports of the Inter-American Commission on Human Rights concluding that Argentine and Uruguayan amnesty laws violated not only the obligation of states to 'respect and ensure' the human rights contained in Article 1 of the Inter-American Convention on Human Rights, but interestingly also its Article 8 granting '[e]very person . . . the right to a hearing, with due guarantees and within a reasonable time, by a competent, independent and impartial tribunal, previously established by law, in the substantiation of any accusation of a criminal nature made against him or for the

There are, of course, important differences between impunity, and thus substantive exemption from criminal prosecution, and procedural immunity from civil liability. However, the examples cited appear to evidence a growing consensus that measures aimed at, or at least having the effect of, insulating – 'immunizing' – certain persons from their accountability or responsibility become less and less acceptable under current human rights standards. Considering that the fair trial provisions of the ICCPR, the Universal Declaration and the European Convention on Human Rights are almost identically worded, the transfer of these European standards to the universal plane and *vice versa* does not appear to be excluded.

Even if one does not accept this 'dynamic interpretation' argument requiring an evolutionary reconsideration of the proper immunity standard, it appears that the notion of an original implied exception for immunity against the plain wording of the applicable human rights instruments is more problematic than one might think. Why should, in case of a conflict between two international rules, the human rights obligation give way to the immunity obligation of a forum state? Even without referring to any argument of a higher value of human rights norms[169] or their potential *ius cogens* character,[170] one could ask why the human rights norm should not prevail in such a conflict.[171]

One of the reasons why this apparent contradiction of individual rights to pursue one's civil rights and obligations in court and immunity under

    determination of his rights and obligations of a civil, labor, fiscal, or any other nature'. Inter-American Commission on Human Rights, Report No. 28/92 *Annual Report*, 41*ff* (Argentina); Inter-American Commission on Human Rights, Report No. 29/92, 2 October 1992, *Annual Report*, 154*ff* (Uruguay).

[169] On the domestic legal level such a solution is certainly conceivable. For instance, in the Austrian legal system the provisions of the European Convention on Human Rights are directly applicable treaty norms of constitutional law status. *Bundesgesetzblatt* No. 59/ 1964. *Cf.* Rudolf Bernhardt, 'The Convention and Domestic Law' in Macdonald, Matscher and Petzold (eds.), *The European System for the Protection of Human Rights*, 25–40 at 27. In cases of conflict with other international norms that are incorporated into the domestic legal order, the fundamental rights of constitutional rank will prevail.

[170] Even the *Restatement (Third)*, § 702, Reporters' Note 11, claiming the *ius cogens* quality of a number of human rights, does not consider a right of access to court to be one of them.

[171] This is exactly the question that has been posed – though not answered – by the French Cour de Cassation in its annual report, commenting on the *Hintermann* case (see p. 298 below). The court considered that an organization's immunity may lead to a denial of justice and asked whether '[c]e déni de justice peut-il être évité par la primauté de la convention européenne des droits de l'homme, qui garantit le libre accès au juge et le procès équitable?' ('whether this denial of justice could be avoided by recognizing the primacy of the European Convention on Human Rights which guarantees the free access to a judge and to a just procedure'). Cour de Cassation, *Rapport annuel* (1995), 418, cited by Byk, 'Case Note', 142.

international law has not given rise to more controversy might lie in the fact that a number of potential cases will no longer arise because of the change of the international rules on state immunity. In a way, the standard of the European Convention on State Immunity, which codified the European trend of restrictive immunity, implicitly acknowledged the human rights concerns raised above. By allowing suits against states in certain types of actions, generally relating to their *iure gestionis* activities, a broad range of claims concerning at least the core of civil rights and obligations seems to be possible. The same is, of course, true in all other countries adhering to a restrictive immunity concept. Where states deny the jurisdiction of their judicial fora over lawsuits against a foreign state only with regard to the latter's *iure imperii* acts, their obligation to provide access to court in cases concerning the determination of 'civil rights and obligations' can be largely fulfilled.

Even if the law has not yet moved towards a higher standard of protection for individuals seeking redress against sovereigns or international organizations in matters concerning their 'civil rights and obligations', the policy argument remains valid that a wholesale exemption of a particular class of potential defendants from the jurisdiction of domestic courts severely curtails the affected individuals' right to have their day in court.[172] If one accepts the proposition that human rights considerations should restrict the scope of sovereign immunity, the same would appear to be true with regard to the immunity of international organizations.

The right of access to court as discussed in case law

It is important to realize that the issue of the immunity of international organizations and the right of access to court of individuals involves a complex three-party relationship, comprising:

(1)   an individual's substantive entitlement *vis-à-vis* an international organization and his or her human right of access to court *vis-à-vis* a forum state;

---

[172]   *Cf.* the reasoning of the judge in the court of first instance in *Trawnik and another v. Ministry of Defence*, High Court, Chancery Division, 16 April 1984, a case brought by German citizens against UK officers complaining against the erection of a shooting range in West Berlin by the British armed forces stationed there: 'I do not need the European Convention on Human Rights to tell me that it is deplorable that . . . there is no court with power to decide whether the plaintiffs are entitled to the remedy that they seek. If heard their claim might fail . . . but at least the plaintiffs would have had their day in court.' In *Trawnik and another v. Lennox and another*, Court of Appeal, 1984, the Court of Appeal was less impressed with such arguments and disallowed the action: 'The plaintiffs may be suffering a wrong for which there is no remedy in our courts. This is to be regretted; but sympathy for the plaintiffs is no justification for adding as a defendant an officer of state who, as a matter of law, has no interest in the proceedings.'

(2) the forum state's obligation *vis-à-vis* the individual to provide access to court and its potential obligation *vis-à-vis* the defendant international organization to grant immunity; and

(3) the international organization's substantive obligation *vis-à-vis* the individual and its potential right to immunity *vis-à-vis* the forum state.

What is important but frequently overlooked is the fact that the right of access to court is an individual's right *vis-à-vis* the forum state and not *vis-à-vis* the international organization intended to be sued. This is exactly the point that seems to have been confused by the Belgian court in the *Manderlier* v. *Organisation des Nations Unies and Etat Belge (Ministre des Affaires Etrangères)*[173] case. There the Civil Tribunal of Brussels disposed of the argument that the UN's immunity from suit in Belgium would violate Article 6 of the European Convention on Human Rights which it qualified as completely effective and applicable under Belgian law, by asserting that 'the Convention was concluded between fourteen European States only, and cannot be applied to and imposed upon the United Nations'.[174] It was, however, not a question of the UN's allegiance to the principles of the European Convention on Human Rights, but rather of Belgium's obligation, as party to a human rights instrument, to provide access to its courts in a dispute involving the UN as defendant.

Express pleas for a limitation of an international organization's immunity from suit based on human rights concerns are rarely found in legal writing.[175] This does not alter the strength of the argument that an

---

[173] Civil Tribunal of Brussels, 11 May 1966; Brussels Appeals Court, 15 September 1969.

[174] (1972) 45 ILR 446 at 452.

[175] One of the few examples is Hammerschlag's case note on *Morgan* v. *IBRD*, US District Court DC, 13 September 1990. On *Morgan*, see pp. 165 and 200 above. This author openly deplores the District of Columbia district court's decision to dismiss a suit brought against the World Bank for reasons of immunity and harshly criticizes this result whereby 'fundamental rights of individuals have been compromised in favor of the expansion of global economic interest', since the court 'based its decision on economic rationales, entirely disregarding human rights issues'. Daniel Hammerschlag, '*Morgan* v. *International Bank for Reconstruction and Development*' (1992) 16 *Maryland Journal of International Law and Trade* 279–303 at 280, note 9. The suit for intentional infliction of emotional distress, false imprisonment, libel and slander brought by an employee of a temporary employment agency who worked for a two-and-a-half-year period for IBRD was certainly not one of the 'ordinary' employment disputes encountered within international organizations. Morgan, who was suspected of having stolen money from within the premises of the IBRD, was interrogated and forcibly detained by IBRD officials and security guards. When they could not produce any evidence, but rather continued to harass him, Morgan in return sought compensatory and punitive damages. Hammerschlag, however, does not pursue the issue of a possible friction with the human rights guarantee of access to court in civil matters as embodied in Article 14 of the International Covenant on Civil and Political Rights, Article 6 of the European Convention on

international organization's immunity should not cover all those cases which determine the civil rights and obligations of individuals – an argument that appears to be equally valid whether it relates to the rights and obligations *vis-à-vis* states, diplomats or international organizations.

Although there is not much discussion in the literature, some national court decisions seem to refer – at least in passing – to the potential friction with constitutional guarantees as a result of excluding international organizations from the adjudicative power of domestic courts. There are a number of serious attempts to address the problem of access to judicial dispute settlement and immunity under fundamental rights guarantees; the discussion is particularly highly developed in the framework of domestic constitutional guarantees.[176]

In Germany the arguments circle around Articles 19(4) and 101(1) of the Basic Law. Article 19(4) provides:

Should any person's rights be violated by public authority, recourse to court shall be open to him. Where no other jurisdiction has been established, recourse to the courts of ordinary jurisdiction is available.

Article 101(1) provides:

Extraordinary courts are inadmissible. No one may be removed from the jurisdiction of his lawful judge (*gesetzlicher Richter*).

Two well-known decisions of the German Constitutional Court involving Eurocontrol mainly concern Article 19(4) of the Basic Law and recourse against administrative acts, and are thus only indirectly relevant to the

Human Rights, etc., but rather focuses on the issue of whether international organizations should be answerable for human rights violations. He immediately links this issue with the question of whether such accountability should be determined by US courts and thus lead to the forfeiture of immunity. Although he does not mention this line of case law, Hammerschlag seems to rely heavily on US court decisions denying immunity from suit to foreign sovereigns in certain tort cases. Cf. *Filartiga* v. *Peña-Irala*, 630 F. 2d 876 (2d Cir. 1980); *Forti* v. *Suarez-Mason*, 672 F. Supp. 1531 (NDC 1987). More recently, Michael Singer, 'Jurisdictional Immunity of International Organizations: Human Rights and Functional Necessity Concerns' (1995) 36 *Virginia Journal of International Law* 53–165, calls for a reappraisal of the law of immunity from suit of international organizations. Like Hammerschlag, he is primarily concerned about human rights violations perpetrated by international organizations and the lack of available fora to remedy such wrongs. He does not address the possible human rights friction resulting from a state's obligation to grant immunity and at the same time to give access to its courts in the determination of civil rights and obligations.

[176] Cf. Mauro Cappelletti, *The Judicial Process in Comparative Perspective* (Oxford, 1989), 226*ff*; and Karl Heinz Schwab and Peter Gottwald, 'Verfassung und Zivilprozeß' in Walther J. Habscheid (ed.), *Effektiver Rechtsschutz und verfassungsmäßige Ordnung* (Bielefeld, 1983), 1–89 at 37*ff* for an overview on national constitutional provisions guaranteeing access to courts.

present problem. The court stated in those cases that Eurocontrol exercised 'foreign' public authority when setting the rates of the applicable flight charges (*Eurocontrol-Flight Charges II*)[177] or when regulating the legal relationship with its employees (*Hetzel* v. *Eurocontrol*).[178] Thus, it was not amenable to suit as a matter of constitutional law since Article 19(4) of the Basic Law provided for legal recourse only against acts of German authorities. Accordingly, the constitutional claims failed. However, these cases also suggest that there might be implicit limits to the abandonment of legal remedies resulting from the grant of immunity to international organizations.

In *Hetzel* v. *Eurocontrol II*,[179] the Federal Constitutional Court clearly stated that, if the legal protection against acts of international institutions proved 'insufficient', this in itself might constitute a violation of the implicit constitutional limitation to the transfer of sovereign powers according to Article 24(1) of the Basic Law.[180] In particular, it thought that the lack of an effective legal remedy against the acts of a public authority

---

[177] Federal Constitutional Court, 23 June 1981. The same qualification of the flight invoicing was reached in *Trans-Mediterranean Airways* v. *Eurocontrol*, Royal Decree (administrative decision of the Crown), 16 January 1974. In an attempt to dispute flight charges invoiced from Eurocontrol, a Lebanese airline appealed to the Dutch Crown. The appeal was rejected since 'Eurocontrol invoices could not be regarded as decisions of an administrative body of the Netherlands Government within the meaning of the Administrative Decisions Appeal Act'. (1977) 8 *Netherlands Yearbook of International Law* 258. In a preliminary ruling the ECJ also held that flight charges set by Eurocontrol are *iure imperii* activities. Thus, the Brussels Convention covering civil and commercial matters was not applicable. *LTU* v. *Eurocontrol*, Case 29/76, ECJ, 14 October 1976. This view was confirmed in *SAT Fluggesellschaft mbH* v. *Eurocontrol*, Case 364/92, ECJ, 19 January 1994, where a German airline had challenged the flight charging methods of the organization, alleging that they infringed the competition rules of the EC. The Belgian courts had doubts as to whether this activity could fall under the competition rules and, in particular, whether Eurocontrol could be regarded as an 'undertaking' in the sense of Article 85*ff* of the EC Treaty. The Belgian Cour de Cassation, 10 September 1992, referred the question to the ECJ. In its preliminary ruling, the ECJ stated: 'Taken as a whole, Eurocontrol's activities, including the collection of route charges on behalf of the Contracting States, are connected with their nature, their aim and the rules to which they are subject, to the exercise of powers relating to the control and supervision of air space which are typically those of a public authority and are not of an economic nature justifying the application of the Treaty rules of competition'. [1994] ECR I-43 at 44. This ruling was followed in *Irish Aerospace (Belgium) NV* v. *European Organisation for the Safety of Air Navigation and Civil Aviation Authority*, Queen's Bench Division (Commercial Court), 6 June 1991, stating that 'Eurocontrol's public service assignment of ensuring the safety of air navigation could not be deemed to be an economic or commercial activity'. [1992] 1 *Lloyd's Reports* 383.

[178] Administrative Court Karlsruhe, 5 July 1979; Appellate Administrative Court Baden-Württemberg, 7 August 1979; Federal Constitutional Court, 10 November 1981.

[179] Federal Constitutional Court, 10 November 1981.

[180] Article 24(1) of the Basic Law provides: 'The Federation may by legislation transfer sovereign powers to intergovernmental institutions.'

could be such a violation.[181] Though the court did not consider it necessary to embark on a discussion of where the exact constitutional limits of Article 24 were and what kind of guarantees had to be fulfilled, it seems to follow quite clearly that at least the existence and availability of an alternative dispute settlement procedure can be seen as a constitutionally mandated minimum. In *Hetzel* v. *Eurocontrol*, the plaintiffs also tried to argue that the fact that Eurocontrol enjoyed immunity from suit in Germany and offered legal recourse for aggrieved employees only to an administrative tribunal violated the constitutional law prohibition of 'exceptional/extraordinary courts' (*Ausnahmegerichte*) enshrined in Article 101(1), first sentence of the Basic Law.[182] The Constitutional Court rejected this claim as well and held that the exclusive competence of the ILO Administrative Tribunal for labour disputes between Eurocontrol and its employees did not deprive the affected individual of his or her right to access to court, because the procedure and jurisprudence of that tribunal satisfied the principles of the rule of law/legality.[183]

In *Eurocontrol-Flight Charges II*,[184] the Federal Constitutional Court rejected the contention of the claimants that the exclusive jurisdiction of Belgian courts violated the principles of the German Basic Law. It held that the German Constitution did not provide a subsidiary jurisdiction for German courts over disputes concerning flight charges of Eurocontrol since the provision allegedly infringed, Article 19(4) of the Basic Law, provided for legal recourse against acts of German authorities only, not against acts of intergovernmental institutions.[185] What is important to note, however, is the fact that the Federal Constitutional Court reiterated its view – already enunciated in the famous *Solange* decisions[186] – accord-

---

[181] '[M]it Blick auf die Grundprinzipien der Verfassung bestehende Grenzen dieser Übertragungsermächtigung könnten überschritten sein, wenn bei der Schaffung einer zwischenstaatlichen Einrichtung und bei ihrer organisatorischen und rechtlichen Ausgestaltung der – schon im Rechtsstaatsprinzip verankerten – Gewährleistung eines wirksamen Rechtsschutzes gegen Akte der öffentlichen Gewalt nicht hinreichend Rechnung getragen wurde.' Federal Constitutional Court, 10 November 1981, BVerfGE 59, 63 at 86.

[182] See p. 290 above.

[183] Federal Constitutional Court, Second Chamber, 10 November 1981, 2 BvR 1058/79, BVerfGE 59, 63 at 91. Also in *Strech* v. *Eurocontrol*, Labour Court Karlsruhe, 5 December 1978; State Labour Court Baden-Württemberg, 28 September 1979, a related labour dispute, the State Labour Court of Baden-Württemberg considered that the procedure of the ILO tribunal conformed to the principles of democracy and the rule of law.

[184] Federal Constitutional Court, 23 June 1981.   [185] BVerfGE 58, 1 at 26.

[186] *Internationale HandelsgesellschaftmbH* v. *Einfuhr- und Vorratstelle für Getreide und Futtermittel*, Federal Constitutional Court, 29 May 1974; *Re Application of Wünsche Handelsgesellschaft*, Federal Constitutional Court, 22 October 1986. See also p. 311 below. Also, in this respect, the German Constitutional Court has recently quite clearly affirmed its *Solange* jurisprudence by stating its willingness to scrutinize acts of European Community

ing to which the constitutional license to transfer sovereign powers to international organizations under Article 24(1) of the Basic Law is limited by the necessity to respect the core elements of the German Constitution. Among those core elements are the fundamental rights of individuals which may not be removed by such a transfer of sovereignty.[187] The Federal Constitutional Court was, however, clearly of the opinion that the option of legal recourse that was offered by Belgian courts satisfied the basic rights requirement of an effective legal protection.[188]

In this respect it confirmed what the German Federal Administrative Court had already stated in *Eurocontrol-Flight Charges I*.[189] In this earlier decision arising from the same dispute, a German air transportation company brought suit against Eurocontrol challenging the legality of its competence to collect flight charges. The German Federal Administrative Court upheld the reasoning of the lower courts which had decided that German courts had no jurisdiction to scrutinize the flight charges of Eurocontrol because such jurisdiction vested exclusively in Belgian courts as a result of Eurocontrol's internal law. The highest German administrative court emphasized that – since the Belgian courts would adequately guarantee a fair trial – the resulting lack of jurisdiction of the German courts posed no constitutional law problems.[190]

In another German decision, *X* v. *Y* (the *ESRO* case),[191] the plaintiff specifically attacked the grant of immunity to officers of the European Space Research Organization as a violation of Article 101 of the German Basic Law. The court, however, thought that the constitutional prohibition of 'exceptional/extraordinary courts' did not guarantee the access to German courts, but rather presupposed the jurisdiction of German courts. Thus, a total exemption from German jurisdiction was held to be

organs that threaten to infringe basic rights of German citizens: 'Acts done under a special power, separate from national powers of Member States, exercised by a supra-national organization also affect the holders of basic rights in Germany. They therefore affect the guarantees of the Constitution and the duties of the Constitutional Court, the object of which is the protection of constitutional rights in Germany – in this respect not merely as against German state bodies.' *Brunner et al.* v. *European Union Treaty (Constitutionality of the Maastricht Treaty)*, German Federal Constitutional Court, 12 October 1993, (1994) 31 *Common Market Law Review* 251 at 253.

[187] BVerfGE 58, 1 at 40: 'Allerdings läßt [Article 24] die Übertragung von Hoheitsrechten auf zwischenstaatliche Einrichtungen nicht schrankenlos zu ... Ein unaufgebbarer Bestandteil des Verfassungsgefüges sind die fundamentalen Rechtsgrundsätze, die in den Grundrechten des Grundgesetzes anerkannt und verbürgt sind.'

[188] BVerfGE 58, 1 at 42.   [189] Federal Administrative Court, 16 September 1977.

[190] BVerwGE 54, 291 at 304.

[191] Federal Labour Court, 25 January 1973. An employment dispute brought against an officer of ESRO was dismissed because the court considered the actions complained of to be covered by the defendant's functional immunity.

compatible with the constitutional prohibition of exceptional courts and not to violate the German constitutional principles of democracy and the rule of law.

Although these decisions have given rise to a number of scholarly comments,[192] they seem to confine themselves to the narrow issue of the applicability of Article 19(4) of the Basic Law to acts of international organizations and do not deal with the problem of 'non-sovereign' or 'non-public' acts of international organizations and the legal protection against such acts by the German courts.[193] However, under the three-party relationship, outlined above, it would be exactly this aspect which is of interest in the present context, i.e. whether individuals have a right to go to court over private law disputes with international organizations and not whether German administrative/constitutional law controls should extend over non-German official acts.

Some Italian cases seem to be relevant to this discussion.[194] They

---

[192] Bleckmann, *Internationale Beamtenstreitigkeiten*; A. E. du Perron, 'Eurocontrol, Liability and Jurisdiction' in J. W. E. Storm van's Gravesande and A. van der Veen Vonk (eds.), *AirWorthy. Liber Amicorum I. H. P. Diederiks-Verschoor* (Deventer, Antwerp, London, Frankfurt, New York and Boston, 1985), 135–49; Ludwig Gramlich, 'Innerstaatlicher Rechtsschutz für internationale Bedienstete?' (1985) 6 *Juristische Rundschau* 221–8; Christoph H. Schreuer, 'Eurocontrol: Wechselwirkungen staatlicher und innerstaatlicher Jurisdiktion' in Rechtswissenschaftliche Fakultät der Universität Salzburg (ed.), *Aus Österreichs Rechtsleben in Geschichte und Gegenwart. Festschrift für Ernst C. Hellbling* (Berlin, 1981), 371–82; Seidl-Hohenveldern, *Die Immunität internationaler Organisationen*; and Ignaz Seidl-Hohenveldern, 'Zur internationalen Zuständigkeit deutscher Gerichte für Rechtsstreitigkeiten über Gebührenforderungen der Eurocontrol' (1982) 31 *Zeitschrift für Luft- und Weltraumrecht* 111–15.

[193] Gramlich, 'Innerstaatlicher Rechtsschutz', 221*ff*; and Manfred Wenckstern, 'Verfassungsrechtliche Fragen der Immunität internationaler Organisationen' (1987) *Neue Juristische Wochenschrift* 1113–18 at 1114. In his short article on constitutional questions of the jurisdictional immunity of international organizations, Wenckstern only briefly touches upon the issue of a potential conflict of this international norm with the rule of law principle as codified in the German Constitution. He merely cites the famous *Eurocontrol-Flight Charges II* case as evidence of the proposition that the strict rules of Article 19(4) of the Basic Law are applicable only *vis-à-vis* acts of German authorities, not acts of international organizations. In his view the requirements of the rule of law principle can be fulfilled by a minimum standard of jurisdictional protection afforded by arbitral tribunals or international courts as long as a minimum protection is guaranteed and as long as the transfer to non-German dispute settlement organs is justified by material reasons (*sachliche Gründe*). Wenckstern, 'Verfassungsrechtliche Fragen', 1114. However, Wenckstern does not mention the European Convention on Human Rights dimension or other human rights concerns.

[194] See also *Astrup* v. *Presidente Consiglio ministri*, Constitutional Court, 27 June 1973; *FAO* v. *Colagrossi*, Corte di Cassazione, 18 May 1992; *Luggeri* v. *ICEM*, Tribunale Santa Maria Capua Vetere, 20 June 1966; Court of Appeals of Naples, 18 December 1970, discussed at p. 310 below.

sometimes refer to the right to a 'natural judge' contained in Article 25(1)[195] of the Italian Constitution and sometimes to Article 24(1) of the Italian Constitution according to which '[e]veryone is entitled to institute legal proceedings for the protection of his rights and legitimate interests'. In *Food and Agriculture Organization* v. *Istituto Nazionale di Previdenze per i Dirigenti di Aziende Industriali (INPDAI)*,[196] the Italian Supreme Court reasoned that this constitutional requirement has to be taken into consideration when assessing the scope of immunity of an international organization.[197] Although the court referred to Article 24 only in passing, it seems relevant that it denied the FAO's claim to absolute immunity and subjected the organization to the jurisdiction of Italian courts as far as private law disputes arising from a lease agreement were concerned.[198]

Among the many US cases dealing with the jurisdictional immunity of international organizations only a few consider its implication for a right of access to courts. This may have to do with the fact that – apart from the trial-by-jury requirement of the Seventh Amendment[199] – the US Constitution does not contain a right of access to court comparable to the strong formulation of the German, Italian or even the Japanese one.[200] In *People* v. *Mark S. Weiner*,[201] criminal proceedings were brought against a private individual accused of having sprayed paint on an outside wall of the UN headquarters building. The defendant alleged that he had been assaulted and harassed by the UN security officer who reported the incident to the police and that he intended to file a counterclaim. In

---

[195] 'No one shall be denied the right to be tried by his natural judge pre-established by law.' This principle requires that in any lawsuit the competent judge will not be chosen *ad hoc* but rather be determined by legislation. *Cf.* Cappelletti, *The Judicial Process*, 220.

[196] Supreme Court, 18 October 1982. See pp. 187*f* above for details of the case.

[197] (1983) 66 *Rivista di diritto internazionale* 187 at 189. The Supreme Court rejected the FAO's claim to immunity observing that under the FAO's constitutive treaty member states were only required to undertake to accord to the organization immunities 'in so far as it may be possible under their own constitutional procedure'. In the court's view, the Italian Constitution requires that such immunity from suit as may be granted to international organizations should take into account the principle laid down in Article 24 of the Constitution that the legitimate interests of citizens should be afforded judicial protection.

[198] (1983) 66 *Rivista di diritto internazionale* 187 at 190*ff*.

[199] Amendment VII: 'In suits at common law, where the value in controversy shall exceed twenty dollars, the right of trial by jury shall be preserved and no fact tried by a jury, shall be otherwise re-examined in any Court of the United States, than according to the rules of the common law.'

[200] Article 32 of the Constitution of Japan provides 'No person shall be denied the right of access to the courts.'

[201] Criminal Court of the City of New York, New York County, 19 January 1976.

anticipating this potential 'counter complaint', the Criminal Court of the City of New York held that the defence of immunity would not be granted. The court reasoned that since the UN and its officials enjoyed only functionally limited immunity the reporting security officer could not claim immunity for acts in excess of his authority. The court, however, did not stop here, but rather relied on an additional line of reasoning, in the court's words on 'equitable considerations which motivate this court to reach its conclusions'[202] – considerations which basically balance the UN's right to immunity with the constitutional right of US citizens of access to court. The court found that '[t]here is a limit to which the international agreement creating the United Nations can inure to the detriment, disadvantage, and unequal protection of a citizen of the United States' and that '[a] basic concept and motivating factor of the founders of this Republic was the absolute right of every citizen to petition for redress in its courts'.[203] In *Urban* v. *United Nations*,[204] the District of Columbia Court of Appeals recognized that a 'court must take great care not to "unduly impair [a litigant's] constitutional right of access to the courts"'.[205] Apparently, however, it did not consider it an impairment to issue an injunction against a frivolous 'litigant flooding the court with meritless, fanciful claims',[206] enjoining him from filing any more lawsuits without obtaining prior leave from the court. There was no need for the court to reach the issue of immunity from suit, since it held that this particular denial of a litigant's access to court was justified 'to protect the integrity of the courts and the orderly and expeditious administration of justice'.[207]

The French case of *Ministre des Affaires étrangères* v. *Dame Burgat et autres*[208] might lend itself in a very indirect way to support the argument that wholesale exemptions of a class of persons from the jurisdiction of domestic courts may pose a problem under domestic legal principles of equality and fairness and may even ultimately entail the forum state's responsibility.[209] The owners of an apartment in Paris, which was leased to a person enjoying absolute immunity under the UNESCO headquarters agreement, had unsuccessfully brought a claim for a rent increase. Subsequently, they brought suit against the French state claiming that the said immunity had made it impossible for them to vindicate their rights against the tenant. In a remarkable decision, the Conseil d'Etat held that the principle of equality concerning public expenses led to the French state's responsibility because the conclusion of the UNESCO head-

---

[202] 378 NYS 2d 966 at 975.   [203] *Ibid.*   [204] US Court of Appeals DC Cir., 2 August 1985.
[205] 768 F. 2d 1497 at 1500 (DC Cir. 1985).   [206] *Ibid.*, 1499.   [207] *Ibid.*, 1500.
[208] Conseil d'Etat, 29 October 1976.   [209] See also p. 329 below.

quarters agreement deprived the plaintiffs of a judicial forum to pursue their rights.[210]

Sometimes, however, the manner in which domestic courts handle these issues reflects their superficial approach. In *Girod de l'Ain*,[211] one of the grounds to challenge a governmental decree enabling France compulsorily to acquire land in order to lease it subsequently to CERN was an alleged violation of the preamble of the French Constitution and of the European Convention on Human Rights. The Conseil d'Etat recognized that:

[the] decree being challenged does not contain any rule with regard to the exercise of means of redress available to persons who suffered damage caused by CERN, with a view to obtaining compensation. It follows that on the ground based on the alleged violation by the decree of the provisions of the European Convention on Human Rights which recognize every person as having the right to seek legal redress before a national tribunal, as well as the principle contained in the preamble of the Constitution according to which every person is entitled to compensation for damage engaging the civil liability of natural or legal persons under private law, must be rejected.[212]

It has been rightly said that the Conseil d'Etat's conclusion is a *non sequitur* because it is exactly this lack of redress procedures which raises a fundamental rights problem.[213]

---

[210] The Conseil d'Etat concluded 'qu'ainsi la responsabilité de l'Etat se trouve engagée sur le fondement du principe de l'égalité des citoyens devant les charges publiques'. (1977) 104 *Journal de droit international* 631.

[211] Conseil d'Etat, 25 July 1986. Mr Girod de l'Ain and other individuals as well as environmental groups tried to challenge the French decision to declare certain parts of French territory for public use and to rent them to CERN in order to enable that international organization to built a particle accelerator there. The Conseil d'Etat rejected the challenges based on various constitutional and administrative law arguments, holding, *inter alia*, that the lease of part of French territory to CERN under the circumstances in question did not constitute a cession of territory under Article 53 of the French Constitution; that an environmental impact study had in fact been properly conducted; etc. Since the relief sought was not directed against CERN, but rather against the French state, CERN's immunity was not directly in issue. The Conseil d'Etat, however, had to consider the consequences of the declaration of public use for the immunities of CERN. The petitioners had claimed, *inter alia*, that the declaration would have had to be made in the form of a law, instead of a mere administrative decree, because it enlarged CERN's immunities. The Conseil d'Etat rejected this claim holding that 'cette declaration d'utilité publique n'ayant ni pour objet, ni pour effet, d'étendre les prérogatives ou les immunités, notamment l'immunité de juridiction, dont beneficie le CERN en tant qu'organisation internationale' ('this declaration of public utility does not have either the object or the effect of extending the prerogatives or immunities, in particular the immunity from jurisdiction, which CERN enjoys as an international organization'). (1987) 33 *Annuaire français de droit international* 905.

[212] (1990) 82 ILR 89*ff*.

[213] *Cf.* David Ruzié, 'La France et l'Organisation européenne de recherche nucléaire' (1986) 2 *Revue française de droit administratif* 956–60 at 960.

In the more recent case of *Hintermann* v. *Union de l'Europe occidentale*,[214] a human rights challenge to the lack of jurisdiction of French courts over suits against international organizations is taken more seriously by the Cour de Cassation. The court rejected the claim by Mr Hintermann, former Vice-Secretary-General of the Western European Union (WEU), that the organization's immunity from suit violated his rights under Article 6(1) of the European Convention on Human Rights in a laconic fashion typical for French courts. It did not address the potential conflict of treaty norms stemming from the European Convention's right of access to court and the grant of immunity to the defendant organization in the WEU Treaty. What are important, however, are the court's reflections in its annual report concerning the *Hintermann* case. There it recognized the potential denial of justice stemming from an organization's immunity and asked whether such denial of justice could be avoided by according primacy to the European Convention on Human Rights.[215] Although the court's 'timidity' prevented it from addressing or even solving this issue in its own decision,[216] it noted in its report that '[i]l appartiendra, éventuellement, à la Cour européenne des droits de l'homme, de trancher le conflit'.[217]

The Spanish Constitutional Court was faced with a similar factual situation and reached a similar result to the French court in *Ministre des Affaires étrangères* v. *Dame Burgat et autres*.[218] In *X* v. *Deodato*,[219] a Spanish landlady had unsuccessfully tried to recover rent arrears from an Italian diplomat. The Constitutional Court rejected her claim that the immunity granted to a foreign diplomat from civil proceedings violated Article 24 of the Spanish Constitution which provides for a right of access to courts in the vindication of one's legitimate rights and interests. In justifying this

---

[214] Cour d'appel de Paris, 10 April 1990, Cour de Cassation, 14 November 1995.

[215] 'Les immunités de juridiction des organisations internationales . . . ont, pour conséquence, lorsque n'est pas organisé au sein de chaque organisation un mode de règlement arbitral ou juridictionnel des litiges, de créer un déni de justice . . . Ce déni de justice peut-il être évité par la primauté de la convention européenne des droits de l'homme, qui garantit le libre accès au juge et le procès équitable?' Cour de Cassation, *Rapport annuel* (1995), 418, cited by Byk, 'Case Note', 142.

[216] In a reasoning which reminds of the separation-of-powers justification for the act of state doctrine (*cf.* p. 86 above), the court noted that it did not want to take 'la responsabilité de perturber le droit des relations internationales en mettant pratiquement à néant les privilèges et immunités juridictionnels des nombreuses organisations internationales auxquelles la France est partie'. Cour de Cassation, Rapport annuel (1995), cited by Byk, 'Case Note', 142.

[217] *Ibid.*, 149 ('it is incumbent on the European Court of Human Rights to eventually settle the conflict').

[218] Conseil d'Etat, 29 October 1976.   [219] Tribunal Constitucional, 28 September 1995.

result, it referred to the alternative remedies available to a plaintiff in such a situation and held that such a claimant could demand that the Spanish Government declare a defaulting diplomat *persona non grata*. If such a request were rejected, the Spanish Government would have to pay compensation for all damages arising for the plaintiff. What is most interesting, however, is the Spanish court's lengthy reasoning concerning the potential friction between a constitutional right of access to court and an internationally agreed upon immunity for certain persons. It thought that Article 31(1) of the applicable Vienna Convention on Diplomatic Relations 1961, which restricted Article 24 of the Spanish Constitution, did not violate constitutional principles because it served a legitimate purpose and because it did so in a proportionate manner leaving the core of the constitutional right under Article 24 untouched. It saw a legitimate purpose of immunity in the effective performance of diplomatic representation according to the principle *ne impediatur legatio*; as to the second requirement, the court thought that immunity could only be reconciled with an individual's right of access to court if he or she had appropriate procedural alternatives in order to guard his or her legitimate interests. In the court's view these alternatives were available since the plaintiff could either sue in the courts of the diplomat's sending state or ask Spain to declare him *persona non grata*.

Turning to international judicial organs, it is surprising that they too seem to be very reluctant to state an incompatibility between the granting of immunity to international organizations and constitutional or, for that matter, human rights guarantees. It seems that also the European Commission of Human Rights disposed of the very few true cases involving the immunity of international organizations too expeditiously because it did not pay sufficient attention to the difference between the individual *vis-à-vis* the member state refusing access to its courts, and the individual *vis-à-vis* the international organization infringing human rights.[220] In *Ary Spaans* v. *The Netherlands*,[221] the applicant expressly invoked Article 6(1) of the European Convention on Human Rights. He complained that the final Dutch immunity decision in *AS* v. *Iran–United States Claims Tribunal*[222] deprived him of his right of access to a court or tribunal in the determination of the legal validity of the unilateral termination of his employment contract with the Iran–United States Claims Tribunal. The Commission, however, declared the application

---

[220] *Cf.* pp. 288*f* above.
[221] European Commission of Human Rights, Application No. 12516/86, 12 December 1988.
[222] Supreme Court, 20 December 1985. See pp. 157 and 208 above.

inadmissible. It thought that according to Article 1 of the European Convention on Human Rights the member states were responsible for securing the rights and freedoms defined in the Convention only to 'everyone within their jurisdiction'. Since the Netherlands granted immunity to the Tribunal, the acts of the latter were considered to be outside the jurisdiction of the Netherlands. Thus, no issue of responsibility involving the Netherlands could arise.[223] If one followed the reasoning of the Commission, a state party to the Convention could avoid its responsibility simply by limiting its jurisdiction through grants of immunity. However, it seems that this approach, based on a preliminary division of jurisdiction, is misleading. The precise question is whether under Article 6(1) of the Convention a state is obliged to provide a forum for certain kinds of disputes (concerning civil rights and obligations) and whether this obligation may be limited in certain situations (because the disputes are directed against a certain class of persons, such as international organizations, diplomats etc.). The question is not whether Article 6(1) might be inapplicable because a state has chosen to relinquish its 'jurisdiction' to the benefit of an international organization or other immune person – a situation that might arise from a transfer of state powers.[224]

It is clear from the existing case law that the Convention organs regularly do not consider themselves competent to decide upon alleged infringements of human rights by international organizations or other inter-state entities which are not parties to the respective human rights instrument, even if all or some of its member states are. The cases *Ilse Hess* v. *United Kingdom*,[225] *Heinz* v. *Contracting Parties who are also Parties to the European Patent Convention*[226] and *M(elchers) & Co.* v. *Federal Republic of*

---

[223] 'Because of the immunity enjoyed by the Tribunal, the administrative decisions of the Tribunal are not acts which occur within the jurisdiction of the Netherlands within the meaning of Article 1 of the Convention and thus do not engage the responsibility of the Netherlands under the Convention.' (1988) 58 *Decisions and Reports* 119 at 122.

[224] The declaration of inadmissibility of the *Spaans* application, qualifying it as incompatible *ratione personae* within the meaning of Article 27(2) of the Convention, resembles the Commission's decision in *Ilse Hess* v. *United Kingdom*, European Commission of Human Rights, Application No. 6231/63, 28 May 1975. See p. 301 below. The important difference between the two situations is, however, that in the *Hess* application it was unclear whether the alleged violation of the Convention could be attributed to the UK individually or only to the Four Powers jointly, whereas in the *Spaans* application there was no issue of attributing the responsibility for a violation of Article 6(1). It was clear that this was an obligation incumbent upon the Netherlands and not upon the Tribunal. Still, the Commission relied on the same reasoning for its inadmissibility decision.

[225] European Commission of Human Rights, Application No. 6231/63, 28 May 1975.

[226] European Commission of Human Rights, Application No. 12090/92, 10 January 1994.

Germany[227] are illustrative of this view. They form part of the accepted case law of the European Commission of Human Rights that decisions taken by an international organization, of which states parties to the European Convention on Human Rights are members, do not involve the exercise of national jurisdiction within the meaning of Article 1 of the Convention and thus cannot, in principle, lead to a violation of the Convention by the member states.[228] In the *Hess* case,[229] the complaint, alleging that the continued imprisonment of the applicant's husband Rudolf Hess at Spandau prison violated the Convention, was declared inadmissible because the responsibility for the prison was held not to be 'a matter within the jurisdiction of the United Kingdom within the meaning of Article 1 [of the Convention]'. Spandau prison was administered jointly by the Four Powers, and in the Commission's view this joint authority could not be divided into four separate jurisdictions.[230] In *Heinz* v. *Contracting Parties who are also Parties to the European Patent Convention*,[231] a complaint claiming that the European Patent Organization member states – bound by the European Convention on Human Rights – were responsible for an alleged property rights violation of that organization was declared inadmissible. In the Commission's view decisions taken by the European Patent Office did not involve the exercise of national jurisdiction within the meaning of Article 1 of the Convention.[232] One of the precedents relied upon in *Heinz* was *M(elchers) & Co.* v. *Federal Republic of Germany*,[233] where the Commission held that 'it is in fact not competent *ratione personae* to examine proceedings before or decisions of organs of the European Communities, the latter not being a

---

[227] European Commission of Human Rights, Application No. 13258/77, 9 February 1990.

[228] See pp. 304 and 311*f* below for potential exceptions.

[229] European Commission of Human Rights, Application No. 6231/63, 28 May 1975.

[230] In its more recent decision in *Vearncombe* v. *Federal Republic of Germany and United Kingdom*, European Commission of Human Rights, Application No. 12816/87, 18 January 1989, the Commission did not resolve the issue of whether the nuisance caused by the construction and use of a shooting range by the British military authorities in Berlin could be attributed to the UK. The Commission observed, however, that 'authorised agents of a State (including armed forces) not only remain under the jurisdiction of that State when abroad, they also bring other persons or property with the jurisdiction of that State to the extent that they exercise authority over such persons or property' and it expressed its opinion that 'there is in principle, from a legal point of view, no reason why acts of the British authorities in Berlin should not entail the liability of the United Kingdom under the Convention'. (1989) 59 *Decisions and Reports* 186 at 194.

[231] European Commission of Human Rights, Application No. 12090/92, 10 January 1994.

[232] (1994) 76-A *Decisions and Reports* 125 at 127.

[233] European Commission of Human Rights, Application No. 13258/77, 9 February 1990.

party to the Convention on Human Rights'.[234] Similarly, in *Conféderation Francaise démocratique du Travail* v. *European Communities*,[235] a complaint against the European Communities was rejected because they were not parties to the European Convention on Human Rights. The dismissal was also based on the ground that the member states when cooperating to adopt a decision within the EC Council did not exercise 'their jurisdiction' in the sense of Article 1 of the Convention.

A Communication of the UN Human Rights Committee in *HvdP* v. *The Netherlands*[236] confirms this view. There an employee of the European Patent Office, with its headquarters in Munich, claimed that he had been treated in a discriminatory fashion by his employer. After having exhausted the internal administrative remedies provided by the European Patent Organization and after having had recourse to the ILO Administrative Tribunal, the complainant applied to the UN Human Rights Committee, arguing that his rights according to Article 25 of the International Covenant on Civil and Political Rights (ICCPR), pursuant to which every citizen should have access, on general terms of equality, to a public service, had been violated and that the internal administrative review procedure did not constitute an effective remedy in the sense of Article 2 of the ICCPR. He claimed that the European Patent Organization 'though a public body common to the Contracting States, constitutes a body exercising Dutch public authority'. The UN Human Rights Committee rejected this claim. In explaining its inadmissibility decision it stated that 'the recruitment policies of an international organization . . . cannot, in any way, be construed as coming within the jurisdiction of the Netherlands or of any other State party to the [ICCPR]'.[237]

It is rather curious to note that an application by the same person in the same matter to the European Commission of Human Rights was declared inadmissible on a rather different ground in *HvdP* v. *The Netherlands*.[238] Relying on its previous case law according to which 'litigation concerning access to, or dismissal from, civil service falls outside the scope of Article 6(1) of the Convention', the Commission held that 'litigation concerning the modalities of employment as a civil servant, on either the national or international level, falls outside the scope of Article

---

[234] See, however, pp. 304ff and 311f below concerning the important qualification regarding the circumstances under which member states might become indirectly responsible for acts of international organizations.

[235] European Commission of Human Rights, Application No. 8030/77, 10 July 1978.

[236] UN Human Rights Committee, Communication No. 217/1986, 8 April 1987.

[237] (1988) 9 *Human Rights Law Journal* 255.

[238] European Commission of Human Rights, Application No. 11056/84, 15 May 1986.

6(1)'[239] and that applications relating thereto were thus inadmissible *ratione materiae.*

It is submitted that, contrary to these cases concerning alleged human rights violations by international organizations, which have been regularly held by the Convention's organs not to entail the responsibility of their member states as a matter of principle, the issue of a potential violation of the duty to provide access to courts by states parties to human rights obligations that may result from their granting immunity to international organizations cannot be properly regarded as a question of dividing spheres of 'jurisdictions' between states and organizations. As already mentioned, this approach – apparently pursued in the *Spaans* decision[240] – would leave it to the member states to limit their responsibility under the Convention by reducing their 'jurisdiction' through the grant of immunity.[241] This, however, would seem to run counter to the interpretation of and the importance accorded to the right of access to court in the jurisprudence of the Court and the Commission. In its judgment in the *Golder* case,[242] the European Court of Human Rights made it quite plain that states parties to the Convention were not wholly free to exclude certain types of actions from the jurisdiction of their courts.[243] In decisions like *Graham Dyer* v. *United Kingdom*[244] and *Kaplan* v. *United Kingdom*,[245] the Commission also demonstrated its awareness that the 'immunization' of certain groups in respect of their actions[246] as well as the elimination of the jurisdiction of courts beyond a certain point[247]

---

[239] (1988) 9 *Human Rights Law Journal* 265 at 266.

[240] European Commission of Human Rights, Application No. 12516/86, 12 December 1988.

[241] See pp. 286 and 300 above.

[242] European Court of Human Rights, 21 February 1975, Series A, No. 18.

[243] 'Were Article 6 § 1 to be understood as concerning exclusively the conduct of an action which had already been initiated before a court, a Contracting State could, without acting in breach of that text, do away with its courts, or take away their jurisdiction to determine certain classes of civil actions and entrust it to organs dependent on the Government.' *Golder*, European Court of Human Rights, 21 February 1975, Series A, No. 18, para. 35.

[244] European Commission of Human Rights, Application No. 10475/83, 9 October 1984.

[245] European Commission of Human Rights, Application No. 7598/76, 17 July 1980.

[246] 'Were Article 6, para. 1 to be interpreted as enabling a State Party to remove the jurisdiction of the courts to determine certain classes of civil claim or to confer immunities from liability on certain groups in respect of their actions, without any possibility of control by the Convention organs, there would exist no protection against the danger of arbitrary power.' *Graham Dyer* v. *United Kingdom*, European Commission of Human Rights, Application No. 10475/83, 9 October 1984, (1984) 39 *Decisions and Reports* 246 at 252.

[247] '[T]he jurisdiction of the courts cannot be removed altogether or limited beyond a certain point.' *Kaplan* v. *United Kingdom*, European Commission of Human Rights, Application No. 7598/76, 17 July 1980, (1981) 21 *Decisions and Reports* 5 at 33.

would be contrary to the Convention. On the other hand, it is part of the settled case law of the Court that the right of access to court as embodied in Article 6 of the Convention is not absolute or unlimited. It is clear, however, that any limitation of that right may not destroy its 'very essence'[248] and that the degree of access to court provided for by national legislation has to have regard to the principle of the 'pre-eminence of law in a democratic society'.[249] These requirements taken together imply that any restriction of the right of access to court has to satisfy the principle of proportionality.[250] At this point it seems appropriate to reconsider the substantive policy reasons discussed above in favour and against the adjudication of disputes involving international organizations by national courts.[251] It is submitted that it would not be inconceivable that the legitimate interests of individuals to have their civil rights and obligations determined by an independent court may outweigh the justifiable concern of international organizations to function freely and independently. It seems plausible that the availability of alternative dispute settlement fora would be one of the crucial elements within such a balancing approach.[252] If a balancing of interests in certain cases turned out in favour of having domestic courts adjudicating claims brought against international organizations, this would clearly run counter to a wholesale exemption of international organizations from the jurisdiction of national courts as a result of their immunity from suit or legal process.

As far as true immunity of international organizations cases are concerned, the European Commission of Human Rights recently used a similar balancing test and slightly modified its *Spaans* approach without, however, reaching a different result. *Karlheinz Beer and Philip Regan* v. *Germany*[253] and *Richard Waite and Terry Kennedy* v. *Germany*[254] both concerned the compatibility of a sweeping grant of immunity to the European Space Agency (ESA) by German legislation. In lawsuits brought by employees of private companies claiming that pursuant to the Ger-

---

[248] *Ashingdane*, European Court of Human Rights, 28 May 1985, Series A, No. 93, para. 57; *Lithgow and others*, European Court of Human Rights, 8 July 1986, Series A, No. 102, para. 194(b); *Philis*, European Court of Human Rights, 27 August 1991, Series A, No. 209, para. 59; *Fayed*, European Court of Human Rights, 21 September 1994, Series A, No. 294-B, para. 65.

[249] *Ashingdane*, European Court of Human Rights, 28 May 1985, Series A, No. 93, para. 24.

[250] *Cf.* Christoph Grabenwarter, *Verfahrensgarantien in der Verwaltungsgerichtsbarkeit* (Vienna and New York, 1997), 444.   [251] See pp. 252*ff* and pp. 233*ff* above.

[252] See pp. 366*f* below.

[253] European Commission of Human Rights, Application No. 28934/95, 2 December 1997.

[254] European Commission of Human Rights, Application No. 26083/94, 2 December 1997.

man Provision of Labour Act they had acquired the status of employees of the defendant organization, ESA successfully relied upon its immunity from German jurisdiction. Thereon applicants complained under Article 6(1) of the European Convention on Human Rights that they did not have a hearing by a court on the question of whether a contractual relationship had existed between them and ESA. While the German Government relied on the existing case law of the Convention organs and maintained that 'the right of access to court is subject to inherent limitations which include the traditional and generally recognised principle of parliamentary and diplomatic immunity and also the immunity of international organisations' the Commission was no longer satisfied with such an easy explanation. Contrary to its reasoning in the *Spaans* decision, it saw a potential violation of Article 6(1) of the Convention and considered that any limitation of the right of access to court would have to 'pursue a legitimate aim and [that there had to be] a reasonable relationship of proportionality between the means employed and the aim sought to be achieved'.[255] It found the legitimate aim in the independence and protection of the proper functioning rationale and concluded that the 'legal impediment to bringing litigation before the German courts, namely the immunity of the European Space Agency from German jurisdiction, [was] only permissible under the Convention if there [was] an equivalent legal protection'.[256] In an interesting final twist to this decision, which was secured by a close vote of seventeen to fifteen, the European Commission of Human Rights – while acknowledging that the applicants 'did not . . . receive a legal protection within the European Space Agency which could be regarded as equivalent to the jurisdiction of the German labour courts'[257] and probably inspired by the peculiar circumstances of the case – concluded that it could not 'apply the test of proportionality in such a way as to force an international organisation to be a party to domestic litigation on a question of employment governed by domestic law'.[258] It is submitted, however, that this apparently crucial issue of whether German labour legislation would be binding for an international organization is not an issue of judicial jurisdiction proper but rather a question of the applicable law.[259] Taking the 'equivalent legal protection' requirement seriously could have resulted in a different finding.

---

[255] *Ibid.*, para. 65.   [256] *Ibid.*, para. 74.   [257] *Ibid.*, para. 79.   [258] *Ibid.*, para. 80.

[259] This view seems to be alluded to by the dissenting opinion of Mr G. Ress who found that 'the question as to whether and to what extent domestic legislation of this kind can be held against an international organisation, which regularly enacts its own staff regulations, cannot be resolved in removing such matters from judicial review' *Ibid.*

Are alternative fora sufficient to guarantee the right of access to courts?

From a human rights policy perspective, the crucial question seems to be whether the existence and/or particular arrangement of alternative dispute settlement procedures can justify immunity from suit. Frequently the availability of alternative dispute settlement procedures is discussed as a necessary requirement for justifying immunity for certain entities in order at the same time to uphold basic considerations of fairness – considerations that also underlie the concept of a right of access to court as an expression of due process/fair trial rights.[260] However, as already mentioned,[261] the obligation to provide for access to court in determining civil rights and obligations of individuals is one of the forum state where immunity might be invoked and not of the international organization invoking immunity. Thus, technically, it is a different legal relationship that is in issue. It is the forum state that has an obligation to provide access to its courts regardless of whether other fora may be available.[262]

Even if one does not consider immunity rules to be implicit limitations of a right of access to court which can be historically explained, one may contemplate legitimate exceptions to this apparently very strict human rights demand. One such exception could result from the availability of alternative fora. The purpose of guaranteeing access to court seems to lie in the idea to give 'enforceable rights' to those falling under the protection of human rights instruments. If alternative dispute settlement fora provide for means to enforce rights, one might consider this form of institutional relief for the regular national adjudicative bodies justified. The problem is best known in the context of arbitral proceedings where – in a similar way – the determination of civil rights and obligations is transferred from state organs, the domestic judiciary, to arbitral bodies, non-state 'private' institutions. It seems that *prima facie* the reasons advanced to justify the derogation from an unlimited duty to provide access to court by allowing arbitral procedures might be equally applicable to the problem of administrative tribunals as a substitute for access to domestic courts and its human rights conformity. Thus a glance at the

---

[260] See pp. 262*ff* above.

[261] *Cf.* the reference to the three-party relationship at pp. 288*f* above.

[262] See also Pahr's argument that the possibility of suing a foreign sovereign state, that enjoys immunity in the forum state, before its own courts would not satisfy the requirements of Article 6(1) of the European Convention on Human Rights (imposed on the forum state). Pahr, *Die Staatenimmunität*, 231*ff*.

arguments used in upholding the permissibility of arbitration in the face of due process guarantees appears useful.

In the international human rights debate this problem finds remarkably little attention.[263] Probably the most advanced considerations can be found in the context of the European Convention on Human Rights, although the Convention organs, in interpreting the conventional obligations of the contracting states, have not yet squarely addressed the issue. They seem to agree, however, on the principle that a derogation from the jurisdiction of domestic courts as a result of the provision for private arbitration is not contrary to Article 6(1) of the Convention.[264] In general, two aspects seem to be of crucial importance: whether arbitral tribunals operate according to fair trial principles; and whether they could be viewed as 'tribunal[s] established by law'.[265]

Although the European Court of Human Rights qualified the right of access to court in Article 6(1) of the Convention as 'not absolute' and acknowledged 'implicit limitations' to it,[266] the Court insisted that such limitations may not deprive the right of its substance.[267] Thus, one would have to scrutinize strictly the proportionality of any restriction of Article 6(1) inherent in a provision for arbitration. In this respect, the Convention organs seem to be prepared to accept private arbitration, as long as it provides judicial guarantees of independence and impartiality, as an alternative 'tribunal' for access to court purposes. They also appear to take into account the fact that parties to arbitral proceedings regularly freely consent to arbitration in advance.[268] Similarly, they seem to con-

---

[263] The few exceptions all relate to the European system of human rights: Jean-Francois Flauss, 'L'application de l'art. 6(1) de la Convention européenne des Droits de l'Homme aux procédures arbitrales', *Gazette du Palais*, 2 July 1986, 2–4; Olivier Jacot-Guillarmod, 'L'arbitrage privé face à l'Article 6, § 1er de la Convention européenne des droits de l'homme' in *Protecting Human Rights: The European Dimension. Studies in Honour of Gérard J. Wiarda* (Cologne, Berlin, Bonn and Munich, 1988), 281–95 at 281*ff*; Franz Matscher, 'Schiedsgerichtsbarkeit und EMRK, in Beiträge zum internationalen Verfahrensrecht und zur Schiedsgerichtsbarkeit' in Walter Habscheid and Karl Heinz Schwab (eds.), *Beiträge zum Internationalen Verfahrensrecht und zur Schiedsgerichtsbarkeit. Festschrift Nagel* (Münster, 1987), 227–45 at 227*ff*. See also Schwab and Gottwald, 'Verfassung und Zivilprozeß', 43.

[264] *Deweer*, European Court of Human Rights, 27 February 1980. See note 268 below.

[265] See also Jacot-Guillarmod, 'L'arbitrage privé', 281.

[266] For instance in *Lithgow*, European Court of Human Rights, 8 July 1986, Series A, No. 102, 71, para. 194(a), as well as in other cases. See p. 282 note 148 above.

[267] *Ibid.*, para. 194(b).

[268] In its *Deweer* judgment of 27 February 1980, Series A, No. 35, para. 49, the European Court of Human Rights held that a 'waiver' of one's right of access to court 'frequently encountered . . . in the shape of arbitration clauses in contracts . . . does not in principle offend against the Convention'.

sider the submission to arbitration as a waiver or renunciation of one's right of access to a state court.[269]

An important element of accepting arbitration as alternative access to court lies in the residual control regularly exercised by domestic courts. Most national laws reserve a certain supervisory power over arbitral proceedings to their judiciary.[270] This power allows them to deny recognition to arbitral awards procured as a result of gross procedural defects or which contain unacceptable results. Usually the standard of review is limited to a very high level of *ordre public* scrutiny. Through this residual control mechanism, states parties to the European Convention on Human Rights can effectively remedy any infringement of the substance of Article 6(1) by decentralized alternative dispute settlement procedures in the form of arbitration and thus avoid accountability as primary obligor under the Convention to guarantee access to court and a fair trial.[271]

When transposing these considerations to the problem of administrative tribunals of international organizations, the parallel situation is evident. As long as such alternative dispute settlement mechanisms guarantee basic procedural standards, the implicit result of limiting the jurisdiction of a state's regular judiciary seems unproblematic. It is crucial, however – although in the context of certain international organizations sometimes unclear – that an alternative mechanism does in fact exist. Furthermore, there seems to be a growing awareness not only that alternative fora must be available in order to justify a grant of immunity

---

[269] In *X v. Federal Republic of Germany*, European Commission of Human Rights, Application No. 1197/61, 5 March 1962, (1962) 5 *Yearbook of the European Convention on Human Rights* 88 at 94, the Commission said: '[T]he inclusion of an arbitration clause in an agreement between individuals amounts legally to partial renunciation of the exercise of those rights defined by Article 6(1); [however] nothing in the text of that Article nor of any other Article of the Convention explicitly prohibits such renunciation.'

[270] In most countries arbitral decisions may be judicially set aside if they are the product of a gross miscarriage of justice or misconduct by an arbitrator, or are in manifest disregard of the law. This supervisory control is not intended to be an indirect appeals mechanism, but should correct only grave wrongs. See Peter Gottwald, 'Die sachliche Kontrolle internationaler Schiedssprüche durch staatliche Gerichte' in Habscheid and Schwab, *Beiträge zum Internationalen Verfahrensrecht*, 54ff; Andreas F. Lowenfeld, *International Litigation and Arbitration* (St Paul, MN, 1993), 342ff. *Cf.* also section 595 of the Austrian Code of Civil Procedure providing for judicial annulment of arbitral awards.

[271] *Cf.* Matscher, 'Schiedsgerichtsbarkeit und EMRK', 244, who regards private arbitration as compatible with the European Convention of Human Rights but underlines, however, the necessity of state control over arbitration.

to international organizations,[272] but that they have to conform to international standards of due process.[273]

The growing awareness of the importance attached to the guarantee of fundamental rights by alternative dispute settlement fora is also evident in diplomatic and judicial practice relating to the issue of the jurisdictional immunity of international organizations. For instance, in the exchange of notes between Italy and the FAO,[274] wherein the two sides agreed upon 'Modes of Settlement of Disputes' of a private character, the FAO reaffirmed its willingness to set up procedures 'safeguarding the fundamental principles on which judicial proceedings are based both under national legal systems and international law'. It went on to specify some of those principles, such as 'the independence and impartiality of those charged with adjudicating the dispute, the right of defence, the right of both parties to state their cases, and the practicality of the proceedings and the possibility of having recourse to them at reasonable cost'.[275]

In *FAO* v. *Colagrossi*,[276] the Italian Supreme Court rejected the argument that Article 24 of the Italian Constitution, guaranteeing access to court, would prevent an Italian court from granting immunity to the FAO. It considered it 'sufficient to observe' that the dispute settlement obligation incumbent upon the FAO 'would effectively guarantee the right of an employee of the organization to bring an action against it in order to protect his or her rights'.[277] In *Astrup* v. *Presidente Consiglio ministri*[278] the Constitutional Court had already held that the jurisdiction of a 'foreign judge' can be sufficient to guarantee the constitutional principle of the natural judge. Although the case did not raise issues of jurisdictional

---

[272] In defending absolute immunity in employment matters, Seidl-Hohenveldern writes that 'it would be unthinkable to exempt acts by an organization in these matters from all jurisdictional scrutiny. It would be absurd to assume that organizations established to promote a progressive cooperation between their member States should hold absolute power over their staff, like some medieval tyrant.' Seidl-Hohenveldern, 'Jurisdiction over Employment Disputes', 360.

[273] Seidl-Hohenveldern, 'Die internationalen Beamten', 443.

[274] Reprinted in FAO, 'Constitutional and General Legal Matters, Annex I' (1986) *United Nations Juridical Yearbook* 156*ff*. See also pp. 131*ff* above.

[275] *Ibid.*, 157.   [276] Corte di Cassazione, 18 May 1992.

[277] (1992) 75 *Rivista di diritto internazionale* 407 at 411. Similar to the reasoning employed by the German Constitutional Court in *Hetzel* v. *Eurocontrol II*, Federal Constitutional Court, 10 November 1981 (see pp. 291*f* above), the Italian Supreme Court concluded that a limitation of the sovereignty of Italy – resulting from the partial transfer of jurisdiction to the ILO Administrative Tribunal – was constitutional as long as the resulting interference with the rights of citizens did not infringe upon a constitutional guarantee.

[278] Constitutional Court, 27 June 1973.

immunity, it is of interest in so far as it dealt with the question of whether a treaty-based exclusion of Italian territorial jurisdiction might violate the principle of judicial guarantees to be provided by states.[279] In *Luggeri v. ICEM*,[280] however, an Italian court affirmed its jurisdiction over an employment dispute between an international organization and one of its employees, basically because it found a waiver on the part of the ICEM. The interesting aspect of this decision is revealed in the court's alternative justification. It thought that a derogation from the jurisdiction of national courts could not take place if that would lead to a situation where the underlying dispute could not be referred to a settlement procedure before an impartial judicial organ at all. Given the constitutional mandate, the court thought it 'absurd' to think that Italy would have agreed to immunity from suit of an international organization without a minimum guarantee of jurisdictional protection for its employees.[281]

The German Constitutional Court satisfied itself that the two alternative fora in its Eurocontrol cases, the Belgian courts in *Eurocontrol-Flight Charges II*,[282] and the ILO Administrative Tribunal in *Hetzel v. Eurocontrol*

---

[279] The Corte Costituzionale was asked for a ruling on whether the possibility of a waiver of jurisdiction as foreseen in the Italian implementing legislation of the NATO Status of Forces Agreement was in conformity with Italian constitutional law, in particular with the principle of the natural judge contained in Article 24(1) of the Constitution. The reason for this question was a criminal proceeding brought against a US NATO force member arising from a car accident in connection with his official functions. According to the NATO Status of Forces Agreement, Italian courts should (but were not obliged to) waive their jurisdiction to the benefit of the sending state's courts. The court denied the alleged infringement considering that the priority to be accorded in such situations to the jurisdiction of the sending state conformed to international customs and that these customs could serve as yardsticks for Italian law which according to Article 10 of the Italian Constitution conforms with the generally accepted rules of international law. In the court's view an Italian waiver would only lead to a change of jurisdiction between two judicial bodies envisaged *a priori* by the respective legal systems. It held that the 'possibility, in virtue of the contested rule, that competence is passed to another judge who is also pre-constituted, does not amount to a violation of [the principle of the natural judge]'. (1976) 2 *Italian Yearbook of International Law* 354 at 358.

[280] Tribunale Santa Maria Capua Vetere, 20 June 1966; Court of Appeals of Naples, 18 December 1970.

[281] 'Sarebbe, infatti, assurdo che lo Stato italiano, nello stipulare [immunity from every form of legal process] abbia inteso includervi i rapporti di lavoro sorti tra l'ente e i cittadini italiani in territorio italiano e abbia inteso abbandonare la regolazione delle relative controversie al mero arbitrato del rappresentante dell'organismo internazionale contraente, senza alcuna anche minima garanzia di carattere giurisdizionale.' Tribunale Santa Maria Capua Vetere, (1968) 51 *Rivista di diritto internazionale* 143.

[282] Federal Constitutional Court, 23 June 1981.

II,[283] clearly provided a minimum of judicial protection that would equal what is constitutionally guaranteed in Germany under the Basic Law. This reliance on the adequacy of judicial guarantees provided by non-German courts seems to be largely inspired by the Constitutional Court's *Solange* jurisprudence. There, in the context of European Community law, the German highest court generally accepted a splitting of competence between the ECJ and national courts in the field of human rights protection. While in *Solange I*[284] the court upheld the admissibility of a human rights scrutiny by the German Constitutional Court as long as Community law does not contain a comparably adequate fundamental rights protection, *Solange II*[285] reversed the reasoning and justified the lack of competence of the German judiciary over acts of Community organs as long as an equal human rights protection is guaranteed by the ECJ.

The organs of the European Convention on Human Rights seem to rely on a similar reasoning. In particular the European Commission of Human Rights, in two decisions on the admissibility of complaints brought against member states of international organizations, which were also parties to the European Convention on Human Rights, in *Heinz v. Contracting Parties who are also Parties to the European Patent Convention*[286] and in *M(elchers) & Co. v. Federal Republic of Germany*,[287] held that the transfer of powers by them to an international organization was compatible with the Convention, provided that fundamental rights received an equivalent protection within the organization.[288] The latter decision in particular reflects the ECJ's case law on the relevance of human rights mandates for Community organs. The applicant's claim that its fundamental rights had been infringed by the EC Commission in the course of competition proceedings had already been rejected both by the ECJ and by the German

---

[283] Federal Constitutional Court, 10 November 1981.

[284] *Internationale HandelsgesellschaftmbH* v. *Einfuhr- und Vorratstelle für Getreide und Futtermittel*, Federal Constitutional Court, 29 May 1974.

[285] *Re Application of Wünsche Handelsgesellschaft*, Federal Constitutional Court, 22 October 1986.

[286] European Commission of Human Rights, Application No. 12090/92, 10 January 1994. See p. 301 above.

[287] European Commission of Human Rights, Application No. 13258/77, 9 February 1990.

[288] 'The object and purpose of the Convention as an instrument for the protection of individual human beings requires that its provisions be interpreted and applied so as to make its safeguards practical and effective . . . Therefore the transfer of powers to an international organisation is not incompatible with the Convention provided that within that organisation fundamental rights will receive an equivalent protection.' *Heinz* v. *Contracting Parties who are also Parties to the European Patent Convention*, European Commission of Human Rights, Application No. 12090/92, 10 January 1994, (1994) 76-A *Decisions and Reports* 125 at 127.

courts, including the German Constitutional Court. Before the Convention's organs Melchers & Co. argued that, by issuing a writ for the execution of a judgment of the ECJ (which had allegedly violated the principle of the presumption of innocence as well as the applicant's right to defend itself in person), the German authorities had incurred Germany's responsibility for violating its obligation to secure the rights contained in the Convention. The Commission here clearly went beyond the *Hess*[289] and *Spaans*[290] cases where it had simply held that acts of international organizations fell outside its competence *ratione personae*.[291] Rather, it stated that the 'transfer of powers [to organisations did] not necessarily exclude a State's responsibility under the Convention with regard to the transferred powers'.[292] In the Commission's view, such a transfer of powers would be incompatible with the Convention if fundamental rights would not receive an equivalent protection within the organization. This led the Commission to scrutinize the fundamental rights protection within the organization in question. In its view, the Community system of protection of such rights, mainly based on the ECJ's case law, provided such an equivalent protection.

There is, of course, an important distinction between the *Solange* and this European Commission jurisprudence and the problem at hand: while the German Constitutional Court and the European Commission of Human Rights address the availability of the proper forum to redress human rights violations by an international organization, in particular the EC, the problem of the immunity of international organizations under the perspective of the guarantees of access to court focuses on the availability of a proper forum to determine one's 'civil rights and obligations'. Recently, however, in *Karlheinz Beer and Philip Regan* v. *Germany*[293] and *Richard Waite and Terry Kennedy* v. *Germany*[294] the European Commission of Human Rights also adopted this 'equivalent protection' approach for determining whether the grant of jurisdictional immunity to an international organization would be compatible with Article 6(1) of the Convention. Although finding no violation[295] this may have laid the basis for a change of the traditional view on jurisdictional immunity.

---

[289] European Commission of Human Rights, Application No. 6231/63, 28 May 1975.

[290] European Commission of Human Rights, Application No. 12516/86, 12 December 1988.

[291] See pp. 299*ff* above.

[292] *M(elchers) & Co.* v. *Federal Republic of Germany*, European Commission on Human Rights, Application No. 13258/77, 9 February 1990, (1990) 64 *Decisions and Reports* 138 at 145.

[293] European Commission of Human Rights, Application No. 28934/95, 2 December 1997.

[294] European Commission of Human Rights, Application No. 26083/94, 2 December 1997.

[295] See pp. 304*f* above.

Conclusion

An interpretation of the domestic and international fundamental rights guarantees calling for a right of access to court in all 'civil rights and obligations' cases even against international organizations would at least mandate a restriction of the scope of immunity to issues other than those concerning the civil rights and obligations of potential adversaries of international organizations before national courts in cases where no alternative dispute settlement fora are available. The result of such a limitation would come close to a restrictive immunity standard for international organizations.

Although human rights complaints claiming an infringement of the right of access to court by the presently predominant sweeping grants of immunity to international organizations have not been successful to date, a reconsideration of the underlying commonly held view would not be undesirable.

Part III
Future developments

6 Do national courts provide an appropriate forum for disputes involving international organizations?

The final chapter of this study is intended to provide at least some tentative suggestions of how courts should approach disputes involving international organizations as parties before them, and whether and under what conditions they should use their adjudicative power or abstain from doing so. Such an attempt can only be based on the firm ground provided for by the existing case law analyzed in Part I and the rationales for and against adjudication addressed in these cases and discussed in Part II.

Critical appraisal of the quality of the existing case law

As far as the rationales for and against adjudication are concerned, to build upon the reasons advanced in the decisions of national courts in an uncritical way would be irresponsible. Although the analysis in Part II has probably demonstrated the predominance of certain arguments (e.g., guaranteeing the independent functioning of international organizations, requiring abstention or fairness to third parties calling for adjudication, etc.), national idiosyncrasies as well as the difference in the 'objective' quality of the legal reasoning used by different courts make a cautious approach towards the reasons advanced advisable.[1]

A critical distance in the evaluation of the case law and its rationales will also contribute to a better appraisal of the issues involved. Such a viewpoint seems to be particularly appropriate in order to draw final conclusions from the wide and sometimes confusing range of options offered in the cases analyzed.

[1] *Cf.*, in general, Ian Brownlie, *Principles of Public International Law* (4th edn, 1990), 23, deploring the 'narrow national outlook' and 'inadequate use of the sources' by many national courts diminishing the value of their decisions as evidence of international law.

The broader framework

With this critical distance in mind, it seems useful to position the issue of international organizations before domestic courts in a broader context in order to draw the appropriate conclusions from the existing law and to propose certain alternatives that might possibly deal more adequately with the problems described.

International organizations and the rule of law

The exemption of international organizations from the adjudicative power of national courts and the availability of alternative fora to settle disputes is embedded in the broader issue of the accountability of international organizations. Lawyers of all legal traditions are familiar with the basic distinction between the existence of an obligation and its enforceability, between substantive rights and the availability of procedural rights to enforce them. It still seems generally accepted that there is an important interrelation between the two, i.e. that the constant denial of the enforceability of substantive rights may cast doubts on the legal quality of these 'rights'. To arrive at such a conclusion, one need not recur to a strict Austinian or Kelsenian view denying the legal character of every norm not guarded by an effective sanction in case of its breach.[2]

The issue of accountability arises on different levels. Basically, one can differentiate between accountability on the level of international law, usually referred to as international 'responsibility', and accountability on the level of a specific domestic law. Today doubts whether an international organization can become internationally responsible have been largely removed;[3] it is also generally accepted that international organizations may become legally liable according to domestic law.[4] The enforcement aspect, however, is in many cases far more controversial. The obvious reason for this legal insecurity as far as the availability of an adjudicative organ to determine and enforce legal accountability is concerned lies in the lack of explicit provisions for such organs or in the

---

[2] John Austin, *The Province of Jurisprudence Determined* (London, 1954), 134*ff*; Hans Kelsen, *Reine Rechtslehre* (2nd edn, Vienna, 1960), 51*ff*; Hans Kelsen, *Allgemeine Theorie der Normen* (Vienna, 1979), 3.

[3] Mario Bettati, *Le droit des organisations internationales* (Paris, 1987), 111; Konrad Ginther, *Die völkerrechtliche Verantwortlichkeit internationaler Organisationen gegenüber Drittstaaten* (Vienna and New York, 1969); Konrad Ginther, 'International Organizations, Responsibility' in Rudolf Bernhardt (ed.), *Encyclopedia of Public International Law* (2nd edn, 1995), vol. II, 1336–40; Mosche Hirsch, *The Responsibility of International Organizations Toward Third Parties* (Dordrecht, Boston and London, 1995).

[4] Henry G. Schermers, *International Institutional Law* (Alphen aan den Rijn and Rockville, 2nd edn, 1980), 780.

explicit exclusion of possible fora. The former is true primarily on the international level where international courts regularly lack competence to adjudicate disputes involving international organizations[5] or are simply not set up at all, while the latter is the predominant situation on the domestic level where existing courts are frequently expressly deprived of their adjudicative power as far as international organizations are concerned.

One of the more fundamental reasons for this lack of available fora might lie in the particular emphasis laid by functionalism on the workability of international organizations neglecting the accountability aspect of the carrying out of their functions. The debate between 'functionalists' and 'constitutionalists' on international organizations certainly focuses on other aspects. Part of this debate, however, and in particular, the predominance of 'functionalist' arguments, might be responsible for the current emphasis on independence to the detriment of accountability.

The basic difference of emphasis between functionalists and constitutionalists becomes evident in the approaches used to secure peace and order through international organizations. Functionalists stress that the peace-securing goal of international organizations can be best achieved through the functional cooperation of states in organizations focusing on essentially economic and technical cooperation and not on a primarily political one. It is based on an evolutionary concept assuming that political cooperation and harmonization – as the ultimate peace-securing goal – will follow as a beneficial side-effect of the economic and technical one.[6] Constitutionalists, on the other hand, put a political consensus first and want to build their peace edifice on a solid legal basis. Part of this legal framework would be legal rules concerning the relationship between members states, between members and the organization or organs of it, or between the organs among themselves, as well as between the organization and third parties. In an ideal case not only accountability but also enforceability would be guaranteed, i.e. the legal rights and obligations resulting from such rules should also give rise to adjudication in competent fora. In the constitutionalists' view, only such proper constitutional groundwork will guarantee peace among its members.

---

[5] In this regard Article 34 of the Statute of the ICJ, according to which only states are competent to appear before it, is a topical example. The ECJ's various competencies to decide disputes involving the European Communities are the exceptions to the rule.

[6] Cf. A. LeRoy Bennett, *International Organizations: Principles and Issues* (6th edn, Englewood Cliffs, NJ, 1995), 16ff; See also David Mitrany, *A Working Peace System* (Chicago, 1966); and Ernst Haas, *Beyond the Nation-State* (Stanford, 1964).

While functionalists underline the 'positive' aspect of the tasks of international organizations and their contribution to a shared exercise of functions traditionally carried out by individual states, the debate among constitutionalists focuses more on the consequential issues of accountability, the other side of the same coin. Put more precisely, constitutionalism looks for legal restraints on the activities of international organizations. These restraints result primarily from the legal position and rights of member states. However, an increasing awareness emerges that the rights of individuals might also be affected by the activities of international organizations.

One of the most visible aspects of constitutionalism in the field of international organizations concerns the relationship between international organizations and the rule of law, in particular, the question of which legal rules the international organizations are bound to respect and the extent to which they are so bound. This issue becomes pertinent with the recognition of international organizations as independent international actors and not as mere fora for states, or as regimes, etc.[7] It certainly presupposes the result of the growing acceptance of international organizations as subjects of international law and deals with the particular consequences of recognizing this independent personality.

'Constitutional' problems of international organizations have gained prominence in international law theory during recent years. A growing literature evidences this trend.[8] The increased awareness of constitutional problems of this kind is particularly visible in the UN context.[9] This is undoubtedly a consequence of the increased activities of the UN, which after the end of the Cold War has become more operative and thus more active. The current debate on legal restraints concerning the activities of international organizations is not limited to the UN, although it probably

---

[7] Frequently, of course, the 'double nature' of international organizations, both as actors and fora remains explicit. *Cf.* Article III(2) of the Agreement Establishing the World Trade Organization stating that the WTO, finally established as a fully fledged international organization, shall provide the 'forum' for negotiations among its member states.

[8] Ernst-Ulrich Petersmann, *The GATT/WTO Dispute Settlement System* (London, The Hague and Boston, 1997), 34*ff*; and Ernst-Ulrich Petersmann, 'The Transformation of the World Trading System Through the 1994 Agreement Establishing the World Trade Organization' (1995) 6 *European Journal of International Law* 161–221 at 161*ff*. The term 'constitutionalism' is not understood in a strict technical sense, but rather in a broader political one. No one suggests that international organizations are states requiring a 'constitution', but functions and powers similar to those of states require similar checks and balances and, in particular, the protection of persons affected by such activities of international organizations.

[9] *Cf.* Gaetano Arangio-Ruiz, 'The "Federal Analogy" and UN Charter Interpretation: A Crucial Issue' (1997) 8 *European Journal of International Law* 1–28 at 1*ff*.

has its most prominent place there.[10] It finds its counterpart in the discussion of the accountability of large multilateral financial organizations,[11] international commodity agreements, etc. A number of recent attempts to challenge measures of international organizations before international human rights organs also witnesses this growing tendency of trying to hold international organizations accountable.[12] Although they have been largely unsuccessful – to date – there is an increased awareness that member states of international organizations should not be allowed to use the latter as vehicles to evade their international responsibilities.[13]

The most advanced and sophisticated discussion of constitutional problems can be found within the framework of the European Community. It is in Community law that the awareness is probably best articulated that constitutionalism not only refers to the protection of the

[10] Most recently it has been primarily the activity of the UN Security Council with regard to the Lockerbie affair, the creation of criminal tribunals for the former Yugoslavia and Rwanda, etc. which has given rise to a discussion of the UN's competence. *Cf.* Mohammed Bedjaoui, *The New World Order and the Security Council. Testing the Legality of its Acts* (Dordrecht, Boston and London, 1994).

[11] *Cf.* Daniel D. Bradlow, 'International Organizations and Private Complaints: The Case of the World Bank Inspection Panel' (1994) 34 *Virginia Journal of International Law* 553–613 at 553*ff*; Daniel D. Bradlow and Sabine Schlemmer-Schulte, 'The World Bank's New Inspection Panel: A Constructive Step in the Transformation of the International Legal Order' (1994) 54 *Zeitschrift für ausländisches öffentliches Recht und Völkerrecht* 392–415 at 392*ff*; and Ibrahim F. I. Shihata, *The World Bank Inspection Panel* (Oxford, 1994).

[12] *Cf. Confédération Francaise démocratique du Travail v. European Communities*, European Commission of Human Rights, Application No. 8030/77, 10 July 1978. See also various attempts to invoke human rights violations of international organizations in legal proceedings brought against their member states. *HvdP v. The Netherlands*, UN Human Rights Committee, Communication No. 217/1986, 8 April 1987, alleging a violation of Articles 2 and 25 of the International Covenant on Civil and Political Rights by the European Patent Organization. See p. 302 above. *Heinz v. Contracting Parties who are also Parties to the European Patent Convention*, European Commission of Human Rights, Application No. 10475/83, 9 October 1984; *M(elchers) & Co. v. Federal Republic of Germany*, European Commission of Human Rights, Application No. 13258/77, 9 February 1990. See pp. 301*f* and 311*f* above.

[13] *Cf. Melchers* holding that the 'transfer of powers [to international organizations] does not necessarily exclude a State's responsibility under the Convention with regard to the transferred powers. Otherwise the guarantees of the Convention could wantonly be limited or excluded and thus be deprived of their peremptory character.' *M(elchers) & Co. v. Federal Republic of Germany*, European Commission of Human Rights, Application No. 13258/77, 9 February 1990, (1990) 64 *Decisions and Reports* 138 at 145. See also August Reinisch, 'Das Jugoslawientribunal der Vereinten Nationen und die Verfahrensgarantien des II. VN-Menschenrechtspaktes. Ein Beitrag zur Frage der Bindung der Vereinten Nationen an nicht-ratifiziertes Vertragsrecht' (1995) 47 *Austrian Journal of Public and International Law* 173–213 at 191, arguing against the possibility of a collective opting-out of member states from their human rights obligations by transferring certain tasks to international organizations.

legal position of the members of an organized community, the states, but also refers to the position of individuals potentially affected by Community action. The ECJ recognized that issues of accountability of international organizations *vis-à-vis* individuals for infringements of their fundamental rights go to the core of an organization's constitutional problems.[14]

The quest for a forum

Constitutionalism, however, is not limited to the substantive issue of how far international organizations are restrained by rules of law in their actions. There is an increasingly important discussion on the compliance/surveillance problems following the affirmation of substantive limitations. The question of the appropriate judicial or quasi-judicial fora competent to scrutinize the activities of international organizations, whether these should be 'internal' or 'external' fora, international or national ones, is of course linked to, and has become more relevant in, organizations which engage in activities that might infringe upon member states' or even individuals' rights. Again the debate involving the UN has probably attracted most controversy and interest. It mainly revolves around the issue of the reviewability of Security Council decisions[15] which lies at the heart of the still pending ICJ case of *Question of Interpretation and Application of the 1971 Montreal Convention Arising from the Aerial Incident at Lockerbie (Libyan Arab Jamahiriya v. United Kingdom; Libyan Arab Jamahiriya v. United States).*[16] There Libya basically challenges the legality of UN Security Council Resolution 748 which imposed economic sanctions to compel Libya to comply with UK and US requests to extradite Libyan nationals suspected of the Lockerbie bombing. The claim of Bos-

---

[14] Cf. *Accession by the Communities to the Convention for the Protection of Human Rights and Fundamental Freedoms*, Opinion 2/94, ECJ, 28 March 1996, [1996] ECR I-1759, para. 35, where the ECJ considered that despite the current practice of guaranteeing the core of the fundamental rights contained in the European Convention on Human Rights, a formal accession of the Community would imply a change of Community law of a 'constitutional dimension' which could only be achieved by treaty revision. See also Christoph Vedder, 'Die verfassungsrechtliche Dimension – die bisher unbekannte Grenze für Gemeinschaftshandeln? Anmerkung zum Gutachten 2/94, EMRK, des EuGH' (1996) 31 *EuropaRecht* 309–19 at 309*ff.*

[15] Jose E. Alvarez, 'Judging the Security Council' (1996) 90 *American Journal of International Law* 1–39 at 1; Bedjaoui, *The New World Order*; Thomas M. Franck, 'The "Powers of Appreciation": Who is the Ultimate Guardian of UN Legality?' (1992) 86 *American Journal of International Law* 519–23 at 519; and W. Michael Reisman, 'The Constitutional Crisis in the United Nations' (1993) 87 *American Journal of International Law* 83–100 at 83.

[16] ICJ, 14 April 1992, Provisional Measures, Order, (1992) *ICJ Reports* 3; ICJ, 27 February 1998, Preliminary Objections, Judgment, (1988) *ICJ Reports* 115.

nia-Herzegovina in *Application of the Convention on the Prevention and Punishment of the Crime of Genocide*[17] also originally included a request to determine that Security Council resolutions imposing an arms embargo on all former provinces of Yugoslavia be construed as not impairing Bosnia's right of individual or collective self-defence, which amounted to a challenge of the legality of Security Council decisions.[18]

The rule of law and national courts

The search for a forum to adjudicate disputes involving international organizations in order to secure adherence to their legal obligations – other than obligations under public international law – does not necessarily lead to domestic courts being the most appropriate fora. Frequently, internal courts or tribunals will have been established to adjudicate disputes involving international organizations – as is the case with administrative tribunals deciding staff disputes of international organizations.[19]

'Constitutional' considerations may also require international organizations to provide a forum to adjudicate disputes arising from their contacts with private parties. Specific obligations of this kind may result as a matter of treaty law which is evident from a number of agreements on privileges and immunities.[20] It is likely that the inclusion of such a duty was a matter of political necessity when granting immunity from domestic adjudication. Whether it could also be regarded as a legal requirement under general international law is discussed by some authors reflecting on an obligation of international organizations to create administrative tribunals or a duty, at least, to agree upon arbitration in cases of claims brought against them.[21]

Even if there were such an obligation, however, this would not imply a duty for international organizations to submit to the jurisdiction of national courts. All one could draw from it would be an obligation to make some kind of dispute settlement forum available. Domestic fora as the appropriate ones to adjudicate disputes of international organizations enter the scene where their potential opponents may rely on a specific right to petition them. Such a right may be contained in a fundamental rights guarantee to provide access to court as is provided for

---

[17] ICJ, 8 April 1993, Provisional Measures, Order, (1993) *ICJ Reports* 3.
[18] Alvarez, 'Judging the Security Council', 1.   [19] See pp. 267*ff* above.
[20] A duty to arbitrate such disputes is contained in the General Convention and the Special Convention as well as in many headquarters agreements. See p. 267 note 70 above.
[21] See pp. 270*f* and 275*ff* above.

in most human rights instruments.[22] It is important to note, however, that the corresponding obligation is addressed to the respective forum state, not to international organizations. Thus, it is primarily a state's domestic judiciary that should be open to recourse. As outlined above, such a right of access to court may entail a human rights mandate for states to limit the immunity they grant to international organizations before their own national courts.[23]

From a policy perspective – to be taken into consideration in a discussion on the future development of this part of the law – it appears to be crucial that both requirements, if not obligations (the one requiring a state to provide access to court in certain situations and the other requiring an international organization to provide legal redress for claims against it) are interrelated and work in the same direction which might increase the argumentative value of a call for stronger judicial fora. The European Court of Human Rights succinctly made this point in the *Golder* case where it reasoned that '[i]n civil matters one can scarcely conceive of the rule of law without there being a possibility of access to courts'.[24]

The parameters

The analysis in Part II described the reasons for abstention and engagement in adjudicating disputes involving international organizations as they are advanced by legal doctrine, diplomatic practice and their adoption, modification or (sometimes) rejection by the judiciary. The merits of the arguments have already been briefly discussed. This section will not repeat this debate, but rather will try to build on the most important and truly justifiable rationales for and against adjudication by domestic courts. These appear to be the protection of the independent functioning of international organizations, on the one hand, and the right of access to court by individuals, on the other.

At the same time, less legitimate reasons sometimes used by courts in order to engage in, but mostly to abstain from, adjudication should be identified.

The protection of the independence and functioning of an international organization

It is beyond doubt that international organizations have a legitimate interest in being able to fulfil their tasks and carry out their functions

---

[22] See p. 281 above.   [23] See pp. 282ff above.
[24] *Golder*, European Court of Human Rights, 21 February 1975, Series A, No. 18, para. 34.

without undue interference from outside, including from domestic courts of member or non-member states. This basic rationale for immunity (or other legal techniques removing international organizations from the adjudicative power of domestic courts) is largely undisputed.[25] It becomes problematic when one focuses on the extent of the protection needed, in particular on the question of what should be interpreted as interference and what degree of interference should be viewed as tolerable. In differentiating between illegitimate and tolerable interference, one has to balance the competing arguments.

On a spectrum of possible types of interference, one can probably discern more and less tolerable ones, in turn giving rise to less or more legitimate claims to be protected against them. One can also discern the unacceptable ones, such as attacks on the very existence or the principal activity of an international organization. The most radical form of interference with an organization would be to seek its dissolution through judicial order.[26] Intolerable interference could also result from efforts directly to influence policy decisions of international organizations *via* court order. This may take the form of an attempt by member states, third states or even private parties. For instance, if one such party tried to enjoin the UN from carrying out a particular peacekeeping mission,[27] or an international development bank from disbursing a particular loan to a member country or individual,[28] such an action is likely directly to conflict with the functioning of an international organization.

On the other side of the spectrum, if an individual, on the merits clearly entitled to a sum of money as a result of a contractual or tort claim, wanted to enforce such a claim through a domestic court, the organization would certainly be burdened to some degree: it would have to defend itself; it would incur external and/or internal costs for doing so, etc. However, this slight interference would hardly ever be substantial enough to touch upon the ability of an international organization to fulfil its functions. The only scenario where this could be envisaged

---

[25] See pp. 233*ff* above.

[26] *Cf.* the winding-up petitions directed against the Tin Council in *Re International Tin Council*, High Court, 22 January 1987. See pp. 118 and 240 above for details of this decision.

[27] *Cf.* the claim put forward in *Abdi Hosh Askir* v. *Boutros Boutros-Ghali, Joseph E. Connor et al.*, US District Court SDNY, 29 July 1996; see pp. 201*f* above. Although the plaintiff did not ask the court to enjoin the UN from its activities, he based his claim for damages on the argument that the 'United Nations did not have the authority to adopt the resolution passed in connection with the peacekeeping operation in Somalia'. 933 F. Supp. 368 at 373.

[28] *Cf.* the facts of *Lutcher SA Celulose e Papel* v. *Inter-American Development Bank*, US Court of Appeals DC Cir., 13 July 1967; see p. 216 above.

would be the forced fulfilment of substantive obligations to such an extent as to threaten the entire financial capacity of an international organization.

Protecting access-to-court expectations of third parties

It may be doubtful whether a fundamental right of access to national courts, as is contained in many international human rights instruments as well as in national constitutional documents, could be interpreted to restrict the immunity of international organizations as a matter of *lex lata*.[29] It is important, however, to recognize that the rationale behind such a claim is probably the overriding policy argument for having domestic courts decide certain types of disputes even if they involve international organizations as parties. The relative value of access-to-court claims has to be weighed against a number of factors. Among such factors, the most important ones are aspects of foreseeability, alternative remedies, and basic fairness considerations.

As a matter of practice, the largest group of persons seeking legal redress against international organizations before domestic courts are their employees. The fact that their employment relationship with an international organization is their primary source of income will give them a very strong interest in having a forum to adjudicate disputes that might involve a loss of their job, of financial or other benefits. However, the legitimacy of their interest in finding a domestic court competent to hear their claims is, or may be, weakened by a number of aspects. International officials are usually aware – or at least should be aware – of the immunity of the international organization they are working for; they usually know that in most cases alternative dispute settlement organs in the form of administrative tribunals are exclusively competent and frequently they have expressly consented to such alternative fora in their contracts of employment; further, employees voluntarily choose to accept a job the financial attractiveness of which might compensate for the lack of certain otherwise available remedies. Of course, situations where no alternative dispute settlement is available at all will increase the legitimacy of an employee's interest in access to a national forum.

Another large group of persons who may seek the jurisdiction of domestic courts are those who render services to an international organization on the basis of contracts regularly governed by a domestic law. Since they are usually not integrated into the administrative structure of

---

[29] See p. 313 above.

an international organization, their employment contracts are normally outside the scope of jurisdiction of administrative tribunals. Thus, their interest in the availability of a domestic court to hear their claims against an international organization might carry a relatively higher legitimacy. Further, they are regularly not 'compensated' for this loss of available remedies, e.g. financially through tax exemptions, etc., and since they have normally contracted on the basis of a domestic law, one might well regard a national court as the most appropriate and (in a material sense) the most 'competent' forum to apply that law. Only where such persons have expressly agreed to a different dispute settlement forum or expressly accepted the immunity of an international organization, is the strength of their interest weakened. However, even the express renunciation of a right to petition a domestic court might be outweighed by the fact that the much greater bargaining power of an organization may have induced the weaker party to agree. Similar considerations apply to persons providing property, by selling or leasing goods or office space, etc., to international organizations who regularly do so on the basis of private law contracts governed by a national law.

Persons suffering harm by the tortious behaviour of international organizations probably have the greatest legitimate interest in having their claim brought before ordinary domestic courts. They did not agree to or assume a risk of being unable to bring their claim because they could not anticipate who would commit a tort against them. There is no reason why they should have to accept alternative dispute settlement mechanisms even if these could be extended to cover their claims.

Illegitimate reasons: lack of personality, lack of functional capacity, non-application of international law

The survey of judicial practice has shown that courts occasionally have recourse to very technical legal concepts forcing them to abstain from the adjudication of a dispute involving an international organization. Two of these seemingly compelling abstention grounds relate to the specific personality of international organizations: the lack of legal personality under domestic law; and the lack of specific legal capabilities in case of activities *ultra vires* an organization.[30] Both reasons are not directly linked to a legitimate interest of international organizations in adjudicative abstention of domestic courts, but rather apply 'interest blind' which sometimes even clearly contravenes the interests of an international

---

[30] See pp. 37*ff* and 70*ff* above.

organization, as, for instance, when an organization tries to bring suit.[31] The non-application of international law as a result of domestic legal doctrines, such as the doctrine of incorporation in English law, is also not related to any interests in abstaining or adjudicating. It precludes English courts from applying treaty norms which have not been incorporated through statutory law in general. In the Tin Council cases[32] it has, however, gained a disproportionate importance. Its use in the context of international organizations before domestic courts is problematic because the rationale of such a doctrine, which lies in the domestic separation-of-powers requirements, is wholly unrelated to legitimate policy grounds in favour or against adjudication as outlined above.[33]

Possible solutions

After assessing the value and relative strength of the arguments for and against adjudication by national courts, and after having noted that the legitimacy of these rationales might vary according to different factual situations, it seems appropriate to seek and to propose solutions which would adequately take into account the legal interests involved.

In this situation one is confronted with a basic choice between acceptance, in principle, of the legal *status quo* or its outright rejection. The former approach would attempt to muddle through with existing legal concepts, in a field dominated by express exemptions from the adjudicative power of domestic courts, in particular with the prevalent concept of immunity. It would try slowly to reinterpret the existing law in a way better to take into account of the policy considerations involved. A more radical solution, leaving the *lex lata* partly behind, would be to look for conceptual alternatives to the existing law dominated as it is by immunity concepts. Of course, it should not attempt to build on a legal vacuum. It should rather search for traits already inherent in the existing case law and examine their usefulness for solving the underlying conflicts of legitimate interests.

---

[31] *Cf.* the problems resulting for the Arab Monetary Fund from its disputed legal personality under UK law. *Arab Monetary Fund* v. *Hashim (No. 3)*. See pp. 65*ff* above. *Cf.* also the opinion of a Dutch court involving a non-governmental international organization considering that 'if an international organisation operating independently in a legal capacity . . . appears before the courts to answer for its actions or omissions, it is undesirable to deem the organisation incompetent to put forward a defence at law on the ground of its not possessing legal personality'. *FO* v. *VK and Fédération Internationale des Echecs and AK*, Amsterdam Court of Appeal, 21 January 1981.
[32] See pp. 118*ff* above.   [33] See pp. 324*ff* above.

Maintaining immunity

One option that would certainly protect the interest of international organizations in being shielded from lawsuits in national courts to a maximum extent would be to maintain or even enlarge their presently enjoyed jurisdictional immunity. In order to compensate for the corresponding loss of access to a national forum for individuals and where alternative fora, such as arbitral or internal tribunals of organizations, are not available or not adequately protective, one would have to consider the creation of a subsidiary mechanism to protect and eventually satisfy the interests of persons having claims against international organizations. Since it is primarily the responsibility of a state to provide dispute settlement facilities,[34] usually in the form of national courts, one could consider whether the withholding of such dispute settlement institutions as a consequence of the grant of immunity from suit to international organizations should not in turn lead to the responsibility of the state granting immunity.

The seemingly far-fetched idea of the subsidiary responsibility of the state granting immunity is not as far from reality as one might think. It finds some support in certain French cases reflecting a rudimentary jurisprudence of state liability for refusing recourse to French courts. In a 1977 decision, in *Ministre des Affaires étrangères* v. *Dame Burgat et autres*,[35] the Conseil d'Etat even went so far as to state the principle that individuals were entitled to damages because they were deprived of the possibility of suing a person enjoying jurisdictional immunity as a result of the headquarters agreement between France and UNESCO. It is surprising, however, that this precedent, this judicial invitation to litigation, apparently was not pursued by individual litigants in France.[36]

There is a similar line of jurisprudence in Spain. In *X* v. *Deodato*,[37] the Spanish Constitutional Court rejected the appellant's claim that the immunity granted to a foreign diplomat from civil proceedings violated Article 24 of the Spanish Constitution which provided for a subjective right of access to courts.[38] In justifying this result, it referred to the

[34] *Cf.* the discussion on a constitutional or human rights requirement to provide access to courts to individuals. See pp. 278*ff* and 288*f* above.

[35] Conseil d'Etat, 29 October 1976. See pp. 296*ff* above.

[36] For instance, in the relatively recent case of *Hintermann* v. *Union de l'Europe occidentale*, Cour d'appel de Paris, 10 April 1990, Cour de Cassation, 14 November 1995, the French Cour de Cassation noted the lack of alternative remedies and the possible human rights dimension; it did not, however, touch on the liability jurisprudence of *Ministre des Affaires étrangères* v. *Dame Burgat et autres*.

[37] Tribunal Constitucional, 28 September 1995.   [38] See pp. 298*f* above.

alternative remedies available to a plaintiff in such a situation and held that such a claimant could demand from the Spanish Government a declaration that the defaulting diplomat was *persona non grata*. If such a request were rejected, the Spanish Government would have to pay compensation for all damages arising to the plaintiff.

The jurisprudence of the European Commission of Human Rights concerning complaints alleging fundamental rights infringements by international organizations brought against their member states in decisions like *Heinz v. Contracting Parties who are also Parties to the European Patent Convention*[39] or *M(elchers) & Co. v. Federal Republic of Germany*[40] can also be taken as additional corroboration for a subsidiary responsibility of that kind. Although the Commission has not yet found a violation in a particular case, it has reiterated its view that the transfer of powers to an international organization does not thereby remove the responsibility of a contracting party to the European Convention on Human Rights with regard to the exercise of such transferred powers.[41] In other words, the member state remains subsidiarily responsible where fundamental rights do not receive an equivalent protection with the organization.

Reinterpreting immunity

It is evident that in most cases international organizations will, as a matter of law, enjoy immunity. The standard or scope of the immunity will vary according to the legal regime applicable; the existence of immunity, however, is normally a given reality. The analysis of the relevant case law demonstrates that the precise content of the applicable immunity standard is open to wide interpretation.[42] By using this broad 'margin of appreciation' in determining the exact scope of immunity, it might be possible properly to take into account the legitimate interests involved.

Finding a 'proportionate' functional immunity standard below absolute immunity

Accepting that the protection of the independent functioning of international organizations is the main justification for granting immunity from suit to international organizations, it is obvious that an absolute immunity of international organizations will guarantee this aim. It appears doubtful, however, whether this undoubtedly effective remedy can be considered necessary under a proportionality test. Even the most

---

[39] European Commission of Human Rights, Application No. 12090/92, 10 January 1994.
[40] European Commission of Human Rights, Application No. 13258/77, 9 February 1990.
[41] For more detail, see pp. 311f above.   [42] See pp. 140*ff* and 185*ff* above.

conservative defenders of absolute immunity for international organizations will probably acknowledge that it is not the adjudication of ordinary, everyday disputes involving international organizations that might
hamper the independent functioning of organizations, but rather the
exceptional potential of harassment and prejudice[43] that might endan-
ger their smooth operation. Thus, the traditional interpretation of functional immunity as a standard requiring absolute immunity from suit
illustrates that courts may protect the interests of international organizations in a manner that is almost too effective. Therefore, it seems
necessary to search for a genuine meaning of a functionally limited
immunity of international organizations. In order to make sense of such
a functional immunity it is probably necessary to go back to the roots of
this concept.

The meaning of functional immunity

The notion of functional immunity is a very elusive one. Although very
appealing at face value for its apparent reasonableness, the precise application of a functional standard is less than clear. Moreover, the idea of
functional immunity is rather imprecise in so far as it could refer both to
the rationale of granting immunity at all (because it is necessary for the
proper functioning of an international organization) as well as to a
certain content of immunity to be accorded (the immunity necessary for
an international organization's functioning).[44] While in the first case it
refers only to the fact that immunity is accorded to international organizations, in the second instance it provides a criterion for the proper scope
of immunity.

   Probably as a consequence of this 'rationale-oriented' understanding of
functional immunity, another ambiguity of the notion of 'functional
necessity' becomes evident. 'Functional necessity' might relate to the
scope of immunity from legal process. However, it may also refer to the
selection of possible privileges and immunities for a specific international organization justified by such functional criteria. Many commentators fail to differentiate between those two fundamentally different
problems. The discussion of the ILC Draft Articles on relations between
states and international organizations by the special rapporteur is a good

---

[43] The dreaded 'unilateral and sometimes irresponsible interference by individual governments'. Paul C. Szasz, 'International Organizations, Privileges and Immunities' in Rudolf
Bernhardt (ed.), *Encyclopedia of Public International Law* (2nd edn, 1995), vol. II, 1325–33 at
1326.
[44] See p. 334 below.

example. Draft Article 5 speaks of immunity from 'every form of legal process', Draft Article 11 seems to open the possibility of limiting such absolute immunity only 'by mutual agreement of the parties concerned', and the special rapporteur in his commentary on these proposals believes that the right approach concerning the scope of immunities granted to international organizations is 'to consider what degree of immunity from legal process ought to be granted to a given international organization in the light of its functional requirements'.[45] The special rapporteur then, however, shifts from the scope of jurisdictional immunity argument to the range of privileges and immunities problem by asserting that those 'functional requirements' must be 'one of the main criteria, if not the only one, used in determining the extent and range of the privileges and immunities that are to be accorded to a given organization' because the 'functions and purposes' of an international organization were its main *raison d'être*.[46] Clearly, it is only the first type of 'functionally limited immunity' that interests us in the present context, i.e. whether the scope of immunity from suit may justifiably be limited by functional criteria.

The origin of the functional immunity standard: Article 105 UN Charter

The functional necessity concept of immunity can be traced back to the establishment of the UN and the Organization of American States in the 1940s.[47] Indeed, the UN Charter's language, for the first time, clearly sets out a standard of immunity 'based on the necessity of realizing the purposes of the Organization' by choosing the formulation of Article 105(1) that: 'The Organization shall enjoy in the territory of each of its Members such privileges and immunities as are necessary for the fulfilment of its purposes.' That this 'necessity' standard is an expression of the UN's functional immunity was affirmed by the ICJ in the *Reparations* case.[48]

Is 'functional' synonymous with 'absolute' immunity?

Apparently many scholars and judges consider the immunity from legal process of international organizations to be 'absolute' and 'functional' at the same time. Thereby they, at least implicitly, assert that for the purposes of jurisdictional immunity 'functional' and 'absolute' are syn-

---

[45] Leonardo Díaz-González (Special Rapporteur), 'Fourth Report on Relations Between States and International Organizations (Second Part of the Topic)' (UN Doc. A/CN.4/424) *Yearbook of the International Law Commission* (1989), vol. II, Part One, 153–68 at 157.   [46] *Ibid.*, 158.

[47] Peter H. F. Bekker, *The Legal Position of Intergovernmental Organizations. A Functional Necessity Analysis of Their Legal Status and Immunities* (Dordrecht, Boston and London, 1994), 110.

[48] *Reparation for Injuries Suffered in the Service of the United Nations*, Advisory Opinion, (1949) *ICJ Reports* 174; cf. Bekker, *The Legal Position*, 111.

onymous qualifications. Indeed, a number of good reasons support the widely held belief that functional immunity in fact means, or at least meant, absolute immunity.

First, from a historical perspective, it appears that what has been intended to be conferred upon international organizations when granting them functional immunity was in most cases absolute immunity. The jurisdictional immunities of the UN, for instance, as originally envisaged, suggest that functional immunity – as far as immunity from legal process was concerned – meant absolute immunity.[49] This view is corroborated by the fact that both international and domestic legal instruments attributed immunity from suit to international organizations under the assumption of treating them like states, conferring the same immunity as enjoyed by states.[50] Although sovereign states are nowadays largely considered to be entitled to restrictive immunity only, a historic understanding of sovereign immunity, coupled with an approximation of the status of international organizations to that of states as far as immunity from suit was concerned, might account for their claim to absolute immunity. It rests on the equating of international organizations with states which have traditionally enjoyed absolute immunity.

Secondly, the 'context' of a grant of functional immunity to an international organization may indicate that what is meant by functional immunity is really absolute immunity. This 'context' against which functional immunity must be interpreted consists of the different, though frequently simultaneously applicable international instruments and domestic laws providing, on the one hand, for functional and, on the other, for absolute immunity.[51] Although there might be different approaches to correctly assessing and interpreting this apparent discrepancy, the majority of writers – there are hardly any court decisions dealing with this question[52] – seems to view the absolute immunity standard as an explanation, illustration or specification of functional immunity regularly

---

[49] For instance, the UN Charter Drafting Committee's report clarifying the standard of immunity suggests that 'immunity from jurisdiction', in an unqualified way, i.e. absolute immunity, is one of the privileges and immunities 'necessary for the realization of the purposes of the organization'. 13 UNCIO, Doc. 933, IV/2/42(2) (1945), 704.

[50] The best-known and probably most fiercely litigated example of such legislation is Title I, section 2(b) of the US IOIA. See p. 134 note 516 above for the text.

[51] Cf. the UN where the UN Charter provides for 'functional' immunity, while the General Convention states that the organization shall enjoy absolute immunity. The situation is similar for many other organizations.

[52] One might have expected, for instance, in the Belgian *Manderlier* case a discussion of the issue, but the court did not recognize any conflict that had to be solved. See pp. 279f above.

provided for in the constituent text.[53] This phenomenon has been reinforced by scholarly writings largely perceiving absolute immunity as the necessary ingredient for the functioning of international organizations. This last argument leads to a semantic clarification.

Thirdly, it might be argued that any attempt to read a limitation into the term 'functional immunity' is inherently flawed in so far as it misapprehends the original meaning of the term. The qualifying adjective 'functional' could be understood as relating exclusively to the rationale for immunity of international organizations, not to its scope. There is no doubt that the protection of the independent functioning of international organizations is the pre-eminent reason for granting immunity to them.[54] In a nearly unanimous fashion courts, national legislators, scholarly commentators, international law textbooks, codification attempts and diplomatic correspondence refer to the protection of the (independent) functioning of international organizations as the primary rationale for exempting them from the jurisdiction of domestic courts.[55] If indeed 'functional' related exclusively to the purpose of the immunity and not to its extent, a case could be made that the resulting unqualified immunity should be regarded absolute.

Fourthly, it has been argued that, because of the functional character of the legal personality of an international organization, all actions must be closely connected with the international organization's purpose.[56] If

---

[53] *Annual Report of the Secretary-General*, 13 GAOR, Supp. 1 (A/7201), 208*ff*, reprinted in Louis Henkin, Richard C. Pugh, Oscar Schachter and Hans Smit, *International Law* (2nd edn, St Paul, MN, 1987), 963; the UN Office of Legal Affairs stated that the 'detailed application' of the principle contained in Article 105 of the UN Charter 'was effected *inter alia* through the [General Convention]'. UN Office of Legal Affairs, 'Opinion Prepared at the Request of the Committee on Relations with the Host Country' (1983) *United Nations Juridical Yearbook* 222. Others regard the multilateral instruments as 'implementation of the brief and general provisions of the constituent instrument of the organization'. Bekker, *The Legal Position*, 129*ff*; see also Elisabeth Zoller, 'The National Security of the United States as the Host State for the United Nations' (1989) 1 *Pace Yearbook of International Law* 127–61 at 134.

[54] See pp. 324*ff* above.

[55] See pp. 233*ff* above.

[56] Ignaz Seidl-Hohenveldern and Gerhard Loibl, *Das Recht der Internationalen Organisationen einschließlich der Supranationalen Gemeinschaften* (6th edn, Cologne, Berlin, Bonn and Munich, 1996), 275; and Kurt Herndl, 'Zur Problematik der Gerichtsbarkeit über fremde Staaten' in Herbert Miehsler, Erhard Mock, Bruno Simma and Ilmar Tammelo (eds.), *Ius Humanitatis. Festschrift Alfred Verdross* (Berlin, 1980), 421–43 at 439. Bekker seems to rely on a similar concept. In regarding the immunity standard as applied to states as inappropriate for international organizations, he argues: 'Whereas States can act *jure gestionis* in the same way as any private individual, all activities of an international organization – its acts *jure imperii* as well as its acts *jure gestionis* – must relate as closely as possible to the purposes of the organization.' Bekker, *The Legal Position*, 165. See also Morgenstern, who

all actions of an international organization were indeed functionally justified, then this would lead to an immunity protection of all those activities, to the same result as under absolute immunity.[57]

All four arguments, though attractive on their face, have some inherent weaknesses. It might be true that in the 1940s or even earlier, everybody agreed that when a jurisdictional immunity status comparable to that enjoyed by sovereign states was conferred on an international organization, this in effect meant absolute immunity from suit. However, it is not persuasive to think that the changing perception of the scope of sovereign immunity (as unforeseeable as it might have been)[58] should have had no influence on the extent of immunity of international organizations. The 'contextual' argument attempting to understand absolute immunity as a clarification of the vague term 'functional' immunity is also not wholly convincing: the term 'functional' apparently has a different meaning from the expression 'absolute' and, although the different instruments containing such different terms may all be treaties, these treaties belong to differing legal levels. As far as the third argument is concerned, even its premise of relating functional exclusively to the rationale and not to the scope of immunity is questionable. The wording of some functional immunity clauses clearly indicates that they qualify the scope of the immunity. It seems to be a common understanding among many scholars and courts that functional immunity contains an inherently limiting element.[59] In other contexts, functional immunity

thinks that the fact 'that the capacity of international organizations is directly related to their public functions seems to imply that, as a matter of principle, the problem of acts *iure gestionis* should remain unimportant'. Felice Morgenstern, *Legal Problems of International Organizations* (Cambridge, 1986), 6.

[57] 'La justification classique de cette attitude qui continue de traiter les organisations à l'instar du traitement dont profitaient également les Etats au 19e siècle, réside dans le fait, qu'en vertu de la limitation de la personnalité des organisations à la réalisation des buts de l'organisation, toute leur activité commerciale demeure liée intimement à la réalisation des buts jure imperii de l'organisation.' Ignaz Seidl-Hohenveldern, 'L'immunité de juridiction des Communautés européennes' (1990) *Revue du Marché Commun* No. 338, 475–9 at 477.

[58] In fact, many states have restricted sovereign immunity since the turn of the century, or even in the late nineteenth century. *Cf.* the overview of the early restrictive state immunity cases in Belgium, Italy and Egypt in the ILC commentary to the Draft Articles on 'Jurisdictional immunities of states and their property', *Yearbook of the International Law Commission* (1991), vol. II, Part Two, 12 at 36*ff.*

[59] *United States ex relatione Casanova* v. *Fitzpatrick*, US District Court SDNY, 16 January 1963, qualified the 'functional immunity' standard in Article 105 of the UN Charter as 'limited immunity'. Similarly, in *People* v. *Mark S. Weiner*, Criminal Court of the City of New York, New York County, 19 January 1976, a US court saw in Article 105 an 'intentional limitation of immunity'.

– while undoubtedly also explaining the need for exemption from jurisdiction – is equally used as a qualification of the scope of the immunity enjoyed. The best example is probably consular law, but to a certain extent also diplomatic law where, as a rule, the persons specially protected enjoy (functional) immunity from the courts of the host state only with regard to acts they perform in the exercise of their official functions.[60] Finally, concerning the intrinsic link between all acts of an international organization and its functional tasks claimed, if one accepts that 'not all activities undertaken by international organizations are within their principal functions', it seems correct to conclude that immunity 'does not necessarily mean "absolute" immunity'.[61]

Functional immunity as immunity for 'official activities'

Recognizing that any references to absolute or restrictive immunity (as remnants of the sovereign immunity doctrine) are inappropriate for international organizations, many commentators seek an alternative immunity standard that could be applied as functional immunity.

It has been suggested that another 'nature' test, based on a strict 'official' activity concept, could provide 'a means for measuring the legitimate incidence of privileges and immunities of international organizations'.[62] This might be inspired by the examples of some more recent immunity instruments linking privileges and immunities to official acts of an international organization,[63] which in turn are restricted to those

[60] A certain group of persons of less than full diplomatic rank (covered by the Vienna Convention on Diplomatic Relations 1961) as well as consular officers enjoy immunity from suit in principle only for '[official] acts performed in the exercise of [their] functions'. Article 43 of the Vienna Convention on Consular Relations 1963 and Articles 37 and 38 of the Vienna Convention on Diplomatic Relations 1961. The immunity of diplomats – which is frequently considered absolute in its scope – is also in fact limited along functional considerations. However, diplomatic law, instead of relying on a flexible (but also rather indeterminate) functionality standard, typifies situations clearly lying beyond functional necessity for which no immunity has to be granted to diplomats. Article 31(1) of the Vienna Convention on Diplomatic Relations 1961 lists among these real actions, actions relating to succession, and commercial activities outside official functions. See also p. 363 below.

[61] Mahnoush H. Arsanjani, 'Claims Against International Organizations – *Quis Custodiet Ipsos Custodes*' (1980–1) 7 *Yale Journal of World Public Order* 131–76 at 163.

[62] Bekker, *The Legal Position*, 163, concluding that '[t]he immunities enjoyed by an international organization are thus confined to their "official activities" which are strictly necessary to the exercise of functions in fulfilment of the organization's purposes'. *Ibid.*, 165.

[63] *Cf.* the European Patent Organization's immunity clause: 'Within the scope of its official activities the Organization shall have immunity from jurisdiction and execution.' Article 3(1) of the EPO Privileges and Immunities Protocol.

of its activities which 'are strictly necessary for its administrative and technical operation, as set out in the Convention'.[64]

The difficulty of ascertaining the precise content of official acts, however, makes the concept appear merely to shift the problem of definition from one undetermined expression to another.[65] The 'official activities' of an international organization are regularly determined by its purposes and functions and, normally, the constitutional texts of international organizations contain only vague and general descriptions of an organization's purposes and functions. In the absence of clear criteria, the dichotomy between official and non-official acts as a basis for deciding immunity problems will lead to difficulties in its practical application. The notion of official acts is clearly related to the 'statutory' functions of an international organization. Thus, 'official activity' has a clear purpose link which is definitely harder to apply in an abstract fashion – without any reference to constituent treaties – than, for instance, the nature-based test of the determination of commercial activity.

The arbitral award in *European Molecular Biology Laboratory* v. *Germany*[66] tried to elaborate on the meaning of 'official activities', although this was not related to the issue of jurisdictional immunity, but rather to the question of tax privileges. The EMBL's headquarters agreement provided that '[w]hen the Laboratory makes substantial purchases or uses substantial services, *strictly necessary for the exercise of its official activities*, in the price of which taxes or duties are included, appropriate measures shall be taken by the Federal Republic of Germany, whenever possible, to remit or reimburse the amount of such taxes or duties'.[67] According to the agreement 'official activities of the Laboratory shall include its administrative activities and those undertaken in pursuance of the purposes of the Laboratory as defined in the Laboratory Agreement'.[68] The arbitral tribunal held that on the basis of these provisions the organization did not

---

[64] E.g., Article 3(4) of the EPO Privileges and Immunities Protocol.

[65] While Bekker acknowledges that '[t]here might, however, in some instances be difficulties in deciding what is to be considered an official activity of an organization', he thinks that these hard cases would be limited to instances where the 'constitutional framework of the organization describes the organization's functions and purposes in general terms only, thereby leaving considerable scope for extending its boundaries in practice'. Bekker, *The Legal Position*, 163ff.

[66] Arbitration Award, 29 June 1990.

[67] Article 7(2) of the Headquarters Agreement Between the Federal Republic of Germany and the European Molecular Biology Laboratory (emphasis added).

[68] Article 9 of the Headquarters Agreement Between the Federal Republic of Germany and the European Molecular Biology Laboratory.

enjoy all the fiscal privileges claimed in connection with the operation of a canteen and guest-house used by staff and visiting scientists of the EMBL. In trying to distinguish between 'official' and 'non-official' activities the tribunal came to the following conclusions:

The realization of scientific events such as courses, seminars, workshops etc. has to be classified as an official activity. The same applies to the meals and accommodation put at the disposal of the participants in the course of these activities . . . For the supply of meals and accommodation nowadays is largely part of the obvious standard of scientific activities . . . This does however not apply when the supply of meals and accommodation is done against payment. For it cannot be deduced from the Establishing Agreement that the functions of the EMBL include the sale of goods or services. None of the functions conferred upon the EMBL is directed at making a profit and the financing of the mentioned activities is done by way of the budget of the EMBL and not of receipts from the sale of goods or services. Therefore such a sale cannot be counted as being among the official activities of the EMBL within the meaning of Article 9 [of the headquarters agreement].[69]

The advantage of a concept of immunity for official activities could lie in the fact that it makes clear that not all activities contributing to the functioning of an international organization, but rather only such acts that are intrinsically related to its official functions, merit exemption from the adjudicative power of a domestic court. Such a restrictive approach would probably exclude those 'instrumental' activities such as renting office space, contracting for secretarial services, etc., which undoubtedly contribute to the functioning of an international organization, but are far from the core of its functional tasks. It would therefore in many cases allow suits to be brought and decided upon in matters that concern issues of the 'civil rights and obligations' of private parties.

A strict functional necessity concept

Certain authors advocate a strict 'functional necessity concept' – which they find embodied in the ILC Draft Articles on relations between states and international organizations – according to which any immunity has to be expressly justified:[70]

The functional necessity concept can be said to dictate that the scope of the privileges and immunities of international organizations shall be *limited* to only

---

[69] (1997) 105 ILR 1 at 43ff.
[70] Peter H. F. Bekker, 'The Work of the International Law Commission on "Relations Between States and International Organizations" Discontinued: An Assessment' (1993) 6 *Leiden Journal of International Law* 3–16 at 9.

those *necessary* for the exercise of the organization's functions in the fulfilment of its purposes.[71]

In a similar vein it has been proposed that states should grant international organizations only those privileges and immunities which are 'indispensable' for the fulfilment of their purposes and the exercise of their tasks.[72]

---

[71] Bekker, *The Legal Position*, 152. According to Bekker, the fine-tuning of immunities for specific international organizations will be achieved by a three-step 'functional necessity analysis'. After first determining the legal status of an international organization, in terms of its functions, and secondly viewing the possible privileges and immunities enumerated in the Draft Articles of the ILC, the third step applies the functional necessity concept as a yardstick for determining the extent or scope of selected privileges and immunities of international organizations. Thus, it should be the international organization's functions as expressed in its founding treaty or other constituent instrument that will determine the precise extent of immunities to be enjoyed by the international organization. Bekker tries to corroborate this interpretation of the ILC Draft Articles by referring to Draft Article 11, which expressly provides that 'the scope of the rights accorded may be limited, in the light of the functional requirements of the organization in question, by mutual agreement of the parties concerned', and to Draft Article 22, which states that 'for the purposes of the foregoing articles, the terms "official activity" or "official use" shall mean those relating to the accomplishment of the purposes of the organization'. Bekker, *The Legal Position*, 166*ff*. In a footnote Bekker expressly applies these criteria to the issue of jurisdictional immunity of an international organization, according to which the functions of a particular organization may make it eligible for such immunity. The third step may then dictate that such immunity be restricted to non-commercial transactions, etc. Bekker, 'The Work of the International Law Commission', 12, note 46. It seems, however, that the ILC Draft Articles do not smoothly fit into this interpretation. Draft Article 7, dealing with jurisdictional immunity, is a mirror to section 2 of the General Convention providing for 'immunity from every form of legal process' which has been generally interpreted as absolute immunity. While it is true that Draft Article 11, which is also relevant to interpreting Draft Article 7, makes it possible to limit such immunity in a flexible and preferably 'functional' way, it still appears crucial to secure the international organization's and the forum state's consent (*argumento* 'by mutual agreement of the parties concerned'). Thus, one can hardly speak of an automatic functional necessity concept operating under the Draft Articles. Equally, the second piece of evidence, Draft Article 22, in its present form rather a definition than an operative limitation, does not prove very useful. As long as it is not incorporated in a substantive Draft Article – such as the one suggested by Bekker, 'The Work of the International Law Commission', 13 ('The scope of privileges and immunities granted shall be limited to the "official activities" of the organization, which shall, for the purposes of this Protocol/ Convention, be such as are strictly necessary for the exercise of its functions and the fulfillment of its purposes, as set out in the organization's constituent instruments, such to be determined ultimately and conclusively and in good faith by [the chief administrative officer of] the organization itself') – it will not serve to limit the (unrestricted) immunity provided for in Draft Article 7.

[72] In its policy analysis on whether and which privileges and immunities should be accorded to international organizations, the Council of Europe recommends that 'les Etats membres devraient procéder à l'examen détaillé des privilèges et immunités indispensables à cette organisation pour la réalisation de ses objectifs et pour l'exercice des ses fonctions'. Conseil de l'Europe, 16.

The *J. J. Zwartveld and others*[73] case decided by the ECJ demonstrates an interesting interpretation of a functionally restricted immunity concept in very peculiar circumstances. This was not a suit brought against the EEC before a domestic court, but rather the request of a national court that the ECJ order the Commission to produce certain evidence and to permit Commission officials to testify in national criminal proceedings. The Commission had previously denied such a request from a Dutch court investigating fraudulent violations of legislation implementing the Community's Common Fisheries Policy. The Commission based its refusal on seemingly unlimited immunity provisions according to the Protocol on the Privileges and Immunities of the European Communities of 1965.[74] In particular, it referred to Article 2 of the Protocol which contained the inviolability of the Community's archives and did not mention any possibility of lifting that inviolability. It further contended that Article 12 of the Protocol did not permit the lifting of the immunity of Community officials with regard to hearing them as witnesses. The ECJ rejected these formally compelling arguments. Invoking Article 5 of the EEC Treaty, the ECJ found that the principle enshrined therein 'imposes on Member States and the Community institutions mutual duties of sincere cooperation'.[75] This duty of cooperation carried particular weight *vis-à-vis* judicial authorities of member states. The ECJ continued to deduce from this principle of cooperation a functionally limited immunity standard which overrode the unqualified and absolute language of the Protocol: 'When analysed in the light of these principles, the privileges and immunities which the Protocol grants to the European Communities have a purely functional character, inasmuch as they are intended to avoid any interference with the functioning and independence of the Communities.'[76] In applying this functional immunity standard the ECJ ordered the Commission to produce the documents sought by the Dutch court 'unless it presents to the Court imperative reasons relating to the need to avoid any interference with the functioning and independence of the Communities justifying its refusal to do so'.[77] In *Ufficio Imposte di Consumo di Ispra* v. *Commission of the European Communities*,[78] the ECJ also affirmed the principle of functionally justified privileges and immunities and applied it in an interesting way.[79]

---

[73] Case 2/88, ECJ, 13 July 1990.   [74] EC Privileges and Immunities Protocol of 1965.
[75] [1990] ECR I-3365 at 3372.   [76] *Ibid.*   [77] *Ibid.*, 3373.
[78] Case 2/68, ECJ Order, 17 December 1968.
[79] The Nuclear Research Centre at Ispra in Italy, an establishment of the Joint Nuclear Research Centre set up by the Commission under Article 8 of the Euratom Treaty, had erected at its premises a club house and sports centre. In 1965 the Ufficio Imposte di Consumo di Ispra, the Excise Duty Office of Ispra, wanted to inspect the construction in

Unfortunately, however, most lawyers advocating a strict 'functional requirements' test do not give any examples of applying this test in order to determine the precise scope of immunity to be granted to an international organization. In fact, it seems that the functional necessity concept – as embodied in the work of the ILC – relates rather to a selection of privileges and immunities than to the scope of jurisdictional immunity.[80]

That the majority of the existing agreements provide for an unqualified (absolute) immunity from suit of international organizations unless expressly waived indeed does not fit neatly into the theory of functional necessity. Article 7 of the ILC Draft Articles on relations between states and international organizations which provides for 'immunity from every form of legal process' also does not in any way restrict the jurisdictional immunity itself. Even proponents of the view that functional necessity underlies the basic concept of the ILC's Draft Articles have to recognize this and acknowledge that functional necessity as chosen in Draft Article 11 is 'subject to an explicit agreement of the parties and not, as [they] propose, [as] an "invisible hand" that is inherent to the subject matter'.[81] According to Draft Article 11, international organizations would enjoy absolute immunity from suit if it is not 'limited, in the light of the functional requirements of the organization in question, by mutual agreement of the parties concerned'.[82]

The fact that even under a functional necessity concept international organizations regularly enjoy absolute immunity is acknowledged by the ILC special rapporteur himself as an 'exceptional situation [that] may

order to assess Euratom's local excise duty on the use of building materials. The administration of the Nuclear Research Centre refused such access to the Italian authorities claiming that according to the agreement between Italy and the Commission for the establishment of the Centre only the Commission could grant access. Since the Commission thought that it was exempt from the duty in question, it refused the permission asked for. Thereupon the Excise Duty Office applied to the ECJ to authorize the intended inspection. The ECJ rejected both the Commission's challenges as to the admissibility and to the substance of the claim. It construed the Excise Duty Office's request '[i]n view of the true nature of its subject matter' as a request for authorization of an administrative measure of constraint within the meaning of Article 1 of the agreement between Italy and the Commission and of Article 1 of the EC Privileges and Immunities Protocol of 1965, over which it had jurisdiction. On the merits, the ECJ held that, since under the governing rules the tax exemption of the Community was subject to certain conditions (which would result in the duty to pay taxes in some situations), the applicant had a legal interest in carrying out the necessary checks for the purpose of establishing the basis of assessment to the duty. Consequently, the ECJ authorized the inspection of building materials requested by the Excise Duty Office.

[80] See pp. 331f above.   [81] Bekker, *The Legal Position*, 166ff.
[82] Díaz-González, 'Fourth Report', 168.

seem excessive'.[83] It is notable, however, he does not seem to be troubled with this inconsistency of theory and practice, when he goes on to say that 'although' this may seem excessive, 'it is expressly limited by the obligation imposed on international organizations to institute a judicial system for the settlement of conflicts or disputes in which they may become involved'.[84] Of course, the question of a potential 'functional' limitation of the scope of judicial immunity of international organizations is abandoned when the special rapporteur turns towards alternative dispute settlement fora mitigating the result of absolute immunity. While one would have expected that a potential excessive absolute immunity should have been restricted by the 'functional necessity' criterion advocated by the special rapporteur, he seems to be content to quote from a 1985 Secretariat study stating that the immunity of the UN as well as that of most of its specialized agencies and the IAEA 'had been fully respected and recognized by the competent national authorities' and that the UN had 'continued to enjoy unrestricted immunity from legal process' in the US even after the enactment of the FSIA in 1976.[85]

The crucial test: what happens to non-functional acts?

As was the case with legal consequences for the domestic personality of international organizations,[86] the issue of non-functional acts is also of crucial importance in the context of immunity from suit. Unfortunately, most authors do not expressly discuss the consequences of acts beyond the functional capacity of international organizations for immunity purposes.

If the *ultra vires* doctrine is to be strictly applied, in the sense of rendering the act or frequently the contract concerned void *ab initio*, the subject matter of a potential lawsuit would disappear and the result would be the same as if absolute immunity was granted. By eliminating *ultra vires* acts from the scope of acts attributable to an international organization, a functional concept would thus protect – literally 'immunize' – an international organization in its dealings instead of limiting its immunity to certain functional fields.

If, however, immunity were to be denied for non-functional acts of international organizations, this might serve as an additional incentive for international organizations to limit their activities to the field of their functional personality where they justly enjoy immunity.

---

[83] *Ibid.*, 161.   [84] *Ibid.*

[85] United Nations Secretariat, The Practice of the United Nations, the Specialized Agencies and the International Atomic Energy Agency Concerning Their Status, Privileges and Immunities, *Yearbook of the International Law Commission* (1985), vol. II, Part One, 145–210.

[86] See pp. 77*ff* above.

To view non-functional acts of international organizations as legally non-existent would probably have a similar effect to allowing absolute immunity. By denying the legal existence of non-functional acts or their attributability to them,[87] international organizations could in effect avoid being sued. This concept seems to underlie some theories regarding absolute immunity as the proper functional immunity standard for international organizations. In fact, the notions of functional immunity and absolute immunity can be best reconciled if non-functional acts are viewed as legally non-existent: under this premise, the scope of functional and absolute immunity would coincide, since international organizations would be legally capable of performing only functional acts all of which would be protected by immunity.[88]

---

[87] *Cf.* pp. 82*ff* above.

[88] The assumption in the textbook on international organizations by Seidl-Hohenveldern and Loibl obviously is that other acts (i.e., not functionally justifiable acts) are beyond the international organization's capacities. Seidl-Hohenveldern and Loibl, *Das Recht der Internationalen Organisationen*, 275, refer to the sale of books by international organizations – an activity which, if carried out by a state press, would certainly be qualified as a private undertaking not giving rise to immunity. The authors reason that no rule of international law exists which would restrict the range of possible publications by a state press. Such a rule, however, could be deduced for international organizations which enjoyed legal personality – both under international and domestic law – only for the fulfilment of their purposes. Thus, only such publications which are closely related to the aims of the organization could be printed. This example, however, seems to rely upon the generally discarded notion of determining the character of state or organizational actions according to their purpose, not their nature, although it purports to illustrate the concept of absolute immunity for international organizations. One might add that the reason for denying immunity for a state press selling books should not lie in the purpose of selling books or the content of the books sold, but rather in the nature of selling books – an action which could and actually is carried out in the same way by private persons. By arguing in favour of immunity for international organizations selling books Seidl-Hohenveldern and Loibl recur to the purposes of these sales which in their view can only be 'public'. If the authors' statement that international organizations enjoy immunity for all actions is correct, then this reasoning seems superfluous. If an international legal entity enjoys absolute immunity, this applies to all actions regardless of their character and regardless of whether they are determined according to their nature or purpose. If, on the other hand, immunity depends upon the purpose of the act, a general immunity can only be claimed if actions not conforming to the purposes of the international organization are regarded as legally impossible or at least non-attributable to the international organization. Such an assumption, however, would deny the possibility of international organizations acting in areas not closely related to the international organization's statutory purposes and thus severely limit its scope of activities and, more importantly, the protection for third parties against such acts. See, however, Ignaz Seidl-Hohenveldern, 'Eurocontrol und EWG-Wettbewerbsrecht' in Konrad Ginther, Gerhard Hafner, Winfried Lang, Hanspeter Neuhold and Lilly Sucharipa-Beermann (eds.), *Völkerrecht zwischen normativem Anspruch und politischer Realität. Festschrift für Karl Zemanek* (Berlin, 1994), 251–73 at 261, clarifying that there could be no immunity for *ultra vires* acts of an international organization.

However, reaffirming that their activities have to be based on their functional tasks does not secure that non-functional acts do not occur. The question remains what happens if, in a specific case, an international organization's action was clearly not connected with the international organization's purpose (regardless whether this might be public or private), e.g. *ultra vires* acts, tortious acts. It is submitted that a different way of interpreting the consequences of non-functional acts would be more appropriate than to deny their (legal) existence.

It seems that the better view, rather than incorporating the 'non-attributability' rationale from the functional personality concept to the immunity field, would be to deny immunity for non-functional acts, in other words, to understand the 'functional immunity standard' as a criterion 'limiting the scope of their potential immunity'.[89] Although frequently rather cautiously formulated, this seems to be the prevailing view of commentators trying to make sense of a perceived functional limitation of immunity.[90]

An analogous reasoning, justifying a loss of immunity as a consequence of non-functional acts, can be found in diplomatic law: one of the exceptions to a diplomat's immunity from suit relates to disputes concerning his or her private professional or commercial activities.[91] Article 42 of the Vienna Convention on Diplomatic Relations 1961 prohibits exactly this kind of conduct. If a diplomat chooses to disregard this prohibition and engages in – from the diplomatic service point of view – non-functional, professional or commercial activities, such – prohibited – activities are not regarded as legally non-existent. The solution is rather

---

[89] ILA, *Report of the 66th Conference, Buenos Aires* (1994), 474.

[90] *Cf.* Bekker's example for delimiting the scope of immunity along an international organization's official activities. Referring to ELDO's Protocol on Privileges and Immunities of 1965 which defined the organization's official activities as probably excluding the commercial production of launchers, he argues that if ELDO decided to commercially produce launchers, 'it could no longer, under the Protocol, rely on its immunity'. Bekker, *The Legal Position*, 165. He fails to explain, however, how ELDO could do so in the first place, if its status, i.e. personality, were functionally determined along the purposes of the organization as Bekker maintained earlier in his book. Arsanjani, 'Claims Against International Organizations', 153, is more outspoken: 'Whatever immunity [an international organization] may enjoy will not extend to acts which exceed its jurisdiction or powers, acts commonly described as *ultra vires* or in *excès de pouvoir*.' Seidl-Hohenveldern, 'Eurocontrol and EWG-Wettbewerbsrecht', 261 states: 'Für *Ultra vires*-Akte kann es . . . keine Immunität geben.' Similarly the 1994 ILA Report on state immunity, in its chapter dealing with immunity of international organizations, might be understood in this sense when it speaks of 'functions' of the international organization 'thus limiting the scope of their potential immunity'. ILA, *Report of the 66th Conference, Buenos Aires* (1994), 474.

[91] Article 31(1)(c) of the Vienna Convention on Diplomatic Relations 1961.

found in depriving the diplomat of immunities he or she would otherwise enjoy. Article 31(1)(c) of the Vienna Convention expressly excludes his or her immunity from suit in such cases.[92] The problem remains whether this rationale can properly be transferred to the international organizations plane, since there is a critical difference: in the context of international organizations it is a question of legal capacity to act in a certain way, whereas in diplomatic law the issues raised by Articles 31 and 42 of the Vienna Convention concern the permissibility of certain activities which diplomats are undoubtedly legally capable of performing. However, if one considers the underlying rationale of denying immunity in accordance with Article 31 of the Vienna Convention as an attempt indirectly to sanction a wrongful conduct, it becomes evident that the idea is not to let diplomats acting outside the functional scope of their diplomatic activities profit from immunity from suit. The other exceptions to diplomatic immunity enshrined in Article 31, relating to real property and succession matters, also evidence this notion of refusing immunity protection for non-functional acts.[93] It seems that this policy rationale is very well transferable to other immunity contexts.

It would be inconsistent with these considerations to grant an international organization immunity in situations where it acts outside its functions. Some support for this idea of a 'loss of immunity' in cases of non-functional acts can be also found in judicial practice:

The issue of a potential immunity from suit in the case of an *ultra vires* action was addressed in *Pilger* v. *United States Steel Corporation et al.*[94] Although it did not involve an international organization, but rather a corporation as an instrumentality of a foreign state, the reasoning is interesting for present purposes. A German citizen brought suit against the defendant company alleging unlawful seizure and withholding of certain shares of stock. The defendant moved to dismiss, claiming that it was acting as an agent of the Government of the United Kingdom and that as such it enjoyed immunity from suit. The court denied this motion holding that – while it was true that the defendant was indeed a governmental agency – it was immune from legal process only for acts performed within the scope of powers vested in it, not for acts beyond and in

---

[92] One could view this provision of the Vienna Convention on Diplomatic Relations 1961 as an 'indirect' sanction for wrongful conduct. According to Denza, this 'exception to immunity is needed to cover cases where the ban [to engage in commercial activities] is disregarded or over-ridden by agreement with the receiving State'. Eileen Denza, 'Diplomatic Agents and Missions, Privileges and Immunities' in Rudolf Bernhardt (ed.), *Encyclopedia of Public International Law* (2nd edn, 1992), vol. I, 1040–5 at 1043.

[93] See also pp. 362f below.   [94] Court of Errors and Appeals New Jersey, 1925.

violation of its authority. The court went on to state the principle of personal liability of agents for acts in excess of their authority which are not shielded by sovereign immunity:

An instrumentality of government ... does not cease to be personally answerable for acts done under color of the authority conferred upon it, but, in fact, in excess of that authority and without legal justification. The immunity of a sovereign against suits arising out of the unlawful acts of its representatives does not extend to those who acted in its name, and cannot be set up by them as a bar to suits brought against them for the doing of such unlawful acts.[95]

In the Belgian *Manderlier v. Organisation des Nations Unies and Etat Belge (Ministre des Affaires Etrangères)*[96] case, the claim brought against the UN was dismissed on the basis of the 'general and absolute' immunity from jurisdiction accorded to the organization in the General Convention. In an *obiter dictum*, however, the court of first instance hinted at the possibility that it would not have granted immunity for the acts complained of had it applied the functional immunity standard of the UN Charter since the court of first instance expressly qualified the tortious acts committed by the UN to be outside of the organization's functions.[97]

An even more striking example of a national court actually denying immunity for an international organization's *ultra vires* act is the German appellate decision in *X et al. v. European School Munich II*.[98] The administrative court found that the functionally limited immunity of the European School did not cover acts *ultra vires* this organization's capacity to act. The court expressly held that the European School did not have the capacity to issue administrative tuition decisions and that the German courts had jurisdiction to identify such a transgression of an international organization's powers where the act's *ultra vires* character was manifest.[99]

---

[95] Green Haywood Hackworth, *Digest of International Law* (Washington DC, 1941), vol. II, 492.
[96] Civil Tribunal of Brussels, 11 May 1966.
[97] (1972) 45 ILR 446 at 453.
[98] Administrative Court Munich, 29 June 1992, Bavarian Administrative Court Munich, 15 March 1995, Federal Administrative Court, 9 October 1995. See pp. 150f above.
[99] 'Mit dem Erlaß von als Verwaltungsakte zu verstehenden Bescheiden über die Erhebung von Schulgeld gegenüber den Eltern "anderer Kinder", die nicht Angehörige der Europäischen Patentorganisation sind, überschreitet die Europäische Schule München offenkundig die ihr nach den ihr zugrundeliegenden völkerrechtlichen Verträgen zustehende Rechtsmacht (Handeln "*ultra vires*"); sie unterliegt insoweit der deutschen Gerichtbarkeit; die Offenkundigkeit dieser Befugnisüberschreitung kann jedenfalls dann von den nationalen Gerichten festgestellt werden, wenn sie sich aus dem eigenen Vortrag der internationalen Organisation ergibt.' Bavarian Administrative Court, 7th Chamber, Munich, 15 March 1995, (1996) *Deutsches Verwaltungsblatt* 448.

Functional immunity as restrictive immunity

The 'obvious' possibility to assimilate the jurisdictional immunity standard of international organizations to that of states – although apparently eagerly pursued by some courts[100] – finds less of an enthusiastic echo
among scholars. To treat international organizations, immunity-wise,
like states has rather been anathema to many international lawyers and
certainly to most organizations which regularly benefit from a far
broader absolute immunity shield. With changing patterns of tasks and
performances of international organizations, however, it is not certain
whether this accepted paradigm will continue. Thus, some authors seem
to acknowledge that a restrictive immunity concept might satisfy the
functional necessity criterion relevant for international organizations.[101]
Others have proposed singling out the activities of international organizations 'of a so-called private law nature that only minimally affect their
major functions, but that may have adverse impact on the public order of
a particular State'.[102] This in fact combines a *iure gestionis/iure imperii*
dichotomy with an impact or effects balancing.

Some critics appear to think that *iure gestionis* acts of international
organizations do not give rise to problems in practice.[103] However, given
the various treaty provisions enabling international organizations to
enter into private law contracts, etc., and the ensuing practice, this seems
to understate the potential problems arising from the acts clearly envisaged by the organizations' founders. Even declared defenders of an
absolute immunity standard for international organizations implicitly
recognize that international organizations perform commercial acts and
that the conditions pertinent at the time when absolute immunity was
granted to international organizations might have changed by now.[104]
Thus, *iure gestionis* acts of international organizations do indeed pose a
challenge for drafting an adequate immunity standard.

In the academic discussion the applicability of a restrictive immunity
standard – as it is currently largely accepted in state immunity practice –

---

[100] See pp. 192*ff* and 199*ff* above, in particular the Italian case law and also some US
decisions.
[101] Bekker, *The Legal Position*, 164*ff*, when proposing his functional immunity standard along
the official/non-official differentiation, suddenly re-introduces the commercial activity
exception, albeit qualified by the additional requirement of profit-making as a means of
delimiting the spheres of official and non-official activities. See also Zemanek, 'Réponse',
in (1995 I) 66 *Annuaire de l'Institut de Droit International* 327, who regards the *iure gestionis/
iure imperii* distinction as relevant to the immunity of international organizations.
[102] Arsanjani, 'Claims Against International Organizations', 163.
[103] *Cf.* Morgenstern, *Legal Problems*, 6.   [104] Seidl-Hohenveldern, 'L'immunité', 477.

to cases involving international organizations seems to depend mainly upon two aspects: on the possibility of transferring the concept of state sovereignty; and on the related issue of the correct interpretation of what it means to accept that international organizations enjoy international legal personality. Beyond these premises, the search for an adequate adaptation of the *iure imperii/iure gestionis* dichotomy to be applied to international organizations has not yet produced convincing results.

Traditional reasons for differentiating from states

In order to confirm the absolute immunity from suit for international organizations and to refute any parallel drawn from state immunity to restrict such exemption from domestic courts, commentators often stress the lack of sovereignty of international organizations. The statement that organizations are not sovereign and thus could not develop any tradition of sovereign immunity (nor rely on reciprocity) is frequently made.[105] Normally the assumption seems to be that any doctrines delimiting the sovereign immunity of states should thus become inapplicable.[106]

Given the true impact of restrictive immunity – which shifts the emphasis from the person of the defendant, the sovereign, to his, her or its activities, which may be sovereign or not – this seems surprising. One might therefore ask whether it would not be more appropriate to investigate whether the *iure imperii/iure gestionis* distinction can be applied to international organizations as a matter of comparing their activities.

Under prevailing international law doctrine, as elaborated by Jean Bodin in his 1583 classic *Six livres de la République*,[107] there are two main external characteristics of sovereignty on the international level: one is equality; the other is independence.[108] Sovereigns are – at least in a legal

---

[105] See e.g. *Restatement (Third) of the Law, The Foreign Relations Law of the United States* (ed. American Law Institute, St Paul, MN, 1987), Introductory Note to § 467. In the – frequently rather cautious – *Restatement*, no explanations are given as to what follows from this. ILA, *Report of the 66th Conference, Buenos Aires* (1994), 474.

[106] In its *amicus curiae* brief in the *Broadbent* case, the UN, in urging the court to adopt a functional immunity standard implying absolute immunity from suit in domestic courts, listed the key differences between sovereign and organizational immunities, ranking the lack of sovereignty of international organizations as the principal difference. (1980) *United Nations Juridical Yearbook* 224 at 230.

[107] See Helmut Quaritsch, *Staat und Souveränität* (Frankfurt am Main, 1970), 251ff.

[108] See Hanspeter Neuhold, 'Abgrenzungen, Strukturmerkmale und Besonderheiten der Völkerrechtsordnung' in Hanspeter Neuhold, Waldemar Hummer and Christoph Schreuer (eds.), *Österreichisches Handbuch des Völkerrechts* (2nd edn, Vienna, 1991), 2–12 at 7; and *Oppenheim's International Law* (9th edn, ed. by Robert Jennings and Arthur Watts, 1992), vol. I, 125.

sense – equal to each other and they are independent from each other. The concept of sovereignty does not deny the existing inequalities of states nor their factual interdependence.[109] It rather stresses their equal claim to independence, in the sense of autonomy, from the will of other 'equals'. Thus, equality is probably just a subordinate qualifying criterion of the main feature of sovereignty, i.e. independence.[110] Accordingly, in the famous arbitral award in the *Island of Palmas Case* (*The Netherlands* v. *USA*)[111] it was pronounced that '[s]overeignty in the relations between States signifies independence'.[112]

The doctrine of sovereign immunity – even in its modern restrictive scope – can be viewed as a clear expression of this claim to independence. The exemption of states from the jurisdiction of the courts of other states seeks to prevent subjecting one sovereign to the authority of the organs of another sovereign and thus to the will of another 'equal'. The classical notion, justifying state immunity, of *par in parem non habet imperium*[113] or *par in parem non habet iurisdictionem*[114] aptly illustrates this idea. The modern view of restrictive immunity only seemingly contradicts this requirement to exempt foreign states from a state's courts. It merely narrows down the necessity to grant such exemption to the sovereign acts of a state, excluding its other activities. This presupposes, of course, that not all state actions are sovereign actions. If this differentiation is accepted, the limitation on immunity can be correctly upheld without infringing the *par in parem* principle. Only in so far as a state acts as an equal, i.e. in its sovereign capacity, it has a claim to be independent from the jurisdiction of another state. Under this approach, of course, sovereignty is not a general qualification of a state which – once established – always attaches to it, but rather becomes an attribute of certain activities of a state. Thus, 'sovereignty' is important in the immunity context, less in order to determine the persons having a claim to such immunity, more to determine the kinds of actions for which such persons have such a

---

[109] *Cf.* Karl Zemanek, 'Interdependence' in Rudolf Bernhardt (ed.), *Encyclopedia of Public International Law* (2nd edn, 1995), vol. II, 1021–3 at 1022.

[110] See the definition of the contemporary principle by Helmut Steinberger, 'Sovereignty' in Rudolf Bernhardt (ed.), *Encyclopedia of Public International Law* (1987), vol. X, 397–418 at 408, as 'the basic international legal status of a State that is not subject, within its territorial jurisdiction, to the governmental, executive, legislative, or judicial jurisdiction of a foreign State or to foreign law other than public international law'.

[111] Arbitration Award. 4 April 1928.

[112] (1949) 2 *United Nations Reports of International Arbitral Awards* 831 at 838.

[113] *Cf.* Ignaz Seidl-Hohenveldern, 'Die Staaten' in Neuhold, Hummer and Schreuer, *Österreichisches Handbuch des Völkerrechts*, 152.

[114] *Cf.* Brownlie, *Principles*, 324.

claim. Under the modern restrictive immunity doctrine, sovereigns enjoy immunity for their sovereign acts only – as opposed to their private or commercial acts. This reflects a shift in emphasis from the static 'person-based' classical concept of absolute state immunity to a modern 'activity-oriented' concept of restrictive immunity. It is not the person, but rather the acts of certain persons that are exempted from the jurisdiction of national courts.[115]

It is important to realize that in this context the meaning – or at least the emphasis – of the notion of 'sovereignty' has slightly shifted. It no longer merely signifies 'independence' in an abstract sense. Even when acting commercially, states are independent in the sense that they freely choose to negotiate or deal on the marketplace and are not dependent on the will of any other 'equal'. 'Sovereign' seems rather to be tantamount to 'governmental' or 'official' in the exercise of public authority, as distinct from 'in the exercise of a state's capacity to act like a private person'. Under this modern sovereign immunity perception, sovereignty stresses less the (external) independence,[116] but rather the (internal) exercise of authority element.[117]

It might well be that, against this background, a parallel between states and international organizations is easier to draw than to regard the latter as sovereign entities.[118] First, however, one should contemplate whether international organizations could not be viewed as 'sovereign' or 'quasi-sovereign' in a sense that would allow the application of principles of sovereign immunity to them.

One of the problems surrounding the sovereignty discourse is the fact that the notion of sovereignty itself is based on frequently strongly predetermined legal concepts. The term 'sovereignty' is almost *per defini-*

---

[115] See the English decision *Buck* v. *Attorney-General* [1965] 1 All ER 882 at 877, stating that 'the basis of the sovereign immunity does not depend on the persons between whom the issue is joined, but on the subject matter of the issue'.

[116] The external aspect of 'sovereignty' is mostly 'defensive'. It stresses the claim to be independent from the will of other states.

[117] Internally 'sovereignty' is largely understood as the highest jurisdictional power (*Befehls-gewalt*) of a state, be it to prescribe, to adjudicate or to enforce, within its sphere of competence (which in turn is largely determined territorially or on the basis of some other jurisdictional nexus). It is more or less an acknowledgment of a state's power to regulate its internal affairs. *Cf. Oppenheim's International Law*, 125. *Cf.* also the *Island of Palmas Case* (*The Netherlands* v. *USA*), Arbitration Award, 4 April 1928, (1949) 2 *United Nations Reports of International Arbitral Awards* 831 at 838, defining sovereignty/independence (in regard to a portion of the globe) as 'the right to exercise therein, to the exclusion of any other State, the functions of a state'.

[118] See pp. 353*ff* below.

tionem seen as a state attribute.[119] Thus, any discussion of the sovereignty of international organizations seems to be precluded from the outset. If viewed from a functional perspective, however, the constitutive characteristics of sovereignty, i.e. equality and independence, might serve as less obviously predetermined expressions that could better describe the position of other subjects of international law, including international organizations.

It is as true as it is quite commonplace to note that international organizations are different from states. However, the determination as to whether they could be viewed as equal (in a sense to underline their potential quality of being sovereign) needs a certain common yardstick in order to ascertain the equality or inequality between states and international organizations. By choosing a particular relative aspect by which to compare states and international organizations, instead of comparing them *in toto*, one might observe their similarity rather than their differences. For instance, the recognition of international organizations as persons of international law evidences that they are viewed as equal to states in relation to their common claim to international personality.[120]

As far as the internal and external aspects of sovereignty are concerned, it is apparent that there are important dissimilarities between states and international organizations. While a state's internal sovereignty, in the sense of supreme jurisdictional power, is largely taken for granted, conceived as a natural attribute of its existence, this is not so with international organizations. As outlined above, the notion of 'derivative' subjects of international law largely stems from the idea that states – as 'primary' subjects of international law – delegate powers to international organizations which the latter do not originally possess.[121] This clearly underlines an important difference *vis-à-vis* states in relation to their exercise of jurisdictional power. Furthermore, the influence of member states is not limited to the initial transfer of powers, but rather a continuing process which casts doubt upon the 'external' independence of international organizations. Member states constantly and lawfully determine the activities of international organizations, mainly through their voting behaviour.[122] In addition, according to the traditional view,

---

[119] E.g., Helmut Steinberger, 'Sovereignty' in Rudolf Bernhardt (ed.), *Encyclopedia of Public International Law* (1987), vol. X, 397–418 at 408*ff*. There is no doubt, however, that other entities, such as the Sovereign Order of Malta, are considered to enjoy this quality as well. *Cf.* Béat de Fischer, 'L'Ordre Souverain de Malte' (1979 II) 163 *Recueil des Cours* 1–46.

[120] *Cf.* pp. 53*ff* above.   [121] *Cf.* pp. 57*ff* above.

[122] Christoph H. Schreuer, 'Internationale Organisationen' in Neuhold, Hummer and Schreuer, *Österreichisches Handbuch des Völkerrechts*, 182.

member states always have the power to dissolve the international organizations they created.[123]

On the other hand, the idea of a certain legal independence of international organizations from their members lies at the core of the idea of international organizations leading some to define an international organization as an entity capable of forming a will separate and independent of the will of its members.[124] Some courts have expressly recognized the 'sovereign' independence of international organizations from the will of its member states and thereby rejected the latter's liability for the former's activities.[125]

When ascertaining the 'sovereignty' of international organizations as far as their independence from the will of their member states is concerned, one could soon be trapped in the 'still organization' or 'already state' query familiar to students of international organizations from the debate on the European Community/Union.[126] The external aspect of independence might have been achieved where the delegation or initial

---

[123] Rudolf Bindschedler, 'International Organizations, General Aspects' in Rudolf Bernhardt (ed.), Encyclopedia of Public International Law (2nd edn, 1995), vol. II, 1289–309 at 1289. See, however, Schermers, International Institutional Law, 813, and, in particular, the persistent discussion on the legal (im-)possibility to dissolve the European Communities/ European Union.

[124] Most radically by Seyersted on objective international personality. According to him, international organizations are 'sovereign' in so far as no one 'above' them determines their actions; they are able to perform their own acts according to their own will which can be distinguished from the will or the sum of the wills of the member states. Finn Seyersted, 'Jurisdiction over Organs and Officials of States, the Holy Sea and Intergovernmental Organisations' (1965) 14 International and Comparative Law Quarterly 31–82 and 493–527 at 31ff; and Finn Seyersted, 'International Personality of Intergovernmental Organizations: Do Their Capacities Really Depend upon Their Constitutions?' (1964) 4 Indian Journal of International Law 1–74 at 1ff. See also the definition of an international organization in Article 2(b) of the IDI draft resolution on 'The legal consequences for member states of the non-fulfilment by international organizations of their obligations toward third parties' requiring the existence of an organization's 'volonté distincte' from the will of its member states. Draft Resolution, (1995 I) 66 Annuaire de l'Institut de Droit International 465.

[125] In Edison Sault Electric Co. v. United States, US Court of Claims, 23 March 1977, the US Court of Claims held that the International Joint Commission, established in 1909 to regulate the water levels in the Great Lakes, was a 'sovereign body which was free to reject the application of the United States if it had so decided'. 552 F. 2d 326 at 333 (Ct Cl. 1977). Although the 'sovereignty' of the Commission could have been held to stem from the transfer of governmental regulatory authority, the court stressed the independence aspect of sovereignty. The fact that it formed its own decision, independent from the will of the US, one of its member states, seemed crucial.

[126] Albert Bleckmann, Europarecht (5th edn, Cologne, Berlin, Bonn and Munich, 1990), 409; and Werner Meng, Das Recht der internationalen Organisationen – eine Entwicklungsstufe des Völkerrechts, Zugleich eine Untersuchung zur Rechtsnatur des Rechts der Europäischen Gemeinschaften (1979).

conferment of powers has become irreversible; it undoubtedly will where the point of transformation of a federation of states into a federal entity has been crossed. Before that, however, and where the member states remain the 'masters of the treaties'[127] establishing an international organization, international organizations will remain largely dependent upon the will of their members and are thus hardly fully independent.[128] Accordingly, one could only speak of the 'sovereignty' of international organizations in a metaphorical way, or should perhaps rather use the term 'quasi-sovereignty'.[129]

Still, this sovereignty or quasi-sovereignty appears particularly evident as far as the internal aspect of sovereignty, the exercise of jurisdictional power and authority, is concerned. The transfer of sovereignty to international organizations, not in the sense of independence (which would probably conflict with the idea of transfer of powers), but rather as a transfer of the power to exercise (parts of) official/governmental authority is a common feature of the constituent agreements of international organizations. In addition, the possibility of delegating 'sovereign powers' to international organizations is provided for in many domestic legal systems, mostly in a national constitutional framework.[130] That

[127] Ulrich Everling, 'Sind die Mitgliedstaaten der Europäischen Gemeinschaft noch Herren der Verträge?' in Bernhardt, Geck, Jaenicke and Steinberger (eds.), *Völkerrecht als Rechtsordnung, Internationale Gerichtsbarkeit, Menschenrechte, Festschrift Mosler* (Berlin, Heidelberg and New York, 1983), 173–91.

[128] The ECJ initiated this discussion by an *obiter dictum* in the *Defrenne* case, where, in effect, it denied the possibility of treaty revision through common accord – which would include the possibility of dissolving the organization through *contrarius actus* – by stating that 'apart from any specific provisions, the Treaty can only be modified by means of the amendment procedure carried out in accordance with Article 236'. *Defrenne* v. *Sabena*, Case 43/75, ECJ, 8 April 1976, [1976] ECR 455 at 478. For a recent contrary opinion, see the German Constitutional Court's *Maastricht* decision which confirmed the view that 'Germany is one of the Masters of the Treaties, which . . . could also ultimately revoke that adherence [to the Union Treaty] by a contrary act'. *Brunner et al.* v. *European Union Treaty (Constitutionality of the Maastricht Treaty)*, German Federal Constitutional Court, 12 October 1993, (1994) 31 *Common Market Law Review* 251 at 258.

[129] See, however, Seyersted, 'Jurisdiction', 522, speaking of 'organic jurisdiction of states, intergovernmental organisations and other *sovereign* communities' (emphasis added).

[130] For instance, Article 24(1) of the Basic Law provides: 'The Federation may by legislation transfer sovereign powers to intergovernmental institutions.' Similarly, Article 9(2) of the Austrian Constitution provides that '[t]hrough law or . . . treaty single sovereign powers of the Federation can be transferred to inter-state institutions and their organs'. Less explicit is Article 11 of the Italian Constitution, according to which '[Italy] agrees . . . to such limitation of sovereignty as may be necessary for a system calculated to ensure peace and justice between Nations; it promotes and encourages international organizations having such ends in view'. Also Article 20 of the Danish Constitution of 1953 authorizes the delegation of governmental powers to international bodies set up 'to promot[e] . . . international rules of law and cooperation'. Comparable provisions can be found in other constitutions.

states do actually transfer 'sovereignty' to international organizations is widely acknowledged.[131] The reasons for such a transfer of sovereign powers, mostly legislative and executive, from individual states to international organizations appears to be an ever growing awareness of the necessity of regional or global administration/governance of tasks which were formerly within the domestic sphere of states.[132]

As the example of the European Union shows, a large-scale, wide-ranging transfer of state powers to international organizations is possible. Although the discussion about the delegation of sovereignty is probably most prominent in the EU context, it is not limited to it. It can also be found in relation to other international organizations. It has been rightly stressed that some 'technical' or 'instrumental' international organizations or programmes of international organizations such as the WHO, the UNDP, etc. can be regarded as exercising a kind of 'public administration normally associated with States'.[133]

In the UN context – although it is apparent that from its own perspective the UN has not and does not attempt to assume some kind of 'super-state' position[134] – there is still a potential for an evolution in the direction of softer forms of 'world government' or 'global governance' that would imply the exercise of some sovereign or quasi-sovereign authority. A future 'world government' underlies not only some overly utopian views for the future of the UN. Even persons, who could be hardly regarded utopians or idealists of international law, expressed the belief that the establishment of the UN presented a particular innovative opportunity in this direction: 'The development of the organization of the

---

[131] E.g., *Eckhardt* v. *Eurocontrol* acknowledges the transfer of sovereignty to international organizations: 'Eurocontrol is a public international organization established by treaty by the Member States for the safety of air navigation in areas of air space which extend beyond the limits of a single State's territory . . . which implies that Member States, as Contracting Parties, have to that extent transferred their sovereignty to Eurocontrol.' District Court of Maastricht, 12 January 1984, (1985) 16 *Netherlands Yearbook of International Law* 464 at 468. See, however, Ignaz Seidl-Hohenveldern, *Corporations in and under International Law* (Cambridge, 1987), 71*ff*, who rejects the idea of a true transfer of sovereign rights to international organizations. In his view, the allegedly 'transferred' power is retained by the states but is dormant. This 'temporary vacuum' is filled by the organization, 'which thereby avails itself of a legislative and executive power of its own'. In his view these 'rights of the organization are parallel to dormant rights *jure imperii* of the member States'.

[132] *Cf.* Susan Strange, *The Retreat of the State* (Cambridge, 1996), 3*ff*.

[133] *Cf.* Christoph H. Schreuer, 'The Waning of the Sovereign State: Towards a New Paradigm for International Law?' (1993) 4 *European Journal of International Law* 447–71 at 452.

[134] *Cf. Reparation for Injuries Suffered in the Service of the United Nations*, Advisory Opinion, (1949) *ICJ Reports* 174 at 179.

international community suggests the ultimate possibility of substituting some kind of joint sovereignty, the supremacy of the common will, for the old single state sovereignty.'[135] There is no need to equalize the actions of international organizations with governmental actions, but one could at least regard some of them, for instance 'the UN as a form of government'.[136] More futuristic thoughts appear to be particularly *en vogue* at a time when the UN – having just celebrated its first fifty years – sets out to prepare for the next fifty years, even though – at the same time – it faces one of its most troubling financial crises.[137] For instance, the Center for War/Peace Studies, under a 'Binding Triad Concept', calls for a far-reaching delegation of legislative powers upon the UN General Assembly, etc.[138] Also more cautious, 'realistic' voices – calling for a change in the UN system as a matter of 'global survival' – advocate the transfer of powers to international organizations.[139]

The current discussion on the issue of 'global governance' is also illustrative in this respect. By propagating this term, the report of the UN Commission on Global Governance takes great care to avoid the expression 'government'. 'Governance' is obviously meant to supplant the notion of 'government' by a more horizontal, issue-related way of tackling modern-day problems. According to the report, '[g]overnance is the sum of the many ways individuals and institutions, public and private, manage their common affairs'.[140] Thus, it rather appears like a regime, a system whereby interested players interact in solving problems. However, a closer description of what is meant by governance points in the direction of regulatory action. The examples given by the Commission range from local waste-recycling schemes and multi-urban transport plans, to regional initiatives to control deforestation, culminating in 'effective

---

[135] Philip C. Jessup, *A Modern Law of Nations* (New York, 1956), 13.

[136] Ian Brownlie, 'The United Nations as a Form of Government' in J. E. S. Fawcett and R. Higgins (eds.), *International Organization. Law in Movement. Essays in Honour of John McMahon* (London, New York and Toronto, 1974), 26–36 at 26*ff*.

[137] See Ruben P. Mendez, 'Financing the United Nations and the International Public Sector: Problems and Reform' (1997) 3 *Global Governance* 283–310 at 283*ff*.

[138] Under its most recent version the Binding Triad concept calls for an amendment of Article 13 of the UN Charter, which would bestow the General Assembly with legislative powers requiring a two-thirds majority of its members' votes, a simple majority of votes assigned according to the population of the members and a simple majority of votes assigned according to the members' financial contributions. *Cf.* Richard Hudson, *Quick Calculator for Estimating Outcomes of Votes in the UN General Assembly under the Binding Triad System for Global Decision-Making* (CW/PS Special Study No. 8, New York, 1995), 1*ff*.

[139] *Cf.* Benjamin B. Ferencz, *New Legal Foundations for Global Survival* (Dobbs Ferry, NY, 1994).

[140] Commission on Global Governance, *Our Global Neighborhood. The Report of the Commission on Global Governance* (Oxford, 1995), 2.

global decision-making'.[141] The report clearly disclaims any super-state tendencies by stating that, even if global necessity requires closer international cooperation, '[t]his does not imply, however, world government or world federalism'.[142] Elsewhere the less authority-based aspect of governance has also been stressed while at the same time maintaining that it has to do with tasks of governing.[143]

Against this background it appears plausible to regard international organizations as sovereign or at least quasi-sovereign in a sense that would make the application of state immunity principles plausible.

A sovereign immunity standard for international organizations exercising sovereign powers?

If one accepts that the modern restrictive state immunity standard *ratione materiae* protects exactly those state powers of a 'public', 'governmental', '*iure imperii*', or 'administrative' nature (as opposed to commercial activities) and if one realizes that many international organizations largely engage in such 'sovereign' or 'quasi-sovereign' activities, it appears difficult to maintain that the 'lack of sovereignty of international organizations', as a conceptual matter of principle, should prevent the application of sovereign immunity standards.

Another development seems to have been even more important for the possibility to 'transfer' the rationale for state immunity to the problem of the immunity of international organizations: the emergence of a restrictive sovereign immunity concept which underlines the predominance of the 'internal' authority aspect of sovereignty over the 'external' equality and independence aspect. It seems that, historically, the justification of sovereign immunity shifted from protecting the equality aspect to protecting the internal authority element of sovereignty. It is no longer the state's formal existence as a state or its existence as an 'equal' that mandates immunity, but rather the exercise of a state's internal authority that requires domestic courts of other states to refrain from adjudication.[144]

---

[141] *Ibid.*, at 2 and 4.   [142] *Ibid.*, 4.

[143] *Cf.* Rosenau speaking of '*control* or *steering* mechanisms, terms that highlight the purposeful nature of governance without presuming the presence of hierarchy'. James N. Rosenau, 'Governance in the Twenty-First Century' (1995) 1 *Global Governance* 13–43 at 14. See also Lawrence S. Finkelstein, 'What is Global Governance' (1995) 1 *Global Governance* 367–72 at 369: 'Global governance is governing, without sovereign authority, relationships that transcend national frontiers. Global governance is doing internationally what governments do at home.'

[144] See p. 373 below.

To regard the distinction between sovereign states and international organizations, which are not sovereign entities, as a primary justification for not applying sovereign immunity principles to international organizations would leave a certain logical inconsistency. Such a reasoning tried to justify a broader scope of jurisdictional immunity for organizations than for states, although the former do not come close to the plenitude of sovereignty of the latter. Of course, there might be different reasons for providing for a larger scope of immunity (to protect their weakness,[145] because they act in the common interest,[146] in order to compensate for their lesser status,[147] etc.), but – to remain in an intra-systematic critique – it is hard to understand how and why the lack of sovereignty should lead to a broader scope of immunity.

Sometimes the fact that international organizations act in the common interest – be it of its member states or of the international community at large – also serves as a justification for regarding their immunity protection as an absolute one. In rejecting the possibility of adopting a restrictive immunity standard from state immunity for international organizations, some authors explicitly refer to the non-egotistic purpose of an international organization's activities.[148] It appears, however, that these views rely heavily on the old 'purpose test' justifying sovereign immunity for activities believed to be 'in the general interest'.[149] Under the modern 'nature' test, the common interest of state or organizational activity should not be a decisive factor when delimiting the scope of jurisdictional immunity.

In a somewhat related reasoning, some authors maintain that the

---

[145] See p. 238 above.   [146] See below on this page.   [147] See pp. 248ff above.

[148] For Dominicé, for instance, it is 'déterminant' that international organizations are 'organismes de service' and not political bodies only pursuing their own interests in order to justify their different treatment. Christian Dominicé, 'L'immunité de juridiction et d'exécution des organisations internationales' (1984 IV) 187 *Recueil des Cours* 145–238 at 179. Similarly, and partly relying on Dominicé, the ILC Special Rapporteur believes that the 'ample immunity' granted to international organizations – in contrast to the increasingly restricted immunity of states – is fully justified, because international organizations are 'service agencies operating on behalf of all their member states'. Díaz-González, 'Fourth Report', 158.

[149] *Cf.* the argument by Balanda in the course of the ILC deliberations on the subject: 'whenever states established an international organization in order to engage in an activity at the international level, they did so in the general interest, which might of course be of a commercial nature. The fact that an international organization engaged in commercial activities did not, however, mean that it was not performing an international public service, and it was precisely because it performed such a service that it required protection.' *Yearbook of the International Law Commission* (1985), vol. I, 294, para. 44.

'functionally limited personality' of international organizations justifies an absolute immunity standard because international organizations can only act within the scope of their functional personality and because they enjoy functional immunity for these acts.[150] Sometimes there seems to be an underlying notion that international organizations – as opposed to states – do not engage in commercial activities at all.[151] Thus, it is argued, there should be no need at all to adapt principles developed in the context of state immunity. However, this argument is open to factual falsification and has in fact been contradicted. Most international organizations do engage in some kind of commercial activity, some – like commodity agreements – even in order to carry out their main functions.

In other instances, practical difficulties likely to be encountered in the application of a sovereign immunity standard led commentators to the conclusion that the, admittedly easier, rule of absolute immunity should govern.[152] This reason for upholding an absolute immunity standard, however, is far from convincing. One could equally well argue that sovereign immunity should revert to the more 'user-friendly' rule of absolute immunity.

Turning now to actual practice, cases decided so far on the basis of an

---

[150] *Cf.* Seidl-Hohenveldern and Loibl, *Das Recht der Internationalen Organisationen*, 275. See p. 343 note 88 above.

[151] See Morgenstern arguing that the fact 'that the capacity of international organizations is directly related to their public functions seems to imply that, as a matter of principle, the problem of acts *iure gestionis* should remain unimportant'. Morgenstern, *Legal Problems*, 6. A version of that attitude finds its expression within the UN. In advising against a profit-making joint venture with a private publishing firm, the Office of Legal Affairs noted that – given that the UN is an international organization 'with a noble mandate of immense importance set out in the Charter of the United Nations' – the planned joint venture 'could put the status and character of the Organization in question'. UN Office of Legal Affairs, 'Memorandum to the Executive Officer, Department of Public Information of 23 July 1990' (1990) *United Nations Juridical Yearbook* 257 at 258.

[152] Harders, for instance, writes that the adoption of the categories of public (*hoheitliche*) and commercial (*fiskalische*) acts for the evaluation of the liability of international organizations under domestic law would lead to substantial difficulties; consequently, it would not be clear why the treaty- and custom-based, well-accepted unlimited (absolute) immunity standard should not remain in force. In his view, the classic international organization could not sufficiently fulfil its task, if its commercial acts were not protected by immunity. Enno J. Harders, 'Haftung und Verantwortlichkeit Internationaler Organisationen' in Rüdiger Wolfrum (ed.), *Handbuch Vereinte Nationen* (2nd edn, Munich, 1991), 248–58 at 256. The practical difficulty in adopting the official/commercial activity distinction for international organizations is also underlined by Bekker who – for other reasons – dismisses such a possibility. He notes 'the puzzling ambiguities caused by applying this concept (i.e., the commercial activity concept) of sovereign immunity law to international organizations'. Bekker, *The Legal Position*, 160.

approximation between functional and restrictive immunity[153] show that the principal danger, possibly rendering a *iure imperii/iure gestionis* test for international organizations worthless, lies in its uncontrolled affirmation of official purposes justifying immunity from jurisdiction. Attempts that tried to assimilate 'functional' to *iure imperii* standards were frequently very broad in their application. Such an encompassing cloak of immunity is in effect spread over international organizations when courts return to a purpose test in order to determine the *iure imperii* character of the basis of a dispute.[154] As in older state immunity cases there will almost always be an official purpose to justify a specific legal relationship's *iure imperii* character. Thus, it may be more promising to revert to attempts to restrict immunity like that of the Italian Supreme Court in *United States* v. *Porciello*[155] which has held that one cannot maintain 'that any act whatsoever of a foreign State, or of an international organization which is endowed with sovereign powers, which has any connection at all, even if only indirectly (as is the case with the procurement of goods and services), with the functioning of the organs of that State or organization in Italy ought to be considered as exempt from the jurisdiction of an Italian court'.[156]

The existing case law demonstrates that the most problematic aspect of the equation of functional to restrictive immunity lies in the fact that a simple parallel between functional and *iure imperii* acts, as well as between non-functional and *iure gestionis* acts, cannot be drawn. Certainly, *iure imperii* activity can be identified as the main purpose of most traditional international/intergovernmental organizations. As far as such organizations are concerned, one could rather easily differentiate between functional/official (*iure imperii*) acts and *iure gestionis* acts also for immunity purposes. The differentiation between *iure gestionis* and public activities becomes more problematic where the tasks to be fulfilled by an international organization are mainly of a private nature, i.e. activities normally described as *acta iure gestionis*. This is apparent in a number of instrumental international organizations in the economic and develop-

---

[153] See pp. 192ff above.
[154] See for example the *ICEM* v. *Di Banella Schirone* case, Corte di Cassazione, 8 April 1975. See p. 190 above.
[155] Corte di Cassazione, 27 January 1977. This unfair dismissal action by an Italian employee of the US forces stationed in Italy under the NATO agreement was upheld despite the defendant's claim to immunity; the Italian Supreme Court qualified the plaintiff as part of the local civilian labour force whose employment relationships were subject to Italian jurisdiction.
[156] (1978–9) 4 *Italian Yearbook of International Law* 174 at 175.

ment sphere. Among their official functions may be the conclusion of sales contracts, loans, etc. with private parties under an applicable private law. The fact that some organizations' instruments expressly provide for partial exceptions from immunity in such situations[157] appears to evidence that these activities are considered *iure gestionis*, not requiring immunity from suit. Considering the activities of some of the international commodity organizations, the differentiation between official and non-official functions along the private/public activity distinction becomes even more problematic. They regularly serve a public purpose (stabilization of world market prices) by carrying out private acts (buying and selling).[158] This insight points towards the distinction between purpose and nature of the acts in question. If one followed a 'nature' test, prevailing among Western states' interpretation of sovereign immunity standards, one would thus deny immunity for the main activities of such organizations. If one adhered to a 'purpose' approach, one might at least qualify the activities concerning a specific commodity covered by the respective organization's immunity. Furthermore – what is true for all types of international organizations – commercial activities are normally complementary to the fulfilment of official functions.[159] Thus, many activities clearly of a *iure gestionis* character might easily be qualified as 'necessary' for the fulfilment of an international organization's functions. This leads to another problem of delimiting the functional scope of such international organizations along lines alien to traditional *iure gestionis/iure imperii* distinctions. The fact that they are regularly established with regard to a specific commodity implies that only activities concerning this commodity could be regarded as covered by their functional purposes. For instance, the International Tin Council would act within its functions only if it engaged in commercial transactions involving tin; if it chose to deal in coffee or sugar, it would act non-functionally. Granting immunity in the first case and denying it in the second, appar-

---

[157] *Cf.* the provisions allowing lawsuits brought by private creditors of international financial institutions such as the World Bank and other international banks. See p. 141 note 545 above.

[158] Pierre Michel Eisemann, 'Crise du conseil international de l'etain et insolvabilité d'une organisation intergouvernmental' (1985) 31 *Annuaire français de droit international* 730–46 at 743.

[159] One only needs to be reminded of Szasz's characterization of the UN 'which, *inter alia*, is a large multinational enterprise, operating in well over a hundred countries and carrying out many types of transactions involving money or goods valued at some billions of dollars and employing tens of thousands of staff members, plus a multitude of contractors'. Paul C. Szasz, 'The United Nations Legislates to Limit its Liability' (1987) 81 *American Journal of International Law* 739–44 at 740.

ently required by a functional concept, would hardly fit into a differentiation along the normal *iure gestionis/iure imperii* distinction.

These considerations demonstrate how difficult the distinction may become in the specific case; they cannot contradict, however, the basic premise that a large number of ordinary *iure gestionis* acts performed by international organizations in their dealings with private parties hardly merit immunity from suit.

Alternative functional restrictions of the scope of immunity: analogies to diplomatic and consular law

The law of diplomatic and consular immunities may be a source of inspiration in order to find a meaningful interpretation of the scope of functional immunity. In particular, one might consider applying some of the highly developed rules of the law of diplomatic immunity to international organizations. Such an approach seems to be justified if similar or at least comparable rationales for the two kinds of immunity regimes can be ascertained. Contrary to the *iure imperii/iure gestionis* distinction, the applicability of which to international organizations has been repeatedly discussed,[160] the potential guidance of the functional immunity rationale stemming from diplomatic and consular law is only rarely addressed in legal writing. This is surprising, even more so in view of the fact that they share the same notion of functionally restricted immunity. In one of the few exceptions, a textbook on international institutional law, an analogy is drawn from diplomatic law to international organizations by suggesting that a customary 'refinement of the law' stemming from diplomatic law precludes the invocation of immunity even without a waiver in cases concerning counterclaims.[161] A casebook on international law, explaining the term 'functional immunities' from the fact that such immunities are 'normally limited to the extent necessary for the fulfillment of the purposes of the organization',[162] further acknowledges that there are parallels between the immunities of international organizations and the privileges and immunities of consuls.[163] Thus, one might consider whether a closer consideration of consular immunity, as a true expression of functionally limited immunity, might prove useful.

---

[160] See pp. 198*ff*, 347*ff* and 356*ff* above.

[161] Schermers, *International Institutional Law*, 796, referring to Article 32 of the Vienna Convention on Diplomatic Relations 1961.

[162] C. T. Oliver, E. B. Firmage, C. L. Blakesley, R. F. Scott and S. A. Williams, *The International Legal System: Cases and Materials* (4th edn, Westbury, NY, 1995), 614.

[163] *Ibid.*

The functional immunity rationale, the idea of protecting the functioning of an organization, finds a parallel in the principle *ne impediatur
legatio* and the concept that immunities are necessary to protect the task
of diplomats and consuls.[164] If one looks at the resulting immunity,
however, one realizes that the scope of diplomatic immunities is rather
broad, while that of consular immunities comes closer to the concept of
functional limitation.

Functional necessity standard in diplomatic and consular law

Diplomatic and consular law broadly differentiates between persons
enjoying functional immunity only (consuls and certain staff at diplomatic missions) and persons enjoying absolute immunity (diplomats).
This perception, however, somewhat oversimplifies and neglects the fact
that diplomats, seemingly enjoying absolute immunity, are also limited
in this enjoyment along certain functional lines.

For the first group of persons, persons of less than full diplomatic rank
(covered by the Vienna Convention on Diplomatic Relations) as well as
consular officers, it is clear that they enjoy immunity from suit in principle only for '[official] acts performed in the exercise of [their] functions'[165] which has been characterized as an 'extremely restricted form of
immunity'.[166] Linked to the diplomatic functions listed in Article 3 of the
Vienna Convention on Diplomatic Relations or to the consular functions
in Article 5 of the Vienna Convention on Consular Relations, it would
seem that other acts would be regarded as not 'functional' and thus not
giving rise to immunity. In particular, illegal or tortious acts would fall
outside a potential immunity cover.[167] Some of the espionage cases
involving UN staff or members of diplomatic missions to the UN are
illustrative of this fact.[168] For instance, in *United States ex relatione Casanova*

---

[164] For a recent survey of the importance of functional acts for diplomatic immunities, see
Jean J. A. Salmon, 'Immunités et actes de fonction' (1992) 38 *Annuaire français de droit
international* 314–57 at 314ff.

[165] Article 43 of the Vienna Convention on Consular Relations 1963 and Articles 37 and 38 of
the Vienna Convention on Diplomatic Relations 1961.

[166] Jonathan Brown, 'Diplomatic Immunity: State Practice Under the Vienna Convention on
Diplomatic Relations' (1988) 37 *International and Comparative Law Quarterly* 53–88 at 76.

[167] Thus, for instance, in *L v. The Crown*, New Zealand Supreme Court, 12 September 1977, a
vice-consul charged for assault on a national of his sending state applying for passport
renewal enjoyed no immunity from suit since '[s]uch an act is as unconnected with the
duty to be performed by the consular officer as an act of murder. It was not required of
him in the exercise of his functions.' (1985) 68 ILR 175 at 179.

[168] See also *United States v. Egorov*, US District Court EDNY, 7 October 1963; *United States v.
Coplon et al.*, US District Court SDNY, 10 May 1949; *United States v. Melekh*, US District Court
SDNY, 28 November 1960.

v. *Fitzpatrick*,[169] a US court held that a member of the Cuban mission to the UN, who was not granted diplomatic immunity, enjoyed only functional immunity in the sense of Article 105(2) of the UN Charter and that '[c]onspiracy to commit sabotage against the Government of the United States is not a function of any mission or member of a mission to the United Nations'.[170] In a similar vein, the English Court of Appeal recently held in *Arab Monetary Fund* v. *Hashim and others*[171] that the 'plea of immunity . . . could at best only apply to official acts . . . [T]he proposition that Dr Hashim was engaged in official acts for the AMF when secretly agreeing and accepting a bribe for his own benefit (and not that of the AMF) has only to be stated to be rejected'.[172]

The immunity of diplomats – which is frequently considered absolute in its scope – is also in fact limited along functional considerations. Diplomatic law, however, instead of relying on a flexible (but also rather indeterminate) functionality standard, typifies situations clearly lying beyond functional necessity for which diplomats are not granted immunity. Article 31(1) of the Vienna Convention on Diplomatic Relations 1961 lists among these real actions, actions relating to succession and commercial activities outside official functions. Although these relatively minor exceptions to immunity from suit of diplomats are certainly narrower than the functional restriction of the immunity of consular officers, the underlying acknowledgment of denying immunity for patently non-functional acts is an important fact for immunity theory in general. The major advantage for the 'administration of justice' of such topical exceptions to diplomatic immunity as contained in Article 31(1) of the Vienna Convention on Diplomatic Relations 1961 lies in the fact that they are generally more accessible and applicable for domestic courts than abstract principles.

Transferability of the rationale for diplomatic and consular immunity

It appears plausible that the rationale of functional immunity common to diplomatic and consular law and the law of international organizations may justify the transfer or incorporation of certain features of the former to the latter. From a historical point of view, privileges and immunities of international organizations are sometimes viewed as a development of diplomatic law. Indeed, diplomatic law served as an important point of reference and analogy for the development

---

[169] US District Court SDNY, 16 January 1963.   [170] 214 F. Supp. 425 at 431 (SDNY 1963).
[171] Court of Appeal (Civil Division), 1 February 1996.
[172] [1996] 1 *Lloyd's Reports* 589 at 596.

and emergence of privileges and immunities of international organizations.[173] Some relevant constitutional texts even expressly referred to
diplomatic law.[174] However, these parallels primarily concern the privileges and immunities enjoyed by officials of international organizations.
There an analogy can be easily seen, so that the rationale for according
diplomatic privileges and immunities seems to be applicable to international civil servants.[175] On the other hand, a broad analogy between
diplomatic (or consular) law and the immunities of international organizations themselves – despite some national courts calling the immunity
of international organizations 'diplomatic immunity'[176] – is no longer
generally accepted. This rejection of the principles of diplomatic immunities with respect to international organizations is, however, based on the
understanding that the former require absolute immunity from suit. In
this context, it is frequently stressed that the limitation of the immunity
of international organizations to the extent necessary for the fulfilment
of its functions and purposes is clearly intended. For instance, when
drafting the appropriate wording for the UN's immunity, the notion of
'diplomatic' privileges and immunities was deliberately avoided and a
more appropriate standard was chosen 'based, for the purposes of the
Organization, on the necessity of realizing its purposes'.[177]

The most plausible justification, possibly allowing analogies to diplomatic and consular law, which seems more important than historical
parallels, might lie in their common 'functional necessity' rationale.
When looking for a modern justification for the grant of privileges and

---

[173] In surveying the subject, Kunz thought that 'the problem of privileges and immunities
of international organizations started historically, by analogy, as an extension of diplomatic privileges to non-diplomats'. Kunz, 'Privileges and Immunities', 842.

[174] For instance, Article 7(4) of the League of Nations Covenant provided that representatives and officials 'when engaged on the business of the League shall enjoy diplomatic
privileges and immunities'.

[175] Of course, here also times have changed. *Cf.* Jenks stating that '[t]he law governing
international immunities no longer consists primarily of a general principle resting on
the questionable analogy of diplomatic immunities'. C. Wilfred Jenks, *International
Immunities* (London and New York, 1961), xxxv.

[176] For instance, the Nigerian Supreme Court in *African Reinsurance Corporation* v. *Abate
Fantaye*, Supreme Court, 20 June 1986, (1991) 86 ILR 655–91 at 691.

[177] *Cf.* the drafting history of Article 105 of the UN Charter in Report of the Rapporteur of
Committee IV/2, as approved by the Committee, 13 UNCIO Doc. 933, IV/2/42(2) (1945),
704, where a clear distinction between diplomatic and organizational immunity law
seems to have been intended: 'In order to determine the nature of the privileges and
immunities, the Committee has seen fit to avoid the term "diplomatic" and has preferred to substitute a more appropriate standard, based, for the purposes of the Organization, on the necessity of realizing its purposes.'

immunities to diplomats, the traditional exterritoriality theory[178] and doctrines stressing their representative character are clearly no longer prevalent. They have been largely replaced by a 'functional necessity theory', the principle of *ne impediatur legatio*.[179] Thus, a comparable principle of *ne impediatur officia* for international organizations could well be justifiable[180] and lead to the adoption of diplomatic immunity principles in the context of international organizations.

A result-oriented immunity standard protecting the functioning of international organizations

In trying to ascertain the scope of an international organization's functional immunity, commentators usually focus on the activity in question and attempt to determine whether it falls within the tasks of the organization. Considering that a major rationale for granting immunity from suit lies in the purpose of protecting an organization's functioning, one might wonder whether the question could not be put differently. Instead of looking at the act of the international organization in question (whether it is necessary to fulfil its official functions, etc.), it might be more appropriate to concentrate on the (anticipated) consequences of denying immunity. If those consequences would impede the organization's activities (e.g., court orders to perform specific acts as distinguished from mere orders to make payment) and thereby threaten its proper functioning, then they should be refrained from.[181]

Such a result-oriented immunity test would focus less on the functions than on the underlying non-interference rationale as a yardstick for the

---

[178] *Cf.* Brownlie, *Principles*, 348.

[179] *Cf. Yearbook of the International Law Commission* (1958), vol. II, 95. See also Denza, 'Diplomatic Agents and Missions', 1041, characterizing the codification results of the Vienna Convention on Diplomatic Relations 1961 as rules 'justified by the functional need for ambassadors and their staffs to act without fear of coercion or harassment by enforcement of local laws and to communicate freely and securely with their sending governments'.

[180] Bekker, *The Legal Position*, 155. See also Max Egger, *Die Vorrechte und Befreiungen zugunsten internationaler Organisationen und ihrer Funktionäre* (dissertation, Berne, 1953) (Vienna, 1954), 149; ILC Report of its 41st Session, *Yearbook of the International Law Commission* (1989), vol. II, Part Two, 136.

[181] Cully introduces in her 'Proposal for Restricted Immunity under the IOIA' elements of such a non-interference yardstick. In her plea for restricted immunity for international organizations she would include only suits for money damages: 'Because injunctions by their very nature interfere (or have the appearance and capability of interfering) with the organization's conduct of its public affairs, even restricted immunity should allow only money damages, not injunctive relief.' Kathleen Cully, 'Jurisdictional Immunities of Intergovernmental Organizations' (1982) 91 *Yale Law Journal* 1167–95 at 1179, note 106.

scope of immunity. It would certainly exclude many petty claims from immunity, giving access to court and thereby a means to pursue the rights of contractors, persons injured by tortious acts of international organizations, etc. At the same time, it could ensure that no judicial action will be taken that might threaten the work of an international organization. Although certainly somewhat unorthodox in the context of jurisdictional immunity, such a balancing test is not wholly unknown to domestic courts in deciding jurisdictional issues. In particular, US courts, when called upon to decide act of state or jurisdiction to adjudicate questions, are familiar with balancing tests specifically taking into consideration the consequences of their jurisdictional decisions.[182] If it were applied as the sole criterion, however, it might lead to problematic, even arbitrary results: in two otherwise substantially identical claims against an organization, one might be excluded if it involves a large sum of money potentially endangering the functioning of the organization, while the other would be allowed if it concerned only a small sum of money.

The grant of immunity made dependent upon alternative dispute resolution procedures

Another result-oriented method of determining whether immunity should be granted to an international organization in a particular case would focus on the availability of alternative means of judicial or quasi-judicial dispute settlement in a specific situation. One of the major advantages of such an approach seems to lie in the fact that it could adequately address two important concerns stemming from the grant or denial of immunity: it might satisfy constitutional or human rights concerns for the protection of the private parties involved, in particular their right to access to court; and equally it might enable international organizations to protect their interests.

Similar balancing of interests tests are used in other jurisdictional fields. For instance, the question of whether domestic courts should uphold the extraterritorial jurisdiction to prescribe of the forum state is frequently determined by a number of factors balanced against each other. Among the factors whether or not, and sometimes to what degree, such legislative jurisdiction should be exercised are considerations con-

---

[182] *Cf.* the US Supreme Court's opinion on the applicability of the act of state doctrine: 'the less important the implications of an issue are for our foreign relations, the weaker the justification for exclusivity in the political branches.' *Banco Nacional de Cuba* v. *Sabbatino*, 376 US 398 at 428 (1964). See also pp. 86 and 92 above.

cerning the potential interference with other states' jurisdictions, comity considerations, etc.[183] However, there are only few and very cautious examples of the exercise of a 'vicarious jurisdiction' in other fields. For instance, in the litigation following the disaster at Bhopal, a US district court in *Re Union Carbide Corp. Gas Plant Disaster* declared itself a *forum non-conveniens* on a conditional basis as long as adequate judicial protection was guaranteed in Indian courts which it considered the appropriate ones to exercise jurisdiction.[184]

To date only a few courts have shown a certain awareness of the lack of an alternative forum in determining immunity issues.[185] In practice, most courts have not been impressed by the argument that they should avoid a situation where an aggrieved party would be left without any forum to which he or she could address his or her complaint and that they should therefore declare themselves competent in the absence of an alternative forum.[186] In other words, the jurisdictional *horror vacui* of

---

[183] According to *Restatement (Third)*, § 403, the exercise of jurisdiction to prescribe is always limited by a reasonableness test 'determined by evaluating [a list of] relevant factors'. *Restatement (Third)*, § 403, para. 2.

[184] On the basis of *forum non conveniens*, the district court dismissed the action on three conditions: (1) that the defendant consented to the jurisdiction of the Indian courts and waived any possible statute of limitations defence; (2) that the defendant agreed to satisfy any Indian judgment rendered according to 'minimal requirements of due process'; and (3) that the defendant agreed to be subject to US discovery rules. 634 F. Supp. 842 (SDNY 1986). The circuit court, however, revoked the second and third of these conditions. The revocation of the second condition was based not on a perception that this kind of supervisory jurisdiction might impose US due process concepts upon the Indian courts, but rather on the concern that the condition 'as it is written ... imposed on the erroneous assumption that such a judgment might not otherwise be enforceable in the United States, may create misunderstandings and problems of construction'. In particular, the court feared that the reference to 'minimal requirements of due process' might lessen the 'due process' standard required to enforce an Indian judgment in New York courts as a matter of statutory law. It thus considered the district court's condition superfluous. 809 F. 2d 195 (2d Cir. 1987).

[185] See pp. 263*ff* above.

[186] Critics of *Mendaro* v. *World Bank*, US Court of Appeals, 27 September 1983, conclude that in this particular case, the US court should have exercised jurisdiction 'especially since Mendaro had nowhere else to turn due to the World Bank's lack of an internal dispute settlement mechanism at the time'. Norman G. Abrahamson, 'International Organizations – International Organizations Immunity Act – Waiver of Immunity for World Bank Denied, *Mendaro* v. *The World Bank* . . .' (1984) 8 *Suffolk Transnational Law Journal* 413–22 at 422. In 1985 the World Bank Administrative Tribunal rejected Mendaro's complaint as inadmissible because most events giving rise to the applicant's complaint had occurred before the entry into force of the Tribunal's Statute and because, to the extent they arose subsequently, the complaint was filed three years after the time limit had expired. *Mendaro* v. *IBRD*, World Bank Administrative Tribunal, 4 September 1985, (1985) *World Bank Administrative Tribunal Reports*, Decision No. 26.

those courts does not appear to be very strong. Sometimes they assure themselves of the existence of an alternative forum and sometimes – usually in a very generous fashion – they assume that due process is guaranteed by them, but they hardly scrutinize these requirements in a more thorough manner.[187] It is submitted, however, that courts should not only take into account the availability of alternative dispute settlement mechanisms as such, but also ascertain their appropriateness and fairness.[188] Thereby national courts would have to engage in a meritorious interest-balancing process.

What is required is a more imaginative use of legal possibilities. When courts relinquish their adjudicative power over a specific case, they normally do so on the basis of an *ex ante* evaluation of what standard of procedural fairness they expect the alternative forum to provide. There is usually no possibility of resuming jurisdiction where that expectation has been disappointed. Exactly this kind of fall-back guarantee, however, would be of crucial importance for individual litigants. It is clear that this might ultimately imply a danger of domestic supervision of international tribunals. However, what is legitimately supervised is only the guarantee of fair judicial proceedings and not the outcome. It should, at the most, correspond to the exercise of supervisory powers by the German Constitutional Court over the ECJ's fundamental rights guarantees according to its *Solange* jurisprudence[189] or to the very restricted supervision of inter-

---

[187] For instance, in *Hetzel v. Eurocontrol II*, Federal Constitutional Court, 10 November 1981, BVerfGE 59, 63, the German Constitutional Court did not think that the exclusive competence of the ILO Administrative Tribunal for labour disputes of Eurocontrol with its employees would deprive the affected individual of his or her right to access to court, because the procedure and jurisprudence of that tribunal satisfied the principles of the rule of law/legality. See pp. 292 and 310 above.

[188] In *Marré v. Istituto internazionale per l'unificazione del diritto privato (Unidroit)*, Tribunale Roma, 12 June 1965, the existence of an administrative tribunal competent to handle employment disputes was one of the reasons taken into consideration by the Tribunale Roma in upholding Unidroit's immunity from suit. It specifically held that the fact that Unidroit was not subject to Italian jurisdiction did not result in its 'immunity from any jurisdiction' since such relations could be validly and effectively dealt with by competent organs of international jurisdiction (i.e., Unidroit's administrative tribunal). In the earlier case of *Institut international pour l'agriculture v. Profili*, Corte di Cassazione, 26 February 1931 (see pp. 117 and 183 above) the Italian Supreme Court – evaluating the Institute's internal administrative dispute settlement mechanism – noted that '[o]pinions may be divided about the adequacy of such a remedy'. It nevertheless refrained from adjudicating concluding that 'though it may be evident that there is a need for a more progressive system, there is nothing which authorises the intervention of an external jurisdiction'. (1929–30) 5 *Annual Digest of Public International Law Cases* 415.

[189] See pp. 292f and 311 above.

national arbitration by domestic courts.[190] If a conditional renunciation of jurisdiction like the one used by the US court in the *Bhopal* case would be procedurally impossible in many other jurisdictions, a similar balancing could be undertaken by a more serious *ex ante* evaluation of the judicial guarantees provided by an alternative forum.

In this sense the question of whether a sort of vicarious jurisdiction of domestic courts over disputes involving international organizations should be upheld is certainly worth discussing. In the final consequence, the legitimate interests of private persons in a judicial forum competent to decide their claims against an organization may be satisfied in a subsidiary mode by national courts depending on the availability of internal procedures. Where they are not available or do not offer sufficiently fair remedies, domestic courts should step in and engage in vicarious dispute settlement. This would not only satisfy human rights concerns over a right of access to court but would also sufficiently protect the independence and functioning of international organizations which are regularly in a position to provide for alternative dispute settlement.

Substituting immunity by other concepts

As a radical alternative to attempts to find an appropriate standard of immunity below absolute immunity – one that would satisfy the competing interests of international organizations and their potential opponents before a national court – one could look beyond the currently prevailing paradigm of immunity and try to discover whether other legal concepts might form a substitute for immunity.

A plea for privileges

Immunity from suit and/or enforcement has the particularly irritating characteristic that the person enjoying such a prerogative cannot be held to perform whatever he or she may be legally obliged to do. The severance of the usual legal consequence of non-performance of a legal duty, i.e. enforcement through state organs, from the 'naked legal duty' leads to situations which appear even less acceptable than the lack of any substantial right *vis-à-vis* certain privileged persons.[191] Thus, one should consider whether – from a policy perspective – it would not be better to extend, where appropriate, the scope of privileges – in the sense of substantive exemptions from the law otherwise applicable[192] – while at the same time reducing the scope of jurisdictional immunity. Such an approach would have the clear advantage that the law is 'fully' applied. Private parties

---

[190] See pp. 306*ff* above.   [191] *Oppenheim's International Law*, 342.
[192] See the discussion on the terminology at pp. 13*ff* above.

would no longer be left with the unsatisfactory situation of holding a right against an immune person which they cannot procedurally pursue and enforce. The substantive exemptions should sufficiently guarantee that international organizations can function independently.

The granting of privileges to international organizations might also lead to a more equitable distribution of the overall burden on third parties. A comparison between the effects of a privilege and an immunity clearly demonstrates this relationship. In the case of fiscal privileges, the burden falls on the domestic community as a whole – to all the taxpayers in an equitable share.[193] Immunity from legal process, on the other hand, tends to lack such an equitable distributive element, because it burdens single persons, those dealing with international organizations, or in the case of torts even less justifiably third persons, at random. Even within these groups, not all members will be negatively affected to the same degree. In most cases international organizations will fulfil the obligations they owe as a matter of substantive law. Only the normally very small and – for that matter – accidentally determined group of persons whose rights are not satisfied will carry a disproportionate share of the burden. By eliminating immunity this danger of burdening third parties by chance would be clearly avoided.

An example of an area where privileges should be extended to – and as a matter of *lex lata* are regularly accorded – are the regulative aspects of employment law, law based on national policy considerations concerning the job market, affirmative action programmes, collective bargaining rights, etc.[194] International organizations should remain exempted from such national rules in order to prevent individual attempts to enforce rights based on this body of law. The exemption from another type of regulative legislation, from antitrust law, might equally be a proper example. Although private parties may suffer economic harm from the anti-competitive behaviour of international organizations as much as from any other competitors, a clarification that national law is not applicable would clearly be 'fairer' than its mere non-enforcement – as a result of jurisdictional immunity or another jurisdictional abstention rationale – as practised in *International Association of Machinists* v. *OPEC*.[195] A

---

[193] See also p. 241 above.   [194] See pp. 101*ff* above.

[195] US District Court CD Cal., 18 September 1979, *affirmed on other grounds*, US Court of Appeals 9th Cir., 6 July–24 August 1981. See pp. 90*ff* above for the details of this case. The district court's decision was based, *inter alia*, on the fact that certain material anti-trust law requirements were not met. The court held that foreign states were not persons amenable to suit under US anti-trust law; and that indirect purchasers, like plaintiffs, could not seek damages. 477 F. Supp. 553 at 572 and 574.

number of national competition laws make a similar public policy choice evident by exempting certain economic sectors or public bodies from the application of their competition rules.[196] Such a clarification on the basis of substantive law would have the additional advantage of avoiding the difficult *iure imperii/gestionis* distinction raised in anti-trust/competition law cases involving states and/or international organizations.[197]

The view defending (the traditional absolute) immunity as being re-quired to guarantee the independent functioning of an international organization (and thereby accepting that substantive obligations cannot be enforced) displays some similarities to an argument raised before, but rejected by, the ICJ in the *Effect of Awards* case.[198] It was claimed that, even if one conceded that the UN General Assembly had the implied power to establish an administrative tribunal, this could not limit the General Assembly's independent discretion in approving the organization's budget. As in the case of a domestic court's adjudication against an international organization, the independent decision of an organization to make payments according to a substantive obligation would surely also be limited by an administrative tribunal's decision. However, in the *Effect of Awards* opinion itself, the ICJ rejected the claim that the budgetary power of the General Assembly was 'absolute' because 'some part of [the UN's] expenditure arises out of obligations already incurred by the organ-ization, and to this extent the General Assembly has no alternative but to honour these engagements'.[199] This shows that the ICJ considered the substantive obligation already incurred by the UN (and as expressed in a

---

[196] For instance, section 5 of the Austrian Cartel Law exempts, *inter alia*, state monopolies from its scope of application.

[197] The distinction between *iure imperii* and *iure gestionis* acts of international organizations in competition cases has posed considerable difficulties for domestic courts. Frequently the courts focus on the underlying activity rather than on the anti-competitive behav-iour itself and thereby qualify what would otherwise be a 'commercial' activity (if performed by a private person) as *iure imperii* activity. In *International Association of Machinists* v. *OPEC*, US District Court CD Cal., 18 September 1979, *affirmed on other grounds*, US Court of Appeals 9th Cir., 6 July–24 August 1981, OPEC's activities of controlling their natural resources were considered fundamentally governmental, a qualification that was not changed by the fact that they formed a 'cartel'. Focusing more on the cartel aspect of OPEC's activities, Seidl-Hohenveldern still characterizes them as *iure imperii* acts (meriting immunity) for the reason that OPEC obliges its member states to make the price fixed by it binding on all oil-selling companies within their territories. Seidl-Hohenveldern, *Corporations*, 111. See also p. 291 note 177 above for cases concerning the qualification of the activities of Eurocontrol.

[198] *Effect of Awards of Compensation Made by the United Nations Administrative Tribunal*, (1954) *ICJ Reports* 47.

[199] *Ibid.*, 59.

binding decision of the UN administrative tribunal) more important than
the organization's independence to decide what kind of expenditure it
wished to make. It is submitted that one might expand this holding and
consider the honouring of substantive obligations more important than
the fully independent functioning of organizations. If an 'expenditure' is
really so substantial as to impede the functioning of an international
organization, one should rather try to eliminate it as a matter of substantive law. This, however, leads back to an issue of applicable law.[200] The
result again supports the idea that an exemption from the substantive
legal rules may be fairer to international organizations and third parties
than a procedural impediment of their enforcement.

Immunity or lack of adjudicative power

As already noted, the general development of the law of immunity from
jurisdiction – be it in the field of sovereign immunity or of diplomatic
immunities – seems to evidence a trend away from the personal 'prerogative' of potential defendants to the protection of a certain kind of activity.[201] In the sovereign immunity context, the notion of shielding the
foreign sovereign from any submission to a domestic court of another
sovereign (*par in parem non habet imperium*) has been largely replaced by a
perception that only a foreign state's public/sovereign acts require immunity. Even in the realm of diplomatic law, the idea that certain
persons are under no condition amenable to legal proceedings before the
courts of host states remains in force only for a small group of persons, i.e.
for diplomats,[202] while most of the staff working at embassies and, as a
matter of principle, all consular officers enjoy only functional immunity,[203] an immunity limited to acts performed in the course of their
official functions. In essence, this functional immunity standard limits
immunity to acts which could be qualified as acts performed in the
fulfilment of official tasks as opposed to private acts of diplomats.

These developments seem to evidence a shift from – what might be

---

[200] The UN's legislation in order to limit its tort liability by its 1986 Regulation No. 4 can
serve as an illustration for a 'substantive' attempt to protect the independent functioning of an international organization. See pp. 15f above.

[201] See p. 349 above.

[202] See Articles 31 and 37(1) of the Vienna Convention on Diplomatic Relations 1961
providing for a sweeping immunity from suit for members of the diplomatic staff and
their families.

[203] See Articles 37(2)–(4) and 38 of the Vienna Convention on Diplomatic Relations 1961 and
Article 43 of the Vienna Convention on Consular Relations 1963, basically limiting
immunity to acts 'performed in the course of their duties', and, 'in the exercise of
consular functions'.

called in traditional terminology – immunity *ratione personae* to immunity *ratione materiae*.[204] If one takes the emerging paramount standard of an immunity *ratione materiae* seriously it may be replaced by a concept of certain activities that will be beyond the adjudicative power of national courts rather than a concept of certain persons beyond their jurisdictional reach. This in turn might lead to a situation where traditional immunity thinking – which is still linked to categories of persons enjoying such immunity – might be replaced by a lack-of-jurisdiction doctrine based on material reasons.[205]

The evolution of the law of state immunity illustrates this shift from a personal prerogative of immunity to a rule of adjudicative abstention depending upon the substance of the underlying dispute in an exemplary fashion. According to the restrictive theory of immunity *acta iure gestionis* as determined by the nature of the act do not give rise to immunity from domestic legal proceedings.[206] These are by definition acts where an international legal person acts in the same way as a (legal) person of domestic law. They are thus governed by a specific national law. At the core of the restrictive theory of immunity lies the idea that the mere fact that the defendant in legal proceedings is a subject of international law by itself should not exclude legal recourse against it. This theory does, however, grant immunity for *acta iure imperii*, acts of a public character which can be performed only by someone with official authority. Where a state acts with public authority by granting licences, imposing taxes, etc., a legal relationship of subordination of the individual legal person of domestic law and a subject of international law is in question. In the context of internationally relevant immunity claims, these are normally issues of foreign public law relating to the state claiming immunity. Here, a correct understanding of the domestic tribunal's adjudicative power would normally lead to the conclusion that this power is lacking

---

[204] *Cf.* Brownlie, *Principles*, 331.

[205] James Crawford, 'International Law and Foreign Sovereigns: Distinguishing Immune Transactions' (1983) 54 *British Yearbook of International Law* 75–118 at 81; Richard A. Falk, *The Role of Domestic Courts in the International Legal Order* (Syracuse, NY, 1964), 139*ff.*

[206] *Cf.* Gamal Moursi Badr, *State Immunity* (The Hague, 1984); Helmut Damian, *Staatenimmunität und Gerichtszwang. Grundlagen und Grenzen der völkerrechtlichen Freiheit fremder Staaten von inländischer Gerichtsbarkeit in Verfahren der Zwangsvollstreckung oder Anspruchssicherung* (Berlin, Heidelberg, New York and Tokyo, 1985); Donald W. Greig, 'Forum State Jurisdiction and Sovereign Immunity Under the International Law Commission's Draft Articles' (1989) 38 *International and Comparative Law Quarterly* 243–76 at 243*ff*; Charles J. Lewis, *State and Diplomatic Immunity* (3rd edn, 1990); Christoph H. Schreuer, *State Immunity: Some Recent Developments* (Cambridge, 1988); and Ian Sinclair, 'The Law of Sovereign Immunity: Recent Developments' (1980 II) 167 *Recueil des Cours* 113–284.

when confronted with such issues of foreign public law. However, if there is no such adjudicative competence, the issue of immunity does not arise any more. Thus, the restrictive theory of immunity – understood as a question basically related to a tribunal's adjudicative power – may ultimately render any questions of immunity *ratione personae* superfluous.

If, on the other hand, a tribunal is competent to adjudicate a private law dispute involving a subject of international law as defendant, the restrictive theory of immunity would only affirm this result by denying a potential immunity for such acts *iure gestionis*. Here again a separate immunity test becomes superfluous.

Lessons for international organizations: which issues should be excluded from domestic adjudication?

The crucial question – if one tried to substitute a lack-of-jurisdiction rationale for immunity – is which issues should be excluded from domestic adjudication. Again one may seek guidance from inter-state relations and scrutinize which types of disputes domestic courts usually regard as not appropriate for them to decide.

Lack of jurisdiction over foreign public law

As a rule – in most domestic legal systems – courts will decline to hear cases involving disputes of a 'constitutional' law character of foreign states or 'administrative' law cases concerning, for instance, civil servants of another state, etc.[207] The legal reasons for this jurisdictional abstention may be manifold. In some countries, particularly in common

---

[207] *Cf.* Brownlie, *Principles*, 334; Otto Kahn-Freund, 'Review of Foreign Law?' in Flume, Hahn, Kegel and Simmonds (eds.), *Internationales Recht und Wirtschaftsordnung. Festschrift für F. A. Mann* (Munich, 1977), 207–25 at 207; and Ignaz Seidl-Hohenveldern, 'Jurisdiction over Employment Disputes in International Organizations' in University of Oviedo (ed.), *Colección de Estudios Jurídicos en Homenaje al Prof. Dr D. José Pérez Montero* (1988), vol. III, Oviedo, 359–72 at 367; *cf.* also Sucharitkul, 'Fifth Report on Jurisdictional Immunities of States and Their Property' in *Yearbook of the International Law Commission* (1985), vol. II, Part One, 25 at 36, surveying the current practice of states and concluding that '[t]here appears to be a general absence of jurisdiction or reluctance to exercise jurisdiction in the field of labour relations'. See also Michael Akehurst, *The Law Governing Employment in International Organizations* (Cambridge, 1967), 12, stressing the parallel between employment relations within international organizations and the civil service of foreign states: 'Courts in all countries usually refuse to handle questions of foreign public law and, in the same way, a number of municipal courts have held themselves incompetent to judge claims brought by international civil servants against the organizations which employ then, not on the ground of immunity, but on the grounds of the special law applicable.' Similarly, see Jean Duffar, *Contribution à l'étude des privilèges et immunités des organisations internationales* (Paris, 1982), 61.

law jurisdictions, it may be the result of a domestic rule such as the judge-made act of state and non-justiciability doctrines,[208] or it could be the consequence of the application of a 'foreign revenue law' principle.[209] According to the classic eighteenth-century formulation of this principle in *Holman* v. *Johnson*,[210] 'no country ever takes notice of the revenue laws of another'. Subsequently, the scope of 'revenue laws' has been broadly understood covering various kinds of 'public' (or sometimes 'political') law – as distinct from private law which is and remains a proper body of law to be applied by foreign courts as is evidenced by the rules of conflict of laws. Next to fiscal provisions, penal laws, expropriation legislation, etc., have been denied application/recognition by foreign courts.[211] The revenue rule has been limited, however, in so far as it has been construed by courts to exclude only the direct or indirect 'enforcement' of foreign public laws, which means that they need not always be totally ignored.[212]

In civil law countries the non-application of foreign public law is probably a consequence rather of the general dichotomy of public and private law and of the particular scope of conflict of laws.[213] International private law (the civil law equivalent to conflict of laws) is considered to be a part of private law. It contains conflict rules determining which (foreign or domestic) private law should be applied in a particular situation. As a

---

[208] See pp. 85*ff* and 96*ff* above. *Cf.* also the English decision *Buck* v. *Attorney-General* [1965] 1 All ER 882 at 887, characterizing as one of the rules of comity the principle that one state 'does not purport to exercise jurisdiction over the internal affairs of any other independent state, or to apply measures of coercion to it or to its property, except in accordance with the rules of public international law'. See also the broad abstention rationale relied upon by the court in *Westland Helicopters Ltd* v. *Arab Organisation for Industrialisation*, High Court, Queen's Bench Division, 3 August 1994, [1995] 2 All ER 387 at 397, according to which the 'adjudication of the question of the validity of the act of a foreign sovereign state measured by the principles of public international law is no more appropriate in the English courts than is adjudication of the validity of the acts within its territory of a foreign sovereign state by reference to its own constitutional powers'.

[209] *Cf.* P. B. Carter, 'Rejection of Foreign Law: Some Private International Law Inhibitions' (1984) 55 *British Yearbook of International Law* 111–31 at 114*ff*; Andreas F. Lowenfeld, *International Litigation and Arbitration* (St Paul, MN, 1993), 7*ff*; and Wilhelm Wengler, 'Über die Maxime von der Unanwendbarkeit ausländischer politischer Gesetze' (1956) 1 *Internationales Recht und Diplomatie* 191–206 at 191*ff*.

[210] King's Bench, 1775.

[211] Cheshire and North, *Private International Law* (ed. by P. M. North and J. J. Fawcett, 11th edn, London, 1987), 112*ff*.

[212] *Ibid.*, 115; Kegel, *Internationales Privatrecht*, 673. *Cf.* also P. B. Carter, 'Transnational Recognition and Enforcement of Foreign Public Laws' (1989) 48 *Cambridge Law Journal* 417–35 at 417*ff*, as to the problematic distinction between mere (permitted) 'recognition' and (prohibited) 'indirect enforcement' of foreign public law under the revenue rule.

[213] Kegel, *Internationales Privatrecht*, 675.

rule, public law (foreign or domestic) remains outside its perspective. Even where public law may be taken into consideration, civil law countries also frequently follow an (at least presumed[214]) conflicts rule of the non-application of foreign public law.[215] It seems that this rule is sometimes derived from the concept of a purely territorial scope of public law.[216]

The political reasons for this – almost universally applied – jurisdictional abstention principle are easier to explain than its precise content. Claims based on public law are usually closely connected to the interests of the respective *res publica* (whether the state is a republic or not is irrelevant), and it would not serve any self-serving interests of one state to enforce the public laws (serving the public interests) of another state.[217]

These exclusionary rules are normally special domestic rules of conflict of laws. It is doubtful whether one could argue that they form part of international law, in particular whether one could deduce an international duty of domestic courts to abstain from handling disputes involving foreign public law.[218] However, the assertion that there is no duty under international law to enforce the public law of another state usually

---

[214] *Cf.* the scepticism shown in the IDI Resolution on 'The Application of Foreign Public Law', adopted at its Wiesbaden Session 1975, (1975) 56 *Annuaire de l'Institut de Droit International* 551, speaking of a 'so-called principle of the inapplicability *a priori* of foreign public law' (Article II).

[215] Bernhard Grossfeld, *Praxis des Internationalen Privat- und Wirtschaftsrechts* (Hamburg, 1975), 95.

[216] Pierre Lalive, 'L'application du droit public étranger, Rapport préliminaire' (1975) 56 *Annuaire de l'Institut de Droit International* 157–83 at 168; Kegel, *Internationales Privatrecht*, 673; see also the cases discussed by F. A. Mann, *Zu den öffentlichrechtlichen Ansprüchen ausländischer Staaten, ein Rückblick nach 30 Jahren, Festschrift Kegel* (1987), 365–88 at 380. It has been concluded by Seidl-Hohenveldern, 'Jurisdiction over Employment Disputes', 367, that '[d]omestic courts enjoying jurisdiction on [sic!] disputes concerning acts of a public law nature possess such power only concerning acts under their domestic public law'. See also the IDI Resolution on 'The Application of Foreign Public Law', which opposes not only the 'so-called principle of the inapplicability *a priori* of foreign public law', but also 'that of its absolute territoriality' (Article II). Nevertheless, its Article IV recognizes among the reasons why 'foreign law which is regarded as public law is still applied less frequently [are] because the foreign provision is restricted in its scope to the territory of the legislator from whom it originates and because such restriction is in principle respected'. (1975) 56 *Annuaire de l'Institut de Droit International* 553.

[217] Kegel, *Internationales Privatrecht*, 674.

[218] Accordingly, Article I(1) of the IDI Resolution on 'The Application of Foreign Public Law' denies such a duty to abstain: 'The public law character attributed to a provision of foreign law which is designated by the rule of conflict of laws shall not prevent the application of that provision, subject however to the fundamental reservation of public policy.'

rests upon the assumption that it is the foreign state or its organs seeking such enforcement.[219] It may well be that, where an individual seeks to enforce a public law claim against a foreign state, the exercise of jurisdiction over such a claim might interfere with that foreign state's rights and thus warrant an obligation of the forum state to abstain from adjudicating.[220]

Internal law of international organizations as a taboo for national courts

A possible justification for excluding lawsuits against international organizations without recurring to a wholesale immunity concept might lie in a kind of specific choice-of-law rule with jurisdictional effect. According to this rule, the internal (i.e., the constitutional and administrative[221]) law of international organizations could be viewed as unsuited for adjudication by domestic courts. Such a rule of excluding the internal law of an international organization cannot be justified by the formal argument that it is a particular kind of international law. Quite a substantial part of international law in fact relies on its enforcement (and thus its application) by national courts. Sometimes there is even a constitutional law obligation for domestic organs to do so.[222] A norm requiring abstention from applying certain parts of international law has to find some distinguishing trait. The non-application or abstention rationale is more likely to be based on the materially analogous character of an international organization's internal law to the constitutional and administrative law rules of states. There are two basic types of international norms in connection with international organizations which may require judicial abstention by national courts: on the one hand, those of an 'administrative' quality; and, on the other hand, those of a 'constitutional' character. Both could be considered to form

---

[219] See the IDI Resolution on 'Public Law Claims Instituted by a Foreign Authority or a Foreign Public Body', adopted at its Oslo Session 1977, (1977 II) 57 *Annuaire de l'Institut de Droit International* 329, whose Article I(a) states that '[p]ublic law claims instituted in legal proceedings by a foreign authority or a foreign public body should, in principle, be considered inadmissible in so far as, from the viewpoint of the State of the forum, the subject matter of such claims is related to the exercise of Governmental power'.

[220] See Crawford, 'International Law and Foreign Sovereigns', 88, mentioning the 'principle that some matters are exclusively or primarily matters for a particular State to determine ... relat[ing] particularly to the organization and legal relations of the State' as one of 'a number of established international law rules [which] can be regarded as underlying the notion of restrictive immunity'.

[221] *Cf.* pp. 378*ff* below.

[222] E.g., custom and general principles form part of the 'law of the land' in Austria and Germany and, through judicial construction, in the US and other states; similarly, treaties are to be directly applied in many legal systems. See also pp. 46*f* above.

part of an international organization's 'internal law'[223] or 'internal relations'.[224]

The 'administrative' aspect of the internal law of an international organization would probably find a parallel – if other states were concerned and not international organizations – in the concept that a foreign state's public law or other governmental act cannot be questioned by the courts of another state, thus leading to the incompetence/lack of jurisdiction, etc., of such national courts. As already noted above, a wholesale and unqualified exclusion of foreign public law from the application and recognition by domestic courts no longer seems tenable as such.[225] Equally, a broad exclusion of everything that might be termed the 'administrative law of international organizations' may lead to unwelcome results.[226] It appears correct, however, to maintain that – parallel to the development between states[227] – the administrative law of international organizations *stricto sensu*, i.e. employment issues governed by staff rules and regulations,[228] should be excluded from domestic

---

[223] As to the 'internal law' of international organizations, see in general Rudolph Bernhardt, 'International Organizations, Internal Law and Rules' in Rudolf Bernhardt (ed.), *Encyclopedia of Public International Law* (2nd edn, 1995), vol. II, 1314–18 at 1315, who defines it as the 'norms for the internal order of the organization contained in the basic treaty as well as the "secondary" rules enacted by the organization'. Although hesitant to describe its content in an abstract and general fashion, he counts among its typical content the purposes and principles of a given organization, its powers and organizational structure, the status and number of its officials and functionaries, etc.

[224] Seyersted subsumes under 'internal relations *stricto sensu*' over which international organizations exercise 'inherent jurisdiction' 'in the first place all relations between and within the organisation and its organs and officials as such. It comprises also relations with member States (and their representatives) in their capacity as members of the organs of the organisation.' Seyersted, 'Jurisdiction over Organs', 69.

[225] See pp. 374*ff* above.

[226] Sometimes the technical rules developed by international administrative unions are characterized as 'international administrative law' leading to broad definitions encompassing the law of functional cooperation between states. *Cf.* Hans-Joachim Priess, *Internationale Verwaltungsgerichte und Beschwerdeausschüsse, Eine Studie zum gerichtlichen Rechtsschutz für Beamte internationaler Organisationen* (Berlin, 1989), 166*ff*. This notion of 'international administrative law' would clearly transgress the scope of an organization's internal law.

[227] See p. 374 note 207 above.

[228] *Cf.* Wolfgang Friedmann and Arghyrios A. Fatouros, 'The United Nations Administrative Tribunal' (1957) 11 *International Organization* 13–29 at 29, speaking of 'international administrative law in the narrow sense'; see also Georges Langrod, *The International Civil Service* (Leiden and Dobbs Ferry, NY, 1963), 85; Priess, *Internationale Verwaltungsgerichte*, 168; and Thomas G. Weiss, *International Bureaucracy* (Lexington, Toronto and London, 1975), xvi. It is clear, however, that the exact borderline between 'administrative' and 'private' issues involving staff members of international organizations is not always easy to draw. For instance, it is not so obvious as the court in *Chiriboga v. IBRD*, US District

adjudication.[229] Some national judgments demonstrate that courts are quite able to exempt international organizations from domestic adjudication in such administrative matters without recurring to a concept of immunity.[230] Such decisions have been rightly characterized as 'refusals of the national courts . . . not based upon the immunity of intergovernmental organizations from suit in municipal courts *ratione personae* – but on the fact that the suit concerned matters which were within the exclusive jurisdiction of the organization (incompetence *ratione materiae*)'.[231]

In a similar way, the proposition could be made that 'constitutional' quarrels of or within international organizations are not proper subjects for national courts. Disputes between member states or different organs of an international organization or between members and organs could be seen as such constitutional issues. In this context the non-interference and independence argument in favour of abstention has its just place. In such cases the claim that 'activities of [an] organization should be carried out exclusively under the supervision of its governing bodies and should not be subjected to decisions of the national authorities of any single

Court DC, 29 March 1985, obviously thought that the insurance benefits claim by the beneficiaries of a World Bank employee who died in a plane crash was an employment dispute and therefore fell outside the jurisdiction of a national court. The OECD Administrative Tribunal was recently confronted with a similarly difficult issue. In *Johansson* v. *Secretary-General of the OECD*, OECD Administrative Tribunal, 25 June 1997, Judgment No. 22, it declined to deal with a dispute between the heirs of a deceased OECD employee concerning her legal guardianship.

[229] Akehurst, *The Law Governing Employment*, 12, for instance, is of the opinion that 'the special nature of the law governing employment in international organizations, closely linked as it is with delicate questions of administrative policy, makes municipal tribunals totally unsuited to deal with it'.

[230] See the early Italian Supreme Court judgment in *Institut international pour l'agriculture* v. *Profili*, Corte di Cassazione, 26 February 1931 (see pp. 117 and 183 above) qualifying the Institute as an 'international legal person' whose 'power of self-determination or autonomy . . . include[d] that of arranging its own organisation and controlling the relations of the organisation in their aspects both normal and exceptional, [which] rules out all state interference and all authority of its laws, substantive and procedural'. (1929–30) 5 *Annual Digest of Public International Law Cases* 415. See also the cases discussed at pp. 114*ff* above.

[231] Finn Seyersted, 'Settlement of Judicial Disputes of Intergovernmental Organizations by Internal and External Courts' (1963) 24 *Zeitschrift für ausländisches öffentliches Recht und Völkerrecht* 1–121 at 79. See also Werner Gloor, 'Employeurs titulaires de l'immunité de juridiction' in Universités de Berne, Fribourg, Geneva, Lausanne et Neuchatel, Enseignement de 3e cycle de droit 1987 (eds.), *Le juriste suisse face au droit et aux jugements étrangers, ouverture ou repli?* (1988), 263–89 at 270. Karl Zemanek, 'Die Rechtsstellung der internationalen Organisationen in Osterreich' (1958) 13 *Osterreichische Juristenzeitung* 380–81 at 381, speaks of 'sachliche[n] internationale[n] Unzuständigkeit' in staff disputes of international organizations.

Member State'[232] can be justly based on functional considerations attempting to ensure the independence of an organization.

This proposal for excluding certain constitutional disputes from the adjudicative power of domestic courts also finds some support in treaty practice: for a few international organizations, treaty clauses expressly provide for the possibility to be sued before national courts. Those clauses, however, try to ensure that only traditional private law disputes may reach domestic fora by excluding constitutional disputes from the adjudicative power of the national courts otherwise competent. They regularly do so by specifically excluding actions brought by member states and sometimes aim at channelling disputes concerning the relationship between members and the organization into special (regularly intra-organizational) dispute settlement mechanisms. While, for instance, the constituent regime of the World Bank does not provide for its immunity from suit in domestic courts, it expressly excludes actions 'brought by members or persons acting for or deriving claims from members'.[233] National courts interpreted this exclusion of suits intended as a safeguard to prevent that member states intruded into 'essential policy decisions . . . entrusted to [the Bank's] officers and Board'.[234] Other constituent agreements of international economic organizations – which contain the same exemption clause from the organization's immunity as the World Bank – expressly provide that constitutional disputes should be settled in non-national fora.[235] The immunity regime of the Multilateral Investment Guarantee Agency also demonstrates an increased awareness that next to constitutional disputes administrative ones should also be expressly removed from the adjudicative power of domestic courts.[236]

---

[232] See FAO, Office of the Legal Counsel, 'Constitutional Matters' (1982) *United Nations Juridical Yearbook* 113.

[233] Article VII(3) of the IBRD Articles of Agreement. See p. 141 note 545 above for the entire text.

[234] *Lutcher SA Celulose e Papel* v. *Inter-American Development Bank*, US Court of Appeals DC Cir., 13 July 1967, 382 F. 2d 454 at 458 (DC Cir. 1967).

[235] The Agreement on the Common Fund for Commodities makes this clear: 'Nevertheless, Associated ICOs [International Commodity Organizations], ICBs [International Commodity Boards], or their participants shall have recourse to such special procedures to settle controversies between themselves and the Fund as may be prescribed in agreements with the Fund, and, in the case of Members, in this Agreement and in any rules and regulations adopted by the Fund.' Article 42 of the Common Fund for Commodities Agreement.

[236] Article 44 of the MIGA Convention states: 'Actions other than those within the scope of Articles 57 [disputes between the Agency and members] and 58 [disputes involving holders of a guarantee or reinsurance to be arbitrated] may be brought against the Agency only in a court of competent jurisdiction in the territories of a member in which the Agency has an office or has appointed an agent for the purpose of accepting

The division of adjudicative power between the organization's tribunal and the member states' national courts in the European Community also reflects this basic distinction. It still is one of the most modern solutions creating a viable system protecting the functioning of the organization and at the same time the interests of private parties without granting any immunity from suit. All it provides for is a division of adjudicative power. It basically foresees the ECJ's jurisdiction in constitutional[237] and administrative[238] disputes brought against the Community. With the exception of tort claims against the EC, for which the ECJ has exclusive jurisdiction,[239] other 'private' disputes 'to which the Community is a party shall not on that ground be excluded from the jurisdiction of the courts or tribunals of the Member States'.[240] In other words, this jurisdiction of domestic courts is not limited by the Community's immunity, but only by the exclusivity of the expressly granted scope of jurisdiction of the ECJ. Such a system of a division of adjudicative power between an internal court of an organization and the domestic courts of its members ensures that constitutional and administrative issues, as part of the internal law of an international organization, are removed from the adjudicative competence of domestic courts.

The idea of an exclusion of certain constitutional disputes of international organizations from the adjudicative power of domestic courts is also backed by some national judicial decisions where the applicable rules do not clearly provide for abstention. 'The great care with which the English courts strive to avoid decision-taking which would be likely to involve a determination of issues arising between foreign sovereign states'[241] can be observed, for instance, in Re International Tin Council,[242] the refusal to grant a winding-up petition against the ITC, because:

Any attempt by one of the member states to assume responsibility for the administration and winding up of the organisation would be inconsistent with

---

service or notice of process. No such action against the Agency shall be brought (i) by members or persons acting for or deriving claims from members or (ii) in respect of personnel matters. The property and assets of the Agency shall, wherever located and by whomsoever held, be immune from all forms of seizure, attachment or execution before the delivery of the final judgment or award against the Agency.' (emphasis added).

[237] Articles 173–176 of the EC Treaty concerning annulment actions and actions for failure to act.

[238] Ibid., Article 179 concerning employment disputes.   [239] Ibid., Article 178.

[240] Ibid., Article 183.

[241] Westland Helicopters Ltd v. Arab Organisation for Industrialisation, [1995] 2 All ER 387 at 409.

[242] High Court, Chancery Division, 22 January 1987.

the arrangements made by them as to the manner in which the enterprise is to be carried on and their relations with each other in that sphere regulated.[243]

In *Westland Helicopters Ltd* v. *Arab Organisation for Industrialisation*,[244] an English court held that:

Questions as to the meaning, effect and operation of [the] constitution [of an international organization] in so far as they arise between the parties to the treaty are issues which . . . can only be determined by reference to the treaty and to the principles of public international law. Once the material issues are inter-state issues, they can no longer be resolved by any body of domestic law.[245]

The court concluded that:

Such issues can be decided only by reference to public international law, by a public international law forum and not by an English municipal court, for both issues necessarily involve the determination of whether foreign sovereign states are acting consistently or inconsistently with the rules of public international law.[246]

In 1950 in *Balfour, Guthrie & Co. Ltd et al.* v. *United States et al.*,[247] a US court, while upholding an 'ordinary' action for damages brought by the UN against the US, came to the fundamental conclusion that – with regard to constitutional disputes – it was:

apparent that Article 104 of the Charter of the United Nations [enabling the UN to be a party to legal proceedings before national courts] was never intended to provide a method for settling differences between the United Nations and its members.[248]

However, it clearly did not regard the tort claim brought as a constitutional dispute between a member and the organization. Rather, it thought that:

The wide variety of activities in which [international organizations] engage is likely to give rise to claims against their members that can most readily be disposed of in national courts. The present claim is such a claim. No political overtones surround it. No possible embarrassment to the United States in the conduct of its international affairs could result from such a decree as this court might enter.[249]

---

[243] [1987] 1 All ER 890 at 903.   [244] High Court, Queen's Bench Division, 3 August 1994.
[245] [1995] 2 All ER 387 at 407*ff*.   [246] *Ibid.*, 415.
[247] US District Court ND Cal., 5 May 1950. See pp. 47*f* and 205 above.
[248] (1950) 17 ILR 323 at 325.   [249] *Ibid.*

Testing the result against factual *topoi*

As noted above, it is useful to review the resulting proposals to deal with disputes involving international organizations from the viewpoint of various factual *topoi* in order to see whether the proposed rules would be appropriate in these factual situations.[250]

Personal services rendered to international organizations

The most frequent occasion for national courts to decide whether they should adjudicate a dispute involving an international organization arises from differences concerning personal services rendered to international organizations. As the survey of the existing practice has shown, the predominant conceptual framework of domestic courts to decide this issue is provided by immunity considerations.[251] Judgments basing their decision on other lack-of-adjudicative-power reasons are clearly less common.[252] It seems, however, that concepts of a lack-of-jurisdiction of domestic courts over the internal affairs of an organization might be a more appropriate *ratio decidendi* in such situations.

The lack of adjudicative power of domestic courts in employment-related disputes does not pose any serious problems where an alternative forum is available and where such a forum guarantees a fair procedure. This would not result in any serious human rights concerns and at the same time it would satisfy an international organization's interest in building on a coherent internal employment law unaffected by possibly diverging interpretations of national courts.

However, where – for whatever reason – no alternative forum is available, the individual's interest in having access to court should prevail over an international organization's interest in remaining undisturbed by lawsuits. The protection of the functioning and independence of international organizations does not seem to mandate that domestic courts relinquish their adjudicative power. The reasons usually provided for by domestic courts denying their jurisdiction (either because it involved the application of foreign administrative law or because of functional immunity, etc.) tend to miss the point. They usually refer to choice of law issues, where indeed the application of different employment regimes could hamper the functioning of an international organization because it could lead to a confusing system of partly overlapping and partly contradictory rules governing the various employment relationships between an international organization and its employees. However,

---

[250] See pp. 24*f* and 328 above.   [251] See pp. 157*ff* above.   [252] See pp. 99*ff* above.

to avoid this is a genuine choice of law issue. Different courts in different countries are perfectly able to apply one single uniform employment law of an international organization without necessarily distorting it.[253] To allow the adjudication of employment disputes by national courts would not necessarily mean that international organizations have to tolerate national court judgments that unduly interfere with their employment relations. Certainly, courts might adjudicate in ways that are not in harmony with what the applicable internal law calls for, by either misinterpreting the 'administrative rules' of employment or by wrongly deciding on the basis of domestic employment law instead of the applicable internal law of the organization – for instance, by applying national age discrimination laws where staff rules provide for mandatory retirement, or national paid maternity leave provisions where staff regulations contain no equivalent benefit. This would violate an international organization's right to non-interference with its internal employment policy *vis-à-vis* the forum state. Of course, it would be more convenient not to provide the possibility for such 'mis-judgments' at all. It seems, however, that the price for this convenience is simply too high where there is no other available forum. In such a situation a dispute should rather be settled at the international level where two near-equals confront each other and not on the back of individuals.[254]

Thus, the exclusivity of the jurisdiction of administrative tribunals should be regarded primarily as a matter of convenience – perfectly sensible as a matter of adjudicative efficiency because one can safely assume that administrative tribunals regularly have a higher expertise in applying an international organization's internal law than national courts who might be called to interpret such rules rather infrequently. However, such exclusivity cannot be viewed an inherently required necessity to guarantee the functioning of international organizations.

The second occasion for national courts to decide whether they should

---

[253] *Cf. Eckhardt* v. *Eurocontrol*, Local Court of Sittard, 25 June 1976, where a Dutch court, although it upheld its jurisdiction over an employment dispute, denied the plaintiff's request for relief on the ground that the applicable internal law of the organization did not provide for it. See pp. 106f above. The Belgian case of *Devos* v. *Supreme Headquarters Allied Powers Europe (SHAPE) and Belgium*, Court of Cassation, 13 November 1985, also shows that a national court may arrive at a correct legal assessment on the basis of the applicable law without referring to immunity. It rejected a claim arising under Belgian law as 'unfounded since the relations between the parties are not subject to the application of national law'. (1993) 91 ILR 242 at 245.

[254] See pp. 389f below.

adjudicate a dispute involving an international organization arises where private persons render services to international organizations outside a regular employment relationship. Here, human rights aspects will frequently gain even more weight because administrative tribunals are usually not open to disputes between an international organization and persons who render services to them without being part of the staff and because alternative dispute settlement mechanisms such as arbitration are not always provided for.

Furthermore, since such services are usually provided on the basis of a contract concluded under a domestic private law – normally the law of the country where the services are to be rendered or of the country where the organization has its seat – the argument that a 'foreign public law' like a foreign employment regime would not be properly interpreted and applied by domestic courts is not valid. On the contrary, national courts will normally be in the best position to adjudicate on labour contracts governed by the law of the forum state and they will be able to decide on foreign labour contracts by applying foreign private law. The danger of a misinterpretation of the applicable law, thus, appears to be rather low.

The functioning of international organizations is unlikely to be severely threatened, if domestic courts from time to time find that someone rendering professional or other personal services deserved a higher remuneration than actually paid by the international organization or would be entitled to compensation in case of dismissal. If one took a result-oriented protection-of-functioning rationale very seriously,[255] one could even argue that remedies should be limited to money damages and prohibit any form of injunctive relief that might possibly interfere with the independent functioning of an international organization.

Since claims based on the contractual provision of services by non-staff members fall squarely within the category of private law contracts, non-justiciability considerations based on non-interference rationales vis-à-vis an international organization's 'sovereign' decision-making are also clearly inapposite. On the contrary, the fact that they can usually be qualified as part of a potential claimant's 'civil rights and obligations' is a strong argument in favour of allowing domestic courts to decide such cases.

---

[255] Cf. pp. 365f above.

Provision of movable and immovable property

In the case of contractual relations with international organizations, a preponderance of arguments speaks in favour of having national courts decide disputes arising from the provision of movable and immovable property. Whether it is the determination of rights and obligations flowing from a contractual meeting of the minds or claims to property itself, it is always – as long as there is no private 'property' or 'contract' law of international organizations – an issue governed by the law of a particular country – whether of the forum or another – which a domestic court will be perfectly well suited to apply according to its rules of private international law/conflict of laws.

A lack of adjudicative power of domestic courts would remain to be justified in situations where private parties *inter se* would also have to accept it. Thus, specific choice of forum clauses, such as arbitration clauses or even contractual stipulations calling for adjudication by an administrative tribunal of an international organization,[256] should be honoured on the basis of respecting the autonomy of the contracting parties. In such situations, the issue is, of course, no longer one peculiar to international organizations before national courts.

Claims for damages against international organizations

Where tortious behaviour on the part of an international organization is concerned, the argument in favour of domestic courts is probably most convincing. The individual victim of an international organization's damaging act or activity normally could not foresee the specific status of the tortfeasor. Thus, any assumption-of-risk argument that might be valid for someone who voluntarily enters into legal relations with an international organization would be inapplicable.

However, claims for damages allegedly caused by international organizations are not limited to the simple tort cases such as car accidents, bricks falling from a headquarters building or slippery floors. Sometimes lawsuits are brought in order to dispute the legality of an international organization's core functions before domestic courts or allege the suffering of harm as a direct result of an international organization's activities. It is usually very difficult to differentiate between actions brought for the compensation of damage caused and those that truly aim at controlling the activities of an organization. Some of the really hard cases rest on the

---

[256] See pp. 108 *f* and *266ff* above.

allegation that an individual's rights have been hurt by the acts of an international organization.

What might be termed as a tort action against an organization may in fact sometimes concern human rights violations allegedly perpetrated by international organizations. The availability of remedies for fundamental rights violations – which has been termed a matter of a 'constitutional dimension'[257] – primarily concerns the relationship between an individual and an organization that is legally empowered to take actions which may directly affect his or her legal position. This is also the reason why such questions arise only in highly integrated organizations, usually supranational ones such as the European Communities. They primarily require an internal grievance procedure because it is considered a duty of those infringing fundamental rights to provide an effective remedy.[258] The example of the Communities where the ECJ has taken up this task – even without an express mandate to do so[259] – underlines this political, if not legal necessity. In exceptional cases, because of the serious nature of the damage inflicted, the competence of external courts to adjudicate such disputes would also be conceivable – at least on a vicarious or subsidiary basis. The jurisdiction of domestic courts for such claims could be based on reasons similar to those developed by the German Constitutional Court in its *Solange* cases.[260]

Another group of cases brought to recover damages from an organization which can be identified are those where a tort was committed incidental to the carrying out of official functions, where, for instance, damage was caused to persons and property in the course of peacekeeping activities or as a result of price-fixing activities while trading in certain raw materials. It is certainly true that international tribunals may be better equipped to determine the main activity to which the causing of damage is only incidental. There is no reason, however, why domestic courts should lack adjudicative power to decide the incidental damage

---

[257] *Accession by the Communities to the Convention for the Protection of Human Rights and Fundamental Freedoms*, Opinion 2/94, ECJ, 28 March 1996, [1996] ECR I-1759, para. 35.

[258] *Cf.* the expression of this thought in Article 8 of the Universal Declaration of Human Rights, Article 2(3) of the International Covenant on Civil and Political Rights, Article 13 of the European Convention on Human Rights, etc., requiring states to provide effective remedies for their potential human rights violations.

[259] See pp. 274f above.

[260] *Internationale Handelsgesellschaft mbH* v. *Einfuhr- und Vorratstelle für Getreide und Futtermittel*, Federal Constitutional Court, 29 May 1974; *Re Application of Wünsche Handelsgesellschaft*, Federal Constitutional Court, 22 October 1986. See pp. 292 and 311 above.

question as a matter of principle. They should, however, be prevented from mingling with the intra-organizational issue of the proper course of an organization's activities. Questions like this are usually constitutional matters for an organization. Such issues are, however, certainly matters that could serve as topics for an increased dialogue between domestic and international courts.

The ultimate guarantee of the independent functioning of international organizations: retrospective instead of anticipated protection

When international organizations are subjected to the adjudicative competence of domestic courts they should not remain wholly at the mercy of the latter. The ultimate guarantee of their legitimate interests could lie in an option to complain of eventual barriers and burdens to their independent functioning on the international level. Harassing and unjustified modes and results of adjudication could be regarded as a denial of justice on the part of the forum state of a court exercising jurisdiction over an international organization.

As outlined above the purpose of preventing such excessive judicial activities forms one of the legitimate policy reasons in the traditional context of according immunity.[261] At the core of the major abstention rationale, to protect the functioning of an international organization, appears to lie the notion that domestic courts might cause harm to an international organization's independence by unjustifiably condemning it to something that it is not obliged to do. In this context, it is crucial to differentiate between a legitimate 'protection of functioning' rationale and an overly broad one. Of course, it may be argued that any judgment against an international organization compelling it to do something interferes to a certain extent with its independence. However, if an international organization is – as a matter of substantive law – obliged to do exactly what it is also judicially required to do, the invocation of a procedural obstacle in order to shield it from such obligation does not appear legitimate. From this point of view, it seems that the protection of international organizations against adjudication by domestic courts is necessary only in cases where there is a danger that domestic courts abuse their power, adjudicate wrongly, etc. Assuming that domestic courts normally adjudicate claims brought against international organizations in a 'correct and proper way', i.e. according to the applicable

---

[261] See pp. 235*ff* above.

substantive law, it is hard to see where the harm to the independence and functioning of an international organization might lie. One may, of course, think that the precise content of a correct and proper decision on the merits would be harder to reach for national courts than for other dispute settlement fora. As far as courts have to base their judgments on domestic contract or tort law this concern appears to be unfounded. If they have to decide on the basis of an international organization's internal staff law, however, the correct application of the law, resulting in an adjudication of whatever might be the substance of an international organization's obligation, could be measured by the result reached by alternative fora such as arbitral or administrative tribunals. One should thus consider whether it would not be more appropriate to redress the harassment of international organizations by prejudiced and possibly (in a material sense) 'incompetent' courts only where they actually occur and only *via* 'international mechanisms', rather than by 'preventively' burdening private parties through immunity provisions.

If one looks at the typical interests of the actors involved in immunity situations, the international organization, its opposing party and the forum state,[262] the following might emerge. The private plaintiff clearly has a strong interest in the domestic court's jurisdiction in order to vindicate his or her substantive right. The international organization has a legitimate interest in its independent functioning which includes an interest not to be compelled to fulfil unwarranted judgments, but not in immunity for its own sake, nor – one has to add – in being freed from its substantive liability. The forum state is probably on the whole neutral, since it will have competing interests. It will be interested in the jurisdiction of its court in order to fulfil its general obligation to provide dispute settlement (a policy function in the broadest sense) which may also be a specific domestic constitutional obligation *vis-à-vis* individuals to provide access to court; on the other hand, it will have an interest in avoiding problems with international organizations – a political consideration that might be bolstered by legal obligations the forum state might have entered into requiring its courts to abstain from exercising jurisdiction.

In many situations an evaluation and balancing of those interests, which might be present in different cases to different degrees, will require that national courts uphold their jurisdiction. The protection of the legitimate interest of international organizations in not being harassed by domestic courts, etc. could be guaranteed on the international level

---

[262] See pp. 288f above as to this three-party relationship.

between the international organization and the forum state and need not be anticipated on the level of domestic courts since this normally burdens the individuals involved to an excessive extent. Where a state's judiciary has clearly impeded the independence and hampered the functioning of an international organization, this might give rise to an international claim concerning a denial of justice.[263]

[263] *Cf.* Lauterpacht's argument against state immunity: 'In fact it is not easy to see why the principle of independence and equality should preclude the courts of a state from exercising jurisdiction over a foreign state and its property so long as the state exercising jurisdiction merely applies its ordinary law, including its rules of private international law, and so long as it applies it in an unobjectionable manner not open to the reproach of a denial of justice.' Sir Hersch Lauterpacht, 'The Problem of Jurisdictional Immunities of Foreign States' (1951) 28 *British Yearbook of International Law* 220–72 at 229.

7   Conclusions

A number of conclusions may be drawn from the preceding inquiry, some of them confirming commonly held presumptions and opinions about the topic, while others might lead to a reappraisal of traditional views.

A descriptive analysis of how national courts react to international organizations as parties before them led to the important outcome that national courts do not exclusively 'solve' cases involving international organizations by resorting to the concept of immunity from jurisdiction. It demonstrated that, in fact, courts use a broad range of legal techniques in order to either avoid deciding such cases or to uphold their adjudicative power over such disputes. These methods range, on the one hand, from not recognizing the legal personality or the legal relevance of a particular act of an organization, prudential abstention doctrines, such as act of state, political questions or non-justiciability techniques, lack of adjudicative power theories, to classic immunity from suit concepts. On the other hand, courts may employ various strategies, from refusing to qualify an entity as an international organization, denying the legal relevance and applicability of immunity provisions, and restricting the scope of immunity, to a number of interpretative techniques of regarding the immunity granted waived, in order to assert jurisdiction over disputes involving international organizations.

National courts, on the whole, do not appear to be convinced that international organizations should enjoy absolute immunity from suit. They often find ways to exercise their adjudicative power over disputes involving international organizations. The method most frequently used in order to do so is the application of a restrictive immunity concept based on principles taken from the law of state immunity. This analogous application of sovereign immunity rules sometimes overlaps with the use of a functional immunity concept. Courts generally seem to agree on the need to accord functional immunity to international organizations. They have substantial difficulties, however, in shaping and thus applying the concept of functional immunity. Consequently, courts have interpreted functional immunity as absolute immunity, as immunity for *iure imperii* acts or only as a shield against actions challenging a core of official activities.

This study suggests that in assessing whether or not domestic courts should refrain from adjudicating disputes involving international organizations, policy considerations, in particular the following two, should be taken into account more closely:

1. the prevailing rationale for abstention, on the one hand, is the necessity for ensuring that international organizations are able to fulfil their functions independently without any outside influence; and
2. on the other hand, it seems to be crucial that the vindication of 'civil rights and obligations' of private parties *vis-à-vis* international organizations as well as of international organizations themselves is sufficiently guaranteed.

The fact that these interests are certainly conflicting does not necessarily mean that they both cannot be taken into account.

It appears that, in the majority of cases, a functional immunity rationale taken seriously requires only a relatively low level of immunity protection. Immunity is probably necessary in areas concerning the internal affairs of international organizations, i.e. in particular, in the case of 'constitutional' disputes, disputes between member states and organs, or between organs of an international organization. The subject matter of such disputes is usually an issue of and governed by public international law and involves the basic interests of an organization's member states. Such disputes should not be fought in the domestic forum of one of the member states but should rather be settled according to the internal dispute settlement mechanism provided for in the respective constitution of the international organization concerned or pursuant to traditional international dispute settlement means. On the other hand, abstention is probably not absolutely necessary in employment disputes between an international organization and its staff, although such relations are usually also regarded as part of the internal law of international organizations. There, the lack of jurisdiction of domestic courts – combined with the possibility of access to internal administrative tribunals – appears rather to be a matter of convenience to guarantee the development of a homogeneous case law of the civil service of international organizations.

The majority of disputes between an international organization and private third parties governed by a specific national law clearly does not warrant immunity. The legitimate interest, in particular, of private parties harmed by tortious acts of international organizations but also by the non-fulfilment of contractual obligations of the latter, in having access to domestic courts may not be regarded a fundamental right *de lege lata*. Its underlying policy reasons are strong enough to militate against a wholesale exemption of international organizations from the jurisdiction of national courts in such disputes.

It seems that a reinterpretation of the immunity concept currently applied to international organizations might adequately address the competing interests involved. A proportionate functional immunity standard below absolute immunity may be found in a strict functional immunity, for official acts only, by taking analogies from diplomatic and consular law in order to determine the scope of functional immunity, by using a result-oriented immunity protecting the functioning of international organizations, by applying a restrictive sovereign immunity standard as adequate functional immunity, or by making the grant of immunity to international organizations dependent upon the availability of alternative dispute settlement procedures.

It is, however, also worth considering whether the still very 'party-focused' concept of immunity from jurisdiction could not be replaced by different principles governing the attitude of national courts towards disputes involving international organizations. The gradual development in the field of state immunity, away from immunizing certain persons as potential defendants to granting immunity only for certain of their acts, illustrates a similar evolution. It is conceivable that a broader principle of not adjudicating internal disputes of international organizations, based on concepts such as act of state, the non-application of foreign public law, lack of jurisdiction over certain classes of disputes, etc., might eventually replace immunity by providing the necessary subject matter exemption for certain types of disputes required to guarantee the independent functioning of international organizations. In fact, some court decisions seem to evidence a trend in this direction.

Testing such an alternative concept of judicial activity and restraint against various factual situations and case law demonstrates that by limiting judicial abstention to 'internal matters' of an international organization the latter's independence and functioning could be safeguarded, and by enabling adjudication in 'ordinary' private law disputes involving international organizations the fundamental right of access to court could be guaranteed.

Bibliography

Abi-Saab, Georges (ed.), *The Concept of International Organization* (Paris, 1981)

Abla, Walid, *Les Conditions de recevabilité de la requête devant les tribuneaux administratifs de l'ONU et de l'OIT* (Paris, 1991)

Abrahamson, Norman G., 'International Organizations – International Organizations Immunity Act – Waiver of Immunity for World Bank Denied, *Mendaro v. The World Bank . . .*' (1984) 8 *Suffolk Transnational Law Journal* 413–22

Adam, Henri T., *Les établissements publics internationaux* (Paris, 1957)

    Les organismes internationaux spécialisés (Paris, 1965), vols I and II

    Les organismes internationaux spécialisés (Paris, 1967), vol. III

    Les organismes internationaux spécialisés (Paris, 1977), vol. IV

Ahluwalia, Kuljit, *The Legal Status, Privileges and Immunities of the Specialized Agencies of the United Nations and Certain Other International Organizations* (The Hague, 1964)

Alkema, E. A., 'The EC and the European Convention of Human Rights – Immunity and Impunity for the Community?' (1979) 16 *Common Market Law Review* 501–8

Akehurst, Michael, *The Law Governing Employment in International Organizations* (Cambridge, 1967)

    'Settlement of Claims by Individuals and Companies Against International Organisations' (1967–8) 37–8 *Annuaire de l'Association des auditeurs et anciens auditeurs de l'Académie de droit international de la Haye* 69–98

    A Modern Introduction to International Law (6th edn, London and New York, 1987)

Al-Kadhim, Nouri Mahmoud, *Diplomatic Privileges and Immunities of International Organizations and their Personnel* (unpublished PhD dissertation, University of Southern California, 1958)

Alvarez, Jose E., 'Judging the Security Council' (1996) 90 *American Journal of International Law* 1–39

Amerasinghe, C. F., 'The World Bank Administrative Tribunal' (1982) 31 *International and Comparative Law Quarterly* 748–64

    'Sources of International Administrative Law' in *Le droit international à l'heure de sa codification, Etudes en l'honneur de Roberto Ago* (Milan, 1987), vol. I, 67–96

    'The World Bank Administrative Tribunal: Its Establishment and its Work' in C. de Cooker (ed.), *International Administration* (looseleaf, The Hague, Boston and London, 1989–), V.3/1 to V.3/39

394

'Liability to Third Parties of Member States of International Organizations – Practice, Principle and Judicial Precedent' (1991) 85 *American Journal of International Law* 259–80

The Law of the International Civil Service (As Applied by International Administrative Tribunals), 2 vols (2nd edn, Oxford, 1994)

'International Legal Personality Revisited' (1995) 47 *Austrian Journal of Public and International Law* 123–45

Principles of the Institutional Law of International Organizations (Cambridge, 1996)

Amerasinghe, C. F. and Bellinger, D., 'Non-Confirmation of Probationary Appointments' (1983) 54 *British Yearbook of International Law* 167–207

American Jurisprudence (looseleaf, 2nd edn, Rochester, NY and San Francisco, 1985), vol. 18B, paras 1168–2168, 'Corporations'

Amrallah, B., 'The International Responsibility of the United Nations for Activities Carried out by UN Peace-Keeping Forces' (1976) 32 *Revue egyptienne de droit international* 57–82

Anzilotti, Dionisio, 'Gli organi communi nelle Societa di Stati' (1914) 8 *Rivista di diritto internazionale* 156–64

Cours de droit international (Paris, 1929)

Apprill, Claudette, 'La notion de "droit acquis" dans le droit de la fonction publique internationale' (1983) 87 *Revue générale de droit international public* 315–58

Arangio-Ruiz, Gaetano, *Diritto internazionale e personalità giuridica* (Milan, 1971)

'The "Federal Analogy" and UN Charter Interpretation: A Crucial Issue' (1997) 8 *European Journal of International Law* 1–28

Archer, Clive, *International Organizations* (2nd edn, London and New York, 1992)

Aristodemou, Maria, 'Applicability of Article VI, Section 22, of the Convention on the Privileges and Immunities of the United Nations' (1992) 41 *International and Comparative Law Quarterly* 695–701

Arsanjani, Mahnoush H., 'Claims Against International Organizations – *Quis custodiet ipsos custodes*' (1980–1) 7 *Yale Journal of World Public Order* 131–76

Aufricht, Hans, 'Personality in International Law' (1943) 37 *American Political Science Review* 217–43

'The Expansion of the Concept of Sovereign Immunity: With Special Reference to International Organizations' (1952) 46 *Proceedings of the American Society of International Law* 85–104

Austin, John, *The Province of Jurisprudence Determined* (ed. by H. L. A. Hart, London, 1954)

Baade, Hans W., 'The Acquired Rights of International Public Servants' (1966–7) 15 *American Journal of Comparative Law* 251–300

Badr, Gamal Moursi, *State Immunity* (The Hague, 1984)

Bajons, Ena-Marlies, *Zwischenstaatliches Justizrecht* (Vienna, 1989)

Balladore Pallieri, Giorgio, 'Le droit interne des organisations internationales' (1969 II) 127 *Recueil des Cours* 7–36

Ballreich, Hans, 'Die Europäische Atomgemeinschaft (Euratom)' (1958) 19 *Zeitschrift für ausländisches öffentliches Recht und Völkerrecht* 24–53

Barberis, Julio A., 'La personalidad juridica internacional' in Bernhardt, Geck, Jaenicke and Steinberger (eds.), *Völkerrecht als Rechtsordnung, Internationale Gerichtsbarkeit, Menschenrechte, Festschrift Mosler* (Berlin, Heidelberg and New York, 1983), 25–44

'Nouvelles questions concernant la personalité juridique internationale' (1983 I) 179 *Recueil des Cours* 145–304

'El Comité internacional de la Cruz Roja como sujeto del derecho de gentes' in Swinarski (ed.), *Etudes et essais sur le droit international humanitaire et sur les principes de la Croix-Rouge en l'honneur de Jean Pictet* (Geneva and The Hague, 1984), 635–41

Bardos, Richard, 'Judicial Abstention Through the Act of State Doctrine, *International Association of Machinists and Aerospace Workers* v. *Organization of Petroleum Exporting Countries* . . .' (1981–3) 7 *International Trade Law Journal* 177–92

Barnhoorn, L. A. N. M., 'Lijfsdwang tegen een personeelslid/deskundige van ESTEC' (1979) *De praktijk gids* 378–85

Barton, G. P., 'Foreign Armed Forces: Immunity from Supervisory Jurisdiction' (1949) 26 *British Yearbook of International Law* 380–413

'Foreign Armed Forces: Immunity from Criminal Jurisdiction' (1950) 27 *British Yearbook of International Law* 186–234

'Foreign Armed Forces: Qualified Jurisdictional Immunity' (1954) 31 *British Yearbook of International Law* 341–70

Basdevant, Suzanne, *Les fonctionnaires internationaux* (Paris, 1931)

Basse, Hermann, *Das Verhältnis zwischen der Gerichtsbarkeit des Gerichtshofs der Europäischen Gemeinschaften und der deutschen Zivilgerichtsbarkeit* (Berlin, 1967)

Bastid, Suzanne, *Le Droit des organisations internationales* (Paris, 1952)

'Les tribunaux administratifs internationaux et leur jurisprudence' (1957 II) 92 *Recueil des Cours* 343–517

'Have the UN Administrative Tribunals Contributed to the Development of International Law' in Friedmann, Wolfgang, Henkin, Louis and Lissitzyn, Oliver (eds.), *Transnational Law in a Changing Society. Essays in Honor of Philip C. Jessup* (New York and London, 1972), 298–312

Bastid, Suzanne and Bastid, David, *La personnalité morale et ses limites. Etudes de droit comparé et de droit international public* (Paris, 1960)

Bathurst, M. E., 'Jurisdiction over Friendly Foreign Armed Forces: The American Law' (1946) 23 *British Yearbook of International Law* 338–41

Batiffol, Henri, *Problèmes des contrats privés internationeaux* (Paris, 1961–2)

Baxter, Richard R., 'Jurisdiction Over Visiting Forces and the Development of International Law' (1958) 52 *Proceedings of the American Society of International Law* 174–80

'Multilateral Treaties as Evidence of Customary International Law' (1965–6) 41 *British Yearbook of International Law* 275–300

Treaties and Custom, (1970 I) 129 *Recueil des Cours* 24–105

Battaglia, Rosa Maria, 'Jurisdiction over NATO Employees' (1978–9) 4 *Italian Yearbook of International Law* 166–73

Bayer, W. F., 'Das Privatrecht der Montanunion' (1952) 17 *Rabels Zeitschrift für ausländisches und internationales Privatrecht* 325–81

Bedjaoui, Mohammed, *The New World Order and the Security Council. Testing the Legality of its Acts* (Dordrecht, Boston and London, 1994)

Beigbeder, Yves, *The Role and Status of International Humanitarian Volunteers and Organizations* (Dordrecht, Boston and London, 1991)

Beitzke, Günther, 'Zivilrechtsfähigkeit von auf Staatsvertrag beruhenden internationalen Organisationen und juristischen Personen' (1969) 9 *Berichte der Deutschen Gesellschaft für Völkerrecht* 77–119

Bekker, Peter H. F., 'The Work of the International Law Commission on "Relations Between States and International Organizations" Discontinued: An Assessment' (1993) 6 *Leiden Journal of International Law* 3–16
  The Legal Position of Intergovernmental Organizations. A Functional Necessity Analysis of Their Legal Status and Immunities (Dordrecht, Boston and London, 1994)

Benedek, Wolfgang, *Die Rechtsordnung des GATT aus völkerrechtlicher Sicht* (Berlin *et al.*, 1990)

Bennett, A. LeRoy, *International Organizations: Principles and Issues* (6th edn, Englewood Cliffs, NJ, 1995)

Bentil, J. Kodwo, 'Involvement of an International Organisation in Litigation in England' (1989) 8 *Litigation* 90
  'Suing an International Organisation for Debt Payment' (1990) 134 *Solicitors' Journal* 475–9

Berg, Axel, 'Nordic Council and Nordic Council of Ministers' in Bernhardt, Rudolf (ed.), *Encyclopedia of Public International Law* (1983), vol. VI, 261–3

Berger, Klaus Peter, 'Internationale Schiedsgerichtsbarkeit und Staatsimmunität – Die Revision des US Foreign Sovereign Immunities Act' (1989) 35 *Recht der Internationalen Wirtschaft/Außenwirtschaftsdienst* 956–8

Berman, Harold J., Greiner, William R. and Saliba, Samir N., *The Nature and Functions of Law* (Westbury, NY, 1996)

Bermann, George A., Goebel, Roger J., Davey, William J. and Fox, Eleanor M., *European Community Law* (St Paul, MN, 1993)

Bernardini, Aldo, 'Accordo e contratto di sede tra Italia e FAO' (1963) 46 *Rivista di diritto internazionale* 26–40

Bernhardt, Rudolf, 'Qualifikation und Anwendungsbereich des internen Rechts internationaler Organisationen' (1973) 12 *Berichte der Deutschen Gesellschaft für Völkerrecht* 7–46
  'The Nature and Field of Application of the Internal Law of International Organizations' (1974) 10 *Law and State* 7–26
  'Bundesverfassungsgericht und völkerrechtliche Verträge' in Starck, Christian (ed.) *Bundesverfassungsgericht und Grundgesetz, Festgabe aus Anlaß des 25jährigen Bestehens des Bundesverfassungsgerichts* (Tübingen, 1976), vol. II, *Verfassungsauslegung*, 154–86
  'The Convention and Domestic Law' in Macdonald, R. St. J., Matscher, F. and Petzold, H. (eds.), *The European System for the Protection of Human Rights* (Dordrecht, Boston and London, 1993), 25–40
  'International Organizations, Internal Law and Rules' in Bernhardt, Rudolf (ed.), *Encyclopedia of Public International Law* (2nd edn, 1995), vol. II, 1314–18

Bettati, Mario, *Le droit des organisations internationales* (Paris, 1987)

Beutler, Bengt, Bieber, Roland, Pipkorn, Jörn and Streil, Jochen, *Die Europäische Union. Rechtsordnung und Politik* (Baden-Baden, 4th edn, 1993)

Beutler, L. A., 'The ILO and IMF: Permissibility and Desirability of a Proposal to Meet the Contemporary Realities of the International Protection of Labor Rights' (1988) 14 *Syracuse Journal of International Law and Commerce* 455–77

Biancarelli, Jacques, 'Le Juge Communautaire et le Contentieux de la Fonction Publique Communautaire' in Société Française pour le Droit International (ed.), *Le Contentieux de la fonction publique international* (Paris, 1996), 193–207

Bianchi, Andrea, 'L'immunita delle Organizzazioni Internazionali dalla

Giurisdizione by S. de Bellis' (book review) (1994) 88 *American Journal of International Law* 212–14

Bieber, Roland, 'Der Abgeordnetenstatus im Europäischen Parlament' (1981) 16 *EuropaRecht* 124–38

Bindschedler, Rudolf, 'International Organizations, General Aspects' in Bernhardt, Rudolf (ed.), *Encyclopedia of Public International Law* (2nd edn, 1995), vol. II, 1289–309

Bleckmann, Albert, *Grundgesetz und Völkerrecht* (Berlin, 1975)

'Zur Verbindlichkeit des allgemeinen Völkerrechts für Internationale Organisationen' (1977) 37 *Zeitschrift für ausländisches öffentliches Recht und Völkerrecht* 107–21

'Die Völkerrechtsfreundlichkeit der deutschen Rechtsordnung' (1979) 23 *Die Öffentliche Verwaltung* 309–18

Internationale Beamtenstreitigkeiten vor nationalen Gerichten, Materialien zum Recht der internationalen Organisationen und zur Immunität, Rechtsgutachten für die Union Syndicale, Section Eurocontrol (Berlin, 1981)

'Nongovernmental Organizations' in Zweigert, K. (ed.), *International Encyclopedia of Comparative Law*, vol. XVII, *State and Economy*, chapter 25, 'Universal Economic Organizations', section III (Tübingen and Alphen aan den Rijn, 1981), 75–88

Grundprobleme und Methoden des Völkerrechts (Freiburg and Munich, 1982)

'Self-Executing Treaty Provisions' in Bernhardt, Rudolf (ed.), *Encyclopedia of Public International Law* (1984), vol. VII, 414–17

Europarecht (5th edn, Cologne, Berlin, Bonn and Munich, 1990)

Blix, Hans, 'The Role of the IAEA in the Development of International Law' (1989) 58 *Nordic Journal of International Law* 231–42

Bokor-Szegö, Hanna, 'International Organizations of Universal Character and the Domestic Legal Order of States' (1988) 4 *Questions of International Law* 9–30

Bota, Liviu, 'The Capacity of International Organizations to Conclude Headquarters Agreements and Some Features of These Agreements' in Zemanek, Karl (ed.), *Agreements of International Organizations and the Vienna Convention on the Law of Treaties* (Österreichische Zeitschrift für öffentliches Recht, Supplement 1, 1971), 57–104

Bothe, Michael, 'Die strafrechtliche Immunität fremder Staatsorgane' (1971) 31 *Zeitschrift für ausländisches öffentliches Recht und Völkerrecht* 246–70

'Internationale Organisationen und das Rechtsstaatsprinzip' in Jekewitz, Jürgen, Klein, Karl Heinz, Kühne, Jörg Detlef, Petersmann, Hans and Wolfrum, Rüdiger (eds.), *Des Menschen Recht zwischen Freiheit und Verantwortung, Festschrift für Karl Josef Partsch* (Berlin, 1989), 493–513

Bothe, M., Brink, J., Kirchner, C. and Stockmayer, A., *Rechtsfragen der internationalen Verschuldenskrise* (Frankfurt am Main, 1988)

Bourel, Pierre, 'Immunités' in Francescakis, Phocion (ed.), *Dalloz, Répertoire de droit international* (1969), vol. II, 118–34

Bowett, Derek W., 'Decisions of British Courts During 1963–1964 Involving Questions of Public or Private International Law, A. Public International Law [*Zoernsch v. Waldock*]' (1964) 40 *British Yearbook of International Law* 372–7

'Military Forces Abroad' in Bernhardt, Rudolf (ed.), *Encyclopedia of Public International Law* (1982), vol. III, 266–9

The Law of International Institutions (4th edn, London, 1982)

Böhm, Peter, 'Die Lehre vom Rechtsschutzbedürfnis' (1974) 96 *Juristische Blätter* 1–25

Bradlow, Daniel D., 'International Organizations and Private Complaints: The Case of the World Bank Inspection Panel' (1994) 34 *Virginia Journal of International Law* 553–613

Bradlow, Daniel D. and Schlemmer-Schulte, Sabine, 'The World Bank's New Inspection Panel: A Constructive Step in the Transformation of the International Legal Order' (1994) 54 *Zeitschrift für ausländisches öffentliches Recht und Völkerrecht* 392–415

Brandon, Michael, 'The United Nations Laissez-Passer' (1950) 27 *British Yearbook of International Law* 448–55

    'The Legal Status of the Premises of the United Nations' (1951) 28 *British Yearbook of International Law* 90–113

    'Sovereign Immunity of Government-Owned Corporations and Ships' (1954) 39 *Cornell Law Quarterly* 425–62

Bridge, J. W., 'The United Nations and English Law' (1969) 18 *International and Comparative Law Quarterly* 689–717

Brierly, J. L., 'The Hague Conventions and the Nullity of Arbitral Awards' (1928) *British Yearbook of International Law* 114–17

Broches, Aron, 'International Legal Aspects of the the Operations of the World Bank' (1959 III) 98 *Recueil des Cours* 296–409

Brown, Jonathan, 'Diplomatic Immunity: State Practice under the Vienna Convention on Diplomatic Relations' (1988) 37 *International and Comparative Law Quarterly* 53–88

Brownlie, Ian, 'The United Nations as a Form of Government' in Fawcett, J. E. S. and Higgins, R. (eds.), *International Organization. Law in Movement. Essays in Honour of John McMahon* (London, New York and Toronto, 1974), 26–36

    System of the Law of Nations. State Responsibility: Part I (Oxford, 1983)

    'Contemporary Problems Concerning the Jurisdictional Immunity of States – Supplementary Report' (1989 I) 63 *Annuaire de l'Institut de Droit International* 13–30

    Principles of Public International Law (4th edn, 1990)

Bruns, Viktor, 'Völkerrecht als Rechtsordnung' (1929) 1 *Zeitschrift für ausländisches öffentliches Recht und Völkerrecht* 1–56

Buergenthal, Thomas and Kewenig, Wilhelm A., 'Zum Begriff der Civil Rights in Artikel 6 Absatz 1 der Europäischen Menschenrechtskonvention' (1966–7) 13 *Archiv des Völkerrechts* 393–411

Burst, Jean-Jaques, 'L'arbitrage dans ses rapports avec les Communautés Européennes' (1979) *Revue de l'arbitrage* 105–15

Butkiewicz, Ewa, 'The Premisses of International Responsibility of Inter-Governmental Organizations' (1981–2) 11 *Polish Yearbook of International Law* 117–140

Byk, C., 'Case Note to *Hintermann v. Union de l'Europe occidental*' (1997) 124 *Journal de droit international* 142–51

Cahier, Philippe, *Etude des accords de siège conclus entre les organisations internationales et les états où elles résident* (Milan, 1959)

    Le droit diplomatique contemporain (Geneva and Paris, 1962)

    'Le droit interne des organisations internationales' (1963) 67 *Revue générale de droit international public* 563–602

'Les charactéristiques de la nullité en droit international' (1972) 76 *Revue générale de droit international public* 645–97

Calus, A., *Rechtspersönlichkeit der europäischen Gemeinschaften* (dissertation, University of Saarland, 1960)

Campbell, A. I. L, 'The Limits of the Powers of International Organisations' (1983) 32 *International and Comparative Law Quarterly* 523–33

'The Attitudes and Practices of the Specialised Agencies and UN Organs and the Interpretation of Their Basic Constitutions' (1986) *Juridical Review* 177–91

Cane, Peter, 'Prerogative Acts, Acts of State and Justiciability' (1980) 29 *International and Comparative Law Quarterly* 680–700

Cappelletti, Mauro, *The Judicial Process in Comparative Perspective* (Oxford, 1989)

Cappelletti, Mauro and Garth, Bryant, 'Access to Justice: The Worldwide Movement to Make Rights Effective' in Cappelletti, Mauro and Garth, Bryant (eds.), *Access to Justice* (Alphen aan den Rijn, 1978), vol. I, book II, 5–124

Carabiber, Charles, 'Le concept des immunités de juridiction doit-il être révisé et dans quel sens?' (1952) 79 *Journal de droit international* 440–95

Caron, David D., 'Iraq and the Force of Law: Why Give a Shield of Immunity?' (1991) 85 *American Journal of International Law* 89–92

Carreau, Dominique, 'Les moyens de pression économic au regard du FMI, du GATT et de l'OCDE' (1984–5) 18 *Revue belge de droit international* 20–33

Carroz, Jean and Probst, Yürg, *Personnalité juridique internationale et capacité de conclure des traités de l'ONU et des institutions spécialisées* (Paris, 1953)

Carroz, J. E. and Roche, A. G., 'The Proposed International Commission for the Conservation of Atlantic Tunas' (1967) 61 *American Journal of International Law* 673–702

Carter, Barry E. and Trimble, Phillip R., *International Law* (Boston, New York, Toronto and London, 2nd edn, 1995)

Carter, P. B., 'Rejection of Foreign Law: Some Private International Law Inhibitions' (1984) 55 *British Yearbook of International Law* 111–31

'Transnational Recognition and Enforcement of Foreign Public Laws' (1989) 48 *Cambridge Law Journal* 417–35

'Decisions of British Courts During 1991 Involving Questions of Public or Private International Law, B. Private International Law [AMF v. Hashim]' (1991) 62 *British Yearbook of International Law* 447–64

Carver, Jeremy P., 'International Organisations After Arab Monetary Fund' (1991) 6 *Butterworths Journal of International Banking and Financial Law* 215–18

Cassese, Antonio, 'L'immunité de juridiction civile des organisations internationales dans la jurisprudence italienne' (1984) 30 *Annuaire français de droit international* 556–66

Castberg, Frede, 'L'Excès de pouvoir dans la justice internationale' (1931 I) 35 *Recueil des Cours* 353–472

Chandavarkar, Anand G., *The International Monetary Fund, Its Financial Organization and Activities* (1984)

Chandrasekhar, Sandhya, 'Cartel in a Can: The Financial Collapse of the International Tin Council' (1989) 10 *Northwestern Journal of International Law and Business* 309–32

Charpentier, J., *Institutions internationales* (9th edn, Paris, 1989)

Chaumont, Charles, 'La signification du principe de spécialité des Organisations
    Internationales' in *Mélanges offertes a Henri Rolin* (Paris, 1964), 55–66
Chen, Kwen, 'The Legal Status, Privileges and Immunities of the Specialized
    Agencies' (1948) 42 *American Journal of International Law* 900–6
Cheshire and North, *Private International Law* (ed. by North, P. M. and Fawcett, J. J.,
    11th edn, London, 1987)
Cheyne, Ilona, 'The International Tin Council' (1989) 38 *International and
    Comparative Law Quarterly* 417–24
    'Status of International Organisations in English Law' (1991) 40 *International
    and Comparative Law Quarterly* 981–4
Cheyne, Ilona and Warbrick, Colin, 'The International Tin Council' (1987) 36
    International and Comparative Law Quarterly 931–5
Chiu, Hungdah, 'Succession in International Organisations' (1965) 14
    International and Comparative Law Quarterly 83–120
    *The Capacity of International Organisations to Conclude Treaties, and the Special Legal
    Aspects of the Treaties So Concluded* (The Hague, 1966)
Ciobanu, Dan, 'Objection to Acts Performed *"Ultra Vires"* by the Political Organs
    of the United Nations' (1972) 55 *Rivista di diritto internazionale* 420–53
Clutterbuck, R. G., 'The ITC Affair' (1990) *Journal of Business Law* 12–13
Cohen, Maxwell, 'Espionage and Immunity – Some Recent Problems and
    Developments' (1948) 25 *British Yearbook of International Law* 404–14
    'The United States and the United Nations Secretariat: A Preliminary
    Appraisal' (1953) 1 *McGill Law Journal* 169–98
    'The United Nations Secretariat – Some Constitutional and Administrative
    Developments' (1955) 48 *American Journal of International Law* 295–319
Colin, Sinkondo, 'Les relations contractuelles des organisations internationales
    avec les personnes privées' (1992) 69 Rev. Inst. belge 7–43
Colliard, C. A., 'Le règlement des différends dans les organisations
    intergouvernementales de caractère non politique' in *Hommage d'une
    génération de juristes au Président Basdevant* (Paris, 1960), 152–82
Colombo, Ennio M., 'La personalità giuridica internationale della Communità
    europee e la loro potestà di concludere accordi internazionali' (1965) *Il
    diritto negli scambi internazionali* 23–32
Commission on Global Governance, *Our Global Neighborhood. The Report of the
    Commission on Global Governance* (Oxford, 1995)
Condorelli, Luigi, 'Acts of the Italian Government in International Matters
    Before Domestic Courts' (1976) 2 *Italian Yearbook of International Law* 178–200
Conforti, Benedetto, 'La personalità della Comunità economica europea nel
    diritto statale' (1964) 47 *Rivista di diritto internazionale* 566–72
Conseil de l'Europe (ed.), *Privilèges et immunités des organisations internationales,
    Resolution (69) 29 adoptée par le Comité des Ministres du Conseil de l'Europe le 26
    septembre 1969 et rapport explicatif* (Strasbourg, 1970)
Coussirat-Coustère, Vincent and Eisemann, Pierre Michel, *Repertory of
    International Arbitral Jurisprudence* (Dordrecht, Boston and London, 1991), vol.
    III, *1946–1988*
Crawford, James, 'International Law and Foreign Sovereigns: Distinguishing
    Immune Transactions' (1983) 54 *British Yearbook of International Law* 75–118
Cully, Kathleen, 'Jurisdictional Immunities of Intergovernmental Organizations'
    (1982) 91 *Yale Law Journal* 1167–95

Czempiel, E.-O., 'Möglichkeiten und Grenzen der Internationalen Organisation'
    (1985) 33 *Vereinte Nationen* 154–7
Dahm, Georg, *Völkerrecht*, vol. I (Stuttgart, 1958) and vol. II (Stuttgart, 1960)
    'Völkerrechtliche Grenzen der inländischen Gerichtsbarkeit gegenüber
    ausländischen Staaten', in *Festschrift Nikisch* (Tübingen, 1958), 153–83
Dahm, Georg, Delbrück, Jost and Wolfrum, Rüdiger, *Völkerrecht I/1, Die
    Grundlagen – Die Völkerrechtssubjekte* (2nd edn, Berlin et al., 1989)
Dai, Poeliu, 'The Headquarters Agreement Between Canada and the
    International Civil Aviation Organization' (1964) 2 *Canadian Yearbook of
    International Law* 205–14
Dale, William, 'UNRWA – A Subsidiary Organ of the United Nations' (1974) 23
    International and Comparative Law Quarterly 576–609
    'Is the Commonwealth an International Organization?' (1992) 41 *International
    and Comparative Law Quarterly* 451–73
Dam, Kenneth W., 'The GATT as an International Organization' (1969) 3 *Journal of
    World Trade Law* 374–89
Damian, Helmut, *Staatenimmunität und Gerichtszwang. Grundlagen und Grenzen der
    völkerrechtlichen Freiheit fremder Staaten von inländischer Gerichtsbarkeit in
    Verfahren der Zwangsvollstreckung oder Anspruchssicherung* (Berlin, Heidelberg,
    New York and Tokyo, 1985)
Daubitz, Sigurd, *Zur Gerichtsbarkeit über die Bank für Internationalen
    Zahlungsausgleich* (dissertation, Zürich, 1937)
Daum, Ulrich, 'Interpol – öffentliche Gewalt ohne Kontrolle' (1980) 35
    Juristenzeitung 798–801
David, Eric, 'L'avis consultatif de la Cour internationale de Justice du 15.12.1989
    sur l'applicabilité de la section 22 de l'article VI de la Convention sur les
    privilèges et immunités des Nations Unies (affaire Mazilu)' (1989) 35
    Annuaire français de droit international 298–320
de Bellis, Saverio, *L'immunità delle organizzazioni internazionali dalla giurisdizione*
    (Bari, 1992)
de Cooker, C. (ed.), *International Administration* (looseleaf, The Hague, Boston and
    London, 1989–)
de Fischer, Béat, 'L'Ordre Souverain de Malte' (1979 II) 163 *Recueil des Cours* 1–46
de Visscher, Paul, 'L'interprétation judiciaire des traités d'organisation
    internationale' (1958) 41 *Rivista di diritto internazionale* 177–87
    'De l'immunité de juridiction de l'Organisation des Nations Unies et du
    caractère discrétionnaire de la compétence de protection diplomatique'
    (1971) 25 *Revue critique de jurisprudence belge* 456–62
de Vuyst, Bruno Michel, 'The Use of Discretionary Authority by International
    Organizations in Their Relations with International Civil Servants' (1983) 12
    Denver Journal of International Law and Policy 237–68
de Weck, Christoph, *Vorrechte und Befreiungen zugunsten des IKRK und seiner
    Delegierten, Ein Vergleich mit diplomatischen Missionen und internationalen
    zwischenstaatlichen Organisationen am Beispiel der Rechtsstellung der Vereinten
    Nationen in der Schweiz* (dissertation, Fribourg 1987)
de Zayas, Alfred M., 'United Nations Relief and Rehabilitation Administration' in
    Bernhardt, Rudolf (ed.), *Encyclopedia of Public International Law* (1983), vol. V,
    338–41
Delaume, Georges, 'The Proper Law of Loans Concluded by International

Persons: A Restatement and a Forecast' (1962) 56 *American Journal of International Law* 63–87

Dellapenna, J. W., *Suing Foreign Governments and Their Corporations* (Washington DC, 1988)

Denza, Eileen, *Diplomatic Law, Commentary on the Vienna Convention on Diplomatic Relations* (Dobbs Ferry, NY, 1976)

'Diplomatic Agents and Missions, Privileges and Immunities' in Bernhardt, Rudolf (ed.), *Encyclopedia of Public International Law* (2nd edn, 1992), vol. I, 1040–5

Department of State (ed.), *Foreign Relations of the United States 1946*, vol. I, *General; The United Nations* (Washington DC, 1972)

Díaz-González, Leonardo (Special Rapporteur), 'Fourth Report on Relations Between States and International Organizations (Second Part of the Topic)' (UN Doc. A/CN.4/424) *Yearbook of the International Law Commission* (1989), vol. II, Part One, 153–68

Die Bank für internationalen Zahlungsausgleich und die Baseler Zusammenkünfte, *Herausgegeben zum fünfzigjährigen Bestehen der Bank 1930–1980* (Basel, 1980)

Dilami, Mohamed A., 'Le droit de l'organisation internationale: sous-ensemble du droit international public' (1985) 17 *Revue juridique politique et economique du Maroc* 97–107

Dinh, Nguyen Quoc, 'Les privilèges et immunités des organismes internationaux d'après les jurisprudences nationales depuis 1945' (1957) 3 *Annuaire français de droit international* 262–304

Dobbert, J. P. and Rädler, Peter, 'Food and Agriculture Organization of the United Nations' in Bernhardt, Rudolf (ed.), *Encyclopedia of Public International Law* (2nd edn, 1995), vol. II, 413–19

Doehring, Karl, 'Fordert das allgemeine Völkerrecht innerstaatlichen Gerichtsschutz gegen die Exekutive?' in Max Planck-Institut für ausländisches öffentliches Recht und Völkerrecht (ed.), *Gerichtsschutz gegen die Exekutive* (Cologne, Berlin, Munich and Dobbs Ferry, NY, 1971), vol. III, *Comparative Law – International Law*

'Gewohnheitsrecht aus Verträgen' (1976) 36 *Zeitschrift für ausländisches öffentliches Recht und Völkerrecht* 77–95

Dolzer, Rudolf, 'Diplomatic Protection of Foreign Nationals' in Bernhardt, Rudolf (ed.), *Encyclopedia of Public International Law* (1987), vol. X, 121–4

Dominicé, Christian, 'La nature juridique des actes des organisations et des juridictions internationales et leurs effets en droit interne' in *VIIIe Congrès international de droit comparé* (1970), 249–64

'La personnalité juridique international du CICR' in Swinarski (ed.), *Etudes et essais sur le droit international humanitaire et sur les principes de la Croix-Rouge en l'honneur de Jean Pictet* (Geneva and The Hague, 1984), 663–74

'L'immunité de juridiction et d'exécution des organisations internationales' (1984 IV) 187 *Recueil des Cours* 145–238

'La nature et l'étendue de l'immunité de juridiction des organisations internationales' in Böckstiegel, Karl-Heinz, Folz, Hans-Ernst, Mössner, Jörg Manfred and Zemanek, Karl (eds.), *Völkerrecht – Recht der Internationalen Organisationen – Weltwirtschaftsrecht. Festschrift für Ignaz Seidl-Hohenveldern* (Cologne, Berlin, Bonn and Munich, 1988), 77–93

'Le Tribunal fédéral face à la personnalité juridique d'un organisme international' (1989) 108 *Zeitschrift für Schweizerisches Recht* 517–28

'Le règlement juridictionnel du contentieux externe des organisations internationales' in *Le droit international au service de la paix, de la justice et du développement. Mélanges Michel Virally* (Paris, 1991), 225–38

'L'arbitrage et les immunités des organisations internationales' in Dominicé, Christian, Patry, Robert and Reymond, Claude (eds.), *Etudes de droit international en l'honneur de Pierre Lalive* (Basel and Frankfurt am Main, 1993), 483–97

'L'accord de siège conclu par le Comité international de la Croix-Rouge avec la Suisse' (1995) 99 *Revue générale de droit international public* 5–36

Doxey, Margaret, 'Rule Observance and Rule Making: Growing Problems of Authority and Control for the United Nations' (1987) 42 *International Journal* (Toronto) 413–37

Drobnig, Ulrich, 'Conflict of Laws and the European Economic Community' (1966–7) 15 *American Journal of Comparative Law* 204–29

Dronillat, *L'immunité de juridiction des organismes internationaux* (1954)

du Perron, A. E., 'Eurocontrol, Liability and Jurisdiction' in Storm van's Gravesande, J. W. E. and van der Veen Vonk, A. (eds.), *AirWorthy. Liber Amicorum I. H. P. Diederiks-Verschoor* (Deventer, Antwerp, London, Frankfurt, New York and Boston, 1985), 135–49

Duffar, Jean, *Contribution à l'étude des privilèges et immunités des organisations internationales* (Paris, 1982)

Dufour, Jean-Marie, 'De l'exterritorialité a l'autonomie international: A propos des relations de l'organisation intergouvernementale avec l'etat-hôte' in *Le droit international au service de la paix, de la justice et du développement. Mélanges Michel Virally* (Paris, 1991), 239–56

Dupuy, Pierre-Marie, *Droit international public* (3rd edn, Paris, 1992)

Dupuy, Rene-Jean (ed.), *Manuel sur les organisations internationales, A Handbook on International Organizations* (Dordrecht and Boston, 1988)

Eagleton, Clyde, 'International Organizations and the Law of Responsibility' (1950 I) 76 *Recueil des Cours* 319–425

International Government (3rd edn, New York, 1957)

Ebenroth, Carsten Thomas, 'Shareholders' Liability in International Organizations – The Settlement of the International Tin Council Case' (1991) 4 *Leiden Journal of International Law* 171–83

Ebenroth, Carsten Thomas and Fuhrmann, Lambert, 'Die zivilrechtliche Haftung internationaler Organisationen und ihrer Mitgliedstaaten' (1989) 44 *Juristenzeitung* 211–20

Edwards, Richard W., 'Is an IMF Stand-By Arrangement a "Seal of Approval" on which other Creditors Can Rely?' (1983) 17 *Journal of International Law and Politics* 513–612

'Effectiveness of the UN' (1983) 77 *Proceedings of the American Society of International Law* 191–212

Egger, Max, 'Die Vorrechte und Befreiungen zugunsten internationaler Organisationen und ihrer Funktionäre' (dissertation, Berne, 1953) (Vienna, 1954)

Ehrenfeld, Alice, 'United Nations Immunity Distinguished from Sovereign Immunity' (1958) 52 *Proceedings of the American Society of International Law*

88–94

Eifler, Robert K., 'Privileges and Immunities of United Nations Delegates and Officials – The International Organizations Immunities Act' (1948) 46 *Michigan Law Review* 381–9

Eisemann, Pierre Michel, 'Crise du conseil international de l'etain et insolvabilité d'une organisation intergouvernmental' (1985) 31 *Annuaire français de droit international* 730–46

El-Erian, Abdullah, 'La Conférence et la Convention sur la Représentation des Etats dans leurs relation avec les organisations internationales (un aperçu général)' (1975) 21 *Annuaire français de droit international* 445–70

(Special Rapporteur), 'Preliminary Report on the Second Part of the Topic of Relations Between States and International Organizations' (UN Doc. A/CN.4/304) *Yearbook of the International Law Commission* (1977), vol. II, Part One, 140–55

Engblom, Göran M., 'International Trade Centre UNCTAD/GATT' in Bernhardt, Rudolf (ed.), *Encyclopedia of Public International Law* (2nd edn, 1995), vol. II, 1385–8

Engel, Christoph, 'Wirkung der völkerrechtlichen Normen über die Immunität im deutschen Rechtsraum' (1988) 87 *Zeitschrift für vergleichende Rechtswissenschaft* 33–45

Völkerrecht als Tatbestandsmerkmal deutscher Normen (Berlin, 1989)

Engel, Franz-Wilhelm (ed.), *Handbuch der NATO* (Frankfurt am Main, 1957)

Engel, Salo, '"Living" International Constitutions and the World Court' (1967) 16 *International and Comparative Law Quarterly* 865–910

Ergec, Rusen, 'Le contrôle juridictionnel de l'administration dans les matières qui se rattachent aux rapports internationaux: actes de gouvernement ou réserve du pouvoir discrétionaire' (1986) 68 *Revue de droit international et de droit comparé* 72–134

Ermacora, Felix, 'Völkerrecht und Landesrecht' in Neuhold, Hanspeter, Hummer, Waldemar and Schreuer, Christoph (eds.), *Osterreichisches Handbuch des Völkerrechts* (2nd edn, Vienna, 1991), 115–25

Espósito Massicci, Carlos D. and Garcimartín Alférez, Francisco, 'Grundrechte und Immunität der Angehörigen ausländischer diplomatischer Missionen (zu span. Tribunal Constitucional, 140/1995, 28.9.1995)' (1997) 17 *Praxis des Internationalen Privat- und Verfahrensrechts* 129–32

Everling, Ulrich, 'Sind die Mitgliedstaaten der Europäischen Gemeinschaft noch Herren der Verträge?' in Bernhardt, Geck, Jaenicke and Steinberger (eds.), *Völkerrecht als Rechtsordnung, Internationale Gerichtsbarkeit, Menschenrechte. Festschrift Mosler* (Berlin, Heidelberg and New York, 1983), 173–91

Falk, Richard A., *Essays on International Jurisdiction* (Columbus, OH, 1961)

The Role of Domestic Courts in the International Legal Order (Syracuse, NY, 1964)

Farrugia, Antoinette A., '*Boimah v. United Nations General Assembly* – International Organizations Immunity is Absolutely not Restrictive' (1989) 15 *Brooklyn Journal of International Law* 497–525

Farukowa, 'La contrôle de la Cour internationale de Justice sur les organisations internationales – les actes *ultra vires* des organisations internationales' (1979) 78 *Japanese Journal of International Law and Diplomacy* 133

Fasching, Hans, *Kommentar zu den Zivilprozeßgesetzen*, vol. I (Vienna, 1959)

Lehrbuch des österreichischen Zivilprozeßrechts (Vienna, 1984)

Faßbender, Bardo, 'Die Völkerrechtssubjektivität internationaler Organisationen' (1986) 37 Osterreichische Zeitschrift für öffentliches Recht und Völkerrecht 17–47

Fastenrath, Ulrich, 'Passivlegitimation der EG und ihrer Mitgliedstaaten in Verfahren vor der Europäischen Kommission für Menschenrechte' (1979) Europäische Grundrechte Zeitschrift 534–6

Fatouros, Arghyrios A., 'The World Bank's Impact on International Law – A Case Study in the International Law of Cooperation' in Wilner, Gabriel M. (ed.), Jus et Societas. Essays in Tribute to Wolfgang Friedmann (The Hague, Boston and London, 1979), 62–95
   'On the Hegemonic Role of International Functional Organization' (1980) 23 German Yearbook of International Law 9–36

Fawcett, James E. S., 'Détournement de Pouvoir by International Organizations' (1957) 33 British Yearbook of International Law 311–16
   'The Place of Law in an International Organisation' (1960) 36 British Yearbook of International Law 321–42

Fawcett, James and Schuster, Gunnar, 'Intelsat' in Bernhardt, Rudolf (ed.), Encyclopedia of Public International Law (2nd edn, 1995), vol. II, 1000–4

Fawcett, J. J., Declining Jurisdiction in Private International Law. Reports to the XIVth Congress of the International Academy of Comparative Law – Athens, August 1994 (Oxford, 1995)

Fedder, Edwin H., 'The Functional Basis of International Privileges and Immunities: A New Concept in International Law and Organization' (1960) 9 American University Law Review 60–9

Fedozzi, Prospero, Gli Enti Collectivi nel Diritto Internazionale Privato (Verona and Padova, 1897)

Feld, Werner, 'The Competences of the European Community for the Conduct of External Relations' (1965) 43 Texas Law Review 891–926

Feld, Werner and Jordan, Robert S., International Organizations: A Comparative Approach (2nd edn, New York, 1988)

Ferencz, Benjamin B., New Legal Foundations for Global Survival (Dobbs Ferry, NY, 1994)

Finkelstein, Lawrence S., 'What is Global Governance' (1995) 1 Global Governance 367–72

Fischer, Georges, 'Organisation Internationale du Travail. Privilèges et Immunités' (1955) 1 Annuaire français de droit international 385–92

Fischer, Peter, Die internationale Konzession (Vienna and New York, 1974)
   'Transnational Enterprises' in Bernhardt, Rudolf (ed.), Encyclopedia of Public International Law (1985), vol. VIII, 515–19

Fischer, Peter and Köck, Heribert Franz, Europarecht (3rd edn, Vienna, 1997)

Fisher, Allan G. B., 'International Institutions in a World of Sovereign States' (1944) 59 Political Science Quarterly 1–14

Flauss, Jean-François, 'L'application de l'art. 6 (1) de la Convention européenne des Droits de l'Homme aux procédures arbitrales' Gazette du Palais, 2 July 1986, 2–4

Fleischhauer, Carl-August, 'Die VN und die Bindung an das Recht' (1985) 36 Außenpolitik 223–9

Folsom, Ralph H., European Union Law (St Paul, MN, 1995)

Folz, Hans-Ernst, Die Geltungskraft fremder Hoheitsäußerungen (Baden-Baden, 1975)

Fonteyne, J.-P., 'Acts of State' in Bernhardt, Rudolf (ed.), *Encyclopedia of Public International* (2nd edn, 1992), vol. I, 17–20

Franck, Thomas M., 'Of Gnats and Camels: Is There a Double Standard at the United Nations?' (1984) 78 *American Journal of International Law* 811–33

'Soviet Initiatives: US Responses – New Opportunities for Reviving the United Nations System' (1989) 83 *American Journal of International Law* 531–43

'United Nations Based Prospects for a New Global Order' (1990) 22 *New York University Journal of International Law and Politics* 601–40

'The "Powers of Appreciation": Who is the Ultimate Guardian of UN Legality?' (1992) 86 *American Journal of International Law* 519–23

Franck, Thomas M. and Fox, Gregory H. (eds.), *International Law Decisions in National Courts* (Irvington-on-Hudson, NY, 1996)

Frank, Rainer, 'Öffentlich-rechtliche Ansprüche fremder Staaten vor inländischen Gerichten' (1970) 34 *Rabels Zeitschrift für ausländisches und internationales Privatrecht* 56–75

Freymond, Pierre, 'Remarques sur l'immunité de juridiction des organisations internationales en matière immobilière' (1955–6) 53 *Friedens-Warte* 365–79

Friedmann, Wolfgang, 'International Public Corporations' (1942–3) 6 *Modern Law Review* 185–207

'General Course in Public International Law' (1968 II) 127 *Recueil des Cours* 39–246

Friedmann, Wolfgang and Fatouros, Arghyrios A., 'The United Nations Administrative Tribunal' (1957) 11 *International Organization* 13–29

Frowein, Jochen A., 'Diskussionsbeitrag' in Bernhardt and Miehsler, 'Qualifikation und Anwendungsbereich des internen Rechts internationaler Organisationen' (1973) 12 *Berichte der Deutschen Gesellschaft für Völkerrecht* 111–12

'Europäisches Gemeinschaftsrecht und Bundesverfassungsgericht' in Starck, Christian (ed.) *Bundesverfassungsgericht und Grundgesetz, Festgabe aus Anlaß des 25jährigen Bestehens des Bundesverfassungsgerichts* (Tübingen, 1976), vol. II, *Verfassungsauslegung*, 187–213

'Nullity in International Law' in Bernhardt, Rudolf (ed.), *Encyclopedia of Public International Law* (1984), vol. VII, 361–4

'The Internal and External Effects of Resolutions by International Organizations' (1989) 49 *Zeitschrift für ausländisches öffentliches Recht und Völkerrecht* 778–90

'Das Maastricht-Urteil und die Grenzen der Verfassungsgerichtsbarkeit' (1994) 54 *Zeitschrift für ausländisches öffentliches Recht und Völkerrecht* 1–16

Frowein, Jochen A. and Peukert, Wolfgang, *Europäische MenschenRechtsKonvention. EMRK-Kommentar* (2nd edn, Kehl, Strasbourg and Arlington, 1996)

Furrer, Hans-Peter, 'La protection juridictionnelle du particulier au sein des Organisations internationales' in Max Planck-Institut für ausländisches öffentliches Recht und Völkerrecht (ed.), *Gerichtsschutz gegen die Exekutive* (Cologne, Berlin, Munich and Dobbs Ferry, NY, 1970), vol. II, *National Reports*, 1217–58

Fusinato, Guido, 'La personalità giuridica dell'Istituto Internazionale d'Agricultura' (1914) 8 *Rivista di diritto internazionale* 149–56

Gaia, Giorgio, 'A "New" Vienna Convention on Treaties Between States and International Organizations or Between International Organizations: A

Critical Commentary' (1987) 58 *International and Comparative Law Quarterly* 253–69

Gallas, Andreas, 'Interpol' in Bernhardt, Rudolf (ed.), *Encyclopedia of Public International Law* (2nd edn, 1995), vol. II, 1414–16

Gallozzi, Marialuisa, 'Applying the Foreign Missions Act of 1982 to International Organizations: Reciprocity in the Multilateral Context' (1985) 18 *New York University Journal of International Law and Politics* 229–66

Gasser, Hans-Peter, 'Der Internationale Suchdienst in Arolsen – eine humanitäre Institution im Dienste von Opfern des Zweiten Weltkrieges' in Jekewitz, Jürgen, Klein, Karl Heinz, Kühne, Jörg Detlef, Petersmann, Hans and Wolfrum, Rüdiger (eds.), *Des Menschen Recht zwischen Freiheit und Verantwortung, Festschrift für Karl Josef Partsch* (Berlin, 1989), 389–402

Geck, Wilhelm Karl, 'Konzession' in Strupp and Schlochauer (eds.), *Wörterbuch des Völkerrechts*, (1961), vol. II, 301–7

Die völkerrechtlichen Wirkungen verfassungswidriger Verträge (Cologne and Berlin, 1963)

'Das Bundesverfassungsgericht und die allgemeinen Regeln des Völkerrechts' in Starck, Christian (ed.) *Bundesverfassungsgericht und Grundgesetz, Festgabe aus Anlaß des 25jährigen Bestehens des Bundesverfassungsgerichts* (Tübingen, 1976), vol. II, *Verfassungsauslegung*, 125–53

'Völkerrechtliche Verträge und Kodifikationen' (1976) 36 *Zeitschrift für ausländisches öffentliches Recht und Völkerrecht* 96–146

'Die Ausweitung von Individualrechten durch völkerrechtliche Verträge und der Diplomatische Schutz' in Börner, Bodo, Jahrreiß, Hermann and Stern, Klaus (eds.) *Einigkeit und Recht und Freiheit, Festschrift für Karl Carstens* (Cologne, Berlin, Bonn and Munich, 1984), vol. I, *Europarecht, Völkerrecht*, 339–60

'Diplomatic Protection' in Bernhardt, Rudolf (ed.), *Encyclopedia of Public International Law* (1987), vol. X, 99–121

Geiger, Rudolf, 'Außenbeziehungen der Europäischen Wirtschaftsgemeinschaft und auswärtige Gewalt der Mitgliedstaaten, Zur Entwicklung der Rechtsprechung des Europäischen Gerichtshofs zu den Vertragsschlußkompetenzen der EWG' (1977) 37 *Zeitschrift für ausländisches öffentliches Recht und Völkerrecht* 640–67

Grundgesetz und Völkerrecht, Die Bezüge des Staatsrechts zum Völkerrecht und Europarecht (Munich, 1985)

Geimer, Reinhold, 'Verfassung, Völkerrecht und Internationales Munich, Zivilverfahrensrecht' (1992) 33 *Zeitschrift für Rechtsvergleichung, internationales Privatrecht und Europarecht* 321–47, 401–20

'Internationalrechtliches zum Justizgewährungsanspruch' in Habscheid, Walter and Schwab, Karl Heinz (eds.), *Beiträge zum Internationalen Verfahrensrecht und zur Schiedsgerichtsbarkeit. Festschrift Nagel* (Münster, 1987), 36–53

Internationales Zivilprozeßrecht (2nd edn, Cologne, 1993)

Geißler, Markus, 'Die Geltendmachung und Beitreibung von Ansprüchen aus Truppenschäden nach dem NATO-Truppenstatut' (1980) *Neue Juristische Wochenschrift* 2615–20

Giardina, A., *Comunità europee e stati terzi* (Naples, 1964)

Giegerich, Thomas, 'Luxemburg, Karlsruhe, Straßburg – Dreistufiger Grundrechtsschutz in Europa?' (1990) 50 *Zeitschrift für ausländisches öffentliches Recht und Völkerrecht* 836–68

Ginther, Konrad, *Die völkerrechtliche Verantwortlichkeit internationaler Organisationen gegenüber Drittstaaten* (Vienna and New York, 1969)

'International Organizations, Responsibility' in Bernhardt, Rudolf (ed.), *Encyclopedia of Public International Law* (2nd edn, 1995), vol. II, 1336–40

Glavinis, Panayotis, *Les litiges relatifs aux contrats passés entre organisations internationales et personnes privées, Travaux et recherches Panthéon-Assas, Paris II* (Paris, 1990)

Glenn, H. Patrick, 'Persuasive Authority' (1987) 32 *McGill Law Journal* 261–98

Glenn, Gordon H., Kearney, Mary M. and Padilla, David J., 'Immunities of International Organizations' (1982) 22 *Virginia Journal of International Law* 247–90

Gloor, Werner, 'Employeurs titulaires de l'immunité de juridiction' in Universités de Berne, Fribourg, Geneva, Lausanne et Neuchatel, Ensèignement de 3e cycle de droit 1987 (eds.), *Le juriste suisse face au droit et aux jugements étrangers, ouverture ou repli?* (1988), 263–89

Goettel, James G., 'Is the International Olympic Committee Amenable to Suit in a United States Court?' (1984) 7 *Fordham International Law Journal* 61–82

Gold, Joseph, *Membership and Nonmembership in the IMF, A Study in International Law and Organization* (Washington DC, 1974)

A Second Report on Some Recent Legal Developments in the International Monetary Fund (1977)

'International Monetary Fund' in Bernhardt, Rudolf (ed.), *Encyclopedia of Public International Law* (2nd edn, 1995), vol. II, 1271–7

Golsong, Heribert, 'Regional Development Banks' in Bernhardt, Rudolf (ed.), *Encyclopedia of Public International Law* (1983), vol. VI, 336–45

'International Bank for Reconstruction and Development' in Bernhardt, Rudolf (ed.), *Encyclopedia of Public International Law* (2nd edn, 1995), vol. II, 1057–64

Gomula, Joanna, 'The International Court of Justice and Administrative Tribunals of International Organizations' (1991) 13 *Michigan Journal of International Law* 83–121

Goode, Victor L., 'Procurement, International Organizations, and Minority and Women Contractors' (1985) 10 *Thurgood Marshall Law Review* 483–505

Goodrich, Leland, 'The Changing United Nations' in Friedmann, Wolfgang, Henkin, Louis and Lissitzyn, Oliver (eds.), *Transnational Law in a Changing Society. Essays in Honor of Philip Jessup* (New York and London, 1972), 259–79

Goodrich, Leland and Hambro, Edvard, *Charter of the United Nations. Commentary and Documents* (London, 1964)

Gordon, G. W., 'Recourse Procedures of International Organizations' (1982) 14 *New York University Journal of International Law and Politics* 871–94

Gordon, Mark, 'Recent Developments, International Organizations: Immunity – *Broadbent* v. *Organization of American States*' (1980) 21 *Harvard International Law Journal* 552–61

Gottwald, Peter, 'Die sachliche Kontrolle internationaler Schiedssprüche durch staatliche Gerichte' in Habscheid, Walter and Schwab, Karl Heinz (eds.), *Beiträge zum Internationalen Verfahrensrecht und zur Schiedsgerichtsbarkeit. Festschrift Nagel* (Münster, 1987), 54–69

Grabenwarter, Christoph, *Verfahrensgarantien in der Verwaltungsgerichtsbarkeit*

(Vienna and New York, 1997)

Grabitz, Eberhard (ed.), *Kommentar zum EWG-Vertrag* (2nd edn, Munich, 1989)

Grabitz, Eberhard and Hilf, Meinhard (eds.), *Kommentar zur Europäischen Union* (Munich, 1996)

Gramlich, Ludwig, 'Diplomatic Protection Against Acts of Intergovernmental Organs' (1984) 27 *German Yearbook of International Law* 386–428

'Innerstaatlicher Rechtsschutz für internationale Bedienstete?' (1985) 6 *Juristische Rundschau* 221–8

Gray, Christine, 'The International Court's Advisory Opinion on the WHO–Egypt Agreement of 1951' (1983) 32 *International and Comparative Law Quarterly* 534–41

Green, L. C., 'The Status of the International Civil Service' (1954) 7 *Current Legal Problems* 192–211

Greenwood, Christopher, 'Decisions of British Courts During 1989 Involving Questions of Public or Private International Law, A. Public International Law' (1989) 60 *British Yearbook of International Law* 461–82

'Put Not Your Trust in Princes: The Tin Council Appeals' (1989) 48 *Cambridge Law Journal* 46–54

'The Tin Council Litigation in the House of Lords' (1990) 49 *Cambridge Law Journal* 8–13

Gregorides, Franz, *Die Privilegien und Immunitäten der internationalen Beamten mit besonderer Berücksichtigung der Rechtslage in Österreich* (Vienna, 1972)

Greig, Donald W., 'Forum State Jurisdiction and Sovereign Immunity Under the International Law Commission's Draft Articles' (1989) 38 *International and Comparative Law Quarterly* 243–76

'Specific Exceptions to Immunity Under the International Law Commission's Draft Articles' (1989) 38 *International and Comparative Law Quarterly* 560–88

Griffith, John C., 'Restricting the Immunity of International Organizations in Labor Disputes: Reforming an Obsolete Shibboleth' (1984–5) 25 *Virginia Journal of International Law* 1007–33

Griller, Stefan, *Die Übertragung von Hoheitsrechten auf zwischenstaatliche Einrichtungen: eine Untersuchung zu Art. 9 Abs. 2 des Bundes-Verfassungsgesetzes* (Vienna, 1989)

Grimes, David M., 'The OAS Administrative Tribunal: Proposals for Appellate Review' (1987) 1 *Emory Journal of International Dispute Resolution* 257–74

Groeben, Hans von der, Thiesing, Jochen and Ehlermann, Claus-Dieter, *Kommentar zum EWG-Vertrag* (Baden-Baden, 4th edn, 1991)

Gross, Leo, 'States as Organs of International Law and the Problem of Autointerpretation' in Lipsky, George A. (ed.), *Law and Politics in the World Community. Essays on Hans Kelsen's Pure Theory and Related Problems in International Law* (Berkeley and Los Angeles, 1953), 59–74

'Immunities and Privileges of Delegations to the United Nations' (1962) 16 *International Organizations* 483–520; reprinted in Gross, Leo, *Essays on International Law and Organization* (1984), 277–310

Grossfeld, Bernhard, *Praxis des Internationalen Privat- und Wirtschaftsrechts* (Hamburg, 1975)

Groux, Jean and Manin, Philippe, *Die Europäischen Gemeinschaften in der Völkerrechtsordnung* (Brussels, 1984)

Guckel, Peter, *Die Streitbeilegungsvorschriften in den Satzungen der Internationalen*

Organisationen mit Ausnahme der Vereinten Nationen und der Europäischen Gemeinschaften (dissertation, Bonn, 1962)

Guggenheim, Paul, 'La validité et la nullité des actes juridiques internationaux' (1949 I) 74 *Recueil des Cours* 195–263

Traité de droit international public, Avec mention de la pratique internationale et suisse (2nd edn, Geneva, 1967), vol. I

Gutteridge, Frank, 'The ILO Administrative Tribunal' in C. de Cooker (ed.), *International Administration* (looseleaf, The Hague, Boston and London, 1989–), V.2/1-V.2/33

Haas, Ernst, *Beyond the Nation-State* (Stanford, 1964)

Habscheid, Walter J., 'Die Immunität ausländischer Staaten nach deutschem Zivilprozeßrecht' (1968) 8 *Berichte der Deutschen Gesellschaft für Völkerrecht* 159–281

'Anmerkung zu OLG Munich, 27.8.1971 und BayObLG, 30.9.1971' (1972) *Familienrechtszeitschrift* 210–15

'Die Staatenimmunität im Erkenntnis- und Vollstreckungsverfahren' in Habscheid *et al.* (eds.), *Freiheit und Zwang. Rechtliche, wirtschaftliche und gesellschaftliche Aspekte, Festschrift zum 60. Geburtstag von Hans Giger* (Berne, 1989), 213–30

Hackworth, Green Haywood, *Digest of International Law* (Washington DC, 1941), vol. II, chapter VII

Hahn, Hugo J., 'Euratom: The Conception of an International Personality' (1958) 71 *Harvard Law Review* 1001–56

'European Organization for Nuclear Research' in Bernhardt, Rudolf (ed.), *Encyclopedia of Public International Law* (2nd edn, 1995), vol. II, 268–70

Hailbronner, Kay, 'Völkerrechtliche und staatsrechtliche Aspekte fiskalischer Immunität im Sitzstaatabkommen des Europäischen Laboratoriums für Molekularbiologie' (1979) 22 *German Yearbook of International Law* 313–34

'International Air Transport Association' in Bernhardt, Rudolf (ed.), *Encyclopedia of Public International Law* (2nd edn, 1995), vol. II, 1047–50

'International Civil Aviation Organization' in Bernhardt, Rudolf (ed.), *Encyclopedia of Public International Law* (2nd edn, 1995), vol. II, 1070–4

Hambro, Edvard, 'A Case of Development of International Law Through the International Court of Justice' in Lipsky, George A. (ed.), *Law and Politics in the World Community. Essays on Hans Kelsen's Pure Theory and Related Problems in International Law* (Berkeley and Los Angeles, 1953), 243–51

Hamilton, Robert W., *Cases and Materials on Corporations* (4th edn, St Paul, MN, 1990)

Hammarskjöld, Ake, 'Les immunités des personnes investies de fonctions internationales' (1936 II) 56 *Recueil des Cours* 107–211

Hammerschlag, Daniel, '*Morgan v. International Bank for Reconstruction and Development*' (1992) 16 *Maryland Journal of International Law and Trade* 279–303

Harders, Enno J., 'Haftung und Verantwortlichkeit Internationaler Organisationen' in Wolfrum, Rüdiger (ed.), *Handbuch Vereinte Nationen* (2nd edn, Munich, 1991), 248–58

Harms, Thomas, *Die Rechtsstellung der Abgeordneten in der Beratenden Versammlung des Europarates und im Europäischen Parlament* (Hamburg, 1968)

Harpignies, R. H., 'Settlement of Disputes of a Private Law Character to which the United Nations is a Party – A Case in Point – The Arbitral Award of

24.9.1969, In Re Starways Ltd v. the United Nations' (1971) 7 *Revue belge de droit international* 451–68

Harremoes, E., 'Council of Europe' in Bernhardt, Rudolf (ed.), *Encyclopedia of Public International Law* (2nd edn, 1992), vol. I, 843–50

Hartwig, Matthias, *Die Haftung der Mitgliedstaaten für Internationale Organisationen* (Berlin, 1993)

Heidelmeyer, Wolfgang, 'Immunität und Rechtsschutz gegen Akte der Besatzungshoheit in Berlin' (1986) 46 *Zeitschrift für ausländisches öffentliches Recht und Völkerrecht* 519–38

Heinze, Christian, 'Die Rechtsstellung der "Europäischen Schulen" und der an ihnen tätigen deutschen Lehrer' (1969) 14 *Jahrbuch für internationales Recht* 209–24

Heiskanen, Veijo, 'Jurisdiction v. Competence: Revisiting a Frequently Neglected Distinction' (1994) 5 *Finnish Yearbook of International Law* 1–33

Henderson, Frances W., 'How Much Immunity for International Organizations?: *Mendaro v. World Bank*' (1985) 10 *North Carolina Journal of International Law and Commercial Regulation* 487–97

Henkin, Louis, *How Nations Behave* (2nd edn, New York, 1979)
  Foreign Affairs and the United States Constitution (2nd edn, Oxford, 1996)

Henkin, Louis, Pugh, Richard C., Schachter, Oscar and Smit, Hans, *International Law* (2nd edn, St Paul, MN, 1987)

Henrichs, Helmut, 'Die Vorrechte und Befreiungen der Beamten der Europäischen Gemeinschaften' (1987) 22 *EuropaRecht* 75–92
  'Zur rechtlichen Stellung der Europäischen Schulen und ihrer Lehrer' (1994) 29 *EuropaRecht* 358–63

Herdegen, Matthias, 'Erklärungen der englischen Krone vor Gerichten in auswärtigen Fragen' (1980) 40 *Zeitschrift für ausländisches öffentliches Recht und Völkerrecht* 782–802
  'Bemerkungen zur Zwangsliquidation und zum Haftungsdurchgriff bei internationalen Organisationen' (1987) 47 *Zeitschrift für ausländisches öffentliches Recht und Völkerrecht* 537–58
  'The Insolvency of International Organizations and the Legal Position of Creditors: Some Observations in the Light of the International Tin Council Crisis' (1988) 35 *Netherlands International Law Review* 135–44
  'Wirkungen von Schiedssprüchen in Streitigkeiten zwischen Privatpersonen und fremden Staaten' (1989) *Recht der Internationalen Wirtschaft/Außenwirtschaftsdienst* 329–37
  'Maastricht and the German Constitutional Court: Constitutional Restraints for an "Ever Closer Union"' (1994) 31 *Common Market Law Review* 235–49

Herndl, Kurt, 'Zur Problematik der Gerichtsbarkeit über fremde Staaten' in Miehsler, Herbert, Mock, Erhard, Simma, Bruno and Tammelo, Ilmar (eds.), *Ius Humanitatis. Festschrift Alfred Verdross* (Berlin, 1980), 421–43

Herzog, Roman, 'Nochmals – Verfassungsbeschwerde gegen Verletzungen der Menschenrechtskonvention?' (1960) 13 *Die Öffentliche Verwaltung* 775–8

Hess, Burkhard, *Staatenimmunität bei Distanzdelikten. Der private Kläger im Schnittpunkt von zivilgerichtlichem und völkerrechtlichem Rechtsschutz* (Munich, 1992)
  'Zur Zustellung von Klagen gegen fremde Staaten' (1989) *Recht der Internationalen Wirtschaft/Außenwirtschaftsdienst* 254–60

Heusch, A., 'Die Europäische Schule in Luxemburg' (1959–60) 8 *Archiv des Völkerrechts* 71–86

Heydte, Friedrich August Freiherr von der, 'Rechtssubjekt und Rechtsperson im Völkerrecht' in Constantinopoulos, D. S., Eustathiades, C. T. and Fragistas, C. N. (eds.), *Grundprobleme des Internationalen Rechts. Festschrift für Jean Spiropoulos* (Bonn, 1957), 237–55

Higgins, Rosalyn, *Problems and Process. International Law and How We Use It* (Oxford, 1994)

'The Legal Consequences for Member States of the Non-Fulfilment by International Organizations of Their Obligations Toward Third Parties – Preliminary Exposé and Draft Questionnaire' (1995) 66 *Annuaire de l'Institut de Droit International* 249–89

'The Legal Consequences for Member States of the Non-Fulfilment by International Organizations of Their Obligations Toward Third Parties – Provisional Report' (1995) 66 *Annuaire de l'Institut de Droit International* 373–420

Hilf, Meinhard, *Die Auslegung mehrsprachiger Staatsverträge, Eine Untersuchung zum Völkerrecht und zum Staatsrecht der Bundesrepublik Deutschland* (Berlin, Heidelberg and New York, 1974)

Die Organisationstruktur der Europäischen Gemeinschaften (Berlin, Heidelberg and New York, 1982)

'European Company for the Chemical Processing of Irradiated Fuels (EUROCHEMIC)' in Bernhardt, Rudolf (ed.), *Encyclopedia of Public International Law* (2nd edn, 1995), vol. II, 176–8

Hill, Jonathan, 'International Corporations in the English Courts [AMF v. Hashim]' (1992) 12 *Oxford Journal of Legal Studies* 135–48

Hill, Martin, *Immunities and Privileges of International Officials, The Experience of the League of Nations* (Washington DC, 1947)

Hill, Norman L., *International Administration* (New York and London, 1931)

'Diplomatic Privileges and Immunities in International Organizations' (1931–2) 20 *Georgetown Law Journal* 44–56

Hirsch, Mosche, *The Responsibility of International Organizations Toward Third Parties* (Dordrecht, Boston and London, 1995)

Hoffmann, Gerhard, 'Der Durchgriff auf die Mitgliedstaaten internationaler Organisationen für deren Schulden' (1988) *Neue Juristische Wochenschrift* 585–90

Hubbard, H. K., 'Separation of Powers Within the United Nations: A Revised Role for the International Court of Justice' (1985) 38 *Stanford Law Review* 165–94

Hudson, Richard, *Quick Calculator for Estimating Outcomes of Votes in the UN General Assembly under the Binding Triad System for Global Decision-Making* (CW/PS Special Study No. 8, New York, 1995)

Hug, Dieter, *Die Rechtsstellung der in der Schweiz niedergelassenen internationalen Organisationen* (Berne, Frankfurt am Main, Nancy and New York, 1984)

Hummer, Waldemar, 'Reichweite und Grenzen unmittelbarer Anwendbarkeit der Freihandelsabkommen' in Koppensteiner, Hans-Georg (ed.), *Rechtsfragen der Freihandelsabkommen der Europäischen Wirtschaftsgemeinschaft mit den EFTA-Staaten* (Vienna, 1987), 43–83

'Politisch bedeutsame transnationale Akteure an oder unter der Schwelle der Völkerrechtssubjektivität' in Neuhold, Hanspeter, Hummer, Waldemar and

Schreuer, Christoph (eds.), *Österreichisches Handbuch des Völkerrechts* (2nd edn, Vienna, 1991), 201–16

Hummer, Waldemar, Simma, Bruno, Vedder, Christoph and Emmert, Frank, *Europarecht in Fällen* (2nd edn, Baden-Baden, 1994)

Hutchinson, D. N., 'Decisions of British Court During 1987 Involving Questions of Public International Law' (1987) 59 *British Yearbook of International Law* 399–454

'Decisions of British Court During 1988 Involving Questions of Public or Private International Law, A. Public International Law' (1988) 58 *British Yearbook of International Law* 267–341

Ignarski, Jonathan S., 'North Atlantic Treaty Organization' in Bernhardt, Rudolf (ed.), *Encyclopedia of Public International Law* (1983), vol. VI, 264–70

Ijalaye, David Adedayo, *The Extension of Corporate Personality in International Law* (New York and Leiden, 1978)

ILA, *Report of the 65th Conference, Cairo* (1992)

Report of the 66th Conference, Buenos Aires (1994)

Imhoof, Rodolphe, 'La personnalité et le statut des institutions de caractère international – Exemples tirés de la pratique suisse' (1989) 46 *Schweizerisches Jahrbuch für Internationales Recht* 93–115

Institut de droit international, 'Recours judiciaire à instituter contre les décisions d'organes internationales' (1957) 47 *Annuaire de l'Institut de Droit International* 274–327

'The Activities of National Judges and the International Relations of Their State' (1993 I) 65 *Annuaire de l'Institut de Droit International* 327–448

Iovane, Massimo, 'In tema di immunità dei quartieri generali della NATO dall'esecuzione forzata' (1985) 68 *Rivista di diritto internazionale* 326–38

Ipsen, Knut, *Völkerrecht* (3rd edn, Munich, 1990)

Isicoff, Eric D., 'An Alternative Justification for Judicial Abstention in Politically Sensitive Disputes Involving Acts of Foreign States. *International Association of Machinists* v. *Organization of Petroleum Exporting Countries* . . .' (1982) 14 *Lawyer of the Americas* 85–90

Ivrakis, Solon Cleanthe, *Privileges and Immunities of the United Nations. Precedents and Present Day Developments* (unpublished PhD dissertation, Cambridge, 1954)

'Speculations Around the Privileges and Immunities of the United Nations' (1954) 7 *Revue Hellenique de Droit International* 175–93

'The Regulation-Making Power of the United Nations' (1956) 9 *Revue Hellenique de Droit International* 80–92

Jacobs, Francis G. and White, Robin C. A., *The European Convention on Human Rights* (2nd edn, Oxford, 1996)

Jacot-Guillarmod, Olivier, 'L'arbitrage privé face à l'Article 6, § 1er de la Convention européenne des droits de l'homme' in *Protecting Human Rights: The European Dimension. Studies in Honour of Gérard J. Wiarda* (Cologne, Berlin, Bonn and Munich, 1988), 281–95

Jaenicke, Günther, 'Die Sicherung des übernationalen Charakters der Organe internationaler Organisationen' (1951–2) 14 *Zeitschrift für ausländisches öffentliches Recht und Völkerrecht* 46–117

Jahn, Eberhard, 'Intergovernmental Committee for Migration' in Bernhardt, Rudolf (ed.), *Encyclopedia of Public International Law* (2nd edn, 1995), vol. II,

1023–5

'International Refugee Organization' in Bernhardt, Rudolf (ed.), *Encyclopedia of Public International Law* (2nd edn, 1995), vol. II, 1351–4

Jenks, C. Wilfred, 'Some Constitutional Problems of International Organizations' (1945) 22 *British Yearbook of International Law* 11–72

'The Legal Personality of International Organizations' (1945) 22 *British Yearbook of International Law* 267–75

The Headquarters of International Intitutions: A Study of their Location and Status (London, 1945)

'The Impact of International Organizations on Public and Private International Law' (1951) 37 *Transactions of the Grotius Society* 23–49

International Immunities (London and New York, 1961)

The Proper Law of International Organizations (London and Dobbs Ferry, NY, 1962)

'Due Process of Law in International Organizations' (1965) 19 *International Organization* 163–8

'Multinational Entities in the Law of Nations' in Friedmann, Wolfgang, Henkin, Louis and Lissitzyn, Oliver (eds.), *Transnational Law in a Changing Society. Essays in Honor of Philip Jessup* (New York and London, 1972), 70–83

Jennings, Robert Y., 'The Progress of International Law' (1958) 34 *British Yearbook of International Law* 334–55

'Nullity and Effectiveness in International Law' in *Cambridge Essays in International Law – Essays in Honour of Lord McNair* (London and New York, 1965), 64–87

'Report' in Max Planck Institut (ed.), *Judicial Settlement of International Disputes: An International Symposium* (Berlin, Heidelberg and New York, 1974), 35–48

Jessup, Philip C., 'Status of International Organizations: Privileges and Immunities of their Officials' (1944) 38 *American Journal of International Law* 658–62

A Modern Law of Nations (New York, 1956)

Transnational Law (New Haven, CT, 1956)

Jiménez de Aréchaga, Eduardo, 'International Responsibility of States for Acts of the Judiciary' in Friedmann, Wolfgang, Henkin, Louis and Lissitzyn, Oliver (eds.), *Transnational Law in a Changing Society. Essays in Honor of Philip Jessup* (New York and London, 1972), 171–87

'The World Bank Administrative Tribunal' (1982) 14 *New York University Journal of International Law and Politics* 895–909

Johnson, Earl, *et al.*, 'Access to Justice in the United States: The Economic Barriers and Some Promising Solutions' in Cappelletti, Mauro and Garth, Bryant (eds.), *Access to Justice* (Alphen aan den Rijn, 1978), vol. I, book II, 915–1023

Kahn-Freund, Otto, 'Review of Foreign Law?' in Flume, Hahn, Kegel and Simmonds (eds.), *Internationales Recht und Wirtschaftsordnung. Festschrift für F. A. Mann* (Munich, 1977), 207–25

Karcewski, Christoph, 'Das Europäische Übereinkommen über Staaten-immunität vom 16.5.1972' (1990) 54 *Rabels Zeitschrift für ausländisches und internationales Privatrecht* 533–50

Kegel, Gerhard, *Internationales Privatrecht* (5th edn, Munich, 1985)

Kegel, Gerhard and Seidl-Hohenveldern, Ignaz, 'Zum Territorialitätsprinzip im internationalen öffentlichen Recht' in Heldrich, Andreas, Henrich, Dieter and Sonnenberger, Hans Jürgen (eds.), *Konflikt und Ordnung, Festschrift für Murad Ferid* (Munich, 1978), 233–77

Kelsen, Hans, *The Law of the United Nations. A Critical Analysis of its Fundamental Problems* (London, 1950)

Recent Trends in the Law of the United Nations: A Supplement (London, 1951)

Principles of International Law (New York, 1952)

Reine Rechtslehre (2nd edn, Vienna, 1960)

Allgemeine Theorie der Normen (Vienna, 1979)

Kenny, Michael, 'European Company for the Financing of Railway Rolling Stock (EUROFIMA)' in Bernhardt, Rudolf (ed.), *Encyclopedia of Public International Law* (2nd edn, 1995), vol. II, 178–80

Kerno, Ivan S., 'Legal Activities of the United Nations' (1949) 16 *Journal of the Bar Association of the District of Columbia* 441–7

Kewenig, Wilhelm A., 'Der Internationale Zinnrat – Ein Lehrstück des Wirtschaftsvölkerrechts' (1990) *Recht der Internationalen Wirtschaft/Außenwirtschaftsdienst* 781–8

Kiesgen, Karl Heinz, *Sachliche Indemnität der Staaten, internationalen Organisationen und ihrer Organe* (dissertation, Bonn, 1970)

King, John Kerry, *The Privileges and Immunities of the Personnel of International Organizations* (Odense, 1949)

International Administrative Jurisdiction (Brussels, 1952)

Kirgis, Frederic L., 'Alien Tort Claims, Sovereign Immunity and International Law in US Courts [*Amerada Hess Shipping Corp* v. *Argentine Republic*]' (1988) 82 *American Journal of International Law* 323–30

International Organizations in Their Legal Setting (2nd edn, St Paul, MN, 1993)

Teacher's Manual to International Organizations in Their Legal Setting (2nd edn, St Paul, MN, 1993)

Klein, Hans H. and Lauff, Werner, 'Inter-Parliamentary Union' in Bernhardt, Rudolf (ed.), *Encyclopedia of Public International Law* (2nd edn, 1995), vol. II, 1016–18

Klotz, Erhard, 'Beschränkter Wirkungskreis der juristischen Personen des öffentlichen Rechts. Grenzen der privatrechtlichen Rechtsfähigkeit der juristischen Personen des öffentlichen Rechts' (1964) 17 *Die Offentliche Verwaltung* 181–9

Knapp, Blaise, 'Les privilèges et immunités des organisations internationales et de leurs agents devant les tribunaux internationaux' (1965) 69 *Revue générale de droit international public* 615–81

'Questions juridiques relatives à la construction d'immeubles par les organisations internationales' (1977) 33 *Schweizerisches Jahrbuch für Internationales Recht* 51–80

'International Labour Organisation Administrative Tribunal' in Bernhardt, Rudolf (ed.), *Encyclopedia of Public International Law* (2nd edn, 1995), vol. II, 1156–9

Knipping, Franz, von Mangoldt, Hans and Rittberger, Volker (eds.), *The United Nations System and its Predecessors. Statutes and Legal Acts*, 3 vols (Berne and Munich, 1995)

Knitel, Hans, 'Les délégations du Comité international de la Croix-Rouge' (1966) 19 *Osterreichische Zeitschrift für öffentliches Recht* 304–91

Köck, Heribert Franz, 'Multinational Diplomacy and Progressive Development of

International Law' (1977) 28 *Osterreichische Zeitschrift für öffentliches Recht und Völkerrecht* 51–105

'Die "implied powers" der Europäischen Gemeinschaften als Anwendungsfall der "implied powers" internationaler Organisationen überhaupt' in Böckstiegel, Karl-Heinz, Folz, Hans-Ernst, Mössner, Jörg Manfred and Zemanek, Karl (eds.), *Völkerrecht – Recht der Internationalen Organisationen – Weltwirtschaftsrecht. Festschrift für Ignaz Seidl-Hohenveldern* (Cologne, Berlin, Bonn and Munich, 1988), 279–99

Köck, Heribert Franz and Fischer, Peter, *Internationale Organisationen* (3rd edn, Eisenstadt, 1997)

Koenig, Eric S., 'Treaties – Agreements Between the United States and the United Nations Regarding UN Headquarters – Reconciliation of Provisions of US Statutes and Treaties – Congressional Intent, United States v. Palestine Liberation Organization . . .' (1988) 82 *American Journal of International Law* 833–7

Kolasa, Jan, 'Capacity to Acquire and Dispose of Immovable and Movable Property' in Dupuy, Rene-Jean (ed.), *Manuel sur les organisations internationales, A Handbook on International Organizations* (Dordrecht and Boston, 1988), 232–6

Kordt, Erich, 'Privilegien und Immunitäten internationaler Organisationen' in Strupp, K. and Schlochauer, H.-J. (eds.), *Wörterbuch des Völkerrechts* (1961), vol. II, 804–7

Koskenniemi, Martti, *From Apology to Utopia* (Helsinki, 1989)

Kraatz, Horst, 'Durchsetzbarkeit zivilrechtlicher Forderungen und Schuldtitel aus Vertrags- und Schadensersatzrecht gegen Mitglieder der Stationierungsstreitkräfte in der Bundesrepublik Deutschland' (1987) *Neue Juristische Wochenschrift* 1126–8

Krafft, Mathias-Charles, 'Les privilèges et immunités diplomatiques en droit international – Leur conséquences pour l'instruction pénale' (1984) 101 *Schweizerische Zeitschrift für Strafrecht* 141–51

Kranz, J., 'Les pays socialistes, le Fonds monétaire international et la Banque mondiale' (1985) 23 *Archiv des Völkerrechts* 270–93

Krieger, Albrecht and Rogge, Dirk, 'Die neue Verwaltungsstruktur der Pariser und Berner Union und die Weltorganisation für geistiges Eigentum' (1967) *Gewerblicher Rechtsschutz und Urheberrecht (Internationaler Teil)* 462–89

Kropholler, Jan, *Internationales Privatrecht* (Tübingen, 1994)

Kuhn, Arthur K., 'United Nations Monetary Conference and the Immunity of International Agencies' (1944) 38 *American Journal of International Law* 662–7

Kunz, Josef L., 'The Pan American Union in the Field of International Administration' (1945) 31 *Iowa Law Review* 58–89
'Vienna as Headquarters of the New League' (1945) 39 *American Journal of International Law* 309–14
'Privileges and Immunites of International Organizations' (1947) 41 *American Journal of International Law* 828–62
'The Secretary General on the Role of the United Nations' (1958) 52 *American Journal of International Law* 300–4

Kunz-Hallstein, Hans Peter, 'Die Beteiligung Internationaler Organisationen am Rechts- und Wirtschaftsverkehr, unter besonderer Berücksichtigung der Probleme des Schutzes des geistigen und gewerblichen Eigentums' (1987) *Gewerblicher Rechtsschutz und Urheberrecht (Internationaler Teil)* 819–33

'Privilegien und Immunitäten internationaler Organisationen im Bereich nicht hoheitlicher Privatrechtsgeschäfte' (1992) *Neue Juristische Wochenschrift* 3069–73

Kwaw, Edmund M. A., 'International Organizations as Foreign Entities: *AMF* v. *Hashim (No. 3)*' (1992) 7 *Banking and Finance Law Review* 453–61

Lachs, Manfred, 'The Judiciary and the International Civil Service – Some Suggestions' in Böckstiegel, Karl-Heinz, Folz, Hans-Ernst, Mössner, Jörg Manfred and Zemanek, Karl (eds.), *Völkerrecht – Recht der Internationalen Organisationen – Weltwirtschaftsrecht. Festschrift für Ignaz Seidl-Hohenveldern* (Cologne, Berlin, Bonn and Munich, 1988), 301–13

Lafferranderie, Gabriel, 'L'immunité de juridiction des organisations internationales, l'exemple de l'Agence spatiale européenne' (1983) 37 *Revue français de droit aérien* 13–27

Lalive, Jean-Flavien, 'L'immunité de juridiction des états et des organisations internationales' (1953 III) 84 *Recueil des Cours* 205–396

Lalive, Pierre, 'L'application du droit public étranger, Rapport préliminaire' (1975) 56 *Annuaire de l'Institut de Droit International* 157–83

Lamoureux, Pierre, 'Cour de justice des Communautés européennes – 13 mars 1962 et 25 septembre 1963' (1965) 54 *Revue critique de droit international privé* 386–402

Lang, Winfried, 'Der Grundsatz der nationalen Differenzierungen im UNIDO-Amtssitzabkommen' (1968) 18 *Österreichische Zeitschrift für öffentliches Recht* 281–306

Langkeit, Jochen, *Staatenimmunität und Schiedsgerichtsbarkeit, Verzichtet ein Staat durch Unterzeichnung einer Schiedsgerichtsvereinbarung auf seine Immunität?* (Heidelberg, 1989)

Langrod, Georges, *The International Civil Service* (Leiden and Dobbs Ferry, NY, 1963)

Larger, Dominique-Pierre, 'L'affaire Klarsfeld devant les tribunaux français' (1968) 14 *Annuaire français de droit international* 369–76

Lashbrooke, E. C., 'Suits Against International Organizations in Federal Court: OPEC, A Case Study' (1982) 12 *California Western International Law Journal* 305–24

Lauterpacht, Elihu, 'The Legal Effects of Illegal Acts of International Organisations' in *Cambridge Essays in International Law – Essays in Honour of Lord McNair* (London and New York, 1965), 88–121
'Implementation of Decisions of International Organization Through National Courts' in Schwebel, S. M. (ed.), *The Effectiveness of International Decisions* (Leiden, 1971), 57–65
'The Development of the Law of International Organisations by the Decisions of International Tribunals' (1976 IV) 152 *Recueil des Cours* 377–478

Lauterpacht, Sir Hersch, 'Decisions of Municipal Courts as a Source of International Law' (1929) 10 *British Yearbook of International Law* 65–95
'The Subjects of the Law of Nations' (1947) 63 *Law Quarterly Review* 438–60
'The Subjects of the Law of Nations' (1948) 64 *Law Quarterly Review* 97–119
'The Problem of Jurisdictional Immunities of Foreign States' (1951) 28 *British Yearbook of International Law* 220–72

Lauwaars, R. H., 'The Interrelationship Between United Nations Law and the Law of other International Organizations' (1984) 82 *Michigan Law Review* 1604–19

Lavigne, Marie, 'Les pays socialistes européens et le Fonds Monetaire

International' in *Problèmes Economiques* (1985), 25–32

Lee, Kenneth R., 'Recent Developments, International Organizations – Immunity – Personnel Decisions of an International Organizations Are Not "Commercial Activities" and Thus May Not Form the Basis for an Action Against the Organization' (1980) 20 *Virginia Journal of International Law* 913–23

Leigh, Monroe, 'International Organizations Immunities Act – Foreign Sovereign Immunities Act – Restrictive Immunity – Commercial Activity, Tuck v. Pan American Health Organization . . .' (1982) 76 *American Journal of International Law* 623–4

   'Immunity of International Organizations – Waiver of Immunity – International Organizations Immunities Act, Mendaro v. World Bank . . .' (1984) 78 *American Journal of International Law* 221–3

Lémonon, Ernest, 'L'immunité de juridiction et d'exécution forcée des Etats étrangers' (1952 I) 44 *Annuaire de l'Institut de Droit International* 5–35

Leopold, Patricia, 'Privileges and Immunities of MEPs' (1981) 6 *European Law Review* 275–8

'Les institutions financières internationales de développement (IFID)' (1986) 40 *Revue juridique et politique, indépendance et coopération* 16–36

Lewis, Charles J., *State and Diplomatic Immunity* (3rd edn, London, 1990)

Lewis, Robert P., 'Sovereign Immunities and International Organizations' (1979) 13 *Journal of International Law and Economics of George Washington University* 675–93

Liang, Yuen-Li, 'The Legal Status of the United Nations in the United States' (1948) 2 *International Law Quarterly* 577–602

   'United Nations Headquarters Agreement' (1948) 42 *American Journal of International Law* 445–7

   'The Question of Access to the United Nations Headquarters of Representatives of Non-Governmental Organizations in Consultative Status' (1954) 48 *American Journal of International Law* 434–50

Lichtenstein, Cynthia C., 'Does International Human Rights Law Have Something To Teach Monetary Law?' (1989) 10 *Michigan Journal of International Law* 225–30

Liermann, H., 'Der Völkerbund als Privatrechtssubjekt' (1930) 15 *Zeitschrift für Völkerrecht* 20–47

Ling, Yu-Long, 'A Comparative Study of the Privileges and Immunities of United Nations Member Representatives and Officials with the Traditional Privileges and Immunities of Diplomatic Agents' (1976) 33 *Washington and Lee Law Review* 91–160

Lister, F., 'The Role of International Organizations in the 1990s and Beyond' (1990) 10 *International Relations* (London) 101–16

Lowenfeld, Andreas F., *International Litigation and Arbitration* (St Paul, MN, 1993)

Lucas, Michael, 'The IMF's Conditionality and the ICESCR: An Attempt to Define the Relation' (1992) 25 *Revue belge de droit international* 104–35

Lüke, Gerhard and Walchshöfer, Alfred (eds.), *Münchner Kommentar zur Zivilprozeßordnung* (Munich, 1992), vol. III

Lyons, A. B., 'Was the League of Nations a Charity?' (1950) 27 *British Yearbook of International Law* 434–9

Macalister-Smith, Peter, 'Western European Union' in Bernhardt, Rudolf (ed.),

Encyclopedia of Public International Law (1983), vol. VI, 366–70

'United Nations Relief and Works Agency for Palestine Refugees in the Near East' in Bernhardt, Rudolf (ed.), *Encyclopedia of Public International Law* (1985), vol. VIII, 519–22

Macdonald, R. St. J., 'Reflections on the Charter of the United Nations' in Jekewitz, Klein, Kühne, Petersmann and Wolfrum (eds.), *Des Menschen Recht zwischen Freiheit und Verantwortung, Festschrift für Karl Josef Partsch* (Berlin, 1989), 29–45

Macdonald, R. St. J., Matscher, F. and Petzold, H. (eds.), *The European System for the Protection of Human Rights* (Dordrecht, Boston and London, 1993)

MacGlashan, M. E., 'The International Tin Council: Should a Trading Organization Enjoy Immunity?' (1987) 46 *Cambridge Law Journal* 193–5

Madders, Kevin J., 'European Space Agency' in Bernhardt, Rudolf (ed.), *Encyclopedia of Public International Law* (2nd edn, 1995), vol. II, 273–98

Makarczyk, Jerzy, 'The International Court of Justice on the Implied Powers of International Organizations' in Makarczyk, J. (ed.), *Essays in Honour of Judge Manfred Lachs* (The Hague, Boston and Lancaster, 1984), 501–18

Mallory, I. A., 'Conduct Unbecoming: The Collapse of the International Tin Agreement' (1990) 5 *American University Journal of International Law and Policy* 835–92

Mangoldt, Hans von, *Die Schiedsgerichtsbarkeit als Mittel internationaler Streitschlichtung* (Berlin, Heidelberg and New York, 1974)

Manin, Philippe, *Droit international public* (Paris, 1979)

Mann, F. A., 'International Corporations and National Law' (1967) 42 *British Yearbook of International Law* 145–74

'Zu den öffentlichrechtlichen Ansprüchen ausländischer Staaten, ein Rückblick nach 30 Jahren' in *Festschrift Kegel* (1987), 365–88

'Die juristische Person des Völkerrechts' (1988) 152 *Zeitschrift für das gesamte Handelsrecht und Wirtschaftsrecht* 303–17

'"Inviolability" and Other Problems of the Vienna Convention on Diplomatic Relations' in Hailbronner, Kay, Ress, Georg and Stein, Torsten (eds.), *Staat und Völkerrechtsordnung. Festschrift für Karl Doehring* (Berlin, Heidelberg, New York, London, Paris, Tokyo and Hong Kong, 1989), 553–65

'The International Enforcement of Public Rights' in Mann, F. A. (ed.), *Further Studies in International Law* (1990), 355–76

'International Organisations as National Corporations' (1991) 107 *Law Quarterly Review* 357–62

Marmorstein, Victoria E., 'Responding to the Call for Order in International Finance: Cooperation Between the IMF and Commercial Banks' (1978) 18 *Virginia Journal of International Law* 445–83

Marston, Geoffrey, 'United Kingdom Materials on International Law 1981' (1981) 52 *British Yearbook of International Law* 361–533

'United Kingdom Materials on International Law 1990 (Privileges of the European School)' (1990) 61 *British Yearbook of International Law* 510–13

'The Arab Monetary Fund: Legal Person or Creature from Outer Space?' (1991) 50 *Cambridge Law Journal* 218–20

'The Origin of Personality of International Organisations in United Kingdom Law' (1991) 40 *International and Comparative Law Quarterly* 403–24

'United Kingdom Materials on International Law 1991 (EBRD–UK

Headquarters Agreement)' (1991) 62 *British Yearbook of International Law* 576–89

Marton, Kati, *A Death in Jerusalem. The Assassination by Jewish Extremists of the First Arab/Israeli Peacemaker* (New York, 1994)

Matscher, Franz, 'Die Verfahrensgarantien der EMRK in Zivilrechtssachen' (1980) 31 *Osterreichische Zeitschrift für öffentliches Recht und Völkerrecht* 1–38

'Schiedsgerichtsbarkeit und EMRK, in Habscheid, Walter and Schwab, Karl Heinz (eds.), *Beiträge zum Internationalen Verfahrensrecht und zur Schiedsgerichtsbarkeit. Festschrift Nagel* (Münster, 1987), 227–45

'Vertragsauslegung durch Vertragsrechtsvergleichung in der Judikatur internationaler Gerichte, vornehmlich vor den Organen der EMRK' in Bernhardt, Geck, Jaenicke and Steinberger (eds.), *Völkerrecht als Rechtsordnung, Internationale Gerichtsbarkeit, Menschenrechte. Festschrift Mosler* (Berlin, Heidelberg and New York, 1983), 545–66

'Methods of Interpretation of the Convention' in Macdonald, R. St. J., Matscher, F. and Petzold, H. (eds.), *The European System for the Protection of Human Rights* (Dordrecht, Boston and London, 1993), 63–81

Maunz, Theodor and Dürig, Günther (eds.), *Grundgesetz Kommentar* (looseleaf, Munich, 1958–)

Max Planck-Institut für ausländisches öffentliches Recht und Völkerrecht (ed.), *Gerichtsschutz gegen die Exekutive – Judicial Protection Against the Executive*, 3 vols (Cologne, Berlin, Munich and Dobbs Ferry, NY, 1979–81)

Mayss, Abia, 'A Breakthrough Toward Recognising the Legal Status of International Organisations?' (1991) 12 *Company Lawyer* 185

McClanahan, Grant V., *Diplomatic Immunity, Principles, Practices, Problems* (1989)

McCormick Croswell, Carol, *Protection of International Personnel Abroad. Law and Practice Affecting the Privileges and Immunities of International Organization* (New York, 1952)

McDougal, Myres S. and Feliciano, Florentino P., *Law and Minimum World Public Order* (New Haven, CT and London, 1961)

McFadden, Eric, 'The Collapse of Tin: Restructuring a Failed Commodity Agreement' (1986) 80 *American Journal of International Law* 811–30

McNair, Arnold D., *The Law of Treaties* (Oxford, 1961)

Mendez, Ruben P., 'Financing the United Nations and the International Public Sector: Problems and Reform' (1997) 3 *Global Governance* 283–310

Meng, Werner, *Das Recht der internationalen Organisationen – eine Entwicklungsstufe des Völkerrechts, Zugleich eine Untersuchung zur Rechtsnatur des Rechts der Europäischen Gemeinschaften* (Baden-Baden, 1979)

'Internationale Organisationen im völkerrechtlichen Deliktsrecht' (1985) 45 *Zeitschrift für ausländisches öffentliches Recht und Völkerrecht* 324–57

Menzel, Eberhard, 'Die Privilegien und Immunitäten der internationalen Funktionäre' in *Verfassung und Verwaltung in Theorie und Wirklichkeit, Festschrift Laforet* (1952), 325–49

Merillat, H. C. C., *Legal Advisers and International Organizations* (Dobbs Ferry, NY, 1966)

Merkatz, H. J. von, 'Les privilèges et immunitès des organisations internationales et de leurs agents' (1968) 46 *Revue de droit international de Sciences Diplomatiques et Politiques* (Geneva) 146–64

Meron, Theodor, 'Status and Independence of the International Civil Servant'

(1980 II) 167 *Recueil des Cours* 285–384

'International Secretariat' in Bernhardt, Rudolf (ed.), *Encyclopedia of Public International Law* (2nd edn, 1995), vol. II, 1376–9

Meron, Theodor and Elder, Betty, 'The New Administrative Tribunal of the World Bank' (1982) 14 *New York University Journal of International Law and Politics* 1

Michaels, David B., *International Privileges and Immunites. A Case for a Universal Statute* (The Hague, 1971)

Miehsler, Herbert, 'Qualifikation und Anwendungsbereich des internen Rechts internationaler Organisationen' (1973) 12 *Berichte der Deutschen Gesellschaft für Völkerrecht* 47–83

Miele, Mario, *Privilèges et immunités des fonctionnaires internationaux* (Milan, 1958)

'Les organisations internationales et le domaine constitutionnel des Etats' (1970 III) 131 *Recueil des Cours* 309–338

Milde, Michael, 'New Headquarters Agreement Between ICAO and Canada' (1992) 17 *Annals of Air and Space Law*, Part II, 305–22

Mitrany, David, *A Working Peace System* (Chicago, 1966)

Monaco, Riccardo, 'Observations sur les contrats conclus par des des organisations internationales. Problèmes des droits de l'homme et de l'unification européenne' in *Mélanges offerts à Polys Modinos* (Paris, 1968), 85–98

'Capacités de droit privé des organisations internationales' in Caemmerer, Ernst von, *et al.* (eds.), *Festschrift für Pan Zepos* (Athens and Freiburg, 1973), 475–90

'Le caractère constitutionnel des actes institutifs d'organisations internationales' in *La Communauté Internationale. Mélanges offerts à Charles Rousseau* (Paris, 1974), 153–72

'Les principes régissants la structure et le fonctionnement des organisations internationales' (1977 III) 156 *Recueil des Cours* 79–223

Lezioni di organizzazione internationale, vol. I (Turin, 1985)

Morawiecki, Wojciech, 'Legal Regime of the International Organization' (1986) 15 *Polish Yearbook of International Law* 71–101

Morgenstern, Felice, 'The Law Applicable to International Officials' (1969) 18 *International and Comparative Law Quarterly* 739–56

'Legality in International Organizations' (1976–7) 48 *British Yearbook of International Law* 241–58

Legal Problems of International Organizations (Cambridge, 1986)

Mosler, Hermann, 'Reflections sur la personnalité juridique en droit international public' in *Mélanges offertes a Henri Rolin* (Paris, 1964), 228–51

'Völkerrecht als Rechtsordnung' (1976) 36 *Zeitschrift für ausländisches öffentliches Recht und Völkerrecht* 6–47

'Subjects of International Law' in Bernhardt, Rudolf (ed.), *Encyclopedia of Public International Law* (1984), vol. VII, 442–59

'Zur Entwicklung des Völkerrechts durch die Vereinten Nationen' (1985) 33 *Vereinte Nationen* 174–9

'General Principles of Law' in Bernhardt, Rudolf (ed.), *Encyclopedia of Public International Law* (2nd edn, 1995), vol. II, 511–27

Muller, A. S., *International Organizations and Their Host States* (The Hague, London and Boston, 1995)

Müller, Hans-Jürgen, 'Grundsätze der völkerrechtlichen Verantwortlichkeit internationaler Organisationen' (1978) 23 *Deutsche Außenpolitik* 89–100

Müller, Wolfgang, 'Trau schau wem! Oder – Von der zivilrechtlichen Verantwortlichkeit der Mitgliedstaaten internationaler Organisationen' (1991) *Neue Juristische Wochenschrift* 2175–81

Münchener Kommentar zur Zivilprozeßordnung mit Gerichtsverfassungsgesetz und Nebengesetzen (1992), vol. III

Myers, R. J. (ed.), *The Political Morality of the International Monetary Fund* (New Brunswick, NJ, 1987)

Nakamura, Osamu, 'The Status, Privileges and Immunities of International Organizations in Japan, An Overview' (1992) 35 *Japanese Annual of International Law* 116–29

Nascimento e Silva, G. E., 'Privileges and Immunities of Permanent Missions to International Organizations' (1978) 21 *German Yearbook of International Law* 9–26

Nash, M. L., 'Contemporary Practice of the United States Relating to International Law, Privileges and Immunities – World Bank' (1980) 74 *American Journal of International Law* 917–34

Nékám, Alexander, *The Personality Conception of the Legal Entity* (Cambridge, 1938)

Neuhold, Hanspeter, 'Abgrenzungen, Strukturmerkmale und Besonderheiten der Völkerrechtsordnung' in Neuhold, Hanspeter, Hummer, Waldemar and Schreuer, Christoph (eds.), *Osterreichisches Handbuch des Völkerrechts* (2nd edn, Vienna, 1991), 2–12

Neuhold, Hanspeter, Hummer, Waldemar and Schreuer, Christoph (eds.), *Osterreichisches Handbuch des Völkerrechts* (2nd edn, Vienna, 1991)

Neumann, Peter, 'The Relationship Between GATT and the United Nations' (1970–1) 3 *Cornell International Law Journal* 63–78

Niboyet, J. P., 'Immunité de juridiction et incompétence d'attribution' (1950) 39 *Revue critique de droit international privé* 139–58

Nicolaysen, Gert, 'Zur Theorie von den implied powers in den Europäischen Gemeinschaften' (1966) 1 *EuropaRecht* 129–42

Niemeyer, T., 'Zur Gerichtsbarkeit über fremde Staaten' (1910) 15 *Deutsche Juristen Zeitung* 105–7

Noll, Alfons and Nolte, Georg, 'International Telecommunication Union' in Bernhardt, Rudolf (ed.), *Encyclopedia of Public International Law* (2nd edn, 1995), vol. II, 1379–85

Nolte, Georg, 'Rechtsschutz gegen Akte der Besatzungsmächte in West-Berlin' (1989) 49 *Zeitschrift für ausländisches öffentliches Recht und Völkerrecht* 499–511

Note, 'Federal Jurisdiction over International Organizations' (1952) 61 *Yale Law Journal* 111–17

Note, 'The Relationship of International Organizations to Municipal Law and their Immunities and Privileges' (1945) 22 *British Yearbook of International Law* 249–51

Note, 'The United Nations and Its Agents. An Evolving Concept' (1949–50) 2 *Stanford Law Review* 193–9

Note, 'The United Nations Under American Municipal Law: A Preliminary Assessment' (1946) 55 *Yale Law Journal* 778–95

Obaid, Ibrahim Ahmed, *The Historical Evolution of the Legal Status of International Organizations* (dissertation, Indiana University, 1970)

O'Connell, D. P., 'La personnalité en droit international' (1963) 67 *Revue générale de droit international public* 5–43

Oellers-Frahm, Karin, 'European Molecular Biology Cooperation' in Bernhardt, Rudolf (ed.), *Encyclopedia of Public International Law* (2nd edn, 1995), vol. II, 259–62

Officier, Lawrence H., 'The International Monetary Fund' (1990) 37 *Proceedings of the Academy of Political Science* 28–36

O'Keefe, Patrick J., 'Privileges and Immunities of the Diplomatic Family' (1976) 25 *International and Comparative Law Quarterly* 329–50

Oliver, C. T., Firmage, E. B., Blakesley, C. L., Scott, R. F. and Williams, S. A., *The International Legal System: Cases and Materials* (4th edn, Westbury, NY, 1995)

Oparil, Richard J., 'Immunity of International Organizations in United States Courts: Absolute or Restrictive?' (1991) 24 *Vanderbilt Journal of Transnational Law* 689–710

Oppenheim's International Law (9th edn, ed. by Jennings, Robert and Watts, Arthur, 1992), vol. I

Orrego Vicuña, Francisco, 'Diplomatic and Consular Immunities and Human Rights' (1991) 40 *International and Comparative Law Quarterly* 34–48

Osakwe, Christopher O., 'Contemporary Soviet Doctrine on the Juridical Nature of Universal International Organizations' (1971) 65 *American Journal of International Law* 502–21

Osieke, Ebere, 'Ultra Vires Acts in International Organizations – The Experience of the International Labour Organisation' (1976–7) 48 *British Yearbook of International Law* 259–80

  'Unconstitutional Acts in International Organizations: The Law and Practice of the ICAO' (1979) 28 *International and Comparative Law Quarterly* 1–26

  'The Legal Validity of Ultra Vires Decisions of International Organizations' (1983) 77 *American Journal of International Law* 239–56

Osmanczyk, E. J., *The Encyclopedia of the United Nations and International Relations* (New York, 1990)

O'Toole, Thomas J., 'Sovereign Immunity Redivivus: Suits Against International Organizations' (1980) 4 *Suffolk Transnational Law Journal* 1–16

Ohlinger, Theo, 'Rechtsfragen des Freihandelsabkommens zwischen Osterreich und der EWG' (1974) 34 *Zeitschrift für ausländisches öffentliches Recht und Völkerrecht* 655–88

Padilla, David J., 'The Administrative Tribunal of the Organization of American States' (1981) 50 *Revista Juridica de la Universidad de Puerto Rico* 479–509

  'Administrative Tribunal of the Organization of American States' (1982) 14 *Lawyer of the Americas* 259–96

Pahr, Willibald P., 'Die Staatenimmunität und Artikel 6 Absatz 1 der Europäischen Menschenrechtskonvention', in *Mélanges offerts à Polys Modinos. Problèmes des droits de l'homme et de l'unification Européenne* (Paris, 1968), 222–32

Panhuys, Jonkheer H. F. van, 'Some Recent Developments of International Law in Respect of the Conflicts of Jurisdiction Resulting from the Presence of Foreign Armed Forces in the Territory of a State' (1955) 2 *Netherlands International Law Review* 253–78

Paone, Pasquale, 'L'organizzazione dell'Atlantico del Nord e la giurisdizione italiana' (1955) 38 *Rivista di diritto internazionale* 358–76

Parry, Clive, 'International Government and Diplomatic Privilege' (1947) 10
    Modern Law Review 97–121
    'The International Public Corporation' in Friedmann, W. (ed.), The Public
    Corporation, A Comparative Symposium (1954), 493
Partan, Daniel G., 'International Administrative Law' (1981) 75 American Journal
    of International Law 639–44
Partsch, Karl Josef, 'Menschenrechtsschutz durch die Vereinten Nationen' (1985)
    36 Außenpolitik 319–27
    'International Law and Municipal Law' in Bernhardt, Rudolf (ed.), Encyclopedia
    of Public International Law (2nd edn, 1995), vol. II, 1183–202
Peaslee, Amos J., International Governmental Organizations, Constitutional Documents
    (3rd edn, The Hague, 1974–9)
Pelikahn, Horst Michael, 'Internationale Rohstoffabkommen – Neuere
    Entwicklungen' (1988) 26 Archiv des Völkerrechts 67–88
Pellet, Alain, 'Les voies de recours ouvertes aux fonctionnaires internationaux'
    (1981) 85 Revue générale de droit international public 253–312, 657–792
Pellet, Alain and Ruzié, David, Les fonctionnaires internationaux (Paris, 1993)
Penfield, Walter Scott, 'The Legal Status of the Pan American Union' (1926) 20
    American Journal of International Law 257–62
Perez Gonzalez, Manuel, 'Les organisations internationales et le droit de la
    responsabilité' (1988) 92 Revue générale de droit international public 63–102
Perez Montero, Jose, 'Algunas consideraciones sobre la proteccion de los
    funcionarios internacionales, especialmente sobre la de los agentes de las
    Naciones Unidas' in Estudios de derecho internacional publico y privado,
    Homenaje al Profesor Luis Sela Sampil (Oviedo, 1970), vol. I, 351–95
Pernice, Ingolf, 'Die Haftung Internationaler Organisationen und ihrer
    Mitarbeiter' (1988) 26 Archiv des Völkerrechts 406–33
Perrenoud, Georges, Régime des Privilèges et Immunités des Missions Diplomatiques
    Etrangères et des Organisations Internationales en Suisse (Lausanne, 1949)
Perrin, Georges, 'Les Privilèges et Immunités des Représentants des Etats auprès
    des Organisations Internationales' (1956) 60 Revue générale de droit
    international public 193–237
Perruchoud, Richard, Les resolutions des Conferences internationales de la Croix-Rouge
    (dissertation, Geneva, 1979)
Pescatore, Pierre, 'Les relations extérieures des Communautés européennes,
    contribution à la doctrine de la personnalité des organisations
    internationales' (1962 II) 103 Recueil des Cours 5–238
    'Les Communautés en tant que personnes de droit international' in Ganshof
    van der Meersch, W. J. (ed.), Les Novelles, Droit des Communautés européennes
    (Brussels, 1969), 107–21
Peter, Manfred, Die Praxis des Europäischen Parlaments in Immunitätssachen,
    Luxemburg, Europäisches Parlament, Juristischer Dienst (DOC-DÈCM85769) (1990)
    Indemnität und Immunität der Mitglieder des Europäischen Parlaments im System des
    Gemeinschaftsrechts, Luxemburg, Europäisches Parlament, Juristischer Dienst
    (DOC-DÈCM85770) (1990)
Petersmann, Ernst-Ulrich, 'The Transformation of the World Trading System
    Through the 1994 Agreement Establishing the World Trade Organization'
    (1995) 6 European Journal of International Law 161–221
    The GATT/WTO Dispute Settlement System (London, The Hague and Boston, 1997)

Petersmann, H. G., 'The World Bank's Contribution to the Law of International Finance and Development (1944–1984)' (1985) 23 *Archiv des Völkerrechts* 241–69

Pettiti, Louis-Edmond, Decaux, Emmanuel and Imbert, Pierre-Henri, *La convention européenne des droits de l'homme* (Paris, 1995)

Pezard, Alice, 'L'organisation internationale de police criminelle et son accord de siège' (1983) 29 *Annuaire français de droit international* 564–75

Picone, Paolo and Conforti, Benedetto, *La giurisprudenza italiana di diritto internazionale pubblico. Repertorio 1960–1987* (Naples, 1988)

Pinto, Roger, 'Some Legal Aspects of International and Multinational Enterprises' in Wilner, Gabriel M. (ed.), *Jus et Societas. Essays in Tribute to Wolfgang Friedmann* (The Hague, Boston and London, 1979), 241–8

'La fermeture du bureau de l'OLP auprès de l'Organisation des Nations Unies à New York' (1989) 116 *Journal de droit international* 329–48

Pisillo Mazzeschi, Riccardo, 'Immunità Giurisdizionale delle Organizzazioni Internazionali e constituzione italiana' (1976) 59 *Rivista di diritto internazionale* 489–521

Plantey, Alain, *Droit et pratique de la fonction publique internationale* (Paris, 1977)
The International Civil Service – Law and Management (New York, 1981)

Plouvier, Liliane, 'L'immunité de contrainte des Communautés européennes' (1973) 9 *Revue belge de droit international* 471–84

Pons Rafols, Francesc-Xavier, 'Aplicabilidad de la seccion 22 del articulo VI de la Convencion sobre los privilegios e immunidades de las Naciones Unidas (Opinión Consulatativa del Tribunal Internacional de Justicia de 15 de diciembre de 1989)' (1991) 43 *Revista Espanola de derecho Internacional* 39–56

Prandler, Árpád, 'The Unchanging Significance of the United Nations Charter and Some International Legal Aspects of its Application' (1986) 3 *Questions of International Law* 191–208

Preibisch, Wolfgang, *Außergerichtliche Vorverfahren in Streitigkeiten der Zivilgerichtsbarkeit* (Berlin, 1982)

Preuss, Lawrence, 'Diplomatic Privileges and Immunities of Agents Invested with Functions of an International Interest' (1931) 25 *American Journal of International Law* 694–710

'The International Organizations Immunities Act' (1946) 40 *American Journal of International Law* 332–45

'Immunity of Officers and Employees of the United Nations for Offcial Acts – The Ranollo Case' (1947) 41 *American Journal of International Law* 555–78

'Privileges and Immunities Accorded by the United States to the United Nations Organization, its Property and its Personnel' (1950) 34 *Minnesota Law Review* 445–63

Priess, Hans-Joachim, *Internationale Verwaltungsgerichte und Beschwerdeausschüsse, Eine Studie zum gerichtlichen Rechtsschutz für Beamte internationaler Organisationen* (Berlin, 1989)

Pugh, Michael, 'Legal Aspects of the "Rainbow Warrior" Affair' (1987) 36 *International and Comparative Law Quarterly* 655–69

Pye, A. Kenneth, 'The Legal Status of the Korean Hostilities' (1956) 45 *Georgetown Law Journal* 45

Quadri, Rolando, 'La personnalité internationale de la Communauté' in Institut des Etudes Juridiques Européennes de la Faculté de Droit de l'Université de

Liège (ed.), *Les relations extérieures de la Communauté Européenne Unifiée – Actes du troisième Colloque sur la Fusion des Communautés Européennes* (1969)

Quaglino, Antonio, 'In Tema di Immunita del CIME dalla Giurisdizione Italiana nelle Controversie in Materia di Lavoro' (1974) 10 *Rivista di Diritto Internazionale Privato e Processuale* 487–500

Quaritsch, Helmut, *Staat und Souveränität* (Frankfurt am Main, 1970)

Rama Montaldo, Manuel, 'International Legal Personality and Implied Powers of International Organizations' (1970) 44 *British Yearbook of International Law* 111–55

Ramboud, Patrick, 'International Law and Municipal Law: Conflicts and Their Review by Third States' in Bernhardt, Rudolf (ed.), *Encyclopedia of Public International Law* (2nd edn, 1995), vol. II, 1202–6

Ramcharan, Bertie G., 'Revitalizing the United Nations' (1986) 55 *Nordic Journal of International Law* 241–61

Randelzhofer, Albrecht, 'Innerstaatlich erforderliche Verfahren für das Wirksamwerden der von der Exekutive abgeschlossenen völkerrechtlichen Vereinbarungen' (1974) 99 *Archiv des öffentlichen Rechts Beiheft* 1, 18–42

'Rechtsschutz gegen Maßnahmen von Interpol vor deutschen Gerichten?' in von Münch (ed.), *Staatsrecht – Völkerrecht – Europarecht. Festschrift für Hans-Jürgen Schlochauer* (Berlin and New York, 1981), 531–55

Raschauer, Bernhard, *Allgemeines Verwaltungsrecht* (Vienna and New York, 1998)

Ratner, Steven R., 'Sovereign Immunity – International Organizations – Act of State Doctrine – Recognition of Foreign Laws – Arbitration Clauses, International Tin Council v. Amalgamet Inc. . . .' (1988) 82 *American Journal of International Law* 837–40

Rauser, Karl T., *Die Übertragung von Hoheitsrechten auf ausländische Staaten, Zugleich ein Beitrag zur Dogmatik des Art. 24 I GG* (Munich, 1991)

Rechberger, Walter (ed.), *Kommentar zur ZPO* (Vienna and New York, 1994)

Reicin, Cheryl V., 'Act of State Doctrine: Applicability of United States Antitrust Laws – *International Association of Machinists & Aerospace Workers* v. *Organization of Petroleum Exporting Countries* . . .' (1982) 23 *Harvard International Law Journal* 117–23

Reinisch, August, 'Zur unmittelbaren Anwendbarkeit von EWR-Recht' (1993) 34 *Zeitschrift für Rechtsvergleichung, internationales Privatrecht und Europarecht* 11–30

'Das Jugoslawientribunal der Vereinten Nationen und die Verfahrensgarantien des II. VN-Menschenrechtspaktes. Ein Beitrag zur Frage der Bindung der Vereinten Nationen an nicht-ratifiziertes Vertragsrecht' (1995) 47 *Austrian Journal of Public and International Law* 173–213

Reisman, W. Michael, 'Dissemination of Information by International Organisations: Reflections on Law and Policy in the Light of Recent Developments' (1987) 17 *Victoria University of Wellington Law Review* 53–70

'The Constitutional Crisis in the United Nations' (1993) 87 *American Journal of International Law* 83–100

Relations Between States and International Organizations (Second Part of the Topic) Copies of Replies to a Questionnaire Concerning the Status, Privileges and Immunities of Regional Organizations (UN Doc. ST/LEG/17) (6 April 1987, unpublished)

'Report of the Commission to the General Assembly, Document A/10010/REV.1, Report of the International Law Commission on the Work of its

Twenty-Seventh Session, 5 May–25 July 1975' *Yearbook of the International Law Commission* (1975), vol. II, 47–187

'Report of the Rapporteur of Committee IV/2, as Approved by the Committee' (1945) 13 *United Nations Conference on International Organization* 703–12

Ress, Georg, 'Die Bedeutung der Rechtsvergleichung für das Recht der Internationalen Organisationen' (1972) 36 *Zeitschrift für ausländisches öffentliches Recht und Völkerrecht* 227–79

'Mangelhafte diplomatische Protektion und Staatshaftung, Überlegungen zum gerichtlichen Rechtsschutz gegen Akte der auswärtigen Gewalt im französischen und deutschen Recht' (1972) 32 *Zeitschrift für ausländisches öffentliches Recht und Völkerrecht* 420–82

'Ex Ante Safeguards Against Ex Post Opportunism in International Treaties: Theory and Practice of International Public Law' (1994) 150 *Journal of Institutional and Theoretical Economics* (formerly *Zeitschrift für die gesamte Staatswissenschaft*) 279–303

Restatement (Third) of the Law, The Foreign Relations Law of the United States (ed. American Law Institute, St Paul, MN, 1987)

Reuter, Paul, *La Communauté Européenne du Charbon et de l'Acier* (Paris, 1953)

Institutions Internationales (7th edn, Paris, 1972)

'Sur quelques limites du droit des organisations internationales' in Diez, Emanuel, Monnier, Jean, Müller, Jörg P., Reimann, Heinrich and Wildhaber, Luzius (eds.), *Festschrift Bindschedler* (Berne, 1980), 491–507

'L'ordre juridique et les traités des organisations internationales' in Bernhardt, Geck, Jaenicke and Steinberger (eds.), *Völkerrecht als Rechtsordnung, Internationale Gerichtsbarkeit, Menschenrechte, Festschrift Mosler* (Berlin, Heidelberg and New York, 1983), 745–57

'La personnalité juridique internationale du Comité international de la Croix-Rouge' in Swinarski (ed.), *Etudes et essais sur le droit international humanitaire et sur les principes de la Croix-Rouge en l'honneur de Jean Pictet* (Geneva and The Hague, 1984), 783–91

Reuterswärd, Reinhold, 'The Legal Nature of International Organizations' (1980) 49 *Nordisk Tidsskrift for International Ret* 14–30

Richter, Stefan, 'Convention on the Privileges and Immunities of the United Nations, Applicability of Article VI, Section 22 (Advisory Opinion)' in Bernhardt, Rudolf (ed.), *Encyclopedia of Public International Law* (2nd edn, 1992), vol. I, 823–5

Rideau, Joël, *Juridictions internationales et contrôle du respect des traités constitutifs des organisations internationales* (Paris, 1969)

Riegel, Reinhard, 'Rechtscharakter der Europäischen Schulen und Befugnis zur Regelung des Rechtsweges für Streitigkeiten mit dem Personal' (1995) 30 *EuropaRecht* 147–9

Riesenfeld, Stefan A., Feldman, Mark B. and Singer, Eric C., 'The Foreign Sovereign Immunities Act. Ten Years Later' (1986) 19 *Vanderbilt Journal of Transnational Law* 1–82

Rittberger, Volker, *Internationale Organisationen – Politik und Geschichte* (Opladen, 1994)

Ritter, Jean-Pierre, 'La protection diplomatique à l'égard d'une organisation internationale' (1962) 8 *Annuaire français de droit international* 427–56

Ritterspach, Theo, 'Corte Costituzionale, Rom – Rechtsprechungsbericht 1984

Nr. 9' (1985) *Europäische Grundrechte Zeitschrift* 352–5

Robertson, A. H., 'Agreement Relating to Persons Participating in Proceedings of the European Commission and Court of Human Rights' in *Miscellanea W. J. Ganshof van der Meersch, Studia ab discipulis amicisque in honorem egregii professoris edita I* (Brussels and Paris, 1972), 545–64

'Some Legal Problems of the UNRRA' (1946) 23 *British Yearbook of International Law* 142–67

Rodgers, Raymond Spencer, 'The Headquarters Agreement of the International Atomic Energy Agency of 1 March 1958 at Vienna' (1958) 34 *British Yearbook of International Law* 391–5

Röhl, Klaus F., *Allgemeine Rechtslehre* (Cologne, Berlin, Bonn and Munich, 1994)

Roffer, Michael H., 'Antitrust Law – International Law – Act of State Doctrine – Foreign Antitrust Violations – *International Association of Machinists & Aerospace Workers* v. *Organization of Petrolcum Exporting Countries (OPEC)*' (1982) 27 *New York Law School Law Review* 1013–41

Rosenau, James N., 'Governance in the Twenty-First Century' (1995) 1 *Global Governance* 13–43

Rosenstock, Robert, 'The Fourty-Fourth Session of the International Law Commission' (1993) 87 *American Journal of International Law* 138–44

Rösgen, Peter, 'Rechtsetzungsakte der Vereinten Nationen und ihrer Sonderorganisationen, Bestandsaufnahme und Vollzug in der Bundesrepublik Deutschland' (dissertation, Bonn, 1985)

Röttinger, Moritz, 'Art. 210–216' in Lenz, Carl Otto (ed.), *Kommentar zu dem Vertrag zur Gründung der Europäischen Gemeinschaften* (Cologne, Basel and Vienna, 1994), 1297–317

Rouhani, Fuad, *A History of OPEC* (New York, 1971)

Rousseau, Charles, *Droit international public* (Paris, 1970–83), vols. I–V

Rouyer-Hameray, Bernard, *Les competénces implicites des organisations internationales* (Paris, 1962)

Roy, Mark A., 'US Loyalty Program for Certain UN Employees Declared Unconstitutional' (1986) 80 *American Journal of International Law* 984–5

Rudolf, Alfred, 'Die außervertragliche Haftung der Europäischen Organisation zur Sicherung der Luftfahrt (Eurocontrol)' (1965) 14 *Zeitschrift für Luftrecht und Weltraumrechtsfragen* 44–64

Rudolf, Walter, *Völkerrecht und deutsches Recht* (Tübingen, 1967)

'Die innerstaatliche Anwendung partikulären Völkergewohnheitsrechts' in Marcic, Mosler *et al.* (eds.), *Festschrift Verdross* (Munich and Saltzburg, 1971), 435–48

Ruffini, Francesco, 'La Natura Giuridica delle Unioni Internazionali Amministrative' (1928) 20 *Rivista di Diritto Pubblico* 241

Rumpf, Helmut, 'Military Bases on Foreign Territory' in Bernhardt, Rudolf (ed.), *Encyclopedia of Public International Law* (1982), vol. III, 260–6

Rüster, Lothar, 'Der völkerrechtliche Status des RGW, Zur neuen Konvention über Rechtsfähigkeit, Privilegien und Immunitäten des RGW' (1987) 41 *Neue Justiz* 176–9

Ruzié, David, 'De l'obligation de réserve des fonctionnaires internationaux et des conditions de leur licenciement à propos de l'affaire Klarsfeld' (1970) 16 *Annuaire français de droit international* 417–28

Les fonctionnaires internationaux (Paris, 1970)

'La France et l'Organisation européenne de recherche nucléaire' (1986) 2 *Revue française de droit administratif* 956–60

'Le recours à l'arbitrage dans le contentieux de la fonction publique internationale: L'exemple du personnel local de l'UNRWA' (1986) 113 *Journal de droit international* 109–21

'L'Avis consultatif de la Cour internationale de justice du 15 décembre 1989 sur la demande du Conseil économique et social des Nations Unies (l'affaire Mazilu)' (1990) 117 *Journal de droit international* 365–79

'Jurisprudence du Tribunal Administratif de l'Organisation Internationale du Travail' (1991) 37 *Annuaire français de droit international* 488–513

'Diversité des juridictions administratives internationales et finalité commune. Rapport général' in Société Française pour le Droit International (ed.), *Le Contentieux de la fonction publique international* (Paris, 1996), 11–65

Sadiq Reza, S., 'Recent Developments – International Agreements: United Nations Headquarters Agreement – Dispute over the United States' Denial of a Visa to Yasir Arafat' (1989) 30 *Harvard International Law Journal* 536–48

Sadurska, Romana and Chinkin, Christine M., 'The Collapse of the International Tin Council: A Case of State Responsibility?' (1990) 30 *Virginia Journal of International Law* 845–90

Salmon, Jean J. A., *Le role des organisations internationales en matière de prets et d'emprunts* (Paris, 1958)

'L'accord ONU-Congo (Léopoldville) du 27 novembre 1961' (1964) 68 *Revue générale de droit international public* 60–109

'Les accords Spaak–U. Thant du février 1965' (1965) 11 *Annuaire français de droit international* 468–97

'De quelques problèmes posés aux tribunaux belges par les actions de citoyens belges contre l'ONU en raison de faits survenus sur le territoire de la République démocratique du Congo' (1966) 81 *Journal des Tribunaux* (Brussels) 713–19

'Les Communautés en tant que personnes de droit interne et leurs privilèges et immunités' in Ganshof van der Meersch, W. J. (ed.), *Les Novelles, Droit des Communautés européennes* (Brussels, 1969), 121–39

'Observations, Quelques réflexions sur l'immunité de juridiction des fonctionnaires internationaux pour actes accomplis en qualité officielle (Apropos de l'affaire Sayag)' (1969) 5 *Cahiers de droit européen* 421–58

'Immunités et actes de fonction' (1992) 38 *Annuaire français de droit international* 314–57

Sanders, A. J. G. M., 'Non-Justiciability of Foreign Policy Matters' in Joubert, W. A. (ed.), *The Law of South Africa* (Durban and Pretoria, 1981), vol. XI, *International Law*, para. 350

Samson, Klaus Theodor, 'International Labour Organisation' in Bernhardt, Rudolf (ed.), *Encyclopedia of Public International Law* (2nd edn, 1995), vol. II, 1150–6

Scelle, Georges, 'Some Reflections on Juridical Personality in International Law' in Lipsky, George A. (ed.), *Law and Politics in the World Community. Essays on Hans Kelsen's Pure Theory and Related Problems in International Law* (Berkeley and Los Angeles, 1953), 49–58

Schatz, Ulrich, 'European Patent Organization' in Bernhardt, Rudolf (ed.), *Encyclopedia of Public International Law* (2nd edn, 1995), vol. II, 273–6

Schaumann, W., 'Die Immunität ausländischer Staaten nach Völkerrecht' in
    (1968) 8 *Berichte der Deutschen Gesellschaft für Völkerrecht* 1–57
Schermers, Henry G., *Judicial Protection in the European Communities* (Deventer, 2nd
    edn, 1979)
    International Institutional Law (Alphen aan den Rijn and Rockville, 2nd edn,
    1980)
    'International Organizations as Members of Other International
    Organizations' in Bernhardt, Geck, Jaenicke and Steinberger (eds.),
    *Völkerrecht als Rechtsordnung, Internationale Gerichtsbarkeit, Menschenrechte,
    Festschrift Mosler* (Berlin, Heidelberg and New York, 1983), 823–37
    'Introduction' in Schermers, Heukels and Mead (eds.), *Non-Contractual Liability
    of the European Communities* (1988), ix–xiv
    'Liability of International Organizations' (1988) 1 *Leiden Journal of International
    Law* 3–14
    'Official Acts of Civil Servants' in Schermers, Heukels and Mead (eds.),
    Non-Contractual Liability of the European Communities (1988), 75–81
    'The European Court of First Instance' (1988) 25 *Common Market Law Review* 541
    'International Organizations, Legal Remedies Against Acts of Organs' in
    Bernhardt, Rudolf (ed.), *Encyclopedia of Public International Law* (2nd edn,
    1995), vol. II, 1318–20
Scheuner, Ulrich, 'Internationale Verträge als Elemente der Bildung von
    völkerrechtlichem Gewohnheitsrecht' in Flume, Hahn, Kegel and
    Simmonds (eds.), *Internationales Recht und Wirtschaftsordnung. Festschrift für F.
    A. Mann* (Munich, 1977), 410–38
Schiemer, Karl, Jabornegg, Peter and Strasser, Rudolf, *Kommentar zum Aktiengesetz*
    (Vienna, 1993)
Schlochauer, Hans-Jürgen, 'Permanent Court of Arbitration' in Bernhardt,
    Rudolf (ed.), *Encyclopedia of Public International Law* (1981), vol. I, 157–63
Schlüter, Bernhard, *Die innerstaatliche Rechtsstellung der internationalen
    Organisationen unter besonderer Berücksichtigung der Rechtslage in der
    Bundesrepublik Deutschland* (Cologne, Berlin, Bonn and Munich, 1972)
Schmid, Franz and Dufour, Jean-Marie, 'Le CERN, exemple de coopération
    scientifique européenne' (1976) 103 *Journal de droit international* 46–104
Schmidt, Claudia, 'Le protocole sur les privileges et immunités des
    Communautés Européennes' (1991) 27 *Cahiers de droit europééne* 67–100
Schmitthoff, Clive, 'The International Corporation' (1944) 30 *Transactions of the
    Grotius Society* 165–83
Schneider, H., 'Gerichtsfreie Hoheitsakte' (1951) 169 *Staat und Recht* 47
Schneider, Michael M., 'International Organizations and Private Persons: The
    Case for a Direct Application of International Law' in Dominicé, Christian,
    Patry, Robert and Reymond, Claude (eds.), *Etudes de droit international en
    l'honneur de Pierre Lalive* (Basel and Frankfurt am Main, 1993), 345–58
Schreuer, Christoph H., 'Concurrent Jurisdiction of National and International
    Tribunals' (1976) 13 *Houston Law Review* 508–26
    Decisions of International Institutions Before Domestic Tribunals (London, Rome and
    New York, 1981)
    'Eurocontrol: Wechselwirkungen staatlicher und innerstaatlicher
    Jurisdiktion' in Rechtswissenschaftliche Fakultät der Universität Salzburg
    (ed.), *Aus Osterreichs Rechtsleben in Geschichte und Gegenwart. Festschrift für Ernst*

C. Hellbling (Berlin, 1981), 371–82

'Staatliche Gerichtsbarkeit und internationale Beamtenstreitigkeiten' (1982) 33 *Osterreichische Zeitschrift für öffentliches Recht und Völkerrecht* 299–306

'Wechselwirkungen zwischen Völkerrecht und Verfassung bei der Auslegung völkerrechtlicher Verträge' (1982) 23 *Berichte der Deutschen Gesellschaft für Völkerrecht* 61–91

'Die Bedeutung internationaler Organisationen im heutigen Völkerrecht' (1984) 22 *Archiv des Völkerrechts* 363–404

State Immunity: Some Recent Developments (Cambridge, 1988)

'Internationale Organisationen' in Neuhold, Hanspeter, Hummer, Waldemar and Schreuer, Christoph (eds.), *Osterreichisches Handbuch des Völkerrechts* (2nd edn, Vienna, 1991), 157–99

'The Waning of the Sovereign State: Towards a New Paradigm for International Law?' (1993) 4 *European Journal of International Law* 447–71

'International Law and Municipal Law: Law and Decisions of International Organizations and Courts' in Bernhardt, Rudolf (ed.), *Encyclopedia of Public International Law* (2nd edn, 1995), vol. II, 1228–33

Schröer, Friedrich, 'Die Anwendung von Landesrecht auf völkerrechtliche Zweckverbände' (1965) 25 *Zeitschrift für ausländisches öffentliches Recht und Völkerrecht* 617–56

'Kollision zwischen internationalem und nationalem Beamtenrecht, insbesondere beim Streik in internationalen Organisationen' (1965) 90 *Archiv des öffentlichen Rechts* 61–80

'Zur Gewährung von Befreiungen und Vorrechten an eine internationale Einrichtung' (1965) 12 *Jahrbuch für Internationales Recht* 207–36

'De l'application de l'immunité juridictionnelle des états étrangers aux organisations internationales' (1971) 75 *Revue générale de droit international public* 712–41

'Zur Anwendung deutscher ordnungs- und sicherheitsrechtlicher Vorschriften auf Truppen der Stationierungsstreitkräfte' (1972) 87 *Deutsches Verwaltungsblatt* 484–9

'Cour d'appel de Colmar (Ch. soc.) – 28 janvier 1971 (Kehren c. Institut franco-allemand de Saint Louis)' (1974) 63 *Revue critique de droit international privé* 514–27

'On the Application of State Immunity from Enforcement Measures to International Organizations' (1974) 30 *Revue egyptienne de droit international* 76–90

Schumann, Ekkehard, 'Das Verhältnis des deutschen Richters zum Gerichtshof der Europäischen Gemeinschaften – Die Anwendung von Gemeinschaftsrecht durch deutsche Gerichte' (1965) 78 *Zeitschrift für Zivilprozeß* 77–130

Schuster, Gunnar, 'Inmarsat' in Bernhardt, Rudolf (ed.), *Encyclopedia of Public International Law* (2nd edn, 1995), vol. II, 991–4

Schütz, Hans-Joachim, 'Host State Agreements' in Wolfrum, Rüdiger (ed.), *United Nations: Law, Policies and Practice* (Dordrecht, London and Boston, 1995), vol. 1, 581–90

Schütze, Rolf A., *Deutsches Internationales Zivilprozeßecht* (Berlin and New York, 1985)

Schwab, Karl Heinz and Gottwald, Peter, 'Verfassung und Zivilprozeß' in Habscheid, Walther J. (ed.), *Effektiver Rechtsschutz und verfassungsmäßige Ordnung* (Bielefeld, 1983), 1–89

Schwartz, Murray L., 'International Law and the Nato Status of Forces Agreement' (1953) 53 *Columbia Law Review* 1091–113

Schwarzenberger, Georg, *International Law as Applied by International Courts and Tribunals* (London, 1976), vol. III, *International Constitutional Law*

Schwebel, Stephen M., 'The International Character of the Secretariat of the United Nations' (1953) 30 *British Yearbook of International Law* 71–115

(ed.), *The Effectiveness of International Decisions* (Dobbs Ferry, NY, 1971)

Schweitzer, Michael and Hummer, Waldemar, *Europarecht* (Frankfurt am Main, 1985)

Schwenk, Walter, 'Rechtsstreitigkeiten über die Erhebung von Flugsicherungsgebühren' (1975) 24 *Zeitschrift für Luft- und Weltraumrecht* 171–82

'Rechtsstreitigkeiten über die Erhebung von Flugsicherungsgebühren II' (1978) 27 *Zeitschrift für Luft- und Weltraumrecht* 71–5

Secrétan, Jacques, 'Les Privilèges et immunités diplomatiques des agents de la Société des Nations' (1925) 20 *Revue de droit international privé* 1–25

Les Privilèges et immunités diplomatiques des représentants des états membres et des agents de la Société des Nations (Lausanne, 1928)

'The Independence Granted to Agents of the International Community in Their Relations with National Public Authorities' (1935) 16 *British Yearbook of International Law* 56–78

'Problèmes de droit diplomatique devant le juge et le gouvermenent suisses' in *Mélanges F. Guisan* (Lausanne, 1950), 364

Seidl-Hohenveldern, Ignaz, 'Rechtsbeziehungen zwischen Internationalen Organisationen und einzelnen Staaten' (1953–4) 4 *Archiv des Völkerrechts* 30–58

'Die völkerrechtliche Haftung für Handlungen internationaler Organisationen im Verhältnis zu Nichtmitgliedstaaten' (1961) 11 *Osterreichische Zeitschrift für öffentliches Recht* 497–506

'The Legal Personality of International and Supranational Organizations' (1965) 21 *Revue egyptienne de droit international* 35–72

'Völkerrechtswidrige Akte fremder Staaten vor innerstaatlichen Gerichten' in Ule, Carl Hermann (ed.), *Recht im Wandel. Festschrift zum 150jährigen Bestehen des Carl Heymanns Verlages* (Cologne, Berlin, Bonn and Munich, 1965), 591–619

'Immunität ausländischer Staaten in Strafverfahren und Verwaltungs- strafverfahren' in Conrad (ed.), *Gedächtnisschrift Peters* (1967), 915–22

'Grenzen rechtlicher Streiterledigung in Internationalen Organisationen' (1969) 9 *Berichte der Deutschen Gesellschaft für Völkerrecht* 45–75

'Gemeinsame zwischenstaatliche Unternehmen' in Baer-Kaupert, Friedrich-Wilhelm, Leistner, Georg and Schwaiger, Herwig (eds.), *Liber Amicorum Bernhard C. H. Aubin* (Kehl am Rhein and Strasbourg, 1979), 193–216

'Les organisations internationales et les actes illicites des fonctionnaires' in *Sciences et actions administratives – Mélanges Georges Langrod* (1980), 385–94

Die Immunität internationaler Organisationen in Dienstrechtsstreitfällen, Rechtsgutachten für Eurocontrol. Schriften zum Völkerrecht (Berlin, 1981), vol. 71

'Dienstrechtliche Klagen gegen Internationale Organisationen' in von Münch (ed.), *Staatsrecht – Völkerrecht – Europarecht. Festschrift für Hans-Jürgen Schlochauer* (Berlin and New York, 1981), 615–34

'L'immunité de juridiction et d'exécution des Etats et des organisations internationales' in Weil (ed.), *Cours et Travaux de l'Institut des Hautes Etudes Internationales de Paris, Droit International 1* (Paris, 1981), 109–67

'Zur internationalen Zuständigkeit deutscher Gerichte für Rechts-streitigkeiten über Gebührenforderungen der Eurocontrol' (1982) 31 *Zeitschrift für Luft- und Weltraumrecht* 111–15

'Der Rückgriff auf die Mitgliedstaaten in Internationalen Organisationen' in Bernhardt, Geck, Jaenicke and Steinberger (eds.), *Völkerrecht als Rechtsordnung, Internationale Gerichtsbarkeit, Menschenrechte. Festschrift für Hermann Mosler* (Berlin, Heidelberg and New York, 1983), 881–90

'Die Entwicklung der Rechtsstellung der Internationalen Beamten' in *Verwaltungsführung, Verwaltungspraxis, Verwaltungswandel, Festschrift für Karl-Heinz Mattern. Regensburg* (1983), 151–9

'Le droit applicable aux entreprises internationales communes, étatiques ou paraétatiques' (1983 I) 60 *Annuaire de l'Institut de Droit International* 1–37, 97–102

Corporations in and under International Law (Cambridge, 1987)

'Die Rechtsstellung der internationalen Beamten' (1987) 124 *Anzeiger der phil.-hist. Klasse der Osterreichischen Akademie der Wissenschaften* 184–99

'Responsibility of Member States of an International Organization for Acts of that Organization' in *Le droit international à l'heure de sa codification. Etudes en l'honneur de Roberto Ago* (Milan, 1987), vol. III, 415–28

Völkerrecht (Cologne, Berlin, Bonn and Munich, 1987)

'Jurisdiction over Employment Disputes in International Organizations' in University of Oviedo (ed.), *Colección de Estudios Jurídicos en Homenaje al Prof. Dr D. José Pérez Montero* (1988), vol. III, Oviedo, 359–72

'Piercing the Corporate Veil of International Organizations – The International Tin Council Case in the English Court of Appeals' (1989) 32 *German Yearbook of International Law* 43–54

'Die Abstellung nationaler Beamter zu Internationalen Organisationen' in Mock, Alois and Schambeck, Herbert (eds.), *Verantwortung in unserer Zeit. Festschrift für Rudolf Kirchschläger* (Vienna, 1990), 211–20

'L'immunité de juridiction des Communautés européennes' (1990) *Revue du Marché Commun* 338, 475–9

'Zur Immunität der EWG' (1990) 1 *Ecolex* 263–4

'Die Staaten' in Neuhold, Hanspeter, Hummer, Waldemar and Schreuer, Christoph (eds.), *Osterreichisches Handbuch des Völkerrechts* (2nd edn, Vienna, 1991), 129–56

'Die internationalen Beamten und ihr Recht auf den gesetzlichen Richter' in Ballon and Hagen (eds.), *Verfahrensgarantien im nationalen und internationalen Prozeßrecht, Festschrift für Franz Matscher* (Vienna, 1993), 441–7

'Eurocontrol und EWG-Wettbewerbsrecht' in Ginther, Konrad, Hafner, Gerhard, Lang, Winfried, Neuhold, Hanspeter and Sucharipa-Beermann, Lilly (eds.), *Völkerrecht zwischen normativem Anspruch und politischer Realität. Festschrift für Karl Zemanek* (Berlin, 1994), 251–73

'Failure of Controls in the Sixth International Tin Agreement' in Blokker and Niels (eds.), *Towards More Effective Supervision by International Organizations.*

Essays in Honour of Henry G. Schermers (Dordrecht, Boston and London, 1994), 255–74

Seidl-Hohenveldern, Ignaz and Loibl, Gerhard, *Das Recht der Internationalen Organisationen einschließlich der Supranationalen Gemeinschaften* (6th edn, Cologne, Berlin, Bonn and Munich, 1996)

Sennekamp, Michael, 'Die völkerrechtliche Stellung der ausländischen Streitkräfte in der Bundesrepublik Deutschland' (1983) *Neue Juristische Wochenschrift* 2731–5

Seyersted, Finn, 'United Nations Forces: Some Legal Problems' (1961) 37 *British Yearbook of International Law* 351–475

'Settlement of Judicial Disputes of Intergovernmental Organizations by Internal and External Courts' (1963) 24 *Zeitschrift für ausländisches öffentliches Recht und Völkerrecht* 1–121

'International Personality of Intergovernmental Organizations: Do Their Capacities Really Depend Upon Their Constitutions?' (1964) 4 *Indian Journal of International Law* 1–74

'Is the International Personality of Intergovernmental Organizations Valid vis-à-vis Non-Members?' (1964) 4 *Indian Journal of International Law* 233–68

'Objective International Personality of Intergovernmental Organizations, Do Their Capacities Really Depend upon the Conventions Establishing Them?' (1964) 34 *Nordisk Tidsskrift for International Ret* 1–112

'Jurisdiction over Organs and Officials of States, the Holy Sea and Intergovernmental Organisations' (1965) 14 *International and Comparative Law Quarterly* 31–82, 493–527

'Applicable Law in Relations Between Intergovernmental Organizations and Private Parties' (1967 III) 122 *Recueil des Cours* 427–616

'Has the Government a Duty to Accord Diplomatic Assistance and Protection to Its Nationals?' (1968) 12 *Scandinavian Studies in Law* 121–49

'The Legal Nature of International Organizations' (1982) 51 *Nordisk Tidsskrift for International Ret* 203–5

'Treaty Making Capacity of Intergovernmental Organizations: Article 6 of the International Law Commission's Draft Articles on the Law of Treaties Between States and International Organizations or Between International Organizations' (1983) 34 *Osterreichische Zeitschrift für öffentliches Recht und Völkerrecht* 261–7

'Binding Authority for the United Nations and Other International Organizations in Limited Functional and Territorial Fields' (1987) 56 *Nordic Journal of International Law* 198–204

Shapiro, Mark J., 'A Search in the Heavens: Should Intelsat be Subject to US Antitrust Laws?' (1985) 24 *Columbia Journal of Transnational Law* 133–64

Shihata, Ibrahim F. I., 'The Role of Law in Economic Development: The Legal Problems of International Public Ventures' (1969) 25 *Revue egyptienne de droit international* 119–28

'The Multilateral Investment Guarantee Agency (MIGA) and the Legal Treatment of Foreign Investment' (1987 III) 203 *Recueil des Cours* 95–320

The European Bank for Reconstruction and Development, A Comparative Analysis of the Constituent Agreement (London and Boston, 1990)

The World Bank Inspection Panel (Oxford, 1994)

Shuster, M. R., *The Public International Law of Money* (Oxford, 1973)

Sieglerschmidt, Hellmut, 'Das Immunitätsrecht der Europäischen Gemeinschaft. Seine Anwendung durch das Europäische Parlament und seine notwendige Weiterentwicklung' (1986) 13 *Europäische Grundrechte Zeitschrift* 445–53

Simma, Bruno, 'The Court of Arbitration for Sport' in Böckstiegel, Karl-Heinz, Folz, Hans-Ernst, Mössner, Jörg Manfred and Zemanek, Karl (eds.), *Völkerrecht – Recht der Internationalen Organisationen – Weltwirtschaftsrecht. Festschrift für Ignaz Seidl-Hohenveldern* (Cologne, Berlin, Bonn and Munich, 1988), 573–85

(ed.), *Charta der Vereinten Nationen, Kommentar* (1991)

(ed.), *The Charter of the United Nations. A Commentary* (Oxford, 1994)

Simma, Bruno and Alston, Philip, 'The Sources of Human Rights Law: Custom, Jus Cogens, and General Principles' (1992) 12 *Australian Yearbook of International Law* 82–108

Simma, Bruno and Vedder, Christoph, 'Art. 210, Art. 211' in Grabitz, Eberhard (ed.), *Kommentar zum EWG-Vertrag* (Munich, 1983)

Simmonds, K. R. and Zimmermann, Andreas, 'International Maritime Organization' in Bernhardt, Rudolf (ed.), *Encyclopedia of Public International Law* (2nd edn, 1995), vol. II, 1262–7

Simmonds, R., 'Status of Locally Recruited Personnel of International Organizations' (1972) 9 *University of Ghana Law Journal* 1

Sinclair, Ian, 'The Law of Sovereign Immunity: Recent Developments' (1980 II) 167 *Recueil des Cours* 113–284

Singer, Michael, 'Abandoning Restrictive Sovereign Immunity: An Analysis in Terms of Jurisdiction to Prescribe' (1985) 26 *Harvard International Law Journal* 1–61

'Jurisdictional Immunity of International Organizations: Human Rights and Functional Necessity Concerns' (1995) 36 *Virginia Journal of International Law* 53–165

Siotto-Pintor, Manfredi, 'Les sujets du droit international autres que les Etats' (1932 III) 41 *Recueil des Cours* 251–361

Skubiszewski, Krzysztof, 'Implied Powers of International Organisations' in Dinstein, Yoram (ed.), *International Law at a Time of Perplexity: Essays in Honour of Shabtai Rosenne* (Dordrecht, Boston and London, 1989), 855–68

Sloan, B., 'The United Nations Charter as a Constitution' (1989) 1 *Pace Yearbook of International Law* 61–126

Slomanson, William R., 'Civil Actions Against Interpol: A Field Compass' (1984) 57 *Temple Law Quarterly* 553–600

Smith, Delbert D., 'The Conclusion of International Agreements by International Organizations: A Functional Analysis Applied to the Agreements of the World Meteorological Organization' (1971) 2 *Loyola University of Chicago Law Journal* 27–68

Smits, 'Rechtspersonen op het snijpunt van (internationaal) privaat- en publiekrecht' (1988) 97 *Mededelingen van de Nederlandse Vereiniging voor Internationaal Recht* 77–195

Société Française pour le Droit International (ed.), *Le Contentieux de la fonction publique international* (Paris, 1996)

Société Française pour le Droit International (ed.), *Les Organisations internationales contemporaines* (Paris, 1988)

Sohn, Louis B., 'Due Process in the United Nations' (1975) 69 *American Journal of International Law* 620–2

Sommereyns, Raymond, 'United Nations Forces' in Bernhardt, Rudolf (ed.),
   Encyclopedia of Public International Law (1982), vol. IV, 253–8
Sørensen, Max, 'Autonomous Legal Orders: Some Considerations Relating to a
   Systems Analysis of International Organisations in the World Legal Order'
   (1983) 32 *International and Comparative Law Quarterly* 559–76
Spencer, Melvin J., 'Jurisdictional Immunity of United Nations Employees – The
   Gubitchev Case' (1950) 49 *Michigan Law Review* 101–10
Staker, Christopher, 'Decisions of British Courts During 1990 Involving
   Questions of Public or Private International Law, A. Public International
   Law [AMF v. Hashim]' (1990) 61 *British Yearbook of International Law* 377–94
   'Decisions of British Courts During 1991 Involving Questions of Public or
   Private International Law, A. Public International Law [AMF v. Hashim]'
   (1991) 62 *British Yearbook of International Law* 433–47
Starck, W. von, 'Internationale und nationale Rechtsstellung des Roten Kreuzes'
   (1967) 13 *Jahrbuch für Internationales Recht* 210–44
Stein, Eric, 'The European Coal and Steel Community: The Beginning of its
   Judicial Process' (1955) 55 *Columbia Law Review* 985–99
   'Application and Enforcement of International Organization Law by National
   Authorities and Courts' in Schwebel, S. M. (ed.), *The Effectiveness of
   International Decisions* (Leiden, 1971), 66–70
Steinberger, Helmut, 'Sovereignty' in Bernhardt, Rudolf (ed.), *Encyclopedia of
   Public International Law* (1987), vol. X, 397–418
Steindorff, Ernst, *Sachnormen im internationalen Privatrecht* (Frankfurt am Main,
   1958)
Steiner, H. J., Vagts, D. F. and Koh, H. H., *Transnational Legal Problems: Materials and
   Text* (4th edn, Westbury, NY, 1994)
Steinmann, Hans Georg, 'Ein Beitrag zu Fragen der zivilrechtlichen Immunität
   von ausländischen Diplomaten, Konsuln und anderen bevorrechtigten
   Personen sowie von fremden Staaten, die durch ihre Missionen oder auf
   ähnliche Weise in der Bundesrepublik Deutschland tätig werden' (1965)
   Monatsschrift für deutsches Recht 706–12, 795–9
Stern, Brigitte, 'L'affaire du Bureau de l'OLP devant les juridictions interne et
   internationale' (1988) 34 *Annuaire français de droit international* 165–94
Strange, Susan, *The Retreat of the State* (Cambridge, 1996)
Strebel, Helmut, 'Staatenimmunität, Die Europaratskonvention und die neuen
   Gesetze der Vereinigten Staaten und Großbritanniens' (1980) 44 *Rabels
   Zeitschrift für ausländisches und internationales Privatrecht* 66–98
Strohl, Pierre, 'The Representation and Professional Protection of the
   International Civil Servant' (1957) 84 *Journal de droit international* 309–59
Struck, Gerhard, *Topische Jurisprudenz* (Frankfurt am Main, 1971)
Strupp, Karl and Schlochauer, Hans-Jürgen (eds.), *Wörterbuch des Völkerrechts* (2nd
   edn, 1960–2), vols. I–III
Sucharitkul, Sompong, 'Immunities of Foreign States Before National
   Authorities' (1976 I) 149 *Recueil des Cours* 87–215
Sundström, G. O. Zacharias, *Public International Utility Corporations* (Leiden, 1972)
Szaniawski, Zbigniew and Forysinski, Wojciech, 'Le problème d'application de la
   Convention sur le statut juridique, les privilèges et les immunités des
   organisations économiques interétatiques fonctionnant dans certains
   domaines de coopération' (1986) 15 *Polish Yearbook of International Law* 29–44

Szasz, Paul C., 'Unions of International Officials: Past, Present and Future' (1982) 14 *New York University Journal of International Law and Politics* 807–39

'The United Nations Legislates to Limit its Liability' (1987) 81 *American Journal of International Law* 739–44

'International Atomic Energy Agency' in Bernhardt, Rudolf (ed.), *Encyclopedia of Public International Law* (2nd edn, 1995), vol. II, 1051–7

'International Organizations, Privileges and Immunities' in Bernhardt, Rudolf (ed.), *Encyclopedia of Public International Law* (2nd edn, 1995), vol. II, 1325–33

Tetzlaff, R., 'Weltbank und Währungsfonds als umstrittene "Krisenmanager" in den Nord-Süd-Beziehungen. Zur Funktionsweise und politischen Bedeutung der beiden Institutionen' (1988) 33/34 *Aus Politik und Zeitgeschichte* 36–46

'The Practice of the United Nations, the Specialized Agencies and the International Atomic Energy Agency Concerning Their Status, Privileges and Immunities – Study Prepared by the Secretariat' (UN Doc. A/CN.4/L.118 and Add. 1 and 2) (1967) *Yearbook of the International Law Commission*, vol. II, 154–324

'The Practice of the United Nations, the Specialized Agencies and the International Atomic Energy Agency Concerning Their Status, Privileges and Immunities – Supplementary Study Prepared by the Secretariat' (UN Doc. A/CN.4/L.383 and Add. 1–3) (1985) *Yearbook of the International Law Commission*, vol. II/1, 145–210

'The United Nations at Forty: The US Policy Perspective' (1985) 79 *Proceedings of the American Society of International Law* 150–69

'The United Nations: Crisis of Confidence or Window of Opportunity?' (1987) 81 *Proceedings of the American Society of International Law* 104–26

Thierry, Hubert, 'Les Voies de recours contre les jugements du tribunal administratif des nations unies et du tribunal administratif de l'OIT' in Société Française pour le Droit International (ed.), *Le Contentieux de la fonction publique international* (Paris, 1996), 121–6

Thompson, Dennis, 'The International Tin Council Litigation' (1988) 22 *Journal of World Trade Law* 103–11

Tomuschat, Christian, 'Die Europäische Union unter der Aufsicht des Bundesverfassungsgerichts' (1993) 20 *Europäische Grundrechte Zeitschrift* 489–96

'International Courts and Tribunals' in Bernhardt, Rudolf (ed.), *Encyclopedia of Public International Law* (2nd edn, 1995), vol. II, 1108–15

Tosato, Gian Luigi, 'L'Istituto internazionale per l'unificazione del diritto privato e la giurisdizione italiana' (1967) 50 *Rivista di diritto internazionale* 150–71

Treves, Tullio, 'Les privilèges et les immunités des membres de la Commission et de la Cour européennes des Droit de l'Homme' in *Multitudo Legum Ius Unum, Festschrift Wengler* (Berlin, 1973), vol. I, *Allgemeine Rechtslehre und Völkerrecht*, 667–84

Trindade, A. A. Cançado, 'Exhaustion of Local Remedies and the Law of International Organizations' (1979) 57 *Revue de droit international* 81–123

Tunkin, Grigory I., 'The Legal Nature of the United Nations' (1966 III) 119 *Recueil des Cours* 7–66

Tyler, Michael Robert, 'IAM v. OPEC: "Acts of States" and "Passive Virtues"' (1982) 5 *Loyola of Los Angeles International and Comparative Law Journal* 159–71

Ule, Carl Hermann, 'Der gerichtliche Rechtsschutz des Einzelnen gegenüber der vollziehenden Gewalt in den Europäischen Gemeinschaften' in Max-Planck-Institut für ausländisches öffentliches Recht und Völkerrecht (ed.), *Gerichtsschutz gegen die Exekutive* (Cologne, Berlin, Bonn, Munich and Dobbs Ferry, NY, 1970), vol. II, *National Reports*, 1179–216

Union of International Associations (ed.), *Yearbook of International Organizations 1984/85* (21st edn, 1984), vol. I, *Organization Descriptions and Index*

United Nations, *Handbook on the Legal Status, Privileges and Immunities of the United Nations* (UN Doc. ST/LEG/2) (1952)

Legislative Texts and Treaty Provisions Concerning the Legal Status, Privileges and Immunities of International Organizations, vol. I (1959) and II (1961) (UN Docs ST/LEG/SER.B/10 and 11)

Relations Between States and International Organizations (Second Part of the Topic) Copies of Replies to a Questionnaire Concerning the Status, Privileges and Immunities of Regional Organizations (UN Doc. ST/LEG/17)

Relations Between States and Intergovernmental Organizations (Second Part of the Topic) The Practice of the United Nations, the Specialized Agencies and the IAEA Concerning their Status, Privileges and Immunities (UN Doc. A/CN.4/L.118 and Add. 1 and 2) (1967) *Yearbook of the International Law Commission* Vol. II, 154–324

Relations Between States and International Organizations (Second Part of the Topic) The Practice of the United Nations, the Specialized Agencies and the IAEA Concerning their Status, Privileges and Immunities (UN Doc. A/CN.4/L.383 and Add. 1–3) (1985) *Yearbook of the International Law Commission* Vol. II, Addendum, 144–210

Report of the Secretary General, Co-ordination of the Privileges and Immunities of the United Nations and the Specialized Agencies (UN Doc. A 339)

Urquhart, Brian, 'The United Nations System and the Future' (1989) 65 *International Affairs* (London) 225–31

Valticos, Nicolas, 'Les contrats conclus par les organisations internationales avec des personnes privées, Rapport provisoire et projet de résolution – Rapport définitif et projet de résolution' (1977) *Annuaire de l'Institut de Droit International* 1–191

'International Organizations and International Law' (1986) 29 *Japanese Annual of International Law* 1–9

van Dijk, Pieter, 'Access to Court' in Macdonald, R. St. J., Matscher, F. and Petzold, H. (eds.), *The European System for the Protection of Human Rights* (Dordrecht, Boston and London, 1993), 345–79

van Hecke, Georges, 'Contracts Between International Organizations and Private Law Persons' in Bernhardt, Rudolf (ed.), *Encyclopedia of Public International Law* (2nd edn, 1992), vol. I, 812–14

'Contracts Between States and Foreign Private Law Persons' in Bernhardt, Rudolf (ed.), *Encyclopedia of Public International Law* (2nd edn, 1992), vol. I, 814–19

Vandersanden, Georges, 'Administrative Tribunals, Boards and Commissions in International Organizations' in Bernhardt, Rudolf (ed.), *Encyclopedia of Public International Law* (2nd edn, 1992), vol. I, 27–31

Vedder, Christoph, 'The International Olympic Committee: An Advanced Non-Governmental Organization and the International Law' (1984) 27 *German Yearbook of International Law* 233–85

'Die verfassungsrechtliche Dimension – die bisher unbekannte Grenze für

Gemeinschaftshandeln? Anmerkung zum Gutachten 2/94, EMRK, des EuGH'
(1996) 31 EuropaRecht 309–19

Venturini, Gabriella, 'Attività di consulenza presso il quartier generale delle
Forze Alleate del Sud Europa e giurisdizione italiana' (1977) 13 Rivista di
Diritto Internazionale Privato e Processuale 564–74

Verdross, Alfred and Simma, Bruno, Universelles Völkerrecht, Theorie und Praxis (3rd
edn, Berlin, 1984)

Verosta, Stephan, 'Exterritorialität' in Strupp and Schlochauer (eds.), Wörterbuch
des Völkerrechts (Berlin, 1968), vol. I, 499–504

Verzijl, J. H. W., 'La validité et la nullité des actes juridiques internationaux'
(1935) 9 Revue de droit international 284–339

Vettovaglia, Jean-Pierre, 'Privileges and Immunities of Members of Permanent
Missions in Geneva and of International Officials in Switzerland' in
Dembinski (ed.), International Geneva Yearbook 1988, Organization and Activities
of International Institutions in Geneva (1988), 71–83

Viehweg, Theodor, Topik und Jurisprudenz (5th edn, Munich, 1974)

Villiger, Mark E., Customary International Law and Treaties (Dordrecht, Boston and
Lancester, 1985)

Virally, Michel, 'De la classification des organisations internationales' in
Miscellanea W. J. Ganshof van der Meersch (Brussels and Paris, 1972), vol. I,
365–82

L'Organisation mondiale (Paris, 1972)

'La notion de fonction dans la théorie de l'organisation internationale' in La
Communauté Internationale. Mélanges offerts à Charles Rousseau (Paris, 1974),
277–300

Vischer, Frank, 'Der ausländische Staat als Kläger (Überlegungen zum Fall
Duvalier v. Haiti)' (1991) 11 Praxis des Internationalen Privat- und
Verfahrensrechts 209–15

Voitovich, S. A., 'Normative Acts of the International Economic Organizations on
International Law-Making' (1990) 24 Journal of World Trade Law 21–38

Vorkink, A. N. and Hakuta, M. C., Lawsuits Against International Organizations –
Cases in National Courts Involving Staff and Employment (Washington DC, World
Bank Legal Department, 1985)

Voskuil, C. C. A., 'The International Law of State Immunity, as Reflected in the
Dutch Civil Law of Execution' (1979) 10 Netherlands Yearbook of International
Law 245–89

Walchshöfer, Alfred, 'Die deutsche internationale Zuständigkeit in der
streitigen Gerichtsbarkeit' (1967) 80 Zeitschrift für Zivilprozeß 165–229

Wassermann, Ursula, 'UNCTAD: Sixth International Tin Agreement' (1981) 15
Journal of World Trade Law 557–8

'Tin and Other Commodities in Crisis' (1986) 20 Journal of World Trade Law
232–5

Watson, Geoffrey R., 'Constitutionalism, Judicial Review, and the World Court'
(1993) 34 Harvard International Law Journal 1–45

Wattles, Gordon W., 'Internal Recourse Procedures of International
Organizations' (1982) 14 New York University Journal of International Law and
Politics 871–94

Weber, Albrecht, 'Der UN-Beamte in den USA – Sein völkerrechtlicher Status
(Vorrechte und Immunitäten)' (dissertation, Würzburg, 1972)

Weber, Ludwig, 'Awards of Compensation Made by UN Administrative Tribunal (Advisory Opinion)' in Bernhardt, Rudolf (ed.), *Encyclopedia of Public International Law* (2nd edn, 1992), vol. I, 312–13

'European Organization for the Safety of Air Navigation (Eurocontrol)' in Bernhardt, Rudolf (ed.), *Encyclopedia of Public International Law* (2nd edn, 1995), vol. II, 270–3

Wehberg, Hans, 'Entwicklungsstufen der internationalen Organisation' (1953–5) 52 *Friedens-Warte* 193–218

Weiss, André, 'Compétence ou incompétence des tribunaux à l'égard des Etats étrangers' (1923) 1 *Recueil des Cours* 521–49

Weiss, Thomas G., *International Bureaucracy* (Lexington, Toronto and London, 1975)

Weissberg, Guenter, *The International Legal Personality of the United Nations* (PhD dissertation, Columbia University, 1959)

The International Status of the United Nations (New York and London, 1961)

Wenckstern, Manfred, 'Verfassungsrechtliche Fragen der Immunität internationaler Organisationen' (1987) *Neue Juristische Wochenschrift* 1113–18

Die Immunität internationaler Organisationen. Handbuch des Internationalen Zivilverfahrensrechts (Tübingen, 1994), vol. II/1

Wengler, Wilhelm, 'Der Begriff des Völkerrechtssubjektes im Lichte der politischen Gegenwart' (1951–2) 51 *Friedens-Warte* 113–42

'Über die Maxime von der Unanwendbarkeit ausländischer politischer Gesetze' (1956) 1 *Internationales Recht und Diplomatie* 191–206

Völkerrecht, 2 vols (Berlin, Göttingen and Heidelberg, 1964)

Whiteman, Marjorie M., *Digest of International Law* (1968), vol. XIII

Wieczorek, Bernhard and Schütze, Rolf A., *Zivilprozeßordnung und Nebengesetze* (3rd edn, Berlin and New York, 1995)

Wildhaber, Luzius, *Treaty-Making Power and Constitution* (Basel and Stuttgart, 1971)

Williams, Sir John Fischer, 'The Status of the League of Nations in International Law' in *Chapters on Current International Law and the League of Nations* (London, 1929), 477

'The Legal Character of the Bank for International Settlements' (1930) 24 *American Journal of International Law* 665–73

Wilmshurst, 'Executive Certificates in Foreign Affairs – The United Kingdom' (1986) 35 *International and Comparative Law Quarterly* 157–69

Winkelmann, Ingo (ed.), *Das Maastricht-Urteil des Bundesverfassungsgerichts vom 12 Oktober 1993. Dokumentation des Verfahrens mit Einführung* (Berlin, 1994)

Winter, L. I., 'Notes on Dutch Judicial Decisions' (1955) 82 *Journal de droit international* 875–903

Wintermeyer, Charles A., 'ICJ Advisory Opinion: 1951 WHO–Egypt Treaty' (1981) 10 *Denver Journal of International Law and Policy* 561–8

Wolf, F., *Le droit aux privilèges et immunités des Institutions spécialisées reliées aux Nations Unies* (1948)

'Le Tribunal Administratif de l'Organisation Internationale du Travail' (1954) 58 *Revue générale de droit international public* 279–314

Wolf, Maurice and Arnold, Elting, *Doing Business with the International Development Organizations in Washington DC* (Washington DC, 1982)

Wolfrum, Rüdiger (ed.), *Handbuch Vereinte Nationen* (2nd edn, Munich, 1991)
  'Eutelsat' in Bernhardt, Rudolf (ed.), *Encyclopedia of Public International Law* (2nd
    edn, 1995), vol. II, 300–2
  'International Administrative Unions' in Bernhardt, Rudolf (ed.), *Encyclopedia
    of Public International Law* (2nd edn, 1995), vol. II, 1041–7
  'International Organizations, Headquarters' in Bernhardt, Rudolf (ed.),
    Encyclopedia of Public International Law (2nd edn, 1995), vol. II, 1309–12
  (ed.), *United Nations: Law, Policies and Practice*, 2 vols (Dordrecht, London and
    Boston, 1995)
Wood, Hugh McKinnon, 'Legal Relations Between Individuals and a World
    Organization of States' (1944) 30 *Transactions of the Grotius Society* 141–64
  'The Dissolution of the League of Nations' (1946) 23 *British Yearbook of
    International Law* 317–23
Wright, Quincy, 'Responsibility for Injuries to United Nations Officials' (1949) 43
    American Journal of International Law 95–104
  'The Jural Personality of the United Nations' (1949) 43 *American Journal of
    International Law* 509–16
Yasseen, Mustafa K., 'La personnalité juridique des organisations
    internationales' in Dupuy, R.-J. (ed.), *Manuel sur les organisations
    internationales, A Handbook on International Organizations* (1988), 33–55
Yokota, Yozo, 'How Useful is the Notion of "International Public Corporation"
    Today?' in Makarczyk (ed.), *Essays in Honour of Judge Manfred Lachs* (The
    Hague, Boston and Lancaster, 1984), 557–71
  'The Effects of International Organizations on the International Law' in
    International Law, UN and Japan, Festschrift Takano (Tokyo, 1988), 123–68
    (Japanese)
Zacklin, Ralph, 'Diplomatic Relations: Status, Privileges and Immunities' in
    Dupuy, R.-J. (ed.), *Manuel sur les organisations internationales, A Handbook on
    International Organizations* (1988), 179–98
Zemanek, Karl, 'Internationale Organisationen als Handlungseinheiten in der
    Völkerrechtsgemeinschaft' (1956) 7 *Osterreichische Zeitschrift für öffentliches
    Recht* 335–72
  Das Vertragsrecht der internationalen Organisationen (Vienna, 1957)
  'Die Rechtsstellung der internationalen Organisationen in Osterreich' (1958)
    13 *Osterreichische Juristenzeitung* 380–1
  'Was kann die Vergleichung staatlichen öffentlichen Rechts für das Recht der
    internationalen Organisationen leisten?' (1964) 24 *Zeitschrift für ausländisches
    öffentliches Recht und Völkerrecht* 453–71
  (ed.), 'Agreements of International Organizations and the Vienna Convention
    on the Law of Treaties' (1971) *Osterreichische Zeitschrift für öffentliches Recht*
    Supplement 1
  'The United Nations Conference on the Law of Treaties Between States and
    International Organizations or Between International Organizations: The
    Unrecorded History of its "General Agreement"' in Böckstiegel, Karl-Heinz,
    Folz, Hans-Ernst, Mössner, Jörg Manfred and Zemanek, Karl (eds.), *Völkerrecht
    – Recht der Internationalen Organisationen – Weltwirtschaftsrecht. Festschrift für
    Ignaz Seidl-Hohenveldern* (Cologne, Berlin, Bonn and Munich, 1988), 665–79
  'Interdependence' in Bernhardt, Rudolf (ed.), *Encyclopedia of Public International
    Law* (2nd edn, 1995), vol. II, 1021–3

'International Organizations, Treaty-Making Power' in Bernhardt, Rudolf (ed.), *Encyclopedia of Public International Law* (2nd edn, 1995), vol. II, 1343–6

'What is "State Practice" and Who Makes It?' in Beyerlin, Ulrich, Bothe, Michael, Hofmann, Rainer and Petersmann, Ernst-Ulrich (eds.), *Recht zwischen Umbruch und Bewahrung. Festschrift für Rudolf Bernhardt* (Berlin, 1995), 289–306

Zoller, Elisabeth, 'The National Security of the United States as the Host State for the United Nations' (1989) 1 *Pace Yearbook of International Law* 127–61

Zuleeg, Manfred, 'International Organizations, Implied Powers' in Bernhardt, Rudolf (ed.), *Encyclopedia of Public International Law* (2nd edn, 1995), vol. II, 1312–14

Index

444

CAMBRIDGE STUDIES IN INTERNATIONAL AND COMPARATIVE LAW

Books in the series

Lightning Source UK Ltd.
Milton Keynes UK
UKOW051427011011

179590UK00001B/80/P